Current Chinese Economic Report Series

For further volumes:
http://www.springer.com/series/11028

Xiaoxi Li • Jiancheng Pan
Editors

China Green Development Index Report 2012

Regional Comparison

BEIJING NORMAL UNIVERSITY PUBLISHING GROUP
BEIJING NORMAL UNIVERSITY PRESS

Springer

Editors
Xiaoxi Li
School of Economics
and Resource Management
Beijing Normal University
Beijing, China

Jiancheng Pan
China Economic Monitoring
and Analysis Center
National Bureau of Statistics of China
Beijing, China

ISSN 2194-7937 ISSN 2194-7945 (electronic)
ISBN 978-3-642-54177-3 ISBN 978-3-642-54178-0 (eBook)
DOI 10.1007/978-3-642-54178-0
Springer Heidelberg New York Dordrecht London

Library of Congress Control Number: 2014936735

Printed on acid-free paper

Springer is part of Springer Science+Business Media (www.springer.com)

Research Group

Research Group Leaders

Xiaoxi Li (Professor, Vice Chairman of Academic Committee of Beijing Normal University, Academic Advisor of Southwestern University of Finance and Economics)

Jiancheng Pan (PhD, Deputy Director-General of China Economic Monitoring and Analysis Center, National Bureau of Statistics of China)

Leaders of Cooperating Institutions

Desheng Lai (Professor, Dean of School of Economics and Business Administration, Beijing Normal University)

Renwu Tang (Professor, Executive Dean of School of Management, Beijing Normal University)

Biliang Hu (Professor, Dean of School of Economics and Resource Management, Beijing Normal University)

Yang Zhifeng (Professor, Dean of School of Environment, Beijing Normal University)

Fangjian Liu (Professor, Executive Dean of School of Economics, Southwestern University of Finance and Economics)

Collaborative and Supporting Institutions

China Economic Monitoring and Analysis Center and Relevant Research Institutes, National Bureau of Statistics of China

Center for Forecasting Science, Chinese Academy of Sciences

Policy Research Center for Environment and Economy, Ministry of Environmental Protection

College of Resources Science and Technology, Beijing Normal University

School of Geography, Beijing Normal University

School of Environment, Beijing Normal University

School of Life Sciences, Beijing Normal University

College of Water Sciences, Beijing Normal University

Institute of National Accounts, Beijing Normal University

China Philanthropy Research Institute, Beijing Normal University

Capital Institute of Science and Technology Development Strategy

School of Public Administration, Southwestern University of Finance and Economics

Institute of Energy Economics, Southwestern University of Finance and Economics

Experimental Economics Laboratory, Southwestern University of Finance and Economics

Coordinators

Junli Zhao, Jiangxue Zhang, Zhao Zheng, Lin Yongsheng

Contact Persons

Tao Song, Ning Cai

Commenting Experts

Wu Jinglian (Professor, Researcher at Development Research Center of the State Council)
Li Yining (Professor, Honorary Dean of Guanghua School of Management, Peking University)
Zhang Zhuoyuan (Professor, Member of Academic Committee, Chinese Academy of Social Sciences)
Wei Liqun (Professor, Vice Chairman of the Committee for Learning and Cultural and Historical Data, National Committee of the Chinese People's Political Consultative Conference)
Chen Xiwen (Professor, Vice Minister of Office of the Central Leading Group on Financial and Economic Affairs)
Liu Shijin (Professor, Vice President of Development Research Center of the State Council)
Lu Zhongyuan (Professor, Vice President of Development Research Center of the State Council)
Gu Shengzu (Professor, Vice Chairman of Internal and Judicial Affairs Committee, the 11th National People's Congress of the People's Republic of China)
Zhou Hongren (Professor, Executive Vice Chairman of the Advisory Committee for State Informatization)
Pan Yue (Professor, Vice Minister of Environmental Protection)
Gan Zangchun (Professor, Vice Minister of Legislative Affairs Office of the State Council)
Liu Wei (Professor, Vice President of Peking University)
Ge Jianping (Professor, Vice President of Beijing Normal University)
Bian Huimin (Professor, Vice President of Southwestern University of Finance and Economics)
Xu Xianchun (Professor, Deputy Commissioner of the National Bureau of Statistics of China)
Zhang Xinshi (Professor, Academician at the Chinese Academy of Sciences)
Niu Wenyuan (Professor, Counselor of the State Council, Researcher at the Chinese Academy of Sciences)

Wang Yi (Professor, Head of Sustainable Development Strategy Study Group, Chinese Academy of Sciences)

Wei Jie (Professor, Director of the National Center for Economic Research, Tsinghua University)

Pan Jiahua (Professor, Director of the Research Center for Sustainable Development, Chinese Academy of Social Sciences)

Fan Hengshan (Professor, Director-General of the Department of Regional Economy, National Development and Reform Commission)

Xia Guang (Professor, Director of Policy Research Center for Environment and Economy, Ministry of Environmental Protection)

Su Wei (Professor, Director-General of the Department of Climate Change, National Development and Reform Commission)

Chen Dongqi (Professor, Vice President of the Academy of Macroeconomic Research, National Development and Reform Commission)

Jia Kang (Professor, Director of the Research Institute for Fiscal Science, Ministry of Finance)

Zhang Jianhua (Professor, Director-General of the Research Bureau of the People's Bank of China)

Qiu Dong (Cheung Kong Scholar Chair Professor at Beijing Normal University)

Chen Zongsheng (Professor, Deputy Secretary-General of Tianjin Municipal People's Government)

Preface 1

In today's world, resources, energy, climate, and ecology are playing an increasingly important role in the development and even survival of mankind. Countries across the globe have chosen to go green and low carbon for sustainable development. Four decades ago, the epoch-making Declaration on the Human Environment was issued at the first United Nations Conference on the Human Environment convened in Stockholm, and the slogan "Only One Earth" was shouted loudly in every corner of the world. The convening of the conference indicated that humans had awakened to the environmental issues, ushering in a new era of green development.

Fostering green development is about reducing the excessive use of resources and energy, enhancing environmental protection and ecological management, and pursing the coordinated and sustainable development of the economy, society, and ecology. Since the policy of reform and opening up was introduced, China has made remarkable achievements in economic and social development; environmental awareness has been improving among the public; party committees and governments at all levels have attached increasing importance to resource conservation, environmental protection, and green development. With the advent of the twenty-first century in particular, environmental protection has been promoted significantly in both theoretical and practical terms, providing strong support for rapid economic growth, response to the international financial crisis, and the development of emerging industries. However, we should also be clear-headed that environmental challenges remain serious and the efforts made in this regard are far from enough given the fast industrialization and urbanization in the country. Changing the growth model, adjusting the economic structure, and promoting green development are tough tasks that concern people's well-being and call for much more efforts.

In light of the growing resource and environmental constraints, it is proposed in the 12th Five-Year Plan that China should continue to pursue green development, prioritize energy conservation and emissions reduction, improve the incentive and restraint mechanisms, step up efforts to develop resource-efficient and environment-friendly patterns of production and consumption, enhance the capacity for sustainable development, and advance ecological progress. It gives full expression to the resolution of the Communist Party of China (CPC) and the Chinese government to lead people of the country to tread a path of development that ensures high productivity, affluent life, and a good ecological environment. Currently, it is an urgent priority to put in place a performance indicator system and an evaluation mechanism conducive to green development and use them to evaluate the level of green development at both national and local levels. It is also part of the efforts to effectively carry out the decisions and policies made by the central authorities.

Beijing Normal University, Southwestern University of Finance and Economics, and China Economic Monitoring and Analysis Center have been publishing China's Green Development Index (GDI) and a related research report annually since 2010. They have made serious attempts to establish a green development evaluation system for China, achieving positive results. The *China Green Development Index Report 2012: Regional Comparison* is built on previous research findings and draws on the views of many experts. The newly introduced "green development checkup tables" for provinces as well as large- and medium-sized cities in China help to improve the evaluation indicator system, and people's opinions on green development in their cities are obtained through survey questionnaires. This report seeks to draw a roadmap for green development in China and give a full and objective account of the realities in this respect across provinces (municipalities/autonomous regions) and major cities of the country. It can be referred to by people from all walks of life for information about the progress China has made in pursuing green development.

We have only one earth. Promoting green development is a time-consuming and arduous task whose accomplishment would be impossible without monitoring and early warning systems. This report is intended to provide valuable information for local authorities to push forward green development based on their realities and to draw more attention to green development so that more people will join the effort to create a livable environment for all!

Commissioner of National Bureau of Statistics of China
Beijing, China

Ma Jiantang

Preface 2

Economic and social development today is faced with resource bottlenecks and serious environmental challenges. Sustainability has become the most important issue related to human survival. In response to the requirements of the central government and to the call of the times, we need to open a new horizon in pursuing development in a scientific way, speed up the change of growth model, and promote the sustainable development of the economy and society.

In 2010 and 2011, led by Professor Li Xiaoxi of Beijing Normal University, experts and scholars in different fields such as economics, management, environment, and resources from Beijing Normal University and Southwestern University of Finance and Economics were brought together to form a research group and work with China Economic Monitoring and Analysis Center to write the *China Green Development Index Report* which is intended to draw a roadmap for green development and give a full and objective account of the progress China has made in this regard. The philosophy of green development has helped to facilitate the change of growth model in this country, causing a real stir in all sectors. The *China Green Development Index Report 2012: Regional Comparison* is another joint effort of the experts and scholars who have pushed the research on the Green Development Index (GDI) a big step forward based on the outcomes in the previous 2 years. This report is of great value in both theoretical and practical terms.

As one of the key universities directly administered by the Chinese Ministry of Education, Beijing Normal University will strive to serve the needs of the country and grow into a world-renowned institution while giving full support to the experts so as to make its due contributions to the faster and healthy development of the economy and society as well as the rejuvenation of the Chinese nation!

Party Secretary of Beijing Normal University
Beijing, China

Liu Chuansheng

Preface 3

Ever since the start of its reform and opening up drive, China has made remarkable achievements in economic development, as evidenced by the world's second largest GDP and largest foreign exchange reserves it has as well as the considerably improved living standards of its people. However, what has come along with its rising economic strength is the growing imbalance between its economic growth and its resources and the ecological environment. Against such a backdrop, the Scientific Outlook on Development and Economic Sustainability Research Base of Beijing Normal University, the Green Economy and Economic Sustainability Research Base of Southwestern University of Finance and Economics, and China Economic Monitoring and Analysis Center, National Bureau of Statistics of China, have jointly launched the annual *China Green Development Index Report* for three consecutive years with a view to sharing constructive ideas about how to correct the imbalance.

The 2010 report was widely acclaimed by all sectors and recognized at the second China Soft Science Awards. The 2011 report was published in the Great Hall of the People on September 24, 2011; covered by many news media agencies including CCTV, Xinhua News Agency, and *People's Daily*; and translated into English with the financial support of the 2011 Classic China International Publishing Project launched by the General Administration of Press and Publication of China. Following the philosophy of green development, the 2012 report has also been prepared based on the views of experts, research institutes, and average people. Apart from the calculations of the Green Development Index (GDI) for all provinces (municipalities/autonomous regions) and 38 cities of China, which can be seen in the previous two reports, this report also includes the "green development checkup tables," green development field surveys, and professors' forum on green development. It gives a full account of green development in China in both theoretical and practical terms. This report of heavy weight and high quality echoes the theme of the times and shows a great sense of responsibility.

A famous institution of higher education in China, Beijing Normal University is on its way to grow into one of the world's leading comprehensive universities with distinctive features and a focus on research. It will give full play to its academic and research strengths, provide strong support for the studies needed by the country, and contribute to the faster change of growth model and sustainable economic and social development in China.

President of Beijing Normal University
Beijing, China

Zhong Binglin

Preface 4

This is the third consecutive time that I have received the invitation to write a preface for the annual *China Green Development Index Report* since 2010. I have accepted every invitation because the theoretical research on green development is of great significance. The green wave is sweeping over the world. Governments and the general public have opted to pursue green development and moved forward steadily. To follow the latest progress, identify the fundamental problems, and figure out the pattern of green development, in-depth theoretical research should be carried out and promoted by theorists at institutions of higher education.

It is heartening to see that the Scientific Outlook on Development and Economic Sustainability Research Base of Beijing Normal University, the Green Economy and Economic Sustainability Research Base of Southwestern University of Finance and Economics, and China Economic Monitoring and Analysis Center, National Bureau of Statistics of China, have jointly launched the *China Green Development Index Report 2012: Regional Comparison*, the third annual report of its kind. Compared with the previous two, this report features improvements and innovations in many aspects. Some indicators and weights are adjusted slightly based on the opinions of authoritative experts, making the report more scientific. In addition to the four cities newly included in the evaluation, survey questionnaires are also used to get the opinions of people in evaluated cities about local green development, making the report more comprehensive. The newly introduced "green development checkup tables" show clearly the strengths, weaknesses, and progress or regression of each province and evaluated city by specific indicators, making the report more instructive. The newly added policy recommendations on China's green development offered by many experts make the report more relevant and helpful for putting theory into practice. The international comparison of green development underscores the Chinese characteristics of the report in a global context.

The 2012 report comes out just before the opening of the 18th CPC National Congress, which adds to its special importance. The *Green Development Index Report* provides the guidelines for party leaders at all levels and the average people to follow the Scientific Outlook on Development, for promoting green development at both national and local levels, and for creating a greener life for the people. I'm convinced that, under the leadership of the CPC, China's great cause of socialism will prosper and burst with vitality on the path of green development.

Party Secretary of Southwestern University
of Finance and Economics
Chengdu, China

Zhao Dewu

Preface 5

The relationship between development and nature has never been so tense as it is today. All countries in the world are faced with the same challenge, i.e., how to promote the harmony between man and nature and achieve sustainable development. As Wen Jiabao said at the Stockholm+40 Partnership Forum for Sustainable Development on April 25, 2012, human beings are neither slaves nor masters of nature; rather, we should be its friends. We should promote sustainable development. To pursue green development is a global trend. It is also a long-term and arduous task and calls for new ideas and new practices.

Led by Professor Li Xiaoxi and Mr. Pan Jiancheng, the Green Economy and Economic Sustainability Research Base of Southwestern University of Finance and Economics, the Scientific Outlook on Development and Economic Sustainability Research Base of Beijing Normal University, and China Economic Monitoring and Analysis Center, National Bureau of Statistics of China, have jointly launched the annual *China Green Development Index Report* for three consecutive years since 2010. The report measures and evaluates the development of green economy in all provinces and major cities of China from three perspectives, i.e., Green Degree of Economic Growth, Carrying Capacity Potential of Natural Resources and Environment, and Support Degree of Government Policies. Widely acclaimed by all sectors, the report stands out as a great example of innovation in the theoretical research on green development. The 2010 report was recognized at the second China Soft Science Awards. The 2011 report was published in the Great Hall of the People; covered by many news media agencies including CCTV, Xinhua News Agency, and *People's Daily*; and translated into English with the financial support of the 2011 Classic China International Publishing Project launched by the General Administration of Press and Publication of China. The 2012 report is another joint effort of all members of the research group. Built on the previous two, this report is improved in many aspects and pushes the research on the Green Development Index (GDI) a big step forward.

Directly administered by the Chinese Ministry of Education, Southwestern University of Finance and Economics is also included in the country's 211 Project and 985 Project to build the platform for developing innovations in advantageous disciplines. It will continue to work together with all stakeholders to advance the research on green development so as to make its due contributions to the sustainability of the Chinese economy and society, the peaceful rise of the country, and the great rejuvenation of the Chinese nation.

President of Southwestern University of Finance
and Economics
Chengdu, China

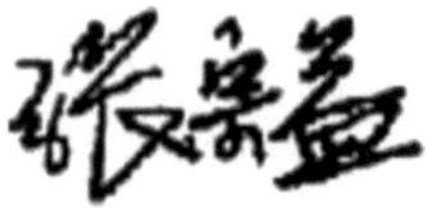

Zhang Zongyi

Expert Comments

Wu Jinglian: While improving the City Green Development Index (CGDI), the *China Green Development Index Report 2012: Regional Comparison* measures the GDI of 30 provinces and 38 cities across China, examines the green development in targeted areas, and points out the progress made in green development and the issues that deserve our attention. Obviously, after continuous efforts, the research on the GDI has become more profound and more practical and will undoubtedly play a significant role in supporting and guiding local green development and accelerating the shift in the philosophy of development. Pursuing green development is an important part of China's economic reform so the research group should continue to follow up the progress. In future research, proper emphasis may be placed on the analysis of the green development mechanism and survey on the factors restricting or even impeding green development, so as to incorporate green development closely into the institutional reform. That's my comment on this report and it is for reference only.

Li Yining: The *China Green Development Index Report 2012: Regional Comparison*, jointly prepared by the Scientific Outlook on Development and Economic Sustainability Research Base of Beijing Normal University, Green Economy and Economic Sustainability Research Base of Southwestern University of Finance and Economics, and China Economic Monitoring Center, National Bureau of Statistics of China, improves China's province and city GDI systems based on the country's GDI in 2011. It is a remarkable progress that makes the GDI more convincing. As far as the provincial study is concerned, the results of the interprovincial GDI comparison are credible because of the improved Province Green Development Index System, and conclusions are thus drawn, such as "eastern provinces are the best in green development and boast an obvious advantage in the green degree of economic growth," "western provinces enjoy a remarkable advantage in resources

To present a full picture of the experts' views, we have made only technical adjustments to the comments. We owe gratitude to these experts for their acknowledgment of and valuable feedback on our research findings.

and the environment but are at quite low levels of economic development," "central provinces have no distinct advantages and their green development level is yet to be improved," and "the three northeast provinces have a low level of green development and differ greatly from one another in this regard." These conclusions are well backed by facts and helpful to improve green development in the abovementioned areas. As to the study on urban GDI, four more cities are included in the evaluation and the analysis of green development in the evaluated cities is made, leading to such conclusions as "green development in eastern cities on the whole remains better," "the green development level in western cities rises steadily," "central cities lag behind in terms of green development," and "the green development level in four northeast cities (Dalian, Harbin, Shenyang, and Changchun) is good." Such analysis is also helpful to facilitate green development in the above cities in the future. Section IV of this report, i.e., Professors' Forum: Proposals for Green Development, is constructive. Experts and professors proceed from their specific field of research and offer their unique insights that are not confined to a particular topic. But it would be better if information about these experts and professors such as the organizations they work with and their fields of study (including major works or research findings) is also provided. In addition, the 2012 report is prepared based on the questionnaire survey organized by the National Bureau of Statistics. That helps to enrich the report with the public opinions on regional green development, which is very good. In the future, the research group may also undertake questionnaire surveys on specific issues. That's my comment on this report and it is for reference only.

Zhang Zhuoyuan: On the one hand, this report is more informative than the previous two (with four more cities covered, three more cities included in the international comparison of green development, and the inspiring part of professors' forum added), and the index systems are improved. It will play a positive role in raising people's green awareness and promoting local green development. On the other hand, it seems to me that some aspects still need to be improved after skimming through the report. First, in the Introduction part, Tianjin ranks 2nd and Shanghai 9th in the interprovincial comparison. But in the comparison between cities, Shanghai ranks 26th, beating Tianjin's 28th. It is understandable that rankings may vary due to the use of different indicators, but an explanation should be given for such a big difference. Moreover, the huge gap between the top two rankings in the interprovincial comparison needs to be explained as well. Second, I suggest adding indicators such as PM2.5 (especially in the city rankings) and precious metal content of land and changing the coverage of water supply to the coverage of clean water supply. Third, the data for some particularly important indicators such as CO_2 emission per capita and CO_2 emission per unit of land area are not provided in the report, and such data should be added once they are announced officially. Fourth, if possible, the evaluation and rankings of China's green development and environmental pollution by international organizations or relevant authorities of other countries might be included in future reports.

Wei Liqun: On the whole, the *China Green Development Index Report 2012: Regional Comparison* is clearly themed and properly structured. Rich in content and data, it provides profound analysis, makes several innovations, and is an outcome of scientific research that applies theory to practice and boasts an important reference mechanism. It has more distinctive features than the previous two reports, with major improvements made in the following four aspects: first, it revises the province and city indicators and includes more cities in the evaluation; second, it draws up special tables to examine the green development in evaluated provinces and cities and provides insightful analyses; third, a questionnaire survey is carried out so the input of public opinions is increased; fourth, it includes an international comparison of green development in the Appendices part. All the changes are necessary and add to the originality and appeal of the report. It is also advisable to: (1) research further into the implications of green development and the indicators to make the report more scientific and feasible, (2) make the measurement of evaluation indicators and data for green development as comparable as possible, and (3) analyze the GDI of cities by category such as provincial capital cities, large cities, medium-sized cities and small cities, to get a clearer picture of the green development levels of cities in the same category. That's my comment on this report and it is for reference only.

Chen Xiwen: In the past two decades, countries around the world have reached a consensus on pursuing sustainability. More and more countries have taken actions to better use resources, promote energy conservation and emissions reduction, facilitate green trade, and follow the path of green development. China is the world's most populous country with a vast territory, which is now at a critical stage in the process of building a moderately prosperous society and modernization. Opting for green development with Chinese characteristics is significant not only for implementing the Scientific Outlook on Development and achieving all-round, balanced, and sustainable development but also for promoting global sustainability and harmony. After years of efforts, the research group has created a cross-sectoral, cross-regional, and cross-disciplinary research network; prepared the basic groundwork; put in place a quite complete system of indicators; and presented some key research findings. The approach to research is maturing, the research methodology is getting more and more scientific, and a pool of highly competent researchers has been developed. In recent years, the social impacts of the report have been growing noticeably. It has played a significant role in promoting the implementation of the Scientific Outlook on Development, energy conservation and emissions reduction, environmental protection, and the development of eco-friendly industries at local level. I would like to make two suggestions for reference only. First, while the scientific development of agriculture promotes ecological protection, energy conservation and emissions reduction, and resource efficiency, irrational approaches to the development of agriculture will cause pollution, soil erosion, and ecological damage. Therefore, I suggest adding one or two indicators reflecting environmental impact and energy conservation and emissions reduction to the Primary Industry Indicators. Second, a summary should be prepared and translated into English to extend the international influence of the report.

Liu Shijin: The research on Green Development Index (GDI), led by Professor Li Xiaoxi, has continued for three consecutive years. By preparing the *China Green Development Index Report*, Prof. Li and his research group provide the guidelines for translating green concepts into green actions, which is significant theoretically and practically. Based on the research findings in the previous 2 years, the *China Green Development Index Report 2012: Regional Comparison* draws fully on the opinions contributed by people from all walks of life and features innovative contents such as "green development checkup" of some provinces and cities, public opinions based on the questionnaire survey, professors' forum, and international comparison of urban green development. Specifically, I think the 2012 report has the following characteristics. First, compared with the previous two, this report is prepared based on a better research approach. Slight adjustments are made to the province and city indicators, and four more cities are evaluated, making the research system more balanced. Second, the quality and depth of research are also improved. In particular, this report includes a section on public opinions, which means that the objective evaluation by indicators and the views of average people are both presented and thus add to the relevance of the report. Third, this report includes the "green development checkup tables" for provinces and cities, which is undoubtedly the biggest highlight of the report. I believe that the "checkup tables" will play an important role in promoting local green development. Besides, I would like to suggest that the research project, a major endeavor in the field of green development, focus on the more specific aspects of the realities about green development, probe deeper into the subject matter, and promote the application of research findings in practice so as to contribute more to China's green development and economic reform.

Lu Zhongyuan: The 2012 report impresses me in the following three aspects. First, the "green development checkup" is innovative in terms of methodology and content. All the provinces and 38 cities of China are involved in the checkup. The changes to their rankings by each indicator are indicated with multidimensional Chernoff faces and their green development is analyzed briefly. Such an approach is a distinct highlight of the report, making it more readable and straightforward. It presents to readers a general picture of how green development goes at local level, which province or city has progressed or regressed, as well as the specific areas calling for improvements. It is helpful for not only ordinary readers but also researchers and local leaders. The purpose of this report is to make local governments become aware of what they have done poorly in green development and consolidate what they have achieved, rather than simply announce the rankings or confuse readers with complicated indicators. Second, the section of professors' forum adds to the academic appeal and influence of the report. In this section, professors in both natural sciences and social sciences are invited to discuss green development broadly yet profoundly. The discussions cover the evolution of green development concepts (comparison of Chinese and foreign concepts and historical and modern concepts), technology and engineering, artifacts and systems, values and methodologies, and development strategies and implementation pathways and show the advantages of multidisciplinary and interdisciplinary researches and the latest development in their respective fields. I believe that it is very helpful to enhance the academic value of this report and stimulate readers to deliberate rationally on the cutting-edge issues and trends of green development. It is fair to say that this section is one of the highlights of the 2012 report. The ultimate purpose of the report, from its preparation to publication, is to allow policy makers, researchers, and all other sectors to build up the concept of promoting green development and ecological progress and translate it into their everyday actions, rather than focus only on the rankings by specific indicators. Third, it is commendable to dedicate a whole section to public opinions. In evaluating the green development level of a province or city, the report mainly uses objective statistical indicators, such as the level of economic and social development, the carrying capacity of the natural environment, and government intervention. It also takes in expert views and values public opinions. It might be hard to accurately describe the green development level by quantifying public perceptions as measurable indicators and using them together with objective indicators for evaluation, but it would be inappropriate to measure the state of green development without considering public opinions. Therefore, the questionnaire survey is conducted to complement the measurement by objective indicators, thus avoiding one-sidedness. It is noteworthy that subjective evaluation indicators such as the "degree of satisfaction" are often not positively, or even negatively, correlated with the economic growth level or green development level, which has been proved in the surveys on "happiness index" or "index of people's welfare" undertaken by some organizations. One possible explanation is that the more developed an area is, the more local people need in terms of public affairs and happiness, and thus the less satisfied they are with the reality. On the contrary, the less developed an area is, the less people need, and the more satisfied they are.

Gu Shengzu: One of the major characteristics of the *China Green Development Index Report 2012: Regional Comparison* is its inclusion of the measurement and comparison of international City Green Development Index. According to the international City Green Development Index System, the data for each indicator, and the method of measuring China's Green Development Index, the Green Development Index and three subindexes, namely, the Green Degree of Economic Growth, Carrying Capacity Potential of Natural Resources and Environment, and Support Degree of Government Policies, for 100 cities worldwide are calculated. The result shows that the top 10 cities are New York, Lille, Barcelona, Geneva, Belfast, Wellington, Busan, Zurich, San Francisco, and Turin; and the last 10 cities are St. Petersburg, Mumbai, Harare, Moscow, New Delhi, Kiev, Ulan Bator, Mexico City, Kolkata, and Rio de Janeiro. Among the 100 sample cities, Beijing ranks 75th and Shanghai 79th. The green development level of the two cities is below the average level of cities in Europe and the United States but far above that of cities in newly industrialized countries and other developing countries. Such an approach puts China's megacities in a global context and the state of their green development clearly depicted. The international comparison and "checkup tables" in this report remind me of WHO's global survey on air pollution and the IBM Global Commuter Pain Survey. According to the survey report released by WHO in

2011, Beijing ranks 1035th among the 1,100 cities surveyed worldwide and is one of the "dirtiest capitals" in the world. In the IBM commuter pain survey, Shenzhen and Beijing rank 2nd and 3rd, respectively, following Mexico City. As Hu Jintao said, "if we fail to protect the ecological environment, people will have no access to clean water, fresh air or safe food, and serious social problems will arise." In the 2012 Report on the Work of the Government, Wen Jiabao said that "we will start monitoring fine particles (PM2.5) in the Beijing-Tianjin-Hebei region, the Yangtze River Delta, the Pearl River Delta and other key areas as well as in municipalities directly under the central government and provincial capital cities." PM2.5 refers to fine particles in the air 2.5 μm or less in diameter, also known as respirable particles, which may cause extreme damage to human body. Statistics show that while the smoking population is decreasing, the incidence rate of lung cancer in Beijing is rising, along with the increased occurrence of foggy weather. The key to controlling the "urban diseases" caused by air pollution and achieving green development is that the government provides the guidance and defines clearly the responsibilities of all parties concerned who work together toward the same goal.

Zhou Hongren: Based on the systems of province and city indicators developed through the 2011 research on the Green Development Index (GDI), the *China Green Development Index Report 2012: Regional Comparison* measures and analyzes in depth the state of green development in provinces, autonomous regions, municipalities directly under the central government, and major cities in China and gives them a "green development checkup." Such measurement, analysis, and comparative studies require the collection of a lot of data and in-depth comparison so the results are hard-earned. Such serious and strenuous efforts have increased the depth of the research on the GDI and are significant in inspiring local governments to devote more attention to green development. I still suggest, as I did in 2011, taking into account the impact of technological advance, IT application in particular, on green development in future studies on the GDI, in order to guide central and local governments to drive green development by promoting technological advance and information technology. That's my comment on this report and it is for reference only.

Pan Yue: Green development is a key path for achieving sustainability and economic transformation and also a major development goal of countries around the world. On the completion of the *China Green Development Index Report 2012: Regional Comparison*, I would like to express my congratulations and make a comment on the report which is intended for reference only. First, the 2012 report, compiled under the leadership of Beijing Normal University, is a major exploration of China's green development, a practice of the Scientific Outlook on Development, and a milestone in the green development studies. The Green Development Index (GDI) represents another major green topic after the green GDP accounting in China. Second, in the principle of seeking truth from facts and improving step by step, the research group has set up the indicator systems based on Green Degree of Economic Growth, Carrying Capacity Potential of Natural Resources and Environment, and Support Degree of Government Policies and the corresponding weighting system to measure provincial and urban green development in China; evaluated the GDI of 30 provinces, autonomous regions, and municipalities directly under the central government as well as 38 cities in China; and produced the *China Green Development Index Report 2012: Regional Comparison*. Third, the indicator system is scientific and rational, so is the use of average value and standard deviation formula in the evaluation. That makes the evaluation results well founded on the whole. The use of average value and standard deviation formula, however, entails the normal distribution of results and implies that “the average value is the target for each green development indicator.” It seems to me that the role of green development policy objectives should be stressed and is worthy of studies. Moreover, the evaluation results might be biased since environmental quality indicators weigh less than enough in the province GDI system, and environmental quality is an important measure of green development. Fourth, I would like to suggest the following in future evaluation: drawing more on international experience, particularly the evaluation indicator systems of international authorities such as the United Nations Environment Programme (UNEP), the Organisation for Economic Co-operation and Development (OECD), and the World Bank; introducing indicators such as the ratio of investment in green development to GDP, the proportion of green energy, the proportion of population exposed to pollution, the quality of water environment, the quality of atmospheric environment, and the quality of soil environment; setting the policy objective for each evaluation indicator instead of replacing it with the “average value”; and comparing the evaluation results with those produced by other organizations (such as the evaluation of regional environmental competitiveness and green economy). Considering that the results are relative, it would be better to present them in arrays and the definition and source of data by each indicator, the method of data quality control, etc. should be clarified.

Gan Zangchun: China’s Green Development Index (GDI) research has continued for three consecutive years. Its research methods and findings have played their due role in facilitating economic and social development, thus receiving great attention and wide recognition from the academia and even the policy implementers. Compared with the previous 2 years, the research group for the 2012 report improved the indicators according to the realities and expert views, added more cities for evaluation and the international comparison of urban green development, and organized a questionnaire survey to increase the impacts of the research and make the research findings more comprehensive, scientific, and relevant. The findings of the 2012 study underscore the harsh fact that regional economic and social development is unbalanced in China: eastern areas enjoy a high level of economic development, value green development, and have made achievements in this regard; western areas are richly endowed with resources but slow in economic development; central areas are picking up the development pace, but the carrying capacity of resources and environment, a key indicator of green economy, has become a major bottleneck in their pursuit of sound and rapid development. The fact deserves the attention of implementers of the Rise of Central China Plan and the Western Development Strategy. We should consider the realities of resources and environment rather than blindly seek growth in quantity. That's a message this report conveys to those engaged in the efforts to promote economic and social development. What's more, the discussions of experts and scholars in different fields on green economy add to the weight of the report from different perspectives and enrich its contents. A global consensus has been reached on green economy, and it has drawn the growing attention of governments around the world. The Chinese government has introduced targets concerning energy conservation, emissions reduction, and ecological protection in the 12th Five-Year Plan, showing how it values green economy and what it has done to promote its growth. Currently, China is on the world's average level in terms of how green economy is valued and promoted and even leads the world theoretically speaking and in some specific fields. To increase the impacts of the report, I suggest that the research group, while continuing to improve the index systems, study the institutional and legal support for green economy or include the degree of legal support as a major part of green economic indicators for analysis and comparison. To achieve healthy growth in the long run, the idea of green development needs to be not only translated into actions but also incorporated into the legal system.

Liu Wei: The *China Green Development Index Report 2012: Regional Comparison* features remarkable improvements in the number of samples, the inclusiveness of data, and the revision of weights, thus being much more convincing. What's more, the newly included international comparison of City Green Development Index not only opens up new horizons for the readers but also enriches the scientific references for China's urban analysis. Notably, the "green development checkup tables" of provinces and cities and the ensuing brief analysis make the report more targeted and relevant. It is a standard and method of applied analysis whose impacts matter much more than the content. The explanation of the methods, indicators, and definitions in this report is necessary but far from enough. Since it is important to the following analysis, arguments, and conclusions, it would be better to cite more materials to back up the explanation. Besides, is it possible to add some correlation analysis, such as the correlation between major selected indicators or between major economic indicators and the core environmental (resource) indicators? Even the analysis of the correlation between only a few indicators (major indicators of course) is helpful for us to identify new issue and strengthen the logic in the analysis. It's worth exploring even if the correlation is not that strong, for we may find something interesting. These are my personal opinions about the report. Some are just rough ideas and thus may not be well grounded.

Ge Jianping: After the Green Index Press Conference at the Great Hall of the People in September 2011, the research group led by Mr. Li Xiaoxi solicited opinions extensively, improved the Green Development Index (GDI) system, and continued to publish the *China Green Development Index Report 2012: Regional Comparison*. After reading the report, I find that this is another upgrade of the GDI. I've read all of the GDI reports published in the past three consecutive years and can tell the proactive and strategic significance of the green development theory and evaluation system developed by Mr. Li and his research group. First, the GDI research is to give an annual "green development checkup" to the governments in a scientific and continued way so as to provide guidance for them. According to the theory of Mr. Li, green economic growth is driven by resources and the environment, and the government should play it due role in facilitating such a process. Second, while there is a need to raise the awareness of the public about green development, their opinions also matter and the effectiveness of government practices in this regard needs to be recognized by them. The two press conferences on the GDI attracted close attention not only from government departments but also from the general public. As far as I know, Mr. Li and his research group are making a questionnaire survey on green development effectiveness to find out how the public are satisfied with green development, which will surely promote green development theoretically and practically. Third, the research group aims to promote the scientific development of governments at all levels and check and advise on the change of growth model. Both green development, a concept proposed by Mr. Li, and the Green New Deal are about pursuing development in a scientific way, so the theory is easy to be recognized by the international community. Fourth, this report includes valuable "checkup" information of different provinces and cities in China. I hope that it will draw the close attention of governments at all levels and that the annual "checkup" will become an integral part of government operations to identify and solve any problems before it's too late and achieve healthy development.

Bian Huimin: I received a phone call from the campus hospital of Southwestern University of Finance and Economics about the annual medical checkup when I had just finished reading the *China Green Development Index Report 2012: Regional Comparison* (draft). What a coincidence! The report is mainly about the "green development checkup" of 30 provinces and 38 cities in China. I am most impressed by the people-oriented mentality displayed in the report which is also core of the spirit of scientific development. I find three characteristics in the report. First, it supplements the Green Development Index (GDI) with the "green development checkup." The GDI is developed not merely for ranking provinces and cities of the country by their performance in promoting green development but to guide the government, enterprises, and the public to think and do in a green way. One of the major innovations of the 2012 report is the introduction of the "green development checkup tables," which are designed to "check the health" of each evaluated province and city based on the GDI indicator system in order to find out their areas for improvement in green development. The smiling and weeping Chernoff faces in the checkup tables are intended to indicate the progress and regression in green development. They make it easier for the readers to compare the yearly data of each province or city surveyed and find out whether it has progressed or regressed compared with the previous year so that the report looks much more accessible than the big subject. Such "green development checkup" will lead China to the path of healthier growth. Second, it presents both experts' views and the perceptions of the public, another innovation of the report. The newly included two sections are entitled "Professors' Forum" and "Public Opinions," respectively. On the one hand, experts carry out an objective analysis of the problems encountered in the process of China's green development from their particular perspectives and put forward their proposals in this regard; on the other hand, both online and field surveys through questionnaires are conducted in cities covered in the evaluation, and the public opinions on regional green development are shown in the survey results. Green development is ultimately for the free development of individuals. The report embodies the spirit of putting people above all by supplementing theoretical research with the perceptions of the general public. Third, it combines statistical calculation and measurement with field surveys. Take Chengdu as an example. Chengdu is recognized as a city which "visitors would never want to leave," but its GDI ranking for the year of 2009 is low in the 2011 report. It also strikes the students and faculty of Southwestern University of Finance and Economics, which is located in Chengdu, that there is a difference between the research finding and public opinions. Therefore, the person responsible for the 2011 report and the research group visited Chengdu and had in-depth discussions with local authorities including the Publicity Department of CPC Chengdu Municipal Committee, Chengdu Municipal Development and Reform Commission, Chengdu Urban and Rural Construction Commission, Chengdu Bureau of Statistics, and Chengdu Bureau of Environmental Protection. It is those discussions that have inspired the research group to add "Green Development Checkup" and "Public Opinions" to the 2012 report. The research group's rigorous and responsible attitude is well displayed in its efforts to supplement authoritative data with the real voice of local people. Thanks to that, this report is made more deindustrialized or more well founded. At the macrolevel, the need to grow green economy has become a global consensus, and China has made it a national strategy to implement the Scientific Outlook on Development, change the growth model, and achieve sustainable development by making the economy green. At the microlevel, however, problems that threat people's well-being such as environmental pollution, traffic congestion, and food safety are still serious. In my opinion, green economy is not only an approach to or a concept of development but also a way of life. It is more than merely reaching the targets for energy conservation and emissions reduction. It is about protecting the environment, resources, and climate while pursuing economic and social development so that the human species will sustain its growth. We need to grow green economy not only because we have to alleviate the immediate impacts of economic growth on resources and the environment but also because "being green" comes with human progress and is indispensable to a better life. "Greenness" is an indication of life, and to some extent, it is life. A healthier life is ensured with "checkup" and likewise China will grow in a healthier way with the "green development checkup."

Xu Xianchun: The *China Green Development Index Report 2012: Regional Comparison* is as scientific and objective as the 2010 and 2011 reports, with detailed data, strong arguments, and richer contents. The 2012 report revises the province and city indicator systems, includes the "checkup tables" on provincial and urban green development, and analyzes the Green Development Index (GDI) of each province and city. In particular, it makes an international comparison of urban green development and ranks the areas at different levels of development. Such an approach helps to find out the development pattern and characteristics of the world's green cities as well as China's strengths and weaknesses compared with them and thus advance the development of green cities in the country. As suggested by the experts, the research group conducted a questionnaire survey on public satisfaction, with the help of the National Bureau of Statistics. The goal of growing green economy is not only to improve people's living standards but also to increase people's sense of happiness and satisfaction. The average people's opinions are the best measure of the progress in promoting green development. Although the survey results are not available yet, I believe that they will provide important information about how local people see the development of green economy and help us get closer to the path of green development that benefits the people. The need to grow green economy has become a global consensus. Governments and enterprises across the globe are taking measures to speed up the growth of green economy featuring low-carbon and high-resource efficiency. One of the two main topics at the UN Conference on Sustainable Development in Rio de Janeiro in June 2012 is the role of green economy in sustainable development and poverty eradication. Green economy, as an important means for achieving sustainability, helps to eradicate poverty and adjust the economic structure. To grow green economy will entail enormous efforts and take a long time. The publication of this annual research report is important for changing China's growth model and inspiring local governments to think differently and step up the efforts to promote green economy. I hope that the research group will continue to study the growth of green economy at home and abroad, keep improving their research methods, and write up more findings in the report.

Zhang Xinshi: It gives me great pleasure to read the *China Green Development Index Report 2012: Regional Comparison* following the 2010 and 2011 reports. Compared with the previous two, this report features improved indicator systems, wider coverage of evaluation, the "green development checkup tables" and analysis, public opinions, and international comparison of urban green development. Besides, it is more practical with a more balanced theoretical framework, more extensive data, more thorough analysis, and more comprehensive contents. But I would like to bring up two questions about the report. Would it be better to consider the differences between evaluated cities in geographical zone when checking their performance by Resource Abundance and Ecological Conservation Indicators, particularly the proportion of area of wetlands in total area of a region? Is it possible to improve the design of evaluation indicators and their weights so as to take into account both subjective and objective factors?

Niu Wenyuan: The first *China Green Development Index Report* was published in 2010. Since then, the report has attracted a lot of media attention at home and abroad. Most of the comments on the report are positive, and it is believed that establishing the Green Development Index (GDI) as a standard will better promote green and sustainable development in China when the country is changing its growth model. My views on the 2012 report are as follows. First, the 2012 report features more balanced indicator systems and better-founded evaluation compared with the 2011 report. The drive to make improvements is embodied throughout the report and makes it more scientific. Second, as China is changing its growth model, the GDI has been taken as a criterion for evaluating local development quantitatively. That makes the report very practical. Over the past three decades, many local governments have been misled by the philosophy of seeking GDP growth at the cost of resources and the environment, and the extensive growth model has undermined the sustainability of development. The introduction of the GDI is conducive to the fast and healthy growth of the economy. Third, based on the its quantitative indicator systems, the 2012 report compares the green development in each province, autonomous region, and municipality directly under the central government in China. The biggest feature of the report is that it recognizes the differences between different parts of the country in terms of the stage of development and geographical features but does not rank them merely by GDP. Therefore, I would suggest that policy makers and administrative departments consult the report. Fourth, it uses weights properly and makes adjustments according to geographical features and the stage of development. Fifth, I suggest including the institutional design for China's green development in future reports.

Wang Yi: More and more countries in the world have opted for green economy, one of the two main topics at the 2012 UN Conference on Sustainable Development, to handle the financial crisis, meet the environmental and resource challenges, and achieve sustainable development. The studies on green development evaluation and related indicators are at the cutting edge of the research on green economy. As the biggest developing country in the world, China is also actively promoting green development and a green transformation and has proposed in the 12th Five-Year Plan to change its growth model by achieving green and low-carbon development so as to build a resource-efficient and environment-friendly society. The *China Green Development Index Report* has been published for three consecutive years. The reports represent the attempts of the research group to help translate the idea of green development into actions based on the continual research on the Green Development Index (GDI). They are strategic, proactive, scientific, and conducive to China's green development in both theoretical and practical terms. A continuation of the previous two, the 2012 report interprets the idea of green development from three aspects, i.e., economy, resources and the environment, and the government, and makes a comprehensive evaluation of the green development levels of provinces and major cities in China. Compared with the 2011 report, the 2012 report takes in expert views and survey results, has some indicators whose weights are adjusted properly, includes four more cities according to relevant rules, and analyzes in detail the green development levels of provinces and 38 major cities and the causes of changes. The depth of the research is increased, and the report is made more balanced, scientific, and inclusive. The 2012 report has two highlights. First, it adds the "green development checkup tables" for cities, which together with the GDI are used to evaluate the green development in those cities. The tables help to identify the problems encountered by the cities in pursuing green development and show them clearly where to improve in this regard. Second, based on the questionnaire survey, the evaluated cities are ranked by public satisfaction to complement the rankings by the GDI, avoiding the one-sidedness caused by objective indicators and statistical data analysis. The solicitation of public opinions helps to increase the relevance of green development evaluation. In addition, I would like to make three suggestions on how to improve the report. First, green development theories should be studied further and the indicator system should be improved based on them. The research on green development is still in its infancy. There is no universally recognized definition or model. Developing related theories based on China's realities is important to China and other developing countries. Second, many studies have been done on the indicator system in China and other countries. I suggest that the research group make a comparative study on all the green development indicator systems to design a better system of indicators for the report and identify the direction and priority of research. Third, comparisons can be made between different areas and different stages of development. I suggest adding the comparison between stages of development to the report so as to give a full account of how green development goes at local level. The suggestions are for reference only.

Wei Jie: In my opinion, the *China Green Development Index Report 2012: Regional Comparison* marks a great stride forward. In particular, the design of "checkup tables" and the international comparison of urban green development make the report more scientific and international. Since the Green Development Index report is an independent evaluation system, free from the impact of power, money, or the media. Its independence is built on scientific indicators and evaluation so it's significant to improve its indicator system and international comparison.

Pan Jiahua: Generally speaking, this report is very informative, valuable, and improved in many aspects compared with the 2011 report. I find the following particularly praiseworthy: first, the index is adjusted to better showcase the reality; second, the newly added "checkup" part gives a clearer picture of the developments at local level; third, the "Professors' Forum" section offers many insights. But for an index report, there is always room for improvement. I would like to make the following suggestions on how to improve the report. The first is about the indicator system. GDP per capita may be changed to disposable income per capita or the disposable income of rural residents; output or emissions per unit area may be changed to output or emissions per unit effective area so as to avoid any error on the Gobi desert on the Tibetan Plateau. If it's too late to make such changes for the 2012 report, they may be taken into account in the next report. The second is about the carrying capacity of resources. Qinghai, Inner Mongolia, and Guizhou all rank high by the Green Development Index (GDI) because of the good carrying capacity of their resources. But the reality is that there is grassland degeneration in Qinghai and Inner Mongolia and desertification and water shortage in Guizhou, which should be explained. Beijing's high ranking also needs extra explanation because the city suffers from groundwater overexploitation and high energy consumption and emissions per capita. It should be explained why Shanghai and Jiangsu rank low by the carrying capacity of resources and environment. External input needs to be considered in checking the carrying capacity of resources and environment in the Yangtze River Delta and the Pearl River Delta. For example, the water resources may be from the Yangtze River Basin and the Pearl River Basin, and pollution may be diluted because of the maritime weather. It is the opposite in Qinghai, Tibet, and Inner Mongolia in Western China. They have small populations due to the low carrying capacity of their resources and environment. The rankings by city seem to make more sense than those by province. The third is about the "Professors' Forum." Its content is commendable, but the background information on the professors should be provided so that readers can know more about them.

Fan Hengshan: Based on the summary of related research findings at home and abroad, the *China Green Development Index Report 2012: Regional Comparison* improves the Green Development Index System based on the realities in China, uses the system to measure and evaluate the green development in different provinces and cities, and analyzes regional differences in green development, providing useful information for better changing the growth model and achieving green economic growth. The 2012 report has a sound structure on the whole, and its indicator system is rationally designed to give a full picture of the realities about green development in China. Its evaluation results are basically in line with the realities in the areas surveyed and point out the direction for future green development in these areas. The 2012 report also features a questionnaire survey on public satisfaction, which is helpful to attract the participation of more stakeholders. The combination of public recognition, public opinions, and theoretical research makes the research findings more representative. The new section of "Professors' Forum" helps to increase the depth of the research and provides different perspectives on path selection and the way to promote green development. The 2012 report compares not only provinces and cities in China but also representative cities worldwide. The international experience in green development is summarized for China to draw on. I would like to suggest improving the report as follows: first, carry out an in-depth analysis of the measurement results and propose more targeted and practical policy recommendations on how to reduce regional disparities; second, make a comparative analysis of different countries, such as the comparison between the BASIC countries and the comparison between developed countries and China, to help China better promote green development; third, design some indicators that are able to distinguish areas with unique features from others.

Xia Guang: The *China Green Development Index Report 2012: Regional Comparison* is about the "green development checkup" of provinces and cities in China. It makes more in-depth analysis based on the 2011 report, has great academic and practical significance, and presents research findings of very high quality. The 2012 report tells readers about the most recent progress in green development all over the world with detailed background information. China has made some progress in promoting green development in implementing the 12th Five-Year Plan, and other countries have also developed massive green investment plans. All these efforts indicate that it is necessary to make a quantitative evaluation of green development. The 2012 report improves the City Green Development Index System, adjusts the weights of indicators, and increases the number of cities for evaluation, making the indicator system better suited to the realities in China. The major part of the 2012 report is about the quantitative comparison of provinces and cities in terms of green development level. Since 60 indicators are applied to the evaluation of each province or city, the workload is huge, which makes the 2012 report valuable and trustworthy. As to the final evaluation results, opinions may vary from person to person, but the rigorous and scientific attitude adopted in preparing the report is widely acknowledged. The conclusions of the 2012 report are on the whole credible. Eastern areas have bigger advantages in green development, the green development level in central areas is below the average, and western areas are weak in green development. These conclusions are generally in line with people's perceptions. In the Appendices part, an explanation is provided specially for the low ranking of Chengdu in the 2011 annual report, which shows the scientific spirit of not evading any question. Beijing is given a score of 0.655, far higher than other provinces (e.g., Tianjin, the runner up, scores only 0.215), so more discussion is recommended. Some basic environmental quality indicators should have the veto power. For example, if the air quality is below a certain level, the green development in that area should be deemed substandard. The "International Comparison of Urban Green Development" is very good, and I suggest moving it from the Appendices part to the main body of the report. The "Analysis of Chengdu's GDI Ranking in 2009" is also very good and I suggest moving it to the third section "Public Opinions."

Su Wei: The report is based on the research on China's Green Development Index (GDI) from three levels: interprovincial comparison, intercity comparison, and public opinions. Based on the research findings in 2010 and 2011, the 2012 report adds the intercity comparison and indicators on public opinions and shows more the part of the GDI system that puts people first and focuses on social progress, further improving the system. With strict logic followed, the report is an academic innovation and has great value in guiding practice. As to how to improve this report, I would like to suggest the following: first, take into account how different parts of China use domestic and international resources in the context of economic globalization, their special roles in the global production landscape, and the possible influences of such roles on the method and results of measuring the GDI; second, in studying the GDI of provinces and cities, I suggest considering how the carrying capacity of resources and environment in some areas, the regional differences in the level of economic development, and the potential for development influence the selection of indicators, the distribution of weights, and the method of measurement, and conducting a targeted comparative analysis. My comment is for reference only.

Chen Dongqi: More and more countries in the world have opted for green development. Human beings are striving to seek a model of green growth which will lead to greater equity and sustainability. To establish such a model and develop more effective strategies and policies, scholars need to provide supporting research data and findings. And the compiling of the *China Green Development Index Report* led by Professor Li Xiaoxi is one of the major academic achievements in this regard. The report provides comparative conclusions based on the systematic survey and analysis of the Green Development Index (GDI) of each province and major city in China. It can be used to inform the formulation of green development policies and lead local governments to grow a green and low-carbon economy. I hope that this annual report will continue to come out in the future.

Jia Kang: With the support and cooperation of several institutions, the research group led by Professor Li Xiaoxi, Vice Chairman of the Academic Committee of Beijing Normal University, and researcher Pan Jiancheng, Deputy Director-General of China Economic Monitoring and Analysis Center of the National Bureau of Statistics, has released the *China Green Development Index Report 2012: Regional Comparison*, the third report of its kind since 2010. Congratulations. After three decades of rapid economic growth since the introduction of the reform and opening up policy, China is faced with strategic opportunities as well as growing challenges in such aspects as resources, the environment, and income distribution. Only by pursuing all-round, balanced, and sustainable development, specifically increasing energy efficiency, reducing emissions, controlling pollution, and implementing the green development strategy, can China break through the bottlenecks, speed up the change of its growth model, promote economic and social transformation, and move closer to the grand goal of building a moderately prosperous society in all respects and completing the modernization drive. Therefore, preparing the *China Green Development Index Report* based on in-depth and detailed research from the perspective of regional comparison is indeed in the interest of the whole country and its sustainable development. Apart from the quantified data for comparison which can also be seen in the previous two reports, the 2012 report covers more evaluated cities, introduces the "checkup tables" for evaluation from multiple perspectives, includes for the first time public opinions obtained from the questionnaire survey with the help of the National Bureau of Statistics, and makes an international comparison of urban green development. All these innovations indicate that this annual research project has been very productive. As a researcher in the field of green development, I would like to express my admiration for the excellent work of the research group, and I'm convinced that the publication of the 2012 report will play a positive role in driving green development at both national and local levels.

Zhang Jianhua: The *China Green Development Index Report 2012: Regional Comparison* presents a scientific and sound system of green development indicators, as well as the in-depth and detailed analysis, comparison, and evaluation of provincial and urban green development in China based on the indicator system so it is important for guiding local practices in making the shift to green development. The 2012 report features breakthroughs in the following aspects. First, the indicator system is improved. As to the Province Green Development Index, the weighting of some Third-Class Indicators is adjusted. For example, the weights of eight subindicators about pollutant emissions per capita and per unit land area under the indicator of "Carrying Capacity Potential of Natural Resources and Environment" are reduced moderately so that weight distribution is more balanced and overweighting caused by the repeated consideration of some factors in different methods of measurement is avoided. As to the City Green Development Index, similar adjustments are also made so that urban green development is better evaluated and compared. Second, it uses Chernoff faces in the analysis of green development at provincial and municipal levels. The report gives a "green development checkup" to 30 provinces and 38 cities and describes their progress or regression in pursing green development, providing very useful information for the provinces and cities to make improvements. Third, it makes an international comparison of green development, which is helpful to improve the green development indicator system and putting China's green development drive in a global context. Moreover, it would be better if the commonalities and differences of different areas in pursuing development are both considered, and the Third-Class Indicators and the weighting are better designed. For example, under the Third-Class Indicator "Support Degree of Provincial Government Policies," "investment in converting cultivated land into forests and grassland per unit of area of cultivated land" might be relevant only to provinces/autonomous regions/municipalities directly under the central government charged with a heavy task of converting cultivated land into forests and grassland.

Chen Zongsheng: After three decades of rapid economic growth, China is faced with growing challenges from resources and the eco-environment and it's urgent to change its growth model. As the idea of green development is being translated into actions worldwide, China has attached more importance to green development. The 12th Five-Year Plan lays down higher requirements for China's green development. The task of saving energy and reducing emissions is challenging. A major focus during the 12th Five-Year Plan period is to truly change the growth model and step up the efforts in building a resource-efficient and environment-friendly society. As scientific and objective as the previous two reports, the *China Green Development Index Report 2012: Regional Comparison* has come out with the joint efforts of scholars such as Li Xiaoxi and Pan Jiancheng. The report seeks to give a comprehensive and objective account of how green development goes in each province and major city in China. A useful supplement to the studies on the change of growth model, the report helps to increase the depth of domestic researches on green development, the Green Development Index (GDI) in particular. The 2012 report differs greatly from the 2011 report in terms of structure. Apart from the "Introduction" part, it has four sections, respectively, on "Provinces," "Cities," "Public Opinions," and "Professors' Forum." The report measures green development at provincial and municipal levels in two separate sections and dedicates three chapters under each section to the measurement by three First-Class Indicators. Based on the comparative analysis of measurement results, the report proposes the approach to promoting green development in each province and major city. "Green development checkup" is introduced to the evaluation of major cities and a brief analysis is given based on ranking changes by each indicator. In addition, feature and theme sections that were used in the 2011 report are replaced by new sections such as "Public Opinions" and "Professors' Forum." Based on the opinions of evaluation and statistical experts, the research group improves the Province and City Green Development Index Systems by taking into account all factors including the macroeconomy, ecological environment, resources and energy, and government policies. Specifically, the weighting of some indicators is adjusted for the Province Green Development Index System, while the weighting of indicators is adjusted properly and four cities are added for the City Green Development Index System. Such changes make the report more useful in informing the policies of each province and major city on achieving scientific development and promoting the harmony between man and nature and expand the scope of domestic research on GDI measurement. As to the research perspective, apart from using objective statistical data to measure and analyze green development, the report presents the opinions of the general public on green development. Since such opinions cannot be directly derived from statistical data, the research group launched a questionnaire survey on public satisfaction with green development in major cities. Such an approach complies with the Scientific Outlook on Development that puts people above all, complements the current GDI research, and helps to raise public awareness about the problems in resources and energy, ecological environment, and green development. Generally speaking, the report is intended to contribute to the green development cause in China. Professors in natural and social sciences have been invited to share their views on green development in China, providing different perspectives for research. It offers more inspirations for promoting green development, helps the general public to have a better and deeper understanding of green development, raises the awareness of investors about the green cost of investment projects, and provides important information for governments to evaluate the performance of local officials in promoting green development. There are also some improvements to be made. For example, while the role of government policies is stressed, attention should also be paid to the role of the market mechanism in reducing pollution and emissions, adjusting industrial structure, and changing the growth model; some environmental quality indicators need to be designed more properly. In short, this report is full of detailed data and thorough analysis, and its conclusions are conducive to future theoretical research and policy making. I would like to recommend it to theoretical researchers and government officials.

Qiu Dong: The *China Green Development Index Report 2012: Regional Comparison*, whose preparation is led by Professor Li Xiaoxi, is the third one of its kind following the 2010 and 2011 reports. The database formed based on the continual empirical research will surely increase the role the report plays in guiding China's green development. It is commendable that the 2012 report introduces the "green development checkup tables" for provinces and cities, the brief analysis of their green development, and the section "Public Opinions," underlining the role of empirical analysis in serving social development. In terms of methodology, the research group has drawn on international experience in the empirical research on the same subject and taken into full account the characteristics of China at the current stage development. Therefore, this report not only bridges empirical analysis and policy making but also provides an example for improving the methodology of multi-indicator evaluation.

Contents

List of Figures

List of Tables

Chapter 1
Introduction

Xiaoxi Li and Jiancheng Pan

The theme of the 42nd World Economic Forum Annual Meeting is "The Great Transformation: Shaping New Models." As Klaus Schwab, Executive Chairman of the World Economic Forum said, "the great transformation is generating tremendous opportunities for humankind to live in a more prosperous, more peaceful world... What we are trying to do at this annual meeting is to re-paint a blueprint for constructive collaborations". At the current stage of economic and social development, only by accelerating transformation of the economic development mode and building up the harmony between humankind and nature can we and our future generations enjoy sustainable development and happiness.

1.1 Growing Green Becomes a Concerted Action Worldwide

So far, the green development concept has been translated into common actions at home and abroad and green actions across the globe are just unfolding. China attaches great importance to green development and its Green Development Index (GDI) has attracted great attention from all sectors.

In recent years, pursuing green development has become a global trend and increasingly a global consensus. Various meetings, forums and reports on this subject have mushroomed. Governments have taken actions one after another, seeking to lead this global trend.

X. Li (✉)
School of Economics and Resource Management, Beijing Normal University, Beijing, China
e-mail: lxx62205058@163.com

J. Pan
China Economic Monitoring and Analysis Center, National Bureau of Statistics of China, Beijing, China
e-mail: panjc@gj.stats.cn

X. Li and J. Pan (eds.), *China Green Development Index Report 2012: Regional Comparison*, Current Chinese Economic Report Series,
DOI 10.1007/978-3-642-54178-0_1,

In February 2011, the United Nations Environment Programme (UNEP) launched a Green Economy Report in Nairobi, the capital city of Kenya. According to the report, from now till 2050, if 2 % of the global GDP is invested in greening 10 central sectors of the economy every year, the global economy will make the transition to a low-carbon and green path. The report also argues that green economy means better utilization of natural resources and sustainable growth and should be more efficient and fairer.[1]

In October 2011, the first Global Green Growth Forum was held in Copenhagen. At the Forum, governments and businesses were called on to work together to seek new approaches to grow green economy and specific public-private actions were scoped or launched in the following areas: sustainable biofuels for civil aviation, green international trades, global green public procurement, energy efficiency and renewable energy. The Forum was intended to expand public-private partnerships, inspire the innovative thinking and actions of all parties concerned to tackle key obstacles, and push the global economy to shift to a green growth model. More than 200 global leaders representing governments, businesses and the financial sector were brought together to talk about the green development of four major industries, namely energy, transport, trade and finance, and the government-business collaboration on promoting global green growth. In addressing the Forum, UN Secretary-General Ban Ki-moon underscored how important it is that the government and businesses work together to green the global economy. He said, "the global green agenda can help drive the advancement of sustainable development for the 21st century. It is good business – good politics – and good for society."[2]

In November 2011, UNEP launched for the first time in Beijing its Green Economy Report entitled "Towards a Green Economy: Pathways to Sustainable Development and Poverty Eradication – A Synthesis for Policy Makers".[3] The report shows that developing green economy has become a global consensus and governments and businesses are taking measures to speed up the shift to a low-carbon, resource-efficient and socially inclusive green economy. The report explains the challenges facing human beings such as the accelerating depletion of natural resources and the worsening food crisis and points out that green economy will become a new engine of growth.

From November to December 2011, the 17th Conference of the Parties (COP17) to the United Nations Framework Convention on Climate Change (UNFCCC) was held in Durban, South Africa.[4] It approved the Durban Package Outcome, set up the Ad Hoc Working Group on the Durban Platform for Enhanced Action, and decided to and begin the second commitment period of the Kyoto Protocol and launch the

---

[1] UNEP. *Towards a Green Economy: Pathways to Sustainable Development and Poverty Eradication.* www.unep.org/greeneconomy. 2011.

[2] http://finance.591hx.com/article/2011-10-13/0000079305s.shtml, October 13, 2011.

[3] UNEP. *Towards a Green Economy: Pathways to Sustainable Development and Poverty Eradication – A Synthesis for Policy Makers.* www.unep.org/greeneconomy. 2011.

[4] Official website of the UNFCCC. http://unfccc.int/meetings/durban_nov_2011/ses-sion/6294.php, 2011.

Green Climate Fund. Germany and Denmark pledged to contribute 40 million euros and 15 million euros respectively as the operating fee and the start-up funding.

The world is paying more and more attention to green development issues. Governments and organizations have taken green actions and the green development concept has been spreading all over the world. It is fair to say that the government sector is leading the green development. In May 2011, the Environment Department of San Francisco, organized the city's first Green Economy Forum, at which participants made greenhouse gas reduction recommendations relating to business, energy independence, transport and etc.[5] By displaying several best practices, Hamburg has proved that ecological sustainability and economic growth can be achieved at the same time even in a highly industrialized port city. It won the 2011 European Green Capital Award created by the European Commission.[6] At the end of 2011, the European Commission indicated that it would invest 32 billion euros in clean energy, energy efficiency and other fields, and the largest part of the investment would go to clean energy technology.[7]

The Chinese government also highly values the development of green economy. The 12th Five-Year Plan stresses the importance of "green development". It is China's first green development plan and marks China's launch and participation in the world green revolution. The year of 2011 is the first year of the 12th Five-Year Plan period. In the 2012 Report on the Work of the Government, Premier Wen Jiabao reviewed the work done in the previous year, saying that "we made progress in conserving energy, reducing emissions and protecting the ecological environment. We adopted and implemented the Comprehensive Work Plan for Conserving Energy and Reducing Emissions and the Work Plan for Controlling Greenhouse Gas Emissions for the 12th Five-Year Plan period, and the Guidelines on Strengthening Key Environmental Protection Tasks. The installed power capacity using clean energy reached 290 million kw, an increase of 33.56 million kw over the previous year. We strengthened the development of major energy conservation and environmental protection projects. We increased daily sewage treatment capacity by 11 million tons in urban areas, and installed desulphurization systems on all new coal-fired power-generating units with a total capacity of over 50 million kw. We tightened controls over industries that are energy intensive, have high emissions or possess excess production capacity, and closed down outdated production facilities whose production capacity amounted to 150 million tons of cement, 31.22 million tons of iron, and 19.25 million tons of coke." He also pointed out the major tasks for 2012, saying that "we will conserve energy, reduce emissions, and protect the ecological environment. The key to conserving energy and reducing emissions is to save energy, improve energy efficiency, and reduce pollution. We will promptly formulate and promulgate a work plan to appropriately control total energy consumption, and move quickly

---

[5] http://news.xinhuanet.com/photo/2011-05/26/c_121461274_2.htm, May 26, 2011.

[6] http://news.qq.com/a/20101123/000787.htm, November 23, 2010.

[7] http://www.in-en.com/capital/html/energy_10561056641226979.html, December 15, 2011.

to overhaul the pricing mechanism of energy. We will use economic, legal and the necessary administrative means to conserve energy and reduce emissions in key areas such as manufacturing, transport, construction, public institutions, households and 1,000 key energy-intensive enterprises; and close down more outdated production facilities. We will tighten supervision of energy use, develop smart power grids and ensure the proper distribution of energy supplies, and implement effective administrative practices such as efficient electricity generation and distribution, energy performance contracting, and government procurement of energy-efficient goods and services".[8] Local governments have developed plans and made investments to implement the central government's strategy of changing the growth mode and develop green economy.

1.2 Improvement of China's Green Development Index (GDI)

Based on the 2011 report, the 2012 report takes into full account the opinions of evaluation and statistical experts and improves the Province Green Development Index (PGDI) and the City Green Development Index (CGDI).

1.2.1 Improvement of the PGDI System

There are still 60 Third-Class Indicators in the PGDI system, including 22 regarding the "Green Degree of Economic Growth", 19 regarding the "Carrying Capacity Potential of Natural Resources and Environment" and 19 regarding the "Support Degree of Government Policies".

Table 1.1 shows all the indicators in the PGDI system.

At the 2012 meeting of experts in the research group, the discussion focused on the following opinions made by evaluation experts in 2011: first, whether to add efficiency indicators to the tertiary industry; second, whether to add indicators related to information technology; third, whether to add indicators reflecting people's green life and related to the people; fourth, whether to make adjustments to the indicator of water resources per capita since Northwest China has the most serious water shortage but it got a high score by the indicator.

After several rounds of discussion, we find it difficult to make revisions. First, we find no suitable statistical indicator for efficiency indicators in the tertiary industry and indicators related to information technology. Second, since the GDI is mainly designed to analyze the economy, the government and the carrying capacity of nature,

[8] Wen Jiabao. *2012 Report on the Work of the Government* (full text). http://www.eeo.com.cn/2012/0305/221970_6.shtml.

Table 1.1 PGDI system

First-Class Indicators	Second-Class Indicators	Third-Class Indicators	
Green Degree of Economic Growth	Green Growth Efficiency Indicators	1. GDP per capita	6. COD emissions per unit of GDP
		2. Energy consumption per unit of GDP	7. Nitrogen oxide emissions per unit of GDP
		3. Ratio of non-fossil energy consumption to total energy consumption	8. Ammonia/nitrogen emissions per unit of GDP
		4. CO_2 emissions per unit of GDP	9. Electricity consumption per capita in urban areas
		5. SO_2 emissions per unit of GDP	
	Primary Industry Indicators	10. Labor productivity of the primary sector	12. Proportion of water-saving irrigated area in effectively irrigated area
		11. Land productivity	13. Proportion of effectively irrigated area in cultivated land area
	Secondary Industry Indicators	14. Labor productivity of the secondary sector	17. Utilization rate of industrial solid waste
		15. Water consumption per unit of value added created by industrial enterprises	18. Recycling rate of industrial water
		15. Energy consumption per unit of value added created by industrial enterprises above designated size	19. Ratio of the output of six energy-intensive industries to gross industrial output
	Tertiary Industry Indicators	20. Labor productivity of the tertiary sector	22. Proportion of tertiary sector employees in the total employed population
		21. Proportion of the value added of the tertiary sector in GDP	
Carrying Capacity Potential of Natural Resources and Environment	Resource Abundance and Ecological Conservation Indicators	23. Water resources per capita	26. Proportion of the area of natural reserves in the total area of a region
		24. Forest area per capita	27. Proportion of the area of wetlands in the total area of a region
		25. Forest coverage rate	28. Growing stock per capita
	Environmental Pressure and Climate	29. CO_2 emissions per unit of land area	36. Nitrogen oxide emissions per capita
		30. CO_2 emissions per capita	37. Ammonia/nitrogen emissions per unit of land area
		31. SO_2 emissions per unit of land area	38. Ammonia/nitrogen emissions per capita

(continued)

Table 1.1 (continued)

First-Class Indicators	Second-Class Indicators	Third-Class Indicators	
	Change Indicators	32. SO_2 emissions per capita	39. Consumption of chemical fertilizers per unit of cultivated land area
		33. COD emissions per unit of land area	40. Consumption of pesticides per unit of cultivated land area
		34. COD emissions per capita	41. Nitrogen oxide emissions per capita from road transport
		35. Nitrogen oxide emissions per unit of land area	
Support Degree of Government Policies	Green Investment Indicators	42. Ratio of environmental spending to government expenditure	45. Investment in converting cultivated land into forests and grassland per unit of cultivated land area
		43. Ratio of the investment in pollution control to GDP	46. Ratio of the spending on science, education, culture, and public health to government expenditure
		44. Government spending per capita on rural water supply system and toilet improvement	
	Infrastructure Indicators	47. Area of green land per capita in urban areas	51. Public buses per 10,000 urban residents
		48. Coverage of water supply in urban areas	52. Length of public transport routes per capita in urban areas
		49. Treatment rate of urban wastewater	53. Ratio of the rural residents benefiting from water supply system improvement to the total rural population
		50. Harmless treatment rate of urban household waste	54. Green coverage of urban built-up areas
	Environmental Management Indicators	55. Newly-added afforestation area of the year per capita	58. Industrial nitrogen oxide removal rate
		56. Industrial SO_2 removal rate	59. Industrial wastewater ammonia/nitrogen removal rate
		57. Industrial wastewater COD removal rate	60. Number of environmental emergencies

Note: The content of this table was finalized after discussions at several seminars in 2012 held by the research group

Table 1.2 First-Class and Second-Class Indicators and their weights in the PGDI system

First-Class Indicators	Weight (%)	Second-Class Indicators	Weight in First-Class Indicators (%)
Green Degree of Economic Growth	30	Green Growth Efficiency Indicators	45
		Primary Industry Indicators	15
		Secondary Industry Indicators	25
		Tertiary Industry Indicators	15
Carrying Capacity Potential of Natural Resources and Environment	40	Resource Abundance and Ecological Conservation Indicators	30
		Environmental Pressure and Climate Change Indicators	70
Support Degree of Government Policies	30	Green Investment Indicators	25
		Infrastructure Indicators	45
		Environmental Management Indicators	30

as well as their relations, experts believe that it would be better to include the indicator of people's green life in the future. Third, the "annual precipitation" in the statistical yearbook is calculated in both cubic meter and millimeter, and the data are not consistent. What's more, the data for "annual precipitation" are not readily available, so it is decided not to include the "annual precipitation" indicator in the PGDI system.

We have made the following adjustments based on experts' opinions concerning the revising the weights of indicators adopted in 2011. Based on the weight distribution in 2011, we have reduced moderately the weights of eight indicators about pollutant emissions per capita and per unit of land area under the indicator "Carrying Capacity Potential of Natural Resources and Environment", so as to reduce the proportion of similar indicators in the indicator system due to the adoption of two ways of measurement. In addition, in the 2012 report, we measure the development in Tibet, but since the data are not complete, we do not include Tibet in the ranking; instead, we analyze the situation of Tibet in the part of "Green Development Checkup" and Analysis by Province. In short, after rounds of discussions, experts believe that the indicators used in 2011 are quite conducive to do comparison and suggest using them all in the 2012 report. If more indicators need to be changed next year, necessary adjustments will be made. Table 1.2 shows the First-Class and Second-Class Indicators and their weights in the 2012 PGDI system.

1.2.2 Improvement of the CGDI System

Since the *China Green Development Index Report 2011: Regional Comparison* was published, the rankings of 34 cities by GDI have captured attention from all sectors and produced huge influence. Moreover, some government officials, experts and common people have offered their opinions concerning how to improve CGDI. The research group has organized rounds of discussions with experts in statistics, ecology, resources and environment on these opinions.

In the first phase of discussion, the research group considered the opinions of evaluation and statistical experts and planned to add three to the 43 Third-Class Indicators, namely, "annual concentration of respirable particles (PM2.5)", "number of city environment cleaning vehicles per 10,000 persons" and "urban recycled water production capacity per capita". The first indicator is under the First-Class Indicator "Carrying Capacity Potential of Natural Resources and Environment" to show "Environmental Pressure and Climate Change"; the other two are under the First-Class Indicator "Support Degree of Government Policies" to show "Infrastructure". In later discussions, experts reached the following consensus: since the data for these three indicators were not available in 2010, and the statistical quality was still to be improved, it is suggested to add these three indicators in 2013. Therefore, the indicator system of 2012 will remain the same as that of 2011, consisting of 3 First-Class Indicators, 9 Second-Class Indicators, and 43 Third-Class Indicators. Among the Third-Class Indicators, 17 are about "Green Degree of Economic Growth", 13 about "Carrying Capacity Potential of Natural Resources and Environment", and 13 about "Support Degree of Government Policies".

Table 1.3 shows the structure of the CGDI system.

The 2012 CGDI system is revised in two aspects: one is the adjustment to the weights, and the other is the inclusion of more cities in the evaluation.

1.2.2.1 Proper Adjustment to the Weights

Since one subject is measured in both per capita and per unit of land area terms in the 2011 CGDI system, such as "nitrogen oxide emissions per capita" and "nitrogen oxide emissions per unit of land area", some officers, experts and common people believe that it will increase the impact factor of this subject in the whole system, and as the indicators are highly correlated, they suggest adjusting indicators using per capita and per unit of land area measures and reducing their weights as appropriate.

After rounds of discussions with statistical experts, the research group adjusted eight Three-Class Indicators using per capita and per unit of land area measures, and reduced their weights. The details are shown in Table 1.4.

The eight Third-Class Indicators measured in per capita and per unit of land area are all under the First-Class Indicator "Carrying Capacity Potential of Natural Resources and Environment" to show the "Environmental Pressure and Climate Change". Before the adjustment, each of the eight indicators took a weight of 2.67 %, and after the adjustment, it fell to 2.50 %, down by 0.17 %.

What needs to be pointed out is that to ensure the objectivity, reliability and stability of measurement, weights of First-Class and Second-Class Indicators

Table 1.3 CGDI system

First-Class Indicators	Second-Class Indicators	Third-Class Indicators	
Green Degree of Economic Growth	Green Growth Efficiency Indicators	1. GDP per capita	5. SO_2 emissions per unit of GDP
		2. Energy consumption per unit of GDP	6. COD emissions per unit of GDP
		3. Electricity consumption per capita in urban areas	7. Nitrogen oxide emissions per unit of GDP
		4. CO_2 emissions per unit of GDP	8. Ammonia/nitrogen emissions per unit of GDP
	Primary Industry Indicators	9. Labor productivity of the primary sector	
	Secondary Industry Indicators	10. Labor productivity of the secondary sector	12. Energy consumption per unit of value added created by industrial enterprises
		11. Water consumption per unit of value added created by industrial enterprises	13. Utilization rate of industrial solid waste 14. Recycling rate of industrial water
	Tertiary Industry Indicators	15. Labor productivity of the tertiary sector	17. Proportion of tertiary sector employees in the total employed population
		16. Proportion of the value added of the tertiary sector in GDP	
Carrying Capacity Potential of Natural Resources and Environment	Resource Abundance and Ecological Conservation Indicators	18. Water resources per capita	
	Environmental Pressure and Climate Change Indicators	19. CO_2 emissions per unit of land area	26. Nitrogen oxide emissions per capita
		20. CO_2 emissions per capita	27. Ammonia/nitrogen emissions per unit of land area
		21. SO_2 emissions per unit of land area	28. Ammonia/nitrogen emissions per capita
		22. SO_2 emissions per capita	29. Percentage of days with air quality at or above level II in a year
		23. COD emissions per unit of land area	

(continued)

Table 1.3 (continued)

First-Class Indicators	Second-Class Indicators	Third-Class Indicators	
		24. COD emissions per capita	30. Percentage of days with respirable suspended particulates as the principal pollutants in a year
		25. Nitrogen oxide emissions per unit of land area	
Support Degree of Government Policies	Green Investment Indicators	31. Ratio of environmental spending to government expenditure	33. Ratio of the spending on science, education, culture, and public health to government expenditure
		32. Ratio of the investment in industrial pollution control to GDP	
	Infrastructure Indicators	34. Area of green land per capita in urban areas	37. Treatment rate of urban household wastewater
		35. Green coverage of urban built-in areas	38. Harmless treatment rate of urban household waste
		36. Coverage of water supply	39. Public buses per 10,000 residents
	Environmental Management Indicators	40. Industrial SO_2 removal rate	42. Industrial nitrogen oxide removal rate
		41. Industrial wastewater COD removal rate	43. Industrial wastewater ammonia/nitrogen removal rate

Note: The content of this table was finalized after discussions at several seminars in 2012 held by the research group

used in the 2012 CGDI system is the same as those in 2011 system. The details are shown in Table 1.5.

1.2.2.2 Inclusion of New Cities in the Evaluation

As experts suggest, four new cities are included in the evaluation. Karamay, Suzhou and Zhuhai are included because they meet the following two requirements: city GDP per capita is among city top 20 in China and city data are complete. As for Urumqi, its data were complete and ready in 2012, so the city was added to the list of cities of its evaluation. But Lhasa is excluded because the data of its some

Table 1.4 Adjustment to the weights of per capita and per unit of land area indicators in the CGDI system

First-Class Indicators	Second-Class Indicators	Third-Class Indicators	Weight after adjustment (%)	Weight before adjustment (%)
Carrying Capacity Potential of Natural Resources and Environment	Resource Abundance and Ecological Conservation Indicators	Water resources per capita	1.70	1.70
		CO_2 emissions per unit of land area	3.08	2.81
		CO_2 emissions per capita	3.08	2.81
	Environmental Pressure and Climate Change Indicators	SO_2 emissions per unit of land area	2.50	2.67
		SO_2 emissions per capita	2.50	2.67
		COD emissions per unit of land area	2.50	2.67
		COD emissions per capita	2.50	2.67
		Nitrogen oxide emissions per unit of land area	2.50	2.67
		Nitrogen oxide emissions per capita	2.50	2.67
		Ammonia/nitrogen emissions per unit of land area	2.50	2.67
		Ammonia/nitrogen emissions per capita	2.50	2.67
		Percentage of days with air quality at or above level II in a year	3.08	2.67
		Percentage of days with respirable suspended particulates as the principal pollutants in a year	3.08	2.67

Table 1.5 First-Class and Second-Class Indicators and their weights in the CGDI system

First-Class Indicators	Weight (%)	Second-Class Indicators	Weight (%)
Green Degree of Economic Growth	33	Green Growth Efficiency Indicators	50
		Primary Industry Indicators	5
		Secondary Industry Indicators	30
		Tertiary Industry Indicators	15
Carrying Capacity Potential of Natural Resources and Environment	34	Resource Abundance and Ecological Conservation Indicators	5
		Environmental Pressure and Climate Change Indicators	95
Support Degree of Government Policies	33	Green Investment Indicators	25
		Infrastructure Indicators	45
		Environmental Management Indicators	30

Table 1.6 Cities Covered in the GDI Evaluation

Province	Number of cities	City name	Province	Number of cities	City name
Beijing	1	Beijing	Henan	1	Zhengzhou
Tianjin	1	Tianjin	Hubei	1	Wuhan
Hebei	1	Shijiazhuang	Hunan	1	Changsha
Shanxi	1	Taiyuan	Guangdong		Guanghzou, Shenzhen, Zhuhai
Inner Mongolia	1	Hohhot	Guangxi	1	Nanning
Liaoning	2	Shenyang, Dalian	Hainan	1	Haikou
Jilin	1	Changchun	Chongqing	1	Chongqing
Heilongjiang	1	Harbin	Sichuan	1	Chengdu
Shanghai	1	Shanghai	Guizhou	1	Guiyang
Jiangsu	2	Nanjing, Suzhou	Yunnan	1	Kunming
Zhejiang	2	Hangzhou, Ningbo	Shaanxi	1	Xi'an
Anhui	1	Hefei	Gansu	1	Lanzhou
Fujian	2	Fuzhou, Xiamen	Qinghai	1	Xining
Jiangxi	1	Nanchang	Ningxia	1	Yinchuan
Shandong	2	Jinan, Qingdao	Xinjiang	2	Urumqi, Karamay

Note: The cities in the table are selected from the 113 key cities subject to environment monitoring with complete data and without singular value announced by the Ministry of Environmental Protection

indicators are still not available. To sum up, four new cities are added to the original 34 cities for evaluation, increasing the total number to 38. The details are shown in Table 1.6.

1.3 GDI Calculation and Result Analysis

Based on the PGDI and CGDI indicators, we have calculated the GDI[9] of 30 provinces/autonomous regions/municipalities directly under the central government (hereinafter referred to as "provinces") (Tibet excluded) and 38 cities for the year of 2010.

1.3.1 Results of PGDI Calculation

Using PGDI system and 2010 data, we have calculated GDI[10] of 30 provinces and measured their performance by the three First-Class Indicators "Green Degree of

[9] The Calculation and analysis of GDI is a joint work of the PGDI Measurement Team and the CGDI Measurement Team.

[10] Due to the lack of data, Tibet, Hong Kong, Macao and Taiwan are not included in the measurement.

Economic Growth", "Carrying Capacity Potential of Natural Resources and Environment" and "Support Degree of Government Policies". The results are shown in Table 1.7.

Since the average value and standard deviation formula are adopted for dimensionless quantities, "0" stands for the average green development level of all the provinces evaluated. When a province scores a point more than "0", it means that its green development level is above the national average; when it scores a point less than "0", it is below the national average.

1.3.2 PGDI Comparison by Region

According to the results of calculations, the top 10 provinces in 2012 in terms of GDP were: Beijing, Tianjin, Guangdong, Hainan, Zhejiang, Qinghai, Yunnan, Fujian, Shanghai and Shandong. Geographically speaking, Qinghai and Yunnan are in Western China[11] while the rest eight provinces are in Eastern China. Among the 10 provinces ranking from 11th to 20th, two (Jiangsu and Hebei, ranking 12th and 17th respectively) are in Eastern China; one (Jiangxi, ranking 18th) is in Central China; five (Inner Mongolia, Guizhou, Shaanxi, Xinjiang and Chongqing, ranking 11th, 13th, 14th, 15th and 19th respectively) in Western China; and two (Heilongjiang and Jilin, ranking 16th and 19th respectively) are in Northeast China. Among the 10 provinces ranking from 21st to 30th, none is in Eastern China; five (Anhui, Hubei, Hunan, Shanxi and Henan, ranking 22nd, 24th, 27th, 29th, and 30th respectively) are in Central China; four (Sichuan, Gansu, Guangxi and Ningxia, ranking 21st, 25th, 26th and 28th respectively) are in Western China; one (Liaoning, ranking 23rd) is in Northeast China. We marked the performance of each region in terms of GDI on the map of China (Fig. 1.1). The top 10 provinces are marked in dark green; those ranking from 11th to 20th are marked in moderate green; and the bottom 10 are marked in light green.

The green development level differs between the four major regions of China (Fig. 1.2), and the PGDI shows the following characteristics:

Eastern provinces have the highest level of green development and stand out in terms of the Green Degree of Economic Growth. Among the 10 provinces in Eastern China, eight rank among the national top 10. Except for Hebei, the rest nine provinces have a green development level above the national average.

[11] The comparison of this report is made between the four regions, namely Eastern China, Central China, Western China and Northeast China, proposed in the Regional Development Strategy of the 11th Five-Year Plan. Eastern China includes 10 provinces: Beijing, Tianjin, Hebei, Shanghai, Jiangsu, Zhejiang, Fujian, Shandong, Guangdong and Hainan; Central China includes six provinces: Shanxi, Anhui, Jiangxi, Henan, Hubei and Hunan; Western China includes 12 provinces : Inner Mongolia, Guangxi, Chongqing, Sichuan, Guizhou, Yunnan, Tibet, Shaanxi, Gansu, Qinghai, Ningxia and Xinjiang; Northeast China includes three provinces: Liaoning, Jilin and Heilongjiang.

Table 1.7 Rankings of China's 30 provinces by GDI

			First-Class Indicators					
	GDI		Green Degree of Economic Growth		Carrying Capacity Potential of Natural Resources and Environment		Support Degree of Government Policies	
Province	Value	Ranking	Value	Ranking	Value	Ranking	Value	Ranking
Beijing	0.655	1	0.465	1	−0.035	14	0.226	1
Tianjin	0.215	2	0.291	3	−0.134	27	0.058	8
Guangdong	0.175	3	0.116	7	−0.086	21	0.145	3
Hainan	0.171	4	0.022	9	0.101	6	0.048	10
Zhejiang	0.160	5	0.158	4	−0.074	19	0.076	4
Qinghai	0.121	6	−0.201	30	0.467	1	−0.145	29
Yunnan	0.109	7	−0.161	27	0.224	3	0.045	11
Fujian	0.100	8	0.091	8	−0.023	13	0.032	14
Shanghai	0.095	9	0.327	2	−0.200	30	−0.032	19
Shandong	0.086	10	0.122	6	−0.099	24	0.063	6
Inner Mongolia	0.075	11	−0.005	11	0.103	5	−0.022	18
Jiangsu	0.062	12	0.149	5	−0.153	28	0.066	5
Guizhou	0.041	13	−0.186	29	0.271	2	−0.044	21
Shaanxi	0.030	14	−0.042	15	0.038	11	0.034	13
Xinjiang	−0.002	15	−0.088	22	0.049	9	0.037	12
Heilongjiang	−0.024	16	−0.043	16	0.181	4	−0.162	30
Hebei	−0.040	17	−0.007	12	−0.095	23	0.062	7
Jiangxi	−0.062	18	−0.078	20	0.021	12	−0.005	16
Chongqing	−0.101	19	−0.104	25	−0.049	16	0.052	9
Jilin	−0.106	20	−0.031	14	0.044	10	−0.119	26
Sichuan	−0.115	21	−0.082	21	0.093	7	−0.127	28
Anhui	−0.122	22	−0.058	18	−0.049	17	−0.016	17
Liaoning	−0.126	23	0.007	10	−0.077	20	−0.056	23
Hubei	−0.173	24	−0.027	13	−0.091	22	−0.055	22
Gansu	−0.176	25	−0.152	26	0.077	8	−0.101	25
Guangxi	−0.179	26	−0.096	24	−0.045	15	−0.037	20
Hunan	−0.188	27	−0.065	19	−0.050	18	−0.073	24
Ningxia	−0.200	28	−0.184	28	−0.181	29	0.164	2
Shanxi	−0.208	29	−0.092	23	−0.124	26	0.007	15
Henan	−0.272	30	−0.048	17	−0.103	25	−0.121	27

Notes: ① The results are obtained based on calculations with 2010 data for each PGDI indicator; ② The provinces (autonomous regions/municipalities directly under the central government) are listed in descending order of GDI value; ③ The value of GDI in this table is the sum of the values by the three First-Class Indicators: Green Degree of Economic Growth, Carrying Capacity Potential of Natural Resources and Environment, and Support Degree of Government Policies; ④ The calculations are based on the *China Statistical Yearbook 2011*, *China Environmental Statistical Yearbook 2011*, *China Environment Annual Report 2010*, *China City Statistical Yearbook 2011*, *China Water Conservancy Statistical Yearbook 2011*, *China Industrial Economy Statistical Yearbook 2011*, and *Deserts in China and Desertification Control*

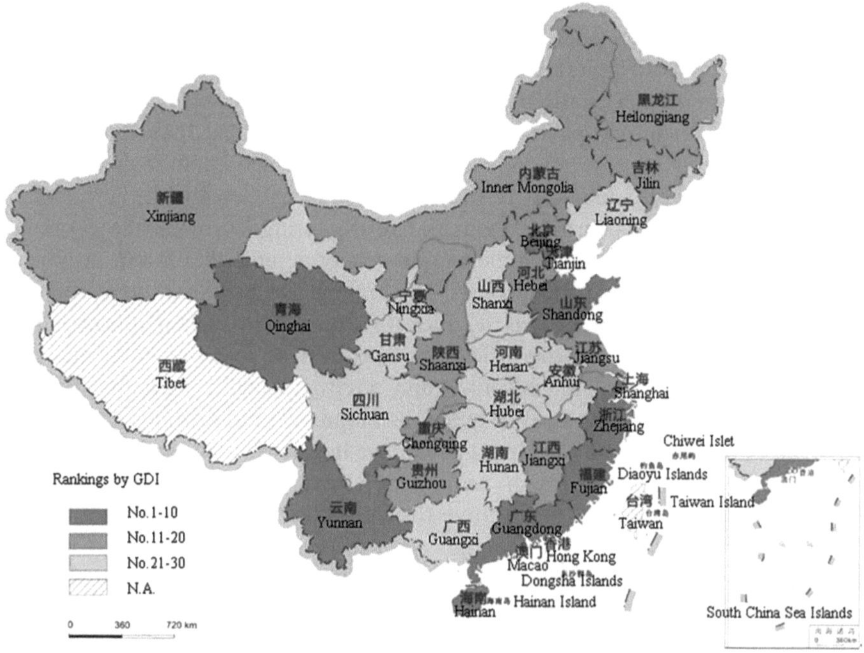

Fig. 1.1 Geographic distribution of GDI rankings (Note: This figure is developed based on data from Table 1.7)

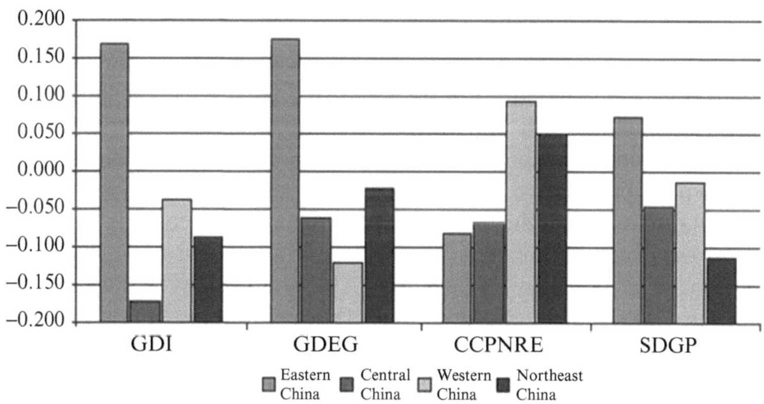

Fig. 1.2 GDI comparison by region (Note: The data of each region in this figure are the arithmetic mean of the scores of all the provinces in the region)

During the three decades of reform and opening up, eastern provinces have grown much faster than other parts of the country due to their own geographical advantages and favorable national policies, and thus gained strengths in promoting growth efficiency, green investment, infrastructure development and environmental management. However, they are also facing resource and environmental constraints, which can be seen from the ranking by the Carrying Capacity Potential of Natural Resources and Environment. Now eastern provinces attach more importance to the balanced development of the economy, resources and the environment and pay more attention to environment friendliness while growing the economy. They advocate "energy conservation and emissions reduction" and try to increase resource efficiency and control environmental pollution and damages through industrial restructuring, to make the economy greener. What's more, thanks to their rapid economic growth, eastern provinces rank higher by the Support Degree of Government Policies than other regions. Local governments have increased green investment, promoted infrastructure construction and improved the efficiency and level of environmental management. Therefore, despite the resource and environmental constraints, Eastern China still enjoys a higher level of green development on the whole.

Western provinces enjoy a distinct advantage in resources and environment but a lower level of economic growth. Among the 11 evaluated provinces in Western China, two rank among the top 10, five from 11th to 20th, and four from 21st to 30th. Western provinces score a higher point in terms of the Carrying Capacity Potential of Natural Resources and Environment, helping to raise their GDI rankings, but they have no advantage in the Green Degree of Economic Growth, by which none of them rank among the top 10; they have little advantage in the terms of Support Degree of Government Policies, only Ningxia (ranking 2nd) and Chongqing (ranking 9th) make it to the top 10, and the rest 10 provinces rank behind 11th, with Qinghai in the 29th place. It shows that despite the abundant resources and high carrying capacity potential of the environment, western provinces have limited financial resources to promote green investment, infrastructure construction and environmental management because of their low level of economic development. They need to do better in greening the economy. Besides, with the economic growth and further development of resources in western provinces, environmental problems will arise. While catching up with eastern and central parts of China in terms of economic development, western provinces should do more to protect the environment and make the economy greener.

Central provinces do not have apparent advantages and their level of green development level is yet to be increased. The results show that among the six provinces in Central China, Jiangxi ranks 18th and the rest five provinces rank behind 20th so the whole region is at a low level. Their development is balanced by the three First-Class Indicators: Green Degree of Economic Growth, Carrying Capacity Potential of Natural Resources and Environment and Support Degree of Government Policies, but the level of development is below the national average. During the "rise of Central China", due to the low efficiency of resource utilization and the absence of advanced technologies for energy conservation & emissions reduction, provinces in the region are facing severe energy shortages, a lot of environmental pressure and many constraints on economic growth. Despite the economic boom in recent years, the six provinces in Central China still lag far behind eastern provinces economically, and they are also far behind western provinces in terms of the Carrying Capacity Potential of Natural Resources and Environment. Restricted by their limited economic strength and resources, central provinces find it hard to strike a balance between growing the economy and going green. In short, green development in Central China is at a low level on the whole and needs to be promoted.

The green development level of the three northeast provinces is low and varies a lot from province to province. The results show that the green development level in Northeast China is below the national average and varies a lot from province to province. As to the three First-Class Indicators, they get low scores for the "Support Degree of Government Policies", below-average scores for the "Green Degree of Economic Growth", and good scores for the "Carrying Capacity Potential of Natural Resources and Environment". Among them, Heilongjiang has the highest green development level, ranking 16th, but it ranks last by the indicator "Support Degree of Government Policies"; Jilin and Liaoning rank 20th and 23rd respectively.

The results show that among the 30 provinces surveyed, 14 have a green development level higher than the national average; they are Beijing, Tianjin, Guangdong, Hainan, Zhejiang, Qinghai, Yunnan, Fujian, Shanghai, Shandong, Inner Mongolia, Jiangsu, Guizhou and Shaanxi (in descending order of GDI value); the rest 16 provinces are below the national average level (Fig. 1.3). To be consistent, and as suggested by many experts, the indicators and calculation method used in 2012 are the same as those in 2011. The top 12 provinces in 2012 are also among the top 12 in 2011, with only a few rankings changed. It shows that the GDI calculation method is stable.

1.3.3 Results of CGDI Calculation

Using the 2010 data and the 2012 CGDI indicators, we have calculated the GDI of 38 cities in China. Their GDI values and rankings are shown in Table 1.8.

The results of calculation are interpreted in the same way used in previous years. If a city's GDI value is higher than "0", it means that its green development level is above the average level of all the evaluated cities; and a GDI value less than "0" means that its green development level is below the average level. Among the 38 cities evaluated, 15 are above the average, including Shenzhen, Haikou, Karamay, Kunming, Guangzhou, Beijing, Dalian, Qingdao, Nanjing, Fuzhou, Zhuhai, Nanning, Changsha, Suzhou and Harbin; and the rest 23 are below the average.

For the readers' convenience, we have drawn the Fig. 1.4 to show the 2012 city rankings by GDI according to Table 1.8.

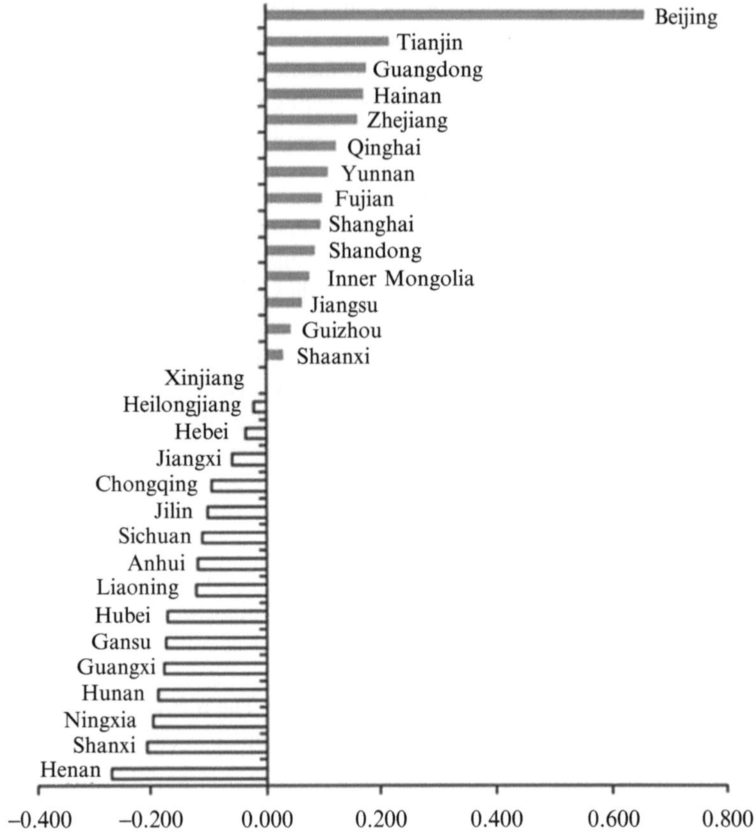

Fig. 1.3 Province rankings by GDI (Note: This figure is developed based on data from Table 1.7)

1.3.4 CGDI Comparison by Region

The evaluation covers 16 eastern cities, including Beijing, Tianjin, Shijiazhuang, Shanghai, Nanjing, Suzhou, Hanghzou, Ningbo, Fuzhou, Xiamen, Jinan, Qingdao, Guangzhou, Shenzhen, Zhuhai and Haikou, six central cities, including Taiyuan, Hefei, Nanchang, Zhengzhou, Wuhan and Changsha, 12 western cities, including Hohhot, Nanning, Chongqing, Chengdu, Guiyang, Kunming, Xi'an, Lanzhou, Xining, Yinchuan, Urumqi and Karamay; and four northeastern cities, including Shenyang, Dalian, Changchun and Harbin.

As shown in Table 1.8, the top 10 cities by GDI are Shenzhen, Haikou, Karamay, Kunming, Guangzhou, Beijing, Dalian, Qingdao, Nanjing and Fuzhou. Geographically, seven of them are in Eastern China, two in Western China, one in Northeast China, and none in Central China. Cities ranking from 11th to 20th are Zhuhai, Nanning, Changsha, Suzhou, Harbin, Yinchuan, Ningbo, Hangzhou, Jinan and

Table 1.8 Rankings of China's 38 Cities by GDI

			First-Class Indicators					
	GDI		Green Degree of Economic Growth		Carrying Capacity Potential of Natural Resources and Environment		Support Degree of Government Policies	
City	Value	Ranking	Value	Ranking	Value	Ranking	Value	Ranking
Shenzhen	1.002	1	0.503	1	0.166	6	0.333	1
Haikou	0.603	2	0.120	3	0.399	2	0.085	10
Karamay	0.403	3	0.044	11	0.227	3	0.132	6
Kunming	0.401	4	−0.087	32	0.416	1	0.072	12
Guangzhou	0.283	5	0.077	8	−0.041	20	0.247	2
Beijing	0.239	6	0.205	2	−0.109	32	0.143	4
Dalian	0.191	7	0.079	7	0.054	9	0.058	14
Qingdao	0.109	8	0.096	6	−0.016	16	0.029	18
Nanjing	0.087	9	0.053	10	−0.056	23	0.090	9
Fuzhou	0.072	10	−0.039	22	0.111	7	−0.001	20
Zhuhai	0.061	11	−0.057	27	−0.048	21	0.166	3
Nanning	0.049	12	−0.073	29	0.190	5	−0.068	24
Changsha	0.044	13	0.100	5	0.057	8	−0.113	32
Suzhou	0.007	14	0.077	9	−0.124	34	0.055	16
Harbin	0.003	15	0.007	16	0.195	4	−0.198	37
Yinchuan	−0.006	16	−0.112	34	−0.035	19	0.141	5
Ningbo	−0.019	17	−0.067	28	−0.032	18	0.080	11
Hangzhou	−0.021	18	0.005	17	−0.058	24	0.032	17
Jinan	−0.029	19	0.032	13	−0.085	28	0.024	19
Guiyang	−0.031	20	−0.168	37	0.046	10	0.091	8
Shenyang	−0.037	21	0.103	4	−0.048	22	−0.091	27
Hefei	−0.048	22	0.018	14	0.011	12	−0.076	26
Taiyuan	−0.057	23	−0.101	33	−0.081	26	0.124	7
Xiamen	−0.059	24	−0.041	23	−0.083	27	0.066	13
Shijiazhuang	−0.093	25	−0.055	26	−0.095	29	0.058	15
Shanghai	−0.093	26	0.039	12	−0.116	33	−0.015	21
Hohhot	0.132	27	0.081	31	0.002	13	−0.053	23
Tianjin	−0.153	28	0.004	18	−0.136	37	−0.022	22
Changchun	−0.164	29	0.000	19	−0.006	15	−0.157	34
Chengdu	−0.172	30	0.008	15	−0.001	14	−0.179	36
Nanchang	−0.175	31	−0.051	25	−0.024	17	−0.100	30
Xi'an	−0.232	32	−0.032	21	−0.107	31	−0.093	28
Chongqing	−0.244	33	−0.161	36	0.035	11	−0.117	33
Wuhan	−0.262	34	−0.021	20	−0.168	38	−0.074	25
Urumqi	−0.274	35	−0.046	24	−0.132	36	−0.096	29
Zhengzhou	−0.284	36	−0.075	30	−0.099	30	−0.110	31
Lanzhou	−0.356	37	−0.121	35	−0.073	25	−0.161	35
Xining	−0.615	38	−0.183	38	−0.132	35	−0.300	38

Notes: ① The results are obtained based on calculations with 2010 data for 2012 CGDI indicators; ② The cities in the table are listed in descending order of GDI value; ③ The calculations are based on the *China City Statistical Yearbook 2011*, *China Environment Annual Report 2010*, *China Urban Construction Statistical Yearbook 2010*, and *China Regional Economic Statistical Yearbook 2011*; ④ Since the data on Lhasa for some indicators are not ready, the city is excluded from the evaluation

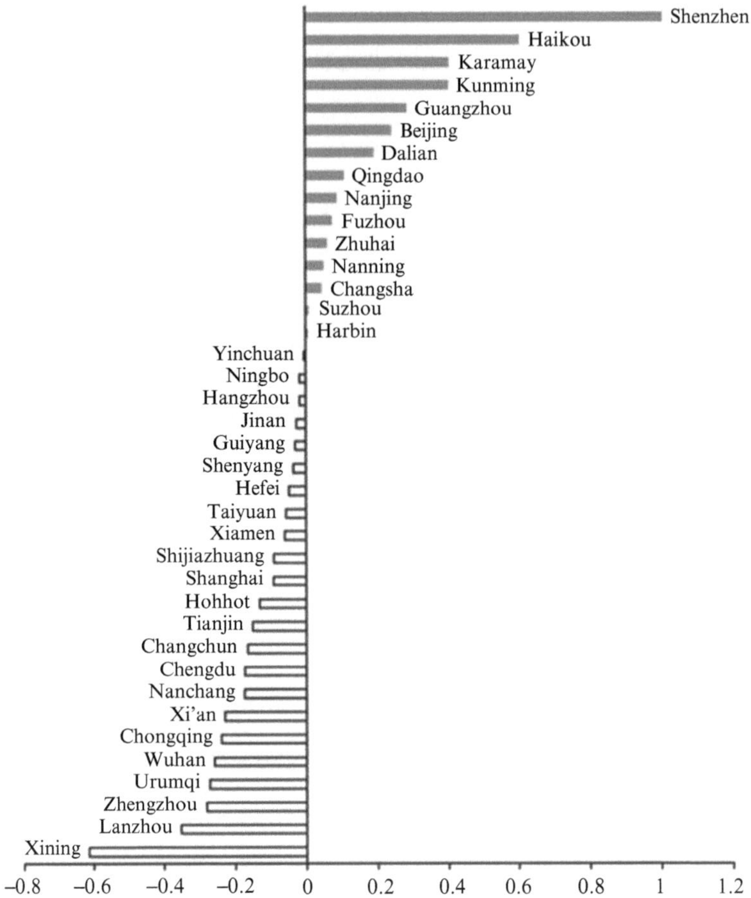

Fig. 1.4 City rankings by GDI (Note: This figure is developed based on data from Table 1.8)

Guiyang. Five of them are in Eastern China one in Central China, three in Western China and one in Northeast China. Among the cities ranking from 21st to 39th, four are in Eastern China five in Central China seven in Western China and two in Northeast China. To give the reader a more direct impression of green development in cities, we have developed the Fig. 1.5 to compare CGDI by region.

Specifically, the CGDI shows the following regional characteristics:

The green development in eastern cities is better on the whole. Among the 16 cities in Eastern China, except for Xiamen, Shijiazhuang, Shanghai and Tianjin, the rest are all above the average level. More than half of the cities among the top 20 are in Eastern China, meaning that this region still leads the country in greening the economy. It shows that these cities are able to achieve growth without causing serious damage to the environment and stands as an evidence of the regional gaps in economic development in China. It is noteworthy that Xiamen, Shanghai and Tianjin, which are usually believed to be good cities, rank below the national average.

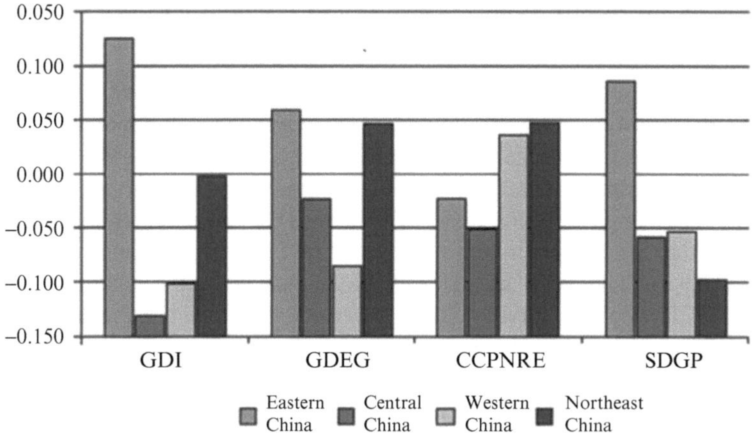

Fig. 1.5 CGDI comparison by region (Note: The data of each region in this figure are the arithmetic mean of the scores of all the cities in the region)

Western cities have made steady progress in pursing green development. In 2011, only Kunming made it to the top 10; in 2012, Karamay, a city in Western China newly included in the evaluation, also made it to the top 10. Moreover, there was only one western city, i.e., Nanning, from the 11th to 20th places but it was joined by Yinchuan and Guiyang in 2012. It shows that western cities have made a big step forward in pursing green development. It is not hard to understand that these cities score high by the indicator "Carrying Capacity Potential of Natural Resources and Environment" because they have natural advantages in this respect, but it deserves our attention that big cities like Chongqing and Chengdu still rank low.

Central cities have fallen behind with the green drive. Among the six cities in Central China, Changsha ranks 13th and the rest are all behind the 20th place, dragging down the green development level of the region as a whole. In 2011, both Hefei and Changsha made it to the top 10. The 2012 rankings of central cities are apparently lower so their green development level is to be increased.

The four northeastern cities have delivered a good performance. Their rankings have not changed too much compared with those in 2011. Dalian and Harbin rank 7th and 15th while Shenyang and Changchun take the 21st and 29th placcs. Thus the overall level of green development is good.

1.4 About the "Green Development Checkup Table" and the "Survey on Public Satisfaction with Urban Green Development"

The "green development checkup table" and the "survey on public satisfaction with urban green development" are specially designed for the 2012 report, which is inspired by field research as well as the questions raised by news media.

1.4.1 About the "Green Development Checkup Table"

After the release of the *China Green Development Index Report: Regional Comparison*, the research group was invited by some provincial and municipal governments to examine local green development. During the field surveys, we found that some local governments cared more about what could be improved specifically than their GDI rankings. Therefore, we have developed the "green development checkup table" for the 2012 report to show the value of Third-Class Indicator values and rankings of provinces and cities as well as the changes in the rankings compared with 2011. During the surveys, local governments expressed the hope that the research group could help them plan for green development. But considering that the research on the GDI is not supported by extensive fieldwork, we are not able to "prescribe" solutions to the problems of local governments with green development yet. The GDI, particularly the Third-Class Indicators, is only used to check up on some projects undertaken by the provinces or cities. That's why the part is called "green development checkup".

There are green development checkup tables for both provinces and cities. The province checkup tables include the GDI information of 31 provinces with 60 Third-Class Indicators and the information is provided in 12 items, namely the serial number, name, unit of measurement, attribute of the indicator, the 2010 mean value of the provinces (excluding Tibet), the 2010 and 2009 indicator values of the province, the 2010 and 2009 rankings of the province by the indicator, the change in the province's ranking, source of data and the Chernoff face to show either progress or regression. The information for six items is the same in each table, including the serial number, name, unit of measurement, attribute of the indicator, the 2010 mean value of 30 provinces (excluding Tibet) and the source of data. The six items are mainly about the 60 Third-Class Indicators in the PGDI system. The information for five items varies from table to table, including the 2010 and 2009 indicator values of the province, the 2010 and 2009 rankings of the province by the indicator and the change in the province's ranking. The five items are mainly about the original data for each province, its rankings and ranking change by each Third-Class Indicator. The last item of Chernoff face is developed according to the ranking change. If the 2010 ranking is higher than the 2009 one by the indicator, a smiling face is given as a sign of encouragement; if it is lower, a crying face is given for stimulation; if there is no change in the ranking, no face is provided. Where the data for an indicator is not available in statistical yearbooks, "NA" is used to specify and data will be provided in future reports. Each province checkup table gives detailed information about the province's performance in every aspect of green development.

The city checkup tables provide details about 39 cities' performances by the 43 Third-Class Indicators. In addition to the 12 items included in the province checkup tables, they have one more item, i.e., the scope of indicator's application, which is designed to make clear whether the data is for the whole city or for municipal districts of the city. Like the province checkup tables, each city checkup table gives detailed information about the city's performance in green development by 43 Third-Class Indicators, including the 2010 and 2009 indicator values, the change in the ranking, the Chernoff face to show either progress or regression, and etc.

Each "green development checkup table" is followed by a brief analysis of the province/city's green development level based on the information provided in the table. Radar charts are developed according to the scores by First-Class and Second-Class Indicators to give the reader a more direct impression of the province/city's good or bad performance by the indicators.

Tibet and Lhasa are two exceptions in this part. Since the data for some indicators are not available, they are not included in the ranking and their checkup tables do not have such items as 2010 and 2009 rankings, change in the ranking and the Chernoff face to show progress or regression. The analysis of their green development levels is only based on available data.

1.4.2 About the "Survey on Public Satisfaction with Urban Green Development"

During the GDI evaluation and at the press conference to launch of the *China Green Development Index Report*, friends of all sectors, the press in particular, shared the same concern with us that the province and city rankings by GDI worked out only based on statistical data might differ from what the public think of green development. In light of that, we have conducted the survey on public satisfaction with urban green development for the 2012 report to obtain local residents' opinions on the green development in their cities, which will help us to get a full picture of how green development goes in the evaluated cities.

The survey was undertaken by China Economic Monitoring and Analysis Center, National Bureau of Statistics of China, with the financial support from the Scientific Outlook on Development and Economic Sustainability Research Base of Beijing Normal University and the Green Economy and Economic Sustainability Research Base of Southwestern University of Finance and Economics. The questionnaire is designed to collect the feedback of local residents on the environment and infrastructure of the city and the green actions taken by the government. The survey was conducted mainly by telephone and 700 urban residents were randomly selected as the respondents in each of the 38 cities covered in the 2012 GDI evaluation. Residents' overall satisfaction with a city's green development is measured by the average degree of their satisfaction with the urban environment, infrastructure and the government's green actions. A positive final score means that the residents are satisfied with the green development in the city while a negative one means that they are dissatisfied with it. The score is between -1 and 1. The closer a score goes to 1, the more satisfied the respondents are; the closer a score goes to -1, the more dissatisfied the respondents are.

The survey results show that: the average satisfaction with green development in the 38 cities is scored 0.121, which means that urban residents have a positive attitude towards the current state of green development. The top 10 cities by public satisfaction are Karamay, Yinchuan, Xining, Xiamen, Hangzhou, Chongqing, Chengdu, Zhuhai, Qingdao, and Ningbo; the bottom 10 are Nanjing, Tianjin, Shenyang, Harbin, Beijing, Hefei, Changsha, Hohhot, Wuhan, and Lanzhou. Specifically, most urban residents are satisfied with the urban environment and infrastructure but less satisfied with the green actions taken by the government.

The survey represents a bold innovation in the research on the theory and practice of green development. Since it has a different focus from that of the GDI evaluation system, its results also differ greatly from the GDI rankings. It is a supplement to the GDI, but it also leaves us many contradictory conclusions to explain. In the next step, we will collect feedback from experts and readers, compare the rankings by public satisfaction with those by the GDI, and carry out special investigations to draw more scientific, objective and reasonable conclusions.

1.5 Structure of the Report

The *China Green Development Index Report 2012: Regional Comparison* consists of the "Prefaces", "Expert Comments", "Introduction", "Provinces", "Cities", "Public Opinions", "Professors' Forum", and "Appendices". Each part measures and analyzes the green development of 31 provinces and 39 cities from different perspectives. The public opinions on regional green development are the results of a questionnaire survey. Moreover, professors and scholars in natural and social sciences involved in writing this report are invited to contribute ideas to green development, which constitute the part of Professors' Forum themed on green development. This report outperforms the previous one in terms of analytical framework.

This report is as scientific and objective as the 2011 report. Twenty-eight experts are invited to comment on this report from their special perspectives. Their valuable suggestions have helped us to improve the report. We have compiled all their views into the "Expert Comments" part and put it before the main body of the report.

The "Introduction" part specifies the improvements made in the 2012 PGDI and CGDI systems, provides the results of calculation and rankings of the 30 provinces and 38 cities, and gives a brief description of the new contents of the report.

The main body of the 2012 report consists of four sections while that of the 2011 report has five, which is the biggest difference between the two years. The sections on the measurement by the three First-Class Indicators are arranged differently in the two reports. In the 2011 report, one section is divided by each indicator and the analysis of provinces and cities are made in each section; in the 2012 report, two separate sections are divided to provinces and cities results respectively, and under each section, there are three chapters divided by the three First-Class

Indicators respectively, which are followed by a chapter on "green development checkup". In addition, the 2012 report has a section of "Public Opinions" based on a questionnaire survey and a section of "Professors' Forum" themed on green development, unlike the feature and theme sections in the 2011 report.

The first section is "Provinces" which has four chapters. The first three chapters measure the green development of provinces by the three First-Class Indicators (Green Degree of Economic Growth, Carrying Capacity Potential of Natural Resources and Environment, and Support Degree of Government Policies), and analyze the results; the fourth chapter is about the "green development checkup and analysis by province" where 31 provinces are given the Chernoff faces of progress or regression according to the changes of their rankings and brief analysis are made. This is a big innovation of the 2012 report.

The second section is "Cities" which has a similar structure as the first section. There are four chapters. The first three measure the green development of cities by the three First-Class Indicators (Green Degree of Economic Growth, Carrying Capacity Potential of Natural Resources and Environment, and Support Degree of Government Policies), and analyze the results; the fourth chapter is about the "green development checkup and analysis by city" where 39 cities are given the Chernoff faces of progress or regression according to the changes of their rankings and brief analysis are made.

The third section is "Public Opinions", which is new in the 2012 report. Considering that public opinions cannot be measured by statistical data, we conducted a questionnaire survey on public satisfaction in selected cities, covering such aspects as air quality and pollution. The section has two chapters. One is the "Questionnaire Design for the Survey on Public Satisfaction with Urban Green Development" and the other is the "Survey on Public Satisfaction with Urban Green Development: Results and Analysis". Some inspirations are drawn from the survey results and provided for reader's reference.

The fourth section "Professors' Forum" is also new. For more extensive discussions on green development, professors in natural and social sciences engaged in the research project are invited to express their views and offer proposals for promoting green development in China from different perspectives.

The last part of the report is the "Appendices". Appendix 1 is about the international comparison of urban green development. The GDI of cities at different levels of development is calculated; they are ranked by the results of calculation; and analysis are made. For the first time that an international comparison has been made in the *China Green Development Index Report*, which helps to improve the GDI system. It is a new attempt and the approach is yet to be improved. Appendix 2 is the "Analysis of Chengdu's 2009 GDI Ranking", which is developed based on the understanding that it is very important to take into account the opinions of local authorities when comparing the GDI of provinces/cities for they will help us push forward the research. Appendix 3 is the "PGDI Indicators and Source of Data". Appendix 4 is the "CGDI Indicators and Source of Data".

The 2012 report is intended to contribute to "the building of a resource-efficient and environment-friendly society and the promotion of ecological progress". In preparing this report, we seek to draw a roadmap for green development, give a full and objective account of the realities across all provinces and major cities, and push the transformation of growth mode by promoting the green development concept. We would like to acknowledge the full support of experts and scholars, local governments, other sectors and the general public. We believe that we can work together and make concerted effort to promote green development.

Part I
Provinces

Based on published statistical yearbooks and the 2010 PGDI system, this part gives a full account of the green development in the 30 evaluated provinces in 2010 and analyzes their rankings in this regard. Three chapters are separately dedicated to the specific performances of the provinces in terms of the three First-Class Indicators of the GDI, namely "Chapter 2 GDEG Measurement and Analysis by Province", "Chapter 3 CCPNRE Measurement and Analysis by Province", and "Chapter 4 SDGP Measurement and Analysis by Province". Chapter 5 explains in detail the green development levels of the provinces in 2010 by providing information including the values of the 60 Third-Class Indicators, their rankings, and the changes in the rankings over the 2 years.

Chapter 2
GDEG Measurement and Analysis by Province

Faqi Shi and Tao Song

As an important component of the GDI, the Green Degree of Economic Growth (GDEG) is the overall evaluation of how green an economy is. According to the criterion of GDEG measurement in the PGDI system, this chapter uses the data for 2010 to measure and analyze the GDEG of 30 provinces/autonomous regions/ municipalities directly under the central government (hereinafter referred to as "provinces")[1] from four perspectives, i.e., Green Growth Efficiency, Primary Industry, Secondary Industry, and Tertiary Industry.

2.1 Results of GDEG Measurement

The GDEG of 30 provinces in China is calculated in line with the related measurement and weighting standards of the PGDI system and the results are shown in Table 2.1 below.

As shown in Table 2.1, the top 10 provinces by GDEG are Beijing, Shanghai, Tianjin, Zhejiang, Jiangsu, Shandong, Guangdong, Fujian, Hainan and Liaoning (Fig. 2.1). Specifically, the top 10 by Green Growth Efficiency Indicators (GGEI) are Beijing, Shanghai, Tianjin, Zhejiang, Jiangsu, Guangdong, Shandong, Fujian, Jiangxi and Hainan; the top 10 by Primary Industry Indicators (PII) are Beijing, Shanghai, Xinjiang, Zhejiang, Fujian, Tianjin, Jiangsu, Hainan, Hebei and Shandong; the top 10 by Secondary Industry Indicators (SII) are Tianjin, Shandong, Shanghai, Inner Mongolia, Guangdong, Jiangsu, Jilin, Zhejiang, Fujian, and Liaoning; the top

[1] Tibet, Hong Kong, Macao and Taiwan are not included in the measurement due to lack of data.

F. Shi (✉)
National Accounts Department, National Bureau of Statistics of China, Beijing, China
e-mail: shifaqi@stats.gov.cn

T. Song
School of Economic Resource and Management, Beijing Normal University, Beijing, China

X. Li and J. Pan (eds.), *China Green Development Index Report 2012: Regional Comparison*, Current Chinese Economic Report Series,
DOI 10.1007/978-3-642-54178-0_2, © Springer-Verlag Berlin Heidelberg 2015

Table 2.1 2010 Rankings of 30 provinces by GDEG

			Second-Class Indicators							
Indicator	Green Degree of Economic Growth		Green Growth Efficiency Indicators		Primary Industry Indicators		Secondary Industry Indicators		Tertiary Industry Indicators	
Province	Score	Ranking	Score	Ranking	Score	Ranking	Score	Ranking	Score	Ranking
Beijing	0.465	1	0.235	1	0.085	1	0.008	11	0.137	1
Shanghai	0.327	2	0.110	2	0.059	2	0.049	3	0.109	2
Tianjin	0.291	3	0.078	3	0.041	6	0.103	1	0.069	3
Zhejiang	0.157	4	0.077	4	0.047	4	0.022	8	0.012	6
Jiangsu	0.149	5	0.074	5	0.038	7	0.023	6	0.015	5
Shandong	0.122	6	0.048	7	0.017	10	0.065	2	−0.009	16
Guangdong	0.116	7	0.057	6	0.003	11	0.034	5	0.022	4
Fujian	0.091	8	0.037	8	0.041	5	0.015	9	−0.002	11
Hainan	0.022	9	0.008	10	0.019	8	−0.014	20	0.009	7
Liaoning	0.007	10	−0.013	14	0.000	12	0.014	10	0.005	8
Inner Mongolia	−0.005	11	−0.043	24	−0.002	13	0.036	4	0.004	9
Hebei	−0.007	12	0.005	12	0.019	9	−0.006	18	−0.025	24
Hubei	−0.027	13	−0.018	18	−0.005	14	0.000	16	−0.004	13
Jilin	−0.031	14	−0.018	19	−0.028	27	0.023	7	−0.007	14
Shaanxi	−0.042	15	−0.019	20	−0.012	16	0.007	13	−0.018	20
Heilongjiang	−0.043	16	−0.015	15	−0.017	18	−0.003	17	−0.007	15

Henan	−0.048	17	0.006	11	−0.011	15	0.004	15	−0.047	30
Anhui	−0.058	18	−0.005	13	−0.025	23	0.004	14	−0.033	28
Hunan	−0.065	19	−0.016	16	−0.013	17	−0.021	22	−0.015	18
Jiangxi	−0.078	20	0.009	9	−0.023	21	−0.035	25	−0.029	27
Sichuan	−0.082	21	−0.020	21	−0.018	20	−0.018	21	−0.026	25
Xinjiang	−0.088	22	−0.081	28	0.052	3	−0.039	26	−0.019	21
Shanxi	−0.092	23	−0.062	26	−0.027	24	0.008	12	−0.011	17
Guangxi	−0.096	24	−0.025	22	−0.023	22	−0.013	19	−0.035	29
Chongqing	−0.104	25	−0.017	17	−0.041	28	−0.031	24	−0.016	19
Gansu	−0.152	26	−0.052	25	−0.028	25	−0.049	28	−0.024	23
Yunnan	−0.160	27	−0.038	23	−0.049	29	−0.047	27	−0.027	26
Ningxia	−0.183	28	−0.133	30	−0.017	19	−0.029	23	−0.004	12
Guizhou	−0.186	29	−0.077	27	−0.055	30	−0.052	29	−0.002	10
Qinghai	−0.201	30	−0.092	29	−0.028	26	−0.061	30	−0.020	22

Note: ① The results are obtained based on calculations with 2010 data for each GDEG indicator; ② The provinces (autonomous regions/municipalities directly under the central government) are listed in descending order of GDEG value; ③ The score by GDEG in this table is the sum of the scores by the four Second-Class Indicators: Green Growth Efficiency Indicators, Primary Industry Indicators, Secondary Industry Indicators, and Tertiary Industry Indicators; ④ The calculations are based on the *China Statistical Yearbook 2011*, *China Environmental Statistical Yearbook 2011*, *China Environment Annual Report 2010*, *China City Statistical Yearbook 2011*, *China Water Conservancy Statistical Yearbook 2011*, *China Industrial Economy Statistical Yearbook 2011*, and *Deserts in China and Desertification Control*

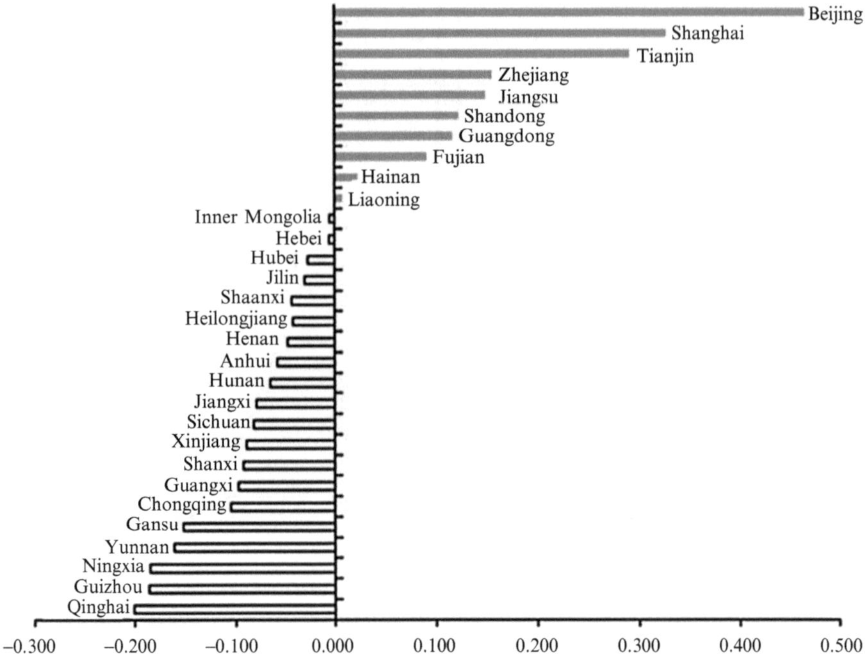

Fig. 2.1 Rankings of provinces by GDEG (Note: This Figure is developed based on relevant data in Table 2.1)

10 by Tertiary Industry Indicators (TII) are Beijing, Shanghai, Tianjin, Guangdong, Jiangsu, Zhejiang, Hainan, Liaoning, Inner Mongolia and Guizhou.

Figure 2.2 is about the rankings of provinces by GDEG. The top 10 provinces are marked with dark green, those ranking 11th–20th with moderate green and the bottom 10 with light green. The darker the green is, the higher the GDEG is. Geographically, "dark green" provinces concentrate in the eastern coastal areas; "moderate green" provinces are mostly in the central eastern region; "light green" provinces are mainly in central western China.

Based on the above table and figures, the following analyses are focused three aspects, namely the regional differences in GDEG, the differences between provinces in GDEG in each region, and the relations between GDEG and GDI.

2.1.1 Regional Differences in GDEG

Generally, measured by GDEG, Eastern China outperforms Northeast and Central China which beat Western China. Of the10 provinces in the eastern region,[2] nine are in the top 10, and the only exception is Hebei (12th). Beijing ranks first with a

[2] Eastern China includes Beijing, Tianjin, Hebei, Shanghai, Jiangsu, Zhejiang, Fujian, Shandong, Guangdong and Hainan; Central China includes Shanxi, Anhui, Jiangxi, Henan, Hubei and Hunan; Western China includes Inner Mongolia, Guangxi, Chongqing, Sichuan, Guizhou, Yunnan, Tibet, Shaanxi, Gansu, Qinghai, Ningxia and Xinjiang; Northeast China includes Liaoning, Jilin and Heilongjiang.

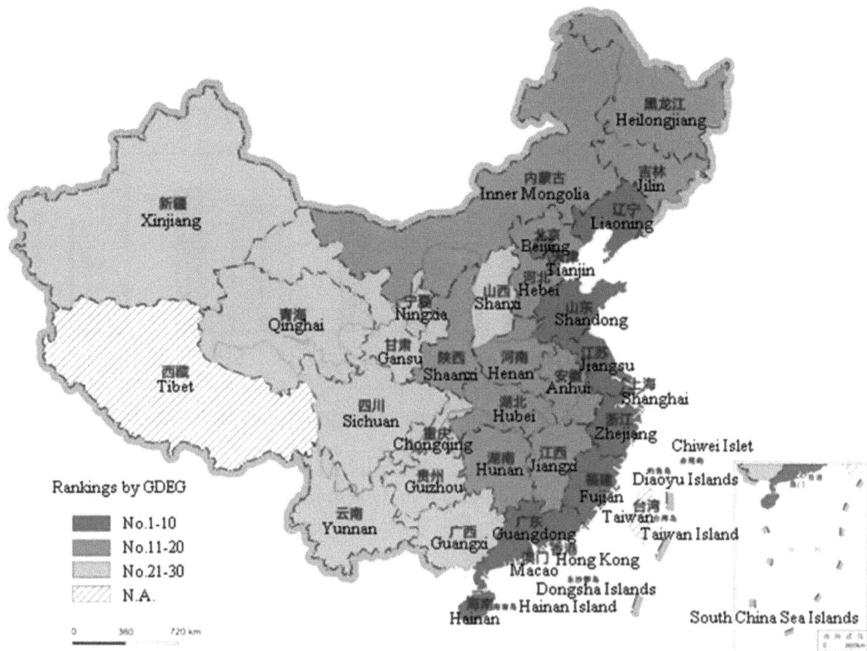

Fig. 2.2 GDEG rankings by region (Note: This Figure is developed based on relevant data in Table 2.1)

high score of 0.465 and also leads the country by all the Second-Class Indicators, except for SII. The three northeastern provinces rank 10th, 14th and 16th respectively, above the average level. As for the central six provinces, Hubei ranks 13th and the remaining five rank between 17th and 23rd, below the average level. Of the 11 provinces in Western China, Inner Mongolia ranks 11th and Shaanxi 15th, while the other eight provinces, including Sichuan, Xinjiang, Guangxi, Chongqing, Gansu, Yunnan, Ningxia, Guizhou and Qinghai, rank from 21st to 30th (Fig. 2.3).

There are also large gaps between the four regions in terms of the four Second-Class Indicators. The largest gap is found in GGEI. Western provinces are far behind eastern ones; while central and northeastern provinces, whose scores are close, are both below the national average, between eastern and western provinces. In terms of PII, eastern provinces stand out, and the rest three regions with narrow gaps in between fail to reach the national average. As for SII where small regional gaps are shown, eastern and northeastern provinces are above the national average while central and western provinces are slightly below the average. By TII, all the four regions score close to the national average. Eastern provinces above the national average are followed closely by northeastern ones, and western provinces beat central ones, unlike the other three Second-Class Indicators of GDEG by which they score the lowest.

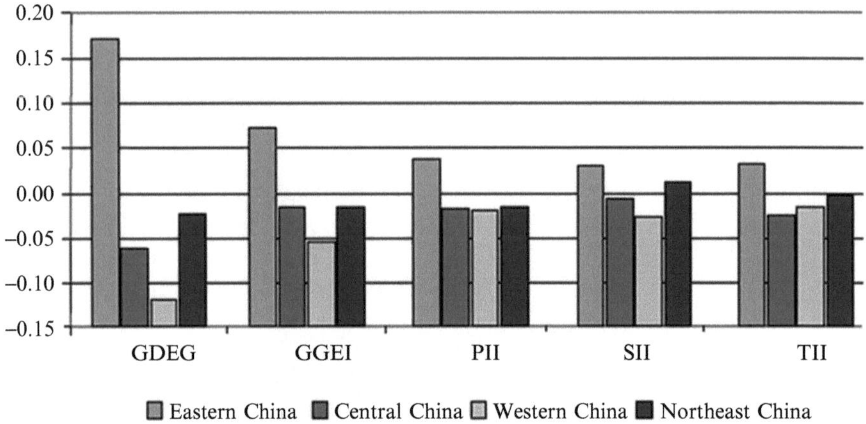

Fig. 2.3 GDEG comparison by region (Note: The data for each region in the figure are the arithmetic mean of the scores of all the provinces in the region)

2.1.2 GDEG in Each Region

Provinces in each region have quite close GDEG. Nine of the 10 eastern provinces (except Hebei) are all above the national average, ranking 1st–9th; Hebei ranks 12th with a score of −0.007, 0.472 lower than Beijing. The six central provinces score between −0.027 and −0.092, all below the national average; and the gap between the highest-ranking Hubei and the lowest-ranking Shanxi is 0.065, indicating that the differences between the six provinces are very small. The 11 western provinces are also below the national average; Inner Mongolia has the highest score of −0.005 and Qinghai has the lowest −0.201, a gap of 0.196. In Northeast China, Liaoning scores 0.007, above the national average; Jilin and Heilongjiang score −0.031 and −0.043 respectively. The details are given in Table 2.2 below.

2.1.3 Impact of GDEG on Green Development

A comparison of the rankings by GDEG and GGEI shows that there is a gap of five places or fewer in 15, or half, of the evaluated provinces; a gap of 10 places or more is seen in six, or one-fifth, of the provinces, including Qinghai, Yunnan, Guizhou, Liaoning, Hubei and Henan (Table 2.3).

GDEG is an integral part of GDI. Table 2.3 shows that, the gaps between the rankings by GDEG and GGEI are generally small in developed eastern provinces. None of the six provinces showing the largest gaps is in Eastern China. It indicates to some extent that GDEG has a considerable impact on green development and increasing GDEG will help to promote green development.

Table 2.2 Regional differences by GDEG

Region	Province	Score	Ranking	Region	Province	Score	Ranking
Eastern China	Beijing	0.465	1	Western China	Inner Mongolia	−0.005	11
	Tianjin	0.291	3		Guangxi	−0.096	24
	Hebei	−0.007	12		Chongqing	−0.104	25
	Shanghai	0.327	2		Sichuan	−0.082	21
	Jiangsu	0.149	5		Guizhou	−0.186	29
	Zhejiang	0.157	4		Yunnan	−0.160	27
	Fujian	0.091	8		Shaanxi	−0.042	15
	Shandong	0.122	6		Gansu	−0.152	26
	Guangdong	0.116	7		Qinghai	−0.201	30
	Hainan	0.022	9		Ningxia	−0.183	28
Central China	Shanxi	−0.092	23		Xinjiang	−0.088	22
	Anhui	−0.058	18	Northeast China	Liaoning	0.007	10
	Jiangxi	−0.078	20		Jilin	−0.031	14
	Henan	−0.048	17		Heilongjiang	−0.043	16
	Hubei	−0.027	13				
	Hunan	−0.065	19				

Note: This table is developed based on Table 2.1

2.2 Inter-provincial Comparison by GDEG

With a 30 % weight in the GDI system, GDEG is composed of 22 Third-Class Indicators, including 12 positive ones and 10 negative ones. We have only measured 20 of the indicators.

2.2.1 Comparison by GGEI

GGEI has a 45 % weight in the GDEG system and 13.5 % in the GDI system, contributing more to GDEG than the other three indicators. GGEI is a weighted combination of nine indicators as shown in Table 2.4.

Among the nine Third-Class Indicators of GGEI, indicator 1 "GDP per capita", indicator 2 "Energy consumption per unit of GDP", and indicator 3 "Ratio of non-fossil energy consumption to total energy consumption" take a weight of 1.70 % each, higher than the weight of the other six indicators (1.40 %). The weighting is made based on the following considerations: indicator 1 is the only one to assess the level of economic development so more weight is given; since local governments have taken reducing energy consumption per unit of GDP as a goal, indicator 2 is given more weight than the other six; increasing the weight of indicator 3, an important criterion for assessing the change of energy mix, helps to make clearer the right direction of pursuing green development. Unfortunately, measurement by indicator 3 is not done due to the lack of data for some provinces. Each of the other six indicators is given a weight of 1.40 %. In short, the nine

Table 2.3 Differences between the rankings by GDI and GDEG

Province	Ranking by GDI	Ranking by GDEG	Difference	Province	Ranking by GDI	Ranking by GDEG	Difference
Beijing	1	1	0	Heilongjiang	16	16	0
Tianjin	2	3	−1	Hebei	17	12	5
Guangdong	3	7	−4	Jiangxi	18	20	−2
Hainan	4	9	−5	Chongqing	19	25	−6
Zhejiang	5	4	1	Jilin	20	14	6
Qinghai	6	30	−24	Sichuan	21	21	0
Yunnan	7	27	−20	Anhui	22	18	4
Fujian	8	8	0	Liaoning	23	10	13
Shanghai	9	2	7	Hubei	24	13	11
Shandong	10	6	4	Gansu	25	26	−1
Inner Mongolia	11	11	0	Guangxi	26	24	2
Jiangsu	12	5	7	Hunan	27	19	8
Guizhou	13	29	−16	Ningxia	28	28	0
Shaanxi	14	15	−1	Shanxi	29	23	6
Xinjiang	15	22	−7	Henan	30	17	13

Note: This table is developed based on Tables 1.5 and 2.1

Table 2.4 GGEI, weights and attributes

No.	Indicator	Weight (%)	Attribute
1	GDP per capita	1.70	Positive
2	Energy consumption per unit of GDP	1.70	Negative
3	Ratio of non-fossil energy consumption to total energy consumption	1.70	Positive
4	CO_2 emissions per unit of GDP	1.40	Negative
5	SO_2 emissions per unit of GDP	1.40	Negative
6	COD emissions per unit of GDP	1.40	Negative
7	Nitrogen oxide emissions per unit of GDP	1.40	Negative
8	Ammonia/nitrogen emissions per unit of GDP	1.40	Negative
9	Electricity consumption per capita in urban areas	1.40	Negative

Note: The content of this table was finalized after discussions at several seminars held by the research group

Table 2.5 2010 rankings of 30 provinces by GGEI

Province	Score	Ranking	Province	Score	Ranking
Beijing	0.235	1	Hunan	−0.016	16
Shanghai	0.110	2	Chongqing	−0.017	17
Tianjin	0.078	3	Hubei	−0.018	18
Zhejiang	0.077	4	Jilin	−0.018	19
Jiangsu	0.074	5	Shaanxi	−0.019	20
Guangdong	0.057	6	Sichuan	−0.020	21
Shandong	0.048	7	Guangxi	−0.025	22
Fujian	0.037	8	Yunnan	−0.038	23
Jiangxi	0.009	9	Inner Mongolia	−0.043	24
Hainan	0.008	10	Gansu	−0.052	25
Henan	0.006	11	Shanxi	−0.062	26
Hebei	0.005	12	Guizhou	−0.077	27
Anhui	−0.005	13	Xinjiang	−0.081	28
Liaoning	−0.013	14	Qinghai	−0.092	29
Heilongjiang	−0.015	15	Ningxia	−0.133	30

Note: The scores and rankings are worked out based on *China Statistical Yearbook 2011*, *China Environmental Statistical Yearbook 2011*, *China Environment Annual Report 2010*, *China City Statistical Yearbook 2011*, *China Water Conservancy Statistical Yearbook 2011*, *China Industrial Economy Statistical Yearbook 2011*, and *Deserts in China and Desertification Control*

indicators are complementary to each other and still are weighted differently with a view to evaluating the efficiency of green growth in a holistic way.

As shown in Table 2.5 and Fig. 2.4, nine of the top 10 provinces by GGEI are in Eastern China, including Beijing, Shanghai, Tianjin, Zhejiang, Jiangsu, Guangdong, Shandong, Fujian and Hainan, and they are also among the top 10 by GDEG. The provinces ranking 11th–20th by GGEI are Henan, Hebei, Anhui, Liaoning, Heilongjiang, Hunan, Chongqing, Hubei, Jilin and Shaanxi. Of them, there is one eastern province, four central ones, two western ones, and all the three northeastern provinces. The bottom 10 are Sichuan, Guangxi, Yunnan, Inner Mongolia, Gansu, Shanxi, Guizhou, Xinjiang, Qinghai and Ningxia, of which only Shanxi is in Central China and the rest nine are all in Western China.

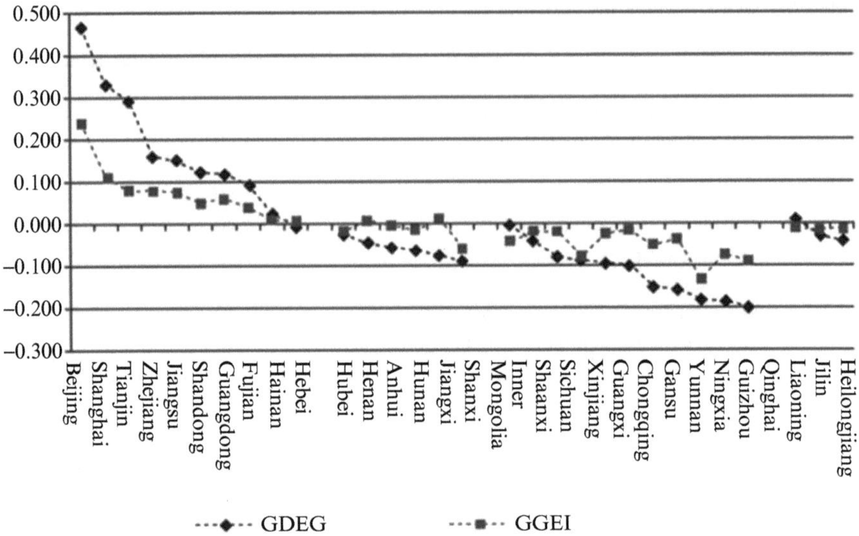

Fig. 2.4 Inter-provincial comparison by GGEI and GDEG (Note: The provinces in the figure are grouped by region, namely Eastern, Central, Western and Northeast China, and arranged from *left* to *right* in descending order of GDEG)

Table 2.6 PII, weights and attributes

No.	Indicator	Weight (%)	Attribute
10	Labor productivity of the primary sector	1.13	Positive
11	Land productivity	1.13	Positive
12	Proportion of water-saving irrigated area in effectively irrigated area	1.13	Positive
13	Proportion of effectively irrigated area in cultivated land area	1.13	Positive

Note: The content of this table was finalized after discussions at several seminars held by the research group

As shown in Fig. 2.4, eastern provinces (except Hebei) are all above the national average by GGEI, but there are big differences between them; Beijing is far ahead of other provinces with a score of 0.235. Slightly below the national average, the six central provinces and three northeastern provinces are quite close to each other. Western provinces as a whole are at a low level and there are some differences between them.

2.2.2 *Comparison by PII*

In the GDEG system, a 15 % weight is given to PII, under which there are four Third-Class Indicators (Table 2.6). Each of the four indicators takes a 1.13 % weight, the lowest among all the Third-Class Indicators.

Table 2.7 2010 rankings of 30 provinces by PII

Province	Score	Ranking	Province	Score	Ranking
Beijing	0.085	1	Shaanxi	−0.012	16
Shanghai	0.059	2	Hunan	−0.013	17
Xinjiang	0.052	3	Heilongjiang	−0.017	18
Zhejiang	0.047	4	Ningxia	−0.017	19
Fujian	0.041	5	Sichuan	−0.018	20
Tianjin	0.041	6	Jiangxi	−0.023	21
Jiangsu	0.038	7	Guangxi	−0.023	22
Hainan	0.019	8	Anhui	−0.025	23
Hebei	0.019	9	Shanxi	−0.027	24
Shandong	0.017	10	Gansu	−0.028	25
Guangdong	0.003	11	Qinghai	−0.028	26
Liaoning	0.000	12	Jilin	−0.028	27
Inner Mongolia	−0.002	13	Chongqing	−0.041	28
Hubei	−0.005	14	Yunnan	−0.049	29
Henan	−0.011	15	Guizhou	−0.055	30

Note: The scores and rankings are worked out based on *China Statistical Yearbook 2011*, *China Environmental Statistical Yearbook 2011*, *China Environment Annual Report 2010*, *China City Statistical Yearbook 2011*, *China Water Conservancy Statistical Yearbook 2011*, *China Industrial Economy Statistical Yearbook 2011*, and *Deserts in China and Desertification Control*

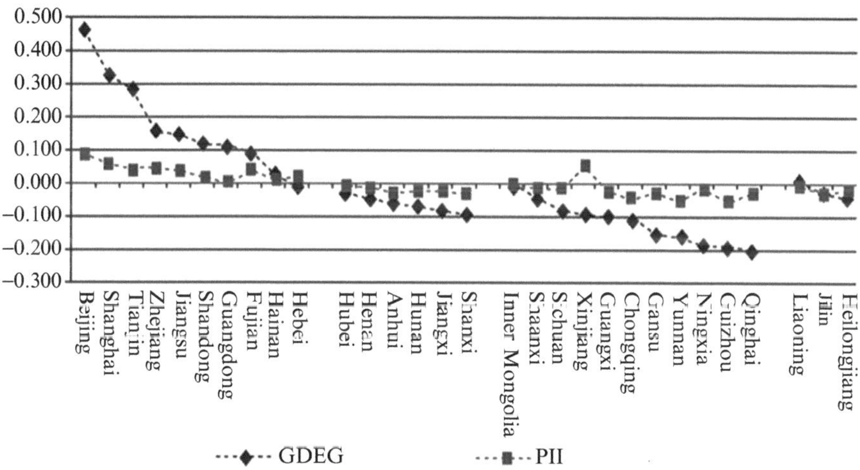

Fig. 2.5 Inter-provincial comparison by PII and GDEG (Note: The provinces in the figure are grouped by region, namely Eastern, Central, Western and Northeast China, and arranged from *left* to *right* in descending order of GDEG)

According to Table 2.7 and Fig. 2.5, the top 10 provinces by PII are Beijing, Shanghai, Xinjiang, Zhejiang, Fujian, Tianjin, Jiangsu, Hainan, Hebei and Shandong, all in Eastern China except the western province Xinjiang. The provinces ranking 11th–20th are Guangdong, Liaoning, Inner Mongolia, Hubei, Henan, Shaanxi, Hunan, Heilongjiang, Ningxia and Sichuan,; of them, Guangdong is in

Table 2.8 SII, weights and attributes

No.	Indicator	Weight (%)	Attribute
14	Labor productivity of the secondary sector	1.25	Positive
15	Water consumption per unit of value added created by industrial enterprises	1.25	Negative
16	Energy consumption per unit of value added created by industrial enterprises above designated size	1.25	Negative
17	Utilization ratio of industrial solid waste	1.25	Positive
18	Recycling rate of industrial water	1.25	Positive
19	Ratio of the output of six energy-intensive industries to gross industrial output	1.25	Negative

Note: The content of this table was finalized after discussions at several seminars held by the research group

Eastern China while three are in Central China, four in Western China and two in Northeast China. The bottom 10 are Jiangxi, Guangxi, Anhui, Shanxi, Gansu, Qinghai, Jilin, Chongqing, Yunnan and Guizhou.

As shown in Fig. 2.5, the eastern provinces are above the national average and the differences between them are small; Beijing ranks No.1 with a score of 0.085. The six central provinces and three northeastern provinces are close to the national average and do not have large differences. Western provinces as a whole are at a low level and there are big differences between them. Xinjiang ranks 3rd with a score of 0.052 while Guizhou is at the bottom with a score of only −0.055 so their difference is larger than 0.1.

2.2.3 Comparison by SII

In the GDEG system, a 25 % weight is given to SII, under which there are six Third-Class Indicators: 14–19. Each of the six indicators takes a 1.25 % weight (Table 2.8).

As shown in Table 2.9 and Fig. 2.6, the top 10 provinces by SII are Tianjin, Shandong, Shanghai, Inner Mongolia, Guangdong, Jiangsu, Jilin, Zhejiang, Fujian and Liaoning; of them, Inner Mongolia is in Western China, Jilin and Liaoning in Northeast China, and the rest seven in Eastern China. The provinces ranking 11th–20th are Beijing, Shanxi, Shaanxi, Anhui, Henan, Hubei, Heilongjiang, Hebei, Guangxi and Hainan. The bottom 10 are Sichuan, Hunan, Ningxia, Chongqing, Jiangxi, Xinjiang, Yunnan, Gansu, Guizhou and Qinghai.

As shown in Fig. 2.6, Eastern provinces as a whole are above the national average except Hainan and Hebei, and there are big differences between them; Tianjin, at 0.103, is far ahead while Hainan, at −0.014, ranks 20th. The six central provinces and three northeastern provinces are close to the national average and do not have big differences. The western provinces at a low level on the whole and the gaps between them are big. Inner Mongolia ranks 4th with a score of 0.036 while Qinghai is at the bottom with a score of only −0.061.

Table 2.9 2010 rankings of 30 provinces by SII

Province	Score	Ranking	Province	Score	Ranking
Tianjin	0.103	1	Hubei	0.000	16
Shandong	0.065	2	Heilongjiang	−0.003	17
Shanghai	0.049	3	Hebei	−0.006	18
Inner Mongolia	0.036	4	Guangxi	−0.013	19
Guangdong	0.034	5	Hainan	−0.014	20
Jiangsu	0.023	6	Sichuan	−0.018	21
Jilin	0.023	7	Hunan	−0.021	22
Zhejiang	0.022	8	Ningxia	−0.029	23
Fujian	0.015	9	Chongqing	−0.031	24
Liaoning	0.014	10	Jiangxi	−0.035	25
Beijing	0.008	11	Xinjiang	−0.039	26
Shanxi	0.008	12	Yunnan	−0.047	27
Shaanxi	0.007	13	Gansu	−0.049	28
Anhui	0.004	14	Guizhou	−0.052	29
Henan	0.004	15	Qinghai	−0.061	30

Note: The scores and rankings are worked out based on *China Statistical Yearbook 2011*, *China Environmental Statistical Yearbook 2011*, *China Environmental Statistical Yearbook 2010*, *China City Statistical Yearbook 2011*, *China Water Conservancy Statistical Yearbook 2011*, *China Industrial Economy Statistical Yearbook 2011*, and *Deserts in China and Desertification Control*

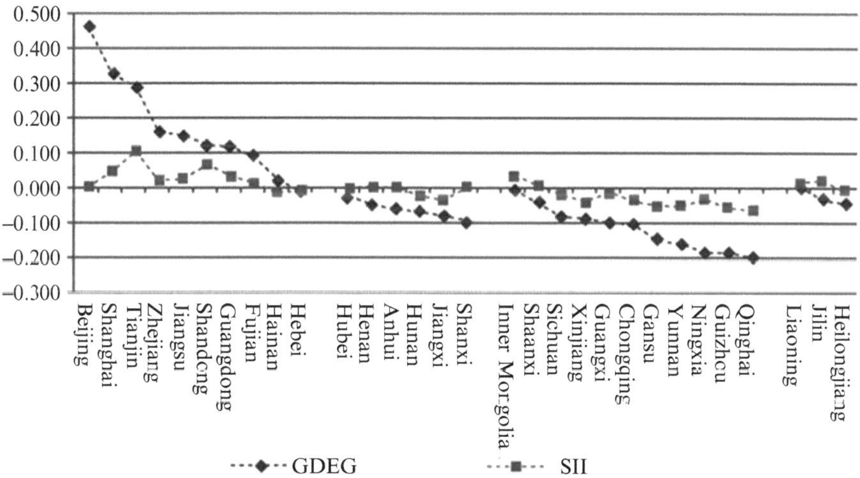

Fig. 2.6 Inter-provincial comparison by SII and GDEG (Note: The provinces in the figure are grouped by region, namely Eastern, Central, Western and Northeast China, and arranged from *left* to *right* in descending order of GDEG)

Table 2.10 TII, weights and attributes

No.	Indicator	Weight (%)	Attribute
20	Labor productivity of the tertiary sector	1.50	Positive
21	Proportion of the value added of the tertiary sector in GDP	1.50	Positive
22	Proportion of tertiary sector employees in the total employed population	1.50	Positive

Note: The content of this table was finalized after discussions at several seminars held by the research group

Table 2.11 2010 rankings of 30 provinces by TII

Province	Score	Ranking	Province	Score	Ranking
Beijing	0.137	1	Shandong	−0.009	16
Shanghai	0.109	2	Shanxi	−0.011	17
Tianjin	0.069	3	Hunan	−0.015	18
Guangdong	0.022	4	Chongqing	−0.016	19
Jiangsu	0.015	5	Shaanxi	−0.018	20
Zhejiang	0.012	6	Xinjiang	−0.019	21
Hainan	0.009	7	Qinghai	−0.020	22
Liaoning	0.005	8	Gansu	−0.024	23
Inner Mongolia	0.004	9	Hebei	−0.025	24
Guizhou	−0.002	10	Sichuan	−0.026	25
Fujian	−0.002	11	Yunnan	−0.027	26
Ningxia	−0.004	12	Jiangxi	−0.029	27
Hubei	−0.004	13	Anhui	−0.033	28
Jilin	−0.007	14	Guangxi	−0.035	29
Heilongjiang	−0.007	15	Henan	−0.047	30

Note: The scores and rankings are worked out based on *China Statistical Yearbook 2011*, *China Environmental Statistical Yearbook 2011*, *China Environment Annual Report 2010*, *China City Statistical Yearbook 2011*, *China Water Conservancy Statistical Yearbook 2011*, *China Industrial Economy Statistical Yearbook 2011*, and *Deserts in China and Desertification Control*

2.2.4 Comparison by TII

In the GDEG system, a 15 % weight is given to TII, under which there are three Third-Class Indicators: 20–22. Each of the three indicators takes a 1.50 % weight. The weights and properties of these indicators are shown in Table 2.10.

As shown in Table 2.11 and Fig. 2.7 show that, the top 10 TII provinces by TII are Beijing, Shanghai, Tianjin, Guangdong, Jiangsu, Zhejiang, Hainan, Liaoning, Inner Mongolia and Guizhou, of which them, Inner Mongolia and Guizhou are from in the Western China, Liaoning from the in Northeast China and the rest seven from the in Eastern China. The top provinces ranking 11th–20th are Fujian, Ningxia, Hubei, Jilin, Heilongjiang, Shandong, Shanxi, Hunan, Chongqing and Shaanxi. The bottom 10 are Xinjiang, Qinghai, Gansu, Hebei, Sichuan, Yunnan, Jiangxi, Anhui, Guangxi and Henan.

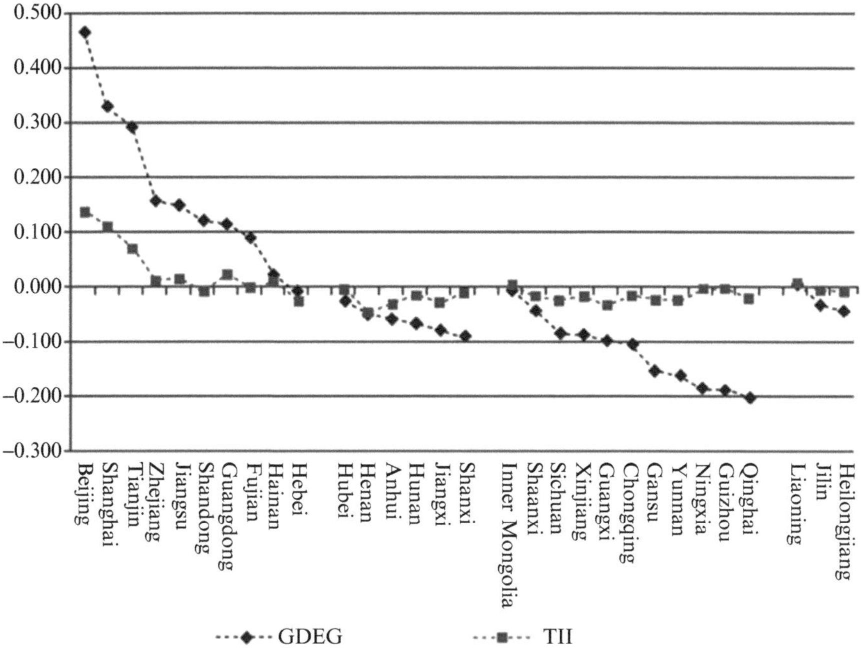

Fig. 2.7 Inter-provincial comparison by TII and GDEG (Note: The provinces in the figure are grouped by region, namely Eastern, Central, Western and Northeast China, and arranged from *left* to *right* in descending order of GDEG)

As shown in Fig. 2.7, eastern provinces as a whole are better but there are wide gaps between them. Beijing, Shanghai and Tianjin are the top three while Shandong, Fujian and Hebei with low scores rank 16th, 11th and 24th respectively. The gaps between the six central provinces are also large. Hubei, at −0.004, ranks 13th while Henan at −0.047 is at the bottom. Western provinces as a whole are at a low level but there are still big gaps. Inner Mongolia ranks 9th with a score of 0.004 while Guangxi, at −0.035, ranks 29th. Comparatively speaking, the three north-eastern provinces are close to the national average and do not show big differences. In short, the development measured by TII is unbalanced in each region.

Chapter 3
CCPNRE Measurement and Analysis by Province

Mingqing Jiang and Yang Liu

The Carrying Capacity Potential of Natural Resources and Environment (CCPNRE) measures how far the economic development and human activities in a region will go given its resource abundance, ecological conservation, environmental pressure and climate change. As an important component of the GDI, CCPNRE reflects how much resources a region is endowed with, how good the ecology is, and how human activities impact its natural resources, ecological environment, and climate.

From the perspective of regional comparison, this chapter uses the PGDI system to calculate the CCPNRE of 30 provinces, analyzes the characteristics of these provinces in two aspects, i.e., Resource Abundance and Ecological Conservation, and Environmental Pressure and Climate Change, and describes their differences in ICCPNRE.

3.1 Results of CCPNRE Measurement

The CCPNRE of 30 provinces in China is calculated in line with the related measurement and weighting standards of the PGDI system and the results are shown in Table 3.1 below.

As shown in Table 3.1, the top 10 provinces by CCPNRE are Qinghai, Guizhou, Yunnan, Heilongjiang, Inner Mongolia, Hainan, Sichuan, Gansu, Xinjiang and Jilin. The top 10 by Resource Abundance and Ecological Conservation Indicators (RAECI) are Qinghai, Inner Mongolia, Heilongjiang, Yunnan, Jilin, Sichuan, Hainan, Jiangxi, Fujian and Guangxi. The top 10 by Environmental Pressure and

M. Jiang (✉)
National Bureau of Statistics of China, Beijing, China
e-mail: jiangmch@gj.stats.cn

Y. Liu
Beijing Normal University, Beijing, China

X. Li and J. Pan (eds.), *China Green Development Index Report 2012: Regional Comparison*, Current Chinese Economic Report Series,
DOI 10.1007/978-3-642-54178-0_3,

Table 3.1 Rankings of 30 provinces by CCPNRE

Indicator	Carrying Capacity Potential of Natural Resources and Environment		Second-Class Indicators: Resource Abundance and Ecological Conservation Indicators		Second-Class Indicators: Environmental Pressure and Climate Change Indicators	
Province	Score	Ranking	Score	Ranking	Score	Ranking
Qinghai	0.466	1	0.160	1	0.307	1
Guizhou	0.271	2	−0.028	20	0.299	2
Yunnan	0.224	3	0.076	4	0.149	3
Heilongjiang	0.181	4	0.114	3	0.067	5
Inner Mongolia	0.103	5	0.125	2	−0.023	15
Hainan	0.101	6	0.046	7	0.055	7
Sichuan	0.093	7	0.050	6	0.043	8
Gansu	0.077	8	−0.021	17	0.098	4
Xinjiang	0.049	9	0.011	11	0.038	9
Jilin	0.044	10	0.060	5	−0.017	12
Shaanxi	0.038	11	−0.022	18	0.060	6
Jiangxi	0.021	12	0.045	8	−0.024	16
Fujian	−0.023	13	0.034	9	−0.057	22
Beijing	−0.035	14	−0.060	23	0.024	10
Guangxi	−0.045	15	0.027	10	−0.072	24
Chongqing	−0.049	16	−0.028	19	−0.021	14
Anhui	−0.049	17	−0.058	22	0.010	11
Hunan	−0.050	18	−0.004	14	−0.047	19
Zhejiang	−0.074	19	−0.009	16	−0.065	23
Liaoning	−0.077	20	−0.002	13	−0.075	26
Guangdong	−0.086	21	−0.008	15	−0.078	27
Hubei	−0.091	22	−0.035	21	−0.056	21
Hebei	−0.094	23	−0.074	29	−0.020	13
Shandong	−0.099	24	−0.065	25	−0.034	18
Henan	−0.103	25	−0.075	30	−0.028	17
Shanxi	−0.124	26	−0.072	28	−0.052	20
Tianjin	−0.134	27	−0.062	24	−0.072	25
Jiangsu	−0.153	28	−0.066	26	−0.087	28
Ningxia	−0.181	29	−0.068	27	−0.112	29
Shanghai	−0.200	30	0.010	12	−0.210	30

Note: ① The results are obtained based on calculations with 2009 and 2010 data for each CCPNRE indicator; ② The provinces (autonomous regions/municipalities directly under the central government) are listed in descending order of CCPNRE value; ③ The calculations are based on the *China Statistical Yearbook 2011*, *China Environmental Statistical Yearbook 2011*, *China Environment Annual Report 2010*, *China City Statistical Yearbook 2011*, *China Water Conservancy Statistical Yearbook 2011*, *China Industrial Economy Statistical Yearbook 2011*, and *Deserts in China and Desertification Control*

Climate Change Indicators (EPCCI) are Qinghai, Guizhou, Yunnan, Gansu, Heilongjiang, Shaanxi, Hainan, Sichuan, Xinjiang, and Beijing.

Figure 3.1 is developed based on Table 3.1. The horizontal axis represents the value of CCPNRE, and "0" stands for the average CCPNRE of 30 provinces.

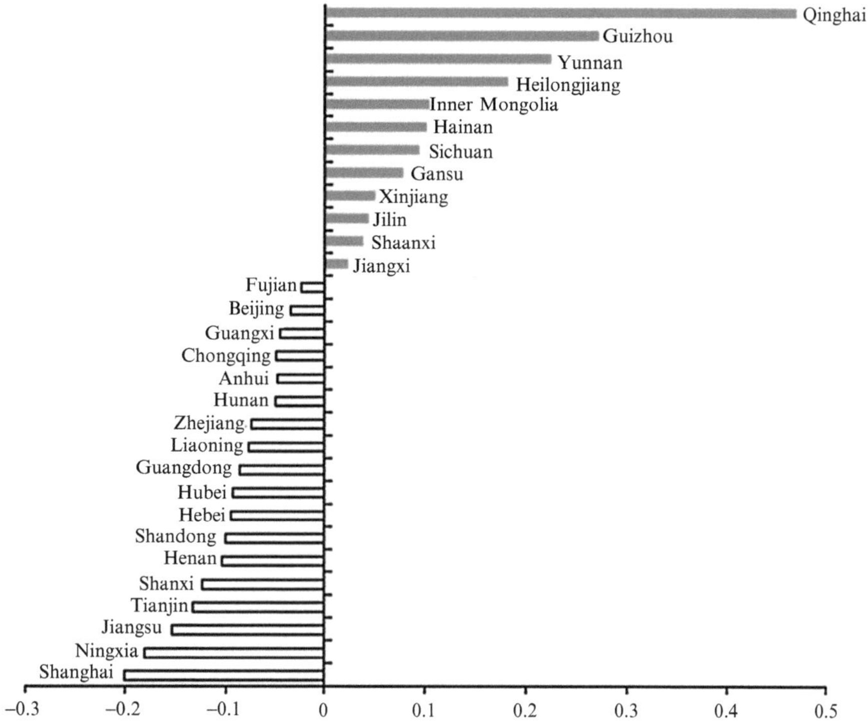

Fig. 3.1 Rankings of provinces by CCPNRE (Note: This figure is developed based on relevant data in Table 3.1)

The colored bars represent the provinces above the average level. The higher the value of CCPNRE is, the longer the colored bar is. The white bars represent those below the average. The lower the value of CCPNRE is, the longer the white bar is.

Figure 3.2 is about the rankings of provinces by CCPNRE. The top 10 provinces are marked with dark green, those ranking 11th–20th with moderate green and the bottom 10 with light green. The darker the green is, the greater the CCPNRE is. Geographically, "dark green" provinces concentrate in Western and Northeast China; "moderate green" provinces are mostly in Central and Eastern China; "light green" provinces are mainly in Eastern China.

Based on the results of measurement, the general features of CCPNRE in each of the 30 provinces are analyzed below.

3.1.1 Regional Differences in CCPNRE

The provincial differences in CCPNRE are notable. The largest difference is 0.66 and the standard deviation is 0.15 among the 30 provinces. The score of

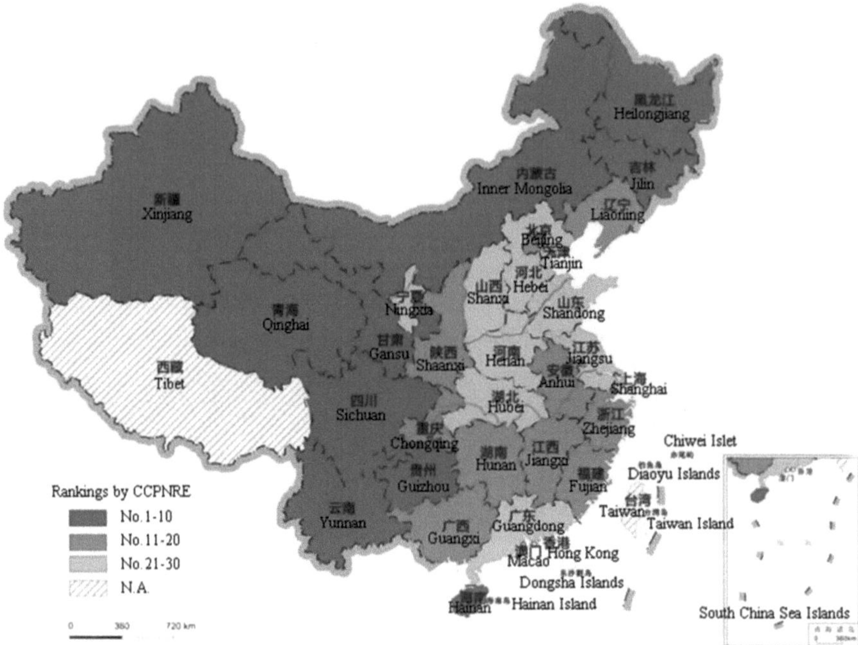

Fig. 3.2 CCPNRE rankings by region (Note: This figure is developed based on relevant data in Table 3.1)

No. 1 province Qinghai is 1.72 times that of No. 2 Guizhou and 2.08 times that of No. 3 Yunnan. In addition, 18 provinces score below the national average.[1]

Considerable differences can also be seen between the four regions, namely Eastern, Central, Northeast and Western China. As shown in Fig. 3.3, the CCPNRE of Western China is the greatest, followed by that of Northeast China and then Eastern and Central China. Specifically, Western and Northeast China score much higher by RAECI than Eastern and Central China do, while Western China is the best by EPCCI (Fig. 3.3 and Table 3.2).

Of the 10 eastern provinces, Hainan ranks No. 6; Fujian, Beijing and Zhejiang rank in the No. 13, 14 and 19 respectively; Guangdong, Hebei, Shandong, Tianjin, Jiangsu and Shanghai all rank low and Shanghai is even at the bottom. Among the six central provinces, Jiangxi ranks the highest at No. 12; Anhui and Hunan are in the middle, ranking No. 17 and 18; Hubei, Henan and Shanxi rank No. 22, 25 and 26. Of the 11 western provinces (Tibet not evaluated), Qinghai, Guizhou, Yunnan, Inner Mongolia, Sichuan, Gansu and Xinjiang all rank among the top 10, and eight of them score higher than the national average. Specifically, Qinghai, Guizhou and Yunnan rank top three; Shaanxi, Guangxi and Chongqing rank in the middle as No. 11, 15 and 16; Ningxia ranks No. 29. Of the three northeastern provinces,

[1] The value of the national average is zero.

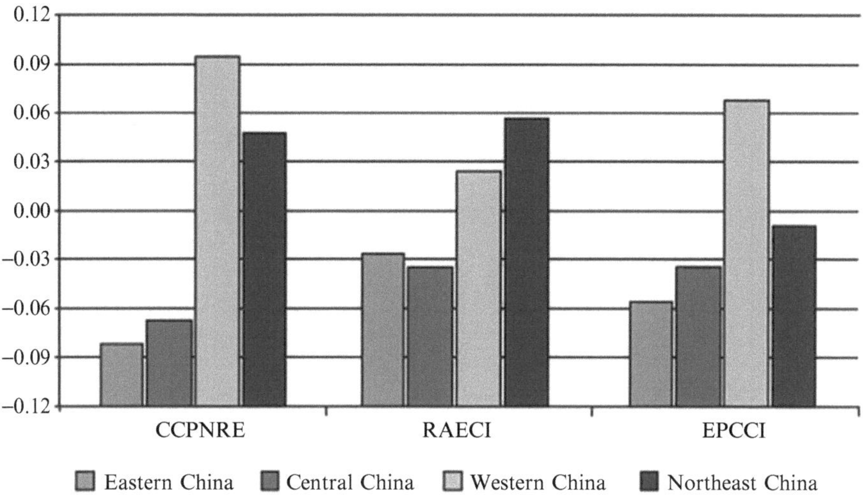

Fig. 3.3 CCPNRE comparison by region (Note: The data for each region in the figure are the arithmetic mean of the scores of all the provinces in the region)

Heilongjiang and Jilin are better and rank No. 4 and 10, but Liaoning lags behind, ranking No. 20.

The above analysis shows that CCPNRE varies greatly from province to province and the differences are apparently caused by regional factors. Identifying such factors will help to make breakthroughs in improving the CCPNRE of each province and minimizing the impact of weaknesses in this regard on development. In developed provinces with CCPNRE burden, restructuring should be accelerated to foster an innovation-driven growth model by reducing energy consumption and promoting energy saving and emissions reduction; less developed provinces with resource and environmental strengths, should learn from the experience and lessons of eastern provinces, and stick to the principle of being green in restructuring and pursuing development. The overall level of green development can only be raised based on the balance between green growth, environment friendliness and policy support. From a macro perspective, to make the Chinese economy greener, China should make the shift to a model of balanced and coordinated development and take more effective measures to promote the collaborations between different regions.

3.1.2 CCPNRE in Each Region

Except Northeast China, provinces in each of other three regions have quite close CCPNRE. Eastern provinces all rank low except Hainan (No. 6). Among them, Fujian, Beijing and Zhejiang rank in the middle as No. 13, 14 and 19; the rest six all rank in the bottom 10, and Shanghai comes last. The six central provinces all score

Table 3.2 CCPNRE rankings by region

Region	Province	Carrying Capacity Potential of Natural Resources and Environment	Resource Abundance and Ecological Conservation	Environmental Pressure and Climate Change	Region	Province	Carrying Capacity Potential of Natural Resources and Environment	Resource Abundance and Ecological Conservation	Environmental Pressure and Climate Change
Eastern China	Beijing	14	23	10	Western China	Inner Mongolia	5	2	15
	Tianjin	27	24	25		Guangxi	15	10	24
	Hebei	23	29	13		Chongqing	16	19	14
	Shanghai	30	12	30		Sichuan	7	6	8
	Jiangsu	28	26	28		Guizhou	2	20	2
	Zhejiang	19	16	23		Yunnan	3	4	3
	Fujian	13	9	22		Shaanxi	11	18	6
	Shandong	24	25	18		Gansu	8	17	4
	Guangdong	21	15	27		Qinghai	1	1	1
	Hainan	6	7	7		Ningxia	29	27	29
Central China	Shanxi	26	28	20		Xinjiang	9	11	9
	Anhui	17	22	11	Northeast China	Liaoning	20	13	26
	Jiangxi	12	8	16		Jilin	10	5	12
	Henan	25	30	17		Heilongjiang	4	3	5
	Hubei	22	21	21					
	Hunan	18	14	19					

Note: This table is developed based on Table 3.1

Table 3.3 Regional differences by CCPNRE

Region	Province	Score	Ranking	Region	Province	Score	Ranking
Eastern China	Beijing	−0.035	14	Western China	Inner Mongolia	0.103	5
	Tianjin	−0.134	27		Guangxi	−0.045	15
	Hebei	−0.094	23		Chongqing	−0.049	16
	Shanghai	−0.200	30		Sichuan	0.093	7
	Jiangsu	−0.153	28		Guizhou	0.271	2
	Zhejiang	−0.074	19		Yunnan	0.224	3
	Fujian	−0.023	13		Shaanxi	0.038	11
	Shandong	−0.099	24		Gansu	0.077	8
	Guangdong	−0.086	21		Qinghai	0.466	1
	Hainan	0.101	6		Ningxia	−0.181	29
Central China	Shanxi	−0.124	26		Xinjiang	0.049	9
	Anhui	−0.049	17	Northeast China	Liaoning	−0.077	20
	Jiangxi	0.021	12		Jilin	0.044	10
	Henan	−0.103	25		Heilongjiang	0.181	4
	Hubei	−0.091	22				
	Hunan	−0.050	18				

Note: This table is developed based on Table 3.1

below the national average except Jiangxi. The 11 western provinces are mostly ahead. Qinghai, Guizhou and Yunnan take the top three places, and eight provinces are above the national average, but Ningxia is next to the last. The three northeastern provinces differ greatly from each other. Heilongjiang ranks No. 4; Jilin ranks No. 10; Liaoning lags behind, ranking No. 20. The details are given in Table 3.3 above.

3.1.3 *Impact of CCPNRE on Green Development*

There is a notable gap between the rankings by GDI and CCPNRE in most provinces. Thirteen provinces have a gap of 10 places or more, and six provinces show a gap of even 15 places or more (Table 3.4).

Of the 13 provinces with a ranking gap of 10 places or more, seven are in Eastern China, including Beijing, Tianjin, Shanghai, Jiangsu, Zhejiang, Shandong and Guangdong; four are in Western China, including Guangxi, Sichuan, Guizhou and Gansu; and two are in Northeast China, including Jilin and Heilongjiang. There is none in Central China. Of the six provinces with a ranking gap of 15 places or more, five are in the eastern region and Gansu is the only western province.

Specifically, the largest gaps are found in the eastern region: Tianjin has a gap of 25 places and Shanghai 21 places.

In short, the largest gaps between CCPNRE and GDI rankings are seen in eastern provinces. Despite the low scores by CCPNRE, these provinces enjoy high GDI rankings because of the high scores by GDEG and SDGP. The Central, Western and Northeast China score high by CCPNRE thanks to their rich resources and

Table 3.4 Differences between the rankings by GDI and CCPNRE

Region	Province	Ranking by GDI	Ranking by CCPNRE	Difference	Region	Province	Ranking by GDI	Ranking by CCPNRE	Difference
Eastern China	Beijing	1	14	13	Western China	Inner Mongolia	11	5	−6
	Tianjin	2	27	25		Guangxi	26	15	−11
	Hebei	17	23	6		Chongqing	19	16	−3
	Shanghai	9	30	21		Sichuan	21	7	−14
	Jiangsu	12	28	16		Guizhou	13	2	−11
	Zhejiang	5	19	14		Yunnan	7	3	−4
	Fujian	8	13	5		Shaanxi	14	11	−3
	Shandong	10	24	15		Gansu	25	8	−17
	Guangdong	3	21	18		Qinghai	6	1	−5
	Hainan	4	6	2		Ningxia	28	29	1
Central China	Shanxi	29	26	−3		Xinjiang	15	9	−6
	Anhui	22	17	−5	Northeast China	Liaoning	23	20	−3
	Jiangxi	18	12	−6		Jilin	20	10	−10
	Henan	30	25	−5		Heilongjiang	16	4	−12
	Hubei	24	22	−2					
	Hunan	27	18	−9					

Note: This table is developed based on Tables 1.5 and 3.1

well-conserved ecological environment, but their unbalanced industrial structure, low economic inefficiency and low GDEG have dragged down their GDI. The differences between GDI and CCPNRE rankings are related to the level of economic development and natural endowments. Fundamentally, they are caused by the regional disparities in economic development and the special realities in China.

3.2 Inter-provincial Comparison by CCPNRE

With a 40 % weight in the GDI system, CCPNRE is composed of two Second-Class Indicators, namely Resource Abundance and Ecological Conservation Indicators (RAECI) and Environmental Pressure and Climate Change Indicators (EPCCI). There are 19 Third-Class Indicators, including 6 positive ones and 13 negative ones. We have only measured 17 of the indicators.

3.2.1 Results and Analysis of RAECI Measurement

RAECI has a 30 % weight in the CCPNRE system and 12 % in the GDI system.

In the selection of Third-Class Indicators of RAECI, considerations are made in the following two aspects: first, resources, namely natural resources that could be developed and used by humans to generate value, are objective reality; and second, ecological conservation is a measure taken by humans to protect the ecological system from damages and ensure its normal functioning.

In terms of composition, RAECI consists of six Third-class Indicators including water resources per capita, forest area per capita, forest coverage rate, proportion of the area of natural reserves in the total area of a region, proportion of the area of wetlands in the total area of a region, and growing stock per capita.

Moreover, the six Third-Class Indicators cover the most important natural resources water, forest and wetland, which enjoy equal significance and the same weight. The weights and attributes of the Third-Class Indicators are shown in Table 3.5.

The performances of all the provinces by RAECI are measured based on the processed data for the Third-Class Indicators and the weighting as shown in Table 3.5. The results are shown in Table 3.6.

As shown in Table 3.6 and Fig. 3.4, the RAECI curve is gentler than the CCPNRE curve, implying that there are no big differences between provinces by RAECI. The scores of provinces range from −0.075 to 0.160, with only three provinces, Qinghai, Inner Mongolia and Heilongjiang scoring higher than 0.1. The largest gap is 0.66 and the standard deviation is 0.062.

The top 10 provinces by RAECI are Qinghai, Inner Mongolia, Heilongjiang, Yunnan, Jilin, Sichuan, Hainan, Jiangxi, Fujian and Guangxi. Of them, five are in Western China, two in Northeast China, one in Central China and two in Eastern

Table 3.5 RAECI, weights and attributes

No.	Indicator	Weight (%)	Attribute
1	Water resources per capita	2.00	Positive
2	Forest area per capita	2.00	Positive
3	Forest coverage rate	**2.00**	Positive
4	Proportion of the area of natural reserves in the total area of a region	**2.00**	Positive
5	Proportion of the area of wetlands in the total area of a region	**2.00**	Positive
6	Growing stock per capita	**2.00**	Positive

Note: The content of this table was finalized after discussions at several seminars held by the research group

Table 3.6 Rankings of 30 provinces by RAECI

Indicator	RAECI		Indicator	RAECI	
Province	Score	Ranking	Province	Score	Ranking
Qinghai	0.160	1	Zhejiang	−0.009	16
Inner Mongolia	0.125	2	Gansu	−0.021	17
Heilongjiang	0.114	3	Shaanxi	−0.022	18
Yunnan	0.076	4	Chongqing	−0.028	19
Jilin	0.060	5	Guizhou	−0.028	20
Sichuan	0.050	6	Hubei	−0.035	21
Hainan	0.046	7	Anhui	−0.058	22
Jiangxi	0.045	8	Beijing	−0.060	23
Fujian	0.034	9	Tianjin	−0.062	24
Guangxi	0.027	10	Shandong	−0.065	25
Xinjiang	0.011	11	Jiangsu	−0.066	26
Shanghai	0.010	12	Ningxia	−0.068	27
Liaoning	−0.002	13	Shanxi	−0.072	28
Hunan	−0.004	14	Hebei	−0.075	29
Guangdong	−0.008	15	Henan	−0.075	30

Note: The scores and rankings are worked out based on *China Statistical Yearbook 2011*, *China Statistical Yearbook 2010*, *Deserts in China and Desertification Control*, *China Environment Annual Report 2010*, and *China Environmental Statistical Yearbook 2011*

China. Of the No. 11–20 provinces, half are in Western China, including No. 11 Xinjiang, No. 17 Gansu, No. 18 Shaanxi, No. 19 Chongqing and No. 20 Guizhou; three are in Eastern China, one in Central China and one in Northeast China. Of the bottom 10 provinces, five are in Eastern China, including No. 23 Beijing, No. 24 Tianjin, No. 25 Shandong, No.26 Jiangsu and No. 29 Hebei; four are in Central China, and one in Western China.

Specifically, the No.1 province is Qinghai whose score is much higher than those of the rest. It ranks first by two Third-Class Indicators: water resources per capita and proportion of the area of natural reserves in the total area of a region, and second by forest area per capita. It is worth mentioning that Qinghai's water

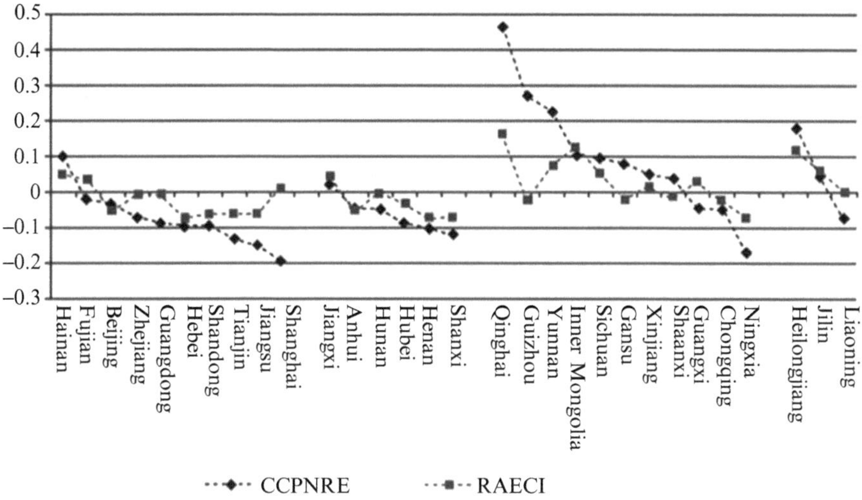

Fig. 3.4 Inter-provincial comparison by RAECI and CCPNRE (Note: The provinces in the figure are grouped by region, namely Eastern, Central, Western and Northeast China, and arranged from *left* to *right* in descending order of CCPNRE)

resources per capita is as high as 13,225.01 cubic meters/person, 2.39 timed that of No. 2 Hainan. Henan comes last by RAECI and ranks among the bottom 10 by all of the six Third-class Indicators, except "proportion of the area of wetlands in the total area of a region".

From a regional perspective, the northeastern provinces score the highest by RAECI, followed by western provinces and then eastern and central provinces with close scores. In Eastern China, the largest gap is 0.12 and Hainan and Hebei are respectively the top and bottom provinces; in Central China, the largest gap is 0.12 and Jiangxi and Henan are respectively the top and bottom provinces; in Western China, the largest gap is 0.228 and Qinghai and Ningxia are respectively the top and bottom provinces; in Northeast China, the largest gap is 0.116, and Heilongjiang and Liaoning are respectively the top and bottom provinces. Generally, the largest gap between the four regions is 0.091, far smaller than that in each region. It indicates that the differences between regions are much larger than those between provinces in a region.

3.2.2 Results and Analysis of EPCCI Measurement

EPCCI has a 70 % weight in the CCPNRE system and 28 % of in the GDI system.

The EPCCI is to measure the pressure on the environment caused by the consumption of natural resources and environmental pollution as result of human activities, and the climate change due to the massive discharge of pollutants, CO_2 emissions in particular.

Table 3.7 EPCCI, weights and attributes

No.	Indicator	Weight (%)	Attribute
1	CO_2 emissions per unit of land area	2.45	Negative
2	CO_2 emissions per capita	2.45	Negative
3	SO_2 emissions per unit of land area	1.97	Negative
4	SO_2 emissions per capita	1.97	Negative
5	COD emissions per unit of land area	1.97	Negative
6	COD emissions per capita	1.97	Negative
7	Nitrogen oxide emissions per unit of land area	1.97	Negative
8	Nitrogen oxide emissions per capita	1.97	Negative
9	Ammonia/nitrogen emissions per unit of land area	1.97	Negative
10	Ammonia/nitrogen emissions per capita	1.97	Negative
11	Consumption of chemical fertilizers per unit of cultivated land area	2.45	Negative
12	Consumption of pesticides per unit of cultivated land area	2.45	Negative
13	Nitrogen oxide emissions per capita from road transport	2.45	Negative

Note: The content of this table was finalized after discussions at several seminars held by the research group

EPCCI consists of 13 Third-Class Indicators, including CO_2 emissions per unit of land area, CO_2 emissions per capita, SO_2 emissions per unit of land area, SO_2 emissions per capita, COD emissions per unit of land area, COD emissions per capita, Nitrogen oxide emissions per unit of land area, Nitrogen oxide emissions per capita, Ammonia/nitrogen emissions per unit of land area, Ammonia/nitrogen emissions per capita, consumption of chemical fertilizers per unit of cultivated land area, consumption of pesticides per unit of cultivated land area, and Nitrogen oxide emissions per capita from road transport.

In addition, the weights of the Third-Class Indicators are adjusted compared with those in 2011. According to the views of evaluation experts in 2011, the eight indicators about pollutant emissions per unit of land area and per capita are correlated so their weights should be lowered. Based on discussions of experts, the research group reduces the weights of consumption of chemical fertilizers per unit of cultivated land area, consumption of pesticides per unit of cultivated land area, and nitrogen oxide emissions per capita from road transport to equal the weight of "CO2 emissions per unit of land area" at 2.45 % in 2011, and the excess weights are evenly shared by the rest eight indicators about pollutant emissions per unit of land area and per capita. Therefore, their average weight is reduced from 2.10 % adopted for 2011 to the 1.97 % for 2012. The weights and attributes of these Third-Class Indicators are shown in Table 3.7.

The performances of all the provinces by EPCCI are measured based on the processed data for the Third-Class Indicators and the weighting as shown in Table 3.7. The results are shown in Table 3.8.

As shown in Table 3.8 and Fig. 3.5, the EPCCI curve goes well with the CCPNRE curve. It implies that, compared with RAECI, EPCCI matters more in the score of CCPNRE.

Table 3.8 Rankings of 30 provinces by EPCCI

Indicator	EPCCI		Indicator	EPCCI	
Province	Score	Ranking	Province	Score	Ranking
Qinghai	0.307	1	Jiangxi	−0.024	16
Guizhou	0.299	2	Henan	−0.028	17
Yunnan	0.149	3	Shandong	−0.034	18
Gansu	0.098	4	Hunan	−0.047	19
Heilongjiang	0.067	5	Shanxi	−0.052	20
Shaanxi	0.060	**6**	Hubei	−0.056	21
Hainan	0.055	7	Fujian	−0.057	22
Sichuan	0.043	8	Zhejiang	−0.065	23
Xinjiang	0.038	9	Guangxi	−0.072	24
Beijing	0.024	10	Tianjin	−0.072	25
Anhui	0.010	11	Liaoning	−0.075	26
Jilin	−0.017	12	Guangdong	−0.078	27
Hebei	−0.020	13	Jiangsu	−0.087	28
Chongqing	−0.021	14	Ningxia	−0.112	29
Inner Mongolia	−0.023	15	Shanghai	−0.210	30

Note: The scores and rankings are worked out based on *China Statistical Yearbook 2011*, *China Statistical Yearbook 2010*, *Deserts in China and Desertification Control*, *China Environment Annual Report 2010*, and *China Environmental Statistical Yearbook 2011*

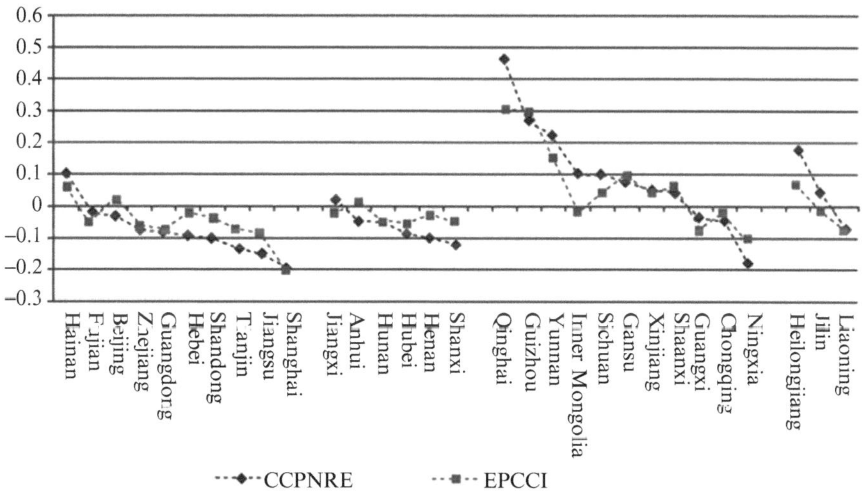

Fig. 3.5 Inter-provincial comparisons by EPCCI and CCPNRE (Note: The provinces in the figure are grouped by region, namely Eastern, Central, Western and Northeast China, and arranged from *left* to *right* in descending order of CCPNRE)

In general, the scores of provinces range from −0.21 to 0.31. Qinghai, Guizhou and Yunnan score higher while Shanghai and Ningxia score lower, showing large gaps. The largest gap between provinces is 0.517 and the standard deviation is 0.106.

The top 10 provinces by EPCCI are Qinghai, Guizhou, Yunnan, Gansu, Heilongjiang, Shaanxi, Hainan, Sichuan, Xinjiang and Beijing. From a regional perspective, seven of the top 10 are western provinces: No.1 Qinghai, No.2 Guizhou, No.3 Yunnan, No.4 Gansu, No.6 Shaanxi, No.8 Sichuan and No. 9 Xinjiang; No. 7 Hainan and No. 10 Beijing are in Eastern China; and No. 5 Heilongjiang is in Northeast China. The provinces ranking from No.11 to No.20 are Anhui, Jilin, Hebei, Chongqing, Inner Mongolia, Jiangxi, Henan, Shandong, Hunan and Shanxi, all of which except Anhui are below the national average and have quite close scores. From a regional perspective, there are five central provinces: No.11 Anhui, No.16 Jiangxi, No.17 Henan, No.19 Hunan and No.20 Shanxi; the two western provinces are No. 14 Chongqing and No. 15 Inner Mongolia; the two eastern provinces are No.13 Hebei and No.18 Shandong; No.12 Jilin is the only northeastern province. The bottom 10 provinces are Hubei, Fujian, Zhejiang, Guangxi, Tianjin, Liaoning, Guangdong, Jiangsu, Ningxia, and Shanghai. From a regional perspective, there are six eastern provinces: No.22 Fujian, No.23 Zhejiang, No.25 Tianjin, No.27 Guangdong, No.28 Jiangsu and No. 30 Shanghai; the one central province is No.21 Hubei; the two western provinces are No.24 Guangxi and No.29 Ningxia; No.26 Liaoning is the only northeastern province.

Specifically, Qinghai ranks No. 1 and Guizhou No.2, with a small gap between their scores. Qinghai leads the country by five of the 11 Third-Class Indicators. It is worth mentioning that, four of the five indicators are about pollutant emissions per unit of land area. While the No.2 Guizhou ranks No.1 by two Third-class Indicators, and No. 2 by one indicator, all of which are about pollutant emissions per capita. Shanghai comes last and scores far less than Ningxia which is next to the last. Shanghai scores the lowest by all the indicators about pollutant emissions per unit of land area, and rank among the bottom by other Third-Class Indicators.

From a regional perspective, western provinces have higher scores, and the scores of other regions are quite close. In Eastern China, the largest gap is 0.264, with the top and bottom provinces being Hainan and Shanghai respectively; in Central China, the largest gap is 0.066, with the top and bottom provinces being Anhui and Hubei; in Western China, the largest gap is 0.419, with the top and bottom provinces being Qinghai and Ningxia; in Northeast China, the largest gap is 0.142, with the top and bottom provinces being Heilongjiang and Liaoning. Generally, western provinces outperform those in other three regions by EPCCI. The largest gap between regions is 0.124, smaller than those between provinces in eastern, western and northeastern regions but larger than that between central provinces.

Chapter 4
SDGP Measurement and Analysis by Province

Junli Zhao and Jiancong Zhou

As an important component of GDI, the Support Degree of Government Policies (SDGP) is the overall evaluation of how much a government values and supports local green development. Based on results of measurement and from a regional perspective, this chapter analyzes the SDGP of 30 provinces in three aspects, i.e., Green Investment, Infrastructure, and Environmental Management, and discusses the relations between the support of government policies and local green development.

4.1 Results of SDGP Measurement

The SDGP of 30 provinces in China is calculated in line with the related measurement and weighting standards of the PGDI system and the results are shown in Table 4.1 below.

According to Table 4.1, Beijing has the highest score of 0.226, 22.6 % higher than the national average; the lowest is −0.162 scored by Heilongjiang, 16.2 % lower than the national average. Provinces differ slight from each other by SDGP, indicating that local governments all give policy support to green development. Fifteen provinces are above the national average.

The top 10 provinces by SDGP are Beijing, Ningxia, Guangdong, Zhejiang, Jiangsu, Shandong, Hebei, Tianjin, Chongqing and Hainan (Fig. 4.1). Specifically, by Green Investment Indicators (GII), the top 10 provinces are Ningxia, Beijing,

J. Zhao (✉)
China Economic Monitoring and Analysis Center,
National Bureau of Statistics of China, Beijing, China
e-mail: zhaojl@stats.gov.cn

J. Zhou
School of Economic Resource and Management, Beijing Normal University, Beijing, China
e-mail: tinycong@163.com

X. Li and J. Pan (eds.), *China Green Development Index Report 2012: Regional Comparison*, Current Chinese Economic Report Series,
DOI 10.1007/978-3-642-54178-0_4,

Table 4.1 2010 rankings of 30 provinces by SDGP

Indicator	Support Degree of Government Policies		Second-Class Indicators: Green Investment Indicators		Infrastructure Indicators		Environmental Management Indicators	
Province	Score	Ranking	Score	Ranking	Score	Ranking	Score	Ranking
Beijing	0.226	1	0.073	2	0.149	1	0.004	17
Ningxia	0.164	2	0.096	1	0.031	12	0.037	5
Guangdong	0.145	3	0.055	3	0.048	9	0.042	3
Zhejiang	0.076	4	0.002	15	0.064	7	0.010	13
Jiangsu	0.066	5	−0.032	23	0.075	3	0.022	10
Shandong	0.063	6	−0.033	24	0.065	6	0.031	7
Hebei	0.061	7	0.016	9	0.033	11	0.012	12
Tianjin	0.058	8	−0.017	19	0.067	4	0.007	14
Chongqing	0.052	9	0.047	4	0.019	14	−0.013	21
Hainan	0.048	10	−0.013	17	0.039	10	0.023	9
Yunnan	0.045	11	0.003	14	−0.007	16	0.049	1
Xinjiang	0.036	12	0.003	13	0.066	5	−0.033	26
Shaanxi	0.034	13	0.039	6	−0.002	15	−0.003	18
Fujian	0.032	14	−0.033	25	0.050	8	0.014	11
Shanxi	0.007	15	0.024	7	−0.046	23	0.029	8
Jiangxi	−0.005	16	−0.018	20	0.028	13	−0.015	22
Anhui	−0.016	17	−0.031	22	−0.022	19	0.037	6
Inner Mongolia	−0.022	18	0.021	8	−0.091	28	0.048	2
Shanghai	−0.032	19	−0.055	30	0.079	2	−0.057	29
Guangxi	−0.037	20	0.016	10	−0.035	21	−0.019	23
Guizhou	−0.044	21	−0.009	16	−0.074	26	0.039	4
Hubei	−0.055	22	−0.014	18	−0.013	18	−0.028	25
Liaoning	−0.056	23	−0.054	29	−0.007	17	0.005	16
Hunan	−0.073	24	−0.030	21	−0.031	20	−0.011	20
Gansu	−0.101	25	0.040	5	−0.147	30	0.005	15
Jilin	−0.119	26	0.007	12	−0.081	27	−0.045	27
Henan	−0.121	27	−0.040	28	−0.054	25	−0.027	24
Sichuan	−0.127	28	−0.034	26	−0.045	22	−0.048	28
Qinghai	−0.145	29	0.008	11	−0.046	24	−0.107	30
Heilongjiang	−0.162	30	−0.040	27	−0.113	29	−0.009	19

Note: ① The results are obtained based on calculations with 2010 data for each SDGP indicator; ② The provinces (autonomous regions/municipalities directly under the central government) are listed in descending order of SDGP value; ③ The score by value of SDGP in this table is the sum of the scores by the three Second-Class Indicators: Green Investment Indicators, Infrastructure Indicators, and Environmental Management Indicators; ④ The calculations are based on the *China Statistical Yearbook 2011*, *China Environmental Statistical Yearbook 2011*, *China Environment Annual Report 2010*, *China City Statistical Yearbook 2011*, *China Water Conservancy Statistical Yearbook 2011*, *China Industrial Economy Statistical Yearbook 2011*, and *Deserts in China and Desertification Control*

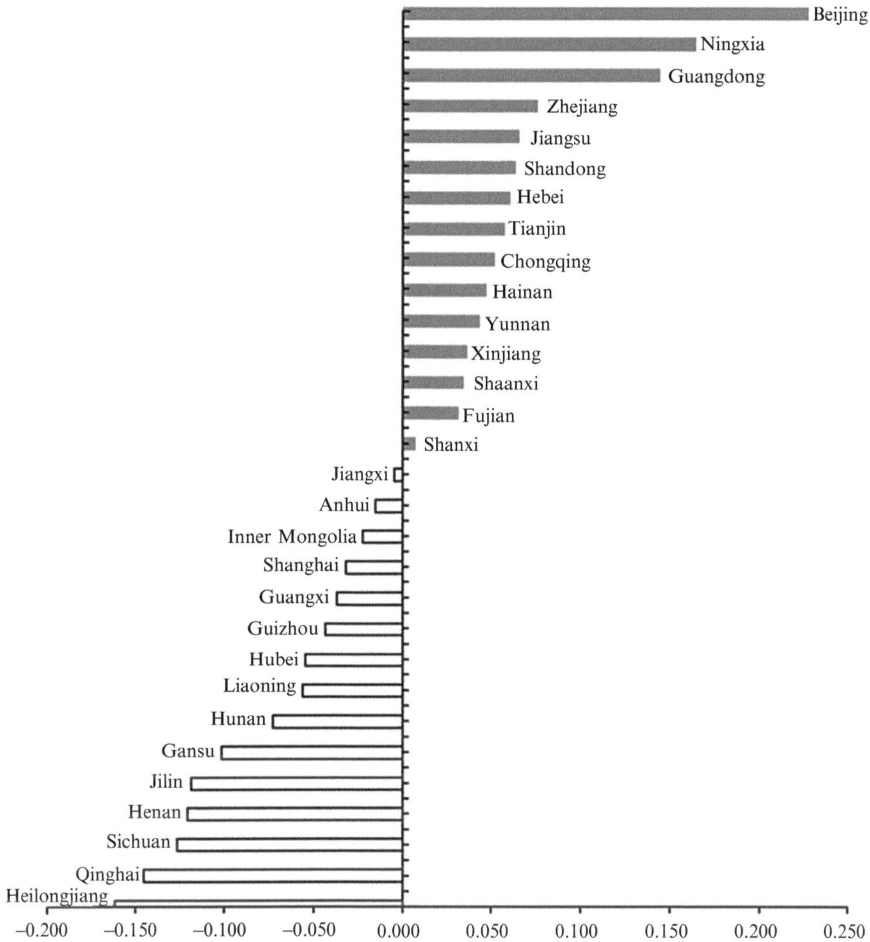

Fig. 4.1 Rankings of provinces by SDGP (Note: This figure is developed based on relevant data in Table 4.1)

Guangdong, Chongqing, Gansu, Shaanxi, Shanxi, Inner Mongolia, Hebei and Guangxi; by Infrastructure Indicators (II), the top 10 provinces are Beijing, Shanghai, Jiangsu, Tianjin, Xinjiang, Shandong, Zhejiang, Fujian, Guangdong and Hainan; by Environmental Management Indicators, the top 10 provinces are Yunnan, Inner Mongolia, Guangdong, Guizhou, Ningxia, Anhui, Shandong, Shanxi, Hainan and Jiangsu.

Figure 4.2 is about the rankings of provinces by SDGP. The top 10 provinces are marked with dark green, those ranking 11th–20th with moderate green and the bottom 10 with light green. The darker the green is, the higher the SDGP is. As shown in the figure, "dark green" provinces concentrate in the eastern coastal areas;

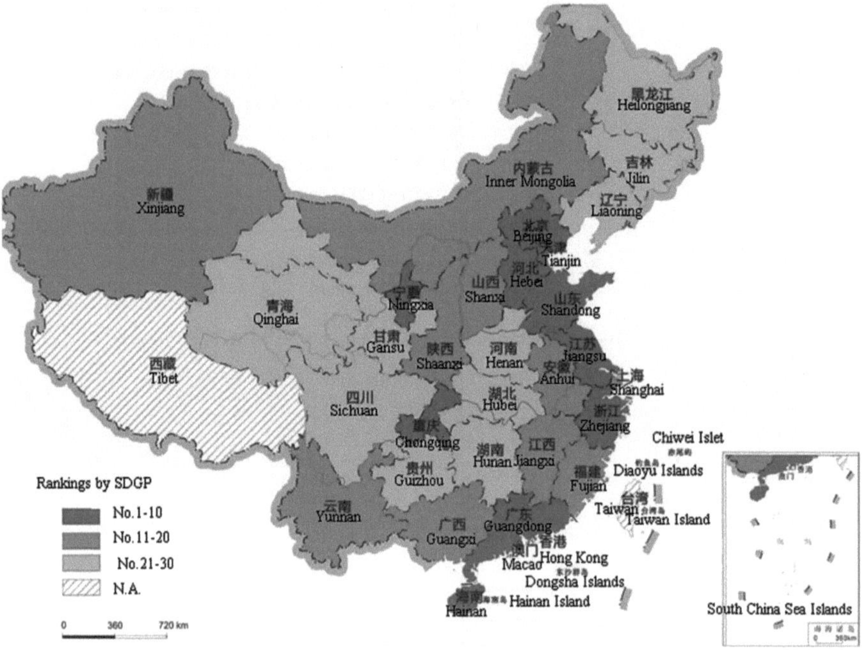

Fig. 4.2 SDGP rankings by region (Note: This figure is developed based on relevant data in Table 4.1)

northeastern provinces are all in light green; different shades of green are used for the central and western provinces which imply large gaps between them. In general, the SDGP of 30 provinces in China shows the following characteristics:

4.1.1 Regional Differences in SDGP

From a regional perspective, the eastern provinces have the highest SDGP, the western provinces have good SDGP, the central provinces lag behind and the northeastern provinces have low SDGP.

The eastern provinces have the highest SDGP. Eight of the ten eastern provinces rank among the top 10 in the country, with the exceptions of No.14 Fujian and No.19 Shanghai. The western provinces have good SDGP but few of the make it to the top 10. Of the 11 western provinces, Ningxia and Chongqing stand at No. 2 and No. 9 respectively; five provinces, Yunnan, Xinjiang, Shaanxi, Inner Mongolia and Guangxi rank No. 11–20 and the rest four, Gansu, Guizhou, Sichuan and Qinghai rank No. 21–30. The central provinces have better SDGP than the northeastern provinces. Shanxi, Jiangxi and Anhui rank No. 15–17, Hubei, Hunan and Henan

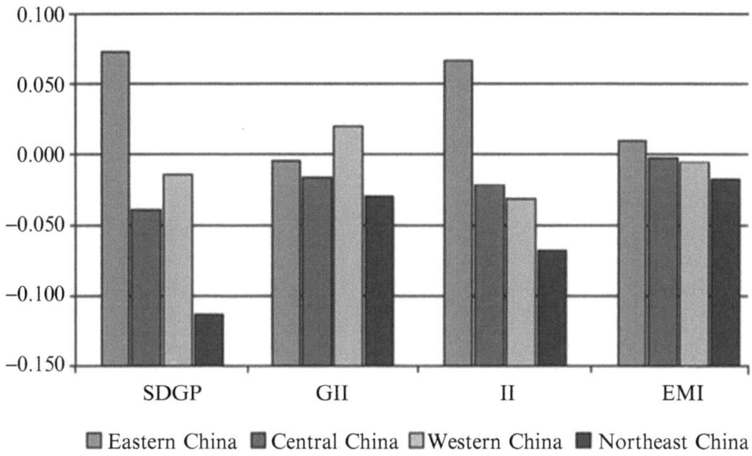

Fig. 4.3 SDGP comparison by region (Note: The data for each region in the figure are the arithmetic mean of the scores of all the provinces in the region)

rank No. 22, 24 and 27. The northeastern provinces are at the bottom, with Liaoning, Jilin and Heilongjiang ranking No. 23, 26 and 30 respectively (Fig. 4.3).

Significant differences are also found by the three Second-Class Indicators. The largest gap is seen in II: the scores of the eastern provinces are remarkably higher than the national average and that of the other provinces; the scores of the central and western provinces are quite close but all below the national average; the northeastern provinces have the lowest scores. In terms of GII, the western provinces have the highest scores which exceed the national average, followed by the eastern, central and northeastern provinces which are all below the national average. The scores by EMI do not vary largely among the four regions which are all close to the national average. The scores of the eastern provinces are slightly higher than the national average; the central and western provinces score similarly; and the northeastern provinces have the lowest scores. In general, the eastern provinces score higher and the northeastern provinces score the lowest by all indicators.

4.1.2 SDGP in Each Region

The scores of eastern and northeastern provinces by SDGP are quite close but the central and western provinces have large gaps (Table 4.2). Nine of the eastern provinces score above the national average and, apart from Beijing and Guangdong which score remarkably higher than the rest provinces, the others all score between 0.076 and 0.032 with a gap of 0.044. The score of Shanghai is only 3.2 % lower than the national average. The northeastern provinces score between −0.056 and −0.162.

Table 4.2 Regional differences by SDGP

Region	Province	Score	Ranking	Region	Province	Score	Ranking
Eastern China	Beijing	0.226	1	Western China	Ningxia	0.164	2
	Guangdong	0.145	3		Chongqing	0.052	9
	Zhejiang	0.076	4		Yunnan	0.045	11
	Jiangsu	0.066	5		Xinjiang	0.036	12
	Shandong	0.063	6		Shaanxi	0.034	13
	Hebei	0.061	7		Inner Mongolia	−0.022	**18**
	Tianjin	0.058	8		Guangxi	−0.037	20
	Hainan	0.048	10		**Guizhou**	−0.044	21
	Fujian	0.032	14		Gansu	***−0.101***	25
	Shanghai	−0.032	19		**Sichuan**	−0.127	28
Central China	Shanxi	0.007	15		Qinghai	−0.145	29
	Jiangxi	−0.005	16	Northeast China	Liaoning	−0.056	23
	Anhui	−0.016	17		Jilin	−0.119	26
	Hubei	−0.055	22		Heilongjiang	−0.162	30
	Hunan	−0.073	24				
	Henan	−**0.121**	27				

Note: This table is developed based on Table 4.1

Of the six central provinces, Shanxi scores 0.007 above the national average and the rest score between −0.005 and −0.121, with a gap of 12 places in ranking, indicating SDGP disparity. The largest SDGP disparity is seen in the 11 western provinces, where five provinces score above the national average. Ningxia has the highest score 0.164 and Qinghai has the lowest −0.145, a gap of 0.309. In terms of ranking, Ningxia ranks No. 2 and Qinghai is next to the last. The 11 western provinces respectively rank among the top 10, No. 11–20 and No. 21–30, showing large regional gaps.

4.1.3 Impact of SDGP on Green Development

SDGP has an impact on green development. The results show that there are gaps between GDI and SDGP rankings in most provinces (Table 4.3). There is a gap of five places or more in 15 provinces, or half, of all the provinces; seven show a gap of ten places or more, including Qinghai, Shanghai, Heilongjiang, Hebei, Chongqing, Ningxia and Shanxi. The high SDGP scores of Shanghai, Hebei, Chongqing, Ningxia and Shanxi contribute significantly to their GDI rankings. In addition, five of the top 10 provinces by GDI have seen their GDI improvement based on high SDGP scores, including Beijing, Tianjin, Guangdong, Zhejiang and Shandong. Their GDI rankings have climbed because they rank among the top 10 by GDEG and SDGP, despite their low rankings by CCPNRE respectively at No. 14, 27, 21, 19 and 24. There are also some provinces whose GDI improvement is hindered

Table 4.3 Differences between the rankings by GDI and SDGP

Province	Ranking by GDI	Ranking by SDGP	Difference	Province	Ranking by GDI	Ranking by SDGP	Difference
Beijing	1	1	0	Heilongjiang	16	30	−14
Tianjin	2	8	−6	Hebei	17	7	10
Guangdong	3	3	0	Jiangxi	18	16	2
Hainan	**4**	10	−6	Chongqing	19	9	10
Zhejiang	5	**4**	1	Jilin	20	26	−6
Qinghai	6	29	−23	Sichuan	21	28	−7
Yunnan	7	11	−4	Anhui	22	17	5
Fujian	8	14	−6	Liaoning	23	23	0
Shanghai	9	19	−10	Hubei	24	22	2
Shandong	10	6	**4**	Gansu	25	25	0
Inner Mongolia	11	18	−7	Guangxi	26	20	6
Jiangsu	12	5	7	Hunan	27	24	3
Guizhou	13	21	−8	Ningxia	28	2	26
Shaanxi	14	13	1	Shanxi	29	15	14
Xinjiang	15	12	3	Henan	30	27	3

Note: This table is developed based on Tables 1.5 and 4.1

by SDGP. Seven of the bottom 10 provinces by GDI are also among the bottom 10 by SDGP. Regardless of the level of economic development and resource abundance, government support promotes local green economy to different extents.

4.2 Inter-provincial Comparison by SDGP

To analyze the SDGP of each province, this part compares their performances by GII, II, and EMI. SDGP has a 30 % weight in the GDI system and the weights of its components GII, II and EMI are 25 %, 45 % and 30 % respectively.

4.2.1 Results and Analysis of GII Measurement

With a 25 % weight in the SDGP system and 7.5 % in the GDI system, GII consists of five Third-Class Indicators, namely the ratio of environmental spending to government expenditure, the ratio of the investment in pollution control to GDP, government spending per capita on rural water supply system and toilet improvement, the investment in converting cultivated land into forests and grassland per unit of cultivated land area, and the ratio of the spending on science, education, culture, and public health to government expenditure, each taking a weigh of 1.5 % (Table 4.4).

The results (Table 4.5 and Fig. 4.4) show slight differences between provinces in GII. Ningxia ranks first with a score at 0.096, 9.6 % higher than the national average, and Shanghai ranks last with a score of −0.055, 5.5 % lower than the national average; 15 provinces are above the national average level. In descending order, the top 10 provinces are Ningxia, Beijing, Guangdong, Chongqing, Gansu, Shaanxi, Shanxi, Inner Mongolia, Hebei and Guangxi, namely three eastern provinces, one central province and six western provinces.

The No. 11–20 are Qinghai, Jilin, Xinjiang, Yunnan, Zhejiang, Guizhou, Hainan, Hubei, Tianjin and Jiangxi, namely three eastern provinces, two central provinces, four western provinces and one northeastern province.

The bottom 10 are Hunna, Anhui, Jiangsu, Shandong, Fujian, Sichuan, Heilongjiang, Henan, Liaoning and Shanghai, namely four eastern provinces, three central province, one western provinces and two northeastern provinces.

In general, the western provinces rank higher, showing higher GII scores above the national average except Sichuan and Guizhou; the scores of central and northeastern provinces do not show large gaps but all at low levels; large gaps are found in eastern provinces, with Beijing, Guangdong and Hebei ranking among top 10, Zhejiang, Hainan and Tianjin ranking in the middle and Jiangsu, Shandong, Fujian and Shanghai in the bottom 10.

Table 4.4 GII, weights and attributes

No.	Indicator	Weight (%)	Attribute
1	Ratio of environmental spending to government expenditure	1.50	Positive
2	Ratio of the investment in pollution control to GDP	1.50	Positive
3	Government spending per capita on rural water supply system and toilet improvement	1.50	Positive
4	Investment in converting cultivated land into forests and grassland per unit of cultivated land area	1.50	Positive
5	Ratio of the spending on science, education, culture, and public health to government expenditure	1.50	Positive

Note: The content of this table was finalized after discussions at several seminars held by the research group

Table 4.5 2010 rankings of 30 provinces by GII

Province	Score	Ranking	Province	Score	Ranking
Ningxia	0.096	1	Guizhou	−0.009	16
Beijing	0.073	2	Hainan	−0.013	17
Guangdong	0.055	3	Hubei	−0.014	18
Chongqing	0.047	4	Tianjin	−0.017	19
Gansu	0.040	5	Jiangxi	−0.018	20
Shaanxi	0.039	6	Hunan	−0.030	21
Shanxi	0.024	7	Anhui	−0.031	22
Inner Mongolia	0.021	8	Jiangsu	−0.032	23
Hebei	0.016	9	Shandong	−0.033	24
Guangxi	0.016	10	Fujian	−0.033	25
Qinghai	0.008	11	Sichuan	−0.034	26
Jilin	0.007	12	Heilongjiang	−0.040	27
Xinjiang	0.003	13	Henan	−0.040	28
Yunnan	0.003	14	Liaoning	−0.054	29
Zhejiang	0.002	15	Shanghai	−0.055	30

Note: The scores and rankings are worked out based on *China Statistical Yearbook 2011*, *China Environmental Statistical Yearbook 2011*, *China Environment Annual Report 2010*, *China City Statistical Yearbook 2011*, *China Water Conservancy Statistical Yearbook 2011*, *China Industrial Economy Statistical Yearbook 2011*, and *Deserts in China and Desertification Control*. Sources: China Statistical Yearbook 2011, China Environmental Statistical Yearbook 2011, Annual Statistical Report on Environment in China 2010, China City Statistical Yearbook 2011, China Water Conservancy Statistical Yearbook 2011, China Industrial Economic Statistical Yearbook 2011, and Desert and Its Treatment in China

4.2.2 Results and Analysis of II Measurement

Weighing 45 % in the SDGP system, II consists of eight Third-Class Indicators, namely area of green land per capita in urban areas, coverage of water supply in urban areas, treatment rate of urban wastewater, harmless treatment rate of urban household waste, public buses per 10,000 urban residents, length of public transport

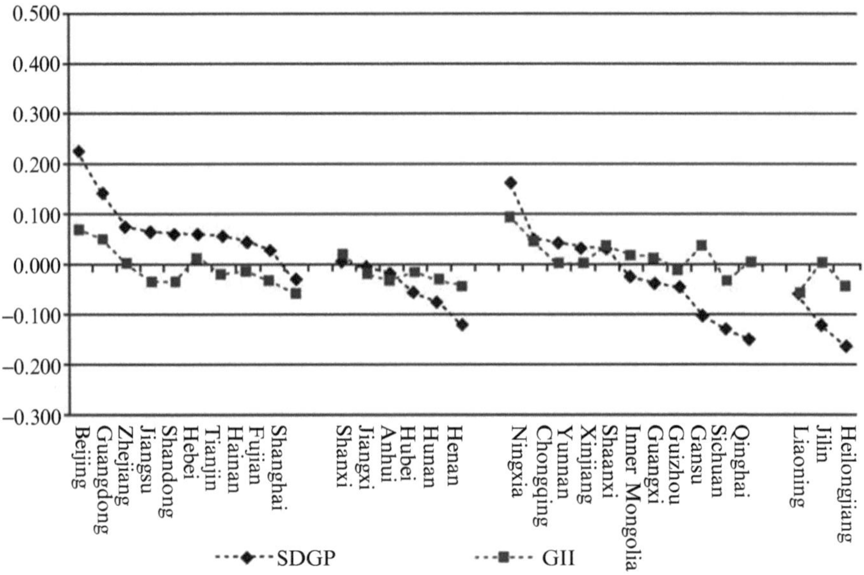

Fig. 4.4 Inter-provincial comparison by GII and SDGP (Note: The provinces in the figure are grouped by region, namely Eastern, Central, Western and Northeast China, and arranged from *left* to *right* in descending order of SDGP)

Table 4.6 II, weights and attributes

No.	Indicator	Weight (%)	Attribute
6	Area of green land per capita in urban areas	1.69	Positive
7	Coverage of water supply in urban areas	1.69	Positive
8	Treatment rate of urban wastewater	1.69	Positive
9	Harmless treatment rate of urban household waste	1.69	Positive
10	Public buses per 10,000 urban residents	1.69	Positive
11	Length of public transport routes in urban areas	1.69	Positive
12	Ratio of the rural residents benefiting from water supply system improvement to total rural population	1.69	Positive
13	Green coverage of urban built-up areas	1.69	Positive

Note: The content of this table was finalized after discussions at several seminars held by the research group

routes per capita in urban areas, ratio of the rural residents benefiting from water supply system improvement to total rural population, and green coverage of urban built-up areas, each taking a weight of 1.69 % (Table 4.6).

Results (Table 4.7 and Fig. 4.5) show large differences between provinces in II. The largest difference is 0.296, larger than the GII gap; Beijing ranks No. 1 with a score of 0.149, 14.9 % higher than the national average. Fourteen provinces score higher than the national average.

Table 4.7 2010 rankings of 30 provinces by II

Province	Score	Ranking	Province	Score	Ranking
Beijing	0.149	1	Yunnan	−0.007	16
Shanghai	0.079	2	Liaoning	−0.007	17
Jiangsu	0.075	3	Hubei	−0.013	18
Tianjin	0.067	4	Anhui	−0.022	19
Xinjiang	0.066	5	Hunan	−0.031	20
Shandong	0.065	6	Guangxi	−0.035	21
Zhejiang	0.064	7	Sichuan	−0.045	22
Fujian	0.050	8	Shanxi	−0.046	23
Guangdong	0.048	9	Qinghai	−0.046	24
Hainan	0.039	10	Henan	−0.054	25
Hebei	0.033	11	Guizhou	−0.074	26
Ningxia	0.031	12	Jilin	−0.081	27
Jiangxi	0.028	13	Inner Mongolia	−0.091	28
Chongqing	0.019	14	Heilongjiang	−0.113	29
Shaanxi	−0.002	15	Gansu	−0.147	30

Note: The scores and rankings are worked out based on *China Statistical Yearbook 2011*, *China Environmental Statistical Yearbook 2011*, *China Environment Annual Report 2010*, *China City Statistical Yearbook 2011*, *China Water Conservancy Statistical Yearbook 2011*, *China Industrial Economy Statistical Yearbook 2011*, and *Deserts in China and Desertification Control*. Sources: China Statistical Yearbook 2011, China Environmental Statistical Yearbook 2011, Annual Statistical Report on Environment in China 2010, China City Statistical Yearbook 2011, China Water Conservancy Statistical Yearbook 2011, China Industrial Economic Statistical Yearbook 2011, and Desert and Its Treatment in China

The top 10 provinces are Beijing, Shanghai, Jiangsu, Tianjin, Xinjiang, Shandong, Zhejiang, Fujian, Guangdong and Hainan, all in Eastern China except Xinjiang in the western region.

The No. 11–20 are Hebei, Ningxia, Jiangxi, Chongqing, Shaanxi, Yunnan, Liaoning, Hubei, Anhui and Hunan, namely one eastern provinces, four central provinces, four western provinces and one northeastern province.

The bottom 10 are Guangxi, Sichuan, Shanxi, Qinghai, Henan, Guizhou, Jilin, Inner Mongolia, Heilongjiang and Gansu, namely two central, six western and two northeastern provinces.

In conclusion, the eastern provinces have the highest scores above the national average and with slight gaps; the central provinces score higher but, except Jiangxi, are lower than the national average; the western and northeastern provinces score low and the western provinces see significant gaps. No. 5 Xinjiang scores 0.066 and No. 30 Gansu scores −0.147, a gap of 0.213.

4.2.3 Results and Analysis of EMI Measurement

Weighing 30 % of SDGP, EMI consists of six Third-Class Indicators, namely newly-added afforestation area of the year per capita, Industrial SO_2 removal rate,

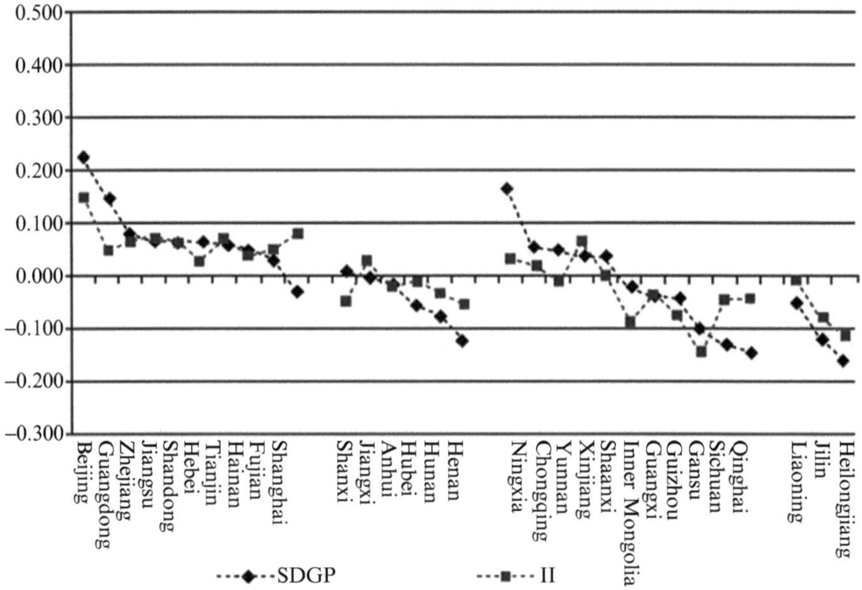

Fig. 4.5 Inter-provincial comparison by II and SDGP (Note: The provinces in the figure are grouped by region, namely Eastern, Central, Western and Northeast China, and arranged from *left* to *right* in descending order of SDGP)

Table 4.8 EMI, weights and attributes

No.	Indicator	Weight (%)	Attribute
14	Newly-added afforestation area of the year per capita	1.50	Positive
15	Industrial SO_2 removal rate	1.50	Positive
16	Industrial wastewater COD removal rate	1.50	Positive
17	Industrial nitrogen oxide removal rate	1.50	Positive
18	Industrial wastewater ammonia/nitrogen removal rate	1.50	Positive
19	Number of environmental emergencies	1.50	Negative

Note: The content of this table was finalized after discussions at several seminars held by the research group

industrial wastewater COD removal rate, industrial nitrogen oxide removal rate, industrial wastewater ammonia/nitrogen removal rate and Number of environmental emergencies, each taking a 1.50 % weight (Table 4.8).

Results (Table 4.9 and Fig. 4.6) show slight differences between provinces in GMI. The largest difference is 0.156. No. 1 Yunnan scores 0.049, 4.9 % higher than the national average. Seventeen provinces score higher than the national average.

The top 10 provinces are Yunnan, Inner Mongolia, Guangdong, Guizhou, Ningxia, Anhui, Shandong, Shanxi, Hainan and Jiangsu, namely four eastern provinces, two central and four western provinces.

Table 4.9 2010 rankings of 30 provinces by EMI

Province	Score	Ranking	Province	Score	Ranking
Yunnan	0.049	1	Liaoning	0.005	16
Inner Mongolia	0.048	2	Beijing	0.004	17
Guangdong	0.042	3	Shaanxi	−0.003	18
Guizhou	0.039	4	Heilongjiang	−0.009	19
Ningxia	0.037	5	Hunan	−0.011	20
Anhui	0.037	6	Chongqing	−0.013	21
Shandong	0.031	7	Jiangxi	−0.015	22
Shanxi	0.029	8	Guangxi	−0.019	23
Hainan	0.023	9	Henan	−0.027	24
Jiangsu	0.022	10	Hubei	−0.028	25
Fujian	0.014	11	Xinjiang	−0.033	26
Hebei	0.012	12	Jilin	−0.045	27
Zhejiang	0.010	13	Sichuan	−0.048	28
Tianjin	0.007	14	Shanghai	−0.057	29
Gansu	0.005	15	Qinghai	−0.107	30

Note: The scores and rankings are worked out based on *China Statistical Yearbook 2011*, *China Environmental Statistical Yearbook 2011*, *China Environment Annual Report 2010*, *China City Statistical Yearbook 2011*, *China Water Conservancy Statistical Yearbook 2011*, *China Industrial Economy Statistical Yearbook 2011*, and *Deserts in China and Desertification Control*. Sources: China Statistical Yearbook 2011, China Environmental Statistical Yearbook 2011, Annual Statistical Report on Environment in China 2010, China City Statistical Yearbook 2011, China Water Conservancy Statistical Yearbook 2011, China Industrial Economic Statistical Yearbook 2011, and Desert and Its Treatment in China

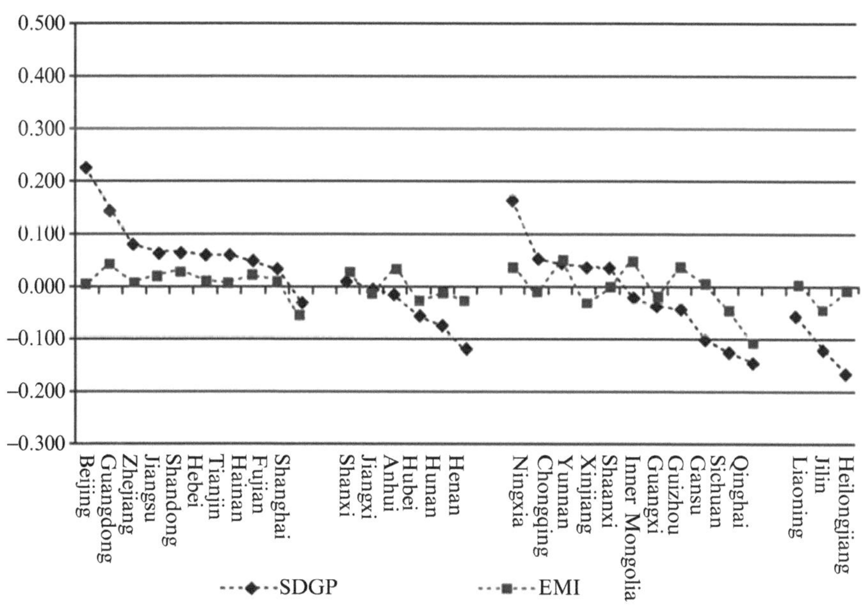

Fig. 4.6 Inter-provincial comparison by EMI and SDGP (Note: The provinces in the figure are grouped by region, namely Eastern, Central, Western and Northeast China, and arranged from *left* to *right* in descending order of SDGP)

No. 11–20 are Fujian, Hebei, Zhejiang, Tianjin, Gansu, Liaoning, Beijing, Shaanxi, Heilongjiang and Hunan, namely five eastern, one central, two western and two northeastern provinces.

The bottom 10 are Chongqing, Jiangxi, Guangxi, Henan, Hubei, Xinjiang, Jilin, Sichuan, Shanghai and Qinghai, namely one eastern, three central, five western and one northeastern provinces.

In conclusion, the eastern provinces have the highest scores above the national average except Shanghai; however, there are differences between eastern provinces, with No. 3 Guangdong scoring 0.042 and No. 29 Shanghai scoring −0.057. The central provinces score higher, with No. 6 Anhui scoring 0.037 and No. 25 Hubei scoring −0.028, showing a gap of 0.065. The western provinces show even larger gaps, with No. 1 Yunnan scoring 0.049 and No. 30 Qinghai scoring −0.107, a gap of 0.156. The northeastern provinces score low, with Liaoning taking the lead and followed by Heilongjiang and Jilin.

Chapter 5
"Green Development Checkup" and Analysis by Province

Faqi Shi, Mingqing Jiang, Hongli Ma, Tao Song, Yang Liu, and Jiancong Zhou

A detailed introduction to the design of the "green development table" has been made in the Introduction part. Based on an overall analysis of the three First-Class Indicators in the first three chapters, this chapter gives more specific analysis to each province according to its "green development table" and to its performance in green development. The provinces appear in the same order as that provided in China's statistical yearbooks, and a list is provided in the Contents part. Explanation to the headers and indicators in "green development table" can be found in the Introduction part. The brief analysis focuses on First- and Second-Class Indicators and mainly covers two aspects: (1) 2010 score of each province by GDI; (2) change in 2009 and 2010 rankings.

F. Shi (✉)
National Accounts Department, National Bureau of Statistics of China, Beijing, China
e-mail: shifaqi@stats.gov.cn

M. Jiang
Integrated Statistics Department, National Bureau of Statistics of China, Beijing, China

H. Ma
Beijing Normal University Publishing House, Beijing, China

T. Song • Y. Liu • J. Zhou
School of Economic Resource and Management, Beijing Normal University, Beijing, China

X. Li and J. Pan (eds.), *China Green Development Index Report 2012: Regional Comparison*, Current Chinese Economic Report Series,
DOI 10.1007/978-3-642-54178-0_5,

Green development checkup-Beijing

No.	Indicator	Unit	Attribute	2010 average of 30 provinces	2010 figure	2009 figure	2010 ranking	2009 ranking	Change in ranking	Source of 2010 data	Chernoff face
1	GDP per capita	Yuan per capita	Positive	33,964.12	75,943	70,452	2	2	0	China Statistics	
2	Energy consumption per unit of GDP	Ton coal equivalent per 10,000 yuan	Negative	1.29	0.58	0.61	1	1	0	China Statistics	
3	Ratio of non-fossil energy consumption to total energy consumption		Positive	NA	NA	NA	NA	NA			
4	CO_2 emissions per unit of GDP		Negative	NA	NA	NA	NA	NA			
5	SO_2 emissions per unit of GDP	Ton per 10,000 yuan	Negative	0.0088	0.0010	0.0011	1	1	0	China Statistics	
6	COD emissions per unit of GDP	Ton per 10,000 yuan	Negative	0.0045	0.0008	0.0009	1	1	0	China Statistics	
7	Nitrogen oxide emissions per unit of GDP	Ton per 10,000 yuan	Negative	0.0068	0.0019	0.0017	1	1	0	Environmental Annual Report; China Statistics	
8	Ammonia/nitrogen emissions per unit of GDP	Ton per 10,000 yuan	Negative	0.0004	0.0001	0.0001	1	1	0	Environmental Annual Report; China Statistics	
9	Electricity consumption per capita in urban areas	kWh per capita	Negative	295.08	1,084.52	857.13	29	29	0	City	
10	Labor productivity of the primary sector	Yuan per capita	Positive	1.61	1.90	1.80	11	8	−3	China Statistics	
11	Land productivity	100 million yuan per 1,000 hectares	Positive	0.26	0.49	0.44	1	1	0	China Statistics	

12	Proportion of water-saving irrigated area in effectively irrigated area		Positive	0.49	1.35	1.26	1	1	0	Water Conservancy; China Statistics	
13	Proportion of effectively irrigated area in cultivated land area	%	Positive	53.55	91.25	94.40	1	1	0	China Statistics	
14	Labor productivity of the secondary sector	10,000 yuan per capita	Positive	12.13	12.56	10.98	8	9	1	China Statistics	☺
15	Water consumption per unit of value added created by industrial enterprises	m^3/yuan	Negative	0.0100	0.0019	0.0023	3	3	0	China Statistics	
16	Energy consumption per unit of value added created by industrial enterprises above designated size (no data)		Negative	NA	NA	NA	NA	NA			
17	Utilization rate of industrial solid waste	%	Positive	69.80	65.80	68.90	17	17	0	Environmental Yearbook	
18	Recycling rate of industrial water	%	Positive	72.90	32.48	96.05	28	2	−26	Environmental Yearbook	☹
19	Ratio of the output of six energy-intensive industries to gross industrial output	%	Negative	39.65	30.66	29.37	8	8	0	Industrial Economy	
20	Labor productivity of the tertiary sector	10,000 yuan per capita	Positive	6.96	11.14	10.33	3	3	0	China Statistics	
21	Proportion of the value added of the tertiary sector in GDP	%	Positive	39.97	75.10	75.50	1	1	0	China Statistics	
22	Proportion of tertiary sector employees in the total employed population	%	Positive	36.67	74.13	73.75	1	1	0	China Statistics	

(continued)

(continued)

No.	Indicator	Unit	Attribute	2010 average of 30 provinces	2010 figure	2009 figure	2010 ranking	2009 ranking	Change in ranking	Source of 2010 data	Chernoff face
23	Water resources per capita	m^3 per capita	Positive	2,419.38	124.19	126.61	29	30	1	China Statistics	☺
24	Forest area per capita	Hectare per capita	Positive	0.19	0.03	0.03	27	26	−1	China Statistics	☹
25	Forest coverage rate	%	Positive	30.63	31.72	31.72	15	15	0	China Statistics	
26	Proportion of the area of natural reserves in the total area of a region	%	Positive	8.60	7.97	7.97	12	11	−1	China Statistics	☹
27	Proportion of the area of wetlands in the total area of a region	%	Positive	7.01	1.93	1.93	25	25	0	China Statistics	
28	Growing stock per capita	m^3 per capita	Positive	10.70	0.66	0.74	27	27	0	China Statistics	
29	CO_2 emissions per unit of land area		Negative	NA	NA	NA	NA	NA			
30	CO_2 emissions per capita		Negative	NA	NA	NA	NA	NA			
31	SO_2 emissions per unit of land area	Ton per km^2	Negative	6.3677	7.0107	7.2389	23	23	0	China Statistics; Deserts	
32	SO_2 emissions per capita	Ton per capita	Negative	0.0191	0.0062	0.0069	2	2	0	China Statistics	
33	COD emissions per unit of land area	Ton per km^2	Negative	3.7722	5.6060	6.0233	27	27	0	China Statistics; Deserts	
34	emissions per capita	Ton per capita	Negative	0.0101	0.0050	0.0057	1	2	1	China Statistics	☺
35	Nitrogen oxide emissions per unit of land area	Ton per km^2	Negative	6.4473	13.5888	11.0295	28	27	−1	China Statistics; Deserts; Environmental Annual Report	☹

36	Nitrogen oxide emissions per capita	Ton per capita	Negative	0.0165	0.0120	0.0105	13	13	0	Environmental Annual Report; China Statistics	
37	Ammonia/nitrogen emissions per unit of land area	Ton per km^2	Negative	0.4164	0.7312	0.7922	28	28	0	China Statistics; Deserts; Environmental Annual Report	
38	Ammonia/nitrogen emissions per capita	Ton per capita	Negative	0.0010	0.0006	0.0008	3	5	2	Environmental Annual Report; China Statistics	☺
39	Consumption of chemical fertilizers per unit of cultivated land area	10,000 ton per hectare	Negative	0.05	0.06	0.06	22	22	0	China Statistics; China Statistics	
40	Consumption of pesticides per unit of cultivated land area	Ton per 1,000 hectares	Negative	17.68	17.14	17.18	19	19	0	Environmental Yearbook; China Statistics	
41	Nitrogen oxide emissions per capita from road transport	Ton per 10,000 persons	Negative	24.07	48.43	59.13	28	27	−1	Environmental Annual Report; China Statistics	☹
42	Ratio of environmental spending to government expenditure	%	Positive	3.35	2.24	2.33	28	25	−3	China Statistics	☹
43	Ratio of the investment in pollution control to GDP	%	Positive	1.40	1.64	1.92	10	6	−4	Environmental Yearbook; China Statistics	☹
44	Government spending per capita on rural water supply system and toilet improvement	Yuan per capita	Positive	57.01	195.25	263.30	1	2	1	China Statistics	☺

(continued)

(continued)

No.	Indicator	Unit	Attribute	2010 average of 30 provinces	2010 figure	2009 figure	2010 ranking	2009 ranking	Change in ranking	Source of 2010 data	Chernoff face
45	Investment in converting cultivated land into forests and grassland per unit of cultivated land area	10,000 yuan per 1,000 hectares	Positive	29.81	25.73	0.00	15	23	8	Environmental Yearbook; China Statistics	☺
46	Ratio of the spending on science, education, culture, and public health to government expenditure	%	Positive	26.10	32.95	31.62	1	2	1	China Statistics	☺
47	Area of green land per capita in urban areas	Hectare per capita	Positive	0.00	0.01	0.00	5	9	4	City	☺
48	Coverage of water supply in urban areas	%	Positive	96.08	100.00	100.00	1	1	0	China Statistics	
49	Treatment rate of urban wastewater	%	Positive	79.18	82.10	80.30	16	9	−7	Environmental Yearbook	☹
50	Harmless treatment rate of urban household waste	%	Positive	78.47	96.95	98.22	4	1	−3	China Statistics	☹
51	Public buses per 10,000 urban residents		Positive	9.86	14.24	24.75	2	1	−1	China Statistics	☹
52	Length of public transport routes per capita in urban areas	km per capita	Positive	0.0006	0.0015	0.0004	4	11	7	China Statistics; City	☺
53	Ratio of the rural residents benefiting from water supply system improvement to the total rural population	%	Positive	94.44	100.00	100.00	1	1	0	Environmental Yearbook	

54	Green coverage of urban built-up areas	%	Positive	37.75	47.69	47.69	1	1	0	China Statistics	
55	Newly-added afforestation area of the year per capita	Hectare per 10,000 persons	Positive	59.50	7.47	10.18	28	26	−2	China Statistics	☹
56	Industrial SO_2 removal rate	%	Positive	59.83	69.56	65.31	7	9	2	China Statistics	☺
57	Industrial wastewater COD removal rate	%	Positive	70.84	88.48	89.09	5	3	−2	Environmental Annual Report; China Statistics	☹
58	Industrial nitrogen oxide removal rate	%	Positive	4.07	1.08	36.27	19	1	−18	Environmental Annual Report	☹
59	Industrial wastewater ammonia/nitrogen removal rate	%	Positive	62.87	76.17	92.84	12	1	−11	Environmental Annual Report; China Statistics	☹
60	Number of environmental emergencies		Negative	14.00	30	31	27	26	−1	China Statistics	☹

Note:
China Statistics: *China Statistical Yearbook 2011*
Environmental Yearbook: *China Environmental Statistical Yearbook 2011*
Environmental Annual Report: *China Environment Annual Report 2010*
City: *China City Statistical Yearbook 2011*
Water Conservancy: *China Water Conservancy Statistical Yearbook 2011*
Industrial Economy: *China Industrial Economy Statistical Yearbook 2011*
Deserts: *Deserts in China and Desertification Control*

5.1 Brief Analysis of Green Development in Beijing

Beijing ranked 1st among the 30 participating provinces by GDI according to 2010 data, as it did in 2009. Following is a brief analysis of its score by each indicator and their changes from 2009 to 2010.

5.1.1 Beijing's 2010 Scores by GDI

Beijing scored 0.655 in 2010. From the three First-Class Indicators including GDEG, CCPNRE, and SDGP as shown in Fig. 5.1, Beijing outstood other provinces in terms of GDEG and SDGP, yet scored lower than the national average in CCPNRE (Note: the national average value of each indicator is 0).

According to Fig. 5.2, Beijing surpassed the national average in eight of Second-Class Indicators in 2010, which are GGEI, PII, SII, TII, EPCCI, GII, EMI, and II, yet scored slightly lower than the national average in RAECI.

5.1.2 Changes in Beijing's GDI Rankings 2009–2010

According to Table 5.1, in First-Class Indicators, the most obvious change occurred in CCPNRE, where Beijing rose as many as 4 places in ranking. It remained the

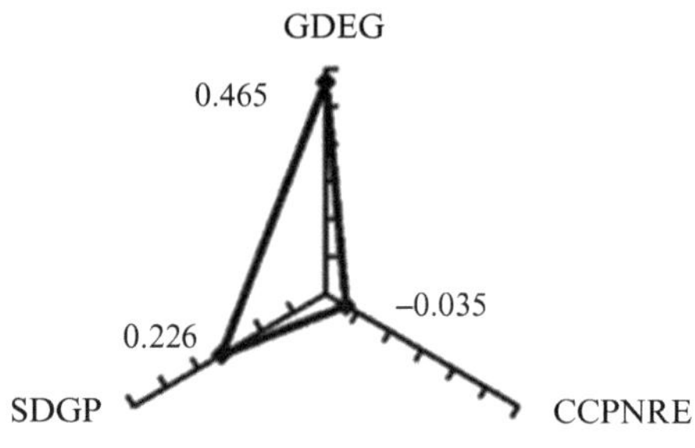

Fig. 5.1 Beijing's scores by First-Class Indicators

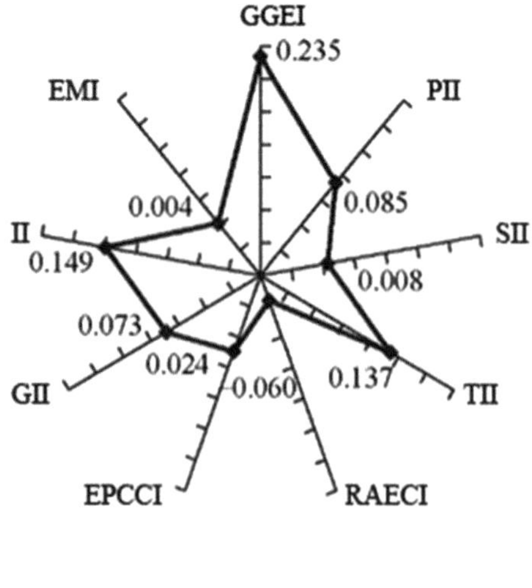

Fig. 5.2 Beijing's scores by Second-Class Indicators

Table 5.1 Changes in Beijing's rankings by First-Class and Second-Class Indicators, 2009–2010

Indicator	2010	2009	Difference	Indicator	2010	2009	Difference
GDI	1	1	0				
GDEG	1	1	0	RAECI	23	26	3
GGEI	1	1	0	EPCCI	10	12	2
PII	1	1	0	SDGP	1	1	0
SII	11	4	−7	GII	2	2	0
TII	1	1	0	II	1	2	1
CCPNRE	14	18	4	EMI	17	1	−16

Note: A positive value in "Difference" means a rise in ranking

Table 5.2 Third-Class Indicators where changes over 3 places occurred in Beijing, 2009–2010

	Original data for 2010 and 2009			Change in ranking		
Third-Class Indicator	Unit	2010	2009	2010	2009	Difference
Labor productivity of the primary sector	Yuan per capita	1.90	1.80	11	8	−3
Recycling rate of industrial water	%	32.48	96.05	28	2	−26
Ratio of environmental spending to government expenditure	%	2.24	2.33	28	25	−3
Ratio of the investment in pollution control to GDP	%	1.64	1.92	10	6	−4
Investment in converting cultivated land into forests and grassland per unit of cultivated land area	10,000 yuan per 1,000 hectares	25.73	0.00	15	23	8
Area of green land per capita in urban areas	Hectare per capita	0.01	0.00	5	9	4
Treatment rate of urban wastewater	%	82.10	80.30	16	9	−7
Harmless treatment rate of urban household waste	%	96.95	98.22	4	1	−3
Length of public transport routes per capita in urban areas	km per capita	0.0015	0.0004	4	11	7
Industrial nitrogen oxide removal rate	%	1.08	36.27	19	1	−18
Industrial wastewater ammonia/nitrogen removal rate	%	76.17	92.84	12	1	−11

Note: A positive value in "Difference" means a rise in ranking

same by GDEG and SDGP. In Second-Class Indicators, Beijing dropped the most in EMI, 16 places lower than last year. It dropped by 7 places in SII ranking. Meanwhile, Beijing rose by 3, 2 and 1 places in RAECI, EPCCI and II respectively. Other indicators remained the same as those in 2009.

To further explain the causes of the changes in the rankings by First- and Second-Class Indicators, we put the Third-Class Indicators where a change of more than 3 places occurred from 2009 to 2010 in Table 5.2. Compared with those in 2009, Beijing dropped by 3 places in Labor productivity of the primary sector, 26 in Recycling rate of industrial water, 3 in Ratio of environmental spending to government expenditure, 4 in Ratio of the investment in pollution control to GDP, 7 in Treatment rate of urban wastewater, 3 in Harmless treatment rate of urban household waste, 18 in Industrial nitrogen oxide removal rate, and 11 in Industrial wastewater ammonia/nitrogen removal rate. It rose by 8 and 4 places respectively in Investment in converting cultivated land into forests and grassland per unit of cultivated land area and Area of green land per capita in urban areas.

Green development checkup-Tianjin

No.	Indicator	Unit	Attribute	2010 average of 30 provinces	2010 figure	2009 figure	2010 ranking	2009 ranking	Change in ranking	Source of 2010 data	Chernoff face
1	GDP per capita	Yuan per capita	Positive	33,964.12	72,994	62,574	3	3	0	China Statistics	
2	Energy consumption per unit of GDP	Ton coal equivalent per 10,000 yuan	Negative	1.29	0.83	0.84	8	7	−1	China Statistics	☹
3	Ratio of non-fossil energy consumption to total energy consumption		Positive	NA	NA	NA	NA	NA			
4	CO_2 emissions per unit of GDP		Negative	NA	NA	NA	NA	NA			
5	SO_2 emissions per unit of GDP	Ton per 10,000 yuan	Negative	0.0088	0.0029	0.0034	5	6	1	China Statistics	☺
6	COD emissions per unit of GDP	Ton per 10,000 yuan	Negative	0.0045	0.0016	0.0019	3	3	0	China Statistics	
7	Nitrogen oxide emissions per unit of GDP	Ton per 10,000 yuan	Negative	0.0068	0.0030	0.0031	3	4	1	Environmental Annual Report; China Statistics	☺
8	Ammonia/nitrogen emissions per unit of GDP	Ton per 10,000 yuan	Negative	0.0004	0.0002	0.0002	7	2	−5	Environmental Annual Report; China Statistics	☹
9	Electricity consumption per capita in urban areas	kWh per capita	Negative	295.08	686.17	692.38	28	28	0	City	
10	Labor productivity of the primary sector	10,000 yuan per capita	Positive	1.61	1.90	1.65	12	12	0	China Statistics	

(continued)

(continued)

No.	Indicator	Unit	Attribute	2010 average of 30 provinces	2010 figure	2009 figure	2010 ranking	2009 ranking	Change in ranking	Source of 2010 data	Chernoff face
11	Land productivity	100 million yuan per 1,000 hectares	Positive	0.26	0.37	0.31	7	7	0	China Statistics	
12	Proportion of water-saving irrigated area in effectively irrigated area		Positive	0.49	0.76	0.72	4	5	1	Water Conservancy; China Statistics	
13	Proportion of water-saving irrigated area in effectively irrigated area	%	Positive	53.55	78.13	78.75	5	5	0	China Statistics	
14	Labor productivity of the secondary sector	10,000 yuan per capita	Positive	12.13	22.89	19.30	2	2	0	China Statistics	
15	Water consumption per unit of value added created by industrial enterprises	m^3/yuan	Negative	0.0100	0.0011	0.0012	1	1	0	China Statistics	
16	Energy consumption per unit of value added created by industrial enterprises above designated size (no data)		Negative	NA	NA	NA	NA	NA			
17	Utilization rate of industrial solid waste	%	Positive	69.80	98.60	98.30	1	1	0	Environmental Yearbook	
18	Recycling rate of industrial water	%	Positive	72.90	95.86	96.40	1	1	0	Environmental Yearbook	
19	Ratio of the output of six energy-intensive industries to gross industrial output	%	Negative	39.65	35.23	34.84	14	13	−1	Industrial Economy	
20	Labor productivity of the tertiary sector	10,000 yuan per capita	Positive	6.96	18.77	15.43	1	2	1	China Statistics	

21	Proportion of the value added of the tertiary sector in GDP	%	Positive	39.97	46.00	45.30	5	5	0	China Statistics	
22	Proportion of tertiary sector employees in the total employed population	%	Positive	36.67	44.43	43.40	3	3	0	China Statistics	
23	Water resources per capita	m^3 per capita	Positive	2,419.38	72.80	126.79	30	29	−1	China Statistics	☹
24	Forest area per capita	Hectare per capita	Positive	0.19	0.01	0.01	29	29	0	China Statistics	
25	Forest coverage rate	%	Positive	30.63	8.24	8.24	28	28	0	China Statistics	
26	Proportion of the area of natural reserves in the total area of a region	%	Positive	8.60	8.06	8.06	11	10	−1	China Statistics	☺
27	Proportion of the area of wetlands in the total area of a region	%	Positive	7.01	14.95	14.95	3	3	0	China Statistics	
28	Growing stock per capita	m^3 per capita	Positive	10.70	0.21	0.23	29	29	0	China Statistics	
29	CO_2 emissions per unit of land area		Negative	NA	NA	NA	NA	NA			
30	CO_2 emissions per capita		Negative	NA	NA	NA	NA	NA			
31	SO_2 emissions per unit of land area	Ton per km^2	Negative	6.3677	19.7318	19.8618	29	29	0	China Statistics; Deserts	
32	SO_2 emissions per capita	Ton per capita	Negative	0.0191	0.0186	0.0197	19	20	1	China Statistics	☺
33	COD emissions per unit of land area	Ton per km^2	Negative	3.7722	11.0737	11.1602	29	29	0	China Statistics; Deserts	
34	COD emissions per capita	Ton per capita	Negative	0.0101	0.0104	0.0111	20	19	−1	China Statistics	☹

(continued)

(continued)

No.	Indicator	Unit	Attribute	2010 average of 30 provinces	2010 figure	2009 figure	2010 ranking	2009 ranking	Change in ranking	Source of 2010 data	Chernoff face
35	Nitrogen oxide emissions per unit of land area	Ton per km^2	Negative	6.4473	20.6422	18.0410	29	29	0	China Statistics; Deserts; Environmental Annual Report	
36	Nitrogen oxide emissions per capita	Ton per capita	Negative	0.0165	0.0195	0.0179	23	24	1	Environmental Annual Report; China Statistics	
37	Ammonia/nitrogen emissions per unit of land area	Ton per km^2	Negative	0.4164	1.6782	1.0069	29	29	0	China Statistics; Deserts; Environmental Annual Report	
38	Ammonia/nitrogen emissions per capita	Ton per capita	Negative	0.0010	0.0016	0.0010	28	17	−11	Environmental Annual Report; China Statistics	
39	Consumption of chemical fertilizers per unit of cultivated land area	10,000 ton per 1,000 hectares	Negative	0.05	0.06	0.06	21	21	0	China Statistics; China Statistics	
40	Consumption of pesticides per unit of cultivated land area	Ton per 1,000 hectares	Negative	17.68	8.44	8.63	11	12	1	Environmental Yearbook; China Statistics	
41	Nitrogen oxide emissions per capita from road transport	Ton per 10,000 persons	Negative	24.07	4.69	4.98	2	2	0	Environmental Annual Report; China Statistics	
42	Ratio of environmental spending to government expenditure	%	Positive	3.35	1.97	1.19	29	29	0	China Statistics	

43	Ratio of the investment in pollution control to GDP	%	Positive	1.40	1.19	1.48	20	15	–5	Environmental Yearbook; China Statistics	☹
44	Government spending per capita on rural water supply system and toilet improvement	Yuan per capita	Positive	57.01	111.83	155.80	3	3	0	Environmental Yearbook	
45	Investment in converting cultivated land into forests and grassland per unit of cultivated land area	10,000 yuan per 1,000 hectares	Positive	29.81	2.57	0.00	24	23	–1	Environmental Yearbook; China Statistics	☹
46	Ratio of the spending on science, education, culture, and public health to government expenditure	%	Positive	26.10	26.67	25.05	14	20	6	China Statistics	☺
47	Area of green land per capita in urban areas	Hectare per capita	Positive	0.00	0.00	0.00	9	26	17	City; China Statistics	☺
48	Coverage of water supply in urban areas	%	Positive	96.08	100.00	100.00	1	1	0	China Statistics	
49	Treatment rate of urban wastewater	%	Positive	79.18	85.30	80.10	10	11	1	Environmental Yearbook	☺
50	Harmless treatment rate of urban household waste	%	Positive	78.47	100.00	94.31	1	4	3	China Statistics	☺
51	Public buses per 10,000 urban residents		Positive	9.86	12.05	15.38	4	3	–1	China Statistics	☹
52	Length of public transport routes per capita in urban areas	km per capita	Positive	0.0006	0.0013	0.0001	5	30	25	China Statistics; City	☺
53	Ratio of the rural residents benefiting from water supply system improvement to the total rural population	%	Positive	94.44	100.00	100.00	1	1	0	Environmental Yearbook	

(continued)

(continued)

No.	Indicator	Unit	Attribute	2010 average of 30 provinces	2010 figure	2009 figure	2010 ranking	2009 ranking	Change in ranking	Source of 2010 data	Chernoff face
54	Green coverage of urban built-up areas	%	Positive	37.75	32.06	30.33	27	27	0	China Statistics	
55	Newly-added afforestation area of the year per capita	Hectare per 10,000 persons	Positive	59.50	8.95	13.02	25	22	−3	China Statistics	☹
56	Industrial SO_2 removal rate	%	Positive	59.83	63.22	59.73	13	14	1	China Statistics	☺
57	Industrial wastewater COD removal rate	%	Positive	70.84	70.22	67.72	18	17	−1	Environmental Annual Report; China Statistics	☹
58	Industrial nitrogen oxide removal rate	%	Positive	4.07	14.78	16.65	2	4	2	Environmental Annual Report	☺
59	Industrial wastewater ammonia/nitrogen removal rate	%	Positive	62.87	24.87	29.79	29	28	−1	Environmental Annual Report; China Statistics	☹
60	Number of environmental emergencies		Negative	14.00	0	0	1	1	0	China Statistics	

Note:
China Statistics: *China Statistical Yearbook 2011*
Environmental Yearbook: *China Environmental Statistical Yearbook 2011*
Environmental Annual Report: *China Environment Annual Report 2010*
City: *China City Statistical Yearbook 2011*
Water Conservancy: *China Water Conservancy Statistical Yearbook 2011*
Industrial Economy: *China Industrial Economy Statistical Yearbook 2011*
Deserts: *Deserts in China and Desertification Control*

5.2 Brief Analysis of Green Development in Tianjin

Tianjin ranked 2nd among the 30 participating provinces by GDI according to 2010 data, two places higher over 2009 (Tianjin ranked 4th in 2009). Following is a brief analysis of its score by each indicator and their changes from 2009 to 2010.

5.2.1 Tianjin's 2010 Scores by GDI

Tianjin scored 0.215 in 2010. From the three First-Class Indicators including GDEG, CCPNRE, and SDGP as shown in Fig. 5.3, Tianjin obviously outshined other provinces in terms of GDEG and SDGP, yet scored lower than the national average in CCPNRE (Note: the national average value of each indicator is 0).

According to Fig. 5.4, Tianjin surpassed the national average by six of Second-Class Indicators in 2010, which are GGEI, PII, SII, TII, II and EMI. Its performance was below the national average in RAECI, EPCCI and GII.

5.2.2 Changes in Tianjin's Rankings by GDI 2009–2010

According to Table 5.3, in First-Class Indicators, the most obvious change occurred in SDGP, where Tianjin rose as many as 9 places in ranking. By CCPNRE, it fell by

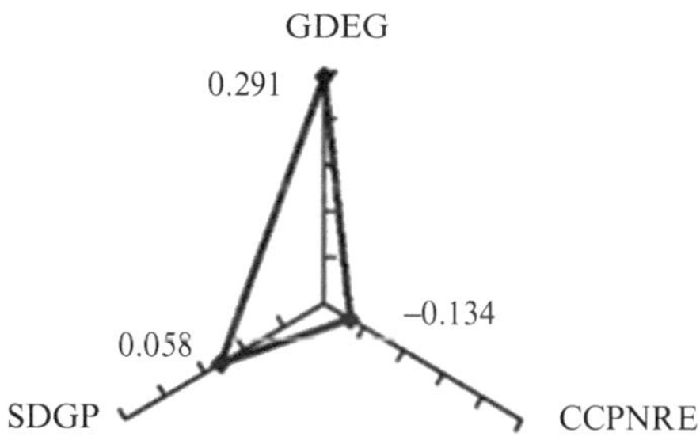

Fig. 5.3 Scores of Tianjin by First-Class Indicators

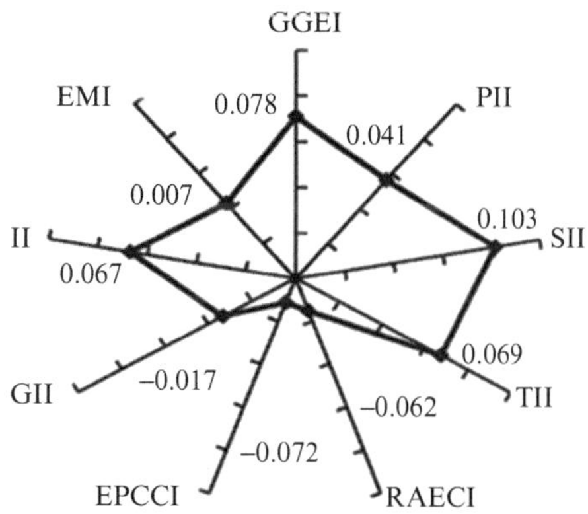

Fig. 5.4 Scores of Tianjin by Second-Class Indicators

Table 5.3 Changes in Tianjin's rankings by First-Class and Second-Class Indicators, 2009–2010

Indicator	2010	2009	Difference	Indicator	2010	2009	Difference
GDI	2	4	2				
GDEG	3	3	0	RAECI	24	22	−2
GGEI	3	3	0	EPCCI	25	22	−3
PII	6	4	−2	SDGP	8	17	9
SII	1	1	0	GII	19	27	8
TII	3	3	0	II	4	11	7
CCPNRE	27	21	−6	EMI	14	13	−1

Note: A positive value in "Difference" means a rise in ranking

Table 5.4 Third-Class Indicators where changes over 3 places occurred in Tianjin, 2009–2010

	Original data for 2010 and 2009			Change in ranking		
Third-Class Indicator	Unit	2010	2009	2010	2009	Difference
Ammonia/nitrogen emissions per unit of GDP	Ton per 10,000 yuan	0.0002	0.0002	7	2	−5
Ammonia/nitrogen emissions per capita	Ton per capita	0.0016	0.0010	28	17	−11
Ratio of the investment in pollution control to GDP	%	1.19	1.48	20	15	−5
Ratio of the spending on science, education, culture, and public health to government expenditure	%	26.67	25.05	14	20	6
Area of green land per capita in urban areas	Hectare per capita	0.00	0.00	9	26	17
Harmless treatment rate of urban household waste	%	100.00	94.31	1	4	3
Length of public transport routes per capita in urban areas	km per capita	0.0013	0.0001	5	30	25
Newly-added afforestation area of the year per capita	Hectare per 10,000 persons	8.95	13.02	25	22	−3

Note: A positive value in "Difference" means a rise in ranking

6 places, and it remained the same by GDEG. In Second-Class Indicators ranking, Tianjin rose the most in GII by 8 places, and 7 in II. Tianjin dropped by 2 places by PII and RAECI, 3 in EPCCI and 1 in EMI. It remained the same in the rankings by other indicators as in 2009.

To further explain the causes of the changes in the rankings by First- and Second-Class Indicators, we put the Third-Class Indicators where a change of more than 3 places occurred from 2009 to 2010 in Table 5.4. Compared with those in 2009, Tianjin rose by 6 places by Ratio of the spending on science, education, culture, and public health to government expenditure, 17 in Area of green land per capita in urban areas, 3 in Harmless treatment rate of urban household waste and 25 in Length of public transport routes per capita in urban areas. Tianjin dropped by 5 places by Ammonia/nitrogen emissions per unit of GDP, 11 in Ammonia/nitrogen emissions per capita, 5 in Ratio of the investment in pollution control to GDP and 3 in Newly-added afforestation area of the year per capita.

Green development checkup-Hebei

No.	Indicator	Unit	Attribute	2010 average of 30 provinces	2010 figure	2009 figure	2010 ranking	2009 ranking	Change in ranking	Source of 2010 data	Chernoff face
1	GDP per capita	Yuan per capita	Positive	33,964.12	28,668	24,581	12	12	0	China Statistics	
2	Energy consumption per unit of GDP	Ton coal equivalent per 10,000 yuan	Negative	1.29	1.58	1.64	24	23	−1	China Statistics	☹
3	Ratio of non-fossil energy consumption to total energy consumption		Positive	NA	NA	NA	NA	NA			
4	CO_2 emissions per unit of GDP		Negative	NA	NA	NA	NA	NA			
5	SO_2 emissions per unit of GDP	Ton per 10,000 yuan	Negative	0.0088	0.0071	0.0081	17	17	0	China Statistics	
6	COD emissions per unit of GDP	Ton per 10,000 yuan	Negative	0.0045	0.0031	0.0037	10	11	1	China Statistics	☺
7	Nitrogen oxide emissions per unit of GDP	Ton per 10,000 yuan	Negative	0.0068	0.0064	0.0064	21	19	−2	Environmental Annual Report; China Statistics	☹
8	Ammonia/nitrogen emissions per unit of GDP	Ton per 10,000 yuan	Negative	0.0004	0.0003	0.0004	9	10	1	Environmental Annual Report; China Statistics	☺
9	Electricity consumption per capita in urban areas	kWh per capita	Negative	295.08	90.06	208.29	1	3	2	City	☺
10	Labor productivity of the primary sector	10,000 yuan per capita	Positive	1.61	1.74	1.49	14	14	0	China Statistics	

(continued)

(continued)

No.	Indicator	Unit	Attribute	2010 average of 30 provinces	2010 figure	2009 figure	2010 ranking	2009 ranking	Change in ranking	Source of 2010 data	Chernoff face
11	Land productivity	100 million yuan per 1,000 hectares	Positive	0.26	0.28	0.22	11	11	0	China Statistics	
12	Proportion of water-saving irrigated area in effectively irrigated area		Positive	0.49	0.59	0.57	12	11	−1	Water Conservancy; China Statistics	☹
13	Proportion of water-saving irrigated area in effectively irrigated area	%	Positive	53.55	71.99	72.07	9	8	−1	China Statistics	☹
14	Labor productivity of the secondary sector	10,000 yuan per capita	Positive	12.13	8.65	7.44	22	21	−1	China Statistics	☹
15	Water consumption per unit of value added created by industrial enterprises	m^3/yuan	Negative	0.0100	0.0027	0.0030	4	4	0	China Statistics	
16	Energy consumption per unit of value added created by industrial enterprises above designated size (no data)		Negative	NA	NA	NA	NA	NA			
17	Utilization rate of industrial solid waste	%	Positive	69.80	56.60	70.90	20	15	−5	Environmental Yearbook	☹
18	Recycling rate of industrial water	%	Positive	72.90	94.64	94.93	3	4	1	Environmental Yearbook	☺
19	Ratio of the output of six energy-intensive industries to gross industrial output	%	Negative	39.65	50.94	53.16	24	25	1	Industrial Economy	☺

20	Labor productivity of the tertiary sector	10,000 yuan per capita	Positive	6.96	6.30	5.59	13	13	0	China Statistics	
21	Proportion of the value added of the tertiary sector in GDP	%	Positive	39.97	34.90	35.20	25	27	2	China Statistics	☺
22	Proportion of tertiary sector employees in the total employed population	%	Positive	36.67	27.95	30.81	27	26	−1	China Statistics	☹
23	Water resources per capita	m^3 per capita	Positive	2,419.38	195.28	201.32	26	27	1	China Statistics	☺
24	Forest area per capita	Hectare per capita	Positive	0.19	0.06	0.06	24	23	−1	China Statistics	☹
25	Forest coverage rate	%	Positive	30.63	22.29	22.29	19	19	0	China Statistics	
26	Proportion of the area of natural reserves in the total area of a region	%	Positive	8.60	3.05	2.97	29	29	0	China Statistics	
27	Proportion of the area of wetlands in the total area of a region	%	Positive	7.01	5.82	5.82	12	12	0	China Statistics	
28	Growing stock per capita	m^3 per capita	Positive	10.70	1.42	1.45	24	24	0	China Statistics	
29	CO_2 emissions per unit of land area		Negative	NA	NA	NA	NA	NA			
30	CO_2 emissions per capita		Negative	NA	NA	NA	NA	NA			
31	SO_2 emissions per unit of land area	Ton per km^2	Negative	6.3677	6.5475	6.6520	20	18	−2	China Statistics; Deserts	☹
32	SO_2 emissions per capita	Ton per capita	Negative	0.0191	0.0173	0.0179	18	17	−1	China Statistics	☹
33	COD emissions per unit of land area	Ton per km^2	Negative	3.7722	2.8979	3.0254	16	16	0	China Statistics; Deserts	

(continued)

(continued)

No.	Indicator	Unit	Attribute	2010 average of 30 provinces	2010 figure	2009 figure	2010 ranking	2009 ranking	Change in ranking	Source of 2010 data	Chernoff face
34	COD emissions per capita	Ton per capita	Negative	0.0101	0.0077	0.0081	8	8	0	China Statistics	
35	Nitrogen oxide emissions per unit of land area	Ton per km^2	Negative	6.4473	5.9225	5.2857	21	20	−1	China Statistics; Deserts; Environmental Annual Report	☹
36	Nitrogen oxide emissions per capita	Ton per capita	Negative	0.0165	0.0157	0.0142	19	18	−1	Environmental Annual Report; China Statistics	☹
37	Ammonia/nitrogen emissions per unit of land area	Ton per km^2	Negative	0.4164	0.2919	0.2919	17	17	0	China Statistics; Deserts; Environmental Annual Report	
38	Ammonia/nitrogen emissions per capita	Ton per capita	Negative	0.0010	0.0008	0.0008	9	8	−1	Environmental Annual Report; China Statistics	☹
39	Consumption of chemical fertilizers per unit of cultivated land area	10,000 ton per 1,000 hectares	Negative	0.05	0.05	0.05	18	17	−1	China Statistics; China Statistics	☹
40	Consumption of pesticides per unit of cultivated land area	Ton per 1,000 hectares	Negative	17.68	13.39	13.69	15	16	1	Environmental Yearbook; China Statistics	☺
41	Nitrogen oxide emissions per capita from road transport	Ton per 10,000 persons	Negative	24.07	10.69	11.37	6	7	1	Environmental Annual Report; China Statistics	☺

42	Ratio of environmental spending to government expenditure	%	Positive	3.35	4.08	4.44	7	5	−2	China Statistics	☹
43	Ratio of the investment in pollution control to GDP	%	Positive	1.40	1.82	1.60	6	9	3	Environmental Yearbook; China Statistics	☺
44	Government spending per capita on rural water supply system and toilet improvement	Yuan per capita	Positive	57.01	6.90	10.35	30	30	0	Environmental Yearbook	
45	Investment in converting cultivated land into forests and grassland per unit of cultivated land area	10,000 yuan per 1,000 hectares	Positive	29.81	31.93	11.99	9	20	11	Environmental Yearbook; China Statistics	☺
46	Ratio of the spending on science, education, culture, and public health to government expenditure	%	Positive	26.10	28.95	28.90	6	7	1	China Statistics	☺
47	Area of green land per capita in urban areas	Hectare per capita	Positive	0.00	0.00	0.00	23	13	−10	City; China Statistics	☹
48	Coverage of water supply in urban areas	%	Positive	96.08	99.97	99.97	4	4	0	China Statistics	
49	Treatment rate of urban wastewater	%	Positive	79.18	92.30	84.50	2	6	4	Environmental Yearbook	☺
50	Harmless treatment rate of urban household waste	%	Positive	78.47	69.82	59.00	23	25	2	China Statistics	☺

(continued)

(continued)

No.	Indicator	Unit	Attribute	2010 average of 30 provinces	2010 figure	2009 figure	2010 ranking	2009 ranking	Change in ranking	Source of 2010 data	Chernoff face
51	Public buses per 10,000 urban residents		Positive	9.86	9.53	9.02	16	22	6	China Statistics	☺
52	Length of public transport routes per capita in urban areas	km per capita	Positive	0.0006	0.0002	0.0003	25	18	−7	China Statistics; City	☹
53	Ratio of the rural residents benefiting from water supply system improvement to the total rural population	%	Positive	94.44	97.46	97.40	14	13	−1	Environmental Yearbook	☹
54	Green coverage of urban built-up areas	%	Positive	37.75	42.73	40.02	3	7	4	China Statistics	☺
55	Newly-added afforestation area of the year per capita	Hectare per 10,000 persons	Positive	59.50	39.90	43.70	15	14	−1	China Statistics	☹
56	Industrial SO_2 removal rate	%	Positive	59.83	63.18	54.28	14	20	6	China Statistics	☺
57	Industrial wastewater COD removal rate	%	Positive	70.84	77.05	76.66	14	12	−2	Environmental Annual Report; China Statistics	☹

58	Industrial nitrogen oxide removal rate	%	Positive	4.07	6.46	4.69	7	12	5	Environmental Annual Report	☺
59	Industrial wastewater ammonia/nitrogen removal rate	%	Positive	62.87	57.57	60.50	18	14	−4	Environmental Annual Report; China Statistics	☹
60	Number of environmental emergencies		Negative	14.00	7	4	17	10	−7	China Statistics	☹

Note:
China Statistics: *China Statistical Yearbook 2011*
Environmental Yearbook: *China Environmental Statistical Yearbook 2011*
Environmental Annual Report: *China Environment Annual Report 2010*
City: *China City Statistical Yearbook 2011*
Water Conservancy: *China Water Conservancy Statistical Yearbook 2011*
Industrial Economy: *China Industrial Economic Statistical Yearbook 2011*
Deserts: *Deserts in China and Desertification Control*

5.3 Brief Analysis of Green Development in Hebei

Hebei ranked 17th among the 30 participating provinces by GDI according to 2010 data, one place higher over 2009 (Hebei ranked 18th in 2009). Following is a brief analysis of its score by each indicator and their changes from 2009 to 2010.

5.3.1 Hebei's 2010 Scores by GDI

Hebei scored −0.040 in 2010. From the three First-Class Indicators including GDEG, CCPNRE, and SDGP as shown in Fig. 5.5, Hebei had advantage in terms of SDGP, yet underperformed compared with the national average in GDEG and CCPNRE (Note: the national average value of each indicator is 0).

According to Fig. 5.6, Hebei surpassed the national average in five of Second-Class Indicators in 2010, which are GGEI, PII, GII, II and EMI. It ranked lower than the national average in terms of SII, TII, RAECI, and EPCCI.

5.3.2 Changes in Hebei's Rankings by GDI 2009–2010

According to Table 5.5, in First-Class Indicators, the most obvious change occurred in SDGP where Hebei's ranking rose 3 places. It rose by 2 places in

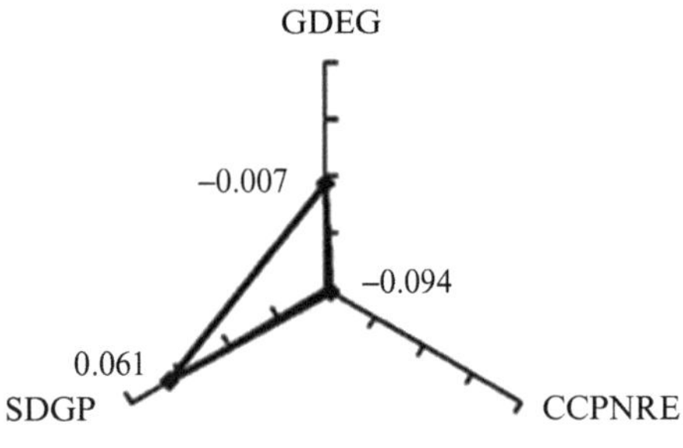

Fig. 5.5 Scores of Hebei by First-Class Indicators

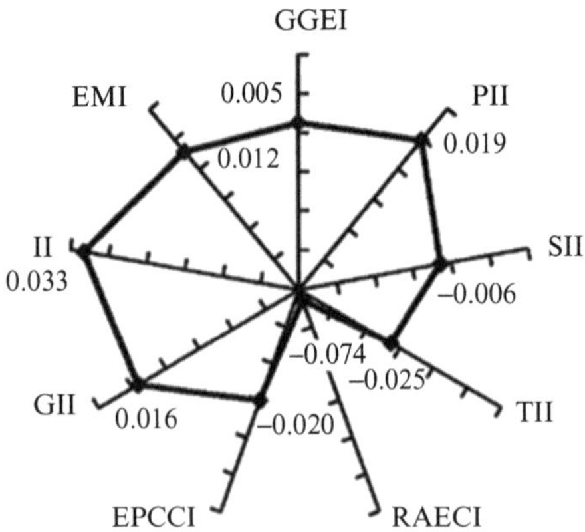

Fig. 5.6 Scores of Hebei by Second-Class Indicators

Table 5.5 Changes in Hebei's rankings by First-Class and Second-Class Indicators, 2009–2010

Indicator	2010	2009	Difference	Indicator	2010	2009	Difference
GDI	17	18	1				
GDEG	12	12	0	RAECI	29	29	0
GGEI	12	11	−1	EPCCI	13	16	3
PII	9	10	1	SDGP	7	10	3
SII	18	16	−2	GII	9	9	0
TII	24	24	0	II	11	10	−1
CCPNRE	23	25	2	EMI	12	12	0

Note: A positive value in "Difference" means a rise in ranking

Table 5.6 Third-Class Indicators where changes over 3 places occurred by Hebei, 2009–2010

	Original data for 2010 and 2009			Change in ranking		
Third-Class Indicator	Unit	2010	2009	2010	2009	Difference
Utilization rate of industrial solid waste	%	56.60	70.90	20	15	−5
Ratio of the investment in pollution control to GDP	%	1.82	1.60	6	9	3
Investment in converting cultivated land into forests and grassland per unit of cultivated land area	10,000 yuan per 1,000 hectares	31.93	11.99	9	20	11
Area of green land per capita in urban areas	Hectare per capita	0.00	0.00	23	13	−10
Treatment rate of urban wastewater	%	92.30	84.50	2	6	4
Public buses per 10,000 urban residents		9.53	9.02	16	22	6
Length of public transport routes per capita in urban areas	km per capita	0.0002	0.0003	25	18	−7
Green coverage of urban built-up areas	%	42.73	40.02	3	7	4
Industrial SO_2 removal rate	%	63.18	54.28	14	20	6
Industrial nitrogen oxide removal rate	%	6.46	4.69	7	12	5
Industrial wastewater ammonia/nitrogen removal rate	%	57.57	60.50	18	14	−4
Number of environmental emergencies		7	4	17	10	−7

Note: A positive value in "Difference" means a rise in ranking

CCPNRE, and remained the same by GDEG and SDGP. In Second-Class Indicators, Hebei rose by 1 and 3 places respectively in PII and EPCCI, and dropped by 1 place by GGEI, 2 in SII and 1 in II. It remained the same in the rankings by other indicators as in 2009.

To further explain the causes of the changes in the rankings by First- and Second-Class Indicators, we put the Third-Class Indicators where a change of more than 3 places occurred from 2009 to 2010 in Table 5.6. Compared with those in 2009, Hebei dropped by 5 places by Utilization rate of industrial solid waste, 10 in Area of green land per capita in urban areas, 7 in Length of public transport routes per capita in urban areas, 4 in Industrial wastewater ammonia/nitrogen removal rate and 7 in Number of environmental emergencies. Hebei rose by 3 places by Ratio of the investment in pollution control to GDP, 11 in Investment in converting cultivated land into forests and grassland per unit of cultivated land area, 4 in Treatment rate of urban wastewater, 6 in Public buses per 10,000 urban residents, 4 in Green coverage of urban built-up areas, 6 in rate of industrial SO_2 emissions and 5 in Industrial nitrogen oxide removal rate.

Green development checkup-Shanxi

No.	Indicator	Unit	Attribute	2010 average of 30 provinces	2010 figure	2009 figure	2010 ranking	2009 ranking	Change in ranking	Source of 2010 data	Chernoff face
1	GDP per capita	Yuan per capita	Positive	33,964.12	26,283	21,522	18	18	0	China Statistics	
2	Energy consumption per unit of GDP	Ton coal equivalent per 10,000 yuan	Negative	1.29	2.24	2.36	27	28	1	China Statistics	
3	Ratio of non-fossil energy consumption to total energy consumption		Positive	NA	NA	NA	NA	NA			
4	CO_2 emissions per unit of GDP		Negative	NA	NA	NA	NA	NA			
5	SO_2 emissions per unit of GDP	Ton per 10,000 yuan	Negative	0.0088	0.0173	0.0201	28	28	0	China Statistics	
6	COD emissions per unit of GDP	Ton per 10,000 yuan	Negative	0.0045	0.0046	0.0054	19	19	0	China Statistics	
7	Nitrogen oxide emissions per unit of GDP	Ton per 10,000 yuan	Negative	0.0068	0.0127	0.0172	27	29	2	Environmental Annual Report; China Statistics	
8	Ammonia/nitrogen emissions per unit of GDP	Ton per 10,000 yuan	Negative	0.0004	0.0006	0.0006	24	24	0	Environmental Annual Report; China Statistics	
9	Electricity consumption per capita in urban areas	kWh per capita	Negative	295.08	134.33	258.36	9	6	−3	City	

(continued)

(continued)

No.	Indicator	Unit	Attribute	2010 average of 30 provinces	2010 figure	2009 figure	2010 ranking	2009 ranking	Change in ranking	Source of 2010 data	Chernoff face
10	Labor productivity of the primary sector	10,000 yuan per capita	Positive	1.61	0.87	0.75	27	27	0	China Statistics	
11	Land productivity	100 million yuan per 1,000 hectares	Positive	0.26	0.18	0.15	21	21	0	China Statistics	
12	Proportion of water-saving irrigated area in effectively irrigated area		Positive	0.49	0.64	0.64	10	10	0	Water Conservancy; China Statistics	
13	Proportion of water-saving irrigated area in effectively irrigated area	%	Positive	53.55	31.42	31.09	25	24	−1	China Statistics	☹
14	Labor productivity of the secondary sector	10,000 yuan per capita	Positive	12.13	12.18	9.55	9	12	3	China Statistics	☺
15	Water consumption per unit of value added created by industrial enterprises	m^3/yuan	Negative	0.0100	0.0035	0.0030	6	5	−1	China Statistics	☹
16	Energy consumption per unit of value added created by industrial enterprises above designated size (no data)		Negative	NA	NA	NA	NA	NA			
17	Utilization rate of industrial solid waste	%	Positive	69.80	65.50	60.10	18	20	2	Environmental Yearbook	☺

18	Recycling rate of industrial water	%	Positive	72.90	94.66	94.99	2	3	1	Environmental Yearbook	☺
19	Ratio of the output of six energy-intensive industries to gross industrial output	%	Negative	39.65	46.00	48.32	21	22	1	Environmental Yearbook; Industrial Economy	☺
20	Labor productivity of the tertiary sector	10,000 yuan per capita	Positive	6.96	6.03	5.41	17	16	−1	China Statistics	☹
21	Proportion of the value added of the tertiary sector in GDP	%	Positive	39.97	37.10	39.20	16	16	0	China Statistics	
22	Proportion of tertiary sector employees in the total employed population	%	Positive	36.67	35.23	34.04	15	18	3	China Statistics	☺
23	Water resources per capita	m^3 per capita	Positive	2,419.38	261.52	250.83	25	25	0	China Statistics	
24	Forest area per capita	Hectare per capita	Positive	0.19	0.06	0.06	22	22	0	China Statistics	
25	Forest coverage rate	%	Positive	30.63	14.12	14.12	23	23	0	China Statistics	
26	Proportion of the area of natural reserves in the total area of a region	%	Positive	8.60	7.40	7.36	14	13	−1	China Statistics	☹
27	Proportion of the area of wetlands in the total area of a region	%	Positive	7.01	3.19	3.19	21	21	0	China Statistics	
28	Growing stock per capita	m^3 per capita	Positive	10.70	2.48	2.58	22	22	0	China Statistics	
29	CO_2 emissions per unit of land area		Negative	NA	NA	NA	NA	NA			
30	CO_2 emissions per capita		Negative	NA	NA	NA	NA	NA			

(continued)

(continued)

No.	Indicator	Unit	Attribute	2010 average of 30 provinces	2010 figure	2009 figure	2010 ranking	2009 ranking	Change in ranking	Source of 2010 data	Chernoff face
31	SO_2 emissions per unit of land area	Ton per km^2	Negative	6.3677	7.9714	8.0940	24	24	0	China Statistics; Deserts	
32	SO_2 emissions per capita	Ton per capita	Negative	0.0191	0.0357	0.0371	28	28	0	China Statistics	
33	COD emissions per unit of land area	Ton per km^2	Negative	3.7722	2.1256	2.1978	11	11	0	China Statistics; Deserts	
34	COD emissions per capita	Ton per capita	Negative	0.0101	0.0095	0.0101	14	16	2	China Statistics	☺
35	Nitrogen oxide emissions per unit of land area	Ton per km^2	Negative	6.4473	5.8388	6.9236	20	22	2	China Statistics; Deserts; Environmental Annual Report	☺
36	Nitrogen oxide emissions per capita	Ton per capita	Negative	0.0165	0.0261	0.0317	27	29	2	Environmental Annual Report; China Statistics	☺
37	Ammonia/nitrogen emissions per unit of land area	Ton per km^2	Negative	0.4164	0.2680	0.2616	15	16	1	China Statistics; Deserts; Environmental Annual Report	☺
38	Ammonia/nitrogen emissions per capita	Ton per capita	Negative	0.0010	0.0012	0.0012	23	22	−1	Environmental Annual Report; China Statistics	☹
39	Consumption of chemical fertilizers per unit of cultivated land area	10,000 ton per 1,000 hectares	Negative	0.05	0.03	0.03	6	6	0	China Statistics; China Statistics	

40	Consumption of pesticides per unit of cultivated land area	Ton per 1,000 hectares	Negative	17.68	6.44	6.24	8	8	0	Environmental Yearbook; China Statistics	
41	Nitrogen oxide emissions per capita from road transport	Ton per 10,000 persons	Negative	24.07	24.52	83.98	19	30	11	Environmental Annual Report; China Statistics	☺
42	Ratio of environmental spending to government expenditure	%	Positive	3.35	4.27	4.52	6	4	–2	China Statistics	☹
43	Ratio of the investment in pollution control to GDP	%	Positive	1.40	2.25	2.49	2	2	0	Environmental Yearbook; China Statistics	
44	Government spending per capita on rural water supply system and toilet improvement	Yuan per capita	Positive	57.01	31.36	27.54	24	27	3	Environmental Yearbook	☺
45	Investment in converting cultivated land into forests and grassland per unit of cultivated land area	10,000 yuan per 1,000 hectares	Positive	29.81	30.76	24.79	10	14	4	Environmental Yearbook; China Statistics	☺
46	Ratio of the spending on science, education, culture, and public health to government expenditure	%	Positive	26.10	25.57	27.24	18	11	–7	China Statistics	☹
47	Area of green land per capita in urban areas	Hectare per capita	Positive	0.00	0.00	0.00	25	24	–1	City; China Statistics	☹
48	Coverage of water supply in urban areas	%	Positive	96.08	97.26	95.38	17	18	1	China Statistics	☺

(continued)

(continued)

No.	Indicator	Unit	Attribute	2010 average of 30 provinces	2010 figure	2009 figure	2010 ranking	2009 ranking	Change in ranking	Source of 2010 data	Chernoff face
49	Treatment rate of urban wastewater	%	Positive	79.18	84.90	75.20	11	15	4	Environmental Yearbook	☺
50	Harmless treatment rate of urban household waste	%	Positive	78.47	73.58	62.89	19	21	2	China Statistics	☺
51	Public buses per 10,000 urban residents		Positive	9.86	6.83	7.09	30	30	0	China Statistics	
52	Length of public transport routes per capita in urban areas	km per capita	Positive	0.0006	0.0004	0.0006	17	3	−14	China Statistics; City	☹
53	Ratio of the rural residents benefiting from water supply system improvement to the total rural population	%	Positive	94.44	87.20	91.40	26	23	−3	Environmental Yearbook	☹
54	Green coverage of urban built-up areas	%	Positive	37.75	38.01	36.49	15	18	3	China Statistics	☺
55	Newly-added afforestation area of the year per capita	Hectare per 10,000 persons	Positive	59.50	80.66	95.53	9	7	−2	China Statistics	☹
56	Industrial SO_2 removal rate	%	Positive	59.83	62.92	58.69	15	15	0	China Statistics	
57	Industrial wastewater COD removal rate	%	Positive	70.84	52.95	51.13	28	27	−1	Environmental Annual Report; China Statistics	☹

58	Industrial nitrogen oxide removal rate	%	Positive	4.07	15.46	16.89	1	3	2	Environmental Annual Report	☺
59	Industrial wastewater ammonia/nitrogen removal rate	%	Positive	62.87	58.57	58.51	17	15	−2	Environmental Annual Report; China Statistics	☹
60	Number of environmental emergencies		Negative	14.00	9	4	19	10	−9	China Statistics	☹

Note:
China Statistics: *China Statistical Yearbook 2011*
Environmental Yearbook: *China Environmental Statistical Yearbook 2011*
Environmental Annual Report: *China Environment Annual Report 2010*
City: *China City Statistical Yearbook 2011*
Water Conservancy: *China Water Conservancy Statistical Yearbook 2011*
Industrial Economy: *China Industrial Economic Statistical Yearbook 2011*
Deserts: *Deserts in China and Desertification Control*

5.4 Brief Analysis of Green Development in Shanxi

Shanxi ranked 29th among the 30 participating provinces by GDI according to 2010 data, one place lower over 2009 (Shanxi ranked 28th in 2009). Following is a brief analysis of its score by each indicator and their changes from 2009 to 2010.

5.4.1 Shanxi's 2010 Scores by GDI

Shanxi scored −0.208 in 2010. From the three First-Class Indicators including GDEG, CCPNRE, and SDGP as shown in Fig. 5.7, Shanxi performed slightly better than the national average in terms of SDGP, yet was relatively weak in GDEG and CCPNRE, much lower than the national average (Note: the national average value of each indicator is 0).

According to Fig. 5.8, Shanxi surpassed the national average by SII, GII and EMI among Second-Class Indicators, but performed worse than the national average in 6 rankings such as GGEI, PII, TII, RAECI, II and EPCCI.

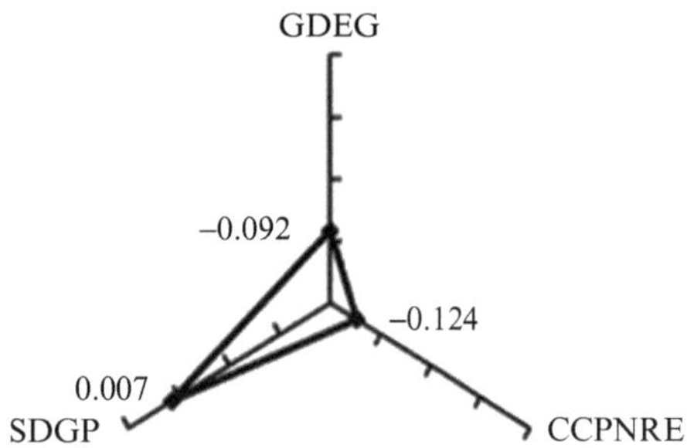

Fig. 5.7 Scores of Shanxi by First-Class Indicators

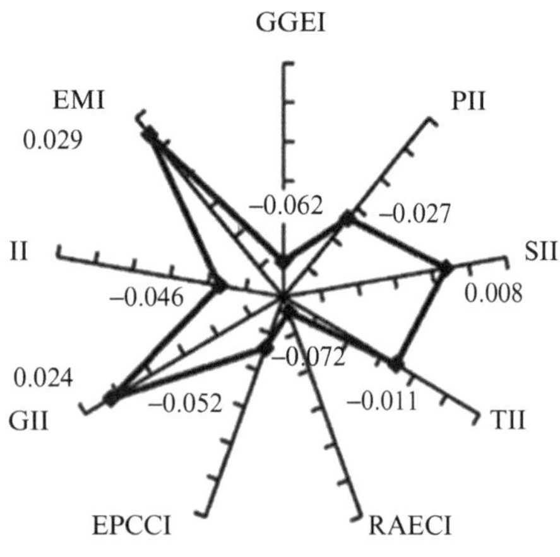

Fig. 5.8 Scores of Shanxi by Second-Class Indicators

Table 5.7 Changes in Shanxi's rankings by First-Class and Second-Class Indicators, 2009–2010

Indicator	2010	2009	Difference	Indicator	2010	2009	Difference
GDI	29	28	−1				
GDEG	23	22	−1	RAECI	28	28	0
GGEI	26	26	0	EPCCI	20	25	5
PII	24	25	1	SDGP	15	11	−4
SII	12	18	6	GII	7	4	−3
TII	17	16	−1	II	23	19	−4
CCPNRE	26	29	3	EMI	8	9	1

Note: A positive value in "Difference" means a rise in ranking

5.4.2 Changes in Shanxi's Rankings by GDI 2009–2010

According to Table 5.7, in First-Class Indicators, the most obvious change occurred in SDGP, where Shanxi dropped by 4 places in ranking, and in GDEG it fell by 1 place too, yet it rose by 3 in CCPNRE. In Second-Class Indicators ranking, Shanxi dropped by 1 place in TII, 3 in GII and 4 in II. It rose by 1 place in PII, 6 in SII, 5 in EPCCI and 1 in EMI. It remained the same in the rankings by other indicators as in 2009.

To further explain the causes of the changes in the rankings by First- and Second-Class Indicators, we put the Third-Class Indicators where a change of more than 3 places occurred from 2009 to 2010 in Table 5.8. Compared with those in 2009, Shanxi dropped by 3 places in Electricity consumption per capita in urban areas, 7 in Ratio of the spending on science, education, culture, and public health to government expenditure, 14 in Length of public transport routes per capita in urban areas, 3 in Ratio of the rural residents benefiting from water supply system improvement to the total rural population and 9 in Number of environmental emergencies. Shanxi rose by 3 places by Labor productivity of the secondary sector, 3 in Proportion of tertiary sector employees in the total employed population, 11 in Nitrogen oxide emissions per capita from road transport, 3 in Government spending per capita on rural water supply system and toilet improvement, 4 in Investment in converting cultivated land into forests and grassland per unit of cultivated land area, 4 in Treatment rate of urban wastewater and 3 in Green coverage of urban built-up areas.

Table 5.8 Third-Class Indicators where changes over 3 places occurred in Shanxi, 2009–2010

	Original data for 2010 and 2009			Change in ranking		
Third-Class Indicator	Unit	2010	2009	2010	2009	Difference
Electricity consumption per capita in urban areas	kWh per capita	134.33	258.36	9	6	−3
Labor productivity of the secondary sector	10,000 yuan per capita	12.18	9.55	9	12	3
Proportion of tertiary sector employees in the total employed population	%	35.23	34.04	15	18	3
Nitrogen oxide emissions per capita from road transport	Ton per 10,000 persons	24.52	83.98	19	30	11
Government spending per capita on rural water supply system and toilet improvement	Yuan per capita	31.36	27.54	24	27	3
Investment in converting cultivated land into forests and grassland per unit of cultivated land area	10,000 yuan per 1,000 hectares	30.76	24.79	10	14	4
Ratio of the spending on science, education, culture, and public health to government expenditure	%	25.57	27.24	18	11	−7
Treatment rate of urban wastewater	%	84.90	75.20	11	15	4
Length of public transport routes per capita in urban areas	km per capita	0.0004	0.0006	17	3	−14
Ratio of the rural residents benefiting from water supply system improvement to the total rural population	%	87.20	91.40	26	23	−3
Green coverage of urban built-up areas	%	38.01	36.49	15	18	3
Number of environmental emergencies		9	4	19	10	−9

Note: A positive value in "Difference" means a rise in ranking

Green development checkup-Inner Mongolia

No.	Indicator	Unit	Attribute	2010 average of 30 provinces	2010 figure	2009 figure	2010 ranking	2009 ranking	Change in ranking	Source of 2010 data	Chernoff face
1	GDP per capita	Yuan per capita	Positive	33,964.12	47,347	40,282	6	7	1	China Statistics	☺
2	Energy consumption per unit of GDP	Ton coal equivalent per 10,000 yuan	Negative	1.29	1.92	2.01	26	26	0	China Statistics	
3	Ratio of non-fossil energy consumption to total energy consumption		Positive	NA	NA	NA	NA	NA			
4	CO_2 emissions per unit of GDP		Negative	NA	NA	NA	NA	NA			
5	SO_2 emissions per unit of GDP	Ton per 10,000 yuan	Negative	0.0088	0.0159	0.0183	26	27	1	China Statistics	☺
6	COD emissions per unit of GDP	Ton per 10,000 yuan	Negative	0.0045	0.0031	0.0036	9	10	1	China Statistics	☺
7	Nitrogen oxide emissions per unit of GDP	Ton per 10,000 yuan	Negative	0.0068	0.0147	0.0134	29	28	−1	Environmental Annual Report; China Statistics	☹
8	Ammonia/nitrogen emissions per unit of GDP	Ton per 10.000 yuan	Negative	0.0004	0.0005	0.0004	21	12	−9	Environmental Annual Report; China Statistics	☹
9	Electricity consumption per capita in urban areas	kWh per capita	Negative	295.08	187.84	244.68	17	5	−12	City	☹

(continued)

(continued)

No.	Indicator	Unit	Attribute	2010 average of 30 provinces	2010 figure	2009 figure	2010 ranking	2009 ranking	Change in ranking	Source of 2010 data	Chernoff face
10	Labor productivity of the primary sector	10,000 yuan per capita	Positive	1.61	1.94	1.67	10	11	1	China Statistics	
11	Land productivity	100 million yuan per 1,000 hectares	Positive	0.26	0.13	0.11	28	28	0	China Statistics	
12	Proportion of water-saving irrigated area in effectively irrigated area		Positive	0.49	0.77	0.73	3	4	1	Water Conservancy; China Statistics	
13	Proportion of water-saving irrigated area in effectively irrigated area	%	Positive	53.55	42.36	41.27	18	18	0	China Statistics	
14	Labor productivity of the secondary sector	10,000 yuan per capita	Positive	12.13	31.88	26.95	1	1	0	China Statistics	
15	Water consumption per unit of value added created by industrial enterprises	m^3/yuan	Negative	0.0100	0.0053	0.0046	8	8	0	China Statistics	
16	Energy consumption per unit of value added created by industrial enterprises above designated size (no data)		Negative	NA	NA	NA	NA	NA			
17	Utilization rate of industrial solid waste	%	Positive	69.80	56.30	52.60	21	23	2	Environmental Yearbook	
18	Recycling rate of industrial water	%	Positive	72.90	84.70	57.52	13	24	11	Environmental Yearbook	

19	Ratio of the output of six energy-intensive industries to gross industrial output	%	Negative	39.65	41.96	44.95	20	20	0	Environmental Yearbook; Industrial Economy	
20	Labor productivity of the tertiary sector	10,000 yuan per capita	Positive	6.96	10.54	9.84	4	4	0	China Statistics	
21	Proportion of the value added of the tertiary sector in GDP	%	Positive	39.97	36.10	38.00	21	19	−2	China Statistics	☹
22	Proportion of tertiary sector employees in the total employed population	%	Positive	36.67	34.40	34.24	17	17	0	China Statistics	
23	Water resources per capita	m^3 per capita	Positive	2,419.38	1,576.08	1,563.88	17	15	−2	China Statistics	☹
24	Forest area per capita	Hectare per capita	Positive	0.19	0.96	0.98	1	1	0	China Statistics	
25	Forest coverage rate	%	Positive	30.63	20.00	20.00	21	21	0	China Statistics	
26	Proportion of the area of natural reserves in the total area of a region	%	Positive	8.60	11.69	11.69	8	7	−1	China Statistics	☹
27	Proportion of the area of wetlands in the total area of a region	%	Positive	7.01	3.66	3.66	19	19	0	China Statistics	
28	Growing stock per capita	m^3 per capita	Positive	10.70	55.04	56.18	1	1	0	China Statistics	
29	CO_2 emissions per unit of land area		Negative	NA	NA	NA	NA	NA			
30	CO_2 emissions per capita		Negative	NA	NA	NA	NA	NA			
31	SO_2 emissions per unit of land area	Ton per km^2	Negative	6.3677	1.8735	1.8798	7	7	0	China Statistics; Deserts	
32	SO_2 emissions per capita	Ton per capita	Negative	0.0191	0.0570	0.0579	30	30	0	China Statistics	

(continued)

(continued)

No.	Indicator	Unit	Attribute	2010 average of 30 provinces	2010 figure	2009 figure	2010 ranking	2009 ranking	Change in ranking	Source of 2010 data	Chernoff face
33	COD emissions per unit of land area	Ton per km^2	Negative	3.7722	0.3697	0.3743	3	3	0	China Statistics; Deserts	
34	COD emissions per capita	Ton per capita	Negative	0.0101	0.0112	0.0115	22	20	−2	China Statistics	☹
35	Nitrogen oxide emissions per unit of land area	Ton per km^2	Negative	6.4473	1.7390	1.3775	10	10	0	China Statistics; Deserts; Environmental Annual Report	
36	Nitrogen oxide emissions per capita	Ton per capita	Negative	0.0165	0.0529	0.0424	29	30	1	Environmental Annual Report; China Statistics	☺
37	Ammonia/nitrogen emissions per unit of land area	Ton per km^2	Negative	0.4164	0.0551	0.0457	4	3	−1	China Statistics; Deserts; Environmental Annual Report	☹
38	Ammonia/nitrogen emissions per capita	Ton per capita	Negative	0.0010	0.0017	0.0014	29	28	−1	China Statistics; Environmental Annual Report	☹
39	Consumption of chemical fertilizers per unit of cultivated land area	10,000 ton per 1,000 hectares	Negative	0.05	0.02	0.02	5	5	0	China Statistics	
40	Consumption of pesticides per unit of cultivated land area	Ton per 1,000 hectares	Negative	17.68	3.40	3.12	4	3	−1	Environmental Yearbook; China Statistics	☹
41	Nitrogen oxide emissions per capita from road transport	Ton per 10,000 persons	Negative	24.07	36.80	25.66	24	20	−4	Environmental Annual Report; China Statistics	☹

42	Ratio of environmental spending to government expenditure	%	Positive	3.35	4.75	5.08	3	3	0	China Statistics	
43	Ratio of the investment in pollution control to GDP	%	Positive	1.40	2.05	2.03	4	3	−1	Environmental Yearbook; China Statistics	☹
44	Government spending per capita on rural water supply system and toilet improvement	Yuan per capita	Positive	57.01	50.67	60.87	14	13	−1	Environmental Yearbook	☹
45	Investment in converting cultivated land into forests and grassland per unit of cultivated land area	10,000 yuan per 1,000 hectares	Positive	29.81	29.97	14.89	12	18	6	Environmental Yearbook; China Statistics	☺
46	Ratio of the spending on science, education, culture, and public health to government expenditure	%	Positive	26.10	22.75	21.37	25	29	4	China Statistics	☺
47	Area of green land per capita in urban areas	Hectare per capita	Positive	0.00	0.00	0.00	11	14	3	City; China Statistics	☺
48	Coverage of water supply in urban areas	%	Positive	96.08	87.97	87.89	30	29	−1	China Statistics	☹
49	Treatment rate of urban wastewater	%	Positive	79.18	80.60	75.20	19	15	−4	Environmental Yearbook	☹
50	Harmless treatment rate of urban household waste	%	Positive	78.47	82.80	72.01	14	15	1	China Statistics	☺
51	Public buses per 10,000 urban residents		Positive	9.86	6.89	7.50	29	29	0	China Statistics	
52	Length of public transport routes per capita in urban areas	km per capita	Positive	0.0006	0.0004	0.0002	13	25	12	China Statistics; City	☺
53	Ratio of the rural residents benefiting from water supply system improvement to the total rural population	%	Positive	94.44	88.35	83.46	25	27	2	Environmental Yearbook	☺

(continued)

(continued)

No.	Indicator	Unit	Attribute	2010 average of 30 provinces	2010 figure	2009 figure	2010 ranking	2009 ranking	Change in ranking	Source of 2010 data	Chernoff face
54	Green coverage of urban built-up areas	%	Positive	37.75	33.35	32.44	26	26	0	China Statistics	
55	Newly-added afforestation area of the year per capita	Hectare per 10,000 persons	Positive	59.50	267.73	356.48	1	1	0	China Statistics	
56	Industrial SO_2 removal rate	%	Positive	59.83	57.33	57.76	22	16	−6	China Statistics	☹
57	Industrial wastewater COD removal rate	%	Positive	70.84	80.22	75.07	8	14	6	Environmental Annual Report; China Statistics	☺
58	Industrial nitrogen oxide removal rate	%	Positive	4.07	0.98	0.28	21	24	3	Environmental Annual Report	☺
59	Industrial wastewater ammonia/nitrogen removal rate	%	Positive	62.87	60.50	61.13	15	13	−2	Environmental Annual Report; China Statistics	☹
60	Number of environmental emergencies		Negative	14.00	5	5	14	13	−1	China Statistics	☹

Note:
China Statistics: *China Statistical Yearbook 2011*
Environmental Yearbook: *China Environmental Statistical Yearbook 2011*
Environmental Annual Report: *China Environment Annual Report 2010*
City: *China City Statistical Yearbook 2011*
Water Conservancy: *China Water Conservancy Statistical Yearbook 2011*
Industrial Economy: *China Industrial Economic Statistical Yearbook 2011*
Deserts: *Deserts in China and Desertification Control*

5.5 Brief Analysis of Green Development in Inner Mongolia

Inner Mongolia ranked 11th among the 30 participating provinces by GDI according to 2010 data, as it did in 2009 (Inner Mongolia ranked 11th in 2009). Following is a brief analysis of its score by each indicator and their changes from 2009 to 2010.

5.5.1 *Inner Mongolia's 2010 Scores by GDI*

Inner Mongolia scored 0.075 in 2010. From the three First-Class as shown in Fig. 5.9, Inner Mongolia had better potential in CCPNRE, and was relatively weak in GDEG and SDGP, lower than the national average (Note: the national average value of each indicator is 0).

According to Fig. 5.10, Inner Mongolia surpassed the national average in 5 of Second-Class Indicators in 2010, which are SII, TII, RAECI, GII, and EMI, yet scored slightly lower than the national average in GGEI, PII, EPCCI, and II.

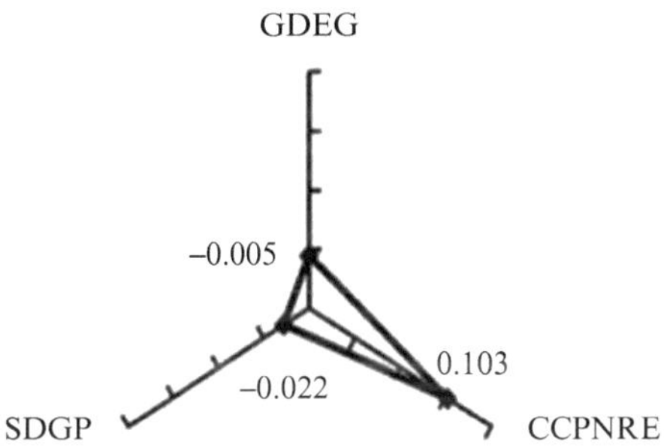

Fig. 5.9 Scores of Inner Mongolia by First-Class Indicators

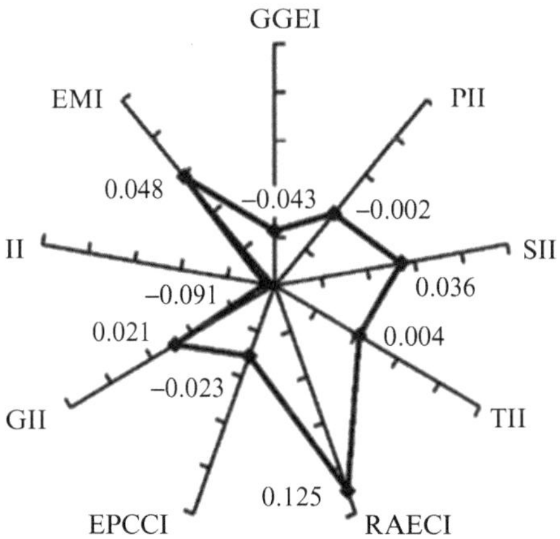

Fig. 5.10 Scores of Inner Mongolia by Second-Class Indicators

Table 5.9 Changes in Inner Mongolia's rankings by First-Class and Second-Class Indicators, 2009–2010

Indicator	2010	2009	Difference	Indicator	2010	2009	Difference
GDI	11	11	0				
GDEG	11	11	0	RAECI	2	2	0
GGEI	24	17	−7	EPCCI	15	10	−5
PII	13	13	0	SDGP	18	19	1
SII	4	11	7	GII	8	12	4
TII	9	7	−2	II	28	27	−1
CCPNRE	5	6	1	EMI	2	2	0

Note: A positive value in "Difference" means a rise in ranking

5.5.2 Changes in Inner Mongolia's Rankings by GDI 2009–2010

According to Table 5.9, in First-Class Indicators, Inner Mongolia rose by 1 place in the rankings by CCPNRE and SDGP. It remained the same in GDEG. In Second-Class Indicators ranking, Inner Mongolia dropped by 7 places by GGEI, 2 in TII, 5 in EPCCI, and 1 in II. It rose by 7 places in SII and 4 in GII. It remained the same in the rankings by other indicators as in 2009.

To further explain the causes of the changes in the rankings by First- and Second-Class Indicators, we put the Third-Class Indicators where a change of more than 3 places occurred from 2009 to 2010 in Table 5.10. Compared with those in 2009, Inner Mongolia dropped by 9 places by Ammonia/nitrogen emissions per unit of GDP, 12 in Electricity consumption per capita in urban areas, 4 in Nitrogen oxide emissions per capita from road transport and Treatment rate of urban wastewater, 6 in Industrial SO_2 removal rate. It rose by 11 places by Recycling rate of industrial water, 6 in Investment in converting cultivated land into forests and grassland per unit of cultivated land area, 4 in Ratio of the spending on science, education, culture, and public health to government expenditure, 3 in Area of green land per capita in urban areas, 12 in Length of public transport routes per capita in urban areas, 6 in Industrial wastewater COD removal rate and 3 in Industrial nitrogen oxide removal rate.

Table 5.10 Third-Class Indicators where changes over 3 places occurred by Inner Mongolia, 2009–2010

	Original data for 2010 and 2009			Change in ranking		
Third-Class Indicator	Unit	2010	2009	2010	2009	Difference
Ammonia/nitrogen emissions per unit of GDP	Ton per 10,000 yuan	0.0005	0.0004	21	12	−9
Electricity consumption per capita in urban areas	kWh per capita	187.84	244.68	17	5	−12
Recycling rate of industrial water	%	84.70	57.52	13	24	11
Nitrogen oxide emissions per capita from road transport	Ton per 10,000 persons	36.80	25.66	24	20	−4
Investment in converting cultivated land into forests and grassland per unit of cultivated land area	10,000 yuan per 1,000 hectares	29.97	14.89	12	18	6
Ratio of the spending on science, education, culture, and public health to government expenditure	%	22.75	21.37	25	29	4
Area of green land per capita in urban areas	Hectare per capita	0.00	0.00	11	14	3
Treatment rate of urban wastewater	%	80.60	75.20	19	15	−4
Length of public transport routes per capita in urban areas	km per capita	0.0004	0.0002	13	25	12
Industrial SO_2 removal rate	%	57.33	57.76	22	16	−6
Industrial wastewater COD removal rate	%	80.22	75.07	8	14	6
Industrial nitrogen oxide removal rate	%	0.98	0.28	21	24	3

Note: A positive value in "Difference" means a rise in ranking

Green development checkup-Liaoning

No.	Indicator	Unit	Attribute	2010 average of 30 provinces	2010 figure	2009 figure	2010 ranking	2009 ranking	Change in ranking	Source of 2010 data	Chernoff face
1	GDP per capita	Yuan per capita	Positive	33,964.12	42,355	35,239	8	9	1	China Statistics	
2	Energy consumption per unit of GDP	Ton coal equivalent per 10,000 yuan	Negative	1.29	1.38	1.44	22	21	−1	China Statistics	
3	Ratio of non-fossil energy consumption to total energy consumption		Positive	NA	NA	NA	NA	NA			
4	CO_2 emissions per unit of GDP		Negative	NA	NA	NA	NA	NA			
5	SO_2 emissions per unit of GDP	Ton per 10,000 yuan	Negative	0.0088	0.0066	0.0078	15	15	0	China Statistics	
6	COD emissions per unit of GDP	Ton per 10,000 yuan	Negative	0.0045	0.0035	0.0042	13	13	0	China Statistics	
7	Nitrogen oxide emissions per unit of GDP	Ton per 10,000 yuan	Negative	0.0068	0.0052	0.0060	17	17	0	Environmental Annual Report; China Statistics	
8	Ammonia/nitrogen emissions per unit of GDP	Ton per 10,000 yuan	Negative	0.0004	0.0004	0.0005	12	15	3	Environmental Annual Report; China Statistics	

9	Electricity consumption per capita in urban areas	kWh per capita	Negative	295.08	258.22	395.64	19	23	4	City	☺
10	Labor productivity of the primary sector	10,000 yuan per capita	Positive	1.61	2.34	2.03	5	4	−1	China Statistics	☹
11	Land productivity	100 million yuan per 1,000 hectares	Positive	0.26	0.28	0.23	12	10	−2	China Statistics	☹
12	Proportion of water-saving irrigated area in effectively irrigated area		Positive	0.49	0.33	0.31	22	22	0	Water Conservancy; China Statistics	
13	Proportion of water-saving irrigated area in effectively irrigated area	%	Positive	53.55	37.64	36.95	20	20	0	China Statistics	
14	Labor productivity of the secondary sector	10,000 yuan per capita	Positive	12.13	17.41	14.45	6	6	0	China Statistics	
15	Water consumption per unit of value added created by industrial enterprises	m^3/yuan	Negative	0.0100	0.0032	0.0035	5	7	2	China Statistics	☺
16	Energy consumption per unit of value added created by industrial enterprises above designated size (no data)		Negative	NA	NA	NA	NA	NA			
17	Utilization rate of industrial solid waste	%	Positive	69.80	46.90	47.20	27	26	−1	Environmental Yearbook	☹

(continued)

(continued)

No.	Indicator	Unit	Attribute	2010 average of 30 provinces	2010 figure	2009 figure	2010 ranking	2009 ranking	Change in ranking	Source of 2010 data	Chernoff face
18	Recycling rate of industrial water	%	Positive	72.90	92.37	91.80	5	6	1	Environmental Yearbook	☺
19	Ratio of the output of six energy-intensive industries to gross industrial output	%	Negative	39.65	38.52	38.90	18	18	0	Industrial Economy	
20	Labor productivity of the tertiary sector	10,000 yuan per capita	Positive	6.96	7.26	6.54	10	11	1	China Statistics	☺
21	Proportion of the value added of the tertiary sector in GDP	%	Positive	39.97	37.10	38.70	16	17	1	China Statistics	☺
22	Proportion of tertiary sector employees in the total employed population	%	Positive	36.67	42.52	42.74	4	4	0	China Statistics	
23	Water resources per capita	m^3 per capita	Positive	2,419.38	1,392.10	396.02	19	22	3	China Statistics	☺
24	Forest area per capita	Hectare per capita	Positive	0.19	0.12	0.12	16	16	0	China Statistics	
25	Forest coverage rate	%	Positive	30.63	35.13	35.13	12	12	0	China Statistics	
26	Proportion of the area of natural reserves in the total area of a region	%	Positive	8.60	12.46	12.46	6	6	0	China Statistics	
27	Proportion of the area of wetlands in the total area of a region	%	Positive	7.01	8.37	8.37	7	7	0	China Statistics	

28	Growing stock per capita	m^3 per capita	Positive	10.70	4.84	4.90	16	16	0	China Statistics	
29	CO_2 emissions per unit of land area		Negative	NA	NA	NA	NA	NA			
30	CO_2 emissions per capita		Negative	NA	NA	NA	NA	NA			
31	SO_2 emissions per unit of land area	Ton per km^2	Negative	6.3677	6.9840	7.1836	22	22	0	China Statistics; Deserts	
32	SO_2 emissions per capita	Ton per capita	Negative	0.0191	0.0235	0.0244	23	23	0	China Statistics	
33	COD emissions per unit of land area	Ton per km^2	Negative	3.7722	3.7004	3.8441	20	21	1	China Statistics; Deserts	☺
34	COD emissions per capita	Ton per capita	Negative	0.0101	0.0125	0.0130	25	24	−1	China Statistics	☹
35	Nitrogen oxide emissions per unit of land area	Ton per km^2	Negative	6.4473	5.5410	5.5956	19	21	2	China Statistics; Deserts; Environmental Annual Report	☺
36	Nitrogen oxide emissions per capita	Ton per capita	Negative	0.0165	0.0187	0.0190	22	25	3	Environmental Annual Report; China Statistics	☺
37	Ammonia/nitrogen emissions per unit of land area	Ton per km^2	Negative	0.4164	0.3826	0.4236	23	23	0	China Statistics; Deserts; Environmental Annual Report	
38	Ammonia/nitrogen emissions per capita	Ton per capita	Negative	0.0010	0.0013	0.0014	25	29	4	Environmental Annual Report; China Statistics	☺

(continued)

(continued)

No.	Indicator	Unit	Attribute	2010 average of 30 provinces	2010 figure	2009 figure	2010 ranking	2009 ranking	Change in ranking	Source of 2010 data	Chernoff face
39	Consumption of chemical fertilizers per unit of cultivated land area	10,000 ton per 1,000 hectares	Negative	0.05	0.03	0.03	10	10	0	China Statistics; China Statistics	
40	Consumption of pesticides per unit of cultivated land area	Ton per 1,000 hectares	Negative	17.68	16.98	13.24	18	15	−3	Environmental Yearbook; China Statistics	☹
41	Nitrogen oxide emissions per capita from road transport	Ton per 10,000 persons	Negative	24.07	12.30	13.42	8	8	0	Environmental Annual Report; China Statistics	
42	Ratio of environmental spending to government expenditure	%	Positive	3.35	2.42	2.08	26	28	2	China Statistics	☺
43	Ratio of the investment in pollution control to GDP	%	Positive	1.40	1.12	1.51	23	12	−11	Environmental Yearbook; China Statistics	☹
44	Government spending per capita on rural water supply system and toilet improvement	Yuan per capita	Positive	57.01	45.43	43.77	15	17	2	Environmental Yearbook	☺

45	Investment in converting cultivated land into forests and grassland per unit of cultivated land area	10,000 yuan per 1,000 hectares	Positive	29.81	17.42	18.86	19	16	−3	Environmental Yearbook; China Statistics	☹
46	Ratio of the spending on science, education, culture, and public health to government expenditure	%	Positive	26.10	21.35	24.00	28	25	−3	China Statistics	☹
47	Area of green land per capita in urban areas	Hectare per capita	Positive	0.00	0.00	0.00	8	10	2	City; China Statistics	☺
48	Coverage of water supply in urban areas	%	Positive	96.08	97.44	97.23	15	15	0	China Statistics	
49	Treatment rate of urban wastewater	%	Positive	79.18	74.90	60.20	22	24	2	Environmental Yearbook	☺
50	Harmless treatment rate of urban household waste	%	Positive	78.47	70.88	59.87	21	24	3	China Statistics	☺
51	Public buses per 10,000 urban residents		Positive	9.86	9.35	10.34	19	15	−4	China Statistics	☹
52	Length of public transport routes per capita in urban areas	km per capita	Positive	0.0006	0.0005	0.0003	12	14	2	China Statistics; City	☺
53	Ratio of the rural residents benefiting from water supply system improvement to the total rural population	%	Positive	94.44	96.68	96.56	17	18	1	Environmental Yearbook	☺
54	Green coverage of urban built-up areas	%	Positive	37.75	39.32	38.33	10	12	2	China Statistics	☺

(continued)

(continued)

No.	Indicator	Unit	Attribute	2010 average of 30 provinces	2010 figure	2009 figure	2010 ranking	2009 ranking	Change in ranking	Source of 2010 data	Chernoff face
55	Newly-added afforestation area of the year per capita	Hectare per 10,000 persons	Positive	59.50	43.86	30.11	14	16	2	China Statistics	☺
56	Industrial SO_2 removal rate	%	Positive	59.83	60.11	52.67	20	21	1	China Statistics	☺
57	Industrial wastewater COD removal rate	%	Positive	70.84	63.82	55.27	22	24	2	Environmental Annual Report; China Statistics	☺
58	Industrial nitrogen oxide removal rate	%	Positive	4.07	4.81	2.29	10	20	10	Environmental Annual Report	☺
59	Industrial wastewater ammonia/nitrogen removal rate	%	Positive	62.87	77.84	76.47	11	10	−1	Environmental Annual Report; China Statistics	☹
60	Number of environmental emergencies		Negative	14.00	10	6	22	14	−8	China Statistics	☹

Note:
China Statistics: *China Statistical Yearbook 2011*
Environmental Yearbook: *China Environmental Statistical Yearbook 2011*
Environmental Annual Report: *China Environment Annual Report 2010*
City: *China City Statistical Yearbook 2011*
Water Conservancy: *China Water Conservancy Statistical Yearbook 2011*
Industrial Economy: *China Industrial Economic Statistical Yearbook 2011*
Deserts: *Deserts in China and Desertification Control*

5.6 Brief Analysis of Green Development in Liaoning

Liaoning ranked 23rd among the 30 participating provinces by GDI according to 2010 data, two provinces higher over 2009 (Liaoning ranked 25th in 2009). Following is a brief analysis of its score by each indicator and their changes from 2009 to 2010.

5.6.1 2010 Scores of Liaoning's 2010 Scores by GDI

Liaoning scored −0.126 in 2010. From the three First-Class Indicators including GDEG, CCPNRE, and SDGP as shown in Fig. 5.11, Liaoning was slightly higher than the national average in GDEG, yet scored lower than the national average in CCPNRE and SDGP (Note: the national average value of each indicator is 0).

According to Fig. 5.12, Liaoning surpassed the national average in four of Second-Class Indicators in 2010, which are PII, SII, TII, and EMI, yet scored lower than the national average in GGEI, RAECI, II, EPCCI and GII.

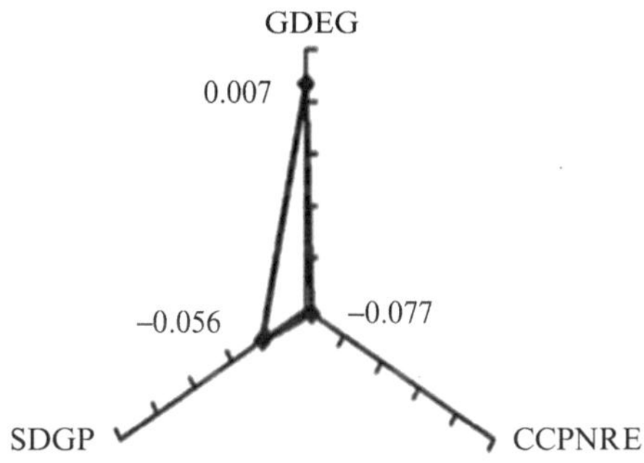

Fig. 5.11 Scores of Liaoning by First-Class Indicators

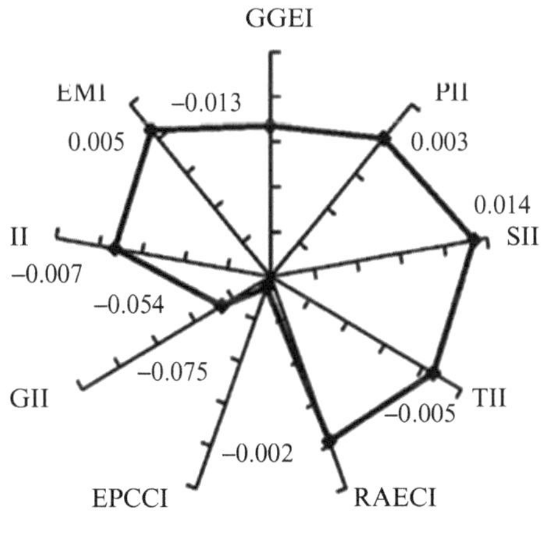

Fig. 5.12 Scores of Liaoning by Second-Class Indicators

Table 5.11 Changes in Liaoning's rankings by First-Class and Second-Class Indicators, 2009–2010

Indicator	2010	2009	Difference	Indicator	2010	2009	Difference
GDI	23	25	2				
GDEG	10	10	0	RAECI	13	16	3
GGEI	14	18	4	EPCCI	26	28	2
PII	12	12	0	SDGP	23	21	−2
SII	10	12	2	GII	29	30	1
TII	8	6	−2	II	17	17	0
CCPNRE	20	27	7	EMI	16	20	4

Note: A positive value in "Difference" means a rise in ranking

5.6.2 Changes in Liaoning's Rankings by GDI 2009–2010

According to Table 5.11, in First-Class Indicators, Liaoning dropped by 2 places by SDGP, and rose by 7 in CCPNRE, and remained the same in GDEG. In Second-Class Indicators ranking, Liaoning rose by 4 places in GGEI, 2 in SII, 3 in RAECI, 2 in EPCCI, 1 in GII, and 4 in EMI. It dropped by 2 places in TII. It remained the same in the rankings by other indicators as in 2009.

To further explain the causes of the changes in the rankings by First- and Second-Class Indicators, we put the Third-Class Indicators where a change of more than 3 places occurred from 2009 to 2010 in Table 5.12. Compared with those in 2009, Liaoning dropped by 11 places in Ratio of the investment in pollution control to GDP, 8 in Number of environmental emergencies, 4 in Public buses per 10,000 urban residents, 3 in Consumption of pesticides per unit of cultivated land area, Investment in converting cultivated land into forests and grassland per unit of area of cultivated and Ratio of the spending on science, education, culture, and public health to government expenditure. It rose by 3 places in Ammonia/nitrogen emissions per unit of GDP, Water resources per capita, Nitrogen oxide emissions per capita and Harmless treatment rate of urban household waste, 4 in Electricity consumption per capita in urban areas and Ammonia/nitrogen emissions per capita, and 10 in Industrial nitrogen oxide removal rate.

Table 5.12 Third-Class Indicators where changes over 3 places occurred by Liaoning, 2009–2010

	Original data for 2010 and 2009			Change in ranking		
Third-Class Indicator	Unit	2010	2009	2010	2009	Difference
Ammonia/nitrogen emissions per unit of GDP	Ton per 10,000 yuan	0.0004	0.0005	12	15	3
Electricity consumption per capita in urban areas	kWh per capita	258.22	395.64	19	23	4
Water resources per capita	m^3 per capita	1,392.10	396.02	19	22	3
Nitrogen oxide emissions per capita	Ton per capita	0.0187	0.0190	22	25	3
Ammonia/nitrogen emissions per capita	Ton per capita	0.0013	0.0014	25	29	4
Consumption of pesticides per unit of cultivated land area	Ton per 1,000 hectares	16.98	13.24	18	15	−3
Ratio of the investment in pollution control to GDP	%	1.12	1.51	23	12	−11
Investment in converting cultivated land into forests and grassland per unit of cultivated land area	10,000 yuan per 1,000 hectares	17.42	18.86	19	16	−3
Ratio of the spending on science, education, culture, and public health to government expenditure	%	21.35	24.00	28	25	−3
Harmless treatment rate of urban household waste	%	70.88	59.87	21	24	3
Public buses per 10,000 urban residents		9.35	10.34	19	15	−4
Industrial nitrogen oxide removal rate	%	4.81	2.29	10	20	10
Number of environmental emergencies		10	6	22	14	−8

Note: A positive value in "Difference" means a rise in ranking

Green development checkup-Jilin

No.	Indicator	Unit	Attribute	2010 average of 30 provinces	2010 figure	2009 figure	2010 ranking	2009 ranking	Change in ranking	Source of 2010 data	Chernoff face
1	GDP per capita	Yuan per capita	Positive	33,964.12	31,599	26,595	11	11	0	China Statistics	
2	Energy consumption per unit of GDP	Ton coal equivalent per 10,000 yuan	Negative	1.29	1.15	1.21	16	17	1	China Statistics	
3	Ratio of non-fossil energy consumption to total energy consumption		Positive	NA	NA	NA	NA	NA			
4	CO_2 emissions per unit of GDP		Negative	NA	NA	NA	NA	NA			
5	SO_2 emissions per unit of GDP	Ton per 10,000 yuan	Negative	0.0088	0.0049	0.0057	10	11	1	China Statistics	
6	COD emissions per unit of GDP	Ton per 10,000 yuan	Negative	0.0045	0.0049	0.0057	20	20	0	China Statistics	
7	Nitrogen oxide emissions per unit of GDP	Ton per 10,000 yuan	Negative	0.0068	0.0078	0.0072	24	22	−2	Environmental Annual Report; China Statistics	
8	Ammonia/nitrogen emissions per unit of GDP	Ton per 10,000 yuan	Negative	0.0004	0.0004	0.0005	15	14	−1	Environmental Annual Report; China Statistics	
9	Electricity consumption per capita in urban areas	kWh per capita	Negative	295.08	179.12	278.77	15	11	−4	City	

10	Labor productivity of the primary sector	10,000 yuan per capita	Positive	1.61	2.02	1.91	9	5	−4	China Statistics	☹
11	Land productivity	100 million yuan per 1,000 hectares	Positive	0.26	0.17	0.15	24	20	−4	China Statistics	☹
12	Proportion of water-saving irrigated area in effectively irrigated area		Positive	0.49	0.15	0.15	28	27	−1	Water Conservancy; China Statistics	☹
13	Proportion of water-saving irrigated area in effectively irrigated area	%	Positive	53.55	31.20	30.44	26	25	−1	China Statistics	☹
14	Labor productivity of the secondary sector	10,000 yuan per capita	Positive	12.13	17.81	15.15	5	5	0	China Statistics	
15	Water consumption per unit of value added created by industrial enterprises	m^3/yuan	Negative	0.0100	0.0080	0.0077	14	15	1	China Statistics	☺
16	Energy consumption per unit of value added created by industrial enterprises above designated size (no data)		Negative	NA	NA	NA	NA	NA			
17	Utilization rate of industrial solid waste	%	Positive	69.80	67.10	64.30	16	19	3	Environmental Yearbook	☺
18	Recycling rate of industrial water	%	Positive	72.90	74.51	72.66	20	19	−1	Environmental Yearbook	☹
19	Ratio of the output of six energy-intensive industries to gross industrial output	%	Negative	39.65	24.13	25.15	2	4	2	Industrial Economy	☺

(continued)

(continued)

No.	Indicator	Unit	Attribute	2010 average of 30 provinces	2010 figure	2009 figure	2010 ranking	2009 ranking	Change in ranking	Source of 2010 data	Chernoff face
20	Labor productivity of the tertiary sector	10,000 yuan per capita	Positive	6.96	7.02	6.62	11	10	−1	China Statistics	
21	Proportion of the value added of the tertiary sector in GDP	%	Positive	39.97	35.90	37.90	22	20	−2	China Statistics	
22	Proportion of tertiary sector employees in the total employed population	%	Positive	36.67	36.64	36.16	10	10	0	China Statistics	
23	Water resources per capita	m^3 per capita	Positive	2,419.38	2,503.32	1,088.93	12	19	7	China Statistics	
24	Forest area per capita	Hectare per capita	Positive	0.19	0.27	0.27	7	6	−1	China Statistics	
25	Forest coverage rate	%	Positive	30.63	38.93	38.93	10	10	0	China Statistics	
26	Proportion of the area of natural reserves in the total area of a region	%	Positive	8.60	12.29	6.75	7	15	8	China Statistics	
27	Proportion of the area of wetlands in the total area of a region	%	Positive	7.01	6.37	6.37	10	10	0	China Statistics	
28	Growing stock per capita	m^3 per capita	Positive	10.70	32.13	32.21	4	4	0	China Statistics	
29	CO_2 emissions per unit of land area		Negative	NA	NA	NA	NA	NA			
30	CO_2 emissions per capita		Negative	NA	NA	NA	NA	NA			

31	SO_2 emissions per unit of land area	Ton per km^2	Negative	6.3677	1.9001	1.9358	8	8	0	China Statistics; Deserts	
32	SO_2 emissions per capita	Ton per capita	Negative	0.0191	0.0130	0.0133	12	11	−1	China Statistics	☹
33	COD emissions per unit of land area	Ton per km^2	Negative	3.7722	1.8780	1.9240	10	10	0	China Statistics; Deserts	
34	COD emissions per capita	Ton per capita	Negative	0.0101	0.0128	0.0132	26	25	−1	China Statistics	☹
35	Nitrogen oxide emissions per unit of land area	Ton per km^2	Negative	6.4473	3.0076	2.4317	15	13	−2	China Statistics; Deserts; Environmental Annual Report	☹
36	Nitrogen oxide emissions per capita	Ton per capita	Negative	0.0165	0.0206	0.0167	25	22	−3	Environmental Annual Report; China Statistics	☹
37	Ammonia/nitrogen emissions per unit of land area	Ton per km^2	Negative	0.4164	0.1600	0.1546	9	9	0	China Statistics; Deserts; Environmental Annual Report	
38	Ammonia/nitrogen emissions per capita	Ton per capita	Negative	0.0010	0.0011	0.0011	20	19	−1	Environmental Annual Report; China Statistics	☹
39	Consumption of chemical fertilizers per unit of cultivated land area	10,000 ton per 1,000 hectares	Negative	0.05	0.03	0.03	8	8	0	China Statistics; China Statistics	
40	Consumption of pesticides per unit of cultivated land area	Ton per 1,000 hectares	Negative	17.68	7.73	7.66	10	10	0	Environmental Yearbook; China Statistics	

(continued)

(continued)

No.	Indicator	Unit	Attribute	2010 average of 30 provinces	2010 figure	2009 figure	2010 ranking	2009 ranking	Change in ranking	Source of 2010 data	Chernoff face
41	Nitrogen oxide emissions per capita from road transport	Ton per 10,000 persons	Negative	24.07	11.02	10.83	7	6	−1	Environmental Annual Report; China Statistics	
42	Ratio of environmental spending to government expenditure	%	Positive	3.35	4.00	3.35	9	14	5	China Statistics	
43	Ratio of the investment in pollution control to GDP	%	Positive	1.40	1.43	1.04	15	24	9	Environmental Yearbook; China Statistics	
44	Government spending per capita on rural water supply system and toilet improvement	Yuan per capita	Positive	57.01	107.78	72.99	4	8	4	Environmental Yearbook	
45	Investment in converting cultivated land into forests and grassland per unit of cultivated land area	10,000 yuan per 1,000 hectares	Positive	29.81	10.69	11.89	20	21	1	Environmental Yearbook; China Statistics	
46	Ratio of the spending on science, education, culture, and public health to government expenditure	%	Positive	26.10	23.12	25.19	24	19	−5	China Statistics	
47	Area of green land per capita in urban areas	Hectare per capita	Positive	0.00	0.00	0.00	16	19	3	City; China Statistics	

48	Coverage of water supply in urban areas	%	Positive	96.08	89.60	88.75	27	27	0	China Statistics	
49	Treatment rate of urban wastewater	%	Positive	79.18	73.90	64.60	25	22	−3	Environmental Yearbook	☹
50	Harmless treatment rate of urban household waste	%	Positive	78.47	44.51	38.39	28	28	0	China Statistics	
51	Public buses per 10,000 urban residents		Positive	9.86	9.75	9.56	13	20	7	China Statistics	☺
52	Length of public transport routes per capita in urban areas	km per capita	Positive	0.0006	0.0004	0.0003	15	15	0	China Statistics; City	
53	Ratio of the rural residents benefiting from water supply system improvement to the total rural population	%	Positive	94.44	99.10	98.13	8	10	2	Environmental Yearbook	☺
54	Green coverage of urban built-up areas	%	Positive	37.75	34.12	32.78	25	25	0	China Statistics	
55	Newly-added afforestation area of the year per capita	Hectare per 10,000 persons	Positive	59.50	30.11	11.05	19	24	5	China Statistics	☺
56	Industrial SO_2 removal rate	%	Positive	59.83	40.32	29.86	27	27	0	China Statistics	
57	Industrial wastewater COD removal rate	%	Positive	70.84	63.74	56.34	23	23	0	Environmental Annual Report; China Statistics	
58	Industrial nitrogen oxide removal rate	%	Positive	4.07	0.00	0.00	29	28	−1	Environmental Annual Report	☹

(continued)

(continued)

No.	Indicator	Unit	Attribute	2010 average of 30 provinces	2010 figure	2009 figure	2010 ranking	2009 ranking	Change in ranking	Source of 2010 data	Chernoff face
59	Industrial wastewater ammonia/nitrogen removal rate	%	Positive	62.87	55.00	62.74	21	12	−9	Environmental Annual Report; China Statistics	☹
60	Number of environmental emergencies		Negative	14.00	3	0	10	1	−9	China Statistics	☹

Note:
China Statistics: *China Statistical Yearbook 2011*
Environmental Yearbook: *China Environmental Statistical Yearbook 2011*
Environmental Annual Report: *China Environment Annual Report 2010*
City: *China City Statistical Yearbook 2011*
Water Conservancy: *China Water Conservancy Statistical Yearbook 2011*
Industrial Economy: *China Industrial Economic Statistical Yearbook 2011*
Deserts: *Deserts in China and Desertification Control*

5.7 Brief Analysis of Green Development in Jilin

Jilin ranked 20th among the 30 participating provinces by GDI according to 2010 data, three places higher over 2009 (Jilin ranked 23rd in 2009). Following is a brief analysis of its score by each indicator and their changes from 2009 to 2010.

5.7.1 Jilin's 2010 Scores by GDI

Jilin scored −0.106 in 2010. From the three First-Class Indicators including GDEG, CCPNRE, and SDGP as shown in Fig. 5.13, Jilin scored slightly higher than the national average in terms of CCPNRE, and lower than the national average in GDEG and SDGP (Note: the national average value of each indicator is 0).

According to Fig. 5.14, Jilin surpassed the national average in 3 of Second-Class Indicators in 2010, which are SII, RAECI and GII. It scored lower than the national average in GGEI, PII, TII, II, EPCCI and EMI.

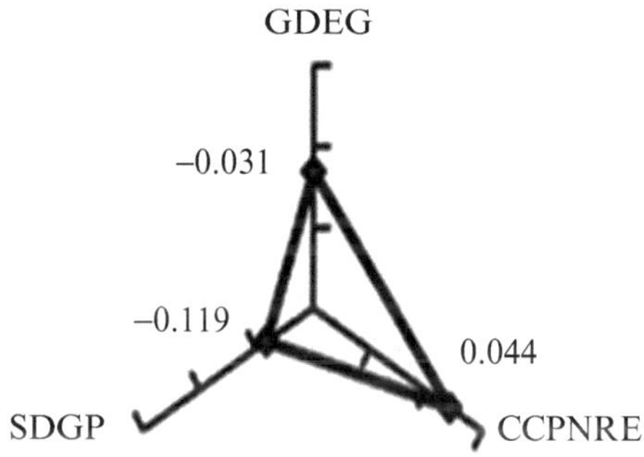

Fig. 5.13 Scores of Jilin by First-Class Indicators

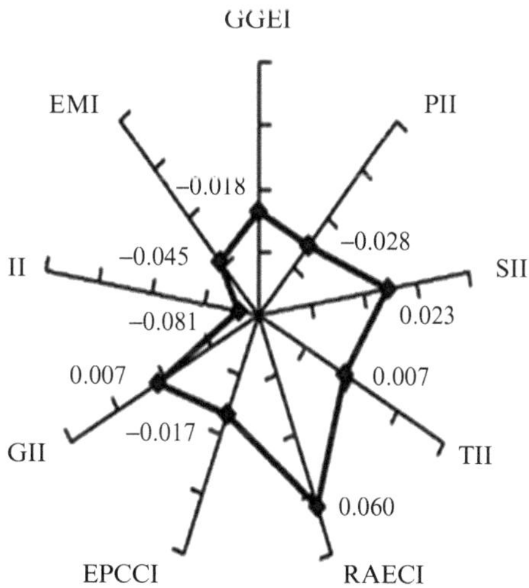

Fig. 5.14 Scores of Jilin by Second-Class Indicators

Table 5.13 Changes in Jilin's rankings by First-Class and Second-Class Indicators, 2009–2010

Indicator	2010	2009	Difference	Indicator	2010	2009	Difference
GDI	20	23	3				
GDEG	14	13	−1	RAECI	5	7	2
GGEI	19	14	−5	EPCCI	12	15	3
PII	27	22	−5	SDGP	26	29	3
SII	7	9	2	GII	12	24	12
TII	14	12	−2	II	27	26	−1
CCPNRE	10	11	1	EMI	27	25	−2

Note: A positive value in "Difference" means a rise in ranking

5.7.2 Changes of Jilin's Rankings by GDI 2009–2010

According to Table 5.13, in First-Class Indicators, Jilin dropped by 1 place by GDEG and rose by 1 in CCPNRE and 3 in SDGP. In Second-Class Indicators ranking, Jilin dropped by 5 places in GGEI and PII, 2 in TII, 1 in II, 2 in EMI. It rose by 2 places in SII and RAECI, 3 in EPCCI, and 12 in Green Investment Indicator. It remained the same in the rankings by other indicators as in 2009.

To further explain the causes of the changes in the rankings by First- and Second-Class Indicators, we put the Third-Class Indicators where a change of more than 3 places occurred from 2009 to 2010 in Table 5.14. Compared with those in 2009, Jilin dropped by 5 places in Ratio of the spending on science, education, culture, and public health to government expenditure, 4 in Electricity consumption per capita in urban areas, Labor productivity of the primary sector and Land productivity, 3 in Nitrogen oxide emissions per capita and Treatment rate of urban wastewater, 9 in Industrial wastewater ammonia/nitrogen removal rate and Number of environmental emergencies. It rose by 3 places in Utilization rate of industrial solid waste, Area of green land per capita in urban areas, 4 in Government spending per capita on rural water supply system and toilet improvement, 5 in Ratio of environmental spending to government expenditure and Newly-added afforestation area of the year per capita, 7 in Public buses per 10,000 urban residents and Water resources per capita, 8 in Proportion of the area of natural reserves in the total area of a region and 9 in Ratio of the investment in pollution control to GDP.

Table 5.14 Third-Class Indicators where changes over 3 places occurred by Jilin, 2009–2010

	Original data for 2010 and 2009			Change in ranking		
Third-Class Indicator	Unit	2010	2009	2010	2009	Difference
Electricity consumption per capita in urban areas	kWh per capita	179.12	278.77	15	11	−4
Labor productivity of the primary sector	10,000 yuan per capita	2.02	1.91	9	5	−4
Land productivity	100 million yuan per 1,000 hectares	0.17	0.15	24	20	−4
Utilization rate of industrial solid waste	%	67.10	64.30	16	19	3
Water resources per capita	m^3 per capita	2,503.32	1,088.93	12	19	7
Proportion of the area of natural reserves in the total area of a region	%	12.29	6.75	7	15	8
Nitrogen oxide emissions per capita	Ton per capita	0.0206	0.0167	25	22	−3
Ratio of environmental spending to government expenditure	%	4.00	3.35	9	14	5
Ratio of the investment in pollution control to GDP	%	1.43	1.04	15	24	9
Government spending per capita on rural water supply system and toilet improvement	Yuan per capita	107.78	72.99	4	8	4
Ratio of the spending on science, education, culture, and public health to government expenditure	%	23.12	25.19	24	19	−5
Area of green land per capita in urban areas	Hectare per capita	0.00	0.00	16	19	3
Treatment rate of urban wastewater	%	73.90	64.60	25	22	−3
Public buses per 10,000 urban residents		9.75	9.56	13	20	7
Newly-added afforestation area of the year per capita	Hectare per 10,000 persons	30.11	11.05	19	24	5
Industrial wastewater ammonia/ nitrogen removal rate	%	55.00	62.74	21	12	−9
Number of environmental emergencies		3	0	10	1	−9

Note: A positive value in "Difference" means a rise in ranking

Green development checkup-Heilongjiang

No.	Indicator	Unit	Attribute	2010 average of 30 provinces	2010 figure	2009 figure	2010 ranking	2009 ranking	Change in ranking	Source of 2010 data	Chernoff face
1	GDP per capita	Yuan per capita	Positive	33,964.12	27,076	22,447	16	15	−1	China Statistics	☹
2	Energy consumption per unit of GDP	Ton coal Equivalent per 10,000 yuan	Negative	1.29	1.16	1.21	17	18	1	China Statistics	☺
3	Ratio of non-fossil energy consumption to total energy consumption		Positive	NA	NA	NA	NA	NA			
4	CO_2 emissions per unit of GDP		Negative	NA	NA	NA	NA	NA			
5	SO_2 emissions per unit of GDP	Ton per 10,000 yuan	Negative	0.0088	0.0050	0.0057	12	10	−2	China Statistics	☹
6	COD emissions per unit of GDP	Ton per 10,000 yuan	Negative	0.0045	0.0046	0.0054	18	18	0	China Statistics	
7	Nitrogen oxide emissions per unit of GDP	Ton per 10,000 yuan	Negative	0.0068	0.0052	0.0055	16	16	0	Environmental Annual Report; China Statistics	
8	Ammonia/nitrogen emissions per unit of GDP	Ton per 10,000 yuan	Negative	0.0004	0.0004	0.0006	19	22	3	Environmental Annual Report; China Statistics	☺
9	Electricity consumption per capita in urban areas	kWh per capita	Negative	295.08	167.65	267.32	13	10	−3	City	☹

10	Labor productivity of the primary sector	10,000 yuan per capita	Positive	1.61	1.67	1.48	15	15	0	China Statistics	
11	Land productivity	100 million yuan per 1,000 hectares	Positive	0.26	0.11	0.10	30	30	0	China Statistics	
12	Proportion of water-saving irrigated area in effectively irrigated area		Positive	0.49	0.69	0.66	7	7	0	Water Conservancy; China Statistics	
13	Proportion of water-saving irrigated area in effectively irrigated area	%	Positive	53.55	32.76	28.79	23	27	4	China Statistics	☺
14	Labor productivity of the secondary sector	10,000 yuan per capita	Positive	12.13	15.28	11.82	7	7	0	China Statistics	
15	Water consumption per unit of value added created by industrial enterprises	m^3/yuan	Negative	0.0100	0.0112	0.0157	20	23	3	China Statistics	☺
16	Energy consumption per unit of value added created by industrial enterprises above designated size (no data)		Negative	NA	NA	NA	NA	NA			
17	Utilization rate of industrial solid waste	%	Positive	69.80	76.50	71.70	14	14	0	Environmental Yearbook	
18	Recycling rate of industrial water	%	Positive	72.90	42.65	41.10	26	26	0	Environmental Yearbook	
19	Ratio of the output of six energy-intensive industries to gross industrial output	%	Negative	39.65	32.25	33.56	11	11	0	Industrial Economy	

(continued)

(continued)

No.	Indicator	Unit	Attribute	2010 average of 30 provinces	2010 figure	2009 figure	2010 ranking	2009 ranking	Change in ranking	Source of 2010 data	Chernoff face
20	Labor productivity of the tertiary sector	10,000 yuan per capita	Positive	6.96	6.47	6.05	12	12	0	China Statistics	
21	Proportion of the value added of the tertiary sector in GDP	%	Positive	39.97	37.20	39.30	15	15	0	China Statistics	
22	Proportion of tertiary sector employees in the total employed population	%	Positive	36.67	36.20	33.34	11	20	9	China Statistics	☺
23	Water resources per capita	m^3 per capita	Positive	2,419.38	2,228.59	2,586.87	13	8	−5	China Statistics	☹
24	Forest area per capita	Hectare per capita	Positive	0.19	0.50	0.50	3	3	0	China Statistics	
25	Forest coverage rate	%	Positive	30.63	42.39	42.39	9	9	0	China Statistics	
26	Proportion of the area of natural reserves in the total area of a region	%	Positive	8.60	14.09	13.60	4	4	0	China Statistics	
27	Proportion of the area of wetlands in the total area of a region	%	Positive	7.01	9.49	9.49	5	5	0	China Statistics	
28	Growing stock per capita	m^3 per capita	Positive	10.70	43.09	43.18	2	2	0	China Statistics	
29	CO_2 emissions per unit of land area		Negative	NA	NA	NA	NA	NA			
30	CO_2 emissions per capita		Negative	NA	NA	NA	NA	NA			
31	SO_2 emissions per unit of land area	Ton per km^2	Negative	6.3677	1.0891	1.0896	4	4	0	China Statistics; Deserts	

32	SO_2 emissions per capita	Ton per capita	Negative	0.0191	0.0128	0.0128	11	10	−1	China Statistics	☹
33	COD emissions per unit of land area	Ton per km^2	Negative	3.7722	0.9875	1.0265	6	6	0	China Statistics; Deserts	
34	COD emissions per capita	Ton per capita	Negative	0.0101	0.0116	0.0121	23	22	−1	China Statistics	☹
35	Nitrogen oxide emissions per unit of land area	Ton per km^2	Negative	6.4473	1.1132	1.0510	4	5	1	China Statistics; Deserts; Environmental Annual Report	☺
36	Nitrogen oxide emissions per capita	Ton per capita	Negative	0.0165	0.0131	0.0124	16	14	−2	Environmental Annual Report; Yearbook	☹
37	Ammonia/nitrogen emissions per unit of land area	Ton per km^2	Negative	0.4164	0.0955	0.1067	7	7	0	China Statistics; Deserts; Environmental Annual Report	
38	Ammonia/nitrogen emissions per capita	Ton per capita	Negative	0.0010	0.0011	0.0013	21	24	3	Environmental Annual Report; China Statistics	☺
39	Consumption of chemical fertilizers per unit of cultivated land area	10,000 ton per 1,000 hectares	Negative	0.05	0.02	0.02	2	2	0	China Statistics; China Statistics	
40	Consumption of pesticides per unit of cultivated land area	Ton per 1,000 hectares	Negative	17.68	6.23	5.65	7	7	0	Environmental Yearbook; China Statistics	
41	Nitrogen oxide emissions per capita from road transport	Ton per 10,000 persons	Negative	24.07	14.50	15.29	9	10	1	Environmental Annual Report; China Statistics	☺
42	Ratio of environmental spending to government expenditure	%	Positive	3.35	3.95	3.15	10	18	8	China Statistics	☺

(continued)

(continued)

No.	Indicator	Unit	Attribute	2010 average of 30 provinces	2010 figure	2009 figure	2010 ranking	2009 ranking	Change in ranking	Source of 2010 data	Chernoff face
43	Ratio of the investment in pollution control to GDP	%	Positive	1.40	1.27	1.25	16	20	4	Environmental Yearbook; China Statistics	
44	Government spending per capita on rural water supply system and toilet improvement	Yuan per capita	Positive	57.01	14.98	19.16	29	29	0	Environmental Yearbook	
45	Investment in converting cultivated land into forests and grassland per unit of cultivated land area	10,000 yuan per 1,000 hectares	Positive	29.81	7.94	16.62	23	17	−6	Environmental Yearbook; China Statistics	
46	Ratio of the spending on science, education, culture, and public health to government expenditure	%	Positive	26.10	22.26	24.26	26	24	−2	China Statistics	
47	Area of green land per capita in urban areas	Hectare per capita	Positive	0.00	0.00	0.00	10	7	−3	City; China Statistics	
48	Coverage of water supply in urban areas	%	Positive	96.08	88.43	86.56	29	30	1	China Statistics	
49	Treatment rate of urban wastewater	%	Positive	79.18	56.70	55.60	28	28	0	Environmental Yearbook	
50	Harmless treatment rate of urban household waste	%	Positive	78.47	40.36	29.86	29	30	1	China Statistics	
51	Public buses per 10,000 urban residents		Positive	9.86	10.00	10.14	12	16	4	China Statistics	
52	Length of public transport routes per capita in urban areas	km per capita	Positive	0.0006	0.0003	0.0003	19	20	1	China Statistics; City	

53	Ratio of the rural residents benefiting from water supply system improvement to the total rural population	%	Positive	94.44	98.57	98.40	12	6	−6	Environmental Yearbook	☹
54	Green coverage of urban built-up areas	%	Positive	37.75	34.89	33.62	24	24	0	China Statistics	
55	Newly-added afforestation area of the year per capita	Hectare per 10,000 persons	Positive	59.50	61.04	55.71	10	11	1	China Statistics	☺
56	Industrial SO_2 removal rate	%	Positive	59.83	20.88	14.99	29	28	−1	China Statistics	☹
57	Industrial wastewater COD removal rate	%	Positive	70.84	77.13	74.89	13	15	2	Environmental Annual Report; China Statistics	☺
58	Industrial nitrogen oxide removal rate	%	Positive	4.07	2.72	3.46	15	16	1	Environmental Annual Report	☺
59	Industrial wastewater ammonia/nitrogen removal rate	%	Positive	62.87	89.37	80.07	2	7	5	Environmental Annual Report; China Statistics	☺
60	Number of environmental emergencies		Negative	14.00	0	0	1	1	0	China Statistics	

Note:
China Statistics: *China Statistical Yearbook 2011*
Environmental Yearbook: *China Environmental Statistical Yearbook 2011*
Environmental Annual Report: *China Environment Annual Report 2010*
City: *China City Statistical Yearbook 2011*
Water Conservancy: *China Water Conservancy Statistical Yearbook 2011*
Industrial Economy: *China Industrial Economic Statistical Yearbook 2011*
Deserts: *Deserts in China and Desertification Control*

5.8 Brief Analysis of Green Development in Heilongjiang

Heilongjiang ranked 16th among the 30 participating provinces by GDI according to 2010 data, one place lower over 2009 (Heilongjiang ranked 15th in 2009). Following is a brief analysis of its score by each indicator and their changes from 2009 to 2010.

5.8.1 Heilongliang's 2010 Scores by GDI

Scored −0.024 in 2010. From the three First-Class Indicators including GDEG, CCPNRE, and SDGP as shown in Fig. 5.15, Heilongjiang had advantage in terms of CCPNRE, yet underperformed compared with the national average in GDEG and SDGP (Note: the national average value of each indicator is 0).

According to Fig. 5.16, Heilongjiang surpassed the national average in 2 of Second-Class Indicators in 2010, which are RAECI and EPCCI, yet ranked lower than the national average in GGEI, PII, SII, TII, II, GII, and EMI.

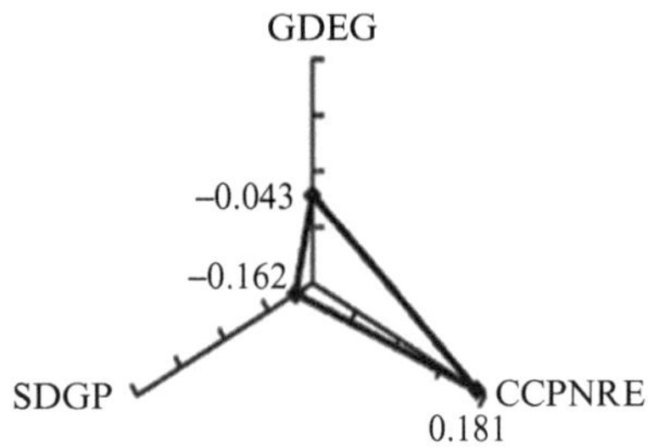

Fig. 5.15 Scores of Heilongjiang by First-Class Indicators

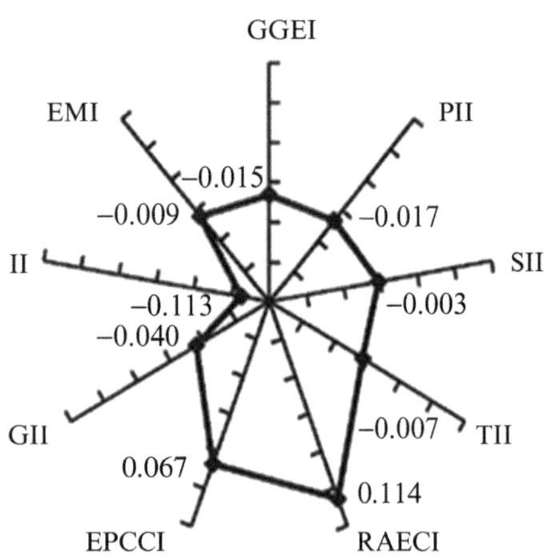

Fig. 5.16 Scores of Heilongjiang by Second-Class Indicators

Table 5.15 Changes in Heilongjiang's rankings by First-Class and Second-Class Indicators, 2009–2010

Indicator	2010	2009	Difference	Indicator	2010	2009	Difference
GDI	16	15	−1				
GDEG	16	16	0	RAECI	3	3	0
GGEI	15	13	−2	EPCCI	5	7	2
PII	18	18	0	SDGP	30	28	−2
SII	17	14	−3	GII	27	29	2
TII	15	15	0	II	29	28	−1
CCPNRE	4	5	1	EMI	19	18	−1

Note: A positive value in "Difference" means a rise in ranking

5.8.2 Changes in Heilongjiang's Rankings by GDI 2009–2010

According to Table 5.15, in First-Class Indicators ranking, Heilongjiang remained the same by GDEG, rose by 1 place in CCPNRE and dropped by 2 in SDGP. In Second-Class Indicators ranking, Heilongjiang dropped by 2 places in GGEI, 3 in SII, and 1 in II and EMI. It rose by 2 places in EPCCI and GII. It remained the same in the rankings by other indicators in 2009.

To further explain the causes of the changes in the rankings by First- and Second-Class Indicators, we put the Third-Class Indicators where a change of more than 3 places occurred from 2009 to 2010 in Table 5.16. Compared with those in 2009, Heilongjiang dropped by 6 places in Investment in converting cultivated land into forests and grassland per unit of cultivated land area and Ratio of the rural residents benefiting from water supply system improvement to the total rural population, 5 in Water resources per capita, 3 in Electricity consumption per capita in urban areas and Area of green land per capita in urban areas. It rose by 3 places in Ammonia/nitrogen emissions per unit of GDP, Water consumption per unit of value added created by industrial enterprises and Ammonia/nitrogen emissions per capita, 4 in Proportion of water-saving irrigated area in effectively irrigated area, Ratio of the investment in pollution control to GDP and Public buses per 10,000 urban residents, 5 in Industrial wastewater ammonia/nitrogen removal rate, 8 in Ratio of environmental spending to government expenditure and 9 in Proportion of tertiary sector employees in the total employed population.

Table 5.16 Third-Class Indicators where changes over 3 places occurred in Heilongjiang, 2009–2010

	Original data for 2010 and 2009			Change in ranking		
Third-Class Indicator	Unit	2010	2009	2010	2009	Difference
Ammonia/nitrogen emissions per unit of GDP	Ton per 10,000 yuan	0.0004	0.0006	19	22	3
Electricity consumption per capita in urban areas	kWh per capita	167.65	267.32	13	10	−3
Proportion of water-saving irrigated area in effectively irrigated area	%	32.76	28.79	23	27	4
Water consumption per unit of value added created by industrial enterprises	m^3/yuan	0.0112	0.0157	20	23	3
Proportion of tertiary sector employees in the total employed population	%	36.20	33.34	11	20	9
Water resources per capita	m^3 per capita	2,228.59	2,586.87	13	8	−5
Ammonia/nitrogen emissions per capita	Ton per capita	0.0011	0.0013	21	24	3
Ratio of environmental spending to government expenditure	%	3.95	3.15	10	18	8
Ratio of the investment in pollution control to GDP	%	1.27	1.25	16	20	4
Investment in converting cultivated land into forests and grassland per unit of cultivated land area	10,000 yuan per 1,000 hectares	7.94	16.62	23	17	−6
Area of green land per capita in urban areas	Hectare per capita	0.00	0.00	10	7	−3
Public buses per 10,000 urban residents		10.00	10.14	12	16	4
Ratio of the rural residents benefiting from water supply system improvement to the total rural population	%	98.57	98.40	12	6	−6
Industrial wastewater ammonia/nitrogen removal rate	%	89.37	80.07	2	7	5

Note: A positive value in "Difference" means a rise in ranking

Green development checkup-Shanghai

No.	Indicator	Unit	Attribute	2010 average of 30 provinces	2010 figure	2009 figure	2010 ranking	2009 ranking	Change in ranking	Source of 2010 data	Chernoff face
1	GDP per capita	Yuan per capita	Positive	33,964.12	76,074	78,989	1	1	0	China Statistics	
2	Energy consumption per unit of GDP	Ton coal equivalent per 10,000 yuan	Negative	1.29	0.71	0.73	3	3	0	China Statistics	
3	Ratio of non-fossil energy consumption to total energy consumption		Positive	NA	NA	NA	NA	NA			
4	CO_2 emissions per unit of GDP		Negative	NA	NA	NA	NA	NA			
5	SO_2 emissions per unit of GDP	Ton per 10,000 yuan	Negative	0.0088	0.0023	0.0027	3	3	0	China Statistics	
6	COD emissions per unit of GDP	Ton per 10,000 yuan	Negative	0.0045	0.0014	0.0017	2	2	0	China Statistics	
7	Nitrogen oxide emissions per unit of GDP	Ton per 10,000 yuan	Negative	0.0068	0.0028	0.0029	2	2	0	Environmental Annual Report; China Statistics	
8	Ammonia/nitrogen emissions per unit of GDP	ton per 10,000 yuan	Negative	0.0004	0.0002	0.0002	3	5	2	Environmental Annual Report; China Statistics	
9	Electricity consumption per capita in urban areas	kWh per capita	Negative	295.08	1,201.20	903.77	30	30	0	City	
10	Labor productivity of the primary sector	10,000 yuan per capita	Positive	1.61	2.72	2.35	2	2	0	China Statistics	

(continued)

(continued)

No.	Indicator	Unit	Attribute	2010 average of 30 provinces	2010 figure	2009 figure	2010 ranking	2009 ranking	Change in ranking	Source of 2010 data	Chernoff face
11	Land productivity	100 million yuan per 1,000 hectares	Positive	0.26	0.39	0.37	6	2	−4	China Statistics	☹
12	Proportion of water-saving irrigated area in effectively irrigated area		Positive	0.49	0.75	0.74	5	3	−2	Water Conservancy; China Statistics	☹
13	Proportion of water-saving irrigated area in effectively irrigated area	%	Positive	53.55	82.39	82.93	3	3	0	China Statistics	
14	Labor productivity of the secondary sector	10,000 yuan per capita	Positive	12.13	20.78	17.16	4	3	−1	China Statistics	☹
15	Water consumption per unit of value added created by industrial enterprises	m^3/yuan	Negative	0.0100	0.0123	0.0156	22	22	0	China Statistics	
16	Energy consumption per unit of value added created by industrial enterprises above designated size (no data)		Negative	NA	NA	NA	NA	NA			
17	Utilization rate of industrial solid waste	%	Positive	69.80	96.20	95.70	2	3	1	Environmental Yearbook	☺
18	Recycling rate of industrial water	%	Positive	72.90	82.40	82.10	16	13	−3	Environmental Yearbook	☹
19	Ratio of the output of six energy-intensive industries to gross industrial output	0/	Negative	39.65	25.84	25.05				Industrial Economy	☹

20	Labor productivity of the tertiary sector	10,000 yuan per capita	Positive	6.96	18.29	17.36	2	1	−1	China Statistics	☹
21	Proportion of the value added of the tertiary sector in GDP	%	Positive	39.97	57.30	59.40	2	2	0	China Statistics	
22	Proportion of tertiary sector employees in the total employed population	%	Positive	36.67	58.50	57.49	2	2	0	China Statistics	
23	Water resources per capita	m^3 per capita	Positive	2,419.38	163.13	218.28	27	26	−1	China Statistics	☹
24	Forest area per capita	Hectare per capita	Positive	0.19	0.00	0.00	30	30	0	China Statistics	
25	Forest coverage rate	%	Positive	30.63	9.41	9.41	27	27	0	China Statistics	
26	Proportion of the area of natural reserves in the total area of a region	%	Positive	8.60	5.22	5.22	22	22	0	China Statistics	
27	Proportion of the area of wetlands in the total area of a region	%	Positive	7.01	53.68	53.68	1	1	0	China Statistics	
28	Growing stock per capita	m^3 per capita	Positive	10.70	0.12	0.14	30	30	0	China Statistics	
29	CO_2 emissions per unit of land area		Negative	NA	NA	NA	NA	NA			
30	CO_2 emissions per capita		Negative	NA	NA	NA	NA	NA			
31	SO_2 emissions per unit of land area	Ton per km^2	Negative	6.3677	43.4639	45.9894	30	30	0	China Statistics; Deserts	
32	SO_2 emissions per capita	Ton per capita	Negative	0.0191	0.0170	0.0199	17	21	4	China Statistics	☺
33	COD emissions per unit of land area	Ton per km^2	Negative	3.7722	26.6779	29.5451	30	30	0	China Statistics; Deserts	
34	COD emissions per capita	Ton per capita	Negative	0.0101	0.0104	0.0128	19	23	4	China Statistics	☺

(continued)

(continued)

No.	Indicator	Unit	Attribute	2010 average of 30 provinces	2010 figure	2009 figure	2010 ranking	2009 ranking	Change in ranking	Source of 2010 data	Chernoff face
35	Nitrogen oxide emissions per unit of land area	Ton per km^2	Negative	6.4473	54.2541	50.8556	30	30	0	China Statistics; Deserts; Environmental Annual Report	
36	Nitrogen oxide emissions per capita	Ton per capita	Negative	0.0165	0.0212	0.0220	26	26	0	Environmental Annual Report; China Statistics	
37	Ammonia/nitrogen emissions per unit of land area	Ton per km^2	Negative	0.4164	3.3985	3.6412	30	30	0	China Statistics; Deserts; Environmental Annual Report	
38	Ammonia/nitrogen emissions per capita	Ton per capita	Negative	0.0010	0.0013	0.0016	26	30	4	Environmental Annual Report; China Statistics	
39	Consumption of chemical fertilizers per unit of cultivated land area	10,000 ton per 1,000 hectares	Negative	0.05	0.05	0.05	15	18	3	China Statistics; China Statistics	
40	Consumption of pesticides per unit of cultivated land area	Ton per 1,000 hectares	Negative	17.68	28.85	29.88	23	24	1	Environmental Yearbook; China Statistics	
41	Nitrogen oxide emissions per capita from road transport	Ton per 10,000 persons	Negative	24.07	52.02	81.63	29	29	0	Environmental Annual Report; China Statistics	
42	Ratio of environmental spending to government expenditure	%	Positive	3.35	1.43	1.14	30	30	0	China Statistics	

43	Ratio of the investment in pollution control to GDP	%	Positive	1.40	0.78	1.12	26	22	−4	Environmental Yearbook; China Statistics	☹
44	Government spending per capita on rural water supply system and toilet improvement	Yuan per capita	Positive	57.01	82.26	352.03	5	1	−4	Environmental Yearbook	☹
45	Investment in converting cultivated land into forests and grassland per unit of cultivated land area	10,000 yuan per 1,000 hectares	Positive	29.81	0.00	0.00	25	23	−2	Environmental Yearbook; China Statistics	☹
46	Ratio of the spending on science, education, culture, and public health to government expenditure	%	Positive	26.10	25.26	25.03	19	21	2	China Statistics	☺
47	Area of green land per capita in urban areas	Hectare per capita	Positive	0.00	0.01	0.01	3	2	−1	City; China Statistics	☹
48	Coverage of water supply in urban areas	%	Positive	96.08	100.00	100.00	1	1	0	China Statistics	
49	Treatment rate of urban wastewater	%	Positive	79.18	83.30	89.00	14	1	−13	Environmental Yearbook	☹
50	Harmless treatment rate of urban household waste	%	Positive	78.47	81.86	78.77	16	13	−3	China Statistics	☹
51	Public buses per 10,000 urban residents		Positive	9.86	8.82	12.76	20	7	−13	China Statistics	☹
52	Length of public transport routes per capita in urban areas	km per capita	Positive	0.0006	0.0017	0.0004	3	7	4	China Statistics; City	☺
53	Ratio of the rural residents benefiting from water supply system improvement to the total rural population	%	Positive	94.44	99.99	99.99	3	3	0	Environmental Yearbook	
54	Green coverage of urban built-up areas	%	Positive	37.75	38.15	38.10	14	14	0	China Statistics	

(continued)

(continued)

No.	Indicator	Unit	Attribute	2010 average of 30 provinces	2010 figure	2009 figure	2010 ranking	2009 ranking	Change in ranking	Source of 2010 data	Chernoff face
55	Newly-added afforestation area of the year per capita	Hectare per 10,000 persons	Positive	59.50	0.64	1.08	30	30	0	China Statistics	
56	Industrial SO_2 removal rate	%	Positive	59.83	61.23	61.64	18	13	−5	China Statistics	☹
57	Industrial wastewater COD removal rate	%	Positive	70.84	92.34	88.48	1	4	3	Environmental Annual Report; China Statistics	☺
58	Industrial nitrogen oxide removal rate	%	Positive	4.07	5.96	6.10	8	10	2	Environmental Annual Report	☺
59	Industrial wastewater ammonia/ nitrogen removal rate	%	Positive	62.87	69.63	77.26	14	9	−5	Environmental Annual Report; China Statistics	☹
60	Number of environmental emergencies		Negative	14.00	161	118	30	30	0	China Statistics	

Note:
China Statistics: *China Statistical Yearbook 2011*
Environmental Yearbook: *China Environmental Statistical Yearbook 2011*
Environmental Annual Report: *China Environment Annual Report 2010*
City: *China City Statistical Yearbook 2011*
Water Conservancy: *China Water Conservancy Statistical Yearbook 2011*
Industrial Economy: *China Industrial Economic Statistical Yearbook 2011*
Deserts: *Deserts in China and Desertification Control*

5.9 Brief Analysis of Green Development in Shanghai

Shanghai ranked 9th among the 30 participating provinces by GDI according to 2010 data, seven places lower over 2009 (Shanghai ranked 2nd in 2009). Following is a brief analysis of its score by each indicator and their changes from 2009 to 2010.

5.9.1 Shanghai's 2010 Scores by GDI

Shanghai scored 0.095 in 2010. From the three First-Class Indicators including GDEG, CCPNRE, and SDGP as shown in Fig. 5.17, Shanghai obviously outshined other provinces in terms of GDEG, yet underperformed compared with the national average in SDGP (Note: the national average value of each indicator is 0).

According to Fig. 5.18, Shanghai surpassed the national average in 6 of Second-Class Indicators in 2010, which are GGEI, PII, SII, TII, RAECI and II, yet ranked lower than the national average in EPCCI, GII and EMI.

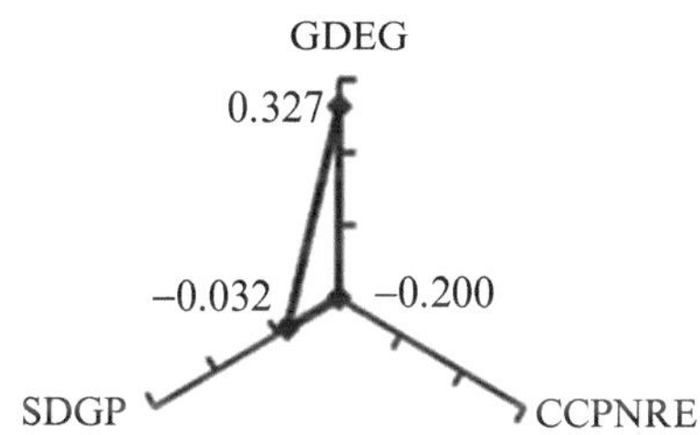

Fig. 5.17 Scores of Shanghai by First-Class Indicators

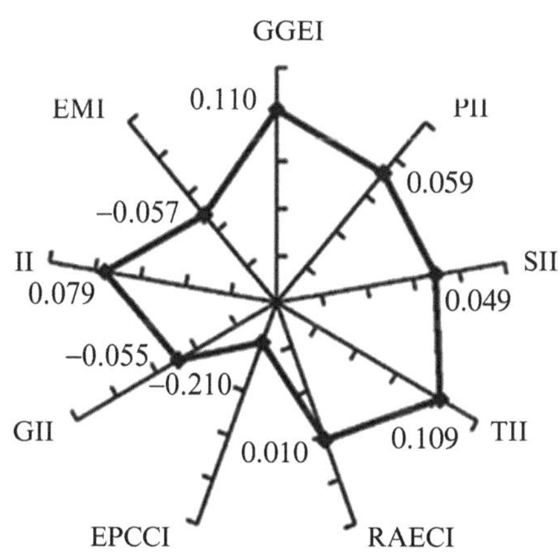

Fig. 5.18 Scores of Shanghai by Second-Class Indicators

Table 5.17 Changes in Shanghai's rankings by First-Class and Second-Class Indicators, 2009–2010

Indicator	2010	2009	Difference	Indicator	2010	2009	Difference
GDI	9	2	−7				
GDEG	2	2	0	RAECI	12	8	−4
GGEI	2	2	0	EPCCI	30	30	0
PII	2	2	0	SDGP	19	3	−16
SII	3	3	0	GII	30	15	−15
TII	2	2	0	II	2	1	−1
CCPNRE	30	24	−6	EMI	29	26	−3

Note: A positive value in "Difference" means a rise in ranking

5.9.2 Changes in Shanghai's GDI Rankings 2009–2010

According to Table 5.17, in First-Class Indicators ranking, the most obvious change occurred in SDGP, where Shanghai dropped as many as 16 places in ranking. Shanghai also dropped 6 places by CCPNRE. In Second-Class Indicators ranking, Shanghai dropped by 15 places in GII, which is very obvious change, 4 in RAECI, 3 in EMI, and 1 in II. It remained the same in the rankings by GGEI, SII, EPCCI in 2009.

To further explain the causes of the changes in the rankings by First- and Second-Class Indicators, we put the Third-Class Indicators where a change of more than 3 places occurred from 2009 to 2010 in Table 5.18. Compared with those in 2009, Shanghai dropped by 13 places in Treatment rate of urban wastewater, 5 in Industrial SO_2 removal rate and Industrial wastewater ammonia/nitrogen removal rate, 4 in Land productivity, Ratio of the investment in pollution control to GDP and Government spending per capita on rural water supply system and toilet improvement, 3 in Recycling rate of industrial water and Harmless treatment rate of urban household waste. It rose by 3 places in Consumption of chemical fertilizers per unit of cultivated land area and Industrial wastewater COD removal rate, 4 in SO_2 emissions per capita, COD emissions per capita, Ammonia/nitrogen emissions per capita and Length of public transport routes per capita in urban areas.

Table 5.18 Third-Class Indicators where changes over 3 places occurred in Shanghai, 2009–2010

	Original data for 2010 and 2009			Change in ranking		
Third-Class Indicator	Unit	2010	2009	2010	2009	Difference
Land productivity	100 million yuan per 1,000 hectares	0.39	0.37	6	2	−4
Recycling rate of industrial water	%	82.40	82.10	16	13	−3
SO_2 emissions per capita	Ton per capita	0.0170	0.0199	17	21	4
COD emissions per capita	Ton per capita	0.0104	0.0128	19	23	4
Ammonia/nitrogen emissions per capita	Ton per capita	0.0013	0.0016	26	30	4
Consumption of chemical fertilizers per unit of cultivated land area	10,000 ton per 1,000 hectares	0.05	0.05	15	18	3
Ratio of the investment in pollution control to GDP	%	0.78	1.12	26	22	−4
Government spending per capita on rural water supply system and toilet improvement	Yuan per capita	82.26	352.03	5	1	−4
Treatment rate of urban wastewater	%	83.30	89.00	14	1	−13
Harmless treatment rate of urban household waste	%	81.86	78.77	16	13	−3
Public buses per 10,000 urban residents		8.82	12.76	20	7	−13
Length of public transport routes per capita in urban areas	km per capita	0.0017	0.0004	3	7	4
Industrial SO_2 removal rate	%	61.23	61.64	18	13	−5
Industrial wastewater COD removal rate	%	92.34	88.48	1	4	3
Industrial wastewater ammonia/nitrogen removal rate	%	69.63	77.26	14	9	−5

Note: A positive value in "Difference" means a rise in ranking

Green development checkup-Jiangsu

No.	Indicator	Unit	Attribute	2010 average of 30 provinces	2010 figure	2009 figure	2010 ranking	2009 ranking	Change in ranking	Source of 2010 data	Chernoff face
1	GDP per capita	Yuan per capita	Positive	33,964.12	52,840	44,744	4	4	0	China Statistics	
2	Energy consumption per unit of GDP	Ton coal equivalent per 10,000 yuan	Negative	1.29	0.73	0.76	5	5	0	China Statistics	
3	Ratio of non-fossil energy consumption to total energy consumption		Positive	NA	NA	NA	NA	NA			
4	CO_2 emissions per unit of GDP		Negative	NA	NA	NA	NA	NA			
5	SO_2 emissions per unit of GDP	Ton per 10,000 yuan	Negative	0.0088	0.0030	0.0035	7	7	0	China Statistics	
6	COD emissions per unit of GDP	Ton per 10,000 yuan	Negative	0.0045	0.0022	0.0026	7	7	0	China Statistics	
7	Nitrogen oxide emissions per unit of GDP	Ton per 10,000 yuan	Negative	0.0068	0.0036	0.0038	8	8	0	Environmental Annual Report; China Statistics	
8	Ammonia/nitrogen emissions per unit of GDP	Ton per 10,000 yuan	Negative	0.0004	0.0002	0.0002	4	4	0	Environmental Annual Report; China Statistics	
9	Electricity consumption per capita in urban areas	kWh per capita	Negative	295.08	271.98	393.35	20	22	2	City	
10	Labor productivity of the primary sector	10,000 yuan per capita	Positive	1.61	2.85	2.49	1	1	0	China Statistics	

11	Land productivity	100 million yuan per 1,000 hectares	Positive	0.26	0.30	0.26	9	9	0	China Statistics	
12	Proportion of water-saving irrigated area in effectively irrigated area		Positive	0.49	0.43	0.42	18	18	0	Water Conservancy; China Statistics	
13	Proportion of water-saving irrigated area in effectively irrigated area	%	Positive	53.55	80.18	80.06	4	4	0	China Statistics	
14	Labor productivity of the secondary sector	10,000 yuan per capita	Positive	12.13	10.43	9.34	15	14	−1	China Statistics	☹
15	Water consumption per unit of value added created by industrial enterprises	m^3/yuan	Negative	0.0100	0.0105	0.0118	17	19	2	China Statistics	☺
16	Energy consumption per unit of value added created by industrial enterprises above designated size (no data)		Negative	NA	NA	NA	NA	NA			
17	Utilization rate of industrial solid waste	%	Positive	69.80	96.10	96.80	3	2	−1	Environmental Yearbook	☹
18	Recycling rate of industrial water	%	Positive	72.90	79.82	79.44	18	15	−3	Environmental Yearbook	☹
19	Ratio of the output of six energy-intensive industries to gross industrial output	%	Negative	39.65	28.76	29.27	7	7	0	Industrial Economy	
20	Labor productivity of the tertiary sector	10,000 yuan per capita	Positive	6.96	10.34	8.71	5	5	0	China Statistics	
21	Proportion of the value added of the tertiary sector in GDP	%	Positive	39.97	41.40	39.60	9	13	4	China Statistics	☺

(continued)

(continued)

No.	Indicator	Unit	Attribute	2010 average of 30 provinces	2010 figure	2009 figure	2010 ranking	2009 ranking	Change in ranking	Source of 2010 data	Chernoff face
22	Proportion of tertiary sector employees in the total employed population	%	Positive	36.67	36.07	35.46	13	12	−1	China Statistics	☹
23	Water resources per capita	m^3 per capita	Positive	2,419.38	489.21	519.82	23	21	−2	China Statistics	☹
24	Forest area per capita	Hectare per capita	Positive	0.19	0.01	0.01	28	28	0	China Statistics	
25	Forest coverage rate	%	Positive	30.63	10.48	10.48	24	24	0	China Statistics	
26	Proportion of the area of natural reserves in the total area of a region	%	Positive	8.60	4.08	4.08	26	26	0	China Statistics	
27	Proportion of the area of wetlands in the total area of a region	%	Positive	7.01	16.32	16.32	2	2	0	China Statistics	
28	Growing stock per capita	m^3 per capita	Positive	10.70	0.64	0.65	28	28	0	China Statistics	
29	CO_2 emissions per unit of land area		Negative	NA	NA	NA	NA	NA			
30	CO_2 emissions per capita		Negative	NA	NA	NA	NA	NA			
31	SO_2 emissions per unit of land area	Ton per km^2	Negative	6.3677	9.8414	10.0631	28	27	−1	China Statistics; Deserts	☹
32	SO_2 emissions per capita	Ton per capita	Negative	0.0191	0.0135	0.0139	13	14	1	China Statistics	☺
33	COD emissions per unit of land area	Ton per km^2	Negative	3.7722	7.3827	7.6979	28	28	0	China Statistics; Deserts	
34	COD emissions per capita	Ton per capita	Negative	0.0101	0.0101	0.0107	17	18	1	China Statistics	☺

35	Nitrogen oxide emissions per unit of land area	Ton per km^2	Negative	6.4473	11.7948	11.0454	27	28	1	China Statistics; Deserts; Environmental Annual Report	☺
36	Nitrogen oxide emissions per capita	Ton per capita	Negative	0.0165	0.0161	0.0153	20	20	0	Environmental Annual Report; China Statistics	
37	Ammonia/nitrogen emissions per unit of land area	Ton per km^2	Negative	0.4164	0.5902	0.6089	26	26	0	China Statistics; Deserts; Environmental Annual Report	
38	Ammonia/nitrogen emissions per capita	Ton per capita	Negative	0.0010	0.0008	0.0008	11	12	1	Environmental Annual Report; China Statistics	☺
39	Consumption of chemical fertilizers per unit of cultivated land area	10,000 ton per 1,000 hectares	Negative	0.05	0.07	0.07	26	26	0	China Statistics; China Statistics	
40	Consumption of pesticides per unit of cultivated land area	ton per 1,000 hectares	Negative	17.68	18.92	19.38	20	21	1	Environmental Yearbook; China Statistics	☺
41	Nitrogen oxide emissions per capita from road transport	Ton per 10,000 persons	Negative	24.07	34.75	33.10	23	22	–1	Environmental Annual Report; China Statistics	☹
42	Ratio of environmental spending to government expenditure	%	Positive	3.35	2.85	3.67	18	12	–6	China Statistics	☹
43	Ratio of the investment in pollution control to GDP	%	Positive	1.40	1.13	1.19	22	21	–1	Environmental Yearbook; China Statistics	☹
44	Government spending per capita on rural water supply system and toilet improvement	Yuan per capita	Positive	57.01	35.68	63.17	21	12	–9	Environmental Yearbook	☹

(continued)

(continued)

No.	Indicator	Unit	Attribute	2010 average of 30 provinces	2010 figure	2009 figure	2010 ranking	2009 ranking	Change in ranking	Source of 2010 data	Chernoff face
45	Investment in converting cultivated land into forests and grassland per unit of cultivated land area	10,000 yuan per 1,000 hectares	Positive	29.81	0.00	0.00	25	23	−2	Environmental Yearbook; China Statistics	☹
46	Ratio of the spending on science, education, culture, and public health to government expenditure	%	Positive	26.10	27.56	26.71	11	13	2	China Statistics	☺
47	Area of green land per capita in urban areas	Hectare per capita	Positive	0.00	0.00	0.01	6	4	−2	City; China Statistics	☹
48	Coverage of water supply in urban areas	%	Positive	96.08	99.56	99.65	8	6	−2	China Statistics	☹
49	Treatment rate of urban wastewater	%	Positive	79.18	87.60	85.40	6	4	−2	Environmental Yearbook	☹
50	Harmless treatment rate of urban household waste	%	Positive	78.47	93.58	90.98	5	6	1	China Statistics	☺
51	Public buses per 10,000 urban residents		Positive	9.86	10.91	13.24	7	6	−1	China Statistics	☹
52	Length of public transport routes per capita in urban areas	km per capita	Positive	0.0006	0.0006	0.0004	10	10	0	China Statistics; City	

53	Ratio of the rural residents benefiting from water supply system improvement to the total rural population	%	Positive	94.44	98.80	98.38	11	8	−3	Environmental Yearbook	☹
54	Green coverage of urban built-up areas	%	Positive	37.75	42.07	41.99	5	3	−2	China Statistics	☹
55	Newly-added afforestation area of the year per capita	hectare per 10,000 persons	Positive	59.50	11.06	10.87	23	25	2	China Statistics	☺
56	Industrial SO_2 removal rate	%	Positive	59.83	68.28	64.71	9	11	2	China Statistics	☺
57	Industrial wastewater COD removal rate	%	Positive	70.84	83.26	82.95	7	6	−1	Environmental Annual Report; China Statistics	☹
58	Industrial nitrogen oxide removal rate	%	Positive	4.07	4.00	6.94	11	9	−2	Environmental Annual Report	☹
59	Industrial wastewater ammonia/nitrogen removal rate	%	Positive	62.87	79.02	78.99	9	8	−1	Environmental Annual Report; China Statistics	☹
60	Number of environmental emergencies		Negative	14.00	7	10	17	18	1	China Statistics	☺

Note:
China Statistics: *China Statistical Yearbook 2011*
Environmental Yearbook: *China Environmental Statistical Yearbook 2011*
Environmental Annual Report: *China Environment Annual Report 2010*
City: *China City Statistical Yearbook 2011*
Water Conservancy: *China Water Conservancy Statistical Yearbook 2011*
Industrial Economy: *China Industrial Economic Statistical Yearbook 2011*
Deserts: *Deserts in China and Desertification Control*

5.10 Brief Analysis of Green Development in Jiangsu

Jiangsu ranked 12th among the 30 participating provinces by GDI according to 2010 data, three places lower over 2009 (Jiangsu ranked 3rd in 2009). Following is a brief analysis of its score by each indicator and their changes from 2009 to 2010.

5.10.1 Jiangsu's 2010 Scores by GDI

Jiangsu scored 0.062 in 2010. From the three First-Class Indicators including GDEG, CCPNRE, and SDGP as shown in Fig. 5.19, Jiangsu had advantage in terms of GDEG and SDGP, yet underperformed compared with the national average in CCPNRE (Note: the national average value of each indicator is 0).

According to Fig. 5.20, Jiangsu surpassed the national average in 6 of Second-Class Indicators in 2010, which are GGEI, PII, SII, TII, II and EMI, yet ranked lower than the national average in RAECI, EPCCI and GII.

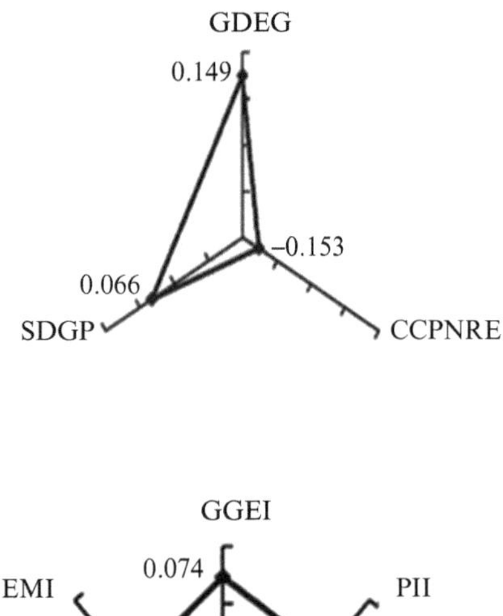

Fig. 5.19 Scores of Jiangsu by First-Class Indicators

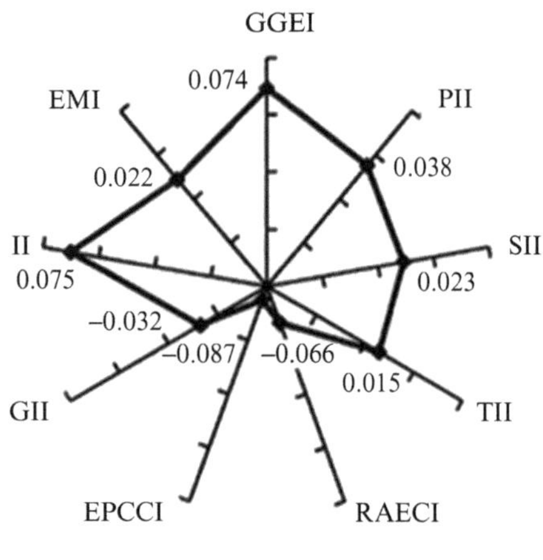

Fig. 5.20 Scores of Jiangsu by Second-Class Indicators

Table 5.19 Changes in Jiangsu's Rankings by First-Class and Second-Class Indicators, 2009–2010

Indicator	2010	2009	Difference	Indicator	2010	2009	Difference
GDI	12	9	−3				
GDEG	5	5	0	RAECI	26	25	−1
GGEI	5	5	0	EPCCI	28	27	−1
PII	7	6	−1	SDGP	5	2	−3
SII	6	6	0	GII	23	20	−3
TII	5	8	3	II	3	3	0
CCPNRE	28	30	2	EMI	10	6	−4

Note: A positive value in "Difference" means a rise in ranking

Table 5.20 Third-Class Indicators where changes over 3 places by Jiangsu, 2009–2010

	Original data for 2010 and 2009			Change in ranking		
Third-Class Indicator	Unit	2010	2009	2010	2009	Difference
Recycling rate of industrial water	%	79.82	79.44	18	15	−3
Proportion of the value added of the tertiary sector in GDP	%	41.40	39.60	9	13	4
Ratio of environmental spending to government expenditure	%	2.85	3.67	18	12	−6
Government spending per capita on rural water supply system and toilet improvement	Yuan per capita	35.68	63.17	21	12	−9
Ratio of the rural residents benefiting from water supply system improvement to the total rural population	%	98.80	98.38	11	8	−3

Note: A positive value in "Difference" means a rise in ranking

5.10.2 Changes in Jiangsu's GDI Rankings 2009–2010

According to Table 5.19, in First-Class Indicators, Jiangsu remained unchanged by GDEG and rose by 2 places in CCPNRE and fell by 3 places in SDGP. In Second-Class Indicators, it fell by 1 place in PII, RAECI and EPCCI, 3 in GII, 4 in EMI and rose by 3 places in TII. Other indicators remained the same as those in 2009.

To further explain the causes of the changes in the rankings by First- and Second-Class Indicators, we put the Third-Class Indicators where a change of more than 3 places occurred from 2009 to 2010 in Table 5.20. Compared with those in 2009, Tianjin dropped by 9 places in Government spending per capita on rural water supply system and toilet improvement, 6 in Ratio of environmental spending to government expenditure, 3 in Recycling rate of industrial water and Ratio of the rural residents benefiting from water supply system improvement to the total rural population. It rose by 4 places in Proportion of the value added of the tertiary sector in GDP.

Green development checkup-Zhejiang

No.	Indicator	Unit	Attribute	2010 average of 30 provinces	2010 figure	2009 figure	2010 ranking	2009 ranking	Change in ranking	Source of 2010 data	Chernoff face
1	GDP per capita	Yuan per capita	Positive	33,964.12	51,711	44,641	5	5	0	China Statistics	
2	Energy consumption per unit of GDP	Ton coal equivalent per 10,000 yuan	Negative	1.29	0.72	0.74	4	4	0	China Statistics	
3	Ratio of non-fossil energy consumption to total energy consumption		Positive	NA	NA	NA	NA	NA			
4	CO_2 emissions per unit of GDP		Negative	NA	NA	NA	NA	NA			
5	SO_2 emissions per unit of GDP	Ton per 10,000 yuan	Negative	0.0088	0.0029	0.0033	6	5	−1	China Statistics	☹
6	COD emissions per unit of GDP	Ton per 10,000 yuan	Negative	0.0045	0.0021	0.0024	5	5	0	China Statistics	
7	Nitrogen oxide emissions per unit of GDP	Ton per 10,000 yuan	Negative	0.0068	0.0040	0.0042	9	10	1	Environmental Annual Report; China Statistics	☺
8	Ammonia/nitrogen emissions per unit of GDP	Ton per 10,000 yuan	Negative	0.0004	0.0002	0.0002	2	3	1	Environmental Annual Report; China Statistics	☺
9	Electricity consumption per capita in urban areas	kWh per capita	Negative	295.08	300.54	423.36	23	24	1	City	☺
10	Labor productivity of the primary sector	10,000 yuan per capita	Positive	1.61	2.10	1.75	8	10	2	China Statistics	☺

11	Land productivity	100 million yuan per 1,000 hectares	Positive	0.26	0.42	0.35	3	5	2	China Statistics	☺
12	Proportion of water-saving irrigated area in effectively irrigated area		Positive	0.49	0.71	0.69	6	6	0	Water Conservancy; China Statistics	
13	Proportion of water-saving irrigated area in effectively irrigated area	%	Positive	53.55	75.54	75.30	6	6	0	China Statistics	
14	Labor productivity of the secondary sector	10,000 yuan per capita	Positive	12.13	7.71	6.78	26	25	−1	China Statistics	☹
15	Water consumption per unit of value added created by industrial enterprises	m^3/yuan	Negative	0.0100	0.0054	0.0053	9	9	0	China Statistics	
16	Energy consumption per unit of value added created by industrial enterprises above designated size (no data)		Negative	NA	NA	NA	NA	NA			
17	Utilization rate of industrial solid waste	%	Positive	69.80	94.30	91.60	5	5	0	Environmental Yearbook	
18	Recycling rate of industrial water	%	Positive	72.90	75.49	77.02	19	16	−3	Environmental Yearbook	☹
19	Ratio of the output of six energy-intensive industries to gross industrial output	%	Negative	39.65	26.03	25.40	6	5	−1	Industrial Economy	☹
20	Labor productivity of the tertiary sector	10,000 yuan per capita	Positive	6.96	8.58	7.42	7	7	0	China Statistics	

(continued)

(continued)

No.	Indicator	Unit	Attribute	2010 average of 30 provinces	2010 figure	2009 figure	2010 ranking	2009 ranking	Change in ranking	Source of 2010 data	Chernoff face
21	Proportion of the value added of the tertiary sector in GDP	%	Positive	39.97	43.50	43.10	7	7	0	China Statistics	
22	Proportion of tertiary sector employees in the total employed population	%	Positive	36.67	36.13	35.83	12	11	−1	China Statistics	☹
23	Water resources per capita	m^3 per capita	Positive	2,419.38	2,608.75	1,808.45	11	12	1	China Statistics	☺
24	Forest area per capita	Hectare per capita	Positive	0.19	0.11	0.11	17	17	0	China Statistics	
25	Forest coverage rate	%	Positive	30.63	57.41	57.41	3	3	0	China Statistics	
26	Proportion of the area of natural reserves in the total area of a region	%	Positive	8.60	1.50	1.47	30	30	0	China Statistics	
27	Proportion of the area of wetlands in the total area of a region	%	Positive	7.01	7.88	7.88	8	8	0	China Statistics	
28	Growing stock per capita	m^3 per capita	Positive	10.70	3.56	3.74	19	19	0	China Statistics	
29	CO_2 emissions per unit of land area		Negative	NA	NA	NA	NA	NA			
30	CO_2 emissions per capita		Negative	NA	NA	NA	NA	NA			
31	SO_2 emissions per unit of land area	Ton per km^2	Negative	6.3677	6.4360	6.6541	18	19	1	China Statistics; Deserts	☺
32	SO_2 emissions per capita	Ton per capita	Negative	0.0191	0.0128	0.0136	10	12	2	China Statistics	☺
33	COD emissions per unit of land area	Ton per km^2	Negative	3.7722	4.6185	4.8749	25	25	0	China Statistics; Deserts	

34	COD emissions per capita	Ton per capita	Negative	0.0101	0.0092	0.0100	13	14	1	China Statistics	☺
35	Nitrogen oxide emissions per unit of land area	Ton per km^2	Negative	6.4473	8.9756	8.3399	26	25	−1	China Statistics; Deserts; Environmental Annual Report	☹
36	Nitrogen oxide emissions per capita	Ton per capita	Negative	0.0165	0.0178	0.0171	21	23	2	Environmental Annual Report; China Statistics	☺
37	Ammonia/nitrogen emissions per unit of land area	Ton per km^2	Negative	0.4164	0.3795	0.3890	22	21	−1	China Statistics; Deserts; Environmental Annual Report	☹
38	Ammonia/nitrogen emissions per capita	Ton per capita	Negative	0.0010	0.0008	0.0008	7	10	3	Environmental Annual Report; China Statistics	☺
39	Consumption of chemical fertilizers per unit of cultivated land area	10,000 ton per 1,000 hectares	Negative	0.05	0.05	0.05	14	16	2	China Statistics; China Statistics	☺
40	Consumption of pesticides per unit of cultivated land area	Ton per 1,000 hectares	Negative	17.68	33.88	34.08	26	26	0	Environmental Yearbook; China Statistics	
41	Nitrogen oxide emissions per capita from road transport	Ton per 10,000 persons	Negative	24.07	43.19	43.48	26	25	−1	Environmental Annual Report; China Statistics	☹
42	Ratio of environmental spending to government expenditure	%	Positive	3.35	2.56	2.09	23	27	4	China Statistics	☺
43	Ratio of the investment in pollution control to GDP	%	Positive	1.40	1.20	0.94	19	25	6	Environmental Yearbook; China Statistics	☺

(continued)

(continued)

No.	Indicator	Unit	Attribute	2010 average of 30 provinces	2010 figure	2009 figure	2010 ranking	2009 ranking	Change in ranking	Source of 2010 data	Chernoff face
44	Government spending per capita on rural water supply system and toilet improvement	Yuan per capita	Positive	57.01	76.20	123.71	7	5	−2	Environmental Yearbook	
45	Investment in converting cultivated land into forests and grassland per unit of cultivated land area	10,000 yuan per 1,000 hectares	Positive	29.81	0.00	0.00	25	23	−2	Environmental Yearbook; China Statistics	
46	Ratio of the spending on science, education, culture, and public health to government expenditure	%	Positive	26.10	32.10	32.40	2	1	−1	China Statistics	
47	Area of green land per capita in urban areas	Hectare per capita	Positive	0.00	0.00	0.00	12	16	4	City; China Statistics	
48	Coverage of water supply in urban areas	%	Positive	96.08	99.79	99.81	6	5	−1	China Statistics	
49	Treatment rate of urban wastewater	%	Positive	79.18	82.70	78.90	15	12	−3	Environmental Yearbook	
50	Harmless treatment rate of urban household waste	%	Positive	78.47	98.30	97.60	3	2	−1	China Statistics	
51	Public buses per 10,000 urban residents		Positive	9.86	11.87	13.70	5	4	−1	China Statistics	
52	Length of public transport routes per capita in urban areas	km per capita	Positive	0.0006	0.0008	0.0007	6	2	−4	China Statistics; City	

53	Ratio of the rural residents benefiting from water supply system improvement to the total rural population	%	Positive	94.44	97.15	96.77	15	16	1	Environmental Yearbook	☺
54	Green coverage of urban built-up areas	%	Positive	37.75	38.30	38.20	12	13	1	China Statistics	☺
55	Newly-added afforestation area of the year per capita	Hectare per 10,000 persons	Positive	59.50	2.86	5.32	29	28	−1	China Statistics	☹
56	Industrial SO_2 removal rate	%	Positive	59.83	66.49	65.85	11	8	−3	China Statistics	☹
57	Industrial wastewater COD removal rate	%	Positive	70.84	85.97	85.53	6	5	−1	Environmental Annual Report; China Statistics	☹
58	Industrial nitrogen oxide removal rate	%	Positive	4.07	3.77	3.23	12	17	5	Environmental Annual Report	☺
59	Industrial wastewater ammonia/nitrogen removal rate	%	Positive	62.87	84.61	81.69	6	6	0	Environmental Annual Report; China Statistics	
60	Number of environmental emergencies		Negative	14.00	35	50	29	29	0	China Statistics	

Note:
China Statistics: *China Statistical Yearbook 2011*
Environmental Yearbook: *China Environmental Statistical Yearbook 2011*
Environmental Annual Report: *China Environment Annual Report 2010*
City: *China City Statistical Yearbook 2011*
Water Conservancy: *China Water Conservancy Statistical Yearbook 2011*
Industrial Economy: *China Industrial Economic Statistical Yearbook 2011*
Deserts: *Deserts in China and Desertification Control*

5.11 Brief Analysis of Green Development in Zhejiang

Zhejiang ranked 5th among the 30 participating provinces by GDI according to 2010 data, one place higher over 2009 (Zhejiang ranked 6th in 2009). Following is a brief analysis of its score by each indicator and their changes from 2009 to 2010.

5.11.1 Zhenjiang's 2010 Scores by GDI

Zhejiang scored 0.160 in 2010. From the three First-Class Indicators including GDEG, CCPNRE, and SDGP as shown in Fig. 5.21, Zhejiang had advantage in terms of GDEG and SDGP, yet underperformed compared with the national average in CCPNRE (Note: the national average value of each indicator is 0).

According to Fig. 5.22, Zhejiang surpassed the national average in 7 of Second-Class Indicators in 2010, which are GGEI, SII, TII, GII, II and EMI, yet ranked lower than the national average in RAECI and EPCCI.

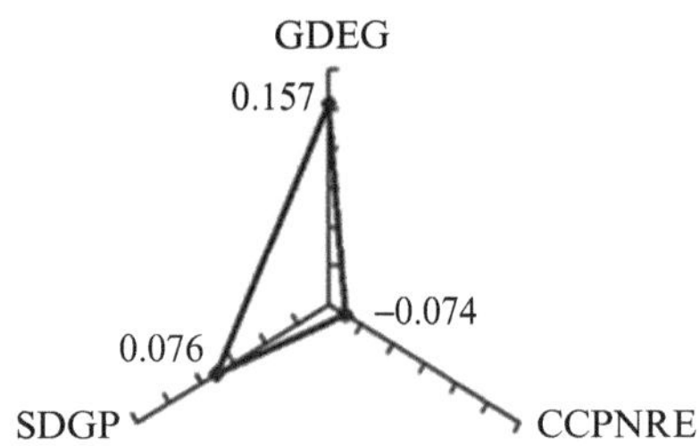

Fig. 5.21 Scores of Zhejiang by First-Class Indicators

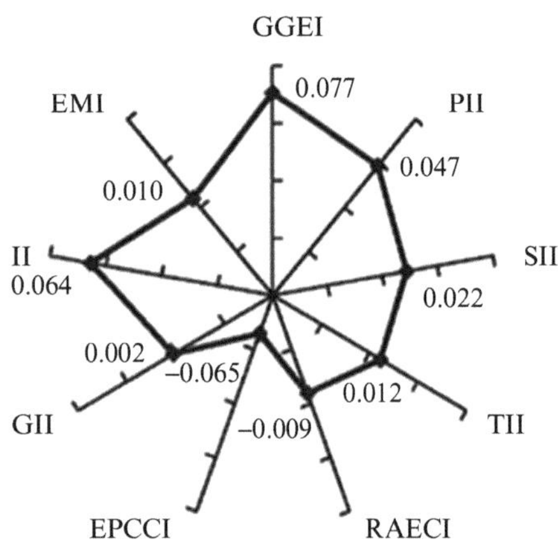

Fig. 5.22 Scores of Zhejiang by Second-Class Indicators

Table 5.21 Changes in Zhejiang's rankings by First-Class and Second-Class Indicators, 2009–2010

Indicator	2010	2009	Difference	Indicator	2010	2009	Difference
GDI	5	6	1				
GDEG	4	4	0	RAECI	16	14	−2
GGEI	4	4	0	EPCCI	23	26	3
PII	4	3	−1	SDGP	4	4	0
SII	8	7	−1	GII	15	16	1
TII	6	5	−1	II	7	4	−3
CCPNRE	19	19	0	EMI	13	15	2

Note: A positive value in "Difference" means a rise in ranking

Table 5.22 Third-Class Indicators where changes over 3 places by Zhejiang, 2009–2010

	Original data for 2010 and 2009			Change in ranking		
Third-Class Indicator	Unit	2010	2009	2010	2009	Difference
Recycling rate of industrial water	%	75.49	77.02	19	16	−3
Ammonia/nitrogen emissions per capita	Ton per capita	0.0008	0.0008	7	10	3
Ratio of environmental spending to government expenditure	%	2.56	2.09	23	27	4
Ratio of the investment in pollution control to GDP	%	1.20	0.94	19	25	6
Area of green land per capita in urban areas	Hectare per capita	0.00	0.00	12	16	4
Treatment rate of urban wastewater	%	82.70	78.90	15	12	−3
Length of public transport routes per capita in urban areas	km per capita	0.0008	0.0007	6	2	−4
Industrial SO_2 removal rate	%	66.49	65.85	11	8	−3
Industrial nitrogen oxide removal rate	%	3.77	3.23	12	17	5

Note: A positive value in "Difference" means a rise in ranking

5.11.2 *Changes in Zhejiang's GDI Rankings 2009–2010*

According to Table 5.21, in First-Class Indicators ranking, Zhejiang remained unchanged in all three indicators, GDEG, CCPNRE and SDGP. In Second-Class Indicators ranking, Zhejiang fell by 1 place in PII, SII and TII and 2 in RAECI. It rose by 3 places in EPCCI and 2 in EMI. It remained the same in the rankings by other indicators in 2009.

To further explain the causes of the changes in the rankings by First- and Second-Class Indicators, we put the Third-Class Indicators where a change of more than 3 places occurred from 2009 to 2010 in Table 5.22. Compared with those in 2009, Zhejiang dropped by 4 places in Length of public transport routes per capita in urban areas, 3 in Recycling rate of industrial water, Treatment rate of urban wastewater and Industrial SO_2 removal rate. It rose by 3 places in Ammonia/nitrogen emissions per capita, 4 in Ratio of environmental spending to government expenditure and Area of green land per capita in urban areas, 5 in Industrial nitrogen oxide removal rate and 6 in Ratio of the investment in pollution control to GDP.

Green development checkup-Anhui

No.	Indicator	Unit	Attribute	2010 average of 30 provinces	2010 figure	2009 figure	2010 ranking	2009 ranking	Change in ranking	Source of 2010 data	Chernoff face
1	GDP per capita	Yuan per capita	Positive	33,964.12	20,888	16,408	26	26	0	China Statistics	
2	Energy consumption per unit of GDP	Ton coal equivalent per 10,000 yuan	Negative	1.29	0.97	1.02	10	10	0	China Statistics	
3	Ratio of non-fossil energy consumption to total energy consumption		Positive	NA	NA	NA	NA	NA			
4	CO_2 emissions per unit of GDP		Negative	NA	NA	NA	NA	NA			
5	SO_2 emissions per unit of GDP	Ton per 10,000 yuan	Negative	0.0088	0.0053	0.0061	13	13	0	China Statistics	
6	COD emissions per unit of GDP	Ton per 10,000 yuan	Negative	0.0045	0.0041	0.0048	15	15	0	China Statistics	
7	Nitrogen oxide emissions per unit of GDP	Ton per 10,000 yuan	Negative	0.0068	0.0063	0.0061	20	18	−2	Environmental Annual Report; China Statistics	☹
8	Ammonia/nitrogen emissions per unit of GDP	Ton per 10,000 yuan	Negative	0.0004	0.0004	0.0005	17	20	3	Environmental Annual Report; China Statistics	☺
9	Electricity consumption per capita in urban areas	kWh per capita	Negative	295.08	122.06	282.79	7	12	5	City	☺
10	Labor productivity of the primary sector	10,000 yuan per capita	Positive	1.61	1.11	0.94	23	22	−1	China Statistics	☹

11	Land productivity	100 million yuan per 1,000 hectares	Positive	0.26	0.17	0.14	22	23	1	China Statistics	☺
12	Proportion of water-saving irrigated area in effectively irrigated area		Positive	0.49	0.23	0.23	24	24	0	Water Conservancy; China Statistics	
13	Proportion of water-saving irrigated area in effectively irrigated area	%	Positive	53.55	61.43	60.80	14	14	0	China Statistics	
14	Labor productivity of the secondary sector	10,000 yuan per capita	Positive	12.13	5.92	4.87	30	30	0	China Statistics	
15	Water consumption per unit of value added created by industrial enterprises	m^3/yuan	Negative	0.0100	0.0210	0.0230	28	29	1	China Statistics	☺
16	Energy consumption per unit of value added created by industrial enterprises above designated size (no data)		Negative	NA	NA	NA	NA	NA			
17	Utilization rate of industrial solid waste	%	Positive	69.80	84.60	83.10	7	9	2	Environmental Yearbook	☺
18	Recycling rate of industrial water	%	Positive	72.90	94.00	93.32	4	5	1	Environmental Yearbook	☺
19	Ratio of the output of six energy-intensive industries to gross industrial output	%	Negative	39.65	34.13	35.60	12	14	2	Industrial Economy	☺
20	Labor productivity of the tertiary sector	10,000 yuan per capita	Positive	6.96	3.74	3.51	27	27	0	China Statistics	
21	Proportion of the value added of the tertiary sector in GDP	%	Positive	39.97	33.90	36.40	27	26	−1	China Statistics	☹

(continued)

(continued)

No.	Indicator	Unit	Attribute	2010 average of 30 provinces	2010 figure	2009 figure	2010 ranking	2009 ranking	Change in ranking	Source of 2010 data	Chernoff face
22	Proportion of tertiary sector employees in the total employed population	%	Positive	36.67	30.57	28.96	26	27	1	China Statistics	☺
23	Water resources per capita	m^3 per capita	Positive	2,419.38	1,526.87	1,195.34	18	17	−1	China Statistics	☹
24	Forest area per capita	Hectare per capita	Positive	0.19	0.06	0.06	23	24	1	China Statistics	☺
25	Forest coverage rate	%	Positive	30.63	26.06	26.06	18	18	0	China Statistics	
26	Proportion of the area of natural reserves in the total area of a region	%	Positive	8.60	3.60	3.60	27	27	0	China Statistics	
27	Proportion of the area of wetlands in the total area of a region	%	Positive	7.01	4.73	4.73	16	16	0	China Statistics	
28	Growing stock per capita	m^3 per capita	Positive	10.70	2.73	2.65	21	21	0	China Statistics	
29	CO_2 emissions per unit of land area		Negative	NA	NA	NA	NA	NA			
30	CO_2 emissions per capita		Negative	NA	NA	NA	NA	NA			
31	SO_2 emissions per unit of land area	Ton per km^2	Negative	6.3677	3.7971	3.8424	14	15	1	China Statistics; Deserts	☺
32	SO_2 emissions per capita	Ton per capita	Negative	0.0191	0.0088	0.0088	3	3	0	China Statistics	
33	COD emissions per unit of land area	Ton per km^2	Negative	3.7722	2.9338	3.0266	17	17	0	China Statistics; Deserts	
34	COD emissions per capita	Ton per capita	Negative	0.0101	0.0068	0.0069	7	7	0	China Statistics	

35	Nitrogen oxide emissions per unit of land area	Ton per km^2	Negative	6.4473	4.5388	3.8465	18	18	0	China Statistics; Deserts; Environmental Annual Report	
36	Nitrogen oxide emissions per capita	Ton per capita	Negative	0.0165	0.0105	0.0088	10	10	0	Environmental Annual Report; China Statistics	
37	Ammonia/nitrogen emissions per unit of land area	Ton per km^2	Negative	0.4164	0.3140	0.3354	19	19	0	China Statistics; Deserts; Environmental Annual Report	
38	Ammonia/nitrogen emissions per capita	Ton per capita	Negative	0.0010	0.0007	0.0008	5	6	1	Environmental Annual Report; China Statistics	☺
39	Consumption of chemical fertilizers per unit of cultivated land area	10,000 ton per 1,000 hectares	Negative	0.05	0.06	0.05	19	20	1	China Statistics; China Statistics	☺
40	Consumption of pesticides per unit of cultivated land area	Ton per 1,000 hectares	Negative	17.68	20.36	19.27	21	20	−1	Environmental Yearbook; China Statistics	☹
41	Nitrogen oxide emissions per capita from road transport	Ton per 10,000 persons	Negative	24.07	15.49	14.18	11	9	−2	Environmental Annual Report; China Statistics	☹
42	Ratio of environmental spending to government expenditure	%	Positive	3.35	2.50	2.77	25	20	−5	China Statistics	☹
43	Ratio of the investment in pollution control to GDP	%	Positive	1.40	1.46	1.58	13	10	−3	Environmental Yearbook; China Statistics	☹
44	Government spending per capita on rural water supply system and toilet improvement	Yuan per capita	Positive	57.01	31.56	35.71	23	20	−3	Environmental Yearbook	☹

(continued)

(continued)

No.	Indicator	Unit	Attribute	2010 average of 30 provinces	2010 figure	2009 figure	2010 ranking	2009 ranking	Change in ranking	Source of 2010 data	Chernoff face
45	Investment in converting cultivated land into forests and grassland per unit of cultivated land area	10,000 yuan per 1,000 hectares	Positive	29.81	10.41	13.32	21	19	−2	Environmental Yearbook; China Statistics	☹
46	Ratio of the spending on science, education, culture, and public health to government expenditure	%	Positive	26.10	26.29	26.52	15	14	−1	China Statistics	☹
47	Area of green land per capita in urban areas	Hectare per capita	Positive	0.00	0.00	0.00	21	17	−4	City; China Statistics	☹
48	Coverage of water supply in urban areas	%	Positive	96.08	96.06	95.25	19	19	0	China Statistics	
49	Treatment rate of urban wastewater	%	Positive	79.18	88.50	83.20	5	8	3	Environmental Yearbook	☺
50	Harmless treatment rate of urban household waste	%	Positive	78.47	64.56	60.91	26	22	−4	China Statistics	☹
51	Public buses per 10,000 urban residents		Positive	9.86	7.73	8.61	25	23	−2	China Statistics	☹
52	Length of public transport routes per capita in urban areas	km per capita	Positive	0.0006	0.0001	0.0002	30	27	−3	China Statistics; City	☹
53	Ratio of the rural residents benefiting from water supply system improvement to the total rural population	%	Positive	94.44	99.56	98.37	6	9	3	Environmental Yearbook	☺

54	Green coverage of urban built-up areas	%	Positive	37.75	37.50	37.16	18	16	−2	China Statistics	☹
55	Newly-added afforestation area of the year per capita	Hectare per 10,000 persons	Positive	59.50	8.06	11.24	27	23	−4	China Statistics	☹
56	Industrial SO_2 removal rate	%	Positive	59.83	76.92	76.88	5	3	−2	China Statistics	☹
57	Industrial wastewater COD removal rate	%	Positive	70.84	78.41	75.27	9	13	4	Environmental Annual Report; China Statistics	☺
58	Industrial nitrogen oxide removal rate	%	Positive	4.07	9.52	11.71	4	5	1	Environmental Annual Report	☺
59	Industrial wastewater ammonia/nitrogen removal rate	%	Positive	62.87	86.04	83.78	5	4	−1	Environmental Annual Report; China Statistics	☹
60	Number of environmental emergencies		Negative	14.00	30	22	27	25	−2	China Statistics	☹

Note:
China Statistics: *China Statistical Yearbook 2011*
Environmental Yearbook: *China Environmental Statistical Yearbook 2011*
Environmental Annual Report: *China Environment Annual Report 2010*
City: *China City Statistical Yearbook 2011*
Water Conservancy: *China Water Conservancy Statistical Yearbook 2011*
Industrial Economy: *China Industrial Economic Statistical Yearbook 2011*
Deserts: *Deserts in China and Desertification Control*

5.12 Brief Analysis of Green Development in Anhui

Anhui ranked 22nd among the 30 participating provinces by GDI according to 2010 data, two places lower over 2009 (Anhui ranked 20th in 2009). Following is a brief analysis of its score by each indicator and their changes from 2009 to 2010.

5.12.1 Anhui's 2010 Scores by GDI

Anhui scored −0.122 in 2010. From the three First-Class Indicators including GDEG, CCPNRE, and SDGP as shown in Fig. 5.23, Anhui underperformed compared with the national average in had advantage in terms of GDEG and SDGP, yet CCPNRE (Note: the national average value of each indicator is 0).

According to Fig. 5.24, Anhui surpassed the national average in 3 of Second-Class Indicators in 2010, which are SII, EPCCI and EMI, yet ranked lower than the national average in GGEI, PII, TII, RAECI, II and GII.

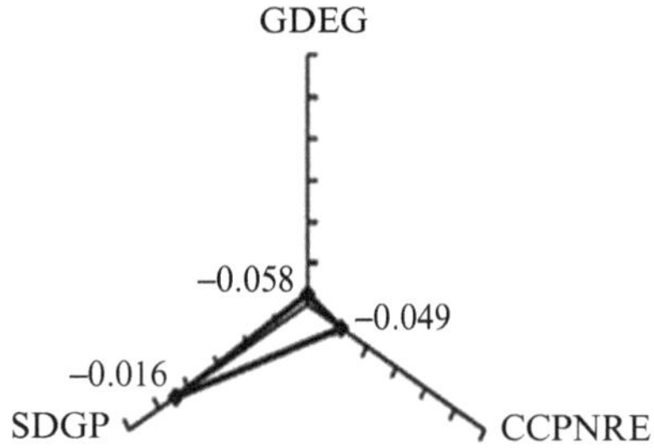

Fig. 5.23 Scores of Anhui by First-Class Indicators

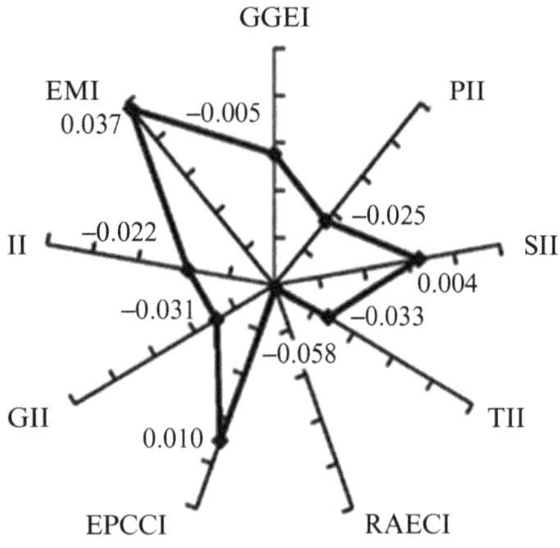

Fig. 5.24 Scores of Anhui by Second-Class Indicators

Table 5.23 Changes in Anhui's rankings by First-Class and Second-Class Indicators, 2009–2010

Indicator	2010	2009	Difference	Indicator	2010	2009	Difference
GDI	22	20	−2				
GDEG	18	19	1	RAECI	22	23	1
GGEI	13	15	2	EPCCI	11	11	0
PII	23	24	1	SDGP	17	15	−2
SII	14	13	−1	GII	22	21	−1
TII	28	28	0	II	19	18	−1
CCPNRE	17	16	−1	EMI	6	5	−1

Note: A positive value in "Difference" means a rise in ranking

5.12.2 Changes in Anhui's GDI Rankings 2009–2010

According to Table 5.23, in First-Class Indicators ranking, Anhui rose by 1 place in GDEG and fell by 1 in CCPNRE and 2 in SDGP. In Second-Class Indicators ranking, Anhui fell by 1 place in SII, GII, II and EMI. It rose by 2 places in GGEI and 1 in RAECI. It remained the same in the rankings by other indicators in 2009.

To further explain the causes of the changes in the rankings by First- and Second-Class Indicators, we put the Third-Class Indicators where a change of more than 3 places occurred from 2009 to 2010 in Table 5.24. Compared with those in 2009, Anhui dropped by 5 places in Ratio of environmental spending to government expenditure, 4 in Area of green land per capita in urban areas, Harmless treatment rate of urban household waste and Newly-added afforestation area of the year per capita, 3 in Ratio of the investment in pollution control to GDP, Government spending per capita on rural water supply system and toilet improvement and Length of public transport routes per capita in urban areas. It rose by 3 places in Ammonia/nitrogen emissions per unit of GDP, Treatment rate of urban wastewater and Ratio of the rural residents benefiting from water supply system improvement to the total rural population, 4 in Industrial wastewater COD removal rate and 5 in Electricity consumption per capita in urban areas.

Table 5.24 Third-Class Indicators where changes over 3 places by Anhui, 2009–2010

	Original data for 2010 and 2009			Change in ranking		
Third-Class Indicator	Unit	2010	2009	2010	2009	Difference
Ammonia/nitrogen emissions per unit of GDP	Ton per 10,000 yuan	0.0004	0.0005	17	20	3
Electricity consumption per capita in urban areas	kWh per capita	122.06	282.79	7	12	5
Ratio of environmental spending to government expenditure	%	2.50	2.77	25	20	−5
Ratio of the investment in pollution control to GDP	%	1.46	1.58	13	10	−3
Government spending per capita on rural water supply system and toilet improvement	Yuan per capita	31.56	35.71	23	20	−3
Area of green land per capita in urban areas	Hectare per capita	0.00	0.00	21	17	−4
Treatment rate of urban wastewater	%	88.50	83.20	5	8	3
Harmless treatment rate of urban household waste	%	64.56	60.91	26	22	−4
Length of public transport routes per capita in urban areas	km per capita	0.0001	0.0002	30	27	−3
Ratio of the rural residents benefiting from water supply system improvement to the total rural population	%	99.56	98.37	6	9	3
Newly-added afforestation area of the year per capita	hectare per 10,000 persons	8.06	11.24	27	23	−4
Industrial wastewater COD removal rate	%	78.41	75.27	9	13	4

Note: A positive value in "Difference" means a rise in ranking

Green development checkup-Fujian

No.	Indicator	Unit	Attribute	2010 average of 30 provinces	2010 figure	2009 figure	2010 ranking	2009 ranking	Change in ranking	Source of 2010 data	Chernoff face
1	GDP per capita	Yuan per capita	Positive	33,964.12	40,025	33,840	10	10	0	China Statistics	
2	Energy consumption per unitof GDP	Ton coal equivalent per 10,000 yuan	Negative	1.29	0.78	0.81	6	6	0	China Statistics	
3	Ratio of non-fossil energy to total energy consumption		Positive	NA	NA	NA	NA	NA			
4	CO_2 emissions per unit of GDP		Negative	NA	NA	NA	NA	NA			
5	SO_2 emissions per unit of GDP	Ton per 10,000 yuan	Negative	0.0088	0.0033	0.0038	8	8	0	China Statistics	
6	COD emissions per unit of GDP	Ton per 10,000 yuan	Negative	0.0045	0.0030	0.0034	8	8	0	China Statistics	
7	Nitrogen oxide emissions per unit of GDP	Ton per 10,000 yuan	Negative	0.0068	0.0035	0.0030	7	3	−4	Environmental Annual Report; China Statistics	☹
8	Ammonia/nitrogen emissions per unit of GDP	Ton per 10,000 yuan	Negative	0.0004	0.0002	0.0003	6	7	1	Environmental Annual Report; China Statistics	☺
9	Electricity consumption per capita in urban areas	kWh per capita	Negative	295.08	300.23	549.44	22	26	4	City	☺
10	Labor productivity of the primary sector	10,000 yuan per capita	Positive	1.61	2.14	1.84	7	6	−1	China Statistics	☹

(continued)

(continued)

No.	Indicator	Unit	Attribute	2010 average of 30 provinces	2010 figure	2009 figure	2010 ranking	2009 ranking	Change in ranking	Source of 2010 data	Chernoff face
11	Land productivity	100 million yuan per 1,000 hectares	Positive	0.26	0.43	0.37	2	4	2	China Statistics	
12	Proportion of water-saving irrigated area in effectively irrigated area		Positive	0.49	0.57	0.54	13	13	0	Water Conservancy; China Statistics	
13	Proportion of water-saving irrigated area in effectively irrigated area	%	Positive	53.55	72.74	72.18	7	7	0	China Statistics	
14	Labor productivity of the secondary sector	10,000 yuan per capita	Positive	12.13	9.45	7.93	17	18	1	China Statistics	
15	Water consumption per unit of value added created by industrial enterprises	m^3/yuan	Negative	0.0100	0.0133	0.0151	23	21	−2	China Statistics	
16	Energy consumption per unit of value added created by industrial enterprises above designated size (no data)		Negative	NA	NA	NA	NA	NA			
17	Utilization rate of industrial solid waste	%	Positive	69.80	82.90	85.40	9	7	−2	Environmental Yearbook	
18	Recycling rate of industrial water	%	Positive	72.90	80.50	80.06	17	14	−3	Environmental Yearbook	
19	Ratio of the output of six energy-intensive industries to gross industrial output	%	Negative	39.65	24.82	24.64	3	2	−1	Industrial Economy	

20	Labor productivity of the tertiary sector	10,000 yuan per capita	Positive	6.96	7.89	6.98	9	8	−1	China Statistics	☹
21	Proportion of the value added of the tertiary sector in GDP	%	Positive	39.97	39.70	41.30	11	10	−1	China Statistics	☹
22	Proportion of tertiary sector employees in the total employed population	%	Positive	36.67	33.42	34.79	21	14	−7	China Statistics	☹
23	Water resources per capita	m^3 per capita	Positive	2,419.38	4,491.74	2,214.94	5	10	5	China Statistics	☺
24	Forest area per capita	Hectare per capita	Positive	0.19	0.21	0.21	9	9	0	China Statistics	
25	Forest coverage rate	%	Positive	30.63	63.10	63.10	1	1	0	China Statistics	
26	Proportion of the area of natural reserves in the total area of a region	%	Positive	8.60	3.23	3.20	28	28	0	China Statistics	
27	Proportion of the area of wetlands in the total area of a region	%	Positive	7.01	3.65	3.65	20	20	0	China Statistics	
28	Growing stock per capita	m^3 per capita	Positive	10.70	14.41	14.67	7	7	0	China Statistics	
29	CO_2 emissions per unit of land area		Negative	NA	NA	NA	NA	NA			
30	CO_2 emissions per capita		Negative	NA	NA	NA	NA	NA			
31	SO_2 emissions per unit of land area	Ton per km^2	Negative	6.3677	3.2984	3.3839	10	11	1	China Statistics; Deserts	☺
32	SO_2 emissions per capita	Ton per capita	Negative	0.0191	0.0112	0.0116	7	7	0	China Statistics	
33	COD emissions per unit of land area	Ton per km^2	Negative	3.7722	3.0048	3.0295	18	18	0	China Statistics; Deserts	

(continued)

(continued)

No.	Indicator	Unit	Attribute	2010 average of 30 provinces	2010 figure	2009 figure	2010 ranking	2009 ranking	Change in ranking	Source of 2010 data	Chernoff face
34	COD emissions per capita	Ton per capita	Negative	0.0101	0.0102	0.0104	18	17	−1	China Statistics	☹
35	Nitrogen oxide emissions per unit of land area	Ton per km^2	Negative	6.4473	3.4996	2.6610	16	15	−1	China Statistics; Deserts; Environmental Annual Report	☹
36	Nitrogen oxide emissions per capita	Ton per capita	Negative	0.0165	0.0119	0.0091	12	11	−1	Environmental Annual Report; China Statistics	☹
37	Ammonia/nitrogen emissions per unit of land area	Ton per km^2	Negative	0.4164	0.2419	0.2419	14	15	1	China Statistics; Deserts; Environmental Annual Report	☺
38	Ammonia/nitrogen emissions per capita	Ton per capita	Negative	0.0010	0.0008	0.0008	12	11	−1	Environmental Annual Report; China Statistics	☹
39	Consumption of chemical fertilizers per unit of cultivated land area	10,000 ton per 1,000 hectares	Negative	0.05	0.09	0.09	30	30	0	China Statistics; China Statistics	
40	Consumption of pesticides per unit of cultivated land area	Ton per 1,000 hectares	Negative	17.68	43.78	43.49	29	29	0	Environmental Yearbook; China Statistics	
41	Nitrogen oxide emissions per capita from road transport	Ton per 10,000 persons	Negative	24.07	24.97	22.02	20	19	−1	Environmental Annual Report; China Statistics	☹

42	Ratio of environmental spending to government expenditure	%	Positive	3.35	2.35	2.40	27	23	−4	China Statistics	☹
43	Ratio of the investment in pollution control to GDP	%	Positive	1.40	0.88	0.79	25	27	2	Environmental Yearbook; China Statistics	☺
44	Government spending per capita on rural water supply system and toilet improvement	Yuan per capita	Positive	57.01	42.91	35.03	16	22	6	Environmental Yearbook	☺
45	Investment in converting cultivated land into forests and grassland per unit of cultivated land area	10,000 yuan per 1,000 hectares	Positive	29.81	0.00	0.00	25	23	−2	Environmental Yearbook; China Statistics	☹
46	Ratio of the spending on science, education, culture, and public health to government expenditure	%	Positive	26.10	29.78	30.07	3	4	1	China Statistics	☺
47	Area of green land per capita in urban areas	Hectare per capita	Positive	0.00	0.00	0.00	17	15	−2	City; China Statistics	☹
48	Coverage of water supply in urban areas	%	Positive	96.08	99.50	99.18	9	9	0	China Statistics	
49	Treatment rate of urban wastewater	%	Positive	79.18	84.40	80.30	12	9	−3	Environmental Yearbook	☹
50	Harmless treatment rate of urban household waste	%	Positive	78.47	91.96	92.53	7	5	−2	China Statistics	☹
51	Public buses per 10,000 urban residents		Positive	9.86	10.32	11.51	9	9	0	China Statistics	
52	Length of public transport routes per capita in urban areas	km per capita	Positive	0.0006	0.0004	0.0004	16	13	−3	China Statistics; City	☹
53	Ratio of the rural residents benefiting from water supply system improvement to the total rural population	%	Positive	94.44	98.81	98.40	10	7	−3	Environmental Yearbook	☹

(continued)

(continued)

No.	Indicator	Unit	Attribute	2010 average of 30 provinces	2010 figure	2009 figure	2010 ranking	2009 ranking	Change in ranking	Source of 2010 data	Chernoff face
54	Green coverage of urban built-up areas	%	Positive	37.75	40.97	39.71	8	8	0	China Statistics	
55	Newly-added afforestation area of the year per capita	Hectare per 10,000 persons	Positive	59.50	8.16	9.20	26	27	1	China Statistics	☺
56	Industrial SO_2 removal rate	%	Positive	59.83	50.86	47.04	25	25	0	China Statistics	
57	Industrial wastewater COD removal rate	%	Positive	70.84	90.55	89.63	3	1	−2	Environmental Annual Report; China Statistics	☹
58	Industrial nitrogen oxide removal rate	%	Positive	4.07	2.32	7.24	17	8	−9	Environmental Annual Report	☹
59	Industrial wastewater ammonia/nitrogen removal rate	%	Positive	62.87	88.33	72.67	3	11	8	Environmental Annual Report; China Statistics	☺
60	Number of environmental emergencies		Negative	14.00	4	6	12	14	2	China Statistics	☺

Note:
China Statistics: *China Statistical Yearbook 2011*
Environmental Yearbook: *China Environmental Statistical Yearbook 2011*
Environmental Annual Report: *China Environment Annual Report 2010*
City: *China City Statistical Yearbook 2011*
Water Conservancy: *China Water Conservancy Statistical Yearbook 2011*
Industrial Economy: *China Industrial Economic Statistical Yearbook 2011*
Deserts: *Deserts in China and Desertification Control*

5.13 Brief Analysis of Green Development in Fujian

Fujian ranked 8th among the 30 participating provinces by GDI according to 2010 data, as it did in 2009 (Fujian ranked 8th in 2009). Following is a brief analysis of its score by each indicator and their changes from 2009 to 2010.

5.13.1 Fujian's 2010 Scores by GDI

Fujian scored 0.100 in 2010. From the three First-Class Indicators including GDEG, CCPNRE, and SDGP as shown in Fig. 5.25, Fujian had advantage in terms of GDEG and SDGP, yet underperformed compared with the national average in CCPNRE (Note: the national average value of each indicator is 0).

According to Fig. 5.26, Fujian surpassed the national average in 6 of Second-Class Indicators in 2010, which are GGEI, PII, SII, RAECI, II and EMI, yet ranked lower than the national average in TII, EPCCI and GII.

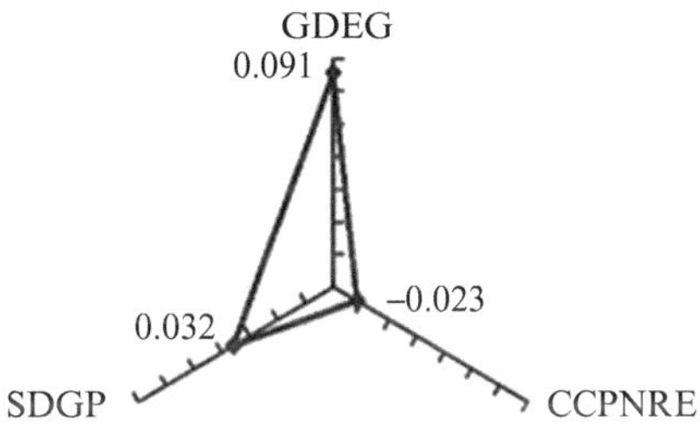

Fig. 5.25 Scores of Fujian by First-Class Indicators

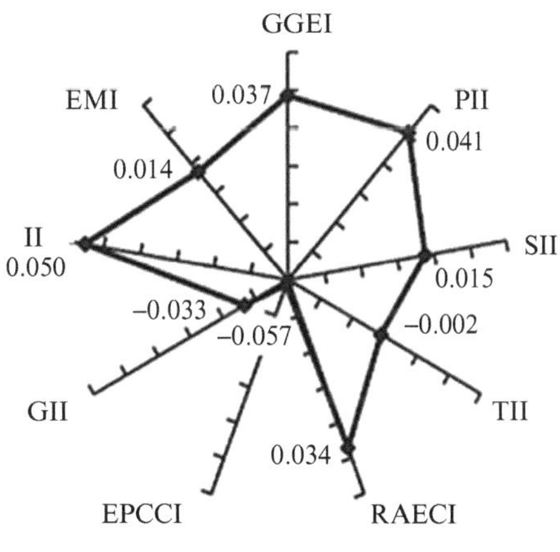

Fig. 5.26 Scores of Fujian by Second-Class Indicators

Table 5.25 Changes in Fujian's rankings by First-Class and Second-Class Indicators, 2009–2010

Indicator	2010	2009	Difference	Indicator	2010	2009	Difference
GDI	8	8	0				
GDEG	8	8	0	RAECI	9	11	2
GGEI	8	8	0	EPCCI	22	21	−1
PII	5	5	0	SDGP	14	8	−6
SII	9	8	−1	GII	25	28	3
TII	11	10	−1	II	8	7	−1
CCPNRE	13	14	1	EMI	11	10	−1

Note: A positive value in "Difference" means a rise in ranking

5.13.2 Changes in Fujian's GDI Rankings 2009–2010

According to Table 5.25, in First-Class Indicators ranking, it fell by 6 places in SDGP and rose by 1 place in CCPNRE. It remained unchanged in GDEG. In Second-Class Indicators ranking, Fujian fell by 1 place in SII, TII, EPCCI, II and EMI. It rose by 2 places in RAECI and 3 in GII. It remained the same in the rankings by other indicators in 2009.

To further explain the causes of the changes in the rankings by First- and Second-Class Indicators, we put the Third-Class Indicators where a change of more than 3 places occurred from 2009 to 2010 in Table 5.26. Compared with those in 2009, Fujian dropped by 9 places in Industrial nitrogen oxide removal rate, 7 in Proportion of tertiary sector employees in the total employed population, 4 in Nitrogen oxide emissions per unit of GDP and Ratio of environmental spending to government expenditure, 3 in Recycling rate of industrial water, Treatment rate of urban wastewater, Length of public transport routes per capita in urban areas and Ratio of the rural residents benefiting from water supply system improvement to the total rural population. It rose by 4 places in Electricity consumption per capita in urban areas, 5 in Water resources per capita, 6 in Government spending per capita on rural water supply system and toilet improvement and 8 in Industrial wastewater ammonia/nitrogen removal rate.

Table 5.26 Third-Class Indicators where changes over 3 places by Fujian, 2009–2010

	Original data for 2010 and 2009			Change in ranking		
Third-Class Indicator	Unit	2010	2009	2010	2009	Difference
Nitrogen oxide emissions per unit of GDP	Ton per 10,000 yuan	0.0035	0.0030	7	3	−4
Electricity consumption per capita in urban areas	kWh per capita	300.23	549.44	22	26	4
Recycling rate of industrial water	%	80.50	80.06	17	14	−3
Proportion of tertiary sector employees in the total employed population	%	33.42	34.79	21	14	−7
Water resources per capita	m^3 per capita	4,491.74	2,214.94	5	10	5
Ratio of environmental spending to government expenditure	%	2.35	2.40	27	23	−4
Government spending per capita on rural water supply system and toilet improvement	Yuan per capita	42.91	35.03	16	22	6
Treatment rate of urban wastewater	%	84.40	80.30	12	9	−3
Length of public transport routes per capita in urban areas	km per capita	0.0004	0.0004	16	13	−3
Ratio of the rural residents benefiting from water supply system improvement to the total rural population	%	98.81	98.40	10	7	−3
Industrial nitrogen oxide removal rate	%	2.32	7.24	17	8	−9
Industrial wastewater ammonia/nitrogen removal rate	%	88.33	72.67	3	11	8

Note: A positive value in "Difference" means a rise in ranking

Green development checkup-Jiangxi

No.	Indicator	Unit	Attribute	2010 average of 30 provinces	2010 figure	2009 figure	2010 ranking	2009 ranking	Change in ranking	Source of 2010 data	Chernoff face
1	GDP per capita	Yuan per capita	Positive	33,964.12	21,253	17,335	24	25	1	China Statistics	☺
2	Energy consumption per unit of GDP	Ton coal equivalent per 10,000 yuan	Negative	1.29	0.85	0.88	9	9	0	China Statistics	
3	Ratio of non-fossil energy consumption to total energy consumption		Positive	NA	NA	NA	NA	NA			
4	CO_2 emissions per unit of GDP		Negative	NA	NA	NA	NA	NA			
5	SO_2 emissions per unit of GDP	Ton per 10,000 yuan	Negative	0.0088	0.0074	0.0085	18	18	0	China Statistics	
6	COD emissions per unit of GDP	Ton per 10,000 yuan	Negative	0.0045	0.0057	0.0066	25	23	−2	China Statistics	☹
7	Nitrogen oxide emissions per unit of GDP	Ton per 10,000 yuan	Negative	0.0068	0.0045	0.0045	13	12	−1	Environmental Annual Report; China Statistics	☹
8	Ammonia/nitrogen emissions per unit of GDP	Ton per 10,000 yuan	Negative	0.0004	0.0005	0.0005	20	18	−2	Environmental Annual Report; China Statistics	☹
9	Electricity consumption per capita in urban areas	kWh per capita	Negative	295.08	96.16	220.79	2	4	2	City	☺
10	Labor productivity of the primary sector	10,000 yuan per capita	Positive	1.61	1.38	1.23	17	17	0	China Statistics	

11	Land productivity	100 million yuan per 1,000 hectares	Positive	0.26	0.15	0.14	26	24	−2	China Statistics	☹
12	Proportion of water-saving irrigated area in effectively irrigated area		Positive	0.49	0.16	0.15	27	28	1	Water Conservancy; China Statistics	☺
13	Proportion of water-saving irrigated area in effectively irrigated area	%	Positive	53.55	65.52	65.10	12	12	0	China Statistics	
14	Labor productivity of the secondary sector	10,000 yuan per capita	Positive	12.13	7.76	6.30	24	26	2	China Statistics	☺
15	Water consumption per unit of value added created by industrial enterprises	m^3/yuan	Negative	0.0100	0.0160	0.0166	24	25	1	China Statistics	☺
16	Energy consumption per unit of value added created by industrial enterprises above designated size (no data)		Negative	NA	NA	NA	NA	NA			
17	Utilization rate of industrial solid waste	%	Positive	69.80	46.50	41.60	28	28	0	Environmental Yearbook	
18	Recycling rate of industrial water	%	Positive	72.90	86.76	64.91	12	20	8	Environmental Yearbook	☺
19	Ratio of the output of six energy-intensive industries to gross industrial output	%	Negative	39.65	48.70	47.34	22	21	−1	Industrial Economy	☹
20	Labor productivity of the tertiary sector	10,000 yuan per capita	Positive	6.96	4.21	3.67	24	24	0	China Statistics	

(continued)

(continued)

No.	Indicator	Unit	Attribute	2010 average of 30 provinces	2010 figure	2009 figure	2010 ranking	2009 ranking	Change in ranking	Source of 2010 data	Chernoff face
21	Proportion of the value added of the tertiary sector in GDP	%	Positive	39.97	33.00	34.40	28	29	1	China Statistics	☺
22	Proportion of tertiary sector employees in the total employed population	%	Positive	36.67	32.73	32.37	22	22	0	China Statistics	
23	Water resources per capita	m^3 per capita	Positive	2,419.38	5,116.68	2,642.46	4	7	3	China Statistics	☺
24	Forest area per capita	Hectare per capita	Positive	0.19	0.22	0.22	8	8	0	China Statistics	
25	Forest coverage rate	%	Positive	30.63	58.32	58.32	2	2	0	China Statistics	
26	Proportion of the area of natural reserves in the total area of a region	%	Positive	8.60	6.69	6.68	17	16	−1	China Statistics	☹
27	Proportion of the area of wetlands in the total area of a region	%	Positive	7.01	5.99	5.99	11	11	0	China Statistics	
28	Growing stock per capita	m^3 per capita	Positive	10.70	10.09	10.16	9	9	0	China Statistics	
29	CO_2 emissions per unit of land area		Negative	NA	NA	NA	NA	NA			
30	CO_2 emissions per capita		Negative	NA	NA	NA	NA	NA			
31	SO_2 emissions per unit of land area	Ton per km^2	Negative	6.3677	3.3379	3.3807	11	10	−1	China Statistics; Deserts	☹
32	SO_2 emissions per capita	Ton per capita	Negative	0.0191	0.0125	0.0128	9	9	0	China Statistics	
33	COD emissions per unit of land area	Ton per km^2	Negative	3.7722	2.5830	2.6077	12	12	0	China Statistics; Deserts	

34	COD emissions per capita	Ton per capita	Negative	0.0101	0.0097	0.0099	15	13	−2	China Statistics	☹
35	Nitrogen oxide emissions per unit of land area	Ton per km^2	Negative	6.4473	2.0312	1.7736	12	12	0	China Statistics; Deserts; Environmental Annual Report	
36	Nitrogen oxide emissions per capita	Ton per capita	Negative	0.0165	0.0076	0.0067	5	5	0	Environmental Annual Report; China Statistics	
37	Ammonia/nitrogen emissions per unit of land area	Ton per km^2	Negative	0.4164	0.2097	0.2037	12	13	1	China Statistics; Deserts; Environmental Annual Report	☺
38	Ammonia/nitrogen emissions per capita	Ton per capita	Negative	0.0010	0.0008	0.0008	10	7	−3	Environmental Annual Report; China Statistics	☹
39	Consumption of chemical fertilizers per unit of cultivated land area	10,000 ton per hectares	Negative	0.05	0.05	0.05	17	15	−2	China Statistics; China Statistics	☹
40	Consumption of pesticides per unit of cultivated land area	Ton per 1,000 hectares	Negative	17.68	37.68	34.52	28	27	−1	Environmental Yearbook; China Statistics	☹
41	Nitrogen oxide emissions per capita from road transport	Ton per 10,000 persons	Negative	24.07	20.83	18.98	18	15	−3	Environmental Annual Report; China Statistics	☹
42	Ratio of environmental spending to government expenditure	%	Positive	3.35	2.56	2.76	24	21	−3	China Statistics	☹
43	Ratio of the investment in pollution control to GDP	%	Positive	1.40	1.66	1.07	9	23	14	Environmental Yearbook; China Statistics	☺

(continued)

(continued)

No.	Indicator	Unit	Attribute	2010 average of 30 provinces	2010 figure	2009 figure	2010 ranking	2009 ranking	Change in ranking	Source of 2010 data	Chernoff face
44	Government spending per capita on rural water supply system and toilet improvement	Yuan per capita	Positive	57.01	29.42	26.50	25	28	3	Environmental Yearbook	☺
45	Investment in converting cultivated land into forests and grassland per unit of cultivated land area	10,000 yuan per 1,000 hectares	Positive	29.81	30.68	36.41	11	9	−2	Environmental Yearbook; China Statistics	☹
46	Ratio of the spending on science, education, culture, and public health to government expenditure	%	Positive	26.10	25.69	26.17	17	17	0	China Statistics	
47	Area of green land per capita in urban areas	Hectare per capita	Positive	0.00	0.00	0.00	24	18	−6	City; China Statistics	☹
48	Coverage of water supply in urban areas	%	Positive	96.08	97.43	98.00	16	12	−4	China Statistics	☹
49	Treatment rate of urban wastewater	%	Positive	79.18	80.80	74.90	18	17	−1	Environmental Yearbook	☹
50	Harmless treatment rate of urban household waste	%	Positive	78.47	85.89	84.40	13	9	−4	China Statistics	☹
51	Public buses per 10,000 urban residents		Positive	9.86	7.61	9.22	26	21	−5	China Statistics	☹
52	Length of public transport routes per capita in urban areas	km per capita	Positive	0.0006	0.0002	0.0002	24	23	−1	China Statistics; City	☹
53	Ratio of the rural residents benefiting from water supply system improvement to the total rural population	%	Positive	94.44	99.64	97.47	4	12	8	Environmental Yearbook	☺

54	Green coverage of urban built-up areas	%	Positive	37.75	46.62	44.36	2	2	0	China Statistics	
55	Newly-added afforestation area of the year per capita	Hectare per 10,000 persons	Positive	59.50	45.15	51.77	13	12	−1	China Statistics	☹
56	Industrial SO_2 removal rate	%	Positive	59.83	77.56	74.46	2	4	2	China Statistics	☺
57	Industrial wastewater COD removal rate	%	Positive	70.84	54.63	62.91	26	21	−5	Environmental Annual Report; China Statistics	☹
58	Industrial nitrogen oxide removal rate	%	Positive	4.07	0.41	0.71	24	23	−1	Environmental Annual Report	☹
59	Industrial wastewater ammonia/nitrogen removal rate	%	Positive	62.87	57.19	57.73	19	16	−3	Environmental Annual Report; China Statistics	☹
60	Number of environmental emergencies		Negative	14.00	9	6	19	14	−5	China Statistics	☹

Note:
China Statistics: *China Statistical Yearbook 2011*
Environmental Yearbook: *China Environmental Statistical Yearbook 2011*
Environmental Annual Report: *China Environment Annual Report 2010*
City: *China City Statistical Yearbook 2011*
Water Conservancy: *China Water Conservancy Statistical Yearbook 2011*
Industrial Economy: *China Industrial Economic Statistical Yearbook 2011*
Deserts: *Deserts in China and Desertification Control*

5.14 Brief Analysis of Green Development in Jiangxi

Jiangxi ranked 18th among the 30 participating provinces by GDI according to 2010 data, one place lower over 2009 (Jiangxi ranked 17th in 2009). Following is a brief analysis of its score by each indicator and their changes from 2009 to 2010.

5.14.1 Jiangxi's 2010 Scores by GDI

Jiangxi scored −0.062 in 2010. From the three First-Class Indicators including GDEG, CCPNRE, and SDGP as shown in Fig. 5.27, Jiangxi had advantage in terms of CCPNRE, yet underperformed compared with the national average in GDEG and SDGP (Note: the national average value of each indicator is 0).

According to Fig. 5.28, Jiangxi surpassed the national average in 3 of Second-Class Indicators in 2010, which are GGEI, PII, SII, RAECI, II and EMI, yet ranked lower than the national average in TII, EPCCI and GII.

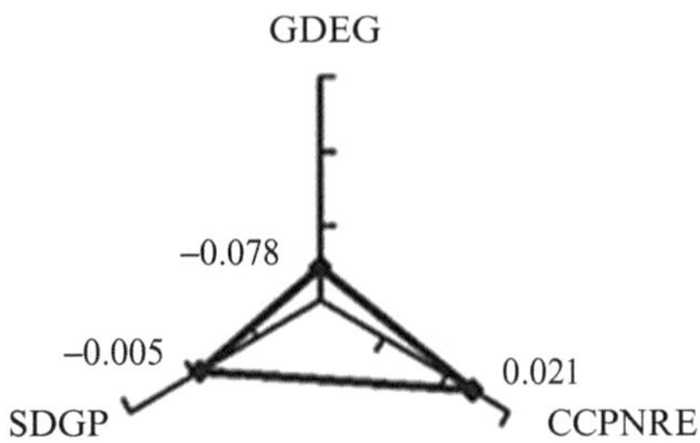

Fig. 5.27 Scores of Jiangxi by First-Class Indicators

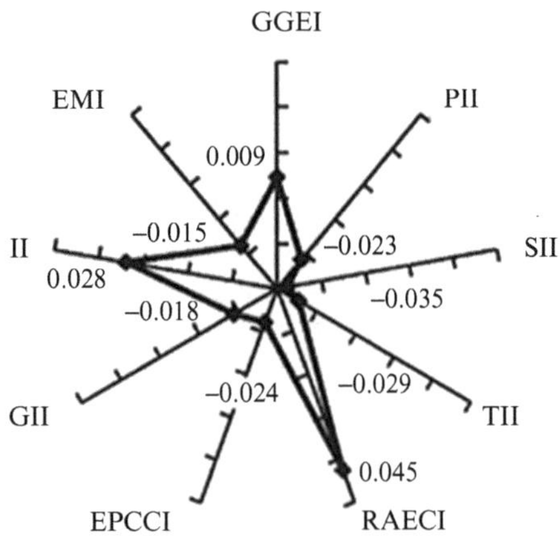

Fig. 5.28 Scores of Jiangxi by Second-Class Indicators

Table 5.27 Changes in Jiangxi's rankings by First-Class and Second-Class Indicators, 2009–2010

Indicator	2010	2009	Difference	Indicator	2010	2009	Difference
GDI	18	17	−1				
GDEG	20	21	1	RAECI	8	9	1
GGEI	9	10	1	EPCCI	16	13	−3
PII	21	20	−1	SDGP	16	14	−2
SII	25	24	−1	GII	20	23	3
TII	27	27	0	II	13	9	−4
CCPNRE	12	10	−2	EMI	22	14	−8

Note: A positive value in "Difference" means a rise in ranking

5.14.2 *Changes in Jiangxi's GDI Rankings 2009–2010*

According to Table 5.27, in First-Class Indicators ranking, it rose by 1 place in GDEG, and fell by 2 places in CCPNRE and SDGP. In Second-Class Indicators ranking, Jiangxi fell by 1 place in PII and SII, 3 in EPCCI, 4 in II, 8 in EMI. It rose by 1 place in GGEI and RAECI and 3 in GII. It remained the same in the rankings by other indicators in 2009.

To further explain the causes of the changes in the rankings by First- and Second-Class Indicators, we put the Third-Class Indicators where a change of more than 3 places occurred from 2009 to 2010 in Table 5.28. Compared with those in 2009, Jiangxi dropped by 6 places in Area of green land per capita in urban areas, 5 in Public buses per 10,000 urban residents, Industrial wastewater COD removal rate and Number of environmental emergencies, 4 in Coverage of water supply in urban areas and Harmless treatment rate of urban household waste, 3 in Ammonia/nitrogen emissions per capita, Nitrogen oxide emissions per capita from road transport, Ratio of environmental spending to government expenditure and Industrial wastewater ammonia/nitrogen removal rate. It rose by 3 places in Water resources per capita and Government spending per capita on rural water supply system and toilet improvement, 8 in Recycling rate of industrial water and Ratio of the rural residents benefiting from water supply system improvement to the total rural population, and 14 in Ratio of the investment in pollution control to GDP.

Table 5.28 Third-Class Indicators where changes over 3 places by Jiangxi, 2009–2010

	Original data for 2010 and 2009			Change in ranking		
Third-Class Indicator	Unit	2010	2009	2010	2009	Difference
Recycling rate of industrial water	%	86.76	64.91	12	20	8
Water resources per capita	m^3 per capita	5,116.68	2,642.46	4	7	3
Ammonia/nitrogen emissions per capita	Ton per capita	0.0008	0.0008	10	7	−3
Nitrogen oxide emissions per capita from road transport	Ton per 10,000 persons	20.83	18.98	18	15	−3
Ratio of environmental spending to government expenditure	%	2.56	2.76	24	21	−3
Ratio of the investment in pollution control to GDP	%	1.66	1.07	9	23	14
Government spending per capita on rural water supply system and toilet improvement	Yuan per capita	29.42	26.50	25	28	3
Area of green land per capita in urban areas	Hectare per capita	0.00	0.00	24	18	−6
Coverage of water supply in urban areas	%	97.43	98.00	16	12	−4
Harmless treatment rate of urban household waste	%	85.89	84.40	13	9	−4
Public buses per 10,000 urban residents		7.61	9.22	26	21	−5
Ratio of the rural residents benefiting from water supply system improvement to the total rural population	%	99.64	97.47	4	12	8
Industrial wastewater COD removal rate	%	54.63	62.91	26	21	−5
Industrial wastewater ammonia/nitrogen removal rate	%	57.19	57.73	19	16	−3
Number of environmental emergencies		9	6	19	14	−5

Note: A positive value in "Difference" means a rise in ranking

Green development checkup-Shandong

No.	Indicator	Unit	Attribute	2010 average of 30 provinces	2010 figure	2009 figure	2010 ranking	2009 ranking	Change in ranking	Source of 2010 data	Chernoff face
1	GDP per capita	Yuan per capita	Positive	33,964.12	41,106	35,894	9	8	−1	China Statistics	
2	Energy consumption per unit of GDP	Ton coal equivalent per 10,000 yuan	Negative	1.29	1.03	1.07	11	12	1	China Statistics	
3	Ratio of non-fossil energy consumption to total energy consumption		Positive	NA	NA	NA	NA	NA			
4	CO_2 emissions per unit of GDP		Negative	NA	NA	NA	NA	NA			
5	SO_2 emissions per unit of GDP	Ton per 10,000 yuan	Negative	0.0088	0.0045	0.0053	9	9	0	China Statistics	
6	COD emissions per unit of GDP	Ton per 10,000 yuan	Negative	0.0045	0.0018	0.0021	4	4	0	China Statistics	
7	Nitrogen oxide emissions per unit of GDP	Ton per 10,000 yuan	Negative	0.0068	0.0041	0.0046	10	14	4	Environmental Annual Report; China Statistics	
8	Ammonia/nitrogen emissions per unit of GDP	Ton per 10,000 yuan	Negative	0.0004	0.0002	0.0002	5	6	1	Environmental Annual Report; China Statistics	
9	Electricity consumption per capita in urban areas	kWh per capita	Negative	295.08	168.44	363.85	14	21	7	City	
10	Labor productivity of the primary sector	10,000 yuan per capita	Positive	1.61	1.79	1.62	13	13	0	China Statistics	

(continued)

(continued)

No.	Indicator	Unit	Attribute	2010 average of 30 provinces	2010 figure	2009 figure	2010 ranking	2009 ranking	Change in ranking	Source of 2010 data	Chernoff face
11	Land productivity	100 million yuan per 1,000 hectares	Positive	0.26	0.34	0.30	8	8	0	China Statistics	
12	Proportion of water-saving irrigated area in effectively irrigated area		Positive	0.49	0.46	0.44	17	17	0	Water Conservancy; China Statistics	
13	Proportion of water-saving irrigated area in effectively irrigated area	%	Positive	53.55	65.94	65.16	11	11	0	China Statistics	
14	Labor productivity of the secondary sector	10,000 yuan per capita	Positive	12.13	11.86	11.01	10	8	−2	China Statistics	
15	Water consumption per unit of value added created by industrial enterprises	m^3/yuan	Negative	0.0100	0.0014	0.0015	2	2	0	China Statistics	
16	Energy consumption per unit of value added created by industrial enterprises above designated size (no data)		Negative	NA	NA	NA	NA	NA			
17	Utilization rate of industrial solid waste	%	Positive	69.80	94.70	94.80	4	4	0	Environmental Yearbook	
18	Recycling rate of industrial water	%	Positive	72.90	92.10	91.45	6	7	1	Environmental Yearbook	
19	Ratio of the output of six energy-intensive industries to gross industrial output	%	Negative	39.65	31.92	31.25	10	10	0	Industrial Economy	
20	Labor productivity of the tertiary sector	10,000 yuan per capita	Positive	6.96	8.14	6.98	8	9	1	China Statistics	

21	Proportion of the value added of the tertiary sector in GDP	%	Positive	39.97	36.60	34.70	18	28	10	China Statistics	☺
22	Proportion of tertiary sector employees in the total employed population	%	Positive	36.67	32.02	31.45	23	24	1	China Statistics	☺
23	Water resources per capita	m^3 per capita	Positive	2,419.38	324.40	301.75	24	24	0	China Statistics	
24	Forest area per capita	Hectare per capita	Positive	0.19	0.03	0.03	26	27	1	China Statistics	☺
25	Forest coverage rate	%	Positive	30.63	16.72	16.72	22	22	0	China Statistics	
26	Proportion of the area of natural reserves in the total area of a region	%	Positive	8.60	4.92	4.89	24	23	−1	China Statistics	☹
27	Proportion of the area of wetlands in the total area of a region	%	Positive	7.01	11.72	11.72	4	4	0	China Statistics	
28	Growing stock per capita	m^3 per capita	Positive	10.70	0.90	0.91	26	26	0	China Statistics	
29	CO_2 emissions per unit of land area		Negative	NA	NA	NA	NA	NA			
30	CO_2 emissions per capita		Negative	NA	NA	NA	NA	NA			
31	SO_2 emissions per unit of land area	Ton per km^2	Negative	6.3677	9.7871	10.1212	27	28	1	China Statistics; Deserts	☺
32	SO_2 emissions per capita	Ton per capita	Negative	0.0191	0.0161	0.0168	16	16	0	China Statistics	
33	COD emissions per unit of land area	Ton per km^2	Negative	3.7722	3.9493	4.1177	24	24	0	China Statistics; Deserts	
34	COD emissions per capita	Ton per capita	Negative	0.0101	0.0065	0.0069	5	6	1	China Statistics	☺
35	Nitrogen oxide emissions per unit of land area	Ton per km^2	Negative	6.4473	8.9609	8.7955	25	26	1	China Statistics; Deserts; Environmental Annual Report	☺

(continued)

(continued)

No.	Indicator	Unit	Attribute	2010 average of 30 provinces	2010 figure	2009 figure	2010 ranking	2009 ranking	Change in ranking	Source of 2010 data	Chernoff face
36	Nitrogen oxide emissions per capita	Ton per capita	Negative	0.0165	0.0148	0.0146	18	19	1	Environmental Annual Report; China Statistics	
37	Ammonia/nitrogen emissions per unit of land area	Ton per km^2	Negative	0.4164	0.4200	0.4264	24	24	0	China Statistics; Deserts; Environmental Annual Report	
38	Ammonia/nitrogen emissions per capita	Ton per capita	Negative	0.0010	0.0007	0.0007	4	3	−1	Environmental Annual Report; China Statistics	
39	Consumption of chemical fertilizers per unit of cultivated land area	10,000 ton per 1,000 hectares	Negative	0.05	0.06	0.06	24	24	0	China Statistics; China Statistics	
40	Consumption of pesticides per unit of cultivated land area	Ton per 1,000 hectares	Negative	17.68	21.95	22.49	22	22	0	Environmental Yearbook; China Statistics	
41	Nitrogen oxide emissions per capita from road transport	Ton per 10,000 persons	Negative	24.07	20.35	20.84	16	18	2	Environmental Annual Report; China Statistics	
42	Ratio of environmental spending to government expenditure	%	Positive	3.35	2.72	2.33	20	24	4	China Statistics	
43	Ratio of the investment in pollution control to GDP	%	Positive	1.40	1.24	1.52	18	11	−7	Environmental Yearbook; China Statistics	

44	Government spending per capita on rural water supply system and toilet improvement	Yuan per capita	Positive	57.01	21.59	32.09	28	24	−4	Environmental Yearbook	☹
45	Investment in converting cultivated land into forests and grassland per unit of cultivated land area	10,000 yuan per 1,000 hectares	Positive	29.81	0.00	0.00	25	23	−2	Environmental Yearbook; China Statistics	☹
46	Ratio of the spending on science, education, culture, and public health to government expenditure	%	Positive	26.10	28.46	28.64	8	8	0	China Statistics	
47	Area of green land per capita in urban areas	Hectare per capita	Positive	0.00	0.00	0.00	13	11	−2	City; China Statistics	☹
48	Coverage of water supply in urban areas	%	Positive	96.08	99.57	99.47	7	7	0	China Statistics	
49	Treatment rate of urban wastewater	%	Positive	79.18	91.10	88.10	4	3	−1	Environmental Yearbook	☹
50	Harmless treatment rate of urban household waste	%	Positive	78.47	91.90	90.54	8	7	−1	China Statistics	☹
51	Public buses per 10,000 urban residents		Positive	9.86	10.18	10.34	10	14	4	China Statistics	☺
52	Length of public transport routes per capita in urban areas	km per capita	Positive	0.0006	0.0004	0.0004	14	8	−6	China Statistics; City	☹
53	Ratio of the rural residents benefiting from water supply system improvement to the total rural population	%	Positive	94.44	99.61	99.60	5	4	−1	Environmental Yearbook	☹
54	Green coverage of urban built-up areas	%	Positive	37.75	41.47	41.18	6	5	−1	China Statistics	☹
55	Newly-added afforestation area of the year per capita	Hectare per 10,000 persons	Positive	59.50	21.53	19.29	21	21	0	China Statistics	

(continued)

(continued)

No.	Indicator	Unit	Attribute	2010 average of 30 provinces	2010 figure	2009 figure	2010 ranking	2009 ranking	Change in ranking	Source of 2010 data	Chernoff face
56	Industrial SO_2 removal rate	%	Positive	59.83	69.51	66.67	8	7	−1	China Statistics	
57	Industrial wastewater COD removal rate	%	Positive	70.84	88.70	89.48	4	2	−2	Environmental Annual Report; China Statistics	
58	Industrial nitrogen oxide removal rate	%	Positive	4.07	0.11	0.21	26	26	0	Environmental Annual Report	
59	Industrial wastewater ammonia/nitrogen removal rate	%	Positive	62.87	91.93	90.00	1	2	1	Environmental Annual Report; China Statistics	
60	Number of environmental emergencies		Negative	14.00	0	19	1	24	23	China Statistics	

Note:
China Statistics: *China Statistical Yearbook 2011*
Environmental Yearbook: *China Environmental Statistical Yearbook 2011*
Environmental Annual Report: *China Environment Annual Report 2010*
City: *China City Statistical Yearbook 2011*
Water Conservancy: *China Water Conservancy Statistical Yearbook 2011*
Industrial Economy: *China Industrial Economic Statistical Yearbook 2011*
Deserts: *Deserts in China and Desertification Control*

5.15 Brief Analysis of Green Development in Shandong

Shandong ranked 10th among the 30 participating provinces by GDI according to 2010 data, two places higher over 2009 (Shandong ranked 12th in 2009). Following is a brief analysis of its score by each indicator and their changes from 2009 to 2010.

5.15.1 Shandong's 2010 Scores by GDI

Shandong scored 0.086 in 2010. From the three First-Class Indicators including GDEG, CCPNRE, and SDGP as shown in Fig. 5.29, Shandong obviously outshined other provinces in terms of GDEG and SDGP, yet underperformed compared with the national average in CCPNRE (Note: the national average value of each indicator is 0).

According to Fig. 5.30, Shandong surpassed the national average in 5 of Second-Class Indicators in 2010, which are GGEI, PII, SII, II and EMI, yet ranked lower than the national average in TII, RAECI, EPCCI and GII.

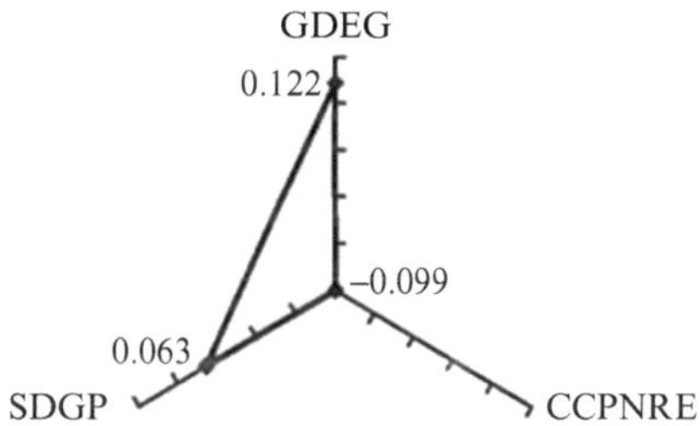

Fig. 5.29 Scores of Shandong by First-Class Indicators

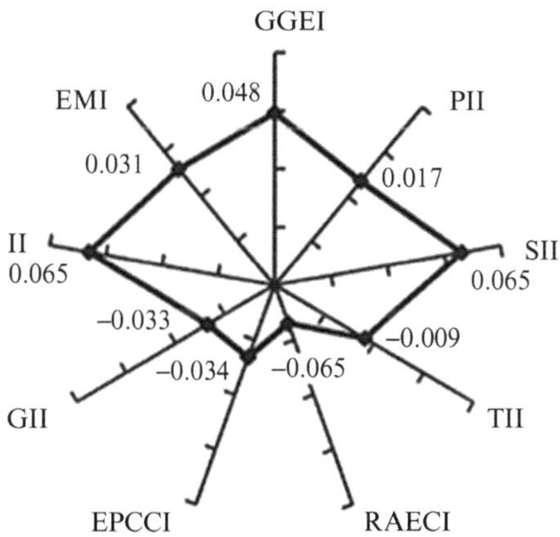

Fig. 5.30 Scores of Shandong by Second-Class Indicators

Table 5.29 Changes in Shandong's rankings by First-Class and Second-Class Indicators, 2009–2010

Indicator	2010	2009	Difference	Indicator	2010	2009	Difference
GDI	10	12	2				
GDEG	6	7	1	RAECI	25	24	−1
GGEI	7	9	2	EPCCI	18	19	1
PII	10	9	−1	SDGP	6	5	−1
SII	2	2	0	GII	24	22	−2
TII	16	20	4	II	6	5	−1
CCPNRE	24	22	−2	EMI	7	7	0

Note: A positive value in "Difference" means a rise in ranking

5.15.2 Changes in Shandong's GDI Rankings 2009–2010

According to Table 5.29, in First-Class Indicators ranking, Shandong rose by 1 place in GDEG, and fell by 2 places and 1 place in CCPNRE and SDGP respectively. In Second-Class Indicators ranking, it dropped by 1 place in PII, RAECI, and II, and 2 places in GII, and rose by 2 places, 4 places, and 1 place respectively in GII, TII, and EPCCI. It remained the same in the rankings by other indicators in 2009.

To further explain the causes of the changes in the rankings by First- and Second-Class Indicators, we put the Third-Class Indicators where a change of more than 3 places occurred from 2009 to 2010 in Table 5.30. Compared with those in 2009, Shandong dropped by 7 provinces in Ratio of the investment in pollution control to GDP, 6 in Length of public transport routes per capita in urban areas and 4 in Government spending per capita on rural water supply system and toilet improvement. It rose by 4 provinces Nitrogen oxide emissions per unit of GDP, Ratio of environmental spending to government expenditure and Public buses per 10,000 urban residents, 7 in Electricity consumption per capita in urban areas, 10 in Proportion of the value added of the tertiary sector in GDP and 23 in Number of environmental emergencies.

Table 5.30 Third-Class Indicators where changes over 3 places by Shandong, 2009–2010

	Original data for 2010 and 2009			Change in ranking		
Third-Class Indicator	Unit	2010	2009	2010	2009	Difference
Nitrogen oxide emissions per unit of GDP	Ton per 10,000 yuan	0.0041	0.0046	10	14	4
Electricity consumption per capita in urban areas	kWh per capita	168.44	363.85	14	21	7
Proportion of the value added of the tertiary sector in GDP	%	36.60	34.70	18	28	10
Ratio of environmental spending to government expenditure	%	2.72	2.33	20	24	4
Ratio of the investment in pollution control to GDP	%	1.24	1.52	18	11	−7
Government spending per capita on rural water supply system and toilet improvement	Yuan per capita	21.59	32.09	28	24	−4
Public buses per 10,000 urban residents		10.18	10.34	10	14	4
Length of public transport routes per capita in urban areas	km per capita	0.0004	0.0004	14	8	−6
Number of environmental emergencies		0	19	1	24	23

Note: A positive value in "Difference" means a rise in ranking

Green development checkup-Henan

No.	Indicator	Unit	Attribute	2010 average of 30 provinces	2010 figure	2009 figure	2010 ranking	2009 ranking	Change in ranking	Source of 2010 data	Chernoff face
1	GDP per capita	Yuan per capita	Positive	33,964.12	24,446	20,597	21	19	−2	China Statistics	☹
2	Energy consumption per unit of GDP	Ton coal equivalent per 10,000 yuan	Negative	1.29	1.12	1.16	13	13	0	China Statistics	
3	Ratio of non-fossil energy consumption to total energy consumption		Positive	NA	NA	NA	NA	NA			
4	CO_2 emissions per unit of GDP		Negative	NA	NA	NA	NA	NA			
5	SO_2 emissions per unit of GDP	Ton per 10,000 yuan	Negative	0.0088	0.0069	0.0079	16	16	0	China Statistics	
6	COD emissions per unit of GDP	Ton per 10,000 yuan	Negative	0.0045	0.0032	0.0036	11	9	−2	China Statistics	☹
7	Nitrogen oxide emissions per unit of GDP	Ton per 10,000 yuan	Negative	0.0068	0.0062	0.0069	19	21	2	Environmental Annual Report; China Statistics	☺
8	Ammonia/nitrogen emissions per unit of GDP	Ton per 10,000 yuan	Negative	0.0004	0.0004	0.0004	13	11	−2	Environmental Annual Report; China Statistics	☹
9	Electricity consumption per capita in urban areas	kWh per capita	Negative	295.08	98.12	262.38	3	7	4	City	☺
10	Labor productivity of the primary sector	10,000 yuan per capita	Positive	1.61	1.19	0.99	20	20	0	China Statistics	

11	Land productivity	100 million yuan per 1,000 hectares	Positive	0.26	0.25	0.20	15	13	−2	China Statistics	☹
12	Proportion of water-saving irrigated area in effectively irrigated area		Positive	0.49	0.30	0.29	23	23	0	Water Conservancy; China Statistics	
13	Proportion of water-saving irrigated area in effectively irrigated area	%	Positive	53.55	64.10	63.50	13	13	0	China Statistics	
14	Labor productivity of the secondary sector	10,000 yuan per capita	Positive	12.13	7.72	6.80	25	24	−1	China Statistics	☹
15	Water consumption per unit of value added created by industrial enterprises	m^3/yuan	Negative	0.0100	0.0054	0.0054	10	10	0	China Statistics	
16	Energy consumption per unit of value added created by industrial enterprises above designated size (no data)		Negative	NA	NA	NA	NA	NA			
17	Utilization rate of industrial solid waste	%	Positive	69.80	77.10	73.70	13	13	0	Environmental Yearbook	
18	Recycling rate of industrial water	%	Positive	72.90	87.09	85.99	10	11	1	Environmental Yearbook	☺
19	Ratio of the output of six energy-intensive industries to gross industrial output	%	Negative	39.65	38.44	38.45	17	17	0	Industrial Economy	
20	Labor productivity of the tertiary sector	10,000 yuan per capita	Positive	6.96	4.28	3.89	23	23	0	China Statistics	
21	Proportion of the value added of the tertiary sector in GDP	%	Positive	39.97	28.60	29.30	30	30	0	China Statistics	

(continued)

(continued)

No.	Indicator	Unit	Attribute	2010 average of 30 provinces	2010 figure	2009 figure	2010 ranking	2009 ranking	Change in ranking	Source of 2010 data	Chernoff face
22	Proportion of tertiary sector employees in the total employed population	%	Positive	36.67	26.09	25.37	29	29	0	China Statistics	
23	Water resources per capita	m^3 per capita	Positive	2,419.38	566.25	347.61	22	23	1	China Statistics	☺
24	Forest area per capita	Hectare per capita	Positive	0.19	0.04	0.04	25	25	0	China Statistics	
25	Forest coverage rate	%	Positive	30.63	20.16	20.16	20	20	0	China Statistics	
26	Proportion of the area of natural reserves in the total area of a region	%	Positive	8.60	4.40	4.41	25	25	0	China Statistics	
27	Proportion of the area of wetlands in the total area of a region	%	Positive	7.01	3.74	3.74	18	18	0	China Statistics	
28	Growing stock per capita	m^3 per capita	Positive	10.70	1.92	1.90	23	23	0	China Statistics	
29	CO_2 emissions per unit of land area		Negative	NA	NA	NA	NA	NA			
30	CO_2 emissions per capita		Negative	NA	NA	NA	NA	NA			
31	SO_2 emissions per unit of land area	Ton per km^2	Negative	6.3677	8.0870	8.1855	25	25	0	China Statistics; Deserts	
32	SO_2 emissions per capita	Ton per capita	Negative	0.0191	0.0142	0.0143	15	15	0	China Statistics	
33	COD emissions per unit of land area	Ton per km^2	Negative	3.7722	3.7436	3.7830	21	20	−1	China Statistics; Deserts	☹
34	COD emissions per capita	Ton per capita	Negative	0.0101	0.0066	0.0066	6	5	−1	China Statistics	☹

35	Nitrogen oxide emissions per unit of land area	Ton per km^2	Negative	6.4473	7.3217	7.2069	23	24	1	China Statistics; Deserts; Environmental Annual Report	☺
36	Nitrogen oxide emissions per capita	Ton per capita	Negative	0.0165	0.0128	0.0126	14	15	1	Environmental Annual Report; China Statistics	☺
37	Ammonia/nitrogen emissions per unit of land area	Ton per km^2	Negative	0.4164	0.4349	0.4531	25	25	0	China Statistics; Deserts; Environmental Annual Report	
38	Ammonia/nitrogen emissions per capita	Ton per capita	Negative	0.0010	0.0008	0.0008	8	9	1	Environmental Annual Report; China Statistics	☺
39	Consumption of chemical fertilizers per unit of cultivated land area	10,000 ton per 1,000 hectares	Negative	0.05	0.08	0.08	28	28	0	China Statistics; China Statistics	
40	Consumption of pesticides per unit of cultivated land area	Ton per 1,000 hectares	Negative	17.68	15.75	15.32	17	18	1	Environmental Yearbook; China Statistics	☺
41	Nitrogen oxide emissions per capita from road transport	Ton per 10,000 persons	Negative	24.07	15.31	19.88	10	17	7	Environmental Annual Report; China Statistics	☺
42	Ratio of environmental spending to government expenditure	%	Positive	3.35	2.82	3.20	19	16	−3	China Statistics	☹
43	Ratio of the investment in pollution control to GDP	%	Positive	1.40	0.57	0.70	29	28	−1	Environmental Yearbook; China Statistics	☹
44	Government spending per capita on rural water supply system and toilet improvement	Yuan per capita	Positive	57.01	27.98	28.50	26	25	−1	Environmental Yearbook	☹

(continued)

(continued)

No.	Indicator	Unit	Attribute	2010 average of 30 provinces	2010 figure	2009 figure	2010 ranking	2009 ranking	Change in ranking	Source of 2010 data	Chernoff face
45	Investment in converting cultivated land into forests and grassland per unit of cultivated land area	10,000 yuan per 1,000 hectares	Positive	29.81	10.25	11.43	22	22	0	Environmental Yearbook; China Statistics	
46	Ratio of the spending on science, education, culture, and public health to government expenditure	%	Positive	26.10	28.67	29.03	7	5	−2	China Statistics	☹
47	Area of green land per capita in urban areas	Hectare per capita	Positive	0.00	0.00	0.00	30	22	−8	City; China Statistics	☹
48	Coverage of water supply in urban areas	%	Positive	96.08	91.03	88.34	25	28	3	China Statistics	☺
49	Treatment rate of urban wastewater	%	Positive	79.18	87.60	83.90	6	7	1	Environmental Yearbook	☺
50	Harmless treatment rate of urban household waste	%	Positive	78.47	82.59	75.33	15	14	−1	China Statistics	☹
51	Public buses per 10,000 urban residents		Positive	9.86	7.58	8.15	27	26	−1	China Statistics	☹
52	Length of public transport routes per capita in urban areas	km per capita	Positive	0.0006	0.0002	0.0003	29	21	−8	China Statistics; City	☹
53	Ratio of the rural residents benefiting from water supply system improvement to the total rural population	%	Positive	94.44	91.19	95.41	23	19	−4	Environmental Yearbook	☹
54	Green coverage of urban built-up areas	%	Positive	37.75	36.56	36.29	21	21	0	China Statistics	

55	Newly-added afforestation area of the year per capita	Hectare per 10,000 persons	Positive	59.50	24.53	44.00	20	13	−7	China Statistics	☹
56	Industrial SO_2 removal rate	%	Positive	59.83	55.21	54.60	23	19	−4	China Statistics	☹
57	Industrial wastewater COD removal rate	%	Positive	70.84	78.02	77.29	11	11	0	Environmental Annual Report; China Statistics	
58	Industrial nitrogen oxide removal rate	%	Positive	4.07	0.42	0.22	23	25	2	Environmental Annual Report	☺
59	Industrial wastewater ammonia/nitrogen removal rate	%	Positive	62.87	53.36	52.08	23	19	−4	Environmental Annual Report; China Statistics	☹
60	Number of environmental emergencies		Negative	14.00	18	10	24	18	−6	China Statistics	☹

Note:
China Statistics: *China Statistical Yearbook 2011*
Environmental Yearbook: *China Environmental Statistical Yearbook 2011*
Environmental Annual Report: *China Environment Annual Report 2010*
City: *China City Statistical Yearbook 2011*
Water Conservancy: *China Water Conservancy Statistical Yearbook 2011*
Industrial Economy: *China Industrial Economic Statistical Yearbook 2011*
Deserts: *Deserts in China and Desertification Control*

5.16 Brief Analysis of Green Development in Henan

Henan ranked 30th among the 30 participating provinces by GDI according to 2010 data, as it did in 2009 (Henan ranked 30th in 2009). Following is a brief analysis of its score by each indicator and their changes from 2009 to 2010.

5.16.1 Henan's 2010 Scores by GDI

Henan scored 0.272 in 2010. From the three First-Class Indicators including GDEG, CCPNRE, and SDGP as shown in Fig. 5.31, Henan underperformed compared with the national average in all these indicators (Note: the national average value of each indicator is 0).

According to Fig. 5.32, Henan surpassed the national average in 2 of Second-Class Indicators in 2010, which are GGEI and SII, yet ranked lower than the national average in PII, TII, RAECI, EPCCI, GII, II and EMI.

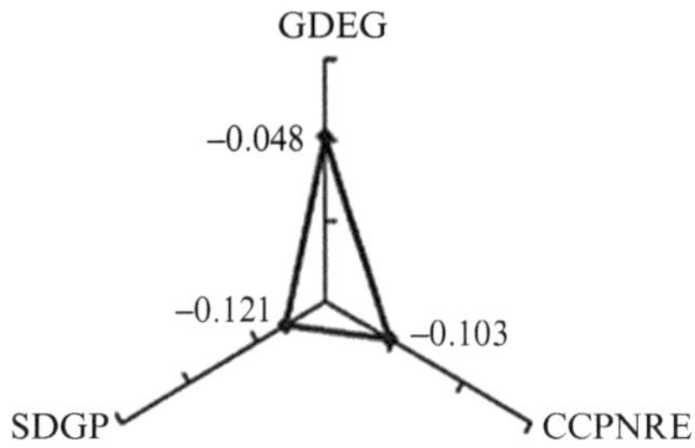

Fig. 5.31 Scores of Henan by First-Class Indicators

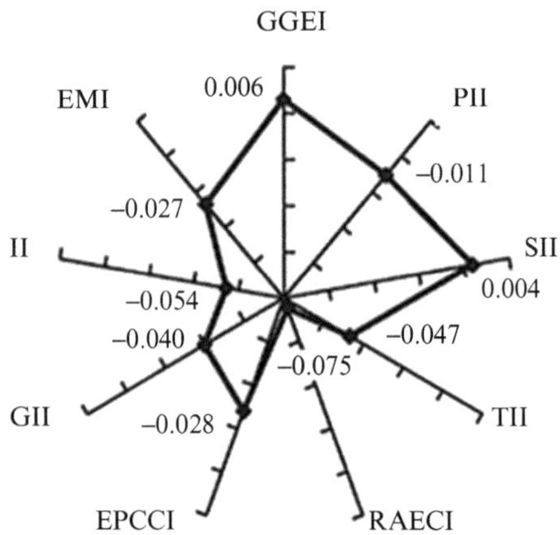

Fig. 5.32 Scores of Henan by Second-Class Indicators

Table 5.31 Changes in Henan's rankings by First-Class and Second-Class Indicators, 2009–2010

Indicator	2010	2009	Difference	Indicator	2010	2009	Difference
GDI	30	30	0				
GDEG	17	20	3	RAECI	30	30	0
GGEI	11	12	1	EPCCI	17	18	1
PII	15	15	0	SDGP	27	25	−2
SII	15	15	0	GII	28	25	−3
TII	30	30	0	II	25	21	−4
CCPNRE	25	26	1	EMI	24	19	−5

Note: A positive value in "Difference" means a rise in ranking

5.16.2 Changes in Henan's GDI Rankings 2009–2010

According to Table 5.31, in First-Class Indicators ranking, it rose by 3 places in GDEG, 1 in CCPNRE and fell by 2 places in SDGP. In Second-Class Indicators ranking, Henan fell by 3 places in GII, 4 in II and 5 in EMI. It rose by 1 place in GGEI and EPCCI. It remained the same in the rankings by other indicators in 2009.

To further explain the causes of the changes in the rankings by First- and Second-Class Indicators, we put the Third-Class Indicators where a change of more than 3 places occurred from 2009 to 2010 in Table 5.32. Compared with those in 2009, Henan dropped by 8 places in Area of green land per capita in urban areas and Length of public transport routes per capita in urban areas, 7 in Newly-added afforestation area of the year per capita, 6 in Number of environmental emergencies, 4 in Ratio of the rural residents benefiting from water supply system improvement to the total rural population, Industrial SO_2 removal rate and Industrial wastewater ammonia/nitrogen removal rate, 3 in Ratio of environmental spending to government expenditure. It rose by 3 places in Coverage of water supply in urban areas, 4 in Electricity consumption per capita in urban areas, and 7 in Nitrogen oxide emissions per capita from road transport.

Table 5.32 Third-Class Indicators where changes over 3 places by Henan, 2009–2010

	Original data for 2010 and 2009			Change in ranking		
Third-Class Indicator	Unit	2010	2009	2010	2009	Difference
Electricity consumption per capita in urban areas	kWh per capita	98.12	262.38	3	7	4
Nitrogen oxide emissions per capita from road transport	Ton per 10,000 persons	15.31	19.88	10	17	7
Ratio of environmental spending to government expenditure	%	2.82	3.20	19	16	−3
Area of green land per capita in urban areas	Hectare per capita	0.00	0.00	30	22	−8
Coverage of water supply in urban areas	%	91.03	88.34	25	28	3
Length of public transport routes per capita in urban areas	km per capita	0.0002	0.0003	29	21	−8
Ratio of the rural residents benefiting from water supply system improvement to the total rural population	%	91.19	95.41	23	19	−4
Newly-added afforestation area of the year per capita	Hectare per 10,000 persons	24.53	44.00	20	13	−7
Industrial SO_2 removal rate	%	55.21	54.60	23	19	−4
Industrial wastewater ammonia/nitrogen removal rate	%	53.36	52.08	23	19	−4
Number of environmental emergencies		18	10	24	18	−6

Note: A positive value in “Difference” means a rise in ranking

Green development checkup-Hubei

No.	Indicator	Unit	Attribute	2010 average of 30 provinces	2010 figure	2009 figure	2010 ranking	2009 ranking	Change in ranking	Source of 2010 data	Chernoff face
1	GDP per capita	Yuan per capita	Positive	33,964.12	27,906	22,677	13	14	1	China Statistics	
2	Energy consumption per unitof GDP	Ton coal equivalent per 10,000 yuan	Negative	1.29	1.18	1.23	19	19	0	China Statistics	
3	Ratio of non-fossil energy consumption to total energy consumption		Positive	NA	NA	NA	NA	NA			
4	CO_2 emissions per unit of GDP		Negative	NA	NA	NA	NA	NA			
5	SO_2 emissions per unit of GDP	Ton per 10,000 yuan	Negative	0.0088	0.0050	0.0059	11	12	1	China Statistics	
6	COD emissions per unit of GDP	Ton per 10,000 yuan	Negative	0.0045	0.0045	0.0052	17	17	0	China Statistics	
7	Nitrogen oxide emissions per unit of GDP	Ton per 10,000 yuan	Negative	0.0068	0.0044	0.0046	12	13	1	Environmental Annual Report; China Statistics	

(continued)

(continued)

No.	Indicator	Unit	Attribute	2010 average of 30 provinces	2010 figure	2009 figure	2010 ranking	2009 ranking	Change in ranking	Source of 2010 data	Chernoff face
8	Ammonia/nitrogen emissions per unit of GDP	Ton per 10,000 yuan	Negative	0.0004	0.0005	0.0006	23	23	0	Environmental Annual Report; China Statistics	
9	Electricity consumption per capita in urban areas	kWh per capita	Negative	295.08	186.68	347.11	16	19	3	City	☺
10	Labor productivity of the primary sector	10,000 yuan per capita	Positive	1.61	2.25	1.79	6	9	3	China Statistics	☺
11	Land productivity	100 million yuan per 1,000 hectares	Positive	0.26	0.24	0.20	16	12	−4	China Statistics	☹
12	Proportion of water-saving irrigated area in effectively irrigated area		Positive	0.49	0.17	0.16	26	26	0	Water Conservancy; China Statistics	
13	Proportion of water-saving irrigated area in effectively irrigated area	%	Positive	53.55	51.02	50.39	15	15	0	China Statistics	
14	Labor productivity of the secondary sector	10,000 yuan per capita	Positive	12.13	9.02	7.94	19	17	−2	China Statistics	☹
15	Water consumption per unit of value added created by industrial enterprises	m^3/yuan	Negative	0.0100	0.0221	0.0194	29	28	−1	China Statistics	☹

16	Energy consumption per unit of value added created by industrial enterprises above designated size (no data)		Negative	NA	NA	NA	NA	NA			
17	Utilization rate of industrial solid waste	%	Positive	69.80	80.50	74.80	11	12	1	Environmental Yearbook	☺
18	Recycling rate of industrial water	%	Positive	72.90	82.57	82.81	15	12	−3	Environmental Yearbook	☹
19	Ratio of the output of six energy-intensive industries to gross industrial output	%	Negative	39.65	36.04	36.96	15	15	0	Industrial Economy	
20	Labor productivity of the tertiary sector	10,000 yuan per capita	Positive	6.96	4.83	4.32	20	20	0	China Statistics	
21	Proportion of the value added of the tertiary sector in GDP	%	Positive	39.97	37.90	39.60	13	13	0	China Statistics	
22	Proportion of tertiary sector employees in the total employed population	%	Positive	36.67	41.33	40.33	5	5	0	China Statistics	
23	Water resources per capita	m^3 per capita	Positive	2,419.38	2,216.51	1,443.94	14	16	2	China Statistics	☺
24	Forest area per capita	Hectare per capita	Positive	0.19	0.10	0.10	18	18	0	China Statistics	
25	Forest coverage rate	%	Positive	30.63	31.14	31.14	17	17	0	China Statistics	
26	Proportion of the area of natural reserves in the total area of a region	%	Positive	8.60	5.16	4.68	23	24	1	China Statistics	☺

(continued)

(continued)

No.	Indicator	Unit	Attribute	2010 average of 30 provinces	2010 figure	2009 figure	2010 ranking	2009 ranking	Change in ranking	Source of 2010 data	Chernoff face
27	Proportion of the area of wetlands in the total area of a region	%	Positive	7.01	4.99	4.99	15	15	0	China Statistics	
28	Growing stock per capita	m^3 per capita	Positive	10.70	4.04	4.04	18	18	0	China Statistics	
29	CO_2 emissions per unit of land area		Negative	NA	NA	NA	NA	NA			
30	CO_2 emissions per capita		Negative	NA	NA	NA	NA	NA			
31	SO_2 emissions per unit of land area	Ton per km^2	Negative	6.3677	3.4030	3.4632	12	12	0	China Statistics; Deserts	
32	SO_2 emissions per capita	Ton per capita	Negative	0.0191	0.0111	0.0113	6	6	0	China Statistics	
33	COD emissions per unit of land area	Ton per km^2	Negative	3.7722	3.0786	3.0970	19	19	0	China Statistics; Deserts	
34	COD emissions per capita	Ton per capita	Negative	0.0101	0.0100	0.0101	16	15	−1	China Statistics	
35	Nitrogen oxide emissions per unit of land area	Ton per km^2	Negative	6.4473	2.9964	2.7005	14	16	2	China Statistics; Deserts; Environmental Annual Report	
36	Nitrogen oxide emissions per capita	Ton per capita	Negative	0.0165	0.0097	0.0088	8	9	1	Environmental Annual Report; China Statistics	
37	Ammonia/nitrogen emissions per unit of land area	Ton per km^2	Negative	0.4164	0.3282	0.3497	20	20	0	China Statistics; Deserts; Environmental Annual Report	

38	Ammonia/nitrogen emissions per capita	Ton per capita	Negative	0.0010	0.0011	0.0011	18	20	2	Environmental Annual Report; China Statistics	☺
39	Consumption of chemical fertilizers per unit of cultivated land area	10,000 ton per 1,000 hectares	Negative	0.05	0.08	0.07	27	27	0	China Statistics; Yearbook	
40	Consumption of pesticides per unit of cultivated land area	Ton per 1,000 hectares	Negative	17.68	30.01	29.78	24	23	−1	Environmental Yearbook; China Statistics	☹
41	Nitrogen oxide emissions per capita from road transport	Ton per 10,000 persons	Negative	24.07	18.77	18.10	15	14	−1	Environmental Annual Report; China Statistics	☹
42	Ratio of environmental spending to government expenditure	%	Positive	3.35	3.85	3.55	11	13	2	China Statistics	☺
43	Ratio of the investment in pollution control to GDP	%	Positive	1.40	0.92	1.37	24	17	−7	Environmental Yearbook; China Statistics	☹
44	Government spending per capita on rural water supply system and toilet improvement	Yuan per capita	Positive	57.01	55.05	69.42	13	10	−3	Environmental Yearbook	☹
45	Investment in converting cultivated land into forests and grassland per unit of cultivated land area	10,000 yuan per 1,000 hectares	Positive	29.81	28.55	32.31	13	10	−3	Environmental Yearbook; China Statistics	☹

(continued)

(continued)

No.	Indicator	Unit	Attribute	2010 average of 30 provinces	2010 figure	2009 figure	2010 ranking	2009 ranking	Change in ranking	Source of 2010 data	Chernoff face
46	Ratio of the spending on science, education, culture, and public health to government expenditure	%	Positive	26.10	24.48	24.77	22	23	1	China Statistics	☺
47	Area of green land per capita in urban areas	Hectare per capita	Positive	0.00	0.00	0.00	20	12	−8	City; China Statistics	☹
48	Coverage of water supply in urban areas	%	Positive	96.08	97.59	97.45	14	14	0	China Statistics	
49	Treatment rate of urban wastewater	%	Positive	79.18	81.00	75.30	17	14	−3	Environmental Yearbook	☹
50	Harmless treatment rate of urban household waste	%	Positive	78.47	61.43	55.65	27	26	−1	China Statistics	☹
51	Public buses per 10,000 urban residents		Positive	9.86	9.47	11.02	18	11	−7	China Statistics	☹
52	Length of public transport routes per capita in urban areas	km per capita	Positive	0.0006	0.0003	0.0005	20	5	−15	China Statistics; City	☹
53	Ratio of the rural residents benefiting from water supply system improvement to the total rural population	%	Positive	94.44	99.17	97.15	7	14	7	Environmental Yearbook	☺

54	Green coverage of urban built-up areas	%	Positive	37.75	37.74	37.79	17	15	−2	China Statistics	☹
55	Newly-added afforestation area of the year per capita	Hectare per 10,000 persons	Positive	59.50	33.58	26.10	16	18	2	China Statistics	☺
56	Industrial SO_2 removal rate	%	Positive	59.83	67.90	62.65	10	12	2	China Statistics	☺
57	Industrial wastewater COD removal rate	%	Positive	70.84	69.63	71.28	19	16	−3	Environmental Annual Report; China Statistics	☹
58	Industrial nitrogen oxide removal rate	%	Positive	4.07	0.98	3.15	20	18	−2	Environmental Annual Report	☹
59	Industrial wastewater ammonia/nitrogen removal rate	%	Positive	62.87	45.78	47.16	26	22	−4	Environmental Annual Report; China Statistics	☹
60	Number of environmental emergencies		Negative	14.00	27	11	26	22	−4	China Statistics	☹

Note:
China Statistics: *China Statistical Yearbook 2011*
Environmental Yearbook: *China Environmental Statistical Yearbook 2011*
Environmental Annual Report: *China Environment Annual Report 2010*
City: *China City Statistical Yearbook 2011*
Water Conservancy: *China Water Conservancy Statistical Yearbook 2011*
Industrial Economy: *China Industrial Economic Statistical Yearbook 2011*
Deserts: *Deserts in China and Desertification Control*

5.17 Brief Analysis of Green Development in Hubei

Hubei ranked 24th among the 30 participating provinces by GDI according to 2010 data, two places lower over 2009 (Hubei ranked 22nd in 2009). Following is a brief analysis of its score by each indicator and their changes from 2009 to 2010.

5.17.1 *Hubei's 2010 Scores by GDI*

Hubei scored −0.173 in 2010. From the three First-Class Indicators including GDEG, CCPNRE, and SDGP as shown in Fig. 5.33, Hubei underperformed compared with the national average in all these indicators (Note: the national average value of each indicator is 0).

According to Fig. 5.34, Hubei surpassed the national average in one of Second-Class Indicators in 2010, which was SII, yet ranked lower than the national average in GGEI, PII, TII, RAECI, EPCCI, GII, II and EMI.

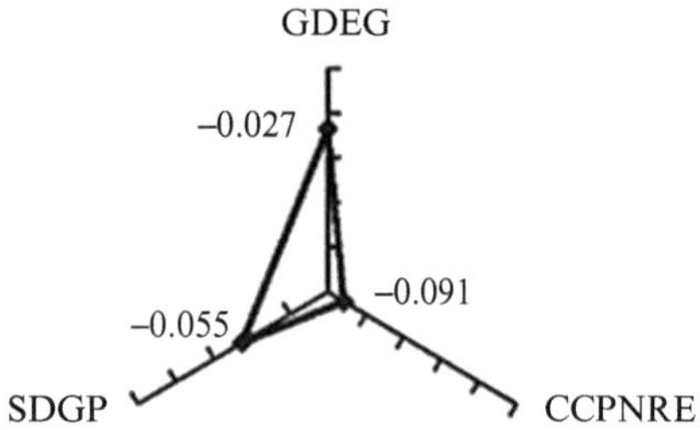

Fig. 5.33 Scores of Hubei by First-Class Indicators

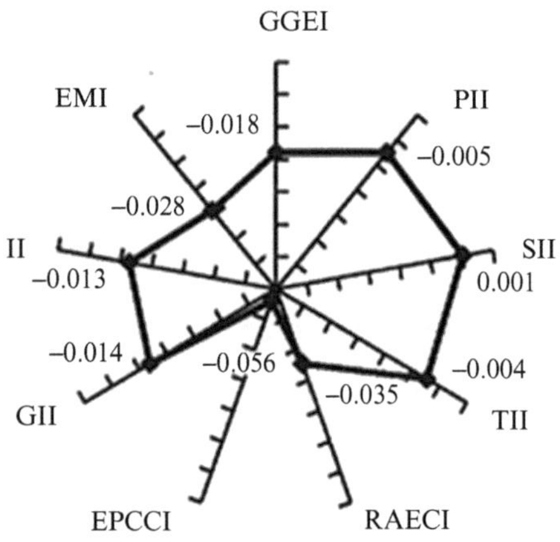

Fig. 5.34 Scores of Hubei by Second-Class Indicators

Table 5.33 Changes in Hubei's rankings by First-Class and Second-Class Indicators, 2009–2010

Indicators	2010	2009	Differences	Indicator	2010	2009	Differences
GDI	24	22	−2				
GDEG	13	15	2	RAECI	21	21	0
GGEI	18	19	1	EPCCI	21	23	2
PII	14	14	0	SDGP	22	16	−6
SII	16	17	1	GII	18	19	1
TII	13	13	0	II	18	13	−5
CCPNRE	22	20	−2	EMI	25	21	−4

Note: A positive value in "Difference" means a rise in ranking

5.17.2 Changes in Hubei's Rankings by GDI 2009–2010

According to Table 5.33, in First-Class Indicators ranking, it rose by 2 places in GDEG, and fell by 2 places in CCPNRE and 6 in Environment SDGP. In Second-Class Indicators ranking, Hubei dropped by 5 places in II, 4 in EMI and rose by 1 in GGEI and SII, 2 in EPCCI, and 1 in GII. It remained the same in the rankings by other indicators in 2009.

To further explain the causes of the changes in the rankings by First- and Second-Class Indicators, we put the Third-Class Indicators where a change of more than 3 places occurred from 2009 to 2010 in Table 5.34. Compared with those in 2009, Hubei dropped by 15 places in Length of public transport routes per capita in urban areas, 8 in Area of green land per capita in urban areas, 7 in Ratio of the investment in pollution control to GDP and Public buses per 10,000 urban residents, 4 in Land productivity, Industrial wastewater ammonia/nitrogen removal rate and Number of environmental emergencies, 3 in Recycling rate of industrial water, Government spending per capita on rural water supply system and toilet improvement, Investment in converting cultivated land into forests and grassland per unit of cultivated land area, Treatment rate of urban wastewater and Industrial wastewater COD removal rate. It rose by 3 places in Electricity consumption per capita in urban areas and Labor productivity of the primary sector, and 7 in Ratio of the rural residents benefiting from water supply system improvement to the total rural population.

Table 5.34 Third-Class Indicators where changes over 3 places occurred by Hubei, 2009–2010

	Original data for 2010 and 2009			Change in ranking		
Third-Class Indicator	Unit	2010	2009	2010	2009	Difference
Electricity consumption per capita in urban areas	kWh per capita	186.68	347.11	16	19	3
Labor productivity of the primary sector	10,000 yuan per capita	2.25	1.79	6	9	3
Land productivity	100 million yuan per 1,000 hectares	0.24	0.20	16	12	−4
Recycling rate of industrial water	%	82.57	82.81	15	12	−3
Ratio of the investment in pollution control to GDP	%	0.92	1.37	24	17	−7
Government spending per capita on rural water supply system and toilet improvement	Yuan per capita	55.05	69.42	13	10	−3
Investment in converting cultivated land into forests and grassland per unit of cultivated land area	10,000 yuan per 1,000 hectares	28.55	32.31	13	10	−3
Area of green land per capita in urban areas	Hectare per capita	0.00	0.00	20	12	−8
Treatment rate of urban wastewater	%	81.00	75.30	17	14	−3
Public buses per 10,000 urban residents		9.47	11.02	18	11	−7
Length of public transport routes per capita in urban areas	km per capita	0.0003	0.0005	20	5	−15
Ratio of the rural residents benefiting from water supply system improvement to the total rural population	%	99.17	97.15	7	14	7
Industrial wastewater COD removal rate	%	69.63	71.28	19	16	−3
Industrial wastewater ammonia/nitrogen removal rate	%	45.78	47.16	26	22	−4
Number of environmental emergencies		27	11	26	22	−4

Note: A positive value in "Difference" means a rise in ranking

Green development checkup-Hunan

No.	Indicator	Unit	Attribute	2010 average of 30 provinces	2010 figure	2009 figure	2010 ranking	2009 ranking	Change in ranking	Source of 2010 data	Chernoff face
1	GDP per capita	Yuan per capita	Positive	33,964.12	24,719	20,428	20	20	0	China Statistics	
2	Energy consumption per unit of GDP	Ton coal equivalent per 10,000 yuan	Negative	1.29	1.17	1.20	18	16	−2	China Statistics	
3	Ratio of non-fossil energy consumption to total energy consumption		Positive	NA	NA	NA	NA	NA			
4	CO_2 emissions per unit of GDP		Negative	NA	NA	NA	NA	NA			
5	SO_2 emissions per unit of GDP	Ton per 10,000 yuan	Negative	0.0088	0.0063	0.0073	14	14	0	China Statistics	
6	COD emissions per unit of GDP	Ton per 10,000 yuan	Negative	0.0045	0.0063	0.0077	26	27	1	China Statistics	
7	Nitrogen oxide emissions perunit of GDP	Ton per 10,000 yuan	Negative	0.0068	0.0032	0.0033	5	6	1	Environmental Annual Report; China Statistics	
8	Ammonia/nitrogen emissions per unit of GDP	Ton per 10,000 yuan	Negative	0.0004	0.0006	0.0008	25	27	2	Environmental Annual Report; China Statistics	
9	Electricity consumption per capita in urban areas	kWh per capita	Negative	295.08	131.14	323.37	8	16	8	City	

(continued)

(continued)

No.	Indicator	Unit	Attribute	2010 average of 30 provinces	2010 figure	2009 figure	2010 ranking	2009 ranking	Change in ranking	Source of 2010 data	Chernoff face
10	Labor productivity of the primary sector	10,000 yuan per capita	Positive	1.61	1.24	1.05	18	18	0	China Statistics	
11	Land productivity	100 million yuan per 1,000 hectares	Positive	0.26	0.25	0.20	14	14	0	China Statistics	
12	Proportion of water-saving irrigated area in effectively irrigated area		Positive	0.49	0.11	0.11	29	29	0	Water Conservancy; China Statistics	
13	Proportion of water-saving irrigated area in effectively irrigated area	%	Positive	53.55	72.28	71.80	8	9	1	China Statistics	☺
14	Labor productivity of the secondary sector	10,000 yuan per capita	Positive	12.13	8.76	7.21	20	22	2	China Statistics	☺
15	Water consumption per unit of value added created by industrial enterprises	m^3/yuan	Negative	0.0100	0.0181	0.0173	26	26	0	China Statistics	
16	Energy consumption per unit of value added created by industrial enterprises above designated size (no data)		Negative	NA	NA	NA	NA	NA			
17	Utilization rate of industrial solid waste	%	Positive	69.80	81.00	76.70	10	11	1	Environmental Yearbook	☺
18	Recycling rate of industrial water	%	Positive	72.90	42.48	30.91	27	28	1	Environmental Yearbook	☺

19	Ratio of the output of six energy-intensive industries to gross industrial output	%	Negative	39.65	37.24	37.62	16	16	0	Industrial Economy	
20	Labor productivity of the tertiary sector	10,000 yuan per capita	Positive	6.96	5.11	4.55	19	19	0	China Statistics	
21	Proportion of the value added of the tertiary sector in GDP	%	Positive	39.97	39.70	41.40	11	9	−2	China Statistics	☹
22	Proportion of tertiary sector employees in the total employed population	%	Positive	36.67	31.81	31.13	24	25	1	China Statistics	☺
23	Water resources per capita	m^3 per capita	Positive	2,419.38	2,938.66	2,190.63	9	11	2	China Statistics	☺
24	Forest area per capita	Hectare per capita	Positive	0.19	0.14	0.15	15	14	−1	China Statistics	☹
25	Forest coverage rate	%	Positive	30.63	44.76	44.76	8	8	0	China Statistics	
26	Proportion of the area of natural reserves in the total area of a region	%	Positive	8.60	5.88	5.42	19	20	1	China Statistics	☺
27	Proportion of the area of wetlands in the total area of a region	%	Positive	7.01	5.79	5.79	13	13	0	China Statistics	
28	Growing stock per capita	m^3 per capita	Positive	10.70	5.81	5.96	15	15	0	China Statistics	
29	CO_2 emissions per unit of land area		Negative	NA	NA	NA	NA	NA			
30	CO_2 emissions per capita		Negative	NA	NA	NA	NA	NA			
31	SO_2 emissions per unit of land area	Ton per km^2	Negative	6.3677	3.7824	3.8305	13	14	1	China Statistics; Deserts	☺
32	SO_2 emissions per capita	Ton per capita	Negative	0.0191	0.0124	0.0127	8	8	0	China Statistics	
33	COD emissions per unit of land area	Ton per km^2	Negative	3.7722	3.7674	4.0044	22	22	0	China Statistics; Deserts	

(continued)

(continued)

No.	Indicator	Unit	Attribute	2010 average of 30 provinces	2010 figure	2009 figure	2010 ranking	2009 ranking	Change in ranking	Source of 2010 data	Chernoff face
34	COD emissions per capita	Ton per capita	Negative	0.0101	0.0123	0.0133	24	26	2	China Statistics	
35	Nitrogen oxide emissions per unit of land area	Ton per km^2	Negative	6.4473	1.9258	1.7134	11	11	0	China Statistics; Deserts; Environmental Annual Report;	
36	Nitrogen oxide emissions per capita	Ton per capita	Negative	0.0165	0.0063	0.0057	2	3	1	Environmental Annual Report; China Statistics	
37	Ammonia/nitrogen emissions per unit of land area	Ton per km^2	Negative	0.4164	0.3540	0.3965	21	22	1	Yearbook Deserts; Environmental Annual Report;	
38	Ammonia/nitrogen emissions per capita	Ton per capita	Negative	0.0010	0.0012	0.0013	22	27	5	Environmental Annual Report; China Statistics	
39	Consumption of chemical fertilizers per unit of cultivated land area	10,000 ton per 1,000 hectares	Negative	0.05	0.06	0.06	23	23	0	Yearbook China Statistics	
40	Consumption of pesticides per unit of cultivated land area	Ton per 1,000 hectares	Negative	17.68	31.34	30.44	25	25	0	Environmental Yearbook; China Statistics	
41	Nitrogen oxide emissions per capita from road transport	Ton per 10,000 persons	Negative	24.07	9.82	9.49	5	4	−1	Environmental Annual Report; China Statistics	

42	Ratio of environmental spending to government expenditure	%	Positive	3.35	3.36	3.33	14	15	1	China Statistics	☺
43	Ratio of the investment in pollution control to GDP	%	Positive	1.40	0.66	1.32	27	19	−8	Environmental Yearbook; China Statistics	☹
44	Government spending per capita on rural water supply system and toilet improvement	Yuan per capita	Positive	57.01	27.46	36.25	27	19	−8	Environmental Yearbook	☹
45	Investment in converting cultivated land into forests and grassland per unit of cultivated land area	10,000 yuan per 1,000 hectares	Positive	29.81	46.35	46.95	8	8	0	Environmental Yearbook; China Statistics	
46	Ratio of the spending on science, education, culture, and public health to government expenditure	%	Positive	26.10	24.36	26.22	23	16	−7	China Statistics	☹
47	Area of green land per capita in urban areas	Hectare per capita	Positive	0.00	0.00	0.00	27	20	−7	City; China Statistics	☹
48	Coverage of water supply in urban areas	%	Positive	96.08	95.17	94.82	20	20	0	China Statistics	
49	Treatment rate of urban wastewater	%	Positive	79.18	75.00	59.20	21	25	4	Environmental Yearbook	☺
50	Harmless treatment rate of urban household waste	%	Positive	78.47	78.99	66.60	18	17	−1	China Statistics	☹
51	Public buses per 10,000 urban residents		Positive	9.86	10.01	10.59	11	12	1	China Statistics	☺
52	Length of public transport routes per capita in urban areas	km per capita	Positive	0.0006	0.0002	0.0002	23	26	3	China Statistics; City	☺
53	Ratio of the rural residents benefiting from water	%	Positive	94.44	94.26	92.98	20	22	2	Environmental Yearbook	☺

(continued)

(continued)

No.	Indicator	Unit	Attribute	2010 average of 30 provinces	2010 figure	2009 figure	2010 ranking	2009 ranking	Change in ranking	Source of 2010 data	Chernoff face
	supply system improvement to the total rural population										
54	Green coverage of urban built-up areas	%	Positive	37.75	36.64	36.59	20	17	−3	China Statistics	☹
55	Newly-added afforestation area of the year per capita	Hectare per 10,000 persons	Positive	59.50	32.90	19.56	17	20	3	China Statistics	☺
56	Industrial SO_2 removal rate	%	Positive	59.83	61.49	56.62	17	18	1	China Statistics	☺
57	Industrial wastewater COD removal rate	%	Positive	70.84	70.96	53.99	17	25	8	Environmental Annual Report; China Statistics	☺
58	Industrial nitrogen oxide removal rate	%	Positive	4.07	3.55	8.72	14	7	−7	Environmental Annual Report	☹
59	Industrial wastewater ammonia/nitrogen removal rate	%	Positive	62.87	46.16	39.88	25	25	0	Environmental Annual Report; China Statistics	
60	Number of environmental emergencies		Negative	14.00	1	0	6	1	−5	China Statistics	☹

Note:
China Statistics: *China Statistical Yearbook 2011*
Environmental Yearbook: *China Environmental Statistical Yearbook 2011*
Environmental Annual Report: *China Environment Annual Report 2010*
City: *China City Statistical Yearbook 2011*
Water Conservancy: *China Water Conservancy Statistical Yearbook 2011*
Industrial Economy: *China Industrial Economic Statistical Yearbook 2011*
Deserts: *Deserts in China and Desertification Control*

5.18 Brief Analysis of Green Development in Hunan

Hunan ranked 27th among the 30 participating provinces by GDI according to 2010 data, one place lower over 2009 (Hunan ranked 26th in 2009). Following is a brief analysis of its score by each indicator and their changes from 2009 to 2010.

5.18.1 Hunan's 2010 Scores by GDI

Hunan scored −0.188 in 2010. From the three First-Class Indicators including GDEG, CCPNRE, and SDGP as shown in Fig. 5.35, Hunan underperformed compared with the national average in all these indicators (Note: the national average value of each indicator is 0).

According to Fig. 5.36, Hunan ranked lower than the national average in GGEI, PII, SII, TII, RAECI, II, EPCCI, GII and EMI.

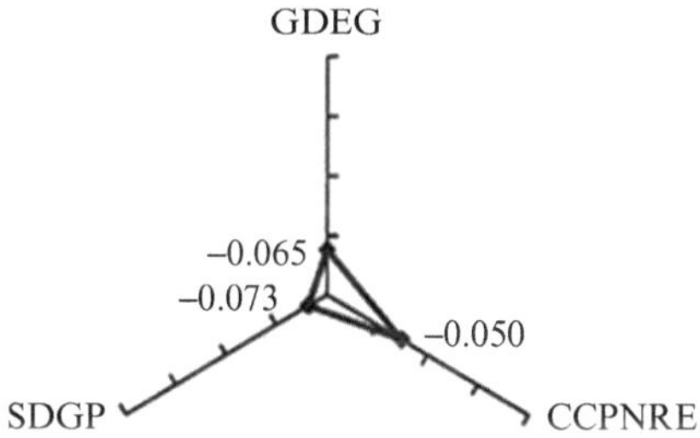

Fig. 5.35 Scores of Hunan by First-Class Indicators

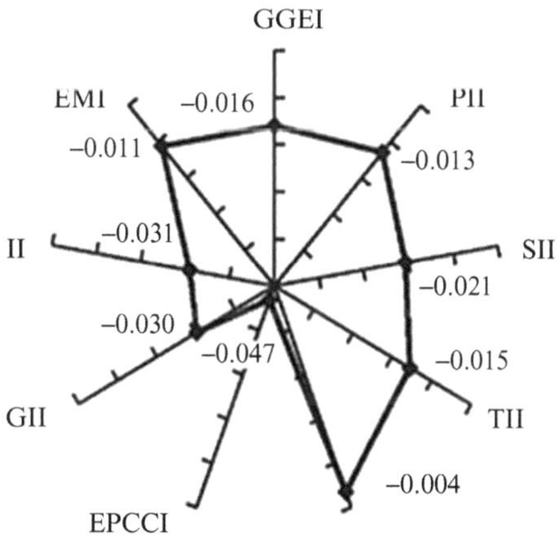

Fig. 5.36 Scores of Hunan by Second-Class Indicators

Table 5.35 Changes in Hunan's rankings by First-Class and Second-Class Indicators, 2009–2010

Indicators	2010	2009	Differences	Indicators	2010	2009	Differences
GDI	27	26	−1				
GDEG	19	18	−1	RAECI	14	13	−1
GGEI	16	16	0	EPCCI	19	17	−2
PII	17	16	−1	SDGP	24	24	0
SII	22	21	−1	GII	21	17	−4
TII	18	18	0	II	20	24	4
CCPNRE	18	15	−3	EMI	20	23	3

Note: A positive value in "Difference" means a rise in ranking

5.18.2 Changes in Hunan's Rankings by GDI 2009–2010

According to Table 5.35, in First-Class Indicators ranking, Hunan dropped by 1 place in GDEG and 3 in CCPNRE. It remained unchanged in SDGP. In Second-Class Indicators ranking, Hunan dropped by 1 place in PII, SII and RAECI, 2 in EPCCI and 4 in GII. It rose by 4 places in II and 3 in EMI. It remained the same in the rankings by other indicators in 2009.

To further explain the causes of the changes in the rankings by First- and Second-Class Indicators, we put the Third-Class Indicators where a change of more than 3 places occurred from 2009 to 2010 in Table 5.36. Compared with those in 2009, Hunan dropped by 8 places in Ratio of the investment in pollution control to GDP and Government spending per capita on rural water supply system and toilet improvement, 7 in Ratio of the spending on science, education, culture, and public health to government expenditure, Area of green land per capita in urban areas and Industrial nitrogen oxide removal rate, 5 in Number of environmental emergencies and 3 in Green coverage of urban built-up areas. It rose by 3 places in Length of public transport routes per capita in urban areas and Newly-added afforestation area of the year per capita, 4 in Treatment rate of urban wastewater, 5 in Ammonia/nitrogen emissions per capita, 8 in Electricity consumption per capita in urban areas and Industrial wastewater COD removal rate.

Table 5.36 Third-Class Indicators where changes over 3 places occurred by Hunan, 2009–2010

	Original data for 2010 and 2009			Change in ranking		
Third-Class Indicator	Unit	2010	2009	2010	2009	Difference
Electricity consumption per capita in urban areas	kWh per capita	131.14	323.37	8	16	8
Ammonia/nitrogen emissions per capita	Ton per capita	0.0012	0.0013	22	27	5
Ratio of the investment in pollution control to GDP	%	0.66	1.32	27	19	−8
Government spending per capita on rural water supply system and toilet improvement	Yuan per capita	27.46	36.25	27	19	−8
Ratio of the spending on science, education, culture, and public health to government expenditure	%	24.36	26.22	23	16	−7
Area of green land per capita in urban areas	Hectare per capita	0.00	0.00	27	20	−7
Treatment rate of urban wastewater	%	75.00	59.20	21	25	4
Length of public transport routes per capita in urban areas	km per capita	0.0002	0.0002	23	26	3
Green coverage of urban built-up areas	%	36.64	36.59	20	17	−3
Newly-added afforestation area of the year per capita	Hectare per 10,000 persons	32.90	19.56	17	20	3
Industrial wastewater COD removal rate	%	70.96	53.99	17	25	8
Industrial nitrogen oxide removal rate	%	3.55	8.72	14	7	−7
Number of environmental emergencies		1	0	6	1	−5

Note: A positive value in "Difference" means a rise in ranking

Green development checkup-Guangdong

No.	Indicator	Unit	Attribute	2010 average of 30 provinces	2010 figure	2009 figure	2010 ranking	2009 ranking	Change in ranking	Source of 2010 data	Chernoff face
1	GDP per capita	Yuan per capita	Positive	33,964.12	44,736	41,166	7	6	−1	China Statistics	☹
2	Energy consumption per unit of GDP	Ton coal equivalent per 10,000 yuan	Negative	1.29	0.66	0.68	2	2	0	China Statistics	
3	Ratio of non-fossil energy consumption to total energy consumption		Positive	NA	NA	NA	NA	NA			
4	CO_2 emissions per unit of GDP		Negative	NA	NA	NA	NA	NA			
5	SO_2 emissions per unit of GDP	Ton per 10,000 yuan	Negative	0.0088	0.0026	0.0030	4	4	0	China Statistics	
6	COD emissions per unit of GDP	Ton per 10,000 yuan	Negative	0.0045	0.0021	0.0025	6	6	0	China Statistics	
7	Nitrogen oxide emissions per unit of GDP	Ton per 10,000 yuan	Negative	0.0068	0.0032	0.0036	4	7	3	Environmental Annual Report; China Statistics	☺
8	Ammonia/nitrogen emissions per unit of GDP	Ton per 10,000 yuan	Negative	0.0004	0.0003	0.0003	8	8	0	Environmental Annual Report; China Statistics	
9	Electricity consumption per capita in urban areas	kWh per capita	Negative	295.08	517.40	673.83	26	27	1	City	☺

10	Labor productivity of the primary sector	10,000 yuan per capita	Positive	1.61	1.51	1.30	16	16	0	China Statistics	
11	Land productivity	100 million yuan per 1,000 hectares	Positive	0.26	0.39	0.35	5	6	1	China Statistics	☺
12	Proportion of water-saving irrigated area in effectively irrigated area		Positive	0.49	0.11	0.10	30	30	0	Water Conservancy; China Statistics	
13	Proportion of water-saving irrigated area in effectively irrigated area	%	Positive	53.55	66.15	66.10	10	10	0	China Statistics	
14	Labor productivity of the secondary sector	10,000 yuan per capita	Positive	12.13	11.68	10.35	12	10	−2	China Statistics	☹
15	Water consumption per unit of value added created by industrial enterprises	m^3/yuan	Negative	0.0100	0.0068	0.0075	12	14	2	China Statistics	☺
16	Energy consumption per unit of value added created by industrial enterprises above designated size (no data)		Negative	NA	NA	NA	NA	NA			
17	Utilization rate of industrial solid waste	%	Positive	69.80	90.20	90.30	6	6	0	Environmental Yearbook	
18	Recycling rate of industrial water	%	Positive	72.90	83.64	75.34	14	18	4	Environmental Yearbook	☺
19	Ratio of the output of six energy-intensive industries to gross industrial output	%	Negative	39.65	21.74	21.32	1	1	0	Industrial Economy	

(continued)

(continued)

No.	Indicator	Unit	Attribute	2010 average of 30 provinces	2010 figure	2009 figure	2010 ranking	2009 ranking	Change in ranking	Source of 2010 data	Chernoff face
20	Labor productivity of the tertiary sector	10,000 yuan per capita	Positive	6.96	9.29	8.44	6	6	0	China Statistics	
21	Proportion of the value added of the tertiary sector in GDP	%	Positive	39.97	45.00	45.70	6	4	−2	China Statistics	☹
22	Proportion of tertiary sector employees in the total employed population	%	Positive	36.67	39.39	38.70	6	6	0	China Statistics	
23	Water resources per capita	m^3 per capita	Positive	2,419.38	1,943.31	1,682.49	15	13	−2	China Statistics	☹
24	Forest area per capita	Hectare per capita	Positive	0.19	0.08	0.09	20	20	0	China Statistics	
25	Forest coverage rate	%	Positive	30.63	49.44	49.44	6	6	0	China Statistics	
26	Proportion of the area of natural reserves in the total area of a region	%	Positive	8.60	6.95	6.68	16	16	0	China Statistics	
27	Proportion of the area of wetlands in the total area of a region	%	Positive	7.01	7.86	7.86	9	9	0	China Statistics	
28	Growing stock per capita	m^3 per capita	Positive	10.70	3.08	3.34	20	20	0	China Statistics	
29	CO_2 emissions per unit of land area		Negative	NA	NA	NA	NA	NA			
30	CO_2 emissions per capita		Negative	NA	NA	NA	NA	NA			
31	SO_2 emissions per unit of land area	Ton per km^2	Negative	6.3677	5.8422	5.9534	17	17	0	China Statistics; Deserts	

32	SO_2 emissions per capita	Ton per capita	Negative	0.0191	0.0105	0.0112	4	5	1	China Statistics	☺
33	COD emissions per unit of land area	Ton per km^2	Negative	3.7722	4.7737	5.0677	26	26	0	China Statistics; Deserts	
34	COD emissions per capita	Ton per capita	Negative	0.0101	0.0085	0.0095	11	12	1	China Statistics	☺
35	Nitrogen oxide emissions per unit of land area	Ton per km^2	Negative	6.4473	7.2131	7.1519	22	23	1	China Statistics; Deserts; Environmental Annual Report	☺
36	Nitrogen oxide emissions per capita	Ton per capita	Negative	0.0165	0.0129	0.0134	15	17	2	Environmental Annual Report; China Statistics	☺
37	Ammonia/nitrogen emissions per unit of land area	Ton per km^2	Negative	0.4164	0.5951	0.6396	27	27	0	China Statistics; Deserts; Environmental Annual Report	
38	Ammonia/nitrogen emissions per capita	Ton per capita	Negative	0.0010	0.0011	0.0012	19	21	2	Environmental Annual Report; China Statistics	☺
39	Consumption of chemical fertilizers per unit of cultivated land area	10,000 ton per 1,000 hectares	Negative	0.05	0.08	0.08	29	29	0	China Statistics; Yearbook	
40	Consumption of pesticides per unit of cultivated land area	Ton per 1,000 hectares	Negative	17.68	36.87	36.64	27	28	1	Environmental Yearbook; China Statistics	☺
41	Nitrogen oxide emissions per capita from road transport	Ton per 10,000 persons	Negative	24.07	43.51	45.53	27	26	−1	Environmental Annual Report; China Statistics	☹
42	Ratio of environmental spending to government expenditure	%	Positive	3.35	4.41	2.33	5	26	21	China Statistics	☺
43	Ratio of the investment in pollution control to GDP	%	Positive	1.40	3.08	0.67	1	29	28	Environmental Yearbook; China Statistics	☺

(continued)

(continued)

No.	Indicator	Unit	Attribute	2010 average of 30 provinces	2010 figure	2009 figure	2010 ranking	2009 ranking	Change in ranking	Source of 2010 data	Chernoff face
44	Government spending per capita on rural water supply system and toilet improvement	Yuan per capita	Positive	57.01	41.60	66.79	17	11	−6	Environmental Yearbook	
45	Investment in converting cultivated land into forests and grassland per unit of cultivated land area	10,000 yuan per 1,000 hectares	Positive	29.81	0.00	0.00	25	23	−2	Environmental Yearbook; China Statistics	
46	Ratio of the spending on science, education, culture, and public health to government expenditure	%	Positive	26.10	29.62	30.82	4	3	−1	China Statistics	
47	Area of green land per capita in urban areas	Hectare per capita	Positive	0.00	0.01	0.01	4	1	−3	City; China Statistics	
48	Coverage of water supply in urban areas	%	Positive	96.08	98.37	97.70	12	13	1	China Statistics	
49	Treatment rate of urban wastewater	%	Positive	79.18	86.10	71.50	9	19	10	Environmental Yearbook	
50	Harmless treatment rate of urban household waste	%	Positive	78.47	72.12	65.49	20	18	−2	China Statistics	
51	Public buses per 10,000 urban residents		Positive	9.86	9.53	10.43	17	13	−4	China Statistics	
52	Length of public transport routes per capita in urban areas	km per capita	Positive	0.0006	0.0008	0.0004	7	9	2	China Statistics; City	
53	Ratio of the rural residents benefiting from water supply system improvement to the total rural population	%	Positive	94.44	98.99	98.57	9	5	−4	Environmental Yearbook	

54	Green coverage of urban built-up areas	%	Positive	37.75	41.31	40.75	7	6	−1	China Statistics	☹
55	Newly-added afforestation area of the year per capita	Hectare per 10,000 persons	Positive	59.50	9.48	2.08	24	29	5	China Statistics	☺
56	Industrial SO_2 removal rate	%	Positive	59.83	59.45	64.92	21	10	−11	China Statistics	☹
57	Industrial wastewater COD removal rate	%	Positive	70.84	76.06	77.55	15	10	−5	Environmental Annual Report; China Statistics	☹
58	Industrial nitrogen oxide removal rate	%	Positive	4.07	13.75	5.98	3	11	8	Environmental Annual Report	☺
59	Industrial wastewater ammonia/nitrogen removal rate	%	Positive	62.87	78.76	83.11	10	5	−5	Environmental Annual Report; China Statistics	☹
60	Number of environmental emergencies		Negative	14.00	2	10	9	18	9	China Statistics	☺

Note:
China Statistics: *China Statistical Yearbook 2011*
Environmental Yearbook: *China Environmental Statistical Yearbook 2011*
Environmental Annual Report: *China Environment Annual Report 2010*
City: *China City Statistical Yearbook 2011*
Water Conservancy: *China Water Conservancy Statistical Yearbook 2011*
Industrial Economy: *China Industrial Economic Statistical Yearbook 2011*
Deserts: *Deserts in China and Desertification Control*

5.19 Brief Analysis of Green Development in Guangdong

Guangdong ranked 3rd among the 30 participating provinces by GDI according to 2010 data, seven places higher over 2009 (Guangdong ranked 10th in 2009). Following is a brief analysis of its score by each indicator and their changes from 2009 to 2010.

5.19.1 Guangdong's 2010 Scores by GDI

Guangdong scored 0.175 in 2010. From the three First-Class Indicators including GDEG, CCPNRE, and SDGP as shown in Fig. 5.37, Guangdong obviously outshined other provinces in terms of GDEG and SDGP, yet underperformed compared with the national average in CCPNRE (Note: the national average value of each indicator is 0).

According to Fig. 5.38, Guangdong surpassed the national average in 7 of Second-Class Indicators in 2010, which are GGEI, PII, SII, GII, II and EMI, yet ranked lower than the national average in RAECI and EPCCI.

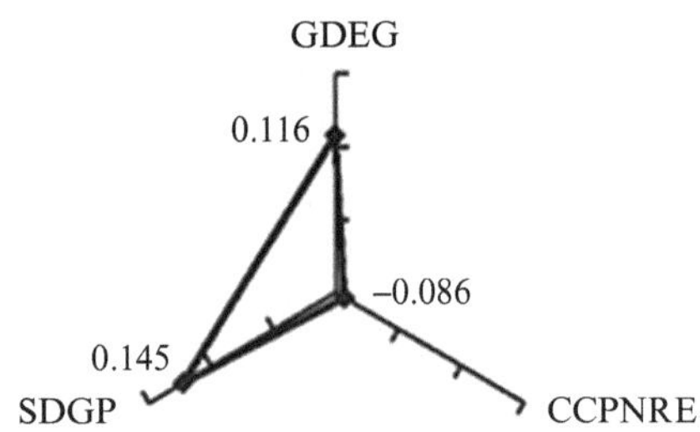

Fig. 5.37 Scores of Guangdong by First-Class Indicators

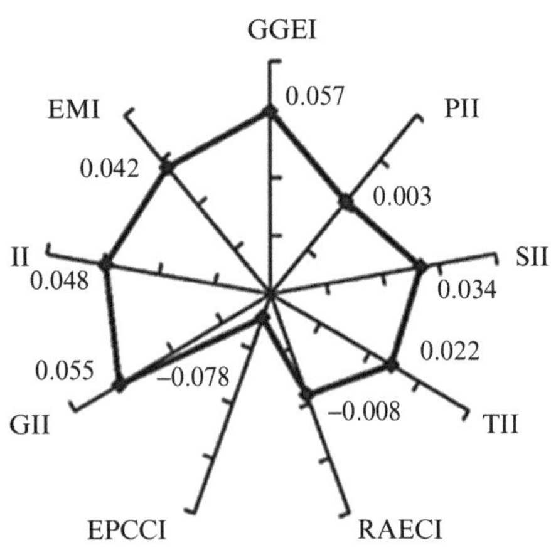

Fig. 5.38 Scores of Guangdong by Second-Class Indicators

Table 5.37 Changes in Guangdong's rankings by First-Class and Second-Class Indicators, 2009–2010

Indicator	2010	2009	Differences	Indicator	2010	2009	Differences
GDI	3	10	7				
GDEG	7	6	−1	RAECI	15	15	0
GGEI	6	7	1	EPCCI	27	29	2
PII	11	11	0	SDGP	3	7	4
SII	5	5	0	GII	3	26	23
TII	4	4	0	II	9	6	−3
CCPNRE	21	23	2	EMI	3	8	5

Note: A positive value in "Difference" means a rise in ranking

5.19.2 Changes in Guangdong's Rankings by GDI 2009–2010

According to Table 5.37, in First-Class Indicators ranking, it fell by 1 place in GDEG and rose by 2 in CCPNRE and 4 in SDGP. In Second-Class Indicators ranking, Guangdong fell by 3 places in II and rose by 1 in GGEI, 2 in EPCCI, 23 in GII and 5 in EMI. It remained the same in the rankings by other indicators in 2009.

To further explain the causes of the changes in the rankings by First- and Second-Class Indicators, we put the Third-Class Indicators where a change of more than 3 places occurred from 2009 to 2010 in Table 5.38. Compared with those in 2009, Guangdong dropped by 11 places in Industrial SO_2 removal rate, 6 in Government spending per capita on rural water supply system and toilet improvement, 5 in Industrial wastewater COD removal rate and Industrial wastewater ammonia/nitrogen removal rate, 4 in Public buses per 10,000 urban residents and Ratio of the rural residents benefiting from water supply system improvement to the total rural population, and 3 in Area of green land per capita in urban areas. It rose by 3 places in Nitrogen oxide emissions per unit of GDP, 4 in Recycling rate of industrial water, 5 in Newly-added afforestation area of the year per capita, 8 in Industrial nitrogen oxide removal rate, 9 in Number of environmental emergencies, 10 in Treatment rate of urban wastewater, 21 in Ratio of environmental spending to government expenditure and 28 in Ratio of the investment in pollution control to GDP.

Table 5.38 Third-Class Indicators where changes over 3 places occurred by Guangdong, 2009–2010

	Original data for 2010 and 2009			Change in ranking		
Third-Class Indicator	Unit	2010	2009	2010	2009	Difference
Nitrogen oxide emissions per unit of GDP	Ton per 10,000 yuan	0.0032	0.0036	4	7	3
Recycling rate of industrial water	%	83.64	75.34	14	18	4
Ratio of environmental spending to government expenditure	%	4.41	2.33	5	26	21
Ratio of the investment in pollution control to GDP	%	3.08	0.67	1	29	28
Government spending per capita on rural water supply system and toilet improvement	Yuan per capita	41.60	66.79	17	11	−6
Area of green land per capita in urban areas	Hectare per capita	0.01	0.01	4	1	−3
Treatment rate of urban wastewater	%	86.10	71.50	9	19	10
Public buses per 10,000 urban residents		9.53	10.43	17	13	−4
Ratio of the rural residents benefiting from water supply system improvement to the total rural population	%	98.99	98.57	9	5	−4
Newly-added afforestation area of the year per capita	Hectare per 10,000 persons	9.48	2.08	24	29	5
Industrial SO_2 removal rate	%	59.45	64.92	21	10	−11
Industrial wastewater COD removal rate	%	76.06	77.55	15	10	−5
Industrial nitrogen oxide removal rate	%	13.75	5.98	3	11	8
Industrial wastewater ammonia/nitrogen removal rate	%	78.76	83.11	10	5	−5
Number of environmental emergencies		2	10	9	18	9

Note: A positive value in "Difference" means a rise in ranking

Green development checkup-Guangxi

No.	Indicator	Unit	Attribute	2010 average of 30 provinces	2010 figure	2009 figure	2010 ranking	2009 ranking	Change in ranking	Source of 2010 data	Chernoff face
1	GDP per capita	Yuan per capita	Positive	33,964.12	20,219	16,045	27	27	0	China Statistics	
2	Energy consumption per unit of GDP	Ton coal equivalent per 10,000 yuan	Negative	1.29	1.04	1.06	12	11	−1	China Statistics	
3	Ratio of non-fossil energy consumption to total energy consumption		Positive	NA	NA	NA	NA	NA			
4	CO_2 emissions per unit of GDP		Negative	NA	NA	NA	NA	NA			
5	SO_2 emissions per unit of GDP	Ton per 10,000 yuan	Negative	0.0088	0.0118	0.0133	23	23	0	China Statistics	
6	COD emissions per unit of GDP	Ton per 10,000 yuan	Negative	0.0045	0.0123	0.0146	30	30	0	China Statistics	
7	Nitrogen oxide emissions per unit of GDP	Ton per 10,000 yuan	Negative	0.0068	0.0045	0.0045	14	11	−3	Environmental Annual Report; China Statistics	
8	Ammonia/nitrogen emissions per unit of GDP	Ton per 10,000 yuan	Negative	0.0004	0.0006	0.0007	26	26	0	Environmental Annual Report; China Statistics	
9	Electricity consumption per capita in urban areas	kWh per capita	Negative	295.08	120.46	309.69	5	15	10	City	

(continued)

(continued)

No.	Indicator	Unit	Attribute	2010 average of 30 provinces	2010 figure	2009 figure	2010 ranking	2009 ranking	Change in ranking	Source of 2010 data	Chernoff face
10	Labor productivity of the primary sector	10,000 yuan per capita	Positive	1.61	1.07	0.94	25	23	−2	China Statistics	
11	Land productivity	100 million yuan per 1,000 hectares	Positive	0.26	0.23	0.19	17	16	−1	China Statistics	
12	Proportion of water-saving irrigated area in effectively irrigated area		Positive	0.49	0.46	0.45	16	16	0	Water Conservancy; China Statistics	
13	Proportion of water-saving irrigated area in effectively irrigated area	%	Positive	53.55	36.11	36.09	21	21	0	China Statistics	
14	Labor productivity of the secondary sector	10,000 yuan per capita	Positive	12.13	7.51	5.91	28	28	0	China Statistics	
15	Water consumption per unit of value added created by industrial enterprises	m^3/yuan	Negative	0.0100	0.0180	0.0188	25	27	2	China Statistics	
16	Energy consumption per unit of value added created by industrial enterprises above designated size (no data)		Negative	NA	NA	NA	NA	NA			

17	Utilization rate of industrial solid waste	%	Positive	69.80	67.80	67.30	15	18	3	Environmental Yearbook	☺
18	Recycling rate of industrial water	%	Positive	72.90	89.19	90.46	9	9	0	Environmental Yearbook	
19	Ratio of the output of six energy-intensive industries to gross industrial output	%	Negative	39.65	41.75	40.93	19	19	0	Industrial Economy	
20	Labor productivity of the tertiary sector	10,000 yuan per capita	Positive	6.96	4.59	4.13	22	21	−1	China Statistics	☹
21	Proportion of the value added of the tertiary sector in GDP	%	Positive	39.97	35.40	37.60	23	22	−1	China Statistics	☹
22	Proportion of tertiary sector employees in the total employed population	%	Positive	36.67	25.62	25.13	30	30	0	China Statistics	
23	Water resources per capita	m^3 per capita	Positive	2,419.38	3,852.88	3,069.30	7	5	−2	China Statistics	☹
24	Forest area per capita	Hectare per capita	Positive	0.19	0.27	0.26	6	7	1	China Statistics	☺
25	Forest coverage rate	%	Positive	30.63	52.71	52.71	4	4	0	China Statistics	
26	Proportion of the area of natural reserves in the total area of a region	%	Positive	8.60	5.97	5.99	18	18	0	China Statistics	
27	Proportion of the area of wetlands in the total area of a region	%	Positive	7.01	2.76	2.76	23	23	0	China Statistics	
28	Growing stock per capita	m^3 per capita	Positive	10.70	11.08	10.51	8	8	0	China Statistics	

(continued)

(continued)

No.	Indicator	Unit	Attribute	2010 average of 30 provinces	2010 figure	2009 figure	2010 ranking	2009 ranking	Change in ranking	Source of 2010 data	Chernoff face
29	CO_2 emissions per unit of land area		Negative	NA	NA	NA	NA	NA			
30	CO_2 emissions per capita		Negative	NA	NA	NA	NA	NA			
31	SO_2 emissions per unit of land area	Ton per km^2	Negative	6.3677	3.8047	3.7485	15	13	−2	China Statistics; Deserts	
32	SO_2 emissions per capita	Ton per capita	Negative	0.0191	0.0191	0.0184	20	18	−2	China Statistics	
33	COD emissions per unit of land area	Ton per km^2	Negative	3.7722	3.9437	4.1097	23	23	0	China Statistics; Deserts	
34	COD emissions per capita	Ton per capita	Negative	0.0101	0.0198	0.0202	30	30	0	China Statistics	
35	Nitrogen oxide emissions per unit of land area	Ton per km^2	Negative	6.4473	1.4565	1.2586	8	8	0	China Statistics; Deserts; Environmental Annual Report	
36	Nitrogen oxide emissions per capita	Ton per capita	Negative	0.0165	0.0073	0.0062	4	4	0	Environmental Annual Report; China Statistics	
37	Ammonia/nitrogen emissions per unit of land area	Ton per km^2	Negative	0.4164	0.1978	0.2021	11	12	1	China Statistics; Deserts; Environmental Annual Report	
38	Ammonia/nitrogen emissions per capita	Ton per capita	Negative	0.0010	0.0010	0.0010	17	16	−1	Environmental Annual Report; China Statistics	

39	Consumption of chemical fertilizers per unit of cultivated land area	10,000 ton per 1,000 hectares	Negative	0.05	0.06	0.05	20	19	−1	China Statistics; China Statistics	☹
40	Consumption of pesticides per unit of cultivated land area	Ton per 1,000 hectares	Negative	17.68	15.28	14.74	16	17	1	Environmental Yearbook; China Statistics	☺
41	Nitrogen oxide emissions per capita from road transport	Ton per 10,000 persons	Negative	24.07	20.47	19.58	17	16	−1	Environmental Annual Report; China Statistics	☹
42	Ratio of environmental spending to government expenditure	%	Positive	3.35	3.19	3.08	16	19	3	China Statistics	☺
43	Ratio of the investment in pollution control to GDP	%	Positive	1.40	1.71	1.98	8	5	−3	Environmental Yearbook; China Statistics	☹
44	Government spending per capita on rural water supply system and toilet improvement	Yuan per capita	Positive	57.01	59.76	52.07	12	15	3	Environmental Yearbook	☺
45	Investment in converting cultivated land into forests and grassland per unit of cultivated land area	10,000 yuan per 1,000 hectares	Positive	29.81	19.78	23.85	17	15	−2	Environmental Yearbook; China Statistics	☹
46	Ratio of the spending on science, education, culture, and public health to government expenditure	%	Positive	26.10	29.23	28.37	5	9	4	China Statistics	☺

(continued)

(continued)

No.	Indicator	Unit	Attribute	2010 average of 30 provinces	2010 figure	2009 figure	2010 ranking	2009 ranking	Change in ranking	Source of 2010 data	Chernoff face
47	Area of green land per capita in urban areas	Hectare per capita	Positive	0.00	0.00	0.00	18	8	−10	City; China Statistics	☹
48	Coverage of water supply in urban areas	%	Positive	96.08	94.65	94.43	21	22	1	China Statistics	☺
49	Treatment rate of urban wastewater	%	Positive	79.18	83.40	73.40	13	18	5	Environmental Yearbook	☺
50	Harmless treatment rate of urban household waste	%	Positive	78.47	91.14	86.32	9	8	−1	Environmental Yearbook; China Statistics	☹
51	Public buses per 10,000 urban residents		Positive	9.86	8.07	9.94	24	18	−6	China Statistics	☹
52	Length of public transport routes per capita in urban areas	km per capita	Positive	0.0006	0.0002	0.0003	28	22	−6	China Statistics; City	☹
53	Ratio of the rural residents benefiting from water supply system improvement to the total rural population	%	Positive	94.44	91.99	87.93	22	25	3	Environmental Yearbook	☺
54	Green coverage of urban built-up areas	%	Positive	37.75	34.96	33.69	23	23	0	China Statistics	
55	Newly-added afforestation area of the year per capita	Hectare per 10,000 persons	Positive	59.50	30.27	28.83	18	17	−1	China Statistics	☹
56	Industrial SO_2 removal rate	%	Positive	59.83	53.72	51.24	24	23	−1	China Statistics	☹

57	Industrial wastewater COD removal rate	%	Positive	70.84	64.16	61.65	21	22	1	Environmental Annual Report; China Statistics	☺
58	Industrial nitrogen oxide removal rate	%	Positive	4.07	8.02	9.71	6	6	0	Yearbook	
59	Industrial wastewater ammonia/nitrogen removal rate	%	Positive	62.87	36.76	39.11	27	26	−1	Environmental Annual Report; China Statistics	☹
60	Number of environmental emergencies		Negative	14.00	4	11	12	22	10	China Statistics	☺

Note:
China Statistics: *China Statistical Yearbook 2011*
Environmental Yearbook: *China Environmental Statistical Yearbook 2011*
Environmental Annual Report: *China Environment Annual Report 2010*
City: *China City Statistical Yearbook 2011*
Water Conservancy: *China Water Conservancy Statistical Yearbook 2011*
Industrial Economy: *China Industrial Economic Statistical Yearbook 2011*
Deserts: *Deserts in China and Desertification Control*

5.20 Brief Analysis of Green Development in Guangxi

Guangxi ranked 26th among the 30 participating provinces by GDI according to 2010 data, two places lower over 2009 (Guangxi ranked 24th in 2009). Following is a brief analysis of its score by each indicator and their changes from 2009 to 2010.

5.20.1 Guangxi's 2010 Scores by GDI

Guangxi scored −0.179 in 2010. From the three First-Class Indicators including GDEG, CCPNRE, and SDGP as shown in Fig. 5.39, Guangxi underperformed compared with the national average in all these indicators (Note: the national average value of each indicator is 0).

According to Fig. 5.40, Guangxi surpassed the national average in 2 of Second-Class Indicators in 2010, which are RAECI and GII, yet ranked lower than the national average in PII, SII, TII, EPCCI, II and EMI.

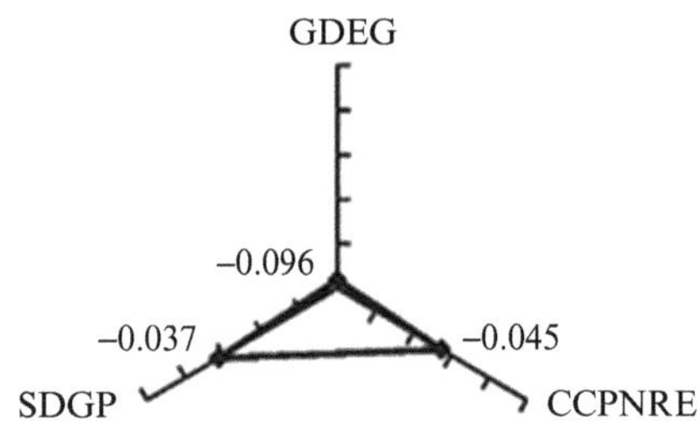

Fig. 5.39 Scores of Guangxi by First-Class Indicators

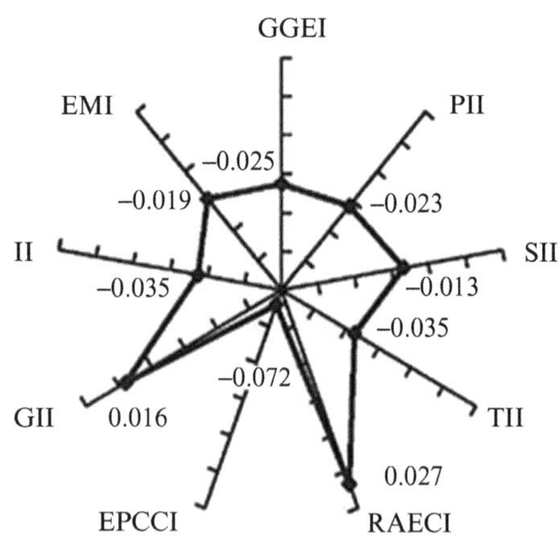

Fig. 5.40 Scores of Guangxi by Second-Class Indicators

Table 5.39 Changes in Guangxi's rankings by First-Class and Second-Class Indicators, 2009–2010

Indicator	2010	2009	Difference	Indicator	2010	2009	Difference
GDI	26	24	−2				
GDEG	24	24	0	RAECI	10	10	0
GGEI	22	25	3	EPCCI	24	20	−4
PII	22	21	−1	SDGP	20	18	−2
SII	19	19	0	GII	10	8	−2
TII	29	29	0	II	21	20	−1
CCPNRE	15	13	−2	EMI	23	24	1

Note: A positive value in "Difference" means a rise in ranking

5.20.2 *Changes in Guangxi's Rankings by GDI 2009–2010*

According to Table 5.39, in First-Class Indicators ranking, it fell by 2 places in SDGP and CCPNRE, and it remained the same by GDEG. In Second-Class Indicators ranking, Guangxi dropped by 1 place in PII, 4 in EPCCI, 2 in GII, 1 in II. It rose by 3 places in GGEI and 1 in EMI.

To further explain the causes of the changes in the rankings by First- and Second-Class Indicators, we put the Third-Class Indicators where a change of more than 3 places occurred from 2009 to 2010 in Table 5.40. Compared with those in 2009, Guangxi dropped by 10 places in Area of green land per capita in urban areas, 6 in Public buses per 10,000 urban residents and Length of public transport routes per capita in urban areas, 3 in Nitrogen oxide emissions per unit of GDP and Ratio of the investment in pollution control to GDP. It rose by 3 places in Utilization rate of industrial solid waste, Ratio of environmental spending to government expenditure, Government spending per capita on rural water supply system and toilet improvement and Ratio of the rural residents benefiting from water supply system improvement to the total rural population, 4 in Ratio of the spending on science, education, culture, and public health to government expenditure, 5 in Treatment rate of urban wastewater, 10 in Electricity consumption per capita in urban areas and 1 in Number of environmental emergencies.

Table 5.40 Third-Class Indicators where changes over 3 places by Guangxi, 2009–2010

Third-Class Indicator	Original data for 2010 and 2009			Change in ranking		
	Unit	2010	2009	2010	2009	Difference
Nitrogen oxide emissions per unit of GDP	Ton per 10,000 yuan	0.0045	0.0045	14	11	−3
Electricity consumption per capita in urban areas	kWh per capita	120.46	309.69	5	15	10
Utilization rate of industrial solid waste	%	67.80	67.30	15	18	3
Ratio of environmental spending to government expenditure	%	3.19	3.08	16	19	3
Ratio of the investment in pollution control to GDP	%	1.71	1.98	8	5	−3
Government spending per capita on rural water supply system and toilet improvement	Yuan per capita	59.76	52.07	12	15	3
Ratio of the spending on science, education, culture, and public health to government expenditure	%	29.23	28.37	5	9	4
Area of green land per capita in urban areas	Hectare per capita	0.00	0.00	18	8	−10
Treatment rate of urban wastewater	%	83.40	73.40	13	18	5
Public buses per 10,000 urban residents		8.07	9.94	24	18	−6
Length of public transport routes per capita in urban areas	km per capita	0.0002	0.0003	28	22	−6
Ratio of the rural residents benefiting from water supply system improvement to the total rural population	%	91.99	87.93	22	25	3
Number of environmental emergencies		4	11	12	22	10

Note: A positive value in “Difference” means a rise in ranking

Green development checkup-Hainan

No.	Indicator	Unit	Attribute	2010 average of 30 provinces	2010 figure	2009 figure	2010 ranking	2009 ranking	Change in ranking	Source of 2010 data	Chernoff face
1	GDP per capita	Yuan per capita	Positive	33,964.12	23,831	19,254	23	23	0	China Statistics	
2	Energy consumption per unit of GDP	Ton coal equivalent per 10,000 yuan	Negative	1.29	0.81	0.85	7	8	1	China Statistics	☺
3	Ratio of non-fossil energy consumption to total energy consumption		Positive	NA	NA	NA	NA	NA			
4	CO_2 emissions per unit of GDP		Negative	NA	NA	NA	NA	NA			
5	SO_2 emissions per unit of GDP	Ton per 10,000 yuan	Negative	0.0088	0.0017	0.0015	2	2	0	China Statistics	
6	COD emissions per unit of GDP	Ton per 10,000 yuan	Negative	0.0045	0.0055	0.0069	23	25	2	China Statistics	☺
7	Nitrogen oxide emissions per unit of GDP	Ton per 10,000 yuan	Negative	0.0068	0.0033	0.0032	6	5	−1	Environmental Annual Report; China Statistics	☹
8	Ammonia/nitrogen emissions per unit of GDP	Ton per 10,000 yuan	Negative	0.0004	0.0005	0.0006	22	21	−1	Environmental Annual Report; China Statistics	☹
9	Electricity consumption per capita in urban areas	kWh per capita	Negative	295.08	467.35	201.67	25	2	−23	City	☹

(continued)

(continued)

No.	Indicator	Unit	Attribute	2010 average of 30 provinces	2010 figure	2009 figure	2010 ranking	2009 ranking	Change in ranking	Source of 2010 data	Chernoff face
10	Labor productivity of the primary sector	10,000 yuan per capita	Positive	1.61	2.41	2.07	4	3	−1	China Statistics	☹
11	Land productivity	100 million yuan per 1,000 hectares	Positive	0.26	0.41	0.37	4	3	−1	China Statistics	☹
12	Proportion of water-saving irrigated area in effectively irrigated area		Positive	0.49	0.47	0.46	15	15	0	Water Conservancy; China Statistics	
13	Proportion of water-saving irrigated area in effectively irrigated area	%	Positive	53.55	33.51	33.43	22	22	0	China Statistics	
14	Labor productivity of the secondary sector	10,000 yuan per capita	Positive	12.13	11.10	9.25	14	15	1	China Statistics	☺
15	Water consumption per unit of value added created by industrial enterprises	m^3/yuan	Negative	0.0100	0.0106	0.0130	18	20	2	China Statistics	☺
16	Energy consumption per unit of value added created by industrial enterprises above designated size (no data)		Negative	NA	NA	NA	NA	NA			

17	Utilization rate of industrial solid waste	%	Positive	69.80	84.10	83.60	8	8	0	Environmental Yearbook	
18	Recycling rate of industrial water	%	Positive	72.90	73.17	75.76	21	17	–4	Environmental Yearbook	☹
19	Ratio of the output of six energy-intensive industries to gross industrial output	%	Negative	39.65	55.62	58.01	26	28	2	Industrial Economy	☺
20	Labor productivity of the tertiary sector	10,000 yuan per capita	Positive	6.96	5.85	4.99	18	18	0	China Statistics	
21	Proportion of the value added of the tertiary sector in GDP	%	Positive	39.97	46.20	45.30	4	5	1	China Statistics	☺
22	Proportion of tertiary sector employees in the total employed population	%	Positive	36.67	38.16	36.18	8	9	1	China Statistics	☺
23	Water resources per capita	m^3 per capita	Positive	2,419.38	5,538.66	5,596.16	2	2	0	China Statistics	
24	Forest area per capita	Hectare per capita	Positive	0.19	0.20	0.20	12	10	–2	China Statistics	☹
25	Forest coverage rate	%	Positive	30.63	51.98	51.98	5	5	0	China Statistics	
26	Proportion of the area of natural reserves in the total area of a region	%	Positive	8.60	7.01	7.20	15	14	–1	China Statistics	☹
27	Proportion of the area of wetlands in the total area of a region	%	Positive	7.01	9.13	9.13	6	6	0	China Statistics	
28	Growing stock per capita	m^3 per capita	Positive	10.70	9.14	9.19	11	11	0	China Statistics	

(continued)

(continued)

No.	Indicator	Unit	Attribute	2010 average of 30 provinces	2010 figure	2009 figure	2010 ranking	2009 ranking	Change in ranking	Source of 2010 data	Chernoff face
29	CO_2 emissions per unit of land area		Negative	NA	NA	NA	NA	NA			
30	CO_2 emissions per capita		Negative	NA	NA	NA	NA	NA			
31	SO_2 emissions per unit of land area	Ton per km^2	Negative	6.3677	0.8149	0.6232				China Statistics; Deserts	
32	SO_2 emissions per capita	Ton per capita	Negative	0.0191	0.0033	0.0026	1	1	0	China Statistics	
33	COD emissions per unit of land area	Ton per km^2	Negative	3.7722	2.6119	2.8364	13	14	1	China Statistics; Deserts	
34	COD emissions per capita	Ton per capita	Negative	0.0101	0.0107	0.0117	21	21	0	China Statistics	
35	Nitrogen oxide emissions per unit of land area	Ton per km^2	Negative	6.4473	1.5840	1.3011	9	9	0	China Statistics; Deserts; Environmental Annual Report	
36	Nitrogen oxide emissions per capita	Ton per capita	Negative	0.0165	0.0065	0.0054	3	1	−2	Environmental Annual Report; China Statistics	
37	Ammonia/nitrogen emissions per unit of land area	Ton per km^2	Negative	0.4164	0.2263	0.2263	13	14	1	China Statistics; Deserts; Environmental Annual Report	
38	Ammonia/nitrogen emissions per capita	Ton per capita	Negative	0.0010	0.0009	0.0009	15	14	−1	Environmental Annual Report; China Statistics	

39	Consumption of chemical fertilizers per unit of cultivated land area	10,000 ton per 1,000 hectares	Negative	0.05	0.06	0.06	25	25	0	China Statistics; China Statistics	
40	Consumption of pesticides per unit of cultivated land area	Ton per 1,000 hectares	Negative	17.68	62.54	64.35	30	30	0	Environmental Yearbook; China Statistics	
41	Nitrogen oxide emissions per capita from road transport	Ton per 10,000 persons	Negative	24.07	26.42	26.70	21	21	0	Environmental Annual Report; China Statistics	
42	Ratio of environmental spending to government expenditure	%	Positive	3.35	2.56	3.81	22	11	−11	China Statistics	☹
43	Ratio of the investment in pollution control to GDP	%	Positive	1.40	1.14	1.36	21	18	−3	Environmental Yearbook; China Statistics	☹
44	Government spending per capita on rural water supply system and toilet improvement	Yuan per capita	Positive	57.01	80.86	101.30	6	6	0	Environmental Yearbook	
45	Investment in converting cultivated land into forests and grassland per unit of cultivated land area	10,000 yuan per 1,000 hectares	Positive	29.81	21.88	25.13	16	12	−4	Environmental Yearbook; China Statistics	☹
46	Ratio of the spending on science, education, culture, and public health to government expenditure	%	Positive	26.10	26.19	24.78	16	22	6	China Statistics	☺

(continued)

(continued)

No.	Indicator	Unit	Attribute	2010 average of 30 provinces	2010 figure	2009 figure	2010 ranking	2009 ranking	Change in ranking	Source of 2010 data	Chernoff face
47	Area of green land per capita in urban areas	Hectare per capita	Positive	0.00	0.02	0.00	1	25	24	City; China Statistics	☺
48	Coverage of water supply in urban areas	%	Positive	96.08	89.43	89.65	28	26	−2	China Statistics	☹
49	Treatment rate of urban wastewater	%	Positive	79.18	54.90	58.40	29	26	−3	Environmental Yearbook	☹
50	Harmless treatment rate of urban household waste	%	Positive	78.47	67.97	64.98	24	20	−4	China Statistics	☹
51	Public buses per 10,000 urban residents		Positive	9.86	8.61	7.77	21	28	7	China Statistics	☺
52	Length of public transport routes per capita in urban areas	km per capita	Positive	0.0006	0.0018	0.0003	2	16	14	China Statistics; City	☺
53	Ratio of the rural residents benefiting from water supply system improvement to the total rural population	%	Positive	94.44	96.41	95.05	18	20	2	Environmental Yearbook	☺
54	Green coverage of urban built-up areas	%	Positive	37.75	42.63	41.88	4	4	0	China Statistics	
55	Newly-added afforestation area of the year per capita	Hectare per 10,000 persons	Positive	59.50	16.35	22.56	22	19	−3	China Statistics	☹
56	Industrial SO_2 removal rate	%	Positive	59.83	75.71	73.73	6	5	−1	China Statistics	☹
57	Industrial wastewater COD removal rate	%	Positive	70.84	90.69	81.78	2	7	5	Environmental Annual Report; China Statistics	☺

58	Industrial nitrogen oxide removal rate	%	Positive	4.07	0.42	1.62	22	21	−1	Environmental Annual Report	☺
59	Industrial wastewater ammonia/nitrogen removal rate	%	Positive	62.87	69.68	56.79	13	18	5	Environmental Annual Report; China Statistics	☺
60	Number of environmental emergencies		Negative	14.00	0	7	1	17	16	China Statistics	☺

Note:
China Statistics: *China Statistical Yearbook 2011*
Environmental Yearbook: *China Environmental Statistical Yearbook 2011*
Environmental Annual Report: *China Environment Annual Report 2010*
City: *China City Statistical Yearbook 2011*
Water Conservancy: *China Water Conservancy Statistical Yearbook 2011*
Industrial Economy: *China Industrial Economic Statistical Yearbook 2011*
Deserts: *Deserts in China and Desertification Control*

5.21 Brief Analysis of Green Development in Hainan

Hainan ranked 4th among the 30 participating provinces by GDI according to 2010 data, one place higher over 2009 (Hainan ranked 5th in 2009). Following is a brief analysis of its score by each indicator and their changes from 2009 to 2010. Following is a brief analysis of its score by each indicator and their changes in 2009 and 2010.

5.21.1 Hainan's 2010 Scores by GDI

Hainan scored 0.171 in 2010. From the three First-Class Indicators including GDEG, CCPNRE, and SDGP as shown in Fig. 5.41, Hainan has better potential in all these indicators, compared with the national average (Note: the national average value of each indicator is 0).

According to Fig. 5.42, Hainan surpassed the national average in 7 of Second-Class Indicators in 2010, which are GGEI, PII, RAECI, EPCCI, II and EMI, yet ranked lower than the national average in SII and GII.

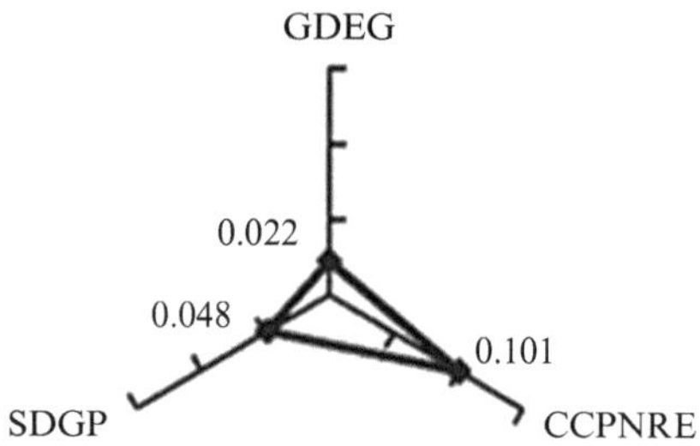

Fig. 5.41 Scores of Hainan by First-Class Indicators

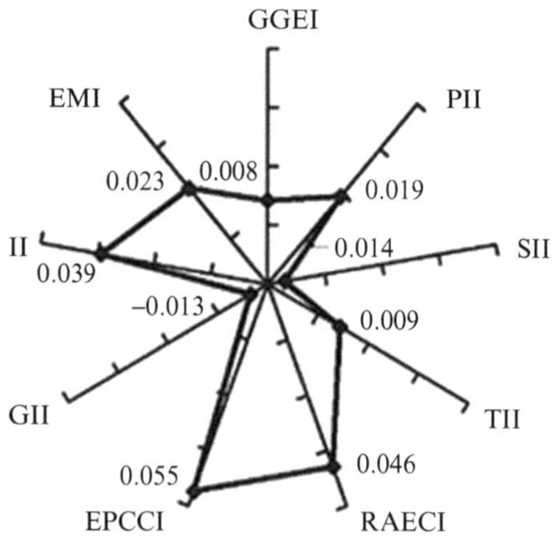

Fig. 5.42 Scores of Hainan by Second-Class Indicators

Table 5.41 Changes in Hainan's rankings by First-Class and Second-Class Indicators, 2009–2010

Indicator	2010	2009	Difference	Indicator	2010	2009	Difference
GDI	4	5	1				
GDEG	9	9	0	RAECI	7	5	−2
GGEI	10	6	−4	EPCCI	7	4	−3
PII	8	8	0	SDGP	10	20	10
SII	20	20	0	GII	17	14	−3
TII	7	9	2	II	10	25	15
CCPNRE	6	4	−2	EMI	9	11	2

Note: A positive value in "Difference" means a rise in ranking

5.21.2 *Changes in Hainan's Rankings by GDI 2009–2010*

According to Table 5.41, in First-Class Indicators ranking, it rose by 10 places in SDGP, dropped by 2 in CCPNRE, and remained unchanged in GDEG. In Second-Class Indicators ranking, Hainan dropped by 4 places in GGEI and RAECI, 3 in EPCCI and GII, rose by 2 in TII, 15 in II, and 2 in EMI. It remained the same in the rankings by other indicators in 2009.

To further explain the causes of the changes in the rankings by First- and Second-Class Indicators, we put the Third-Class Indicators where a change of more than 3 places occurred from 2009 to 2010 in Table 5.42. Compared with those in 2009, Hainan dropped by 23 places in Electricity consumption per capita in urban areas, 11 in Ratio of environmental spending to government expenditure, 4 in Recycling rate of industrial water, Investment in converting cultivated land into forests and grassland per unit of cultivated land area and Harmless treatment rate of urban household waste, 3 in Ratio of the investment in pollution control to GDP, Treatment rate of urban wastewater and Newly-added afforestation area of the year per capita. It rose by 5 places in Industrial wastewater COD removal rate and Industrial wastewater ammonia/nitrogen removal rate, 6 in Ratio of the spending on science, education, culture, and public health to government expenditure, 7 in Public buses per 10,000 urban residents, 14 in Length of public transport routes per capita in urban areas, 16 in Number of environmental emergencies, 24 in Area of green land per capita in urban areas.

Table 5.42 Third-Class Indicators where changes over 3 places by Hainan, 2009–2010

	Original data for 2010 and 2009			Change in ranking		
Third-Class Indicator	Unit	2010	2009	2010	2009	Difference
Electricity consumption per capita in urban areas	kWh per capita	467.35	201.67	25	2	−23
Recycling rate of industrial water	%	73.17	75.76	21	17	−4
Ratio of environmental spending to government expenditure	%	2.56	3.81	22	11	−11
Ratio of the investment in pollution control to GDP	%	1.14	1.36	21	18	−3
Investment in converting cultivated land into forests and grassland per unit of cultivated land area	10,000 yuan per 1,000 hectares	21.88	25.13	16	12	−4
Ratio of the spending on science, education, culture, and public health to government expenditure	%	26.19	24.78	16	22	6
Area of green land per capita in urban areas	Hectare per capita	0.02	0.00	1	25	24
Treatment rate of urban wastewater	%	54.90	58.40	29	26	−3
Harmless treatment rate of urban household waste	%	67.97	64.98	24	20	−4
Public buses per 10,000 urban residents		8.61	7.77	21	28	7
Length of public transport routes per capita in urban areas	km per capita	0.0018	0.0003	2	16	14
Newly-added afforestation area of the year per capita	Hectare per 10,000 persons	16.35	22.56	22	19	−3
Industrial wastewater COD removal rate	%	90.69	81.78	2	7	5
Industrial wastewater ammonia/nitrogen removal rate	%	69.68	56.79	13	18	5
Number of environmental emergencies		0	7	1	17	16

Note: A positive value in "Difference" means a rise in ranking

Green development checkup-Chongqing

No.	Indicator	Unit	Attribute	2010 average of 30 provinces	2010 figure	2009 figure	2010 ranking	2009 ranking	Change in ranking	Source of 2010 data	Chernoff face
1	GDP per capita	Yuan per capita	Positive	33,964.12	27,596	22,920	14	13	−1	China Statistics	☹
2	Energy consumption per unit of GDP	Ton coal equivalent per 10,000 yuan	Negative	1.29	1.13	1.18	14	15	1	China Statistics	☺
3	Ratio of non-fossil energy consumption to total energy consumption		Positive	NA	NA	NA	NA	NA			
4	CO_2 emissions per unit of GDP		Negative	NA	NA	NA	NA	NA			
5	SO_2 emissions per unit of GDP	Ton per 10,000 yuan	Negative	0.0088	0.0103	0.0126	22	22	0	China Statistics	
6	COD emissions per unit of GDP	Ton per 10,000 yuan	Negative	0.0045	0.0034	0.0040	12	12	0	China Statistics	
7	Nitrogen oxide emissions per unit of GDP	Ton per 10,000 yuan	Negative	0.0068	0.0043	0.0040	11	9	−2	Environmental Annual Report; China Statistics	☹
8	Ammonia/nitrogen emissions per unit of GDP	Ton per 10,000 yuan	Negative	0.0004	0.0004	0.0005	11	13	2	Environmental Annual Report; China Statistics	☺

(continued)

(continued)

No.	Indicator	Unit	Attribute	2010 average of 30 provinces	2010 figure	2009 figure	2010 ranking	2009 ranking	Change in ranking	Source of 2010 data	Chernoff face
9	Electricity consumption per capita in urban areas	kWh per capita	Negative	295.08	219.41	463.60	18	25	7	City	☺
10	Labor productivity of the primary sector	10,000 yuan per capita	Positive	1.61	1.06	0.91	26	24	−2	China Statistics	☹
11	Land productivity	100 million yuan per 1,000 hectares	Positive	0.26	0.19	0.16	20	19	−1	China Statistics	☹
12	Proportion of water-saving irrigated area in effectively irrigated area		Positive	0.49	0.22	0.21	25	25	0	Water Conservancy; China Statistics	
13	Proportion of water-saving irrigated area in effectively irrigated area	%	Positive	53.55	30.65	30.06	27	26	−1	China Statistics	☹
14	Labor productivity of the secondary sector	10,000 yuan per capita	Positive	12.13	8.11	6.84	23	23	0	China Statistics	
15	Water consumption per unit of value added created by industrial enterprises	m^3/yuan	Negative	0.0100	0.0186	0.0163	27	24	−3	China Statistics	☹

16	Energy consumption per unit of value added created by industrial enterprises above designated size (no data)		Negative	NA	NA	NA	NA	NA			
17	Utilization rate of industrial solid waste	%	Positive	69.80	80.20	79.80	12	10	−2	Environmental Yearbook	☹
18	Recycling rate of industrial water	%	Positive	72.90	4.14	4.61	30	30	0	Environmental Yearbook	
19	Ratio of the output of six energy-intensive industries to gross industrial output	%	Negative	39.65	25.89	25.52	5	6	1	Industrial Economy	☺
20	Labor productivity of the tertiary sector	10,000 yuan per capita	Positive	6.96	4.04	3.61	25	26	1	China Statistics	☺
21	Proportion of the value added of the tertiary sector in GDP	%	Positive	39.97	36.40	37.90	19	20	1	China Statistics	☺
22	Proportion of tertiary sector employees in the total employed population	%	Positive	36.67	37.85	37.44	9	7	−2	China Statistics	☹
23	Water resources per capita	m^3 per capita	Positive	2,419.38	1,616.75	1,600.27	16	14	−2	China Statistics	☹
24	Forest area per capita	Hectare per capita	Positive	0.19	0.10	0.10	19	19	0	China Statistics	
25	Forest coverage rate	%	Positive	30.63	34.85	34.85	13	13	0	China Statistics	

(continued)

(continued)

No.	Indicator	Unit	Attribute	2010 average of 30 provinces	2010 figure	2009 figure	2010 ranking	2009 ranking	Change in ranking	Source of 2010 data	Chernoff face
26	Proportion of the area of natural reserves in the total area of a region	%	Positive	8.60	9.92	10.18	9	8	−1	China Statistics	
27	Proportion of the area of wetlands in the total area of a region	%	Positive	7.01	0.52	0.52	29	29	0	China Statistics	
28	Growing stock per capita	m^3 per capita	Positive	10.70	4.79	4.83	17	17	0	China Statistics	
29	CO_2 emissions per unit of land area		Negative	NA	NA	NA	NA	NA			
30	CO_2 emissions per capita		Negative	NA	NA	NA	NA	NA			
31	SO_2 emissions per unit of land area	Ton per km^2	Negative	6.3677	8.7446	9.0690	26	26	0	China Statistics; Deserts	
32	SO_2 emissions per capita	Ton per capita	Negative	0.0191	0.0251	0.0262	24	25	1	China Statistics	
33	COD emissions per unit of land area	Ton per km^2	Negative	3.7722	2.8508	2.9148	15	15	0	China Statistics; Deserts	
34	COD emissions per capita	Ton per capita	Negative	0.0101	0.0082	0.0084	9	9	0	China Statistics	
35	Nitrogen oxide emissions per unit of land area	Ton per km^2	Negative	6.4473	3.6466	2.8565	17	17	0	China Statistics; Deserts; Environmental Annual Report	
36	Nitrogen oxide emissions per capita	Ton per capita	Negative	0.0165	0.0104	0.0082	9	7	−2	Environmental Annual Report; China Statistics	

37	Ammonia/nitrogen emissions per unit of land area	Ton per km^2	Negative	0.4164	0.3039	0.3282	18	18	0	China Statistics; Deserts; Environmental Annual Report;	
38	Ammonia/nitrogen emissions per capita	Ton per capita	Negative	0.0010	0.0009	0.0009	14	15	1	Environmental Annual Report; China Statistics; Environmental Annual Report;	☺
39	Consumption of chemical fertilizers per unit of cultivated land area	10,000 ton per 1,000 hectares	Negative	0.05	0.04	0.04	12	12	0	China Statistics; China Statistics	
40	Consumption of pesticides per unit of cultivated land area	Ton per 1,000 hectares	Negative	17.68	9.33	9.84	12	13	1	Environmental Yearbook; China Statistics	☺
41	Nitrogen oxide emissions per capita from road transport	Ton per 10,000 persons	Negative	24.07	16.76	17.47	12	12	0	Environmental Annual Report; China Statistics	
42	Ratio of environmental spending to government expenditure	%	Positive	3.35	4.04	3.87	8	10	2	China Statistics	☺
43	Ratio of the investment in pollution control to GDP	%	Positive	1.40	2.22	1.85	3	7	4	Environmental Yearbook; China Statistics	☺
44	Government spending per capita on rural water supply system and toilet improvement	Yuan per capita	Positive	57.01	60.45	78.03	11	7	–4	Environmental Yearbook	☹

(continued)

(continued)

No.	Indicator	Unit	Attribute	2010 average of 30 provinces	2010 figure	2009 figure	2010 ranking	2009 ranking	Change in ranking	Source of 2010 data	Chernoff face
45	Investment in converting cultivated land into forests and grassland per unit of cultivated land area	10,000 yuan per 1,000 hectares	Positive	29.81	90.92	98.90	2	2	0	Environmental Yearbook; China Statistics	
46	Ratio of the spending on science, education, culture, and public health to government expenditure	%	Positive	26.10	22.07	23.34	27	27	0	China Statistics	
47	Area of green land per capita in urban areas	Hectare per capita	Positive	0.00	0.00	0.01	19	5	−14	City; China Statistics	☹
48	Coverage of water supply in urban areas	%	Positive	96.08	94.05	94.60	23	21	−2	China Statistics	☹
49	Treatment rate of urban wastewater	%	Positive	79.18	91.70	88.40	3	2	−1	Environmental Yearbook	☹
50	Harmless treatment rate of urban household waste	%	Positive	78.47	98.82	95.88	2	3	1	China Statistics	☺
51	Public buses per 10,000 urban residents		Positive	9.86	7.23	7.85	28	27	−1	China Statistics	☹
52	Length of public transport routes per capita in urban areas	km per capita	Positive	0.0006	0.0003	0.0002	18	28	10	China Statistics; City	☺
53	Ratio of the rural residents benefiting from water supply system improvement to the total rural population	%	Positive	94.44	98.55	98.13	13	11	−2	Environmental Yearbook	☹

54	Green coverage of urban built-up areas	%	Positive	37.75	40.57	38.48	9	11	2	China Statistics	☺
55	Newly-added afforestation area of the year per capita	Hectare per 10,000 persons	Positive	59.50	88.88	33.60	8	15	7	China Statistics	☺
56	Industrial SO_2 removal rate	%	Positive	59.83	62.69	57.10	16	17	1	China Statistics	☺
57	Industrial wastewater COD removal rate	%	Positive	70.84	59.29	52.48	24	26	2	Environmental Annual Report; China Statistics	☺
58	Industrial nitrogen oxide removal rate	%	Positive	4.07	3.64	3.64	13	15	2	Environmental Annual Report	☺
59	Industrial wastewater ammonia/nitrogen removal rate	%	Positive	62.87	53.62	47.88	22	20	−2	Environmental Annual Report; China Statistics	☹
60	Number of environmental emergencies		Negative	14.00	23	33	25	27	2	China Statistics	☺

Note:
China Statistics: *China Statistical Yearbook 2011*
Environmental Yearbook: *China Environmental Statistical Yearbook 2011*
Environmental Annual Report: *China Environment Annual Report 2010*
City: *China City Statistical Yearbook 2011*
Water Conservancy: *China Water Conservancy Statistical Yearbook 2011*
Industrial Economy: *China Industrial Economic Statistical Yearbook 2011*
Deserts: *Deserts in China and Desertification Control*

5.22 Brief Analysis of Green Development in Chongqing

Chongqing ranked 19th among the 30 participating provinces by GDI according to 2010 data, two places higher over 2009 (Chongqing ranked 21st in 2009). Following is a brief analysis of its score by each indicator and their changes from 2009 to 2010.

5.22.1 Chongqing's 2010 Scores by GDI

Chongqing scored −0.101 in 2010. From the three First-Class Indicators including GDEG, CCPNRE, and SDGP as shown in Fig. 5.43, Chongqing had advantage in terms of SDGP, yet underperformed compared with the national average in GDEG and CCPNRE (Note: the national average value of each indicator is 0).

According to Fig. 5.44, Chongqing surpassed the national average in 2 of Second-Class Indicators in 2010, which are GII and II, yet ranked lower than the national average in GGEI, PII, SII, TII, EPCCI and EMI.

5.22.2 Changes in Chongqing's Rankings by GDI 2009–2010

According to Table 5.43, in First-Class Indicators ranking, its place remained unchanged by GDEG. It rose by 1 place in CCPNRE and 3 in SDGP. In Second-Class

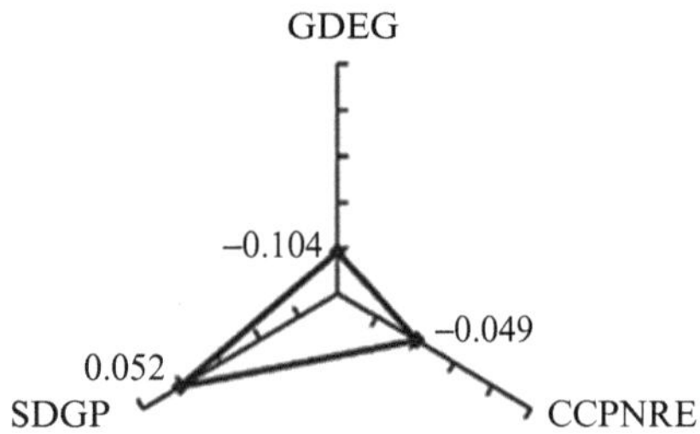

Fig. 5.43 Scores of Chongqing by First-Class Indicators

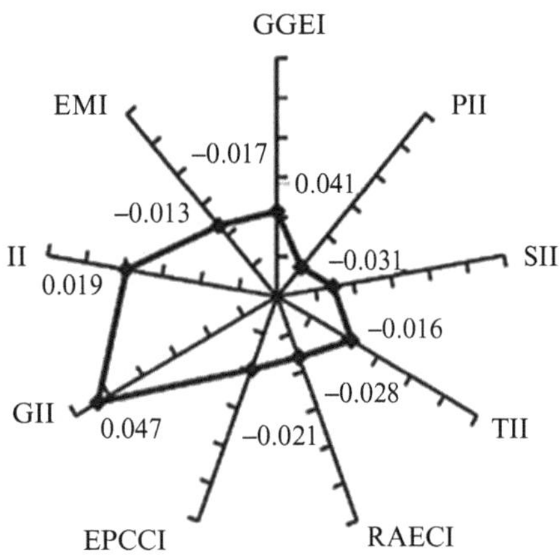

Fig. 5.44 Scores of Chongqing by Second-Class Indicators

Table 5.43 Changes in Chongqing's rankings by First-Class and Second-Class Indicators, 2009–2010

Indicator	2010	2009	Difference	Indicator	2010	2009	Difference
GDI	19	21	2				
GDEG	25	25	0	RAECI	19	17	−2
GGEI	17	20	3	EPCCI	14	14	0
PII	28	28	0	SDGP	9	12	3
SII	24	22	−2	GII	4	5	1
TII	19	19	0	II	14	8	−6
CCPNRE	16	17	1	EMI	21	28	7

Note: A positive value in "Difference" means a rise in ranking

Table 5.44 Third-Class Indicators where changes over 3 places by Chongqing, 2009–2010

	Original data for 2010 and 2009			Change in ranking		
Third-Class Indicator	Unit	2010	2009	2010	2009	Difference
Electricity consumption per capita in urban areas	kWh per capita	219.41	463.60	18	25	7
Water consumption per unit of value added created by industrial enterprises	m^3/yuan	0.0186	0.0163	27	24	−3
Ratio of the investment in pollution control to GDP	%	2.22	1.85	3	7	4
Government spending per capita on rural water supply system and toilet improvement	Yuan per capita	60.45	78.03	11	7	−4
Area of green land per capita in urban areas	Hectare per capita	0.00	0.01	19	5	−14
Length of public transport routes per capita in urban areas	km per capita	0.0003	0.0002	18	28	10
Newly-added afforestation area of the year per capita	Hectare per 10,000 persons	88.88	33.60	8	15	7

Note: A positive value in "Difference" means a rise in ranking

Indicators ranking, Chongqing dropped by 2 places in SII and RAECI, 6 in II, and rose by 3 places in GGEI, 1 in GII, and 7 in EMI. It remained the same in the rankings by other indicators in 2009.

To further explain the causes of the changes in the rankings by First- and Second-Class Indicators, we put the Third-Class Indicators where a change of more than 3 places occurred from 2009 to 2010 in Table 5.44. Compared with those in 2009, Chongqing dropped by 14 places in Area of green land per capita in urban areas, 4 in Government spending per capita on rural water supply system and toilet improvement, and 3 in Water consumption per unit of value added created by industrial enterprises. It rose by 4 places in Ratio of the investment in pollution control to GDP, 7 in Electricity consumption per capita in urban areas and Newly-added afforestation area of the year per capita, 10 in Length of public transport routes per capita in urban areas.

Green development checkup-Sichuan

No.	Indicator	Unit	Attribute	2010 average of 30 provinces	2010 figure	2009 figure	2010 ranking	2009 ranking	Change in ranking	Source of 2010 data	Chernoff face
1	GDP per capita	Yuan per capita	Positive	33,964.12	21,182	17,339	25	24	−1	China Statistics	
2	Energy consumption per unit of GDP	Ton coal equivalent per 10,000 yuan	Negative	1.29	1.28	1.34	20	20	0	China Statistics	
3	Ratio of non-fossil energy consumption to total energy consumption		Positive	NA	NA	NA	NA	NA			
4	CO_2 emissions per unit of GDP		Negative	NA	NA	NA	NA	NA			
5	SO_2 emissions per unit of GDP	Ton per 10,000 yuan	Negative	0.0088	0.0081	0.0093	19	20	1	China Statistics	
6	COD emissions per unit of GDP	Ton per 10,000 yuan	Negative	0.0045	0.0053	0.0061	22	22	0	China Statistics	
7	Nitrogen oxide emissions per unit of GDP	Ton per 10,000 yuan	Negative	0.0068	0.0048	0.0049	15	15	0	Environmental Annual Report; China Statistics	
8	Ammonia/nitrogen emissions per unit of GDP	Ton per 10,000 yuan	Negative	0.0004	0.0004	0.0005	16	17	1	Environmental Annual Report; China Statistics	
9	Electricity consumption per capita in urban areas	kWh per capita	Negative	295.08	121.98	287.94	6	13	7	City	

10	Labor productivity of the primary sector	10,000 yuan per capita	Positive	1.61	1.15	1.03	21	19	−2	China Statistics	☹
11	Land productivity	100 million yuan per 1,000 hectares	Positive	0.26	0.22	0.19	18	18	0	China Statistics	
12	Proportion of water-saving irrigated area in effectively irrigated area		Positive	0.49	0.49	0.47	14	14	0	Water Conservancy; China Statistics	
13	Proportion of water-saving irrigated area in effectively irrigated area	%	Positive	53.55	42.93	42.43	17	17	0	China Statistics	
14	Labor productivity of the secondary sector	10,000 yuan per capita	Positive	12.13	7.66	6.16	27	27	0	China Statistics	
15	Water consumption per unit of value added created by industrial enterprises	m^3/yuan	Negative	0.0100	0.0100	0.0108	16	17	1	China Statistics	☺
16	Energy consumption per unit of value added created by industrial enterprises above designated size (no data)		Negative	NA	NA	NA	NA	NA			
17	Utilization rate of industrial solid waste	%	Positive	69.80	54.80	57.50	22	21	−1	Environmental Yearbook	☹
18	Recycling rate of industrial water	%	Positive	72.90	71.79	38.51	22	27	5	Environmental Yearbook	☺
19	Ratio of the output of six energy-intensive industries to gross industrial output	%	Negative	39.65	31.63	31.22	9	9	0	Industrial Economy	

(continued)

(continued)

No.	Indicator	Unit	Attribute	2010 average of 30 provinces	2010 figure	2009 figure	2010 ranking	2009 ranking	Change in ranking	Source of 2010 data	Chernoff face
20	Labor productivity of the tertiary sector	10,000 yuan per capita	Positive	6.96	3.57	3.16	28	28	0	China Statistics	
21	Proportion of the value added of the tertiary sector in GDP	%	Positive	39.97	35.10	36.70	24	25	1	China Statistics	☺
22	Proportion of tertiary sector employees in the total employed population	%	Positive	36.67	34.05	33.91	19	19	0	China Statistics	
23	Water resources per capita	m^3 per capita	Positive	2,419.38	3,173.51	2,857.51	8	6	−2	China Statistics	☹
24	Forest area per capita	Hectare per capita	Positive	0.19	0.21	0.20	10	12	2	China Statistics	☺
25	Forest coverage rate	%	Positive	30.63	34.31	34.31	14	14	0	China Statistics	
26	Proportion of the area of natural reserves in the total area of a region	%	Positive	8.60	18.42	18.41	2	2	0	China Statistics	
27	Proportion of the area of wetlands in the total area of a region	%	Positive	7.01	1.98	1.98	24	24	0	China Statistics	
28	Growing stock per capita	m^3 per capita	Positive	10.70	20.98	20.62	5	5	0	China Statistics	
29	CO_2 emissions per unit of land area		Negative	NA	NA	NA	NA	NA			
30	CO_2 emissions per capita		Negative	NA	NA	NA	NA	NA			

31	SO_2 emissions per unit of land area	Ton per km^2	Negative	6.3677	2.3364	2.3454	9	9	0	China Statistics; Deserts	
32	SO_2 emissions per capita	Ton per capita	Negative	0.0191	0.0139	0.0139	14	13	−1	China Statistics	☹
33	COD emissions per unit of land area	Ton per km^2	Negative	3.7722	1.5305	1.5446				China Statistics; Deserts	
34	COD emissions per capita	Ton per capita	Negative	0.0101	0.0091	0.0092	12	11	−1	China Statistics	☹
35	Nitrogen oxide emissions per unit of land area	Ton per km^2	Negative	6.4473	1.3965	1.2230	7	7	0	China Statistics; Deserts; Environmental Annual Report	
36	Nitrogen oxide emissions per capita	Ton per capita	Negative	0.0165	0.0083	0.0073	6	6	0	Environmental Annual Report; China Statistics	
37	Ammonia/nitrogen emissions per unit of land area	Ton per km^2	Negative	0.4164	0.1260	0.1240	8	8	0	China Statistics; Deserts; Environmental Annual Report	
38	Ammonia/nitrogen emissions per capita	Ton per capita	Negative	0.0010	0.0008	0.0007	6	4	−2	Environmental Annual Report; China Statistics	☹
39	Consumption of chemical fertilizers per unit of cultivated land area	10,000 ton per 1,000 hectares	Negative	0.05	0.04	0.04	13	13	0	China Statistics; China Statistics	

(continued)

(continued)

No.	Indicator	Unit	Attribute	2010 average of 30 provinces	2010 figure	2009 figure	2010 ranking	2009 ranking	Change in ranking	Source of 2010 data	Chernoff face
40	Consumption of pesticides per unit of cultivated land area	Ton per 1,000 hectares	Negative	17.68	10.46	10.41	14	14	0	Environmental Yearbook; China Statistics	
41	Nitrogen oxide emissions per capita from road transport	Ton per 10,000 persons	Negative	24.07	6.83	10.73	3	5	2	Environmental Annual Report; China Statistics	
42	Ratio of environmental spending to government expenditure	%	Positive	3.35	2.65	3.19	21	17	−4	China Statistics	
43	Ratio of the investment in pollution control to GDP	%	Positive	1.40	0.52	0.85	30	26	−4	Environmental Yearbook; China Statistics	
44	Government spending per capita on rural water supply system and toilet improvement	Yuan per capita	Positive	57.01	67.36	137.13	10	4	−6	Environmental Yearbook	
45	Investment in converting cultivated land into forests and grassland per unit of cultivated land area	10,000 yuan per 1,000 hectares	Positive	29.81	66.60	89.34	5	3	−2	Environmental Yearbook; China Statistics	
46	Ratio of the spending on science, education, culture, and public health to government expenditure	%	Positive	26.10	21.09	20.74	29	30	1	China Statistics	

47	Area of green land per capita in urban areas	Hectare per capita	Positive	0.00	0.00	0.00	26	28	2	City; China Statistics	☺
48	Coverage of water supply in urban areas	%	Positive	96.08	90.80	89.68	26	24	−2	China Statistics	☹
49	Treatment rate of urban wastewater	%	Positive	79.18	74.80	67.50	23	20	−3	Environmental Yearbook	☹
50	Harmless treatment rate of urban household waste	%	Positive	78.47	86.86	83.50	12	10	−2	China Statistics	☹
51	Public buses per 10,000 urban residents		Positive	9.86	9.65	11.18	15	10	−5	China Statistics	☹
52	Length of public transport routes per capita in urban areas	km per capita	Positive	0.0006	0.0002	0.0003	26	19	−7	Yearbook; City	☹
53	Ratio of the rural residents benefiting from water supply system improvement to the total rural population	%	Positive	94.44	92.61	90.95	21	24	3	Environmental Yearbook	☺
54	Green coverage of urban built-up areas	%	Positive	37.75	37.88	36.40	16	19	3	China Statistics	☺
55	Newly-added afforestation area of the year per capita	Hectare per 10,000 persons	Positive	59.50	47.10	59.77	12	10	−2	China Statistics	☹
56	Industrial SO_2 removal rate	%	Positive	59.83	48.07	46.96	26	26	0	China Statistics	
57	Industrial wastewater COD removal rate	%	Positive	70.84	56.57	63.76	25	20	−5	Environmental Annual Report; China Statistics	☹
58	Industrial nitrogen oxide removal rate	%	Positive	4.07	2.42	4.10	16	14	−2	Environmental Annual Report	☹

(continued)

(continued)

No.	Indicator	Unit	Attribute	2010 average of 30 provinces	2010 figure	2009 figure	2010 ranking	2009 ranking	Change in ranking	Source of 2010 data	Chernoff face
59	Industrial wastewater ammonia/ nitrogen removal rate	%	Positive	62.87	30.49	42.70	28	24	−4	Environmental Annual Report; China Statistics	
60	Number of environmental emergencies		Negative	14.00	1	0	6	1	−5	China Statistics	

Note:
China Statistics: *China Statistical Yearbook 2011*
Environmental Yearbook: *China Environmental Statistical Yearbook 2011*
Environmental Annual Report: *China Environment Annual Report 2010*
City: *China City Statistical Yearbook 2011*
Water Conservancy: *China Water Conservancy Statistical Yearbook 2011*
Industrial Economy: *China Industrial Economic Statistical Yearbook 2011*
Deserts: *Deserts in China and Desertification Control*

5.23 Brief Analysis of Green Development in Sichuan

Sichuan ranked 21st among the 30 participating provinces by GDI according to 2010 data, two places lower over 2009 (Sichuan ranked 19th in 2009). Following is a brief analysis of its score by each indicator and their changes from 2009 to 2010.

5.23.1 Sichuan's 2010 Scores by GDI

Sichuan scored −0.115 in 2010. From the three First-Class Indicators including GDEG, CCPNRE, and SDGP as shown in Fig. 5.45, Sichuan had better potential in terms of CCPNRE, yet underperformed compared with the national average in GDEG and SDGP (Note: the national average value of each indicator is 0).

According to Fig. 5.46, Sichuan surpassed the national average in 2 of Second-Class Indicators in 2010, which are RAECI and EPCCI, yet ranked lower than the national average in GGEI, SII, TII, GII, II and EMI.

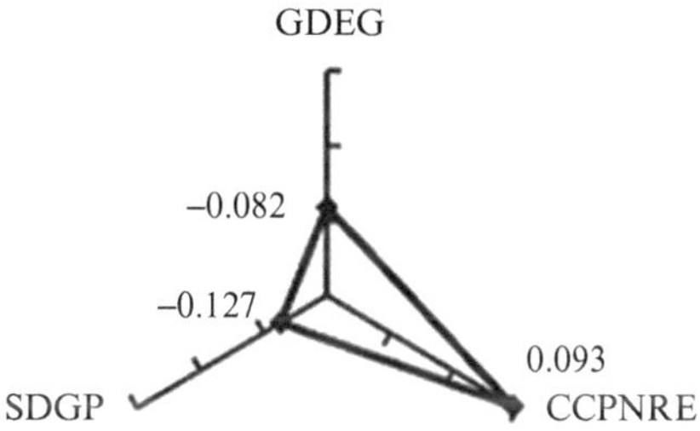

Fig. 5.45 Scores of Sichuan by First-Class Indicators

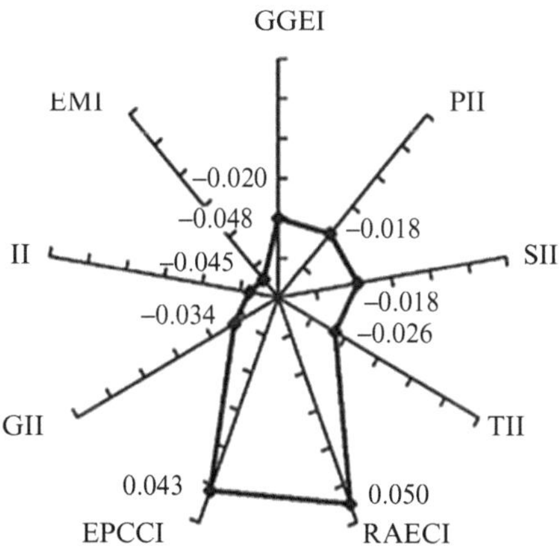

Fig. 5.46 Scores of Sichuan by Second-Class Indicators

Table 5.45 Changes in Sichuan's rankings by First-Class and Second-Class Indicators, 2009–2010

Indicator	2010	2009	Differences	Indicator	2010	2009	Differences
GDI	21	19	−2				
GDEG	21	23	2	RAECI	6	6	0
GGEI	21	21	0	EPCCI	8	8	0
PII	20	19	−1	SDGP	28	23	−5
SII	21	23	2	GII	26	18	−8
TII	25	25	0	II	22	22	0
CCPNRE	7	7	0	EMI	28	22	−6

Note: A positive value in "Difference" means a rise in ranking

5.23.2 Changes in Sichuan's Rankings by GDI 2009–2010

According to Table 5.45, in First-Class Indicators ranking, it rose by 2 places in GDEG, remained unchanged in CCPNRE, and fell by 5 in SDGP. In Second-Class Indicators ranking, Sichuan fell by 1 place in PII, 8 in GII; 6 in EMI and rose by 2 places in SII. It remained the same in the rankings by other indicators in 2009.

To further explain the causes of the changes in the rankings by First- and Second-Class Indicators, we put the Third-Class Indicators where a change of more than 3 places occurred from 2009 to 2010 in Table 5.46. Compared with those in 2009, Tianjin dropped by 7 places in Length of public transport routes per capita in urban areas, 6 in Government spending per capita on rural water supply system and toilet improvement, 5 in Public buses per 10,000 urban residents, Industrial wastewater COD removal rate and Number of environmental emergencies, 4 in Ratio of environmental spending to government expenditure, Ratio of the investment in pollution control to GDP and Industrial wastewater ammonia/nitrogen removal rate, 3 in Treatment rate of urban wastewater. It rose by 3 places in Ratio of the rural residents benefiting from water supply system improvement to the total rural population and Green coverage of urban built-up areas, 5 in Recycling rate of industrial water and 7 in Electricity consumption per capita in urban areas.

Table 5.46 Third-Class Indicators where changes over 3 places by Sichuan, 2009–2010

	Original data for 2010 and 2009			Change in ranking		
Third-Class Indicator	Unit	2010	2009	2010	2009	Difference
Electricity consumption per capita in urban areas	kWh per capita	121.98	287.94	6	13	7
Recycling rate of industrial water	%	71.79	38.51	22	27	5
Ratio of environmental spending to government expenditure	%	2.65	3.19	21	17	−4
Ratio of the investment in pollution control to GDP	%	0.52	0.85	30	26	−4
Government spending per capita on rural water supply system and toilet improvement	Yuan per capita	67.36	137.13	10	4	−6
Treatment rate of urban wastewater	%	74.80	67.50	23	20	−3
Public buses per 10,000 urban residents		9.65	11.18	15	10	−5
Length of public transport routes per capita in urban areas	km per capita	0.0002	0.0003	26	19	−7
Ratio of the rural residents benefiting from water supply system improvement to the total rural population	%	92.61	90.95	21	24	3
Green coverage of urban built-up areas	%	37.88	36.40	16	19	3
Industrial wastewater COD removal rate	%	56.57	63.76	25	20	−5
Industrial wastewater ammonia/nitrogen removal rate	%	30.49	42.70	28	24	−4
Number of environmental emergencies		1	0	6	1	−5

Note: A positive value in "Difference" means a rise in ranking

Green development checkup-Guizhou

No.	Indicator	Unit	Attribute	2010 average of 30 provinces	2010 figure	2009 figure	2010 ranking	2009 ranking	Change in ranking	Source of 2010 data	Chernoff face
1	GDP per capita	Yuan per capita	Positive	33,964.12	13,119	10,309	30	30	0	China Statistics	
2	Energy consumption per unit of GDP	Ton coal equivalent per 10,000 yuan	Negative	1.29	2.25	2.35	28	27	−1	China Statistics	☹
3	Ratio of non-fossil energy consumption to total energy consumption		Positive	NA	NA	NA	NA	NA			
4	CO_2 emissions per unit of GDP		Negative	NA	NA	NA	NA	NA			
5	SO_2 emissions per unit of GDP	Ton per 10,000 yuan	Negative	0.0088	0.0316	0.0365	30	30	0	China Statistics	
6	COD emissions per unit of GDP	Ton per 10,000 yuan	Negative	0.0045	0.0057	0.0067	24	24	0	China Statistics	
7	Nitrogen oxide emissions per unit of GDP	Ton per 10,000 yuan	Negative	0.0068	0.0062	0.0066	18	20	2	Environmental Annual Report; China Statistics	☺
8	Ammonia/nitrogen emissions per unit of GDP	Ton per 10,000 yuan	Negative	0.0004	0.0004	0.0005	18	19	1	Environmental Annual Report; China Statistics	☺
9	Electricity consumption per capita in urban areas	kWh per capita	Negative	295.08	276.16	346.64	21	18	−3	City	☹

10	Labor productivity of the primary sector	10,000 yuan per capita	Positive	1.61	0.52	0.46	30	30	0	China Statistics	
11	Land productivity	100 million yuan per 1,000 hectares	Positive	0.26	0.12	0.10	29	29	0	China Statistics	
12	Proportion of water-saving irrigated area in effectively irrigated area		Positive	0.49	0.35	0.38	21	19	−2	Water Conservancy; China Statistics	☹
13	Proportion of water-saving irrigated area in effectively irrigated area	%	Positive	53.55	25.23	22.65	30	30	0	China Statistics	
14	Labor productivity of the secondary sector	10,000 yuan per capita	Positive	12.13	6.51	5.58	29	29	0	China Statistics	
15	Water consumption per unit of value added created by industrial enterprises	m^3/yuan	Negative	0.0100	0.0260	0.0273	30	30	0	China Statistics	
16	Energy consumption per unit of value added created by industrial enterprises above designated size (no data)		Negative	NA	NA	NA	NA	NA			
17	Utilization rate of industrial solid waste	%	Positive	69.80	50.90	45.60	24	27	3	Environmental Yearbook	☺
18	Recycling rate of industrial water	%	Positive	72.90	59.34	57.99	24	23	−1	Environmental Yearbook	☹

(continued)

(continued)

No.	Indicator	Unit	Attribute	2010 average of 30 provinces	2010 figure	2009 figure	2010 ranking	2009 ranking	Change in ranking	Source of 2010 data	Chernoff face
19	Ratio of the output of six energy-intensive industries to gross industrial output	%	Negative	39.65	50.56	53.00	23	24	1	Industrial Economy	
20	Labor productivity of the tertiary sector	10,000 yuan per capita	Positive	6.96	2.44	2.22	30	30	0	China Statistics	
21	Proportion of the value added of the tertiary sector in GDP	%	Positive	39.97	47.30	48.20	3	3	0	China Statistics	
22	Proportion of tertiary sector employees in the total employed population	%	Positive	36.67	38.51	36.84	7	8	1	China Statistics	
23	Water resources per capita	m^3 per capita	Positive	2,419.38	2,726.76	2,397.65	10	9	−1	China Statistics	
24	Forest area per capita	Hectare per capita	Positive	0.19	0.16	0.15	14	15	1	China Statistics	
25	Forest coverage rate	%	Positive	30.63	31.61	31.61	16	16	0	China Statistics	
26	Proportion of the area of natural reserves in the total area of a region	%	Positive	8.60	5.39	5.41	21	21	0	China Statistics	
27	Proportion of the area of wetlands in the total area of a region	%	Positive	7.01	0.45	0.45	30	30	0	China Statistics	
28	Growing stock per capita	m^3 per capita	Positive	10.70	8.02	7.35	13	14	1	China Statistics	

29	CO_2 emissions per unit of land area		Negative	NA	NA	NA	NA	NA			
30	CO_2 emissions per capita		Negative	NA	NA	NA	NA	NA			
31	SO_2 emissions per unit of land area	Ton per km^2	Negative	6.3677	6.5218	6.6732	19	20	1	China Statistics; Deserts	☺
32	SO_2 emissions per capita	Ton per capita	Negative	0.0191	0.0316	0.0310	27	27	0	China Statistics	
33	COD emissions per unit of land area	Ton per km^2	Negative	3.7722	1.1804	1.2260	7	7	0	China Statistics; Deserts	
34	COD emissions per capita	Ton per capita	Negative	0.0101	0.0057	0.0057	2	1	−1	China Statistics	☹
35	Nitrogen oxide emissions per unit of land area	Ton per km^2	Negative	6.4473	1.2830	1.1978	6	6	0	China Statistics; Deserts; Environmental Annual Report	
36	Nitrogen oxide emissions per capita	Ton per capita	Negative	0.0165	0.0062	0.0056	1	2	1	Environmental Annual Report; China Statistics	☺
37	Ammonia/nitrogen emissions per unit of land area	Ton per km^2	Negative	0.4164	0.0908	0.0965	6	6	0	China Statistics; Deserts; Environmental Annual Report	
38	Ammonia/nitrogen emissions per capita	Ton per capita	Negative	0.0010	0.0004	0.0004	1	2	1	Environmental Annual Report; China Statistics	☺
39	Consumption of chemical fertilizers per unit of cultivated land area	10,000 ton per 1,000 hectares	Negative	0.05	0.02	0.02	4	4	0	China Statistics; China Statistics	

(continued)

(continued)

No.	Indicator	Unit	Attribute	2010 average of 30 provinces	2010 figure	2009 figure	2010 ranking	2009 ranking	Change in ranking	Source of 2010 data	Chernoff face
40	Consumption of pesticides per unit of cultivated land area	Ton per 1,000 hectares	Negative	17.68	2.88	2.78	2	2	0	Environmental Yearbook; China Statistics	
41	Nitrogen oxide emissions per capita from road transport	Ton per 10,000 persons	Negative	24.07	2.51	2.40	1	1	0	Environmental Annual Report; China Statistics	
42	Ratio of environmental spending to government expenditure	%	Positive	3.35	3.33	4.03	15	9	−6	China Statistics	☹
43	Ratio of the investment in pollution control to GDP	%	Positive	1.40	0.65	0.66	28	30	2	Environmental Yearbook; China Statistics	☺
44	Government spending per capita on rural water supply system and toilet improvement	Yuan per capita	Positive	57.01	38.06	33.84	19	23	4	Environmental Yearbook	☺
45	Investment in converting cultivated land into forests and grassland per unit of cultivated land area	10,000 yuan per 1,000 hectares	Positive	29.81	46.60	52.85	7	6	−1	Environmental Yearbook; China Statistics	☹
46	Ratio of the spending on science, education, culture, and public health to government expenditure	%	Positive	26.10	28.22	28.96	9	6	−3	China Statistics	☹

47	Area of green land per capita in urban areas	Hectare per capita	Positive	0.00	0.00	0.00	14	23	9	City; China Statistics	☺
48	Coverage of water supply in urban areas	%	Positive	96.08	94.10	92.09	22	23	1	China Statistics	☺
49	Treatment rate of urban wastewater	%	Positive	79.18	86.80	56.20	8	27	19	Environmental Yearbook	☺
50	Harmless treatment rate of urban household waste	%	Positive	78.47	90.64	81.70	10	11	1	China Statistics	☺
51	Public buses per 10,000 urban residents		Positive	9.86	8.46	8.28	22	24	2	China Statistics	☺
52	Length of public transport routes per capita in urban areas	km per capita	Positive	0.0006	0.0003	0.0002	21	24	3	China Statistics; City	☺
53	Ratio of the rural residents benefiting from water supply system improvement to the total rural population	%	Positive	94.44	81.04	77.14	29	29	0	Environmental Yearbook	
54	Green coverage of urban built-up areas	%	Positive	37.75	29.58	27.44	28	29	1	China Statistics	☺
55	Newly-added afforestation area of the year per capita	Hectare per 10,000 persons	Positive	59.50	56.78	62.21	11	9	–2	China Statistics	☹
56	Industrial SO_2 removal rate	%	Positive	59.83	77.19	67.87	3	6	3	China Statistics	☺
57	Industrial wastewater COD removal rate	%	Positive	70.84	78.41	80.73	10	8	–2	Environmental Annual Report; China Statistics	☹
58	Industrial nitrogen oxide removal rate	%	Positive	4.07	8.53	17.33	5	2	–3	Environmental Annual Report	☹

(continued)

(continued)

No.	Indicator	Unit	Attribute	2010 average of 30 provinces	2010 figure	2009 figure	2010 ranking	2009 ranking	Change in ranking	Source of 2010 data	Chernoff face
59	Industrial wastewater ammonia/nitrogen removal rate	%	Positive	62.87	59.32	57.05	16	17	1	Environmental Annual Report; China Statistics	
60	Number of environmental emergencies		Negative	14.00	5	4	14	10	–4	China Statistics	

Note:
China Statistics: *China Statistical Yearbook 2011*
Environmental Yearbook: *China Environmental Statistical Yearbook 2011*
Environmental Annual Report: *China Environment Annual Report 2010*
City: *China City Statistical Yearbook 2011*
Water Conservancy: *China Water Conservancy Statistical Yearbook 2011*
Industrial Economy: *China Industrial Economic Statistical Yearbook 2011*
Deserts: *Deserts in China and Desertification Control*

5.24 Brief Analysis of Green Development in Guizhou

Guizhou ranked 13th among the 30 participating provinces by GDI according to 2010 data, as it did in 2009 (Guizhou ranked 13th in 2009). Following is a brief analysis of its score by each indicator and their changes from 2009 to 2010.

5.24.1 Guizhou's 2010 Scores by GDI

Guizhou scored 0.041 in 2010. From the three First-Class Indicators including GDEG, CCPNRE, and SDGP as shown in Fig. 5.47, Guizhou had advantage in terms of CCPNRE, yet underperformed compared with the national average in GDEG and SDGP (Note: the national average value of each indicator is 0).

According to Fig. 5.48, Guizhou surpassed the national average in 2 of Second-Class Indicators in 2010, which are EPCCI and EMI, yet ranked lower than the national average in GGEI, PII, TII, RAECI, GII and II.

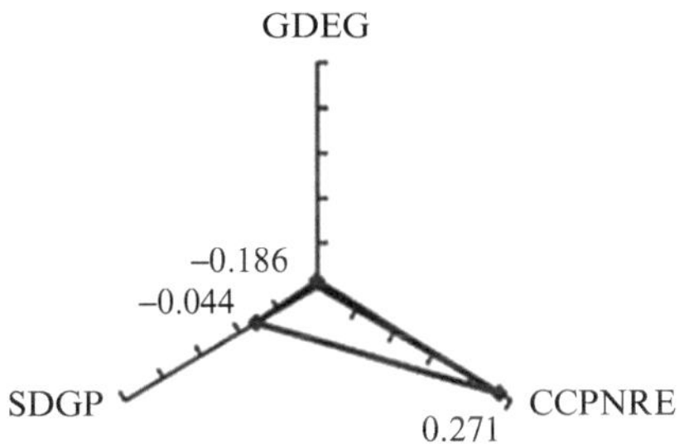

Fig. 5.47 Scores of Guizhou by First-Class Indicators

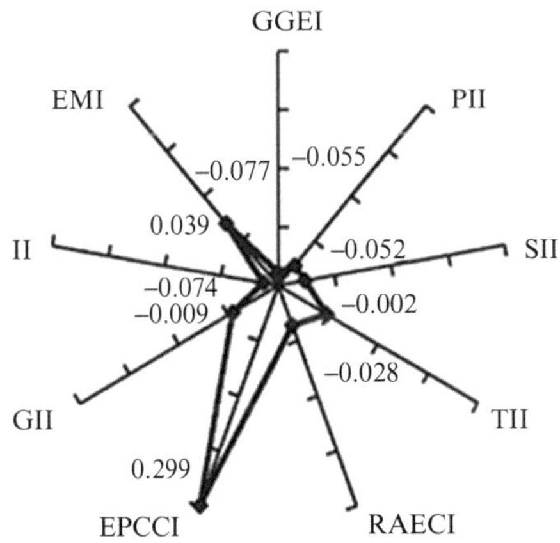

Fig. 5.48 Scores of Guizhou by Second-Class Indicators

Table 5.47 Changes in Guizhou's rankings by First-Class and Second-Class Indicators, 2009–2010

Indicator	2010	2009	Difference	Indicator	2010	2009	Difference
GDI	13	13	0				
GDEG	29	30	1	RAECI	20	20	0
GGEI	27	28	1	EPCCI	2	2	0
PII	30	30	0	SDGP	21	26	5
SII	29	29	0	GII	16	11	−5
TII	10	11	1	II	26	29	3
CCPNRE	2	2	0	EMI	4	4	0

Note: A positive value in "Difference" means a rise in ranking

5.24.2 Changes in Guizhou's Rankings by GDI 2009–2010

According to Table 5.47, in First-Class Indicators ranking, it rose by 1 place in GDEG and 5 in SDGP, and remained unchanged in CCPNRE. In Second-Class Indicators ranking, Guizhou dropped by 5 places in GII and rose by 1 in GGEI and TII and 3 in II. It remained the same in the rankings by other indicators in 2009.

To further explain the causes of the changes in the rankings by First- and Second-Class Indicators, we put the Third-Class Indicators where a change of more than 3 places occurred from 2009 to 2010 in Table 5.48. Compared with those in 2009, Guizhou dropped by 6 places in Ratio of environmental spending to government expenditure, 4 in Number of environmental emergencies, 3 in Electricity consumption per capita in urban areas, Ratio of the spending on science, education, culture, and public health to government expenditure and Industrial nitrogen oxide removal rate. It rose by 3 places in Utilization rate of industrial solid waste, Length of public transport routes per capita in urban areas and Industrial SO_2 removal rate, 4 in Government spending per capita on rural water supply system and toilet improvement, 9 in Area of green land per capita in urban areas and 19 in Treatment rate of urban wastewater.

Table 5.48 Third-Class Indicators where changes over 3 places by Guizhou, 2009–2010

	Original data for 2010 and 2009			Change in ranking		
Third-Class Indicator	Unit	2010	2009	2010	2009	Difference
Electricity consumption per capita in urban areas	kWh per capita	276.16	346.64	21	18	−3
Utilization rate of industrial solid waste	%	50.90	45.60	24	27	3
Ratio of environmental spending to government expenditure	%	3.33	4.03	15	9	−6
Government spending per capita on rural water supply system and toilet improvement	Yuan per capita	38.06	33.84	19	23	4
Ratio of the spending on science, education, culture, and public health to government expenditure	%	28.22	28.96	9	6	−3
Area of green land per capita in urban areas	Hectare per capita	0.00	0.00	14	23	9
Treatment rate of urban wastewater	%	86.80	56.20	8	27	19
Length of public transport routes per capita in urban areas	km per capita	0.0003	0.0002	21	24	3
Industrial SO_2 removal rate	%	77.19	67.87	3	6	3
Industrial nitrogen oxide removal rate	%	8.53	17.33	5	2	−3
Number of environmental emergencies		5	4	14	10	−4

Note: A positive value in "Difference" means a rise in ranking

Green development checkup-Yunnan

No.	Indicator	Unit	Attribute	2010 average of 30 provinces	2010 figure	2009 figure	2010 ranking	2009 ranking	Change in ranking	Source of 2010 data	Chernoff face
1	GDP per capita	Yuan per capita	Positive	33,964.12	15,752	13,539	29	28	−1	China Statistics	
2	Energy consumption per unit of GDP	Ton coal equivalent per 10,000 yuan	Negative	1.29	1.44	1.50	23	22	−1	China Statistics	
3	Ratio of non-fossil energy consumption to total energy consumption		Positive	NA	NA	NA	NA	NA			
4	CO_2 emissions per unit of GDP		Negative	NA	NA	NA	NA	NA			
5	SO_2 emissions per unit of GDP	Ton per 10,000 yuan	Negative	0.0088	0.0083	0.0093	20	19	−1	China Statistics	
6	COD emissions per unit of GDP	Ton per 10,000 yuan	Negative	0.0045	0.0044	0.0051	16	16	0	China Statistics	
7	Nitrogen oxide emissions per unit of GDP	Ton per 10,000 yuan	Negative	0.0068	0.0072	0.0073	23	24	1	Environmental Annual Report; China Statistics	
8	Ammonia/nitrogen emissions per unit of GDP	Ton per 10,000 yuan	Negative	0.0004	0.0003	0.0004	10	9	−1	Environmental Annual Report; China Statistics	
9	Electricity consumption per capita in urban areas	kWh per capita	Negative	295.08	154.07	263.73	11	8	−3	City	

10	Labor productivity of the primary sector	10,000 yuan per capita	Positive	1.61	0.66	0.64	29	29	0	China Statistics	
11	Land productivity	100 million yuan per 1,000 hectares	Positive	0.26	0.14	0.13	27	25	−2	China Statistics	☹
12	Proportion of water-saving irrigated area in effectively irrigated area		Positive	0.49	0.35	0.34	20	20	0	Water Conservancy; China Statistics	
13	Proportion of water-saving irrigated area in effectively irrigated area	%	Positive	53.55	26.16	25.73	29	29	0	China Statistics	
14	Labor productivity of the secondary sector	10,000 yuan per capita	Positive	12.13	8.76	7.58	21	19	−2	China Statistics	☹
15	Water consumption per unit of value added created by industrial enterprises	m^3/yuan	Negative	0.0100	0.0110	0.0107	19	16	−3	China Statistics	☹
16	Energy consumption per unit of value added created by industrial enterprises above designated size (no data)		Negative	NA	NA	NA	NA	NA			
17	Utilization rate of industrial solid waste	%	Positive	69.80	50.80	48.90	25	24	−1	Environmental Yearbook	☹
18	Recycling rate of industrial water	%	Positive	72.90	64.65	62.20	23	22	−1	Environmental Yearbook	☹
19	Ratio of the output of six energy-intensive industries to gross industrial output	%	Negative	39.65	55.63	53.47	27	26	−1	Industrial Economy	☹
20	Labor productivity of the tertiary sector	10,000 yuan per capita	Positive	6.96	3.95	3.66	26	25	−1	China Statistics	☹

(continued)

(continued)

No.	Indicator	Unit	Attribute	2010 average of 30 provinces	2010 figure	2009 figure	2010 ranking	2009 ranking	Change in ranking	Source of 2010 data	Chernoff face
21	Proportion of the value added of the tertiary sector in GDP	%	Positive	39.97	40.00	40.80	10	11	1	China Statistics	
22	Proportion of tertiary sector employees in the total employed population	%	Positive	36.67	27.00	25.79	28	28	0	China Statistics	
23	Water resources per capita	m^3 per capita	Positive	2,419.38	4,233.15	3,459.73	6	4	−2	China Statistics	
24	Forest area per capita	Hectare per capita	Positive	0.19	0.40	0.40	4	4	0	China Statistics	
25	Forest coverage rate	%	Positive	30.63	47.50	47.50	7	7	0	China Statistics	
26	Proportion of the area of natural reserves in the total area of a region	%	Positive	8.60	7.80	7.41	13	12	−1	China Statistics	
27	Proportion of the area of wetlands in the total area of a region	%	Positive	7.01	0.61	0.61	28	28	0	China Statistics	
28	Growing stock per capita	m^3 per capita	Positive	10.70	37.21	37.46	3	3	0	China Statistics	
29	CO_2 emissions per unit of land area		Negative	NA	NA	NA	NA	NA			
30	CO_2 emissions per capita		Negative	NA	NA	NA	NA	NA			
31	SO_2 emissions per unit of land area	Ton per km^2	Negative	6.3677	1.3067	1.3030	5	5	0	China Statistics; Deserts	
32	SO_2 emissions per capita	Ton per capita	Negative	0.0191	0.0109	0.0110	5	4	−1	China Statistics	
33	COD emissions per unit of land area	Ton per km^2	Negative	3.7722	0.7002	0.7126	5	5	0	China Statistics; Deserts	
34	COD emissions per capita	Ton per capita	Negative	0.0101	0.0059	0.0060	3	3	0	China Statistics	

35	Nitrogen oxide emissions per unit of land area	Ton per km^2	Negative	6.4473	1.1352	1.0308	5	4	−1	China Statistics; Deserts; Environmental Annual Report	☹
36	Nitrogen oxide emissions per capita	Ton per capita	Negative	0.0165	0.0095	0.0087	7	8	1	Environmental Annual Report; China Statistics	☺
37	Ammonia/nitrogen emissions per unit of land area	Ton per km^2	Negative	0.4164	0.0548	0.0496	3	4	1	China Statistics; Deserts; Environmental Annual Report	☺
38	Ammonia/nitrogen emissions per capita	Ton per capita	Negative	0.0010	0.0005	0.0004	2	1	−1	Environmental Annual Report; China Statistics	☹
39	Consumption of chemical fertilizers per unit of cultivated land area	10,000 ton per 1,000 hectares	Negative	0.05	0.03	0.03	7	7	0	China Statistics Yearbook	
40	Consumption of pesticides per unit of cultivated land area	Ton per 1,000 hectares	Negative	17.68	7.61	7.01	9	9	0	Environmental Yearbook; China Statistics	
41	Nitrogen oxide emissions per capita from road transport	Ton per 10,000 persons	Negative	24.07	18.26	17.74	14	13	−1	Environmental Annual Report; China Statistics	☹
42	Ratio of environmental spending to government expenditure	%	Positive	3.35	3.78	4.21	12	8	−4	China Statistics	☹

(continued)

(continued)

No.	Indicator	Unit	Attribute	2010 average of 30 provinces	2010 figure	2009 figure	2010 ranking	2009 ranking	Change in ranking	Source of 2010 data	Chernoff face
43	Ratio of the investment in pollution control to GDP	%	Positive	1.40	1.47	1.48	12	14	2	Environmental Yearbook; China Statistics	☺
44	Government spending per capita on rural water supply system and toilet improvement	Yuan per capita	Positive	57.01	37.16	28.38	20	26	6	Environmental Yearbook	☺
45	Investment in converting cultivated land into forests and grassland per unit of cultivated land area	10,000 yuan per 1,000 hectares	Positive	29.81	27.19	28.27	14	11	−3	Environmental Yearbook; China Statistics	☹
46	Ratio of the spending on science, education, culture, and public health to government expenditure	%	Positive	26.10	26.93	26.17	13	18	5	China Statistics	☺
47	Area of green land per capita in urban areas	Hectare per capita	Positive	0.00	0.00	0.00	22	21	−1	City; China Statistics	☹
48	Coverage of water supply in urban areas	%	Positive	96.08	96.50	96.23	18	17	−1	China Statistics	☹
49	Treatment rate of urban wastewater	%	Positive	79.18	93.40	85.30	1	5	4	Environmental Yearbook	☺
50	Harmless treatment rate of urban household waste	%	Positive	78.47	88.28	80.88	11	12	1	China Statistics	☺
51	Public buses per 10,000 urban residents		Positive	9.86	9.74	9.80	14	19	5	China Statistics	☺
52	Length of public transport routes per capita in urban areas	km per capita	Positive	0.0006	0.0005	0.0004	11	12	1	Yearbook City	☺

53	Ratio of the rural residents benefiting from water supply system improvement to the total rural population	%	Positive	94.44	85.05	81.80	27	28	1	Environmental Yearbook	☺
54	Green coverage of urban built-up areas	%	Positive	37.75	37.31	36.29	19	21	2	China Statistics	☺
55	Newly-added afforestation area of the year per capita	Hectare per 10,000 persons	Positive	59.50	144.23	156.57	4	4	0	China Statistics	
56	Industrial SO_2 removal rate	%	Positive	59.83	77.14	77.23	4	2	−2	China Statistics	☹
57	Industrial wastewater COD removal rate	%	Positive	70.84	77.69	78.30	12	9	−3	Environmental Annual Report; China Statistics	☹
58	Industrial nitrogen oxide removal rate	%	Positive	4.07	0.00	0.00	30	28	−2	Environmental Annual Report	☹
59	Industrial wastewater ammonia/nitrogen removal rate	%	Positive	62.87	82.16	85.63	7	3	−4	Environmental Annual Report; China Statistics	☹
60	Number of environmental emergencies		Negative	14.00	0	3	1	9	8	China Statistics	☺

Note:
China Statistics: *China Statistical Yearbook 2011*
Environmental Yearbook: *China Environmental Statistical Yearbook 2011*
Environmental Annual Report: *China Environment Annual Report 2010*
City: *China City Statistical Yearbook 2011*
Water Conservancy: *China Water Conservancy Statistical Yearbook 2011*
Industrial Economy: *China Industrial Economic Statistical Yearbook 2011*
Deserts: *Deserts in China and Desertification Control*

5.25 Brief Analysis of Green Development in Yunnan

Yunnan ranked 7th among the 30 participating provinces by GDI according to 2010 data, as it did in 2009 (Yunnan ranked 7th in 2009). Following is a brief analysis of its score by each indicator and their changes from 2009 to 2010. Following is a brief analysis of its score by each indicator and their changes in 2009 and 2010.

5.25.1 Yunnan's 2010 Scores by GDI

Yunnan scored 0.109 in 2010. From the three First-Class Indicators including GDEG, CCPNRE, and SDGP as shown in Fig. 5.49, Yunnan had advantage in terms of CCPNRE and SDGP, yet underperformed compared with the national average in GDEG (Note: the national average value of each indicator is 0).

According to Fig. 5.50, Yunnan surpassed the national average in 4 of Second-Class Indicators in 2010, which are RAECI, EPCCI, GII and EMI, yet ranked lower than the national average in GGEI, SII, TII and II.

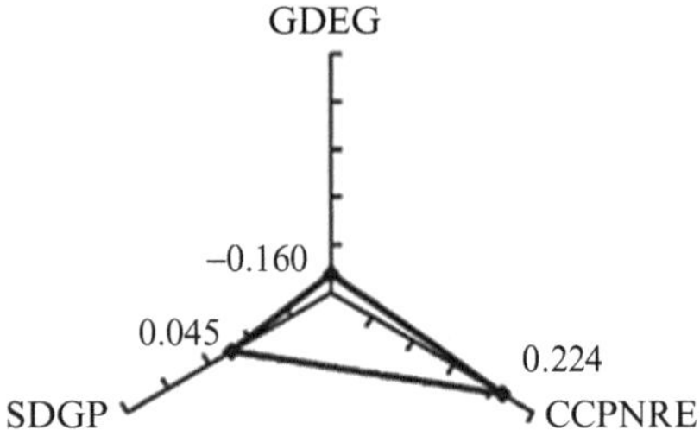

Fig. 5.49 Scores of Yunnan by First-Class Indicators

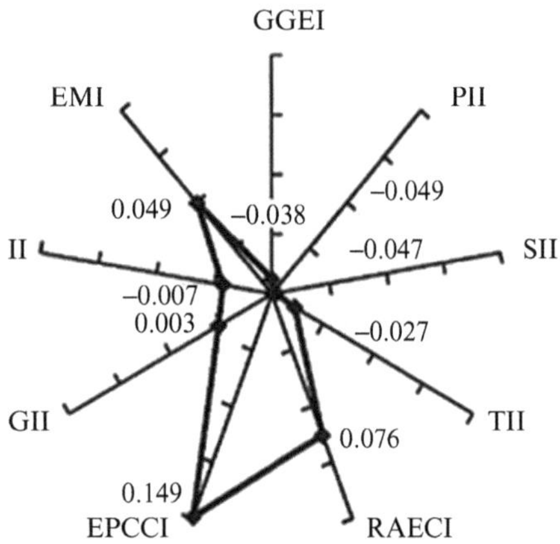

Fig. 5.50 Scores of Yunnan by Second-Class Indicators

Table 5.49 Changes in Yunnan's rankings by First-Class and Second-Class Indicators, 2009–2010

Indicators	2010	2009	Difference	Indicators	2010	2009	Difference
GDI	7	7	0				
GDEG	27	26	−1	RAECI	4	4	0
GGEI	23	24	1	EPCCI	3	3	0
PII	29	29	0	SDGP	11	9	−2
SII	27	27	0	GII	14	13	−1
TII	26	26	0	II	16	15	−1
CCPNRE	3	3	0	EMI	1	3	2

Note: A positive value in "Difference" means a rise in ranking

5.25.2 Changes in Yunnan's Rankings by GDI 2009–2010

According to Table 5.49, in First-Class Indicators ranking, it fell by 1 place in GDEG and 2 in SDGP. It remained unchanged by CCPNRE. In Second-Class Indicators ranking, Yunnan fell by 1 place in GII and II. It rose by 1 place in GGEI and 2 in EMI. It remained the same in the rankings by other indicators in 2009.

To further explain the causes of the changes in the rankings by First- and Second-Class Indicators, we put the Third-Class Indicators where a change of more than 3 places occurred from 2009 to 2010 in Table 5.50. Compared with those in 2009, Yunnan dropped by 4 places in Ratio of environmental spending to government expenditure and Industrial wastewater ammonia/nitrogen removal rate, 3 in Electricity consumption per capita in urban areas, Water consumption per unit of value added created by industrial enterprises, Investment in converting cultivated land into forests and grassland per unit of cultivated land area and Industrial wastewater COD removal rate. It rose by 4 places in Treatment rate of urban wastewater, 5 in Ratio of the spending on science, education, culture, and public health to government expenditure and Public buses per 10,000 urban residents, 6 in Government spending per capita on rural water supply system and toilet improvement and 8 in Number of environmental emergencies.

Table 5.50 Third-Class Indicators where changes over 3 places by Yunnan, 2009–2010

	Original data for 2010 and 2009			Change in ranking		
Third-Class Indicator	Unit	2010	2009	2010	2009	Difference
Electricity consumption per capita in urban areas	kWh per capita	154.07	263.73	11	8	−3
Water consumption per unit of value added created by industrial enterprises	m^3/yuan	0.0110	0.0107	19	16	−3
Ratio of environmental spending to government expenditure	%	3.78	4.21	12	8	−4
Government spending per capita on rural water supply system and toilet improvement	Yuan per capita	37.16	28.38	20	26	6
Investment in converting cultivated land into forests and grassland per unit of cultivated land area	10,000 yuan per 1,000 hectares	27.19	28.27	14	11	−3
Ratio of the spending on science, education, culture, and public health to government expenditure	%	26.93	26.17	13	18	5
Treatment rate of urban wastewater	%	93.40	85.30	1	5	4
Public buses per 10,000 urban residents		9.74	9.80	14	19	5
Industrial wastewater COD removal rate	%	77.69	78.30	12	9	−3
Industrial wastewater ammonia/nitrogen removal rate	%	82.16	85.63	7	3	−4
Number of environmental emergencies		0	3	1	9	8

Note: A positive value in "Difference" means a rise in ranking

Green development checkup-Shaanxi

No.	Indicator	Unit	Attribute	2010 average of 30 provinces	2010 figure	2009 figure	2010 ranking	2009 ranking	Change in ranking	Source of 2010 data	Chernoff face
1	GDP per capita	Yuan per capita	Positive	33,964.12	27,133	21,688	15	17	2	China Statistics	☺
2	Energy consumption per unit of GDP	Ton coal equivalent per 10,000 yuan	Negative	1.29	1.13	1.17	15	14	−1	China Statistics	☹
3	Ratio of non-fossil energy consumption to total energy consumption		Positive	NA	NA	NA	NA	NA			
4	CO_2 emissions per unit of GDP		Negative	NA	NA	NA	NA	NA			
5	SO_2 emissions per unit of GDP	Ton per 10,000 yuan	Negative	0.0088	0.0099	0.0117	21	21	0	China Statistics	
6	COD emissions per unit of GDP	Ton per 10,000 yuan	Negative	0.0045	0.0039	0.0046	14	14	0	China Statistics	
7	Nitrogen oxide emissions per unit of GDP	Ton per 10,000 yuan	Negative	0.0068	0.0066	0.0073	22	23	1	Environmental Annual Report; China Statistics	☺
8	Ammonia/nitrogen emissions per unit of GDP	Ton per 10,000 yuan	Negative	0.0004	0.0004	0.0005	14	16	2	Environmental Annual Report; China Statistics	☺
9	Electricity consumption per capita in urban areas	kWh per capita	Negative	295.08	157.94	323.86	12	17	5	City	☺
10	Labor productivity of the primary sector	10,000 yuan per capita	Positive	1.61	1.14	0.88	22	25	3	China Statistics	☺

(continued)

(continued)

No.	Indicator	Unit	Attribute	2010 average of 30 provinces	2010 figure	2009 figure	2010 ranking	2009 ranking	Change in ranking	Source of 2010 data	Chernoff face
11	Land productivity	100 million yuan per 1,000 hectares	Positive	0.26	0.26	0.20	13	15	2	China Statistics	☺
12	Proportion of water-saving irrigated area in effectively irrigated area		Positive	0.49	0.66	0.66	9	8	−1	Water Conservancy; China Statistics	☹
13	Proportion of water-saving irrigated area in effectively irrigated area	%	Positive	53.55	31.72	31.93	24	23	−1	China Statistics	☹
14	Labor productivity of the secondary sector	10,000 yuan per capita	Positive	12.13	11.83	10.13	11	11	0	China Statistics	
15	Water consumption per unit of value added created by industrial enterprises	m^3/yuan	Negative	0.0100	0.0038	0.0033	7	6	−1	China Statistics	☹
16	Energy consumption per unit of value added created by industrial enterprises above designated size (no data)		Negative	NA	NA	NA	NA	NA			
17	Utilization rate of industrial solid waste	%	Positive	69.80	54.40	54.00	23	22	−1	Environmental Yearbook	☹
18	Recycling rate of industrial water	%	Positive	72.90	91.06	91.11	8	8	0	Environmental Yearbook	
19	Ratio of the output of six energy-intensive industries to gross industrial output	%	Negative	39.65	34.97	34.32	13	12	−1	Industrial Economy	☹

20	Labor productivity of the tertiary sector	10,000 yuan per capita	Positive	6.96	6.06	5.06	15	17	2	China Statistics	☺
21	Proportion of the value added of the tertiary sector in GDP	%	Positive	39.97	36.40	38.50	19	18	−1	China Statistics	☹
22	Proportion of tertiary sector employees in the total employed population	%	Positive	36.67	31.16	31.75	25	23	−2	China Statistics	☹
23	Water resources per capita	m^3 per capita	Positive	2,419.38	1,360.25	1,105.63	20	18	−2	China Statistics	☹
24	Forest area per capita	Hectare per capita	Positive	0.19	0.21	0.20	11	11	0	China Statistics	
25	Forest coverage rate	%	Positive	30.63	37.26	37.26	11	11	0	China Statistics	
26	Proportion of the area of natural reserves in the total area of a region	%	Positive	8.60	5.64	5.62	20	19	−1	China Statistics	☹
27	Proportion of the area of wetlands in the total area of a region	%	Positive	7.01	1.42	1.42	26	26	0	China Statistics	
28	Growing stock per capita	m^3 per capita	Positive	10.70	9.68	9.58	10	10	0	China Statistics	
29	CO_2 emissions per unit of land area		Negative	NA	NA	NA	NA	NA			
30	CO_2 emissions per capita		Negative	NA	NA	NA	NA	NA			
31	SO_2 emissions per unit of land area	Ton per km^2	Negative	6.3677	3.9973	4.1295	16	16	0	Yearbook Desert	
32	SO_2 emissions per capita	Ton per capita	Negative	0.0191	0.0207	0.0214	21	22	1	China Statistics	☺
33	COD emissions per unit of land area	Ton per km^2	Negative	3.7722	1.5794	1.6329	9	9	0	China Statistics; Deserts	

(continued)

(continued)

No.	Indicator	Unit	Attribute	2010 average of 30 provinces	2010 figure	2009 figure	2010 ranking	2009 ranking	Change in ranking	Source of 2010 data	Chernoff face
34	COD emissions per capita	Ton per capita	Negative	0.0101	0.0082	0.0084	10	10	0	China Statistics	
35	Nitrogen oxide emissions per unit of land area	Ton per km^2	Negative	6.4473	2.6592	2.5617	13	14	1	China Statistics; Deserts; Environmental Annual Report	
36	Nitrogen oxide emissions per capita	Ton per capita	Negative	0.0165	0.0138	0.0132	17	16	−1	Environmental Annual Report; China Statistics	
37	Ammonia/nitrogen emissions per unit of land area	Ton per km^2	Negative	0.4164	0.1643	0.1643	10	10	0	China Statistics; Deserts; Environmental Annual Report	
38	Ammonia/nitrogen emissions per capita	Ton per capita	Negative	0.0010	0.0009	0.0008	13	13	0	Environmental Annual Report; China Statistics	
39	Consumption of chemical fertilizers per unit of cultivated land area	10,000 ton per 1,000 hectares	Negative	0.05	0.05	0.04	16	14	−2	China Statistics; China Statistics	
40	Consumption of pesticides per unit of cultivated land area	Ton per 1,000 hectares	Negative	17.68	3.06	3.25	3	4	1	Environmental Yearbook; China Statistics	
41	Nitrogen oxide emissions per capita from road transport	Ton per 10,000 persons	Negative	24.07	6.88	8.59	4	3	−1	Environmental Annual Report; China Statistics	
42	Ratio of environmental spending to government expenditure	%	Positive	3.35	3.74	4.32	13	6	−7	China Statistics	

43	Ratio of the investment in pollution control to GDP	%	Positive	1.40	1.77	1.74	7	8	1	Environmental Yearbook; China Statistics	☺
44	Government spending per capita on rural water supply system and toilet improvement	Yuan per capita	Positive	57.01	69.69	48.21	9	16	7	Environmental Yearbook	☺
45	Investment in converting cultivated land into forests and grassland per unit of cultivated land area	10,000 yuan per 1,000 hectares	Positive	29.81	55.30	58.30	6	5	−1	Environmental Yearbook; China Statistics	☹
46	Ratio of the spending on science, education, culture, and public health to government expenditure	%	Positive	26.10	27.38	27.07	12	12	0	China Statistics	
47	Area of green land per capita in urban areas	Hectare per capita	Positive	0.00	0.00	0.00	28	27	−1	City; China Statistics	☹
48	Coverage of water supply in urban areas	%	Positive	96.08	99.39	98.06	10	11	1	China Statistics	☺
49	Treatment rate of urban wastewater	%	Positive	79.18	74.20	66.40	24	21	−3	Environmental Yearbook	☹
50	Harmless treatment rate of urban household waste	%	Positive	78.47	79.84	69.16	17	16	−1	China Statistics	☹
51	Public buses per 10,000 urban residents		Positive	9.86	12.64	13.36	3	5	2	China Statistics	☺
52	Length of public transport routes per capita in urban areas	km per capita	Positive	0.0006	0.0002	0.0002	22	29	7	China Statistics; City	☺
53	Ratio of the rural residents benefiting from water supply system improvement to the total rural population	%	Positive	94.44	89.27	96.93	24	15	−9	Environmental Yearbook	☹

(continued)

(continued)

No.	Indicator	Unit	Attribute	2010 average of 30 provinces	2010 figure	2009 figure	2010 ranking	2009 ranking	Change in ranking	Source of 2010 data	Chernoff face
54	Green coverage of urban built-up areas	%	Positive	37.75	38.29	38.76	13	9	−4	China Statistics	☹
55	Newly-added afforestation area of the year per capita	Hectare per 10,000 persons	Positive	59.50	97.06	119.31	6	6	0	China Statistics	
56	Industrial SO_2 removal rate	%	Positive	59.83	60.36	50.09	19	24	5	China Statistics	☺
57	Industrial wastewater COD removal rate	%	Positive	70.84	66.81	65.85	20	18	−2	Environmental Annual Report; China Statistics	☹
58	Industrial nitrogen oxide removal rate	%	Positive	4.07	2.22	2.89	18	19	1	Environmental Annual Report	☺
59	Industrial wastewater ammonia/ nitrogen removal rate	%	Positive	62.87	55.47	47.22	20	21	1	Environmental Annual Report; China Statistics	☺
60	Number of environmental emergencies		Negative	14.00	9	10	19	18	−1	China Statistics	☹

Note:
China Statistics: *China Statistical Yearbook 2011*
Environmental Yearbook: *China Environmental Statistical Yearbook 2011*
Environmental Annual Report: *China Environment Annual Report 2010*
City: *China City Statistical Yearbook 2011*
Water Conservancy: *China Water Conservancy Statistical Yearbook 2011*
Industrial Economy: *China Industrial Economic Statistical Yearbook 2011*
Deserts: *Deserts in China and Desertification Control*

5.26 Brief Analysis of Green Development in Shaanxi

Shaanxi ranked 14th among the 30 participating provinces by GDI according to 2010 data, as it did in 2009 (Shaanxi ranked 14th in 2009). Following is a brief analysis of its score by each indicator and their changes from 2009 to 2010.

5.26.1 *Shaanxi's 2010 Scores by GDI*

Shaanxi scored 0.030 in 2010. From the three First-Class Indicators including GDEG, CCPNRE, and SDGP as shown in Fig. 5.51, Shaanxi had advantage in terms of CCPNRE and SDGP, yet underperformed compared with the national average in GDEG (Note: the national average value of each indicator is 0).

According to Fig. 5.52, Shaanxi surpassed the national average in 3 of Second-Class Indicators in 2010, which are SII, EPCCI and GII, yet ranked lower than the national average in GGEI, PII, TII, RAECI, II and EMI.

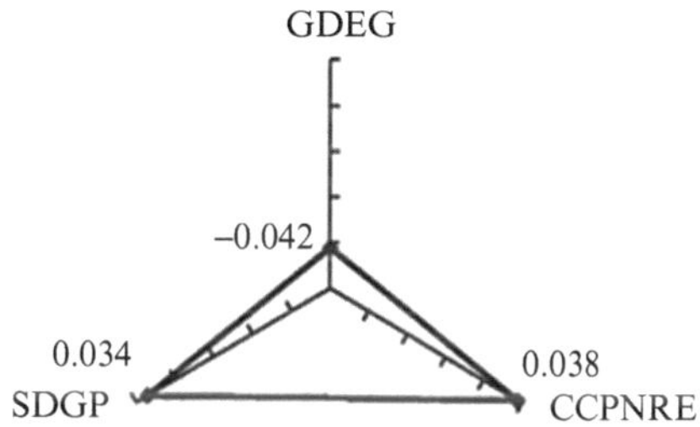

Fig. 5.51 Scores of Shaanxi by First-Class Indicators

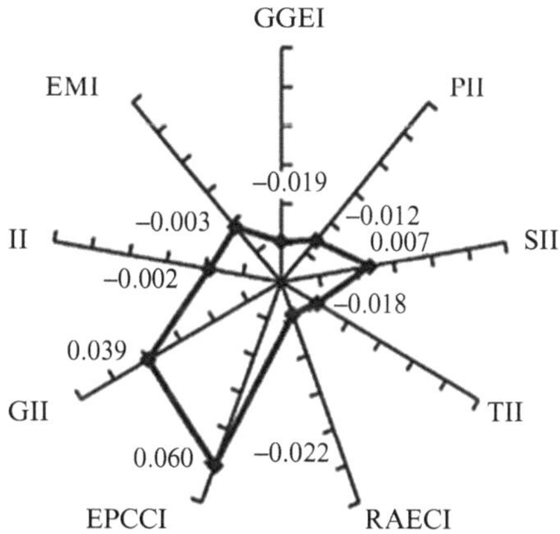

Fig. 5.52 Scores of Shaanxi by Second-Class Indicators

Table 5.51 Changes in Shaanxi's rankings by First-Class and Second-Class Indicators, 2009–2010

Indicator	2010	2009	Difference	Indicator	2010	2009	Difference
GDI	14	14	0				
GDEG	15	14	−1	RAECI	18	19	1
GGEI	20	22	2	EPCCI	6	9	3
PII	16	17	1	SDGP	13	13	0
SII	13	10	−3	GII	6	6	0
TII	20	21	1	II	15	14	−1
CCPNRE	11	12	1	EMI	18	17	−1

Note: A positive value in "Difference" means a rise in ranking

5.26.2 Changes in Shaanxi's Rankings by GDI 2009–2010

According to Table 5.51, in First-Class Indicators ranking, it dropped by 1 place in CCPNRE, rose by 1 place in GDEG and remained unchanged in SDGP. In Second-Class Indicators ranking, Shaanxi dropped by 3 places in SII, 1 in II and EMI. It rose by 2 places in GGEI and 1 in PII, TII and RAECI, 3 in EPCCI. It remained the same in the rankings by other indicators in 2009.

To further explain the causes of the changes in the rankings by First- and Second-Class Indicators, we put the Third-Class Indicators where a change of more than 3 places occurred from 2009 to 2010 in Table 5.52. Compared with those in 2009, Shaanxi dropped by 9 places in Ratio of the rural residents benefiting from water supply system improvement to the total rural population, 7 in Ratio of environmental spending to government expenditure, 4 in Green coverage of urban built-up areas, 3 in Treatment rate of urban wastewater and Labor productivity of the primary sector. It rose by 5 places in Electricity consumption per capita in urban areas and Industrial SO_2 removal rate, 7 in Government spending per capita on rural water supply system and toilet improvement and Length of public transport routes per capita in urban areas.

Table 5.52 Third-Class Indicators where changes over 3 places by Shaanxi, 2009–2010

	Original data for 2010 and 2009			Change in ranking		
Third-Class Indicator	Unit	2010	2009	2010	2009	Difference
Electricity consumption per capita in urban areas	kWh per capita	157.94	323.86	12	17	5
Labor productivity of the primary sector	10,000 yuan per capita	1.14	0.88	22	25	3
Ratio of environmental spending to government expenditure	%	3.74	4.32	13	6	−7
Government spending per capita on rural water supply system and toilet improvement	Yuan per capita	69.69	48.21	9	16	7
Treatment rate of urban wastewater	%	74.20	66.40	24	21	−3
Length of public transport routes per capita in urban areas	km per capita	0.0002	0.0002	22	29	7
Ratio of the rural residents benefiting from water supply system improvement to the total rural population	%	89.27	96.93	24	15	−9
Green coverage of urban built-up areas	%	38.29	38.76	13	9	−4
Industrial SO_2 removal rate	%	60.36	50.09	19	24	5

Note: A positive value in "Difference" means a rise in ranking

Green development checkup-Gansu

No.	Indicator	Unit	Attribute	2010 average of 30 provinces	2010 figure	2009 figure	2010 ranking	2009 ranking	Change in ranking	Source of 2010 data	Chernoff face
1	GDP per capita	Yuan per capita	Positive	33,964.12	16,113	12,872	28	29	1	China Statistics	
2	Energy consumption per unit of GDP	Ton coal equivalent per 10,000 yuan	Negative	1.29	1.80	1.86	25	24	−1	China Statistics	
3	Ratio of non-fossil energy consumption to total energy consumption		Positive	NA	NA	NA	NA	NA			
4	CO_2 emissions per unit of GDP		Negative	NA	NA	NA	NA	NA			
5	SO_2 emissions per unit of GDP	Ton per 10,000 yuan	Negative	0.0088	0.0168	0.0170	27	26	−1	China Statistics	
6	COD emissions per unit of GDP	Ton per 10,000 yuan	Negative	0.0045	0.0051	0.0057	21	21	0	China Statistics	
7	Nitrogen oxide emissions per unit of GDP	Ton per 10,000 yuan	Negative	0.0068	0.0089	0.0087	25	25	0	Environmental Annual Report; China Statistics	
8	Ammonia/nitrogen emissions per unit of GDP	Ton per 10,000 yuan	Negative	0.0004	0.0007	0.0009	28	30	2	Environmental Annual Report; China Statistics	
9	Electricity consumption per capita in urban areas	kWh per capita	Negative	295.08	107.45	266.19	4	9	5	City	
10	Labor productivity of the primary sector	10,000 yuan per capita	Positive	1.61	0.81	0.67	28	28	0	China Statistics	

11	Land productivity	100 million yuan per 1,000 hectares	Positive	0.26	0.19	0.15	19	22	3	China Statistics	☺
12	Proportion of water-saving irrigated area in effectively irrigated area		Positive	0.49	0.67	0.65	8	9	1	Water Conservancy; China Statistics	☺
13	Proportion of water-saving irrigated area in effectively irrigated area	%	Positive	53.55	27.44	27.14	28	28	0	China Statistics	
14	Labor productivity of the secondary sector	10,000 yuan per capita	Positive	12.13	9.43	7.57	18	20	2	China Statistics	☺
15	Water consumption per unit of value added created by industrial enterprises	m^3/yuan	Negative	0.0100	0.0112	0.0109	21	18	−3	China Statistics	☹
16	Energy consumption per unit of value added created by industrial enterprises above designated size (no data)		Negative	NA	NA	NA	NA	NA			
17	Utilization rate of industrial solid waste	%	Positive	69.80	46.30	33.40	29	30	1	Environmental Yearbook	☺
18	Recycling rate of industrial water	%	Positive	72.90	87.09	89.21	10	10	0	Environmental Yearbook	
19	Ratio of the output of six energy-intensive industries to gross industrial output	%	Negative	39.65	67.41	68.92	30	30	0	Industrial Economy	
20	Labor productivity of the tertiary sector	10,000 yuan per capita	Positive	6.96	3.25	2.97	29	29	0	China Statistics	

(continued)

(continued)

No.	Indicator	Unit	Attribute	2010 average of 30 provinces	2010 figure	2009 figure	2010 ranking	2009 ranking	Change in ranking	Source of 2010 data	Chernoff face
21	Proportion of the value added of the tertiary sector in GDP	%	Positive	39.97	37.30	40.20	14	12	−2	China Statistics	☹
22	Proportion of tertiary sector employees in the total employed population	%	Positive	36.67	33.81	32.88	20	21	1	China Statistics	☺
23	Water resources per capita	m^3 per capita	Positive	2,419.38	841.66	794.32	21	20	−1	China Statistics	☹
24	Forest area per capita	Hectare per capita	Positive	0.19	0.18	0.18	13	13	0	China Statistics	
25	Forest coverage rate	%	Positive	30.63	10.42	10.42	25	25	0	China Statistics	
26	Proportion of the area of natural reserves in the total area of a region	%	Positive	8.60	16.17	16.16	3	3	0	China Statistics	
27	Proportion of the area of wetlands in the total area of a region	%	Positive	7.01	2.80	2.80	22	22	0	China Statistics	
28	Growing stock per capita	m^3 per capita	Positive	10.70	8.48	8.24	12	12	0	China Statistics	
29	CO_2 emissions per unit of land area		Negative	NA	NA	NA	NA	NA			
30	CO_2 emissions per capita		Negative	NA	NA	NA	NA	NA			
31	SO_2 emissions per unit of land area	Ton per km^2	Negative	6.3677	1.6418	1.4886	6	6	0	China Statistics; Deserts	
32	SO_2 emissions per capita	Ton per capita	Negative	0.0191	0.0212	0.0190	22	19	−3	China Statistics	☹
33	COD emissions per unit of land area	Ton per km^2	Negative	3.7722	0.4986	0.5002	4	4	0	China Statistics; Deserts	

34	COD emissions per capita	Ton per capita	Negative	0.0101	0.0065	0.0064	4	4	0	China Statistics	
35	Nitrogen oxide emissions per unit of land area	Ton per km^2	Negative	6.4473	0.8688	0.7587	3	3	0	China Statistics; Deserts; Environmental Annual Report	
36	Nitrogen oxide emissions per capita	Ton per capita	Negative	0.0165	0.0112	0.0097	11	12	1	Environmental Annual Report; China Statistics	☺
37	Ammonia/nitrogen emissions per unit of land area	Ton per km^2	Negative	0.4164	0.0714	0.0803	5	5	0	China Statistics; Deserts; Environmental Annual Report	
38	Ammonia/nitrogen emissions per capita	Ton per capita	Negative	0.0010	0.0009	0.0010	16	18	2	Environmental Annual Report; China Statistics	
39	Consumption of chemical fertilizers per unit of cultivated land area	10,000 ton per 1,000 hectares	Negative	0.05	0.02	0.02	3	3	0	China Statistics; China Statistics	
40	Consumption of pesticides per unit of cultivated land area	Ton per 1,000 hectares	Negative	17.68	9.57	8.57	13	11	−2	Environmental Yearbook; China Statistics	☹
41	Nitrogen oxide emissions per capita from road transport	Ton per 10,000 persons	Negative	24.07	17.74	15.54	13	11	−2	Environmental Annual Report; China Statistics	☹
42	Ratio of environmental spending to government expenditure	%	Positive	3.35	4.65	4.26	4	7	3	China Statistics	☺
43	Ratio of the investment in pollution control to GDP	%	Positive	1.40	1.55	1.51	11	13	2	Environmental Yearbook; China Statistics	☺

(continued)

(continued)

No.	Indicator	Unit	Attribute	2010 average of 30 provinces	2010 figure	2009 figure	2010 ranking	2009 ranking	Change in ranking	Source of 2010 data	Chernoff face
44	Government spending per capita on rural water supply system and toilet improvement	Yuan per capita	Positive	57.01	41.06	40.53	18	18	0	Environmental Yearbook	
45	Investment in converting cultivated land into forests and grassland per unit of cultivated land area	10,000 yuan per 1,000 hectares	Positive	29.81	82.80	49.46	4	7	3	Environmental Yearbook; China Statistics	
46	Ratio of the spending on science, education, culture, and public health to government expenditure	%	Positive	26.10	25.15	26.43	20	15	−5	China Statistics	
47	Area of green land per capita in urban areas	Hectare per capita	Positive	0.00	0.00	0.00	29	29	0	City; China Statistics	
48	Coverage of water supply in urban areas	%	Positive	96.08	91.57	89.66	24	25	1	China Statistics	
49	Treatment rate of urban wastewater	%	Positive	79.18	62.60	61.30	27	23	−4	Environmental Yearbook	
50	Harmless treatment rate of urban household waste	%	Positive	78.47	37.95	32.37	30	29	−1	China Statistics	
51	Public buses per 10,000 urban residents		Positive	9.86	8.10	8.20	23	25	2	China Statistics	
52	Length of public transport routes per capita in urban areas	km per capita	Positive	0.0006	0.0002	0.0003	27	17	−10	China Statistics; City	
53	Ratio of the rural residents benefiting from water supply system improvement to the total rural population	%	Positive	94.44	97.09	94.95	16	21	5	Environmental Yearbook	

54	Green coverage of urban built-up areas	%	Positive	37.75	27.12	27.32	30	30	0	China Statistics	
55	Newly-added afforestation area of the year per capita	Hectare per 10,000 persons	Positive	59.50	89.60	80.70	7	8	1	China Statistics	☺
56	Industrial SO_2 removal rate	%	Positive	59.83	79.32	82.68	1	1	0	China Statistics	
57	Industrial wastewater COD removal rate	%	Positive	70.84	54.42	44.71	27	29	2	Environmental Annual Report; China Statistics	☺
58	Industrial nitrogen oxide removal rate	%	Positive	4.07	5.41	4.32	9	13	4	Environmental Annual Report	☺
59	Industrial wastewater ammonia/nitrogen removal rate	%	Positive	62.87	46.38	17.99	24	29	5	Environmental Annual Report; China Statistics	☺
60	Number of environmental emergencies		Negative	14.00	10	36	22	28	6	China Statistics	☺

Note:
China Statistics: *China Statistical Yearbook 2011*
Environmental Yearbook: *China Environmental Statistical Yearbook 2011*
Environmental Annual Report: *China Environment Annual Report 2010*
City: *China City Statistical Yearbook 2011*
Water Conservancy: *China Water Conservancy Statistical Yearbook 2011*
Industrial Economy: *China Industrial Economic Statistical Yearbook 2011*
Deserts: *Deserts in China and Desertification Control*

5.27 Brief Analysis of Green Development in Gansu

Gansu ranked 25th among the 30 participating provinces by GDI according to 2010 data, four places higher over 2009 (Gansu ranked 29th in 2009). Following is a brief analysis of its score by each indicator and their changes from 2009 to 2010.

5.27.1 Gansu's 2010 Scores by GDI

Gansu scored −0.176 in 2010. From the three First-Class Indicators including GDEG, CCPNRE, and SDGP as shown in Fig. 5.53, Gansu had advantage in terms of CCPNRE, yet underperformed compared with the national average in GDEG and SDGP (Note: the national average value of each indicator is 0).

According to Fig. 5.54, Gansu surpassed the national average in 3 of Second-Class Indicators in 2010, which are EPCCI, GII and EMI. It underperformed compared with the national average in 6 indicators including GGEI, PII, SII, TII, RAECI, and II.

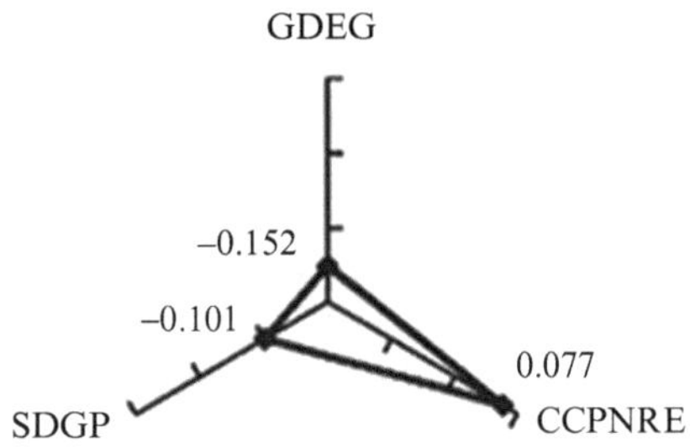

Fig. 5.53 Scores of Gansu by First-Class Indicators

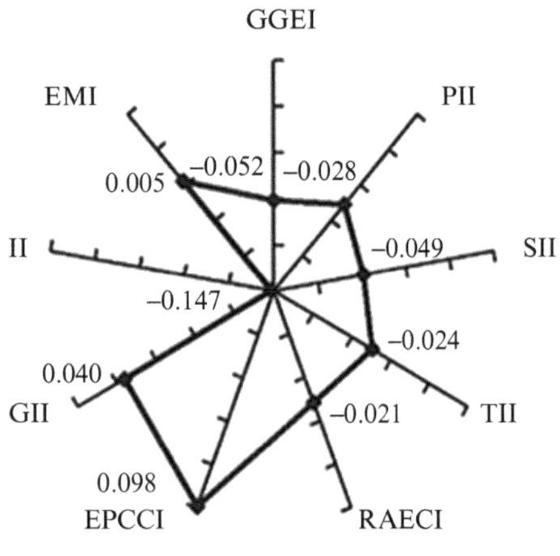

Fig. 5.54 Scores of Gansu by Second-Class Indicators

Table 5.53 Changes in Gansu's rankings by First-Class and Second-Class Indicators, 2009–2010

Indicator	2010	2009	Difference	Indicator	2010	2009	Difference
GDI	25	29	4				
GDEG	26	28	2	RAECI	17	18	1
GGEI	25	27	2	EPCCI	4	5	1
PII	25	26	1	SDGP	25	30	5
SII	28	28	0	GII	5	7	2
TII	23	23	0	II	30	30	0
CCPNRE	8	8	0	EMI	15	27	12

Note: A positive value in "Difference" means a rise in ranking

5.27.2 Changes in Gansu's Rankings by GDI 2009–2010

According to Table 5.53, in First-Class Indicators ranking, it rose by 2 places in GDEG, 5 in SDGP and remained unchanged in CCPNRE. In Second-Class Indicators ranking, Gansu rose by 2 places in GGEI and 1 in PII, RAECI and EPCCI, 2 in GII, and 12 in EMI. It remained the same in the rankings by other indicators in 2009.

To further explain the causes of the changes in the rankings by First- and Second-Class Indicators, we put the Third-Class Indicators where a change of more than 3 places occurred from 2009 to 2010 in Table 5.54. Compared with those in 2009, Gansu dropped by 10 places in Length of public transport routes per capita in urban areas, 5 in Ratio of the spending on science, education, culture, and public health to government expenditure, 4 in Treatment rate of urban wastewater, 3 in Water consumption per unit of value added created by industrial enterprises and SO_2 emissions per capita. It rose by 3 places in Land productivity, Ratio of environmental spending to government expenditure and Investment in converting cultivated land into forests and grassland per unit of cultivated land area, 4 in Industrial nitrogen oxide removal rate, 5 in Electricity consumption per capita in urban areas, Ratio of the rural residents benefiting from water supply system improvement to the total rural population and Industrial wastewater ammonia/nitrogen removal rate, 6 in Number of environmental emergencies.

Table 5.54 Third-Class Indicators where changes over 3 places by Gansu, 2009–2010

	Original data for 2010 and 2009			Change in ranking		
Third-Class Indicator	Unit	2010	2009	2010	2009	Difference
Electricity consumption per capita in urban areas	kWh per capita	107.45	266.19	4	9	5
Land productivity	100 million yuan per 1,000 hectares	0.19	0.15	19	22	3
Water consumption per unit of value added created by industrial enterprises	m^3/yuan	0.0112	0.0109	21	18	−3
SO_2 emissions per capita	Ton per capita	0.0212	0.0190	22	19	−3
Ratio of environmental spending to government expenditure	%	4.65	4.26	4	7	3
Investment in converting cultivated land into forests and grassland per unit of cultivated land area	10,000 yuan per 1,000 hectares	82.80	49.46	4	7	3
Ratio of the spending on science, education, culture, and public health to government expenditure	%	25.15	26.43	20	15	−5
Treatment rate of urban wastewater	%	62.60	61.30	27	23	−4
Length of public transport routes per capita in urban areas	km per capita	0.0002	0.0003	27	17	−10
Ratio of the rural residents benefiting from water supply system improvement to the total rural population	%	97.09	94.95	16	21	5
Industrial nitrogen oxide removal rate	%	5.41	4.32	9	13	4
Industrial wastewater ammonia/nitrogen removal rate	%	46.38	17.99	24	29	5
Number of environmental emergencies		10	36	22	28	6

Note: A positive value in "Difference" means a rise in ranking

Green development checkup-Qinghai

No.	Indicator	Unit	Attribute	2010 average of 30 provinces	2010 figure	2009 figure	2010 ranking	2009 ranking	Change in ranking	Source of 2010 data	Chernoff face
1	GDP per capita	Yuan per capita	Positive	33,964.12	24,115	19,454	22	22	0	China Statistics	
2	Energy consumption per unit of GDP	Ton coal equivalent per 10,000 yuan	Negative	1.29	2.55	2.69	29	29	0	China Statistics	
3	Ratio of non-fossil energy consumption to total energy consumption		Positive	NA	NA	NA	NA	NA			
4	CO_2 emissions per unit of GDP		Negative	NA	NA	NA	NA	NA			
5	SO_2 emissions per unit of GDP	Ton per 10,000 yuan	Negative	0.0088	0.0142	0.0155	25	25	0	China Statistics	
6	COD emissions per unit of GDP	Ton per 10,000 yuan	Negative	0.0045	0.0083	0.0087	28	28	0	China Statistics	
7	Nitrogen oxide emissions per unit of GDP	Ton per 10,000 yuan	Negative	0.0068	0.0109	0.0104	26	26	0	Environmental Annual Report; China Statistics	
8	Ammonia/nitrogen emissions per unit of GDP	Ton per 10,000 yuan	Negative	0.0004	0.0008	0.0008	29	28	−1	Environmental Annual Report; China Statistics	

(continued)

(continued)

No.	Indicator	Unit	Attribute	2010 average of 30 provinces	2010 figure	2009 figure	2010 ranking	2009 ranking	Change in ranking	Source of 2010 data	Chernoff face
9	Electricity consumption per capita in urban areas	kWh per capita	Negative	295.08	351.62	307.41	24	14	−10	City	
10	Labor productivity of the primary sector	10,000 yuan per capita	Positive	1.61	1.10	0.87	24	26	2	China Statistics	
11	Land productivity	100 million yuan per 1,000 hectares	Positive	0.26	0.17	0.12	23	27	4	China Statistics	
12	Proportion of water-saving irrigated area in effectively irrigated area		Positive	0.49	0.35	0.31	19	21	2	Water Conservancy; China Statistics	
13	Proportion of water-saving irrigated area in effectively irrigated area	%	Positive	53.55	46.37	46.37	16	16	0	China Statistics	
14	Labor productivity of the secondary sector	10,000 yuan per capita	Positive	12.13	11.52	9.45	13	13	0	China Statistics	
15	Water consumption per unit of value added created by industrial enterprises	m^3/yuan	Negative	0.0100	0.0073	0.0064	13	11	−2	China Statistics	
16	Energy consumption per unit of value added created by industrial enterprises above designated size (no data)		Negative	NA	NA	NA	NA	NA			

17	Utilization rate of industrial solid waste	%	Positive	69.80	42.20	37.30	30	29	−1	Environmental Yearbook	☹
18	Recycling rate of industrial water	%	Positive	72.90	44.62	42.31	25	25	0	Environmental Yearbook	
19	Ratio of the output of six energy-intensive industries to gross industrial output	%	Negative	39.65	62.22	63.42	29	29	0	Industrial Economy	
20	Labor productivity of the tertiary sector	10,000 yuan per capita	Positive	6.96	4.61	4.10	21	22	1	China Statistics	☺
21	Proportion of the value added of the tertiary sector in GDP	%	Positive	39.97	34.90	36.90	25	24	−1	China Statistics	☹
22	Proportion of tertiary sector employees in the total employed population	%	Positive	36.67	35.47	35.06	14	13	−1	China Statistics	☹
23	Water resources per capita	m^3 per capita	Positive	2,419.38	13,225.01	7,488.50	1	1	0	China Statistics	
24	Forest area per capita	Hectare per capita	Positive	0.19	0.59	0.59	2	2	0	China Statistics	
25	Forest coverage rate	%	Positive	30.63	4.57	4.57	29	29	0	China Statistics	
26	Proportion of the area of natural reserves in the total area of a region	%	Positive	8.60	30.21	30.21	1	1	0	China Statistics	
27	Proportion of the area of wetlands in the total area of a region	%	Positive	7.01	5.72	5.72	14	14	0	China Statistics	

(continued)

(continued)

No.	Indicator	Unit	Attribute	2010 average of 30 provinces	2010 figure	2009 figure	2010 ranking	2009 ranking	Change in ranking	Source of 2010 data	Chernoff face
28	Growing stock per capita	m^3 per capita	Positive	10.70	7.84	7.92	14	13	−1	China Statistics	☹
29	CO_2 emissions per unit of land area		Negative	NA	NA	NA	NA	NA			
30	CO_2 emissions per capita		Negative	NA	NA	NA	NA	NA			
31	SO_2 emissions per unit of land area	Ton per km^2	Negative	6.3677	0.2232	0.2112	1	1	0	China Statistics; Deserts	
32	SO_2 emissions per capita	Ton per capita	Negative	0.0191	0.0256	0.0244	25	24	−1	China Statistics	☹
33	COD emissions per unit of land area	Ton per km^2	Negative	3.7722	0.1293	0.1185	1	1	0	China Statistics; Deserts	
34	COD emissions per capita	Ton per capita	Negative	0.0101	0.0148	0.0137	28	28	0	China Statistics	
35	Nitrogen oxide emissions per unit of land area	Ton per km^2	Negative	6.4473	0.1712	0.1416	1	1	0	China Statistics; Deserts; Environmental Annual Report	
36	Nitrogen oxide emissions per capita	Ton per capita	Negative	0.0165	0.0196	0.0164	24	21	−3	Environmental Annual Report; China Statistics	☹
37	Ammonia/nitrogen emissions per unit of land area	Ton per km^2	Negative	0.4164	0.0125	0.0109	1	1	0	China Statistics; Deserts; Environmental Annual Report	
38	Ammonia/nitrogen emissions per capita	Ton per capita	Negative	0.0010	0.0014	0.0013	27	25	−2	Environmental Annual Report; China Statistics	☹

39	Consumption of chemical fertilizers per unit of cultivated land area	10,000 ton per 1,000 hectares	Negative	0.05	0.02	0.01	1	1	0	China Statistics; China Statistics	
40	Consumption of pesticides per unit of cultivated land area	Ton per 1,000 hectares	Negative	17.68	3.80	3.73	5	5	0	Environmental Yearbook; China Statistics	
41	Nitrogen oxide emissions per capita from road transport	Ton per 10,000 persons	Negative	24.07	40.31	36.18	25	23	−2	Environmental Annual Report; China Statistics	☹
42	Ratio of environmental spending to government expenditure	%	Positive	3.35	4.86	5.95	2	1	−1	China Statistics	☹
43	Ratio of the investment in pollution control to GDP	%	Positive	1.40	1.26	1.41	17	16	−1	Environmental Yearbook; China Statistics	☹
44	Government spending per capita on rural water supply system and toilet improvement	Yuan per capita	Positive	57.01	32.05	35.49	22	21	−1	Environmental Yearbook	☹
45	Investment in converting cultivated land into forests and grassland per unit of cultivated land area	10,000 yuan per 1,000 hectares	Positive	29.81	93.60	113.49	1	1	0	Environmental Yearbook; China Statistics	
46	Ratio of the spending on science, education, culture, and public health to government expenditure	%	Positive	26.10	18.44	23.56	30	26	−4	China Statistics	☹

(continued)

(continued)

No.	Indicator	Unit	Attribute	2010 average of 30 provinces	2010 figure	2009 figure	2010 ranking	2009 ranking	Change in ranking	Source of 2010 data	Chernoff face
47	Area of green land per capita in urban areas	Hectare per capita	Positive	0.00	0.00	0.00	15	30	15	City; China Statistics	☺
48	Coverage of water supply in urban areas	%	Positive	96.08	99.87	99.45	5	8	3	China Statistics	☺
49	Treatment rate of urban wastewater	%	Positive	79.18	43.50	46.40	30	29	−1	Environmental Yearbook	☹
50	Harmless treatment rate of urban household waste	%	Positive	78.47	67.28	65.11	25	19	−6	China Statistics	☹
51	Public buses per 10,000 urban residents		Positive	9.86	18.30	17.62	1	2	1	China Statistics	☺
52	Length of public transport routes per capita in urban areas	km per capita	Positive	0.0006	0.0007	0.0005	8	6	−2	China Statistics; City	☹
53	Ratio of the rural residents benefiting from water supply system improvement to the total rural population	%	Positive	94.44	85.04	84.98	28	26	−2	Environmental Yearbook	☹
54	Green coverage of urban built-up areas	%	Positive	37.75	29.38	29.02	29	28	−1	China Statistics	☹
55	Newly-added afforestation area of the year per capita	Hectare per 10,000 persons	Positive	59.50	210.31	253.07	2	2	0	China Statistics	
56	Industrial SO_2 removal rate	%	Positive	59.83	17.34	9.58	30	29	−1	China Statistics	☹
57	Industrial wastewater COD removal rate	%	Positive	70.84	12.11	16.65	30	30	0	Environmental Annual Report; China Statistics	

58	Industrial nitrogen oxide removal rate	%	Positive	4.07	0.06	0.00	27	27	0	Environmental Annual Report	
59	Industrial wastewater ammonia/nitrogen removal rate	%	Positive	62.87	2.53	17.11	30	30	0	Environmental Annual Report; China Statistics	
60	Number of environmental emergencies		Negative	14.00	1	2	6	8	2	China Statistics	☺

Note:
China Statistics: *China Statistical Yearbook 2011*
Environmental Yearbook: *China Environmental Statistical Yearbook 2011*
Environmental Annual Report: *China Environment Annual Report 2010*
City: *China City Statistical Yearbook 2011*
Water Conservancy: *China Water Conservancy Statistical Yearbook 2011*
Industrial Economy: *China Industrial Economic Statistical Yearbook 2011*
Deserts: *Deserts in China and Desertification Control*

5.28 Brief Analysis of Green Development in Qinghai

Qinghai ranked 6th among the 30 participating provinces by GDI according to 2010 data, three places lower over 2009 (Qinghai ranked 3rd in 2009). Following is a brief analysis of its score by each indicator and their changes from 2009 to 2010.

5.28.1 Qinghai's 2010 Scores by GDI

Qinghai scored 0.121 in 2010. From the three First-Class Indicators including GDEG, CCPNRE, and SDGP as shown in Fig. 5.55, Qinghai obviously outshined other places in terms of CCPNRE, yet underperformed compared with the national average in GDEG and SDGP (Note: the national average value of each indicator is 0).

According to Fig. 5.56, Qinghai surpassed the national average in 3 of Second-Class Indicators in 2010, which are RAECI, EPCCI and GII, yet ranked lower than the national average in GGEI, PII, SII, TII, II and EMI.

5.28.2 Changes in Qinghai's Rankings by GDI 2009–2010

According to Table 5.55, in First-Class Indicators ranking, it fell by 1 by GDEG and 2 in SDGP. It remained unchanged in CCPNRE. In Second-Class Indicators

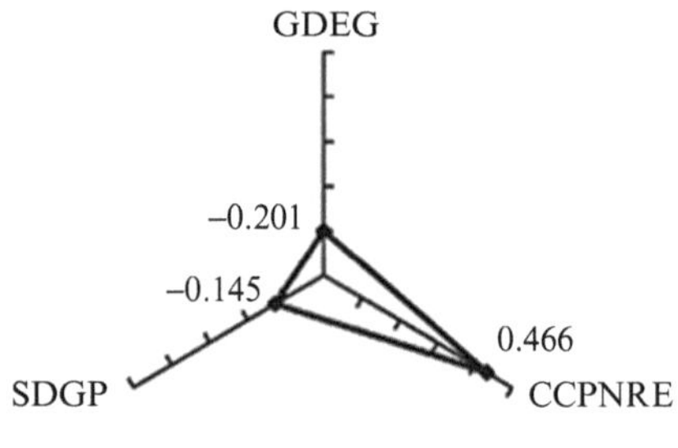

Fig. 5.55 Scores of Qinghai by First-Class Indicators

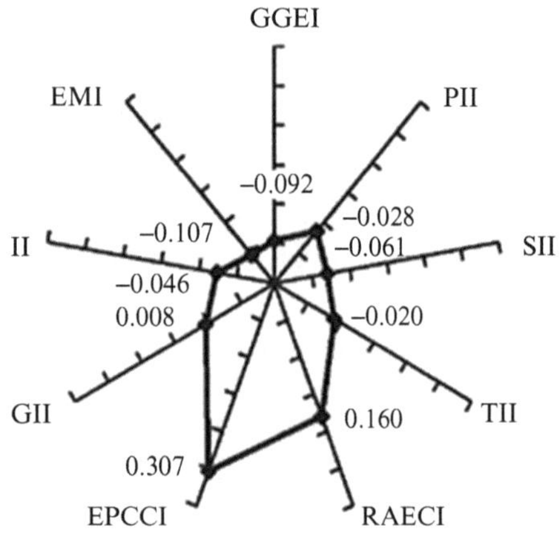

Fig. 5.56 Scores of Qinghai by Second-Class Indicators

Table 5.55 Changes of Qinghai's rankings by First-Class and Second-Class Indicators, 2009–2010

Indicator	2010	2009	Difference	Indicator	2010	2009	Difference
GDI	6	3	−3				
GDEG	30	29	−1	RAECI	1	1	0
GGEI	29	29	0	EPCCI	1	1	0
PII	26	27	1	SDGP	29	27	−2
SII	30	30	0	GII	11	3	−8
TII	22	22	0	II	24	23	−1
CCPNRE	1	1	0	EMI	30	30	0

Note: A positive value in "Difference" means a rise in ranking

Table 5.56 Third-Class Indicators where changes over 3 places by Qinghai, 2009–2010

	Original data for 2010 and 2009			Change in ranking		
Third-Class Indicator	Unit	2010	2009	2010	2009	Difference
Electricity consumption per capita in urban areas	kWh per capita	351.62	307.41	24	14	−10
Land productivity	100 million yuan per 1,000 hectares	0.17	0.12	23	27	4
Nitrogen oxide emissions per capita	Ton per capita	0.0196	0.0164	24	21	−3
Ratio of the spending on science, education, culture, and public health to government expenditure	%	18.44	23.56	30	26	−4
Area of green land per capita in urban areas	Hectare per capita	0.00	0.00	15	30	15
Coverage of water supply in urban areas	%	99.87	99.45	5	8	3
Harmless treatment rate of urban household waste	%	67.28	65.11	25	19	−6

Note: A positive value in "Difference" means a rise in ranking

ranking, Qinghai dropped by 8 places in GII, 1 in II. It rose by 1 place in PII. It remained the same in the rankings by other indicators in 2009.

To further explain the causes of the changes in the rankings by First- and Second-Class Indicators, we put the Third-Class Indicators where a change of more than 3 places occurred from 2009 to 2010 in Table 5.56. Compared with those in 2009, Qinghai dropped by 10 places in Electricity consumption per capita in urban areas, 6 in Harmless treatment rate of urban household waste, 4 in Ratio of the spending on science, education, culture, and public health to government expenditure and 3 in Nitrogen oxide emissions per capita. It rose by 3 places in Coverage of water supply in urban areas, 4 in Land productivity and 15 in Area of green land per capita in urban areas.

Green development checkup-Ningxia

No.	Indicator	Unit	Attribute	2010 average of 30 provinces	2010 figure	2009 figure	2010 ranking	2009 ranking	Change in ranking	Source of 2010 data	Chernoff face
1	GDP per capita	Yuan per capita	Positive	33,964.12	26,860	21,777	17	16	−1	China Statistics	
2	Energy consumption per unit of GDP	Ton coal equivalent per 10,000 yuan	Negative	1.29	3.31	3.45	30	30	0	China Statistics	
3	Ratio of non-fossil energy consumption to total energy consumption		Positive	NA	NA	NA	NA	NA			
4	CO_2 emissions per unit of GDP		Negative	NA	NA	NA	NA	NA			
5	SO_2 emissions per unit of GDP	Ton per 10,000 yuan	Negative	0.0088	0.0279	0.0321	29	29	0	China Statistics	
6	COD emissions per unit of GDP	Ton per 10,000 yuan	Negative	0.0045	0.0109	0.0128	29	29	0	China Statistics	
7	Nitrogen oxide emissions per unit of GDP	Ton per 10,000 yuan	Negative	0.0068	0.0314	0.0181	30	30	0	Environmental Annual Report; China Statistics	
8	Ammonia/nitrogen emissions per unit of GDP	Ton per 10,000 yuan	Negative	0.0004	0.0012	0.0008	30	29	−1	Environmental Annual Report; China Statistics	
9	Electricity consumption per capita in urban areas	kWh per capita	Negative	295.08	151.76	353.92	10	20	10	City	
10	Labor productivity of the primary sector	10,000 yuan per capita	Positive	1.61	1.23	0.95	19	21	2	China Statistics	

11	Land productivity	100 million yuan per 1,000 hectares	Positive	0.26	0.16	0.12	25	26	1	China Statistics	☺
12	Proportion of water-saving irrigated area in effectively irrigated area		Positive	0.49	0.64	0.55	11	12	1	Water Conservancy; China Statistics	☺
13	Proportion of water-saving irrigated area in effectively irrigated area	%	Positive	53.55	41.97	40.97	19	19	0	China Statistics	
14	Labor productivity of the secondary sector	10,000 yuan per capita	Positive	12.13	9.69	8.23	16	16	0	China Statistics	
15	Water consumption per unit of value added created by industrial enterprises	m^3/yuan	Negative	0.0100	0.0088	0.0071	15	13	−2	China Statistics	☹
16	Energy consumption per unit of value added created by industrial enterprises above designated size (no data)		Negative	NA	NA	NA	NA	NA			
17	Utilization rate of industrial solid waste	%	Positive	69.80	57.50	70.60	19	16	−3	Environmental Yearbook	☹
18	Recycling rate of industrial water	%	Positive	72.90	91.18	62.64	7	21	14	Environmental Yearbook	☺
19	Ratio of the output of six energy-intensive industries to gross industrial output	%	Negative	39.65	59.49	57.34	28	27	−1	Industrial Economy	☹
20	Labor productivity of the tertiary sector	10,000 yuan per capita	Positive	6.96	6.26	5.52	14	15	1	China Statistics	☺

(continued)

(continued)

No.	Indicator	Unit	Attribute	2010 average of 30 provinces	2010 figure	2009 figure	2010 ranking	2009 ranking	Change in ranking	Source of 2010 data	Chernoff face
21	Proportion of the value added of the tertiary sector in GDP	%	Positive	39.97	41.60	41.70	8	8	0	China Statistics	
22	Proportion of tertiary sector employees in the total employed population	%	Positive	36.67	34.19	34.39	18	16	−2	China Statistics	☹
23	Water resources per capita	m^3 per capita	Positive	2,419.38	148.18	135.51	28	28	0	China Statistics	
24	Forest area per capita	Hectare per capita	Positive	0.19	0.08	0.08	21	21	0	China Statistics	
25	Forest coverage rate	%	Positive	30.63	9.84	9.84	26	26	0	China Statistics	
26	Proportion of the area of natural reserves in the total area of a region	%	Positive	8.60	9.79	9.79	10	9	−1	China Statistics	☹
27	Proportion of the area of wetlands in the total area of a region	%	Positive	7.01	3.85	3.85	17	17	0	China Statistics	
28	Growing stock per capita	m^3 per capita	Positive	10.70	0.99	1.00	25	25	0	China Statistics	
29	CO_2 emissions per unit of land area		Negative	NA	NA	NA	NA	NA			
30	CO_2 emissions per capita		Negative	NA	NA	NA	NA	NA			
31	SO_2 emissions per unit of land area	Ton per km^2	Negative	6.3677	6.8366	6.9134	21	21	0	China Statistics; Deserts	
32	SO_2 emissions per capita	Ton per capita	Negative	0.0191	0.0494	0.0506	29	29	0	China Statistics	
33	COD emissions per unit of land area	Ton per km^2	Negative	3.7722	2.6772	2.7539	14	13	−1	China Statistics; Deserts	☹
34	COD emissions per capita	Ton per capita	Negative	0.0101	0.0193	0.0201	29	29	0	China Statistics	

35	Nitrogen oxide emissions per unit of land area	Ton per km^2	Negative	6.4473	7.6780	3.8940	24	19	–5	China Statistics; Deserts; Environmental Annual Report	☹
36	Nitrogen oxide emissions per capita	Ton per capita	Negative	0.0165	0.0555	0.0285	30	28	–2	Environmental Annual Report; China Statistics	☹
37	Ammonia/nitrogen emissions per unit of land area	Ton per km^2	Negative	0.4164	0.2860	0.1760	16	11	–5	China Statistics; Deserts; Environmental Annual Report	☹
38	Ammonia/nitrogen emissions per capita	Ton per capita	Negative	0.0010	0.0021	0.0013	30	26	–4	Environmental Annual Report; China Statistics	☹
39	Consumption of chemical fertilizers per unit of cultivated land area	10,000 ton per 1,000 hectares	Negative	0.05	0.03	0.03	9	9	0	China Statistics; China Statistics	
40	Consumption of pesticides per unit of cultivated land area	Ton per 1,000 hectares	Negative	17.68	2.38	2.16	1	1	0	Environmental Yearbook; China Statistics	
41	Nitrogen oxide emissions per capita from road transport	Ton per 10,000 persons	Negative	24.07	33.69	38.28	22	24	2	Environmental Annual Report; China Statistics	☺
42	Ratio of environmental spending to government expenditure	%	Positive	3.35	5.52	5.22	1	2	1	China Statistics	☺
43	Ratio of the investment in pollution control to GDP	%	Positive	1.40	2.04	2.93	5	1	–4	Environmental Yearbook; China Statistics	☹

(continued)

(continued)

No.	Indicator	Unit	Attribute	2010 average of 30 provinces	2010 figure	2009 figure	2010 ranking	2009 ranking	Change in ranking	Source of 2010 data	Chernoff face
44	Government spending per capita on rural water supply system and toilet improvement	Yuan per capita	Positive	57.01	114.06	69.44	2	9	7	Environmental Yearbook	☺
45	Investment in converting cultivated land into forests and grassland per unit of cultivated land area	10,000 yuan per 1,000 hectares	Positive	29.81	88.79	70.39	3	4	1	Environmental Yearbook; China Statistics	☺
46	Ratio of the spending on science, education, culture, and public health to government expenditure	%	Positive	26.10	24.69	23.09	21	28	7	China Statistics	☺
47	Area of green land per capita in urban areas	Hectare per capita	Positive	0.00	0.00	0.01	7	6	−1	City; China Statistics	☹
48	Coverage of water supply in urban areas	%	Positive	96.08	98.23	97.20	13	16	3	China Statistics	☺
49	Treatment rate of urban wastewater	%	Positive	79.18	78.00	42.20	20	30	10	Environmental Yearbook	☺
50	Harmless treatment rate of urban household waste	%	Positive	78.47	92.53	41.96	6	27	21	China Statistics	☺
51	Public buses per 10,000 urban residents		Positive	9.86	10.63	10.06	8	17	9	China Statistics	☺
52	Length of public transport routes per capita in urban areas	km per capita	Positive	0.0006	0.0007	0.0009	9	1	−8	China Statistics; City	☹
53	Ratio of the rural residents benefiting from water supply system improvement to the total rural population	%	Positive	94.44	94.56	96.71	19	17	−2	Environmental Yearbook	☹

54	Green coverage of urban built-up areas	%	Positive	37.75	38.75	38.75	11	10	−1	China Statistics	☹
55	Newly-added afforestation area of the year per capita	Hectare per 10,000 persons	Positive	59.50	150.91	143.99	3	5	2	China Statistics	☺
56	Industrial SO_2 removal rate	%	Positive	59.83	65.41	51.27	12	22	10	China Statistics	☺
57	Industrial wastewater COD removal rate	%	Positive	70.84	72.50	64.66	16	19	3	Environmental Annual Report; China Statistics	☺
58	Industrial nitrogen oxide removal rate	%	Positive	4.07	0.06	0.00	28	28	0	Environmental Annual Report	
59	Industrial wastewater ammonia/nitrogen removal rate	%	Positive	62.87	87.15	43.54	4	23	19	Environmental Annual Report; China Statistics	☺
60	Number of environmental emergencies		Negative	14.00	3	0	10	1	−9	China Statistics	☹

Note:
China Statistics: *China Statistical Yearbook 2011*
Environmental Yearbook: *China Environmental Statistical Yearbook 2011*
Environmental Annual Report: *China Environment Annual Report 2010*
City: *China City Statistical Yearbook 2011*
Water Conservancy: *China Water Conservancy Statistical Yearbook 2011*
Industrial Economy: *China Industrial Economic Statistical Yearbook 2011*
Deserts: *Deserts in China and Desertification Control*

5.29 Brief Analysis of Green Development in Ningxia

Ningxia ranked 28th among the 30 participating provinces by GDI according to 2010 data, one place lower over 2009 (Ningxia ranked 27th in 2009). Following is a brief analysis of its score by each indicator and their changes from 2009 to 2010.

5.29.1 Ningxia's 2010 Scores by GDI

Ningxia scored −0.200 in 2010. From the three First-Class Indicators including GDEG, CCPNRE, and SDGP as shown in Fig. 5.57, Ningxia obviously outshined other places in terms of SDGP, yet underperformed compared with the national average in GDEG and CCPNRE (Note: the national average value of each indicator is 0).

According to Fig. 5.58, Ningxia surpassed the national average in 3 of Second-Class Indicators in 2010, which are GII, II and EMI, yet ranked lower than the national average in GGEI, PII, TII, RAECI and EPCCI.

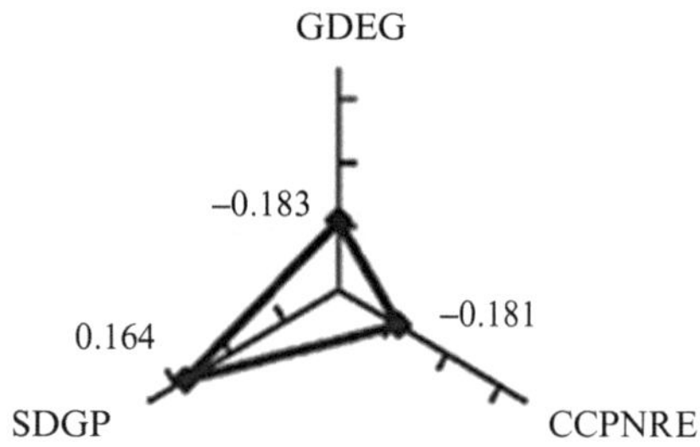

Fig. 5.57 Scores of Ningxia by First-Class Indicators

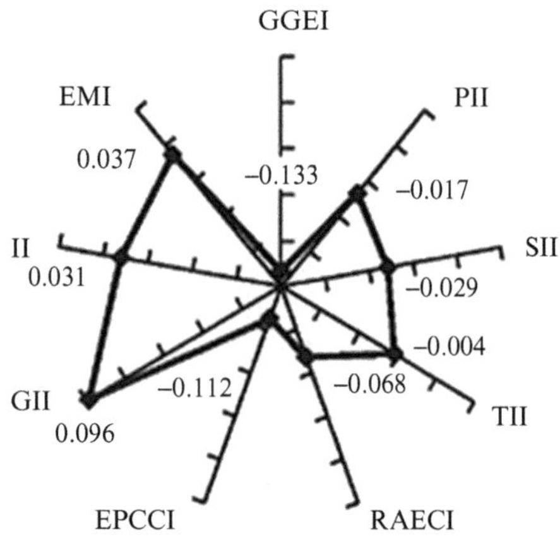

Fig. 5.58 Scores of Ningxia by Second-Class Indicators

Table 5.57 Changes in Ningxia's rankings by First-Class and Second-Class Indicators, 2009–2010

Indicator	2010	2009	Difference	Indicators	2010	2009	Difference
GDI	28	27	−1				
GDEG	28	27	−1	RAECI	27	27	0
GGEI	30	30	0	EPCCI	29	24	−5
PII	19	23	4	SDGP	2	6	4
SII	23	25	2	GII	1	1	0
TII	12	14	2	II	12	12	0
CCPNRE	29	28	−1	EMI	5	16	11

Note: A positive value in "Difference" means a rise in ranking

5.29.2 Changes in Ningxia's Rankings by GDI 2009–2010

According to Table 5.57, in First-Class Indicators ranking, it fell by 1 place in GDEG and 1 in CCPNRE. It rose by 4 places in SDGP. In Second-Class Indicators ranking, Ningxia rose by 4 places in PII, 2 in SII and TII, and 11 in EMI. It dropped by 5 places in EPCCI. It remained the same in the rankings by other indicators in 2009

To further explain the causes of the changes in the rankings by First- and Second-Class Indicators, we put the Third-Class Indicators where a change of more than 3 places occurred from 2009 to 2010 in Table 5.58. Compared with those in 2009, Ningxia dropped by 9 places in Number of environmental emergencies, 8 in Length of public transport routes per capita in urban areas, 5 in Nitrogen oxide emissions per unit of land area and Ammonia/nitrogen emissions per unit of land area, 4 in Ammonia/nitrogen emissions per capita and Ratio of the investment in pollution control to GDP, and 3 in Utilization rate of industrial solid waste. It rose by 3 places in Coverage of water supply in urban areas and Industrial wastewater COD removal rate, 7 in Government spending per capita on rural water supply system and toilet improvement and Ratio of the spending on science, education, culture, and public health to government expenditure, 9 in Public buses per 10,000 urban residents, 10 in Electricity consumption per capita in urban areas, Treatment rate of urban wastewater and Industrial SO_2 removal rate, 14 in Recycling rate of industrial water, 19 in Industrial wastewater ammonia/nitrogen removal rate, and 21 in Harmless treatment rate of urban household waste.

Table 5.58 Third-Class Indicators where changes over 3 places by Ningxia, 2009–2010

	Original data for 2010 and 2009			Change in ranking		
Third-Class Indicator	Unit	2010	2009	2010	2009	Difference
Electricity consumption per capita in urban areas	kWh per capita	151.76	353.92	10	20	10
Utilization rate of industrial solid waste	%	57.50	70.60	19	16	−3
Recycling rate of industrial water	%	91.18	62.64	7	21	14
Nitrogen oxide emissions per unit of land area	Ton per km^2	7.6780	3.8940	24	19	−5
Ammonia/nitrogen emissions per unit of land area	Ton per km^2	0.2860	0.1760	16	11	−5
Ammonia/nitrogen emissions per capita	Ton per capita	0.0021	0.0013	30	26	−4
Ratio of the investment in pollution control to GDP	%	2.04	2.93	5	1	−4
Government spending per capita on rural water supply system and toilet improvement	Yuan per capita	114.06	69.44	2	9	7
Ratio of the spending on science, education, culture, and public health to government expenditure	%	24.69	23.09	21	28	7
Coverage of water supply in urban areas	%	98.23	97.20	13	16	3
Treatment rate of urban wastewater	%	78.00	42.20	20	30	10
Harmless treatment rate of urban household waste	%	92.53	41.96	6	27	21
Public buses per 10,000 urban residents		10.63	10.06	8	17	9
Length of public transport routes per capita in urban areas	km per capita	0.0007	0.0009	9	1	−8
Industrial SO_2 removal rate	%	65.41	51.27	12	22	10
Industrial wastewater COD removal rate	%	72.50	64.66	16	19	3
Industrial wastewater ammonia/nitrogen removal rate	%	87.15	43.54	4	23	19
Number of environmental emergencies		3	0	10	1	−9

Note: A positive value in “Difference” means a rise in ranking

Green development checkup-Xinjiang

No.	Indicator	Unit	Attribute	2010 average of 30 provinces	2010 figure	2009 figure	2010 ranking	2009 ranking	Change in ranking	Source of 2010 data	Chernoff face
1	GDP per capita	Yuan per capita	Positive	33,964.12	25,034	19,942	19	21	2	China Statistics	☺
2	Energy consumption per unit of GDP	Ton coal equivalent per 10,000 yuan	Negative	1.29	1.29	1.93	21	25	4	China Statistics	☺
3	Ratio of non-fossil energy consumption to total energy consumption		Positive	NA	NA	NA	NA	NA			
4	CO_2 emissions per unit of GDP		Negative	NA	NA	NA	NA	NA			
5	SO_2 emissions per unit of GDP	Ton per 10,000 yuan	Negative	0.0088	0.0137	0.0152	24	24	0	China Statistics	
6	COD emissions per unit of GDP	Ton per 10,000 yuan	Negative	0.0045	0.0069	0.0074	27	26	−1	China Statistics	☹
7	Nitrogen oxide emissions per unit of GDP	Ton per 10,000 yuan	Negative	0.0068	0.0140	0.0131	28	27	−1	Environmental Annual Report; China Statistics	☹
8	Ammonia/nitrogen emissions per unit of GDP	Ton per 10,000 yuan	Negative	0.0004	0.0006	0.0007	27	25	−2	Environmental Annual Report; China Statistics	☹
9	Electricity consumption per capita in urban areas	kWh per capita	Negative	295.08	542.41	162.09	27	1	−26	City	☹

(continued)

(continued)

No.	Indicator	Unit	Attribute	2010 average of 30 provinces	2010 figure	2009 figure	2010 ranking	2009 ranking	Change in ranking	Source of 2010 data	Chernoff face
10	Labor productivity of the primary sector	10,000 yuan per capita	Positive	1.61	2.50	1.80	3	7	4	China Statistics	☺
11	Land productivity	100 million yuan per 1,000 hectares	Positive	0.26	0.29	0.19	10	17	7	China Statistics	☺
12	Proportion of water-saving irrigated area in effectively irrigated area		Positive	0.49	0.80	0.77	2	2	0	Water Conservancy; China Statistics	
13	Proportion of water-saving irrigated area in effectively irrigated area	%	Positive	53.55	90.23	89.12	2	2	0	China Statistics	
14	Labor productivity of the secondary sector	10,000 yuan per capita	Positive	12.13	21.96	16.94	3	4	1	China Statistics	☺
15	Water consumption per unit of value added created by industrial enterprises	m^3/yuan	Negative	0.0100	0.0065	0.0065	11	12	1	China Statistics	☺
16	Energy consumption per unit of value added created by industrial enterprises above designated size (no data)		Negative	NA	NA	NA	NA	NA			
17	Utilization rate of industrial solid waste	%	Positive	69.80	47.50	47.30	26	25	−1	Environmental Yearbook	☹

18	Recycling rate of industrial water	%	Positive	72.90	11.96	11.75	29	29	0	Environmental Yearbook	
19	Ratio of the output of six energy-intensive industries to gross industrial output	%	Negative	39.65	51.07	48.84	25	23	−2	Industrial Economy	☹
20	Labor productivity of the tertiary sector	10,000 yuan per capita	Positive	6.96	6.05	5.58	16	14	−2	China Statistics	☹
21	Proportion of the value added of the tertiary sector in GDP	%	Positive	39.97	32.50	37.10	29	23	−6	China Statistics	☹
22	Proportion of tertiary sector employees in the total employed population	%	Positive	36.67	34.79	34.63	16	15	−1	China Statistics	☹
23	Water resources per capita	m^3 per capita	Positive	2,419.38	5,125.24	3,516.60	3	3	0	China Statistics	
24	Forest area per capita	Hectare per capita	Positive	0.19	0.30	0.31	5	5	0	China Statistics	
25	Forest coverage rate	%	Positive	30.63	4.02	4.02	30	30	0	China Statistics	
26	Proportion of the area of natural reserves in the total area of a region	%	Positive	8.60	12.95	12.95	5	5	0	China Statistics	
27	Proportion of the area of wetlands in the total area of a region	%	Positive	7.01	0.86	0.86	27	27	0	China Statistics	
28	Growing stock per capita	m^3 per capita	Positive	10.70	15.52	15.71	6	6	0	China Statistics	
29	CO_2 emissions per unit of land area		Negative	NA	NA	NA	NA	NA			
30	CO_2 emissions per capita		Negative	NA	NA	NA	NA	NA			

(continued)

(continued)

No.	Indicator	Unit	Attribute	2010 average of 30 provinces	2010 figure	2009 figure	2010 ranking	2009 ranking	Change in ranking	Source of 2010 data	Chernoff face
31	SO_2 emissions per unit of land area	Ton per km^2	Negative	6.3677	0.6182	0.6197	2	2	0	China Statistics; Deserts	
32	SO_2 emissions per capita	Ton per capita	Negative	0.0191	0.0271	0.0275	26	26	0	China Statistics	
33	COD emissions per unit of land area	Ton per km^2	Negative	3.7722	0.3110	0.3012	2	2	0	China Statistics; Deserts	
34	COD emissions per capita	Ton per capita	Negative	0.0101	0.0136	0.0134	27	27	0	China Statistics	
35	Nitrogen oxide emissions per unit of land area	Ton per km^2	Negative	6.4473	0.6345	0.5347	2	2	0	China Statistics; Deserts; Environmental Annual Report	
36	Nitrogen oxide emissions per capita	Ton per capita	Negative	0.0165	0.0278	0.0237	28	27	−1	Environmental Annual Report; China Statistics	☹
37	Ammonia/nitrogen emissions per unit of land area	Ton per km^2	Negative	0.4164	0.0284	0.0273	2	2	0	China Statistics; Deserts; Environmental Annual Report	
38	Ammonia/nitrogen emissions per capita	Ton per capita	Negative	0.0010	0.0012	0.0012	24	23	−1	Environmental Annual Report; China Statistics	☹
39	Consumption of chemical fertilizers per unit of cultivated land area	10,000 ton per 1,000 hectares	Negative	0.05	0.04	0.04	11	11	0	China Statistics; China Statistics	

40	Consumption of pesticides per unit of cultivated land area	Ton per 1,000 hectares	Negative	17.68	4.41	4.40	6	6	0	Environmental Yearbook; China Statistics	
41	Nitrogen oxide emissions per capita from road transport	Ton per 10,000 persons	Negative	24.07	70.22	72.34	30	28	−2	Environmental Annual Report; China Statistics	☹
42	Ratio of environmental spending to government expenditure	%	Positive	3.35	3.00	2.70	17	22	5	China Statistics	☺
43	Ratio of the investment in pollution control to GDP	%	Positive	1.40	1.44	2.01	14	4	−10	Environmental Yearbook; China Statistics	☹
44	Government spending per capita on rural water supply system and toilet improvement	Yuan per capita	Positive	57.01	73.80	52.57	8	14	6	Environmental Yearbook	☺
45	Investment in converting cultivated land into forests and grassland per unit of cultivated land area	10,000 yuan per 1,000 hectares	Positive	29.81	17.46	24.92	18	13	−5	Environmental Yearbook; China Statistics	☹
46	Ratio of the spending on science, education, culture, and public health to government expenditure	%	Positive	26.10	27.75	27.81	10	10	0	China Statistics	
47	Area of green land per capita in urban areas	Hectare per capita	Positive	0.00	0.01	0.01	2	3	1	City; China Statistics	☺

(continued)

(continued)

No.	Indicator	Unit	Attribute	2010 average of 30 provinces	2010 figure	2009 figure	2010 ranking	2009 ranking	Change in ranking	Source of 2010 data	Chernoff face
48	Coverage of water supply in urban areas	%	Positive	96.08	99.17	99.03	11	10	−1	China Statistics	
49	Treatment rate of urban wastewater	%	Positive	79.18	73.30	75.40	26	13	−13	Environmental Yearbook	
50	Harmless treatment rate of urban household waste	%	Positive	78.47	70.58	60.63	22	23	1	China Statistics	
51	Public buses per 10,000 urban residents		Positive	9.86	11.66	12.22	6	8	2	China Statistics	
52	Length of public transport routes per capita in urban areas	km per capita	Positive	0.0006	0.0037	0.0005	1	4	3	China Statistics; City	
53	Ratio of the rural residents benefiting from water supply system improvement to the total rural population	%	Positive	94.44	76.97	66.70	30	30	0	Environmental Yearbook	
54	Green coverage of urban built-up areas	%	Positive	37.75	36.42	36.30	22	20	−2	China Statistics	
55	Newly-added afforestation area of the year per capita	Hectare per 10,000 persons	Positive	59.50	115.85	160.19	5	3	−2	China Statistics	
56	Industrial SO_2 removal rate	%	Positive	59.83	25.68	5.43	28	30	2	China Statistics	
57	Industrial wastewater COD removal rate	%	Positive	70.84	50.51	46.42	29	28	−1	Environmental Annual Report; China Statistics	

58	Industrial nitrogen oxide removal rate	%	Positive	4.07	0.21	1.14	25	22	−3	Environmental Annual Report	☹
59	Industrial wastewater ammonia/nitrogen removal rate	%	Positive	62.87	81.87	32.60	8	27	19	Environmental Annual Report; China Statistics	☹
60	Number of environmental emergencies		Negative	14.00	6	0	16	1	−15	China Statistics	☹

Note:
China Statistics: *China Statistical Yearbook 2011*
Environmental Yearbook: *China Environmental Statistical Yearbook 2011*
Environmental Annual Report: *China Environment Annual Report 2010*
City: *China City Statistical Yearbook 2011*
Water Conservancy: *China Water Conservancy Statistical Yearbook 2011*
Industrial Economy: *China Industrial Economic Statistical Yearbook 2011*
Deserts: *Deserts in China and Desertification Control*

5.30 Brief Analysis of Green Development in Xinjiang

Xinjiang ranked 15th among the 30 participating provinces by GDI according to 2010 data, one place higher over 2009 (Xinjiang ranked 16th in 2009). Following is a brief analysis of its score by each indicator and their changes from 2009 to 2010.

5.30.1 Xinjiang's 2010 Scores by GDI

Xinjiang scored −0.002 in 2010. From the three First-Class Indicators including GDEG, CCPNRE, and SDGP as shown in Fig. 5.59, Xinjiang had advantage in terms of CCPNRE and SDGP, yet underperformed compared with the national average in GDEG (Note: the national average value of each indicator is 0).

According to Fig. 5.60, Ningxia surpassed the national average in 5 of Second-Class Indicators in 2010, which are PII, RAECI, EPCCI, GII and II, yet ranked lower than the national average in GGEI, SII, TII and EMI.

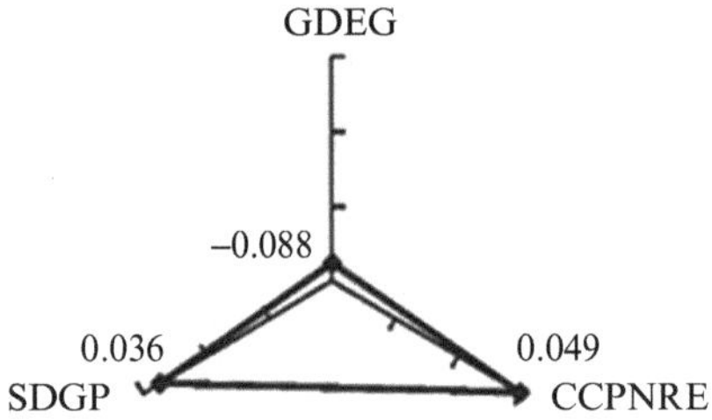

Fig. 5.59 Scores of Xinjiang by First-Class Indicators

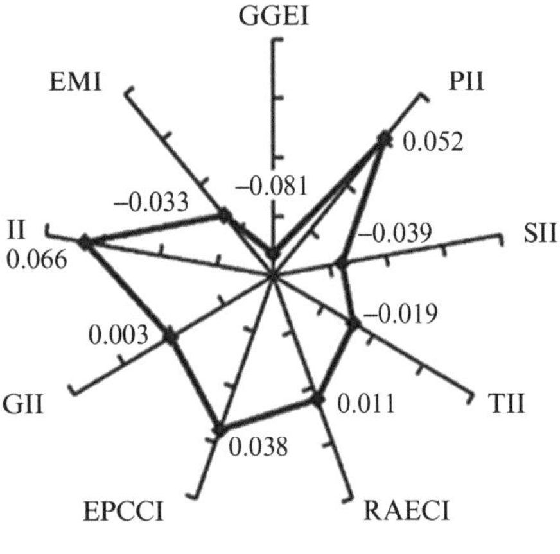

Fig. 5.60 Scores of Xinjiang by Second-Class Indicators

Table 5.59 Changes in Xinjiang's rankings by First-Class and Second-Class Indicators, 2009–2010

Indicator	2010	2009	Difference	Indicator	2010	2009	Difference
GDI	15	16	1				
GDEG	22	17	−5	RAECI	11	12	1
GGEI	28	23	−5	EPCCI	9	6	−3
PII	3	7	4	SDGP	12	22	10
SII	26	26	0	GII	13	10	−3
TII	21	17	−4	II	5	16	11
CCPNRE	9	9	0	EMI	26	29	3

Note: A positive value in "Difference" means a rise in ranking

5.30.2 Changes in Xinjiang's Rankings by GDI 2009–2010

According to Table 5.59, in First-Class Indicators ranking, it fell by 5 places in GDEG and remained unchanged in CCPNRE. It rose by 10 places in SDGP. In Second-Class Indicators ranking, Xinjiang fell by 5 places in GGEI, 4 in TII, and 3 in EPCCI and GII. It rose by 4 places in PII, 1 in RAECI, 11 in II and 3 in EMI. It remained the same in the rankings by other indicators in 2009.

To further explain the causes of the changes in the rankings by First- and Second-Class Indicators, we put the Third-Class Indicators where a change of more than 3 places occurred from 2009 to 2010 in Table 5.60. Compared with those in 2009, Xinjiang dropped by 26 places in Electricity consumption per capita in urban areas, 15 in Number of environmental emergencies, 13 in Treatment rate of urban wastewater, 10 in Ratio of the investment in pollution control to GDP, 6 in Proportion of the value added of the tertiary sector in GDP, 5 in Investment in converting cultivated land into forests and grassland per unit of cultivated land area, 3 in Industrial nitrogen oxide removal rate. It rose by 3 places in Length of public transport routes per capita in urban areas, 4 in Energy consumption per unit of GDP and Labor productivity of the primary sector, 5 in Ratio of environmental spending to government expenditure, 6 in Government spending per capita on rural water supply system and toilet improvement, 7 in Land productivity and 19 in Industrial wastewater ammonia/nitrogen removal rate.

Table 5.60 Third-Class Indicators where changes over 3 places by Xinjiang, 2009–2010

	Original data for 2010 and 2009			Change in ranking		
Third-Class Indicator	Unit	2010	2009	2010	2009	Difference
Energy consumption per unit of GDP	Ton coal equivalent per 10,000 yuan	1.29	1.93	21	25	4
Electricity consumption per capita in urban areas	kWh per capita	542.41	162.09	27	1	−26
Labor productivity of the primary sector	10,000 yuan per capita	2.50	1.80	3	7	4
Land productivity	100 million yuan per 1,000 hectares	0.29	0.19	10	17	7
Proportion of the value added of the tertiary sector in GDP	%	32.50	37.10	29	23	−6
Ratio of environmental spending to government expenditure	%	3.00	2.70	17	22	5
Ratio of the investment in pollution control to GDP	%	1.44	2.01	14	4	−10
Government spending per capita on rural water supply system and toilet improvement	Yuan per capita	73.80	52.57	8	14	6
Investment in converting cultivated land into forests and grassland per unit of cultivated land area	10,000 yuan per 1,000 hectares	17.46	24.92	18	13	−5
Treatment rate of urban wastewater	%	73.30	75.40	26	13	−13
Length of public transport routes per capita in urban areas	km per capita	0.0037	0.0005	1	4	3
Industrial nitrogen oxide removal rate	%	0.21	1.14	25	22	−3
Industrial wastewater ammonia/nitrogen removal rate	%	81.87	32.60	8	27	19
Number of environmental emergencies		6	0	16	1	−15

Note: A positive value in "Difference" means a rise in ranking

Green development checkup-Tibet

No.	Indicator	Unit	Attribute	2010 average of 30 provinces	2010 figure	2009 figure	Growth rate (%)	Difference between Tibet's figure and the average of other provinces	Source of 2010 data
1	GDP per capita	Yuan per capita	Positive	33,964.12	17,319	15,295	13.23	−16,645.12	China Statistics
2	Energy consumption per unit of GDP	Ton coal equivalent per 10,000 yuan	Negative	1.29	1.28	NA	NA	−0.02	China Statistics
3	Ratio of non-fossil energy consumption to total energyconsumption		Positive	NA	NA	NA	NA	NA	
4	CO_2 emissions per unit of GDP		Negative	NA	NA	NA	NA	NA	
5	SO_2 emissions per unit of GDP	Ton per 10,000 yuan	Negative	0.0088	0.0009	0.0005	71.73	−0.01	China Statistics
6	COD emissions per unit of GDP	Ton per 10,000 yuan	Negative	0.0045	0.0064	0.0039	66.52	0.00	China Statistics
7	Nitrogen oxide emissions per unit of GDP	Ton per 10,000 yuan	Negative	0.0068	0.0000	0.0000	NA	−0.01	Environmental Annual Report; China Statistics
8	Ammonia/nitrogen emissions per unit of GDP	Ton per 10,000 yuan	Negative	0.0004	0.0004	0.0003	78.09	0.00	Environmental Annual Report; China Statistics

(continued)

(continued)

No.	Indicator	Unit	Attribute	2010 average of 30 provinces	2010 figure	2009 figure	Growth rate (%)	Difference between Tibet's figure and the average of other provinces	Source of 2010 data
9	Electricity consumption per capita in urban areas	kWh per capita	Negative	295.08	217.37	0.00	NA	−77.71	City
10	Labor productivity of the primary sector	10,000 yuan per capita	Positive	1.61	0.74	0.70	5.42	−0.87	China Statistics
11	Land productivity	100 million yuan per 1,000 hectares	Positive	0.26	0.19	0.17	15.61	−0.06	China Statistics
12	Proportion of water-saving irrigated area in effectively irrigated area		Positive	0.49	0.22	0.17	28.03	−0.27	Water Conservancy; China Statistics
13	Proportion of water-saving irrigated area in effectively irrigated area	%	Positive	53.55	65.55	65.02	0.80	12.00	China Statistics
14	Labor productivity of the secondary sector	10,000 yuan per capita	Positive	12.13	8.73	7.82	11.59	−3.40	China Statistics
15	Water consumption per unit of value added created by industrial enterprises	m^3/yuan	Negative	0.0100	0.0443	0.0416	6.59	0.03	China Statistics
16	Energy consumption per unit of value added created by industrial enterprises above designated size (no data)		Negative	NA	NA	NA	NA	NA	
17	Utilization rate of industrial solid waste	%	Positive	69.80	1.80	1.80	0.00	−68.00	Environmental Yearbook

18	Recycling rate of industrial water	%	Positive	72.90	63.61	NA	NA	−9.29	Environmental Yearbook
19	Ratio of the output of six energy-intensive industries to gross industrial output	%	Negative	39.65	47.51	NA	NA	7.85	Industrial Economy
20	Labor productivity of the tertiary sector	10,000 yuan per capita	Positive	6.96	4.53	4.26	6.32	−2.44	China Statistics
21	Proportion of the value added of the tertiary sector in GDP	%	Positive	39.97	54.20	54.60	−0.73	14.23	China Statistics
22	Proportion of tertiary sector employees in the total employed population	%	Positive	36.67	35.80	34.74	3.06	−0.87	China Statistics
23	Water resources per capita	m^3 per capita	Positive	2,419.38	153,681.86	139,658.8	10.04	151,262.48	China Statistics
24	Forest area per capita	Hectare per capita	Positive	0.19	4.86	5.04	−3.56	4.67	China Statistics
25	Forest coverage rate	%	Positive	30.63	11.91	11.91	0.00	−18.72	China Statistics
26	Proportion of the area of natural reserves in the total area of a region	%	Positive	8.60	34.02	33.94	0.24	25.42	China Statistics
27	Proportion of the area of wetlands in the total area of a region	%	Positive	7.01	4.26	4.26	0.00	−2.75	China Statistics
28	Growing stock per capita	m^3 per capita	Positive	10.70	755.75	783.61	−3.56	745.06	China Statistics
29	CO_2 emissions per unit of land area		Negative	NA	NA	NA	NA	NA	
30	CO_2 emissions per capita		Negative	NA	NA	NA	NA	NA	

(continued)

(continued)

No.	Indicator	Unit	Attribute	2010 average of 30 provinces	2010 figure	2009 figure	Growth rate (%)	Difference between Tibet's figure and the average of other provinces	Source of 2010 data
31	SO_2 emissions per unit of land area	Ton per km^2	Negative	6.3677	0.0032	0.0017	92.85	−6.36	China Statistics; Deserts
32	SO_2 emissions per capita	Ton per capita	Negative	0.0191	0.0013	0.0007	88.37	−0.02	China Statistics
33	COD emissions per unit of land area	Ton per km^2	Negative	3.7722	0.0240	0.0128	87.00	−3.75	China Statistics;
34	COD emissions per capita	Ton per capita	Negative	0.0101	0.0097	0.0053	82.66	0.00	China Statistics
35	Nitrogen oxide emissions per unit of land area	Ton per km^2	Negative	6.4473	0.0000	0.0000	NA	−6.45	China Statistics; Deserts; Environmental Annual Report
36	Nitrogen oxide emissions per capita	Ton per capita	Negative	0.0165	0.0000	0.0000	NA	−0.02	Environmental Annual Report; China Statistics
37	Ammonia/nitrogen emissions per unit of land area	Ton per km^2	Negative	0.4164	0.0017	0.0008	100.00	−0.41	China Statistics; Deserts; Environmental Annual Report
38	Ammonia/nitrogen emissions per capita	Ton per capita	Negative	0.0010	0.0007	0.0003	95.35	0.00	Environmental Annual Report; China Statistics
39	Consumption of chemical fertilizers per unit of cultivated land area	10,000 ton per 1,000 hectares	Negative	0.05	0.01	0.01	1.07	−0.04	China Statistics; China Statistics

40	Consumption of pesticides per unit of cultivated land area	Ton per 1,000 hectares	Negative	17.68	2.86	2.55	12.49	−14.82	Environmental Yearbook; China Statistics
41	Nitrogen oxide emissions per capita from road transport	Ton per 10,000 persons	Negative	24.07	24.59	NA	NA	0.52	Environmental Annual Report; China Statistics
42	Ratio of environmental spending to government expenditure	%	Positive	3.35	2.14	2.07	3.00	−1.21	China Statistics
43	Ratio of the investment in pollution control to GDP	%	Positive	1.40	0.06	0.68	−91.29	−1.34	Environmental Yearbook; China Statistics
44	Government spending per capita on rural water supply system and toilet improvement	Yuan per capita	Positive	57.01	58.56	NA	NA	1.55	Environmental Yearbook
45	Investment in converting cultivated land into forests and grassland per unit of cultivated land area	10,000 yuan per 1,000 hectares	Positive	29.81	20.50	21.84	−6.13	−9.30	Environmental Yearbook; China Statistics
46	Ratio of the spending on science, education, culture, and public health to government expenditure	%	Positive	26.10	19.60	21.10	−7.08	−6.50	China Statistics

(continued)

(continued)

No.	Indicator	Unit	Attribute	2010 average of 30 provinces	2010 figure	2009 figure	Growth rate (%)	Difference between Tibet's figure and the average of other provinces	Source of 2010 data
47	Area of green land per capita in urban areas	Hectare per capita	Positive	0.00	0.00	0.01	−74.54	0.00	City; China Statistics
48	Coverage of water supply in urban areas	%	Positive	96.08	97.42	92.53	5.28	1.34	China Statistics
49	Treatment rate of urban wastewater	%	Positive	79.18	76.57	NA	NA	−2.61	Environmental Yearbook
50	Harmless treatment rate of urban household waste	%	Positive	78.47	80.61	NA	NA	2.15	China Statistics
51	Public buses per 10,000 urban residents		Positive	9.86	20.91	12.60	65.97	11.05	China Statistics
52	Length of public transport routes per capita in urban areas	km per capita	Positive	0.0006	0.0007	0.0011	−38.69	0.00	China Statistics; City
53	Ratio of the rural residents benefiting from water supply system improvement to the total rural population	%	Positive	94.44	89.14	NA	NA	−5.30	Environmental Yearbook
54	Green coverage of urban built-up areas	%	Positive	37.75	25.40	29.62	−14.25	−12.35	China Statistics
55	Newly-added afforestation area of the year per capita	Hectare per 10,000 persons	Positive	59.50	210.91	243.66	−13.44	151.41	China Statistics
56	Industrial SO_2 removal rate	%	Positive	59.83	56.75	NA	NA	−3.08	China Statistics
57	Industrial wastewater COD removal rate	%	Positive	70.84	3.49	5.27	−33.83	−67.35	Environmental Annual Report; China Statistics

58	Industrial nitrogen oxide removal rate	%	Positive	4.07	2.87	NA	NA	−1.20	Environmental Annual Report
59	Industrial wastewater ammonia/nitrogen removal rate	%	Positive	62.87	54.20	NA	NA	−8.67	Environmental Annual Report; China Statistics
60	Number of environmental emergencies		Negative	14.00	6	0	NA	−7.91	China Statistics

Note:
China Statistics: *China Statistical Yearbook 2011*
Environmental Yearbook: *China Environmental Statistical Yearbook 2011*
Environmental Annual Report: *China Environment Annual Report 2010*
City: *China City Statistical Yearbook 2011*
Water Conservancy: *China Water Conservancy Statistical Yearbook 2011*
Industrial Economy: *China Industrial Economic Statistical Yearbook 2011*
Deserts: *Deserts in China and Desertification Control*

5.31 Brief Analysis of Green Development in Tibet

Tibet was excluded from the GDI evaluation due to the lack of too many data, therefore the following is an analysis of the changes in Tibet's Third-Class Indicators from 2009 to 2010, as well as the difference between Tibet's 2010 scores and the national average.[1]

5.31.1 Tibet's Performance by Third-Class Indicators Under GDEG

Of the 22 Third-Class Indicators under GDEG, 12 are positively-correlated indicators and 10 negative. Data of 2 positively-correlated indicators and 4 negative ones are missing.

In 2010, 8 positively-correlated indicators of Tibet had higher value than they did in 2009, 3 with over 10 % growth rate. One indicator remained the same as in 2009 and one dropped in value, which was Proportion of the value added of the tertiary sector in GDP, from 54.6 % in 2009 to 54.2 % in 2010.

In 2010, 5 negatively-correlated indicators of Tibet had higher value than they did in 2009, 3 with over a 10 % growth rate. One indicator remained the same as in 2009, which was Proportion of the value added of the tertiary sector in GDP.

Overall, among 10 positively-correlated indicators where data are available, 8 ranked lower than the national average, and the one with largest Difference was Utilization rate of industrial solid waste, only 2.85 % of the latter. Besides, 2 ranked higher than the national average, which are Proportion of water-saving irrigated area in effectively irrigated area and Proportion of the value added of the tertiary sector in GDP, 1.22 and 1.36 times the national average.

Among the 6 negatively-correlated indicators where data are available, 3 ranked higher than the national average, and Water consumption per unit of value added created by industrial enterprises had the largest difference, 4.4 times the latter. Besides, 3 indicators had lower values than the national average, among which SO_2 emissions per unit of GDP, only 9.79 % of the national average, had the largest difference.

5.31.2 Tibet's Performance by Third-Class Indicators Under CCPNRE

There are 19 Third-Class Indicators under CCPNRE, 6 positive and 13 negative, and data of 3 negatively-correlated indicators are missing.

[1] Tibet data are excluded when calculating the national average.

In 2010, 2 positively-correlated indicators of Tibet valued higher than those in 2009, 1 with growth rate of over 10 %. 2 indicators remained the same with those in 2009, and 2 lower. Forest area per capita fell from 5.00 hectares per capita in 2009 to 4.80 hectares per capita in 2010, and Growing stock per capita fell from 783.61 m^3 per capita in 2009 to 755.75 m^3 per capita in 2010.

In 2010, 8 negatively-correlated indicators of Tibet valued higher than those in 2009, 7 with growth rate of over 10 %. 2 indicators remained he same with those in 2009, which are Nitrogen oxide emissions per unit of land area and Nitrogen oxide emissions per capita.

Among the 6 positively-correlated indicators where data are available, 2 are lower than the national average, and 4 obviously higher: Water resources per capita was 63 times the national average, Forest area per capita 25, Proportion of the area of natural reserves in the total area of a region 3.9, and Growing stock per capita 70.

All the 10 negatively-correlated indicators where data are available ranked lower than the national average. The three indicators with largest Difference are SO_2 emissions per unit of land area, COD emissions per unit of land area and Ammonia/nitrogen emissions per unit of land area, and they took up 0.05 %, 0.64 % and 0.40 % respectively of the national average.

5.31.3 Tibet's Performance by Third-Class Indicators Under SDGP

Under SDGP there are 19 Third-Class Indicators, 18 positive and 1 negative, and data of 7 positively-correlated indicators are missing.

In 2010, 3 positively-correlated indicators of Tibet were higher than those in 2009, 1 with growth rate of over 10 %. 8 indicators fell, among which Ratio of the investment in pollution control to GDP and Area of green land per capita in urban areas were 91.3 % and 74.5 % lower than those in 2009. In 2010, the only negatively-correlated indicator of Tibet was higher than that in 2009 with a relatively high growth rate.

Among the 11 positively-correlated indicators where data were available, 8 were lower than the national average. Ratio of the investment in pollution control to GDP and Industrial wastewater COD removal rate had largest difference with the national average, only 4.21 % and 4.92 % of the average value. 3 indicators valued higher than the national average. Newly-added afforestation area of the year per capita was 3.5 times the national average. The only negatively-correlated indicator, Number of environmental emergencies, was 43.5 % of the national average.

Part II
Cities

Based on published statistical yearbooks and the 2010 CGDI system, this part gives a full account of the green development in the 38 evaluated cities in 2010 and analyzes their rankings in this regard. Three chapters are separately dedicated to the specific performances of the cities in terms of the three First-Class Indicators of the GDI, namely "Chapter 6 GDEG Measurement and Analysis by City", "Chapter 7 CCPNRE Measurement and Analysis by City", and "Chapter 8 SDGP Measurement and Analysis by City". Chapter 9 explains in detail the green development levels of the cities in 2010 by providing information including the values of the 43 Third-Class Indicators, their rankings, and the changes in the rankings over the 2 years.

Chapter 6
GDEG Measurement and Analysis by City

Youjuan Wang, Lei Zhu, and Yilong Shi

As an important component of the GDI, the Green Degree of Economic Growth (GDEG) is the overall evaluation of how green an economy is. According to the criterion of GDEG measurement in the CGDI system, this chapter uses the data for 2010 to measure and analyze the GDEG of 38 large and medium-sized cities[1] from four perspectives, i.e., Green Growth Efficiency, Primary Industry, Secondary Industry, and Tertiary Industry.

6.1 Results of GDEG Measurement

The GDEG of 38 cities in China is calculated in line with the related measurement and weighting standards of the CGDI system and the results are shown in Table 6.1 below.

As shown in Table 6.1, the top 10 cities by GDEG are Shenzhen, Beijing, Haikou, Shenyang, Changsha, Qingdao, Dalian, Guangzhou, Suzhou and Nanjing. Specifically, the top 10 cities by GGEI are Shenzhen, Beijing, Changsha, Qingdao, Haikou, Guangzhou, Dalian, Karamay, Hefei and Suzhou; the top 10 cities by PII are Shenzhen, Suzhou, Dalian, Ningbo, Zhuhai, Karamay, Fuzhou, Shenyang,

[1] Including four municipalities directly under the central government, 26 provincial capitals and 5 cities specifically designated in the state plan, as well as Suzhou, Zhuhai and Karamay; Lhasa, Hong Kong, Macao and Taiwan are not included due to lack of data.

Y. Wang (✉)
National Bureau of Statistics, Beijing, China
e-mail: wangyj@gj.stats.cn

L. Zhu • Y. Shi
Beijing Normal University, Beijing, China

X. Li and J. Pan (eds.), *China Green Development Index Report 2012: Regional Comparison*, Current Chinese Economic Report Series,
DOI 10.1007/978-3-642-54178-0_6,

Table 6.1 2010 rankings of 38cities by GDEG

	First-Class Indicators		Second-Class Indicators							
	Green Degree of Economic Growth		Green Growth Efficiency Indicators		Primary Industry Indicators		Secondary Industry Indicators		Tertiary Industry Indicators	
City	Score	Ranking	Score	Ranking	Score	Ranking	Score	Ranking	Score	Ranking
Shenzhen	0.503	1	0.309	1	0.091	1	0.069	2	0.035	7
Beijing	0.205	2	0.103	2	−0.004	21	−0.008	26	0.115	1
Haikou	0.120	3	0.080	5	−0.004	20	0.000	19	0.043	5
Shenyang	0.103	4	0.026	13	0.002	8	0.057	3	0.018	11
Changsha	0.100	5	0.083	3	−0.006	27	0.038	4	−0.015	26
Qingdao	0.096	6	0.082	4	0.000	14	0.016	11	−0.002	17
Dalian	0.079	7	0.057	7	0.014	3	0.004	16	0.003	15
Guangzhou	0.077	8	0.065	6	−0.002	18	−0.047	35	0.061	3
Suzhou	0.077	9	0.029	10	0.017	2	0.022	7	0.009	14
Nanjing	0.053	10	0.029	11	0.002	9	−0.002	20	0.025	8
Karamay	0.044	11	0.034	8	0.002	6	0.088	1	−0.081	38
Shanghai	0.039	12	−0.019	24	0.000	13	−0.004	23	0.061	2
Ninan	0.032	13	0.000	17	0.001	10	0.019	9	0.012	12
Hefei	0.018	14	0.033	9	−0.006	28	0.018	10	−0.027	33
Chengdu	0.008	15	0.014	15	−0.005	25	0.007	14	−0.008	22
Harbin	0.007	16	0.000	16	0.000	11	0.008	12	−0.002	18
Hangzhou	0.005	17	0.026	12	0.000	12	−0.020	30	−0.001	16
Tianjin	0.004	18	−0.029	26	−0.004	24	0.026	6	0.011	13
Changchun	0.000	19	−0.004	20	−0.004	22	0.035	5	−0.027	32
Wuhan	−0.021	20	−0.060	31	0.000	15	0.019	8	0.020	10
Xi'an	−0.032	21	−0.013	22	−0.009	32	−0.003	21	−0.007	21
Fuzhou	−0.039	22	−0.003	19	0.002	7	−0.022	31	−0.016	27
Xiamen	−0.041	23	−0.040	28	−0.001	17	0.003	17	−0.003	19
Urumqi	−0.046	24	−0.096	36	−0.004	23	0.007	15	0.048	4

Nanchang	−0.051	25	−0.028	25	−0.006	29	0.008	13	−0.024	30
Shijiazhuang	−0.055	26	−0.011	21	−0.001	16	0.003	18	−0.045	35
Zhuhai	−0.057	27	−0.052	30	0.007	5	−0.007	25	−0.005	20
Ningbo	−0.067	28	0.015	14	0.010	4	−0.075	38	−0.016	28
Nanning	−0.073	29	−0.018	23	−0.009	31	−0.007	24	−0.039	34
Zhengzhou	−0.075	30	−0.038	27	−0.009	33	−0.003	22	−0.024	31
Hohhot	−0.081	31	−0.061	32	−0.003	19	−0.053	37	0.037	6
Kunming	−0.087	32	−0.002	18	−0.011	35	−0.053	36	−0.021	29
Taiyuan	−0.101	33	−0.083	34	−0.009	30	−0.032	32	0.023	9
Yinchuan	−0.112	34	−0.081	33	−0.005	26	−0.010	28	−0.015	25
Lanzhou	−0.121	35	−0.091	35	−0.011	37	−0.010	27	−0.009	23
Chongqing	−0.161	36	−0.051	29	−0.011	34	−0.034	33	−0.066	37
Guiyang	−0.168	37	−0.100	37	−0.011	36	−0.045	34	−0.011	24
Xining	−0.183	38	−0.107	38	−0.012	38	−0.012	29	−0.052	36

Note: ① The results are obtained based on calculations with 2010 data for each GDEG indicator; ② The cities are listed in descending order of GDEG value; ③ The score by GDEG in this table is the sum of the scores by the four Second-Class Indicators: Green Growth Efficiency Indicators, Primary Industry Indicators, Secondary Industry Indicators, and Tertiary Industry Indicators; ④ The national average of each indicator is "0". ⑤ The calculations are based on the *China Statistical Yearbook 2011*, *China Environment Annual Report 2010*, *China Environmental Statistical Yearbook 2011*, *China City Statistical Yearbook 2011*, *China Urban Construction Statistical Yearbook 2010*, and *China Regional Economy Statistical Yearbook 2011*

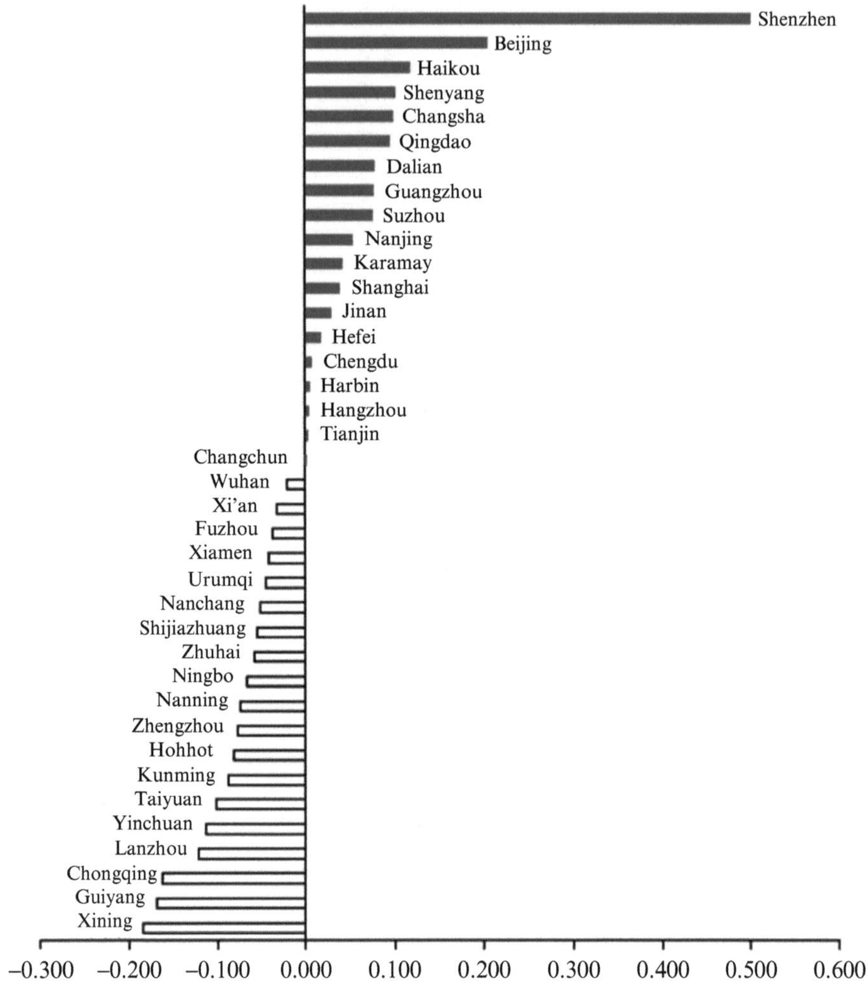

Fig. 6.1 2010 rankings of 38 Cities by GDEG (Note: This figure is developed based on relevant data in Table 6.1)

Nanjing and Jinan; the top 10 cities by SII are Karamay, Shenzhen, Shenyang, Changsha, Changchun, Tianjin, Suzhou, Wuhan, Jinan and Hefei; the top 10 cities by TII are Beijing, Shanghai, Guangzhou, Urumqi, Haikou, Hohhot, Shenzhen, Nanjing, Taiyuan and Wuhan.

Based on Table 6.1 and Fig. 6.1, the following analyses are focused three aspects, namely the regional differences in GDEG, the differences between cities in GDEG in each region, and the relations between GDEG and GDI.

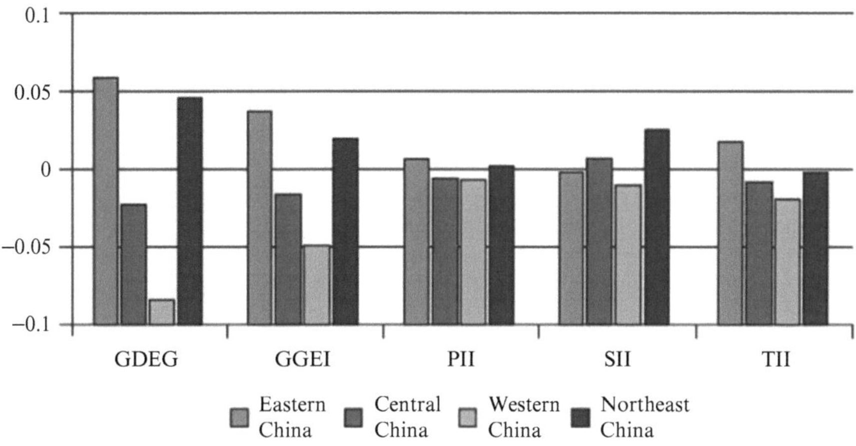

Fig. 6.2 GDEG comparison by region (Note: The data for each region in the figure are the arithmetic mean of the scores of all the cities in the region)

6.1.1 Regional Differences in GDEG

The contribution of GDEG to regional GDI is reflected as follows: the GDEG of eastern cities plays a more significant role in improving GDI than western and central cities, while the GDI of the latter is driven more by the other two Second-Class Indicators, namely Carrying Capacity Potential of Natural Resources and Environment (CCPNRE) and Support Degree of Government Policies (SDGP). Generally, Eastern China has the best GDEG, followed by Northeast China, Central China and Western China (Fig. 6.2).[2] The average score of evaluated eastern cities is 0.060, and that of northeastern cities 0.047, remarkably higher than that of central and western cities which respectively registers −0.022 and −0.084, below the national average.

By comparing the Second-Class Indicators, we find that, in terms of GGEI, eastern cities score 0.037, followed by northeastern cities at 0.020. The GGEI of central and western cities score −0.016 and −0.048 respectively, both below the national average.

In terms of PII, eastern and northeastern cities score 0.007 and 0.003 respectively, slightly above the national average; and central and western cities score −0.006 and −0.007 respectively, below the national average. Generally speaking, there are very small gaps between cities in the four regions.

In terms of SII, northeastern cities score 0.026, followed by 0.008 of central cities; eastern and western cities score −0.002 and −0.010 respectively, below the national average.

[2] Eastern cities include Beijing, Tianjin, Shijiazhuang, Shanghai, Nanjing, Suzhou, Hangzhou, Ningbo, Fuzhou, Xiamen, Jinan, Qingdao, Guangzhou, Shenzhen, Zhuhai and Haikou; central cities include Taiyuan, Hefei, Nanchang, Zhengzhou, Wuhan and Changsha; western cities include Hohhot, Urumqi, Nanning, Chongqing, Chengdu, Guiyang, Kunming, Xi'an, Lanzhou, Xining, Yinchuan and Karamay; northeastern cities include Shenyang, Dalian, Changchun and Harbin.

Table 6.2 2010 rankings of eastern cities by GDEG

City	Score	Ranking in China	Ranking in the region	City	Score	Ranking in China	Ranking in the region
Shenzhen	0.503	1	1	Jinan	0.032	13	9
Beijing	0.205	2	2	Hangzhou	0.005	17	10
Haikou	0.120	3	3	Tianjin	0.004	18	11
Qingdao	0.096	6	4	Fuzhou	−0.039	22	12
Guangzhou	0.077	8	5	Xiamen	−0.041	23	13
Suzhou	0.077	9	6	Shijiazhuang	−0.055	26	14
Nanjing	0.053	10	7	Zhuhai	−0.057	27	15
Shanghai	0.039	12	8	Ningbo	−0.067	28	16

Note: This table is developed based on Table 6.1

In terms of SII, eastern cities score 0.018, and the central, western and northeastern cities all score below the national average, respectively at −0.008, −0.019 and −0.002.

6.1.2 GDEG in Each Region

According to the results of GDEG measurement, there are significant regional gaps between city rankings. Relatively speaking, eastern cities rank ahead, followed by northeastern cities, central cities and western cities. What's more, there are large gaps between the rankings of cities in each region.

6.1.2.1 Rankings of Eastern Cities by GDEG

The 2010 rankings of eastern cities by GDEG are shown in Table 6.2.

Of the 16 eastern cities, Shenzhen, Beijing, Haikou, Qingdao, Guangzhou, Suzhou and Nanjing rank among the national top 10. Shenzhen scores 0.503 and Beijing 0.205, far ahead of other cities. In addition, four cities rank No. 11–20, and the rest five rank No. 21–30. Eleven or 68.7 % of eastern cities score more than 0, i.e. above the national average, implying the leading GDEG of Eastern China.

6.1.2.2 Rankings of Central Cities by GDEG

The 2010 rankings of central cities by GDEG are shown in Table 6.3.

The rankings of the six central cities vary significantly. One is among the top 10; two rank No. 11–20; one stands between No. 25 and No. 30, and one is in No. 31–38. Changsha scores 0.100 and Hefei 0.018, both above the national average, and the rest four cities all score less than 0, indicating large GDEG gaps between central cities in different ranges of rankings.

Table 6.3 2010 rankings of central cities by GDEG

City	Score	Ranking in China	Ranking in the region	City	Score	Ranking in China	Ranking in the region
Changsha	0.100	5	1	Nanchang	−0.051	25	4
Hefei	0.018	14	2	Zhengzhou	−0.075	30	5
Wuhan	−0.021	20	3	Taiyuan	−0.101	33	6

Note: This table is developed based on Table 6.1

Table 6.4 2010 rankings of western cities by GDEG

City	Score	Ranking in China	Ranking in the region	City	Score	Ranking in China	Ranking in the region
Karamay	0.044	11	1	Kunming	−0.087	32	7
Chengdu	0.008	15	2	Yinchuan	−0.112	34	8
Xi'an	−0.032	21	3	Lanzhou	−0.121	35	9
Urumqi	−0.046	24	4	Chongqing	−0.161	36	10
Nanning	−0.073	29	5	Guiyang	−0.168	37	11
Hohhot	−0.081	31	6	Xining	−0.183	38	12

Note: This table is developed based on Table 6.1

Table 6.5 2010 rankings of northeastern cities by GDEG

City	Score	Ranking in China	Ranking in the region	City	Score	Ranking in China	Ranking in the region
Shenyang	0.103	4	1	Harbin	0.007	16	3
Dalian	0.079	7	2	Changchun	0.000	19	4

Note: This table is developed based on Table 6.1

6.1.2.3 Rankings of Western Cities by GDEG

The 2010 rankings of western cities by are shown in Table 6.4.

Western cities have low GDEG rankings. Seven of the 12 cities rank No. 31–38; only Karamay ranks No. 11 and Chengdu No. 15; none of them stand among the top 10. From the perspective of scores, all the cities, except Karamay and Chengdu, score lower than the national average.

6.1.2.4 Rankings of Northeastern Cities by GDEG

The 2010 rankings of northeastern cities by GDEG are shown in Table 6.5.

The four northeastern cities have higher rankings. Shenyang, Dalian and Harbin rank No. 4, No. 7 and No. 16 respectively and score above 0. While Changchun ranks No. 19 with a score close to the national average. This reflects that, though they differ in GDEG, the northeastern cities as a whole rank fairly high.

Table 6.6 Differences between the 2010 rankings by GDI and GDEG

City	Ranking by GDI	Ranking by GDEG	Difference	City	Ranking by GDI	Ranking by GDEG	Difference
Shenzhen	1	1	0	Guiyang	20	37	−17
Haikou	2	3	−1	Shenyang	21	4	17
Karamay	3	11	−8	Hefei	22	14	8
Kunming	4	32	−28	Taiyuan	23	33	−10
Guangzhou	5	8	−3	Xiamen	24	23	1
Beijing	6	2	4	Shijiazhuang	25	26	−1
Dalian	7	7	0	Shanghai	26	12	14
Qingdao	8	6	2	Hohhot	27	31	−4
Nanjing	9	10	−1	Tianjin	28	18	10
Fuzhou	10	22	−12	Changchun	29	19	10
Zhuhai	11	27	−16	Chengdu	30	15	15
Nanning	12	29	−17	Nanchang	31	25	6
Changsha	13	5	8	Xi'an	32	21	11
Suzhou	14	9	5	Chongqing	33	36	−3
Harbin	15	16	−1	Wuhan	34	20	14
Yinchuan	16	34	−18	Urumqi	35	24	11
Ningbo	17	28	−11	Zhengzhou	36	30	6
Hangzhou	18	17	1	Lanzhou	37	35	2
Jinan	19	13	6	Xining	38	38	0

Note: ① This table is developed based on Tables 1.6 and 6.1. ② The "Difference" in the table refers to the gap between the GDEG ranking and the GDI ranking. A positive value indicates how many places GDEG ranking is ahead of GDI ranking, and a negative value indicates how many places GDEG ranking is behind GDI ranking

6.1.3 Impact of GDEG on GDI

According to the results, the GDEG of cities has significant yet largely varied impacts on GDI in different regions. Comparing the rankings by GDEG and GDI, we find that, 16 cities experience a difference of five places or less between their GDEG and GDI rankings, and 25 cities see a gap of 10 places or less. The largest gap, 28 places, is found in Kunming, implying that the city lags behind in terms of GDEG and a good many pollutants are discharged during its development (Table 6.6).

6.2 Inter-city Comparison by GDEG

Using the GDEG measurement system, we have analyzed the GGEI, PII, SII and TII of the 38 cities to evaluate their GDEG. To ensure consistency, we have used the same GDEG indicators and weights as those for the 2011 report. There are 17 Third-class Indicators, including 8 positive ones and 9 negative ones, and two of them have no official data. They take a 33 % weight in the GDI system. The weight of each Third-class Indicator is between 1.65 % and 2.36 %.

Table 6.7 GGEI, weights and attributes

No.	Indicator	Weight (%)	Attribute
1	GDP per capita	2.02	Positive
2	Energy consumption per unit of GDP	2.36	Negative
3	Electricity consumption per capita in urban areas	2.02	Negative
4	CO_2 emissions per unit of GDP	2.02	Negative
5	SO_2 emissions per unit of GDP	2.02	Negative
6	COD emissions per unit of GDP	2.02	Negative
7	Nitrogen oxide emissions per unit of GDP	2.02	Negative
8	Ammonia/nitrogen emissions per unit of GDP	2.02	Negative

Note: The content of this table was finalized after discussions at several seminars held by the research group

6.2.1 Comparison by GGEI

GGEI has a 50 % weight in the GDEG system and 16.5 % in the GDI system, contributing more to GDEG than the other three Second-Class Indicators. The eight Third-Level Indicators under GGEI are shown in Table 6.7 above.

Energy consumption per unit of GDP is a restrictive indicator under key monitoring by the State Council and is more important than the others. This is why its weight is as high as 2.36 %. Each of the other indicators is weighted 2.02 %. Using the processed data for the indicators and their weights shown in Table 6.7, we have worked out the 2010 rankings of cities by GGEI as shown in Table 6.8.

According to Table 6.8, the 38 cities score between −0.107 and 0.309, displaying a large gap. Fifteen or 40 % of all cities score more than the national average, and they are Shenzhen, Beijing, Changsha, Qingdao, Haikou, Guangzhou, Dalian, Karamay, Hefei, Suzhou, Nanjing, Hangzhou, Shenyang, Ningbo and Chengdu, most of them are eastern cities. Twenty-one cities score below the average of all eligible cities and they are Kunming, Fuzhou, Changchun, Shijiazhuang, Xi'an, Nanjing, Shanghai, Nanchang, Tianjin, Zhengzhou, Xiamen, Chongqing, Zhuhai, Wuhan, Hohhot, Yinchuan, Taiyuan, Lanzhou, Urumqi, Guiyang and Xining. Harbin and Jinan score close to the national average.

The GGEI of the cities by region are shown in Fig. 6.3. The 16 eastern cities are Shenzhen, Beijing, Haikou, Qingdao, Guangzhou, Suzhou, Nanjing, Shanghai, Jinan, Hangzhou, Tianjin, Fuzhou, Xiamen, Shijiazhuang, Zhuhai and Ningbo; the six central cities are Changsha, Hefei, Wuhan, Nanchang, Zhengzhou and Taiyuan; the 12 western cities are Karamay, Chengdu, Xi'an, Urumqi, Nanning, Hohhot, Kunming, Yinchuan, Lanzhou, Chongqing, Guiyang and Xining; the four northeastern cities are Shenyang, Dalian, Harbin and Changchun.

As shown in Fig. 6.3, eastern cities display large disparity; northeastern cities score higher than central and western cities. The scores of eastern cities average 0.037, that of central cities −0.016, western cities −0.048 and northeastern cities 0.020. Eastern cities have the best GGEI, followed by northeastern, central and western cities.

In terms of ranking, the top 10 cities include six eastern cities, i.e., Shenzhen, Beijing, Haikou, Qingdao, Guangzhou and Suzhou, as well as two central cities,

Table 6.8 2010 rankings of cities in China by GGEI

Indicator	GGEI		Indicator	GGEI	
City	Score	Ranking	City	Score	Ranking
Shenzhen	0.309	1	Changchun	−0.004	20
Beijing	0.103	2	Shijiazhuang	−0.011	21
Changsha	0.083	3	Xi'an	−0.013	22
Qingdao	0.082	4	Nanning	−0.018	23
Haikou	0.080	5	Shanghai	−0.019	24
Guangzhou	0.065	6	Nanchang	−0.028	25
Dalian	0.057	7	Tianjin	−0.029	26
Karamay	0.034	8	Zhengzhou	−0.038	27
Hefei	0.033	9	Xiamen	−0.040	28
Suzhou	0.029	10	Chongqing	−0.051	29
Nanjing	0.029	11	Zhuhai	−0.052	30
Hangzhou	0.026	12	Wuhan	−0.060	31
Shenyang	0.026	13	Hohhot	−0.061	32
Ningbo	0.015	14	Yinchuan	−0.081	33
Chengdu	0.014	15	Taiyuan	−0.083	34
Harbin	0.000	16	Lanzhou	−0.091	35
Jinan	0.000	17	Urumqi	−0.096	36
Kunming	−0.002	18	Guiyang	−0.100	37
Fuzhou	−0.003	19	Xining	−0.107	38

Note: The scores and rankings are worked out based on *China Statistical Yearbook 2011, China Environment Annual Report 2010, China Environmental Statistical Yearbook 2011, China City Statistical Yearbook 2011, China Urban Construction Statistical Yearbook 2010*, and *China Regional Economy Statistical Yearbook 2011*

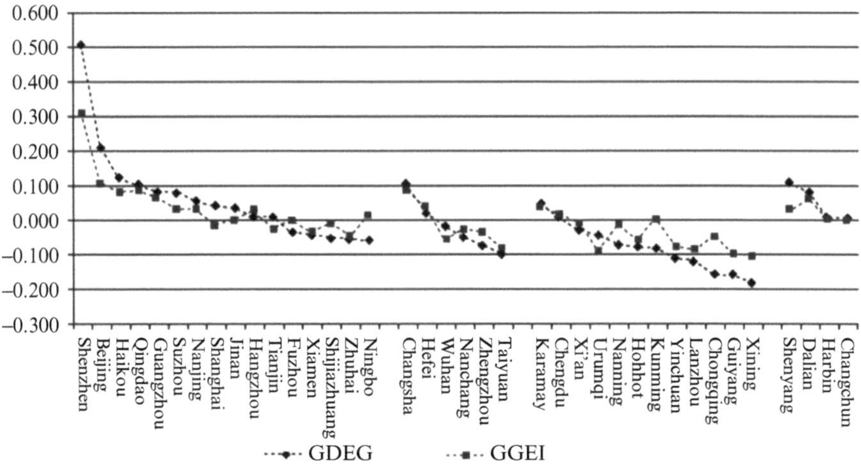

Fig. 6.3 Inter-city comparison by GGEI and GDEG (Note: The cities in the figure are grouped by region, namely Eastern, Central, Western and Northeast China, and arranged from *left* to *right* in descending order of GDEG)

Table 6.9 PII, weight and attribute

No.	Indicator	Weight	Attribute
9	Labor productivity of the primary sector	1.65 %	Positive

Note: The content of this table was finalized after discussions at several seminars held by the research group

Table 6.10 2010 rankings of cities in China by PII

Indicator	PII		Indicator	PII	
City	Score	Ranking	City	Score	Ranking
Shenzhen	0.091	1	Haikou	−0.004	20
Suzhou	0.017	2	Beijing	−0.004	21
Dalian	0.014	3	Changchun	−0.004	22
Ningbo	0.010	4	Urumqi	−0.004	23
Zhuhai	0.007	5	Tianjin	−0.004	24
Karamay	0.002	6	Chengdu	−0.005	25
Fuzhou	0.002	7	Yinchuan	−0.005	26
Shenyang	0.002	8	Changsha	−0.006	27
Nanjing	0.002	9	Hefei	−0.006	28
Jinan	0.001	10	Nanchang	−0.006	29
Harbin	0.000	11	Taiyuan	−0.009	30
Hangzhou	0.000	12	Nanning	−0.009	31
Shanghai	0.000	13	Xi'an	−0.009	32
Qingdao	0.000	14	Zhengzhou	−0.009	33
Wuhan	0.000	15	Chongqing	−0.011	34
Shijiazhuang	−0.001	16	Kunming	−0.011	35
Xiamen	−0.001	17	Guiyang	−0.011	36
Guangzhou	−0.002	18	Lanzhou	−0.011	37
Hohhot	−0.003	19	Xining	−0.012	38

Note: The scores and rankings are worked out based on *China Statistical Yearbook 2011*, *China Environment Annual Report 2010*, *China Environmental Statistical Yearbook 2011*, *China City Statistical Yearbook 2011*, *China Urban Construction Statistical Yearbook 2010*, and *China Regional Economy Statistical Yearbook 2011*

one western and one northeastern cities; while the bottom 10 include Zhuhai in Eastern China, Wuhan and Taiyuan in Central China, and seven western cities, i.e., Urumqi, Hohhot, Yinchuan, Lanzhou, Chongqing, Guiyang and Xining. Generally, western cities lag behind.

6.2.2 Comparison by PII

In the GDEG system, a 5 % weight is given to PII, under which there is only one Third-Class Indicator, taking a 1.65 % weight in the GDI system. It is a positive indicator (Table 6.9).

Using the weights provided in Table 6.9 and processed data for the PII of the 38 cities, we have worked out the 2010 rankings of cities by PII as shown in Table 6.10.

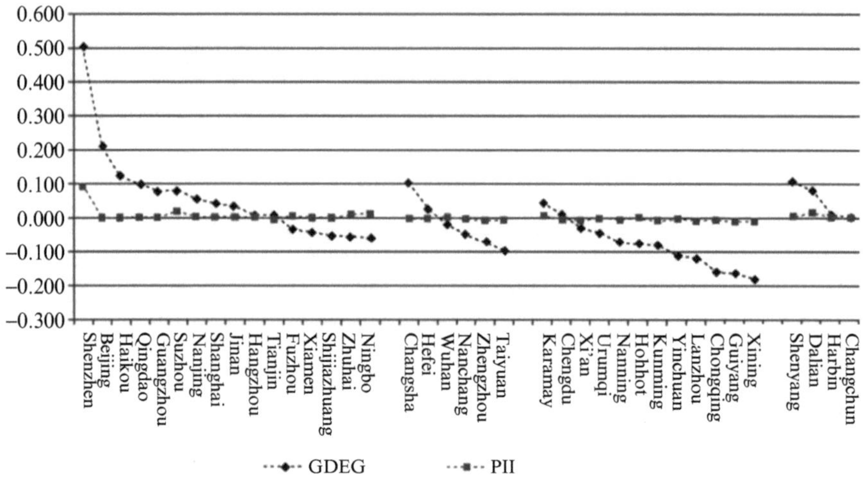

Fig. 6.4 Inter-city Comparison by PII and GDEG (Note: The cities in the figure are grouped by region, namely Eastern, Central, Western and Northeast China, and arranged from *left* to *right* in descending order of GDEG)

According to Table 6.10, there are only 10 cities scoring higher than the national average, and they are Shenzhen, Suzhou, Dalian, Ningbo, Zhuhai, Karamay, Fuzhou, Shenyang, Nanjing and Jinan, most of them are in the eastern region; there are 23 cities scoring lower than the national average and they are Shijiazhuang, Xiamen, Guangzhou, Hohhot, Haikou, Beijing, Changchun, Urumqi, Tianjin, Chengdu, Yinchuan, Changsha, Hefei, Nanchang, Taiyuan, Nanning, Xi'an, Zhengzhou, Chongqing, Kunming, Guiyang, Lanzhou and Xining; 5 cities score close to the national average, which are more in number compared with other Second-class Indicators. The top value of PII registers 0.091 and the bottom −0.012, a small gap of 0.103. Because of its small weight, the scores of PII do not have too much influence on the GDEG ranking.

To illustrate the regional disparity of PII, we have analyzed Fig. 6.4 and found that, among the 38 cities, Shenzhen is the only one with high score and the rest cities are quite close. The PII curve is not highly correlated with the GDEG curve, implying that PII scores do not have significant influences on GDEG.

In terms of average PII scores, the eastern cities average 0.007, followed by 0.003 of the northeastern cities, −0.006 of the central cities and −0.007 of the western cities, showing small gaps.

6.2.3 Comparison by SII

In the GDEG system, SII is given a 30 % weight, only next to GGEI. There are five Third-class Indicators, including three positive ones and two negative ones, and the

Table 6.11 SII, weights and attributes

No.	Indicator	Weight (%)	Attribute
10	Labor productivity of the secondary sector	1.98	Positive
11	Water consumption per unit of value added created by industrial enterprises	1.98	Negative
12	Energy consumption per unit of value added created by industrial enterprises	1.98	Negative
13	Utilization rate of industrial solid waste	1.98	Positive
14	Recycling rate of industrial water	1.98	Positive

Note: The content of this table was finalized after discussions at several seminars held by the research group

indicator "Energy consumption value added created by industrial enterprises" has no official data. Apart from "Labor productivity of the secondary sector", the rest four indicators represent the energy efficiency and recycling rate of resources to reflect the green degree of the secondary industry. Each Third-class Indicator takes a weight of 1.98 % (Table 6.11).

Using the weights provided in Table 6.11 and processed data for the SII of the 38 cities, we have worked out the 2010 rankings of cities by SII as shown in Table 6.12.

As shown in Table 6.12, the cities score between −0.075 and 0.088, with the highest and lowest going to Karamay and Ningbo respectively. 18, nearly half of 38 cities, which score nearly the national average, and they are Karamay, Shenzhen, Shenyang, Changsha, Changchun, Tianjin, Suzhou, Wuhan, Jinan, Hefei, Qingdao, Harbin, Nanchang, Chengdu, Urumqi, Dalian, Xiamen and Shijiazhuang; while 19 cities score lower than the national average, and they are Nanjing, Xi'an, Zhengzhou, Shanghai, Nanning, Zhuhai, Beijing, Lanzhou, Yinchuan, Xining, Hangzhou, Fuzhou, Taiyuan, Chongqing, Guiyang, Guangzhou, Kunming, Hohhot and Ningbo; Haikou scores 0.000, the national average.

According to Fig. 6.5, there are not significant disparities between the 38 cities. In each region, the gaps between cities are also small.

From the perspective of scores, the eastern cities average −0.002, the central cities 0.008, the western cities −0.010, and the northeastern cities 0.026. Eastern cities are no longer leaders as they are by GGEI and PII, while the northeastern and central cities show some strengths.

From the perspective of ranking, the top 10 include four eastern cities—Shenzhen, Tianjin, Suzhou and Jinan, two central cities—Changsha and Wuhan, Karamay from the west which is No. 1, and 2 northeastern cities—Shenyang and Changchun. The bottom 10 include four eastern cities of which Ningbo stayed at the bottom of the list, Taiyuan from the central region, five western cities—Xining, Hohhot, Kunming, Chongqing and Guiyang. Northeastern cities have higher rankings while western cities have lower scores.

Table 6.12 2010 rankings of cities in China by SII

Indicator	SII		Indicator	SII	
City	Score	Ranking	City	Score	Ranking
Karamay	0.088	1	Nanjing	−0.002	20
Shenzhen	0.069	2	Xi'an	−0.003	21
Shenyang	0.057	3	Zhengzhou	−0.003	22
Changsha	0.038	4	Shanghai	−0.004	23
Changchun	0.035	5	Nanning	−0.007	24
Tianjin	0.026	6	Zhuhai	−0.007	25
Suzhou	0.022	7	Beijing	−0.008	26
Wuhan	0.019	8	Lanzhou	−0.010	27
Jinan	0.019	9	Yinchuan	−0.010	28
Hefei	0.018	10	Xining	−0.012	29
Qingdao	0.016	11	Hangzhou	−0.020	30
Harbin	0.008	12	Fuzhou	−0.022	31
Nanchang	0.008	13	Taiyuan	−0.032	32
Chengdu	0.007	14	Chongqing	−0.034	33
Urumqi	0.007	15	Guiyang	−0.045	34
Dalian	0.004	16	Guangzhou	−0.047	35
Xiamen	0.003	17	Kunming	−0.053	36
Shijiazhuang	0.003	18	Hohhot	−0.053	37
Haikou	0.000	19	Ningbo	−0.075	38

Note: The scores and rankings are worked out based on *China Statistical Yearbook 2011*, *China Environment Annual Report 2010*, *China Environmental Statistical Yearbook 2011*, *China City Statistical Yearbook 2011*, *China Urban Construction Statistical Yearbook 2010*, and *China Regional Economy Statistical Yearbook 2011*

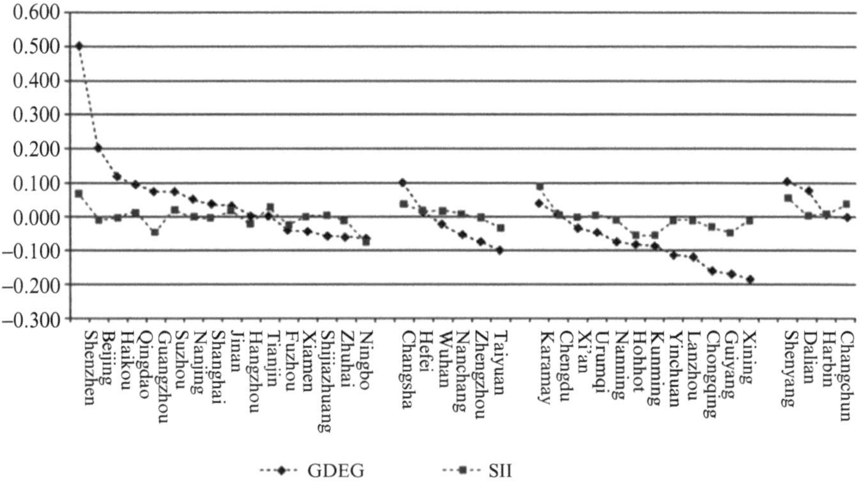

Fig. 6.5 Inter-city Comparison by SII and GDEG (Note: The cities in the figure are grouped by region, namely Eastern, Central, Western and Northeast China, and arranged from *left* to *right* in descending order of GDEG)

Table 6.13 TII, weights and attributes

No.	Indicator	Weight (%)	Attribute
15	Labor productivity of the tertiary sector	1.65	Positive
16	Proportion of the value added of the tertiary sector in GDP	1.65	Positive
17	Proportion of tertiary sector employees in the total employed population	1.65	Positive

Note: The content of this table was finalized after discussions at several seminars held by the research group

Table 6.14 2010 rankings of cities in China by TII

Indicator	TII		Indicator	TII	
City	Score	Ranking	City	Score	Ranking
Beijing	0.115	1	Zhuhai	−0.005	20
Shanghai	0.061	2	Xi'an	−0.007	21
Guangzhou	0.061	3	Chengdu	−0.008	22
Urumqi	0.048	4	Lanzhou	−0.009	23
Haikou	0.043	5	Guiyang	−0.011	24
Hohhot	0.037	6	Yinchuan	−0.015	25
Shenzhen	0.035	7	Changsha	−0.015	26
Nanjing	0.025	8	Fuzhou	−0.016	27
Taiyuan	0.023	9	Ningbo	−0.016	28
Wuhan	0.020	10	Kunming	−0.021	29
Shenyang	0.018	11	Nanchang	−0.024	30
Jinan	0.012	12	Zhengzhou	−0.024	31
Tianjin	0.011	13	Changchun	−0.027	32
Suzhou	0.009	14	Hefei	−0.027	33
Dalian	0.003	15	Nanning	−0.039	34
Hangzhou	−0.001	16	Shijiazhuang	−0.045	35
Qingdao	−0.002	17	Xining	−0.052	36
Harbin	−0.002	18	Chongqing	−0.066	37
Xiamen	−0.003	19	Karamay	−0.081	38

Note: The scores and rankings are worked out based on *China Statistical Yearbook 2011*, *China Environment Annual Report 2010*, *China Environmental Statistical Yearbook 2011*, *China City Statistical Yearbook 2011*, *China Urban Construction Statistical Yearbook 2010*, and *China Regional Economy Statistical Yearbook 2011*

6.2.4 Comparison by TII

TII takes a 15 % weight in the GDEG system and 4.95 % in the GDI system. There are three Third-class Indicators, all of which are positive ones, each taking a weight of 1.65 % (Table 6.13).

TII is not only closely related to the overall economic growth, but also an important factor for measuring industrial structure optimization and green growth of economy. Based on Table 6.13 and related data, we have worked out the 2010 rankings of cities by TII as shown in Table 6.14.

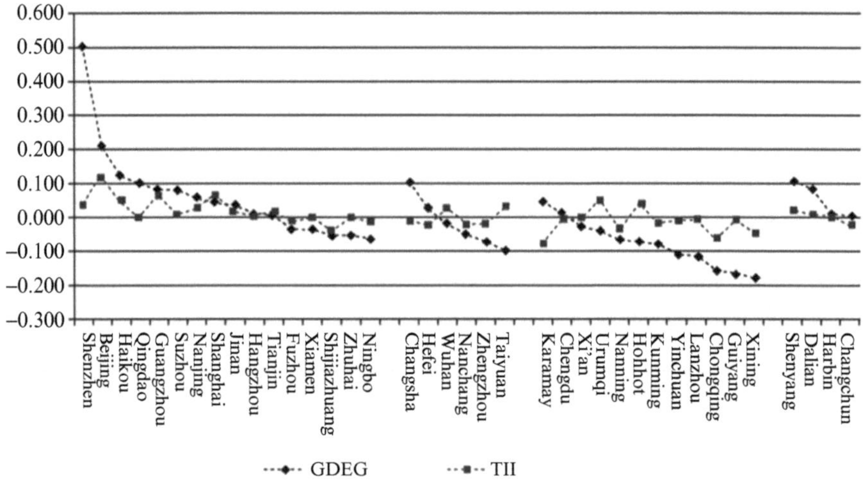

Fig. 6.6 Inter-city comparison by TII and GDEG (Note: The cities in the figure are grouped by region, namely Eastern, Central, Western and Northeast China, and arranged from *left* to *right* in descending order of GDEG)

According to Table 6.14, No. 1 Beijing scores 0.115 and Karamay is at the bottom of the list with a score of −0.081, a gap of 0.196. Of the 38 cities, 15 cities score higher than the national average and they are Beijing, Shanghai, Guangzhou, Urumqi, Haikou, Hohhot, Shenzhen, Nanjing, Taiyuan, Wuhan, Shenyang, Jinan, Tianjin, Suzhou and Dalian; 23 cities score lower than the national average and they are Hangzhou, Qingdao, Harbin, Xiamen, Zhuhai, Xi'an, Chengdu, Lanzhou, Guiyang, Yinchuan, Changsha, Fuzhou, Ningbo, Kunming, Nanchang, Zhengzhou, Changchun, Hefei, Nanning, Shijiazhuang, Xining, Chongqing and Karamay.

From a regional perspective, 9 eastern cities, 2 central, 2 western and 2 northeastern cities score more than the national average; 7 eastern cities, 4 central, 10 western and 2 northeastern cities score less than the national average. Cities scoring higher than the national average are mainly in Eastern China, while those scoring below the national average are mainly in Western China. The following is an analysis of the regional disparity based on Fig. 6.6 above.

As shown in Fig. 6.6, eastern cities as a whole score higher than cities in the other regions. Northeastern cities are next to eastern cities, and western cities are at the bottom.

From the perspective of scores, eastern cities average 0.018, followed by −0.008 of central cities, −0.019 of western cities and −0.002 of northeastern cities.

From the perspective of rankings, the top 10 include 6 eastern cities, of which Beijing, Shanghai and Guangzhou are among top 3 and Beijing in particular scores 0.115, far ahead of No.2 Shanghai; Taiyuan and Wuhan in the central region and Urumqi and Hohhot in the western region also rank among the top 10. The bottom 10 include Shijiazhuang in the eastern region, 3 or half of the central cities—Hefei, Nanchang and Zhengzhou, 5 western cities—Karamay, Nanning, Kunming,

Chongqing and Xining, and Changchun in the northeastern region. This suggests that, eastern cities have absolute advantages; central cities have improvement potential; northeastern cities are not outstanding despite their fairly good TII scores, indicating the necessity to enhance the tertiary industry and foster key cities with good rankings; western cities lag behind in terms of the tertiary industry and should take the development opportunity and attach more importance to support the industry, so as to get closer to the national average.

Chapter 7
CCPNRE Measurement and Analysis by City

Yuru Mao, Jiangxue Zhang, and Shiyao Liu

The Carrying Capacity Potential of Natural Resources and Environment (CCPNRE) measures how far the economic development and human activities in a region will go given its resource abundance, ecological conservation, environmental pressure and climate change. This chapter uses the 2010 data to calculate the CCPNRE of 38 large and medium sized cities in two aspects, i.e., Resource Abundance and Ecological Conservation, and Environmental Pressure and Climate Change.

7.1 Results of CCPNRE Measurement

The CCPNRE of 38 cities in China is calculated in line with the related measurement and weighting standards of the CGDI system and the results are shown in Table 7.1 below.

As shown in Table 7.1, Kunming scores the highest at 0.416 and Wuhan the lowest at −0.168. Thirteen or one-third of the 38 cities score more than the national average. The top 10 cities are Kunming, Haikou, Karamay, Harbin, Nanning, Shenzhen, Fuzhou, Changsha, Dalian and Guiyang. The top 10 cities by Resource Abundance and Ecological Conservation Indicators (RAECI) are Lanzhou, Hangzhou, Fuzhou, Zhuhai, Changsha, Ningbo, Nanning, Harbin, Chongqing and Guiyang; the top 10 cities by Environmental Press and Climate Change Indicators (EPCCI) are Kunming, Haikou, Karamay, Harbin, Nanning, Shenzhen, Fuzhou, Dalian, Changsha and Guiyang. The 2010 rankings of the 38 cities by CCPNRE are shown in Fig. 7.1.

Y. Mao (✉)
Environmental Statistics Division, Department of Total Emission Control,
Ministry of Environmental Protection, Beijing, China
e-mail: mao.yuru@mep.gov.cn

J. Zhang • S. Liu
School of Economics and Resource Management, Beijing Normal University, Beijing, China

X. Li and J. Pan (eds.), *China Green Development Index Report 2012: Regional Comparison*, Current Chinese Economic Report Series,
DOI 10.1007/978-3-642-54178-0_7,

Table 7.1 2010 rankings of 38 cities by CCPNRE

	First-Class Indicator		Second-Class Indicators			
	Carrying Potential of Natural Resources and Environment		Resource Abundance and Ecological Conservation Indicators		Environmental Pressure and Climate Change Indicators	
City	Score	Ranking	Score	Ranking	Score	Ranking
Kunming	0.416	1	0.002	11	0.414	1
Haikou	0.399	2	−0.009	36	0.408	2
Karamay	0.227	3	−0.002	14	0.229	3
Harbin	0.195	4	0.005	8	0.190	4
Nanning	0.190	5	0.006	7	0.184	5
Shenzhen	0.166	6	−0.003	16	0.169	6
Fuzhou	0.111	7	0.011	3	0.100	7
Changsha	0.057	8	0.006	5	0.051	9
Dalian	0.054	9	−0.004	17	0.057	8
Guiyang	0.046	10	0.003	10	0.043	10
Chongqing	0.035	11	0.005	9	0.031	11
Hefei	0.011	12	−0.004	18	0.015	12
Hohhot	0.002	13	−0.005	24	0.007	13
Chengdu	−0.001	14	−0.005	22	0.004	14
Changchun	−0.006	15	−0.005	21	−0.002	15
Qingdao	−0.016	16	−0.008	29	−0.008	16
Nanchang	−0.024	17	−0.008	30	−0.016	17
Ningbo	−0.032	18	0.006	6	−0.038	19
Yinchuan	−0.035	19	−0.010	38	−0.025	18
Guangzhou	−0.041	20	0.001	12	−0.042	20
Zhuhai	−0.048	21	0.008	4	−0.056	23
Shenyang	−0.048	22	−0.005	23	−0.044	21
Nanjing	−0.056	23	−0.005	20	−0.052	22
Hangzhou	−0.058	24	0.018	2	−0.076	25
Lanzhou	−0.073	25	0.094	1	−0.167	38
Taiyuan	−0.081	26	−0.009	33	−0.072	24
Xiamen	−0.083	27	−0.003	15	−0.081	27
Jinan	−0.085	28	−0.008	27	−0.078	26
Shijiazhuang	−0.095	29	−0.009	35	−0.086	28
Zhengzhou	−0.099	30	−0.009	34	−0.090	29
Xi'an	−0.107	31	−0.009	31	−0.099	30
Beijing	−0.109	32	−0.009	32	−0.100	31
Shanghai	−0.116	33	−0.008	28	−0.108	32
Suzhou	−0.124	34	−0.006	26	−0.118	33
Xining	−0.132	35	−0.004	19	−0.127	36
Urumqi	−0.132	36	−0.006	25	−0.126	34
Tianjin	−0.136	37	−0.010	37	−0.126	35
Wuhan	−0.168	38	−0.001	13	−0.167	37

Note: ① The results are obtained based on calculations with 2010 data for each CCPNRE indicator; ② The cities are listed in descending order of GDEG value; ③ The score by CCPNRE in this table is the sum of the scores by the two Second-Class Indicators: Resource Abundance and Ecological Conservation and Environmental Pressure and Climate Change; ④ The national average of each indicator is "0". ⑤ The calculations are based on the *China Statistical Yearbook 2011*, *China Environment Annual Report 2010*, *China Environmental Statistical Yearbook 2011*, *China City Statistical Yearbook 2011*, *China Urban Construction Statistical Yearbook 2010*, and *China Regional Economy Statistical Yearbook 2011*

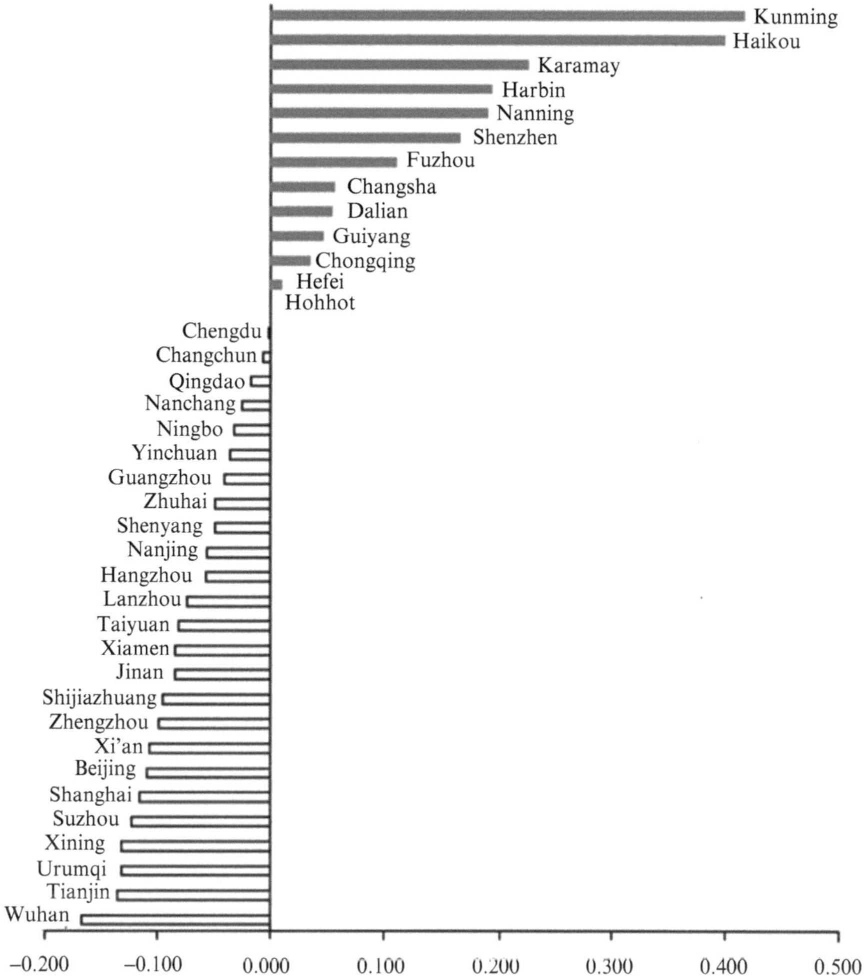

Fig. 7.1 2010 rankings of 38 cities by CCPNRE (Note: This figure is developed based on relevant data in Table 6.1)

Based on Table 7.1 and Fig. 7.1, the following analyses are focused three aspects, namely the regional differences in CCPNRE, the differences between cities in CCPNRE in each region, and the relations between CCPNRE and GDI.

7.1.1 Regional Differences in CCPNRE

As shown in Fig. 7.2, CCPNRE of the northeastern and western cities are remarkably better than that of the eastern and central cities. The average score of northeastern cities reaches 0.048, that of western cities registers 0.036, while those of the

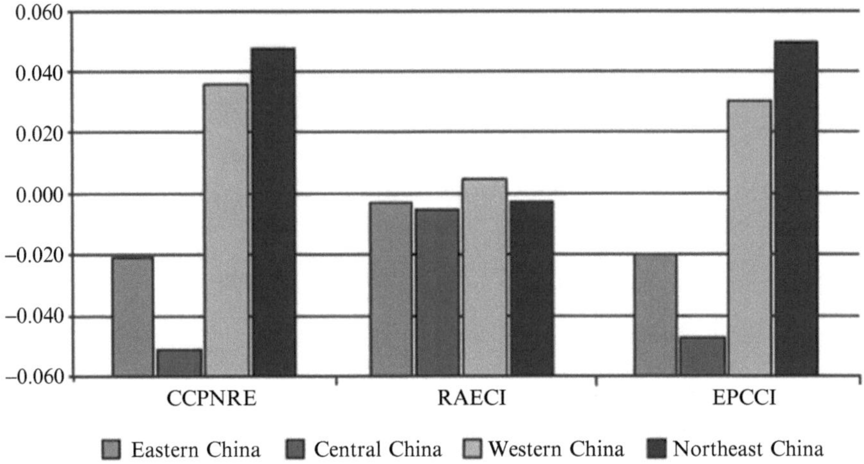

Fig. 7.2 CCPNRE comparison by region (Note: The data for each region in the figure are the arithmetic mean of the scores of all the cities in the region)

eastern and central cities are lower than the national average, respectively −0.020 and −0.051.

By comparing the Second-Class Indicators, we find that, in terms of RAECI, the western cities average 0.004 and led the other regions; the averages of the eastern, central and northeastern cities are all below the national average, with that of the central cities as the lowest at −0.003.

In terms of EPCCI, northeastern cities average 0.050, far ahead of the other regions; the averages of the eastern, central and northeastern cities are all below the national average, with that of the central cities as the lowest at −0.054.

7.1.2 CCPNRE in Each Region

Although northeastern and western regions fair better than eastern and central regions in terms of CCPNRE, there are large gaps between the rankings of cities in each region.

7.1.2.1 Rankings of Eastern Cities by CCPNRE

The 2010 rankings of eastern cities by CCPNRE are shown in Table 7.2.

Only three or 18.75 % of the 16 eastern cities rank among top 10, and they are Haikou, Shenzhen and Fuzhou. Haikou scores 0.399 and ranks No. 2, far ahead of the other eastern cities. Qingdao, Ningbo and Guangzhou rank No. 11–20, but score less than the national average 0. Zhuhai, Nanjing, Hangzhou, Xiamen, Jinan and Shijiazhuang rank No. 21–30, and Beijing, Shanghai, Suzhou and Tianjin rank No. 31–38, all scoring less than 0, suggesting that their CCPNRE are lower than the national average.

Table 7.2 2010 rankings of eastern cities by CCPNRE

City	Score	Ranking in China	Ranking in the region	City	Score	Ranking in China	Ranking in the region
Haikou	0.399	2	1	Hangzhou	−0.058	24	9
Shenzhen	0.166	6	2	Xiamen	−0.083	27	**10**
Fuzhou	**0.111**	7	3	Jinan	−0.085	28	11
Qingdao	−0.016	16	4	Shijiazhuang	−0.095	29	*12*
Ningbo	−0.032	18	5	Beijing	−0.109	32	13
Guangzhou	−0.041	20	6	Shanghai	−0.116	33	14
Zhuhai	−0.048	21	7	Suzhou	−0.124	34	15
Nanjing	−0.056	23	8	Tianjin	−0.136	37	16

Note: This table is developed based on Table 7.1

Table 7.3 2010 rankings of central cities by CCPNRE

City	Score	Ranking in China	Ranking in the region	City	Score	Ranking in China	Ranking in the region
Changsha	0.057	8	1	Nanchang	−0.024	22	4
Hefei	0.011	12	2	Zhengzhou	−0.099	30	5
Taiyuan	−0.081	13	3	Wuhan	−0.168	38	6

Note: This table is developed based on Table 7.1

7.1.2.2 Rankings of Central Cities by CCPNRE

The 2010 rankings of central cities by CCPNRE are shown in Table 7.3.

Only one city, Changsha, or 16.7 % of the six central cities, ranks among top 10 with a score higher than the national average. Hefei ranks No. 12 and score higher than the national average. Taiyuan, Nanchang, Zhengzhou and Wuhan rank No. 13, 22, 30 and 38 respectively, and all score lower than the national average 0.

7.1.2.3 Rankings of Western Cities by CCPNRE

The 2010 rankings of western cities by CCPNRE are shown in Table 7.4.

Four or 33.3 % of the 12 western cities rank among top 10 with scores higher than the national average, and they are Kunming, Karamay, Nanning and Guiyang. Kunming leads the country and scores 0.416. Chongqing and Hohhot score more than the national average and rank respectively No. 11 and 13. Chengdu, Yinchuan, Lanzhou, Xi'an, Xining and Urumqi score between −0.001 and −0.132, lower than the national average.

7.1.2.4 Rankings of Northeastern Cities by CCPNRE

The 2010 rankings of northeastern cities by CCPNRE are shown in Table 7.5.

Harbin ranks No. 4 with a score of 0.195, followed by No. 9 Dalian with a score of 0.054, all above national average. Changchun and Shenyang rank No. 15 and 22 and score −0.006 and −0.048 respectively, lower than the national average.

Table 7.4 2010 rankings of Western cities by CCPNRE

City	Score	Ranking in China	Ranking in the region	City	Score	Ranking in China	Ranking in the region
Kunming	0.416	1	1	Chengdu	**−0.001**	14	7
Karamay	0.227	3	2	Yinchuan	−0.035	19	8
Nanning	0.190	5	3	Lanzhou	−0.073	25	9
Guiyang	0.046	10	4	Xi'an	−0.107	31	10
Chongqing	0.035	11	5	Xining	−0.132	35	11
Hohhot	0.002	13	6	Urumqi	−0.132	36	12

Note: This table is developed based on Table 7.1

Table 7.5 2010 rankings of Northeastern cities by CCPNRE

City	Score	Ranking in China	Ranking in the region	City	Score	Ranking in China	Ranking in the region
Harbin	0.195	4	1	Changchun	−0.006	15	3
Dalian	0.054	9	2	Shenyang	−0.048	22	4

Note: This table is developed based on Table 7.1

7.1.3 Impact of CCPNRE on GDI

By comparing city GDI and CCPNRE of 2010, we find that, 17 or 44.74 % of the 38 cities show a ranking gap of no more than five places between their CCPNRE and GDI rankings, such as Haikou, Karamay and Dalian, suggesting small influences of CCPNRE on GDI; 21 or more than half of the cities see a gap of more than five places, including Guangzhou, Beijing and Nanjing, implying large influences of CCPNRE on GDI. Beijing ranks No. 6 in terms of GDI but No. 32 by CCPNRE, a gap of 26 places. The ranking gaps between GDI and CCPNRE are shown in Table 7.6.

7.2 Inter-city Comparison by CCPNRE

CCPNRE has a 34 % weight in the GDI system. There are 14 Third-Class Indicators, including two positively-correlated indicators and 12 negative ones, of which 3 have no official data.

7.2.1 Results and Analysis of RAECI Measurement

Taking a 5 % weight in CCPNRE, RAECI contributes less to CCPNRE than EPCCI. Under RAECI, there is only one Third-Class Indicator, namely water resources per capita, a positively-correlated indicator taking a 1.70 % weight in the GDI.

Using processed data, we have worked out the 2010 rankings of cities by RAECI as shown in Table 7.7.

Table 7.6 Differences between the 2010 rankings by GDI and CCPNRE

City	Ranking by GDI	Ranking by CCPNRE	Difference	City	Ranking by GDI	Ranking by CCPNRE	Difference
Shenzhen	1	6	−5	Guiyang	20	10	10
Haikou	2	2	0	Shenyang	21	22	−1
Karamay	3	3	0	Hefei	22	12	10
Kunming	4	1	3	Taiyuan	23	26	−3
Guangzhou	5	20	−15	Xiamen	24	27	−3
Beijing	6	32	−26	Shijiazhuang	25	29	−4
Dalian	7	9	−2	Shanghai	26	33	−7
Qingdao	8	16	−8	Hohhot	27	13	14
Nanjing	9	23	−14	Tianjin	28	37	−9
Fuzhou	10	7	3	Changchun	29	15	14
Zhuhai	11	21	−10	Chengdu	30	14	16
Nanning	12	5	7	Nanchang	31	17	14
Changsha	13	8	5	Xi'an	32	31	1
Suzhou	14	34	−20	Chongqing	33	11	22
Harbin	15	4	11	Wuhan	34	38	−4
Yinchuan	16	19	−3	Urumqi	35	36	−1
Ningbo	17	18	−1	Zhengzhou	36	30	6
Hangzhou	18	24	−6	Lanzhou	37	25	12
Jinan	19	28	−9	Xining	38	35	3

Note: ① This table is developed based on Tables 1.6 and 7.1. The "Difference" in the table refers to the gap between the CCPNRE ranking and the GDI ranking. A positive value indicates how many places CCPNRE ranking is ahead of GDI ranking, and a negative value indicates how many places CCPNRE ranking is behind GDI ranking

As shown in Table 7.7, scores of the 38 cities are between −0.10 and 0.094 with small disparities. Twelve or one-third of the cities score above the national average and they are Lanzhou, Hangzhou, Fuzhou, Zhuhai, Changsha, Ningbo, Nanning, Harbin, Chongqing, Guiyang, Kunming and Guangzhou; the other 26 cities score less than the national average.

From a regional perspective, Fig. 7.3 compares CCPNRE and RAECI in the eastern, central, western and northeastern cities in descending order of CCPNRE. In terms of regional disparity, the average scores of the four regions register respectively −0.002, −0.004, 0.006, and −0.002 (three effective digits after the decimal point), showing that western cities have higher scores and central cities have poor scores.

From the perspective of scores, the top 10 include four western cities—Lanzhou, Nanning, Chongqing and Guiyang, and four eastern cities—Hangzhou, Fuzhou, Zhuhai and Ningbo. The bottom 10 include Qingdao, Beijing, Shijiazhuang, Haikou and Tianjin from the eastern region and Nanchang, Taiyuan and Zhengzhou from Central China.

Table 7.7 2010 rankings of cities in China by RAECI

Indicator	RAECI		Indicator	RAECI	
City	Score	Ranking	City	Score	Ranking
Lanzhou	0.094	1	Nanjing	−0.005	20
Hangzhou	0.018	2	Changchun	−0.005	21
Fuzhou	0.011	3	Chengdu	−0.005	22
Zhuhai	0.008	4	Shenyang	−0.005	23
Changsha	0.006	5	Hohhot	−0.005	24
Ningbo	0.006	6	Urumqi	−0.006	25
Nanning	0.006	7	Suzhou	−0.006	26
Harbin	0.005	8	Jinan	−0.008	27
Chongqing	0.005	9	Shanghai	−0.008	28
Guiyang	0.003	10	Qingdao	−0.008	29
Kunming	0.002	11	Nanchang	−0.008	30
Guangzhou	0.001	12	Xi'an	−0.009	31
Wuhan	−0.001	13	Beijing	−0.009	32
Karamay	−0.002	14	Taiyuan	−0.009	33
Xiamen	−0.003	15	Zhengzhou	−0.009	34
Shenzhen	−0.003	16	Shijiazhuang	−0.009	35
Dalian	−0.004	17	Haikou	−0.009	36
Hefei	−0.004	18	Tianjin	−0.010	37
Xining	−0.004	19	Yinchuan	−0.010	38

Note: The scores and rankings are worked out based on *China Statistical Yearbook 2011*, *China Environment Annual Report 2010*, *China Environmental Statistical Yearbook 2011*, *China City Statistical Yearbook 2011*, *China Urban Construction Statistical Yearbook 2010*, and *China Regional Economy Statistical Yearbook 2011*

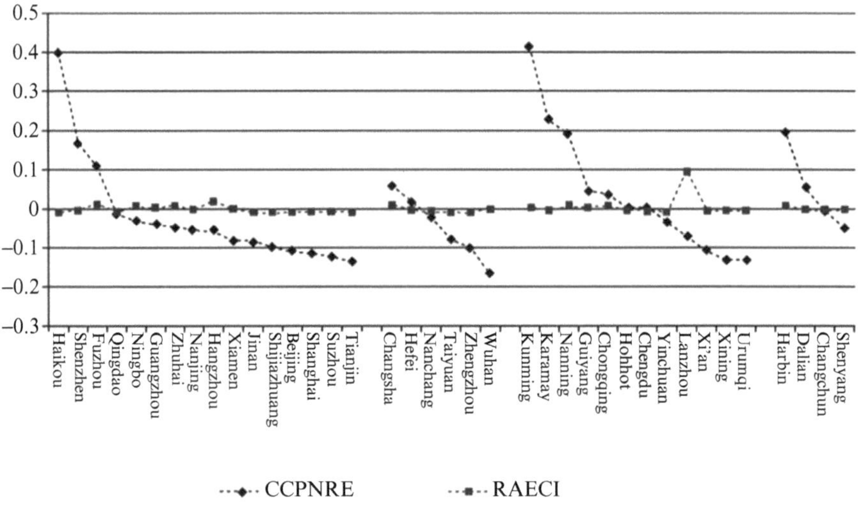

Fig. 7.3 Inter-city Comparison by CCPNRE and RAECI (Note: The cities in the figure are grouped by region, namely Eastern, Central, Western and Northeast China, and arranged from *left* to *right* in descending order of CCPNRE)

Table 7.8 EPCCI, weights and attributes

No.	Indicator	Weight (%)	Attribute
19	CO_2 emissions per unit of land area	3.08	Negative
20	CO_2 emissions per capita	3.08	Negative
21	SO_2 emissions per unit of land area	2.50	Negative
22	SO_2 emissions per capita	2.50	Negative
23	COD emissions per unit of land area	2.50	Negative
24	COD emissions per capita	2.50	Negative
25	Nitrogen oxide emissions per unit of land area	2.50	Negative
26	Nitrogen oxide emissions per capita	2.50	Negative
27	Ammonia/nitrogen emissions per unit of land area	2.50	Negative
28	Ammonia/nitrogen emissions per capita	2.50	Negative
29	Percentage of days with air quality at or above level II in a year	3.08	Positive
30	Percentage of days with respirable suspended particulates as the principal pollutants in a year	3.08	Negative
31	Average value of PM2.5 concentration	0.00	Negative

Note: The content of this table was finalized after discussions at several seminars held by the research group

7.2.2 Results and Analysis of EPCCI Measurement

The most important Second-Class Indicator to measure EPCCI of cities, EPCCI is given the largest weight. There are 13 Third-Class Indicators, namely CO_2 emissions per unit of land area, CO_2 emissions per capita, SO_2 emissions per unit of land area, SO_2 emissions per capita, COD emissions per unit of land area, COD emissions per capita, Nitrogen oxide emissions per unit of land area, Nitrogen oxide emissions per capita, Ammonia/nitrogen emissions per unit of land area, Ammonia/nitrogen emissions per capita, Percentage of days with air quality at or above level II in a year, Percentage of days with respirable suspended particulates as the principal pollutants in a year, and average value of PM2.5 concentration. All the indicators take a total weight of 95 % in CCPNRE system. The weight of each indicator is shown in Table 7.8.

Using processed data for the indicators and their weights shown in Table 7.8, we have worked out the rankings of the 38 cities by EPCCI as shown in Table 7.9.

As shown in Table 7.9, No. 1 Kunming scores 0.414 and No. 38 Lanzhou scores −0.167. The large gap between the two western cities indicates that even the same region sees large disparity in EPCCI. Such a disparity is also found among eastern cities, with Haikou scoring 0.408 and Tianjin scoring −0.126. From the perspective of rankings, 14 cities score more than 0 or above the national average, and they are Kunming, Haikou, Karamay, Harbin, Nanning, Shenzhen, Fuzhou, Dalian, Changsha, Guiyang, Chongqing, Hefei, Hohhot and Chengdu. The other 24 cities score less than the national average.

The comparison of CCPNRE and EPCCI in each region in Fig. 7.4 suggests strong consistency between them, particularly in the eastern, central and

Table 7.9 2010 rankings of cities in China by EPCCI

Indicator	EPCCI		Indicator	EPCCI	
City	Score	Ranking	City	Score	Ranking
Kunming	0.414	1	Guangzhou	−0.042	20
Haikou	0.408	2	Shenyang	−0.044	21
Karamay	0.229	3	Nanjing	−0.052	22
Harbin	0.190	4	Zhuhai	−0.056	23
Nanning	0.184	5	Taiyuan	−0.072	24
Shenzhen	0.169	6	Hangzhou	−0.076	25
Fuzhou	0.100	7	Jinan	−0.078	26
Dalian	0.057	8	Xiamen	−0.081	27
Changsha	0.051	9	Shijiazhuang	−0.086	28
Guiyang	0.043	10	Zhengzhou	−0.090	29
Chongqing	0.031	11	Xi'an	−0.099	30
Hefei	0.015	12	Beijing	−0.100	31
Hohhot	0.007	13	Shanghai	−0.108	32
Chengdu	0.004	14	Suzhou	−0.118	33
Changchun	−0.002	15	Urumqi	−0.126	34
Qingdao	−0.008	16	Tianjin	−0.126	35
Nanchang	−0.016	17	Xining	−0.127	36
Yinchuan	−0.025	18	Wuhan	−0.167	37
Ningbo	−0.038	19	Lanzhou	−0.167	38

Note: The scores and rankings are worked out based on *China Statistical Yearbook 2011*, *China Environment Annual Report 2010*, *China Environmental Statistical Yearbook 2011*, *China City Statistical Yearbook 2011*, *China Urban Construction Statistical Yearbook 2010*, and *China Regional Economy Statistical Yearbook 2011*

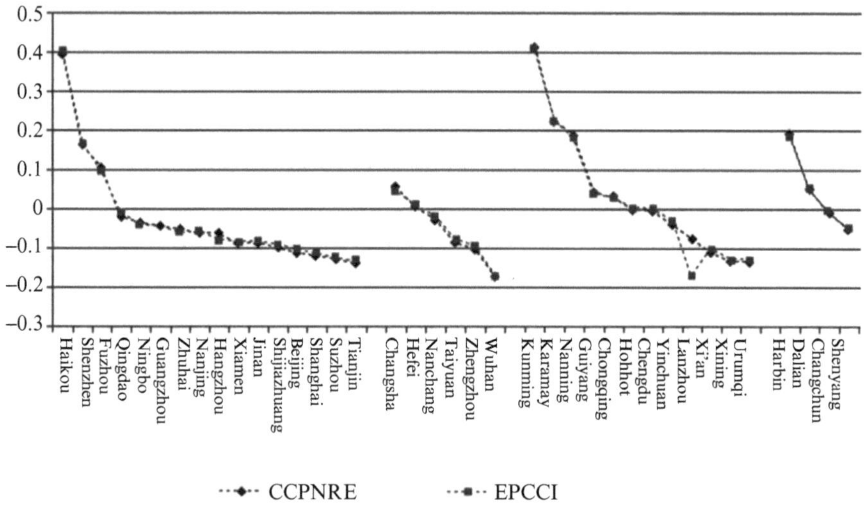

Fig. 7.4 Inter-city Comparison by CCPNRE and EPCCI (Note: The cities in the figure are grouped by region, namely Eastern, Central, Western and Northeast China, and arranged from *left* to *right* in descending order of CCPNRE)

northeastern regions where the latter contributes significantly to the former. The EPCCI of the western city Lanzhou is far behind its CCPNRE.

From the perspective of scores, the eastern, central, western and northeastern cities average respectively −0.018, −0.046, 0.031, and 0.050 (three effective digits after the decimal point), showing that western and northeastern cities have higher scores and eastern and central cities have poor scores. In terms of rankings, the top 10 include six western and northeastern cities and the bottom 10 include six eastern and central cities.

Chapter 8
SDGP Measurement and Analysis by City

Xiaolong Chen, Ning Cai, and Delong Min

The Support Degree of Government Policies (SDGP) is the overall evaluation of the government's green actions in the economic and social development of a city. According to the criterion of SDGP measurement in the CGDI system, this chapter uses the data for 2010 to measure and analyze the SDGP of 38 large and medium-sized cities from three aspects: Green Investment, Infrastructure, and Environmental Management.

8.1 Results of SDGP Measurement

The SDGP of 38 cities in China is calculated in line with the related measurement and weighting standards of the CGDI system and the results are shown in Table 8.1 below.

As shown in Table 8.1, Shenzhen scores the highest at 0.333 and Xining scores the lowest at −0.300. Nineteen or half of the 38 cities score more than the national average. The top 10 cities are Shenzhen, Guangzhou, Zhuhai, Beijing, Yinchuan, Karamay, Taiyuan, Guiyang, Nanjing and Haikou. The top 10 cities by Green Investment Indicators (GII) are Karamay, Zhuhai, Lanzhou, Xining, Taiyuan, Yinchuan, Guiyang, Tianjin, Beijing and Xiamen; the top 10 cities by Infrastructure Indicators (II) are Shenzhen, Beijing, Guangzhou, Dalian, Shijiazhuang, Qingdao, Kunming, Yinchuan, Xiamen and Suzhou; and the top 10 cities by Environmental

X. Chen (✉)
National Bureau of Statistics of China, Beijing, China
e-mail: chenxl@gj.stats.cn

N. Cai • D. Min
Beijing Normal University, Beijing, China
e-mail: ggbnu@163.com; delong.min@gmail.com

X. Li and J. Pan (eds.), *China Green Development Index Report 2012: Regional Comparison*, Current Chinese Economic Report Series,
DOI 10.1007/978-3-642-54178-0_8, © Springer-Verlag Berlin Heidelberg 2015

Table 8.1 2010 rankings of 38 cities by SDGP

	First-Class Indicator		Second-Class Indicators					
	Support Degree of Government Policies		Green Investment Indicators		Infrastructure Indicators		Environmental Management Indicators	
City	Score	Ranking	Score	Ranking	Score	Ranking	Score	Ranking
Shenzhen	0.333	1	−0.020	21	0.331	1	0.022	17
Guangzhou	0.247	2	−0.012	16	0.084	3	0.174	1
Zhuhai	0.166	3	0.142	2	0.032	12	−0.008	23
Beijing	0.143	4	0.028	9	0.088	2	0.027	15
Yinchuan	0.141	5	0.067	6	0.049	8	0.025	16
Karamay	0.132	6	0.175	1	0.028	14	−0.070	35
Taiyuan	0.124	7	0.074	5	−0.020	25	0.071	5
Guiyang	0.091	8	0.053	7	−0.045	32	0.083	4
Nanjing	0.090	9	−0.014	17	0.013	18	0.091	3
Haikou	0.085	10	0.000	13	0.025	15	0.060	6
Ningbo	0.080	11	−0.029	25	0.012	19	0.096	2
Kunming	0.072	12	−0.023	22	0.050	7	0.045	8
Xiamen	0.066	13	0.011	10	0.048	9	0.008	20
Dalian	0.058	14	−0.044	34	0.064	4	0.038	11
Shijiazhuang	0.058	15	−0.019	20	0.060	5	0.017	18
Suzhou	0.055	16	−0.031	26	0.048	10	0.038	10
Hangzhou	0.032	17	0.009	11	0.042	11	−0.019	24
Qingdao	0.029	18	−0.052	35	0.054	6	0.028	14
Jinan	0.024	19	0.001	12	−0.008	24	0.031	12
Fuzhou	−0.001	20	−0.042	32	0.031	13	0.011	19
Shanghai	−0.015	21	−0.008	15	−0.036	31	0.029	13
Tianjin	−0.022	22	0.034	8	−0.036	30	−0.020	25
Hohhot	−0.053	23	−0.018	19	−0.078	34	0.043	9
Nanning	−0.068	24	−0.043	33	0.016	16	−0.042	29
Wuhan	−0.074	25	−0.040	30	−0.029	27	−0.005	21
Hefei	−0.076	26	−0.054	36	0.016	17	−0.039	27
Shenyang	−0.091	27	−0.032	27	0.001	23	−0.060	31
Xi'an	−0.093	28	−0.034	28	0.004	21	−0.063	33
Urumqi	−0.096	29	−0.002	14	−0.087	35	−0.007	22
Nanchang	−0.100	30	−0.040	31	0.004	22	−0.063	32
Zhengzhou	−0.110	31	−0.034	29	−0.030	28	−0.045	30
Changsha	−0.113	32	−0.055	37	0.011	20	−0.069	34
Chongqing	−0.117	33	−0.027	23	−0.051	33	−0.039	28
Changchun	−0.157	34	−0.015	18	−0.030	29	−0.112	37
Lanzhou	−0.161	35	0.111	3	−0.243	38	−0.029	26
Chengdu	−0.179	36	−0.072	38	−0.023	26	−0.085	36
Harbin	−0.198	37	−0.027	24	−0.226	37	0.055	7
Xining	−0.300	38	0.082	4	−0.165	36	−0.217	38

Note: ① The results are obtained based on calculations with 2010 data for each SDGP indicator; ② The cities are listed in descending order of GDEG value; ③ The score by SDGP in this table is the sum of the scores by the three Second-Class Indicators: Green Investment Indicators, Infrastructure Indicators, and Environmental Management Indicators; ④The national average of each indicator is "0". ⑤ The calculations are based on the *China Statistical Yearbook 2011, China Environment Annual Report 2010, China Environmental Statistical Yearbook 2011, China City Statistical Yearbook 2011, China Urban Construction Statistical Yearbook 2010*, and *China Regional Economy Statistical Yearbook 2011*

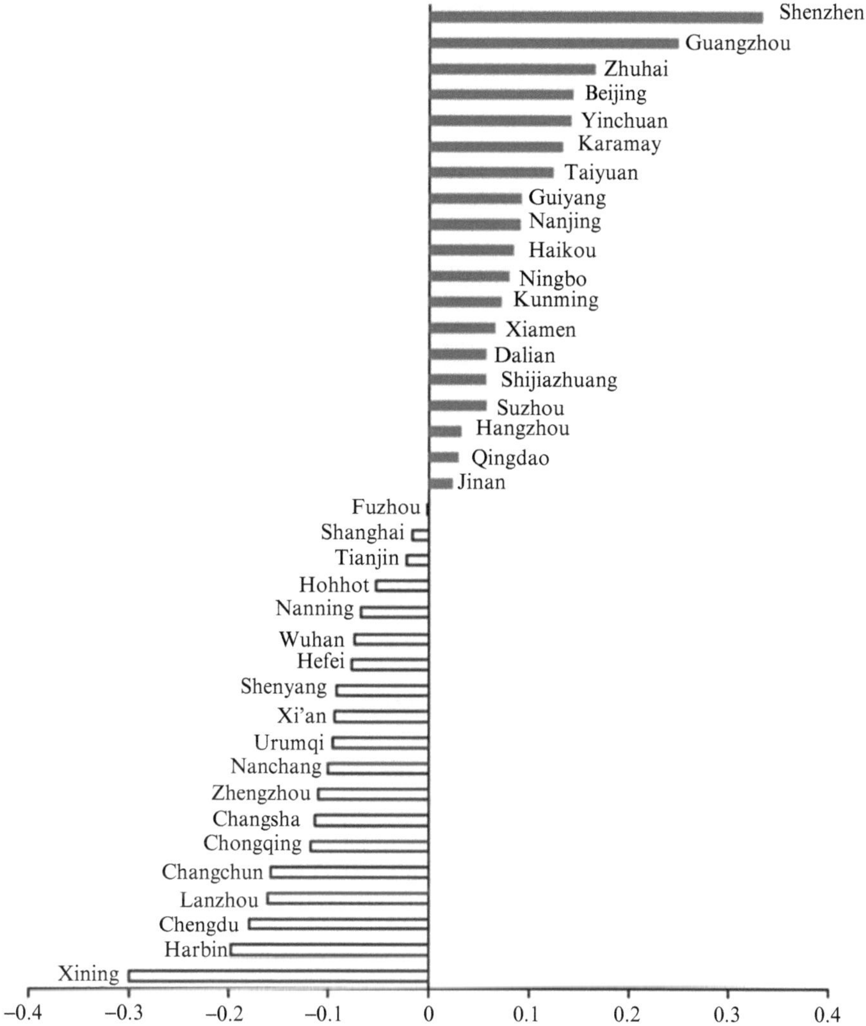

Fig. 8.1 2010 rankings of 38 cities by SDGP (Note: This figure is developed based on relevant data in Table 8.1)

Management Indicators (EMI) are Guangzhou, Ningbo, Nanjing, Guiyang, Taiyuan, Haikou, Harbin, Kunming, Hohhot and Suzhou. The rankings of the 38 cities by SDGP are shown in Fig. 8.1.

Based on Table 8.1 and Fig. 8.1, the following analyses are focused four aspects, namely the regional differences in SDGP, the differences between cities in SDGP in each region, the differences between provinces and cities in SDGP and the relations between SDGP and GDI.

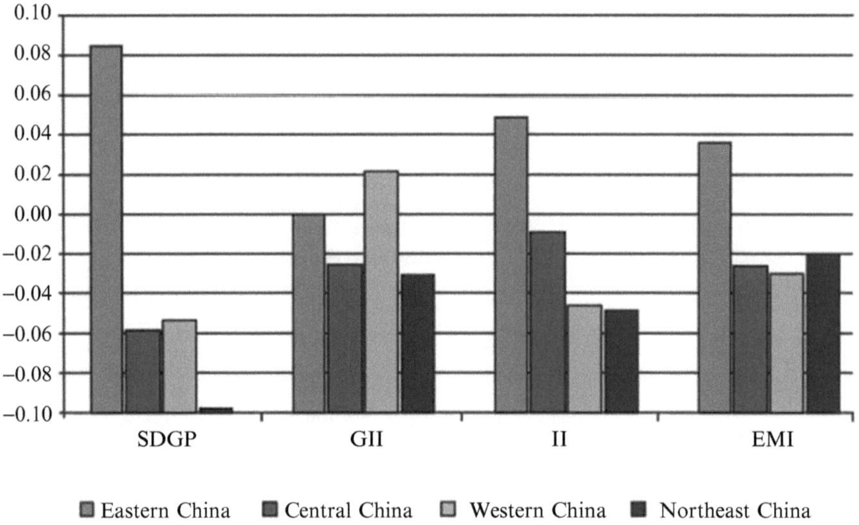

Fig. 8.2 SDGP comparison by region (Note: The data for each region in the figure are the arithmetic mean of the scores of all the cities in the region)

8.1.1 Regional Differences in SDGP

As shown in Fig. 8.2, the eastern cities have the best SDGP, followed by the western and central cities, while the northeastern cities have poor SDGP. The average score of eastern cities reaches 0.086, far ahead that of the rest cities; the average scores of the western and central cities are respectively −0.053and −0.058, lower than that of the eastern cities and the national average; the average score of the northeastern cities is −0.097, staying at the bottom.

By comparing the Second-Class Indicators, we find that, in terms of GII, the western cities average 0.022 and outperform the other regions; the average of the eastern cities reaches the national average and slightly lower than that of the western cities; the averages of the central and northeastern cities are below the national average.

In terms of II, the eastern cities average 0.049, far ahead of the other regions; the central cities come the next with an average score of −0.008, lower than the national average; the averages of the western and northeastern cities respectively register −0.045 and −0.048, suggesting that improvements are needed.

In terms of EII, eastern cities take the lead with an average of 0.037 above the national average; the followers are the northeastern, central and western cities which all stay behind the national average and have close scores.

Table 8.2 2010 rankings of eastern cities by SDGP

City	Score	Ranking in China	Ranking in the region	City	Score	Ranking in China	Ranking in the region
Shenzhen	0.333	1	1	Shijiazhuang	0.058	15	9
Guangzhou	0.247	2	2	Suzhou	0.055	16	10
Zhuhai	0.166	3	3	Hangzhou	0.032	17	11
Beijing	0.143	4	4	Qingdao	0.029	18	12
Nanjing	0.090	9	5	Jinan	0.024	19	13
Haikou	0.085	10	6	Fuzhou	−0.001	20	14
Ningbo	0.080	11	7	Shanghai	−0.015	21	15
Xiamen	0.066	13	8	Tianjin	−0.022	22	16

Note: This table is developed based on Table 8.1

8.1.2 SDGP in Each Region

Although eastern region fairs better than western and central regions and north-easter cities do worst in terms of CCPNRE, there are large gaps between rankings of cities in each region.

8.1.2.1 Rankings of Eastern Cities by SDGP

The 2010 rankings of eastern cities by SDGP are shown in Table 8.2.

Six or 37.5 % of the 16 eastern cities rank among top 10, and they are Shenzhen, Guangzhou, Zhuhai, Beijing, Nanjing and Haikou. Shenzhen scores 0.333 and ranks No.1. Ningbo, Xiamen, Shijiazhuang, Suzhou, Hangzhou, Qingdao and Jinan rank No.11–19 with scores above the national average 0. Fuzhou, Shanghai and Tianjin rank No.21, 22 and 23 with scores lower than the national average.

8.1.2.2 Rankings of Central Cities by SDGP

The 2010 rankings of central cities by SDGP are shown in Table 8.3.

Only one city, Taiyuan, or 16.7 % of the six central cities, ranks among top 10 with a score higher than the national average. Wuhan, Hefei, Nanchang, Zhengzhou and Changsha rank No.25, 26, 30, 31 and 32 respectively, with their scores lower than the national average.

8.1.2.3 Rankings of Western Cities by SDGP

The 2010 rankings of western cities by SDGP are shown in Table 8.4.

Three cities, Yinchuan, Karamay and Guiyang, or 25.0 % of the 12 western cities, rank among top 10. Kunming ranks No.12 with a score of 0.072. While the rest eight cities, including Hohhot, Nanning and Xi'an, score between −0.053 and −0. 300, lower than the national average.

Table 8.3 2010 rankings of eastern cities by SDGP

City	Score	Ranking in China	Ranking in the region	City	Score	Ranking in China	Ranking in the region
Taiyuan	0.124	7	1	Nanchang	−0.100	30	4
Wuhan	−0.074	25	2	Zhengzhou	−0.110	31	5
Hefei	−0.076	26	3	Changsha	−0.113	32	6

Note: This table is developed based on Table 8.1

Table 8.4 2010 rankings of eastern cities by SDGP

City	Score	Ranking in China	Ranking in the region	City	Score	Ranking in China	Ranking in the region
Yinchuan	0.141	5	1	Xi'an	−0.093	28	7
Karamay	0.132	6	2	Urumqi	−0.096	29	8
Guiyang	0.091	8	3	Chongqing	−0.117	33	9
Kunming	0.072	12	4	Lanzhou	−0.161	35	10
Hohhot	−0.053	23	5	Chengdu	−0.179	36	11
Nanning	−0.068	24	6	Xining	−0.300	38	12

Note: This table is developed based on Table 8.1

Table 8.5 2010 rankings of Northeastern cities by SDGP

City	Score	Ranking in China	Ranking in the region	City	Score	Ranking in China	Ranking in the region
Dalian	0.058	14	1	Changchun	−0.157	34	3
Shenyang	−0.091	27	2	Harbin	−0.198	37	4

Note: This table is developed based on Table 8.1

8.1.2.4 Rankings of Northeastern Cities by SDGP

The 2010 rankings of northeastern cities by SDGP are shown in Table 8.5.

Dalian ranks No.14 with a score of 0.058 above the national average. Shenyang, Changchun and Harbin respectively rank No.27, 34 and 37 and score between −0.091 and −0.198, staying below the national average.

8.1.3 Impact of SDGP on GDI

By comparing 2010 city rankings by GDI and SDGP, we find that, 18 or 47.4 % of the 38 cities experience a ranking gap of no more than five places between their SDGP and GDI rankings, such as Shenzhen, Karamay, Guangzhou and Beijing, suggesting small influences of SDGP on GDI; 20 or more than half of the cities show a gap of more than five places, including Haikou, Kunming, Dalian and Qingdao, implying large influences of SDGP on GDI. Harbin ranks No.15 in terms of GDI but No.37 by SDGP, a gap of 22 places. Shenzhen, Nanjing, Jinan, Chongqing and Xining see zero-gap between their SDGP and GDI rankings. The ranking gaps between GDI and SDGP are shown in Table 8.6.

Table 8.6 Differences between the 2010 rankings by GDI and SDGP

City	Ranking by GDI	Ranking by SDGP	Difference	City	Ranking by GDI	Ranking by SDGP	Difference
Shenzhen	1	1	0	Guiyang	20	8	12
Haikou	2	10	−8	Shenyang	21	27	−6
Karamay	3	6	−3	Hefei	22	26	−4
Kunming	4	12	−8	Taiyuan	23	7	16
Guangzhou	5	2	3	Xiamen	24	13	11
Beijing	6	4	2	Shijiazhuang	25	15	10
Dalian	7	14	−7	Shanghai	26	21	5
Qingdao	8	18	−10	Hohhot	27	23	4
Nanjing	9	9	0	Tianjin	28	22	6
Fuzhou	10	20	−10	Changchun	29	34	−5
Zhuhai	11	3	8	Chengdu	30	36	−6
Nanning	12	24	−12	Nanchang	31	30	1
Changsha	13	32	−19	Xi'an	32	28	4
Suzhou	14	16	−2	Chongqing	33	33	0
Harbin	15	37	−22	Wuhan	34	25	9
Yinchuan	16	5	11	Urumqi	35	29	6
Ningbo	17	11	6	Zhengzhou	36	31	5
Hangzhou	18	17	1	Lanzhou	37	35	2
Jinan	19	19	0	Xining	38	38	0

Note: ① This table is developed based on Tables 1.6 and 8.1. The "Difference" in the table refers to the gap between the SDGP ranking and the GDI ranking. A positive value indicates how many places SDGP ranking is ahead of GDI ranking, and a negative value indicates how many places SDGP ranking is behind GDI ranking

8.2 Inter-city Comparison by SDGP

SDGP takes a 33 % weight in the GDI system. There are a total of 13 positive Third-Class Indicators, all of which have no official data.

8.2.1 Results and Analysis of GII Measurement

Taking a 25 % weight in the SDGP system, GII evaluates the financial support of cities for green development from an economic perspective. Green Investment Indicator (GII) consisted There are three Third-Class Indicators, namely Ratio of environmental spending to government expenditure, Ratio of the investment in industrial pollution control to GDP, and Ratio of the spending on science, education, culture, and public health to government expenditure, each taking a weight of 2.75 % (Table 8.7).

Using processed data for the indicators and their weights shown in Table 8.7, we have worked out the 2010 rankings of the 38 cities by GII as shown in Table 8.8.

Table 8.7 GII, weights and attributes

No.	Indicator	Weight (%)	Attribute
31	Ratio of environmental spending to government expenditure	2.75	Positive
32	Ratio of the investment in industrial pollution control to GDP	2.75	Positive
33	Ratio of the spending on science, education, culture, and public health to government expenditure	2.75	Positive

Note: The content of this table was finalized after discussions at several seminars held by the research group

Table 8.8 2010 rankings of cities in China by GII

Indicator	GII		Indicator	GII	
City	Score	Ranking	City	Score	Ranking
Karamay	0.175	1	Shijiazhuang	−0.019	20
Zhuhai	0.142	2	Shenzhen	−0.020	21
Lanzhou	0.111	3	Kunming	−0.023	22
Xining	0.082	4	Chongqing	−0.027	23
Taiyuan	0.074	5	Harbin	−0.027	24
Yinchuan	0.067	6	Ningbo	−0.029	25
Guiyang	0.053	7	Suzhou	−0.031	26
Tianjin	0.034	8	Shenyang	−0.032	27
Beijing	0.028	9	Xi'an	−0.034	28
Xiamen	0.011	10	Zhengzhou	−0.034	29
Hangzhou	0.009	11	Wuhan	−0.040	30
Jinan	0.001	12	Nanchang	−0.040	31
Haikou	0.000	13	Fuzhou	−0.042	32
Urumqi	−0.002	14	Nanning	−0.043	33
Shanghai	−0.008	15	Dalian	−0.044	34
Guangzhou	−0.012	16	Qingdao	−0.052	35
Nanjing	−0.014	17	Hefei	−0.054	36
Changchun	−0.015	18	Changsha	−0.055	37
Hohhot	−0.018	19	Chengdu	−0.072	38

Note: The scores and rankings are worked out based on *China Statistical Yearbook 2011*, *China Environment Annual Report 2010*, *China Environmental Statistical Yearbook 2011*, *China City Statistical Yearbook 2011*, *China Urban Construction Statistical Yearbook 2010*, and *China Regional Economy Statistical Yearbook 2011*

As shown in Table 8.8, the GII scores of the 38 cities vary slightly from −0.072 to 0.175. Twelve or one-third of the cities, namely Karamay, Zhuhai, Lanzhou, Xining, Taiyuan, Yinchuan, Guiyang, Tianjin, Beijing, Xiamen, Hangzhou and Jinan, score more than the national average; 25 cities, namely Urumqi, Shanghai, Guangzhou, Nanjing, Changchun, Hohhot, Shijiazhuang, Shenzhen, Kunming, Chongqing, Harbin, Ningbo, Suzhou, Shenyang, Xi'an, Zhengzhou, Wuhan, Nanchang, Fuzhou, Nanning, Dalian, Qingdao, Hefei, Changsha and Chengdu, score less than the national average. While Haikou scores 0, equaling to the national average.

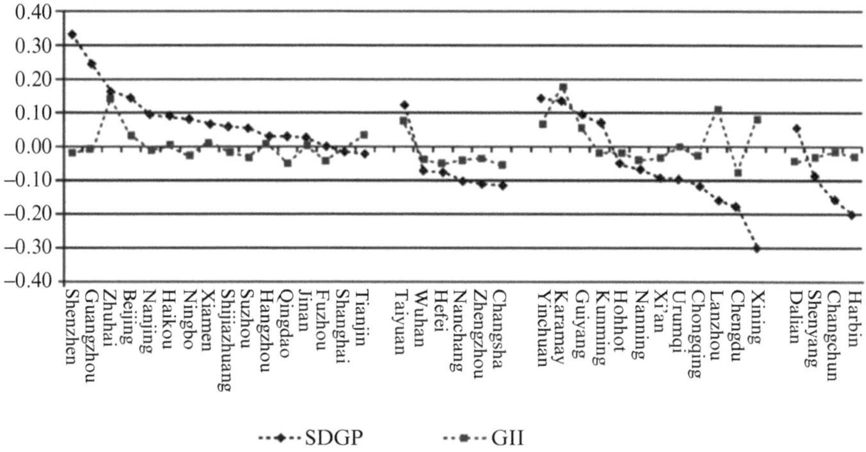

Fig. 8.3 Inter-city comparison by SDGP and GII (Note: The cities in the figure are grouped by region, namely Eastern, Central, Western and Northeast China, and arranged from *left* to *right* in descending order of SDGP)

A comparison of SDGP and GII in each region in Fig. 8.3 shows the correlation between SDGP and GII of cities. We find out that: first, the GII of eastern cities are close to the national average and show small gaps, except Zhuhai; the western cities see large gaps between them, with Karamay, Yinchuan, Guiyang and Lanzhou scoring over the national average and Kunming, Xi'an and Chengdu below the national average; the central and northeastern cities generally score below the national average; second, the scores of the eastern cities in GII are lower than that in SDGP, implying less contribution of GII to local SDGP; and the scores of the central, western and northeastern cities in GII are higher than that in SDGP, suggesting higher contribution of GII to local SDGP.

8.2.2 *Results and Analysis of II Measurement*

The most important Second-Class Indicator to measure SDGP of cities, II takes a weight of 45 % and consists of six Third-Class Indicators, namely Area of green land per capita in urban areas, Green coverage of urban built-in areas, Coverage of water supply, Treatment rate of urban household wastewater, Harmless treatment rate of urban household waste, and Public buses per 10,000 residents, each taking a weight of 2.48 % (Table 8.9).

Using processed data for the indicators and their weights shown in Table 8.9, we have worked out the 2010 rankings of the 38 cities by II as shown in Table 8.10.

As shown in Table 8.10, there is a large gap between No.1 Shenzhen which scores 0.331 and No.38 Lanzhou which scores −0.243. Large gaps are also found even in the same regions such as Western China where Kunming scores 0.050 and

Table 8.9 II, weights and attributes

No.	Indicator	Weight (%)	Attribute
34	Area of green land per capita in urban areas	2.48	Positive
35	Green coverage of urban built-in areas	2.48	Positive
36	Coverage of water supply	2.48	Positive
37	Treatment rate of urban household wastewater	2.48	Positive
38	Harmless treatment rate of urban household waste	2.48	Positive
39	Public buses per 10,000 residents	2.48	Positive

Note: The content of this table was finalized after discussions at several seminars held by the research group

Table 8.10 2010 rankings of cities in China by II

Indicator	II		Indicator	II	
City	Score	Ranking	City	Score	Ranking
Shenzhen	0.331	1	Changsha	0.011	20
Beijing	0.088	2	Xi'an	0.004	21
Guangzhou	0.084	3	Nanchang	0.004	22
Dalian	0.064	4	Shenyang	0.001	23
Shijiazhuang	0.060	5	Jinan	−0.008	24
Qingdao	0.054	6	Taiyuan	−0.020	25
Kunming	0.050	7	Chengdu	−0.023	26
Yinchuan	0.049	8	Wuhan	−0.029	27
Xiamen	0.048	9	Zhengzhou	−0.030	28
Suzhou	0.048	10	Changchun	−0.030	29
Hangzhou	0.042	11	Tianjin	−0.036	30
Zhuhai	0.032	12	Shanghai	−0.036	31
Fuzhou	0.031	13	Guiyang	−0.045	32
Karamay	0.028	14	Chongqing	−0.051	33
Haikou	0.025	15	Hohhot	−0.078	34
Nanning	0.016	16	Urumqi	−0.087	35
Hefei	0.016	17	Xining	−0.165	36
Nanjing	0.013	18	Harbin	−0.226	37
Ningbo	0.012	19	Lanzhou	−0.243	38

Note: The scores and rankings are worked out based on *China Statistical Yearbook 2011*, *China Environment Annual Report 2010*, *China Environmental Statistical Yearbook 2011*, *China City Statistical Yearbook 2011*, *China Urban Construction Statistical Yearbook 2010*, and *China Regional Economy Statistical Yearbook 2011*

Lanzhou scores −0.243. From the perspective of ranking, 23 cities, Shenzhen, Beijing, Guangzhou, Dalian, Shijiazhuang, Qingdao, Kunming, Yinchuan, Xiamen, Suzhou, Hangzhou, Zhuhai, Fuzhou, Karamay, Haikou, Nanning, Hefei, Nanjing, Ningbo, Changsha, Xi'an, Nanchang and Shenyang, score more than 0, and the rest 15 cities, Jinan, Taiyuan, Chengdu, Wuhan, Zhengzhou, Changchun, Tianjin, Shanghai, Guiyang, Chongqing, Hohhot, Urumqi, Xining, Harbin and Lanzhou, score less than the national average.

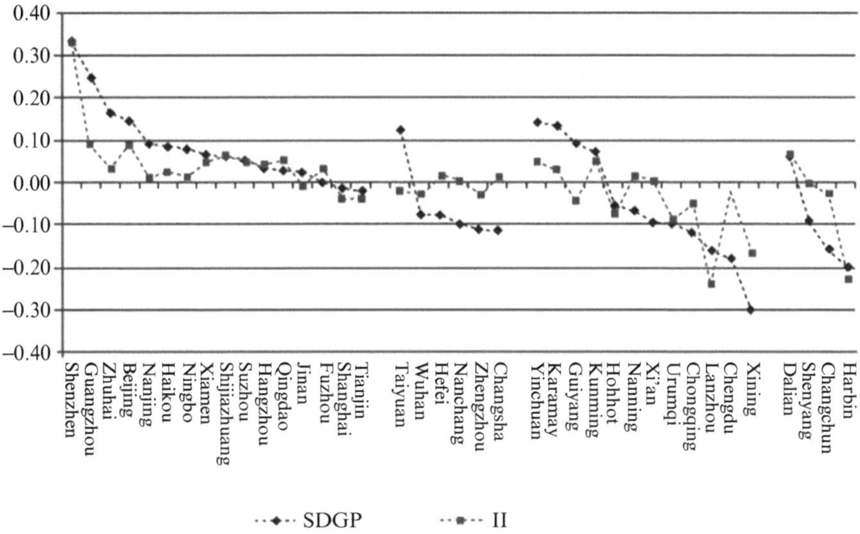

Fig. 8.4 Inter-city Comparison by SDGP and II (Note: The cities in the figure are grouped by region, namely Eastern, Central, Western and Northeast China, and arranged from *left* to *right* in descending order of SDGP)

Figure 8.4 shows the gaps in scores by SDGP and II in each region. First, the eastern cities, except Shenzhen which scores extremely high, have II scores higher than the national average and see small gaps; in the central, western and northeastern regions, some cities score higher and some lower than the national average, showing significant gaps. Second, the II scores of the eastern cities are lower than that in SDGP, implying less contribution of II to local SDGP; the II scores of most central and northeastern cities are higher than those by SDGP, suggesting higher contribution of II to local SDGP; the scores of some western cities such as Nanning, Xi'an and Urumqi by II are higher, and those of some other such as Karamay, Guiyang and Lanzhou are lower than SDGP, reflecting significant regional gaps.

8.2.3 *Results and Analysis of EMI Measurement*

A comprehensive evaluation of the importance attached by cities to environmental management, EMI takes a weight of 30 % in the SDGP system and consists of four Third-Class Indicators, namely Industrial SO_2 removal rate, Industrial wastewater COD removal rate, Industrial nitrogen oxide removal rate, and Industrial wastewater ammonia/nitrogen removal rate, each taking a weight of 2.48 % (Table 8.11).

Based on the weights shown in Table 8.11, we have worked out the 2010 rankings of the 38 cities by EMI as shown in Table 8.12.

Table 8.11 EMI, weights and attributes

No.	Indicator	Weight (%)	Attribute
40	Industrial SO_2 removal rate	2.48	Positive
41	Industrial wastewater COD removal rate	2.48	Positive
42	Industrial nitrogen oxide removal rate	2.48	Positive
43	Industrial wastewater ammonia/nitrogen removal rate	2.48	Positive

Note: The content of this table was finalized after discussions at several seminars held by the research group

Table 8.12 2010 rankings of cities in China by EMI

Indicator	EMI		Indicator	EMI	
City	Score	Ranking	City	Score	Ranking
Guangzhou	0.174	1	Xiamen	0.008	20
Ningbo	0.096	2	Wuhan	−0.005	21
Nanjing	0.091	3	Urumqi	−0.007	22
Guiyang	0.083	4	Zhuhai	−0.008	23
Taiyuan	0.071	5	Hangzhou	−0.019	24
Haikou	0.060	6	Tianjin	−0.020	25
Harbin	0.055	7	Lanzhou	−0.029	26
Kunming	0.045	8	Hefei	−0.039	27
Hohhot	0.043	9	Chongqing	−0.039	28
Suzhou	0.038	10	Nanning	−0.042	29
Dalian	0.038	11	Zhengzhou	−0.045	30
Jinan	0.031	12	Shenyang	−0.060	31
Shanghai	0.029	13	Nanchang	−0.063	32
Qingdao	0.028	14	Xi'an	—0.063	33
Beijing	0.027	15	Changsha	—0.069	34
Yinchuan	0.025	16	Karamay	−0.070	35
Shenzhen	0.022	17	Chengdu	—0.085	36
Shijiazhuang	0.017	18	Changchun	—0.112	37
Fuzhou	0.011	19	Xining	—0.217	38

Note: The scores and rankings are worked out based on *China Statistical Yearbook 2011*, *China Environment Annual Report 2010*, *China Environmental Statistical Yearbook 2011*, *China City Statistical Yearbook 2011*, *China Urban Construction Statistical Yearbook 2010*, and *China Regional Economy Statistical Yearbook 2011*

As shown in Table 8.12, No.1 Guangzhou scores 0.174 and No.38 Xining scores −0.217, displaying a large gap. Twenty cities, namely Guangzhou, Ningbo, Nanjing, Guiyang, Taiyuan, Haikou, Harbin, Kunming, Hohhot, Suzhou, Dalian, Jinan, Shanghai, Qingdao, Beijing, Yinchuan, Shenzhen, Shijiazhuang, Fuzhou and Xiamen, score more than the national average, and 18 cities, including Wuhan, Urumqi, Zhuhai, Hangzhou, Tianjin, Lanzhou, Hefei, Chongqing, Nanning, Zhengzhou, Shenyang, Nanchang, Xi'an, Changsha, Karamay, Chengdu, Changchun and Xining, score less than the national average.

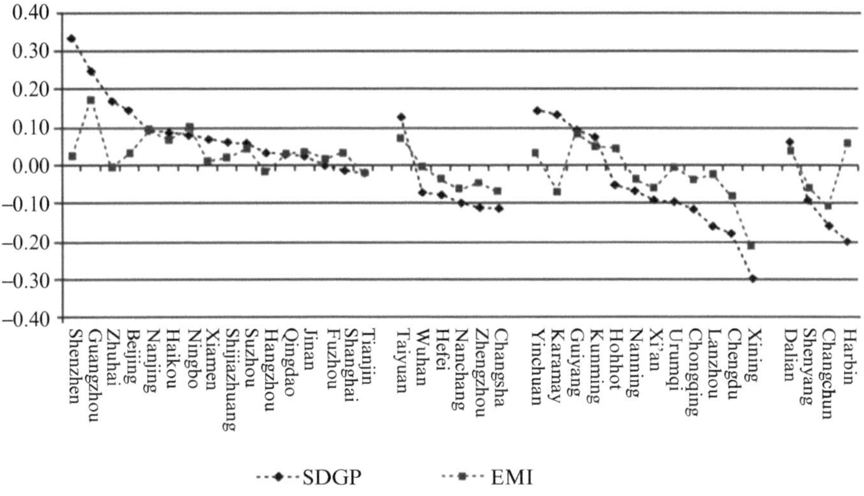

Fig. 8.5 Inter-city Comparison by SDGP and EMI (Note: The cities in the figure are grouped by region, namely Eastern, Central, Western and Northeast China, and arranged from *left* to *right* in descending order of SDGP)

Figure 8.5 shows the gaps between SDGP and EMI scores in each region. First, the eastern cities have their EMI scores higher than the national average but see significant gaps between them; the central cities score lower than the national average and show small gaps between them; in the western and northeastern regions, some cities score higher and some lower than the national average, displaying significant gaps. Second, the EMI scores of the eastern cities are lower than their SDGP scores, implying less contribution of EMI to local SDGP; most central, western and northeastern cities, except Karamay and Yinchuan, have higher EMI scores than SDGP scores, suggesting larger contribution of EMI to local SDGP.

Chapter 9
"Green Development Checkup" and Analysis by City

Youjuan Wang, Yuru Mao, Xiaolong Chen, Jiangxue Zhang, Ning Cai, Lei Zhu, Yilong Shi, Shiyao Liu, and Delong Min

A detailed introduction to the design of the "green development table" has been made in the Introduction part. Based on an overall analysis of the three First-Class Indicators in the first three chapters, this chapter gives more specific analysis to each city according to its "green development table" and to its performance in green development. A list of cities appearing in this part is provided in the Contents part. Explanation to the head.ers and indicators in the "green development table" can be found in the Introduction part. The brief analysis focuses on First- and Second-Class Indicators and mainly covers two aspects: (1) 2010 score of each city by GDI; (2) change in 2009 and 2010 rankings.

Y. Wang (✉) • X. Chen
National Bureau of Statistics, Beijing, China

Y. Mao
Environmental Statistics Division, Department of Total Emission Control,
Ministry of Environmental Protection, Beijing, China

J. Zhang • N. Cai • L. Zhu • Y. Shi • S. Liu • D. Min
Beijing Normal University, Beijing, China

X. Li and J. Pan (eds.), *China Green Development Index Report 2012: Regional Comparison*, Current Chinese Economic Report Series,
DOI 10.1007/978-3-642-54178-0_9,

Green development checkup-Beijing

No.	Indicator	Unit	Scope	Attribute	2010 average of 38 cities	2010 figure	2009 figure	2010 ranking	2009 ranking	Change in ranking	Source of 2010 data	Chernoff face
1	GDP per capita	Yuan	Whole city	Positive	56,231.37	75,943	70,452.35	8	7	−1	Regional Economy; City	☹
2	Energy consumption per unit of GDP	Ton per 10,000 yuan	Whole city	Negative	0.81	0.18	N/A	3	N/A	N/A	Regional Economy; City	
3	Electricity consumption per capita in urban areas	kWh per capita	Whole city	Negative	580.70	1,084.52	1,016.51	34	34	0	City	
4	CO_2 emissions per unit of GDP			Negative	No data			N/A	N/A	N/A		
5	SO_2 emissions per unit of GDP	Ton per 100 million yuan	Whole city	Negative	43.72	9.87	11.24	4	3	−1	Regional Economy; Environment Annual Report	☹
6	COD emissions per unit of GDP	Ton per 100 million yuan	Whole city	Negative	24.81	7.89	9.35	3	3	0	Regional Economy; Environment Annual Report	
7	Nitrogen oxide emissions per unit of GDP	Ton per 100 million yuan	Whole city	Negative	41.71	19.13	17.14	6	4	−2	Regional Economy; Environment Annual Report	☹
8	Ammonia/nitrogen emissions per unit of GDP	Ton per 100 million yuan	Whole city	Negative	2.63	1.04	1.23	6	6	0	Regional Economy; Environment Annual Report	

9	Labor productivity of the primary sector	10,000 yuan per capita	Whole city	Positive	3.03	2.01	1.89	22	19	−3	Regional Economy	☹
10	Labor productivity of the secondary sector	10,000 yuan per capita	Whole city	Positive	17.91	16.85	14.03	10	11	1	Regional Economy	☺
11	Water consumption per unit of value added created by industrial enterprises	10,000 tons per 10,000 yuan	Whole city	Negative	0.03	0.02	0.02	17	18	1	Regional Economy; Environment Annual Report	☺
12	Energy consumption per unit of value added created by industrial enterprises			Negative	No data			N/A	N/A	N/A		
13	Utilization rate industrial solid waste	%	Whole city	Positive	85.58	65.80	68.90	34	32	−2	Environment Annual Report	☹
14	Recycling rate of industrial water	%	Whole city	Positive	83.81	96.30	96.05	3	4	1	Environment Annual Report	☺
15	Labor productivity of the tertiary sector	10,000 yuan per capita	Whole city	Positive	11.40	14.10	12.69	8	9	1	Regional Economy	☺
16	Proportion of value added of tertiary sector in GDP	%	Whole city	Positive	47.97	75.11	75.53	1	1	0	City	
17	Proportion of tertiary sector employees in the total employed population	%	Whole city	Positive	46.44	74.40	73.78	1	1	0	Regional Economy	
18	Water resources per capita	m^3 per capita	Whole city	Positive	1,026.43	190.01	175.30	32	33	1	Environment Annual Report; City	☺

(continued)

(continued)

No.	Indicator	Unit	Scope	Attribute	2010 average of 38 cities	2010 figure	2009 figure	2010 ranking	2009 ranking	Change in ranking	Source of 2010 data	Chernoff face
19	CO_2 emissions per unit of land area			Negative	No data			N/A	N/A	N/A		
20	CO_2 emissions per capita			Negative	No data			N/A	N/A	N/A		
21	SO_2 emissions per unit of land area	Ton per km^2	Whole city	Negative	11.64	7.01	7.24	13	15	2	Environment Annual Report; City	☺
22	SO_2 emissions per capita	Ton per 10,000 persons	Whole city	Negative	216.46	91.91	96.14	6	9	3	Environment Annual Report; City	☺
23	COD emissions per unit of land area	Ton per km^2	Whole city	Negative	7.83	5.61	6.02	20	20	0	Environment Annual Report; City	
24	COD emissions per capita	Ton per 10,000 persons	Whole city	Negative	118.15	73.49	80.00	10	11	1	Environment Annual Report; City	☺
25	Nitrogen oxides emissions per unit of land area	Ton per km^2	Whole city	Negative	15.00	13.59	11.04	26	26	0	Environment Annual Report; City	
26	Nitrogen oxides emissions per capita	Ton per 10,000 persons	Whole city	Negative	237.70	178.17	146.67	17	17	0	Environment Annual Report; City	
27	Ammonia/nitrogen emissions per unit of land area	Ton per km^2	Whole city	Negative	0.86	0.74	0.79	25	25	0	Environment Annual Report; City	
28	Ammonia/nitrogen emissions per capita	Ton per 10,000 persons	Whole city	Negative	12.63	9.69	10.54	15	19	4	Environment Annual Report; City	☺

29	Percentage of the days with air quality at or over level II in a year	%	District	Positive	89.20	78.30	78.02	35	35	0	MEP Data	
30	Percentage of days with respirable suspended particulates as the principal pollutants in a year	%	District	Negative	70.81	84.11	84.38	27	29	2	MEP Data	☺
31	Ratio of environmental spending to government expenditure	%	Whole city	Positive	3.13	2.24	2.33	23	16	−7	China Statistics; City	☹
32	Ratio of the investment in industrial pollution control to GDP	%	Whole city	Positive	0.08	N/A	0.03	N/A	28	N/A	Environment Annual Report; Regional Economy	
33	Ratio of the spending on science, education, culture, and public health to government expenditure	%	Whole city	Positive	21.08	32.32	31.62	2	5	3	China Statistics; City; Regional Economy	☺
34	Area of green land per capita in urban areas	m^2	District	Positive	59.39	53.00	52.52	15	13	−2	City	☹
35	Green coverage of urban built-in areas	%	District	Positive	40.04	55.10	47.69	1	1	0	Urban Construction	
36	Coverage of water supply	%	District	Positive	98.82	100.00	100.00	1	1	0	Urban Construction	

(continued)

(continued)

No.	Indicator	Unit	Scope	Attribute	2010 average of 38 cities	2010 figure	2009 figure	2010 ranking	2009 ranking	Change in ranking	Source of 2010 data	Chernoff face
37	Treatment rate of urban household wastewater	%	District	Positive	86.16	82.09	80.29	30	24	−6	Urban Construction	☹
38	Harmless treatment of urban household waste	%	District	Positive	94.38	96.95	98.22	21	17	−4	Urban Construction	☹
39	Public buses per 10,000 urban residents		District	Positive	15.61	18.15	18.49	7	3	−4	City	☹
40	Industrial SO_2 removal rate	%	Whole city	Positive	57.30	69.56	65.31	11	17	6	Environment Annual Report	☺
41	Industrial wastewater COD removal rate	%	Whole city	Positive	77.86	88.48	89.09	10	9	−1	Environment Annual Report	☹
42	Industrial nitrogen oxide removal rate	%	Whole city	Positive	5.29	1.08	36.27	21	3	−18	Environment Annual Report	☹
43	Industrial waste water ammonia/nitrogen removal rate	%	Whole city	Positive	67.89	76.16	92.84	15	5	−10	Environment Annual Report	☹

Note:
Regional Economy: *China Regional Economy Statistical Yearbook 2011*
City: *China City Statistical Yearbook 2011*
China Statistics: *China Statistical Yearbook 2011*
Urban Construction: *China Urban Construction Statistical Yearbook 2010*
Environment Annual Report: *China Environment Annual Report 2010*
Environmental Yearbook: *China Environmental Statistical Yearbook 2011*
MEP Data: Ministry of Environmental Protection Data Center

9.1 Brief Analysis of Green Development in Beijing

Beijing ranked 6th among the 38 participating cities by GDI according to 2010 data, 1 place lower over 2009 (Beijing ranked 5th in 2009). Following is a brief analysis of its score by each indicator and their changes from 2009 to 2010.

9.1.1 *Beijing's 2010 Scores by GDI*

Beijing scored 0.239 in 2010. From the three First-Class Indicators including GDEG, CCPNRE, and SDGP as shown in Fig. 9.1, Beijing outperformed other cities in terms of GDEG and SDGP, yet scored lower than the national average in CCPNRE (Note: the national average value of each indicator is 0).

According to Fig. 9.2, Beijing surpassed the national average in 5 of Second-Class Indicators in 2010, which were GGEI, TII, GII, II, and EMI, yet scored lower than the national average in 4 indicators including PII, SII, RAECI, and EPCCI.

9.1.2 *Changes in Beijing's GDI Rankings 2009–2010*

According to Table 9.1, in First-Class Indicators, the most obvious change occurred in CCPNRE, where Beijing fell by 5 places in ranking, and 2 in SDGP. It remained the same by GDEG. In Second-Class Indicators, Beijing rose by 4, 3 and 1 place in GGEI, GII and RAECI, and it fell by 13, 5, 3, and 2 places in EMI, EPCCI, SII and PII. It remained the same as those in 2009 in TII and II.

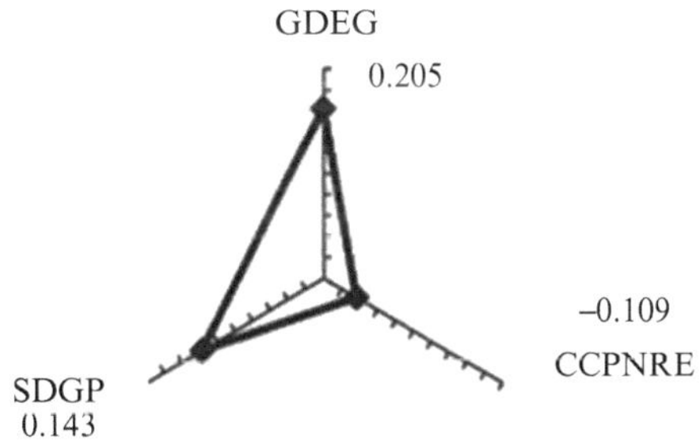

Fig. 9.1 Scores of Beijing by First-Class Indicators

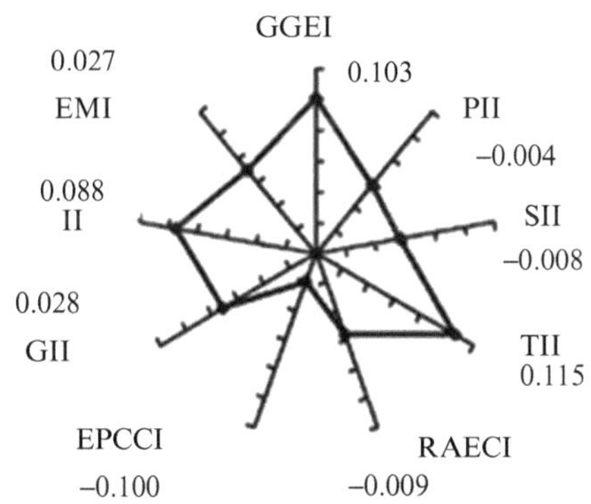

Fig. 9.2 Scores of Beijing by Second-Class Indicators

Table 9.1 Changes in Beijing's rankings by First-Class and Second-Class Indicators, 2009–2010

Indicator	2010	2009	Difference	Indicator	2010	2009	Difference
GDI	6	5	−1				
GDEG	2	2	0	RAECI	32	33	1
GGEI	2	6	4	EPCCI	31	26	−5
PII	21	19	−2	SDGP	4	2	−2
SII	26	23	−3	GII	9	12	3
TII	1	1	0	II	2	2	0
CCPNRE	32	27	−5	EMI	15	2	−13

Note: A positive value in "Difference" means a rise in ranking

Table 9.2 Third-Class Indicators where changes over 3 places occurred in Beijing, 2009–2010

	Original data for 2009 and 2010			Change in ranking		
Third-Class Indicator	2010	2009	Unit	2010	2009	Difference
Labor productivity of the primary sector	2.01	1.89	10,000 yuan per capita	22	19	−3
SO_2 emissions per capita	91.91	96.14	Ton per 10,000 persons	6	9	3
Ammonia/nitrogen emissions per capita	9.69	10.54	Ton per 10,000 persons	15	19	4
Ratio of environmental spending to government expenditure	2.24	2.33	%	23	16	−7
Ratio of the spending on science, education, culture, and public health to government expenditure	32.32	31.62	%	2	5	3
Treatment rate of urban household wastewater	82.09	80.29	%	30	24	−6
Harmless treatment of urban household waste	96.95	98.22	%	21	17	−4
Public buses per 10,000 urban residents	18.15	18.49		7	3	−4
Industrial SO_2 removal rate	69.56	65.31	%	11	17	6
Industrial nitrogen oxide removal rate	1.08	36.27	%	21	3	−18
Industrial waste water ammonia/nitrogen removal rate	76.16	92.84	%	15	5	−10

Note: A positive value in "Difference" means a rise in ranking

To further explain the causes of the changes in the rankings by First- and Second-Class Indicators, we put the Third-Class Indicators where a change of more than 3 places occurred from 2009 to 2010 as follows in Table 9.2. Compared with those in 2009, Beijing both out- and underperformed in ranking in 2010, while the more obvious trend is underperforming compared with the previous year. It dropped by 10 places in Industrial waste water ammonia/nitrogen removal rate, 7 in Ratio of environmental spending to government expenditure, 6 in Treatment rate of urban household wastewater, 4 in Harmless treatment of urban household waste and Public buses per 10,000 urban residents and 3 in Labor productivity of the primary sector; it rose a lot in the 4 indicators including SO_2 emissions per capita, Ammonia/nitrogen emissions per capita, Ratio of the spending on science, education, culture, and public health to government expenditure and Industrial SO_2 removal rate.

Green development checkup-Tianjin

No.	Indicator	Unit	Scope	Attribute	2010 average of 38 cities	2010 figure	2009 figure	2010 ranking	2009 ranking	Change in ranking	Source of 2010 data	Chernoff face
1	GDP per capita	Yuan	Whole city	Positive	56,231.37	72,994	62,574.00	9	11	2	Regional Economy; City	☺
2	Energy consumption per unit of GDP	Ton per 10,000 yuan	Whole city	Negative	0.81	0.88	0.89	25	21	−4	Regional Economy; City	☹
3	Electricity consumption per capita in urban areas	kWh per capita	Whole city	Negative	580.70	686.17	663.10	29	28	−1	City	☹
4	CO_2 emissions per unit of GDP			Negative	No data			N/A	N/A	N/A		
5	SO_2 emissions per unit of GDP	Ton per 100 million yuan	Whole city	Negative	43.72	30.26	35.76	22	22	0	Regional Economy; Environment Annual Report	
6	COD emissions per unit of GDP	Ton per 100 million yuan	Whole city	Negative	24.81	16.98	20.09	16	15	−1	Regional Economy; Environment Annual Report	☹
7	Nitrogen oxide emissions per unit of GDP	Ton per 100 million yuan	Whole city	Negative	41.71	31.62	32.43	18	19	1	Regional Economy; Environment Annual Report	☺
8	Ammonia/nitrogen emissions per unit of GDP	Ton per 100 million yuan	Whole city	Negative	2.63	2.54	1.81	23	12	−11	Regional Economy; Environment Annual Report	☹
9	Labor productivity of the primary sector	10,000 yuan per capita	Whole city	Positive	3.03	1.95	1.70	24	23	−1	Regional Economy	☹

(continued)

(continued)

No.	Indicator	Unit	Scope	Attribute	2010 average of 38 cities	2010 figure	2009 figure	2010 ranking	2009 ranking	Change in ranking	Source of 2010 data	Chernoff face
10	Labor productivity of the secondary sector	10,000 yuan per capita	Whole city	Positive	17.91	16.60	14.42	12	9	−3	Regional Economy	☹
11	Water consumption per unit of value added created by industrial enterprises	10,000tons per 10,000 yuan	Whole city	Negative	0.03	0.03	0.03	22	23	1	Regional Economy; Environment Annual Report	☺
12	Energy consumption per unit of value added created by industrial enterprises			Negative	No data			N/A	N/A	N/A		
13	Utilization rate industrial solid waste	%	Whole city	Positive	85.58	98.60	98.30	6	7	1	Environment Annual Report	☺
14	Recycling rate of industrial water	%	Whole city	Positive	83.81	93.77	94.18	11	12	1	Environment Annual Report	☺
15	Labor productivity of the tertiary sector	10,000 yuan per capita	Whole city	Positive	11.40	12.60	10.99	13	11	−2	Regional Economy	☹
16	Proportion of value added of tertiary sector in GDP	%	Whole city	Positive	47.97	45.95	45.27	23	26	3	City	☺
17	Proportion of tertiary sector employees in the total employed population	%	Whole city	Positive	46.44	48.37	47.32	14	15	1	Regional Economy	☺

18	Water resources per capita	m^3 per capita	Whole city	Positive	1,026.43	93.42	155.54	37	34	−3	Environment Annual Report; City	☹
19	CO_2 emissions per unit of land area			Negative	No data			N/A	N/A	N/A		
20	CO_2 emissions per capita			Negative	No data			N/A	N/A	N/A		
21	SO_2 emissions per unit of land area	Ton per km^2	Whole city	Negative	11.64	20.00	20.13	33	32	−1	Environment Annual Report; City	☹
22	SO_2 emissions per capita	Ton per 10,000 persons	Whole city	Negative	216.46	239.37	242.93	27	27	0	Environment Annual Report; City	
23	COD emissions per unit of land area	Ton per km^2	Whole city	Negative	7.83	11.22	11.31	31	30	−1	Environment Annual Report; City	☹
24	COD emissions per capita	Ton per 10,000 persons	Whole city	Negative	118.15	134.34	136.50	25	23	−2	Environment Annual Report; City	☹
25	Nitrogen oxides emissions per unit of land area	Ton per km^2	Whole city	Negative	15.00	20.89	18.25	30	28	−2	Environment Annual Report; City	☹
26	Nitrogen oxides emissions per capita	Ton per 10,000 persons	Whole city	Negative	237.70	250.12	220.30	29	28	−1	Environment Annual Report; City	☹
27	Ammonia/nitrogen emissions per unit of land area	Ton per km^2	Whole city	Negative	0.86	1.68	1.02	35	30	−5	Environment Annual Report; City	☹
28	Ammonia/nitrogen emissions per capita	Ton per 10,000 persons	Whole city	Negative	12.63	20.13	12.30	32	24	−8	Environment Annual Report; City	☹

(continued)

(continued)

No.	Indicator	Unit	Scope	Attribute	2010 average of 38 cities	2010 figure	2009 figure	2010 ranking	2009 ranking	Change in ranking	Source of 2010 data	Chernoff face
29	Percentage of the days with air quality at or over level II in a year	%	District	Positive	89.20	84.34	84.07	30	29	−1	MEP Data	☹
30	Percentage of days with respirable suspended particulates as the principal pollutants in a year	%	District	Negative	70.81	68.22	71.51	15	14	−1	MEP Data	☹
31	Ratio of environmental spending to government expenditure	%	Whole city	Positive	3.13	1.97	1.19	28	35	7	China Statistics; City	☺
32	Ratio of the investment in industrial pollution control to GDP	%	Whole city	Positive	0.08	0.18	0.24	6	8	2	Environment Annual Report; Regional Economy	☺
33	Ratio of the spending on science, education, culture, and public health to government expenditure	%	Whole city	Positive	21.08	25.06	25.05	7	23	16	China Statistics; City; Regional Economy	☺
34	Area of green land per capita in urban areas		District	Positive	59.39	24.00	21.63	33	35	2	City	☺

35	Green coverage of urban built-in areas	%	District	Positive	40.04	32.06	30.33	37	37	0	Urban Construction	
36	Coverage of water supply	%	District	Positive	98.82	100.00	100.00	1	1	0	Urban Construction	
37	Treatment rate of urban household wastewater	%	District	Positive	86.16	85.30	80.11	26	25	−1	Urban Construction	☹
38	Harmless treatment of urban household waste	%	District	Positive	94.38	100.00	94.31	1	23	22	Urban Construction	☺
39	Public buses per 10,000 urban residents		District	Positive	15.61	8.87	9.84	34	35	1	City	☺
40	Industrial SO_2 removal rate	%	Whole city	Positive	57.30	63.22	59.73	17	21	4	Environment Annual Report	☺
41	Industrial wastewater COD removal rate	%	Whole city	Positive	77.86	70.22	67.72	31	31	0	Environment Annual Report	
42	Industrial nitrogen oxide removal rate	%	Whole city	Positive	5.29	14.78	16.65	6	6	0	Environment Annual Report	
43	Industrial waste water ammonia/nitrogen removal rate	%	Whole city	Positive	67.89	24.86	29.78	35	35	0	Environment Annual Report	

Note:
Regional Economy: *China Regional Economy Statistical Yearbook 2011*
City: *China City Statistical Yearbook 2011*
China Statistics: *China Statistical Yearbook 2011*
Urban Construction: *China Urban Construction Statistical Yearbook 2010*
Environment Annual Report: *China Environment Annual Report 2010*
Environmental Yearbook: *China Environmental Statistical Yearbook 2011*
MEP Data: Ministry of Environmental Protection Data Center

9.2 Brief Analysis of Green Development in Tianjin

Tianjin ranked 28th among the 38 participating cities by GDI according to 2010 data, 3 places higher over 2009 (Tianjin ranked 31st in 2009). Following is a brief analysis of its score by each indicator and their changes from 2009 to 2010.

9.2.1 Tianjin's 2010 Scores by GDI

Tianjin scored −0.153 in 2010. From the three First-Class Indicators including GDEG, CCPNRE, and SDGP as shown in Fig. 9.3, Tianjin showed some advantages in GDEG, yet its performance in CCPNRE and SDGP was relatively weak, both lower than the national average (Note: the national average value of each indicator is 0).

According to Fig. 9.4, Tianjin surpassed the national average in 3 of Second-Class Indicators in 2010, which were SII, TII and GII. It ranked lower than the national average in 6 indicators including GGEI, PII, RAECI, EPCCI, II and EMI.

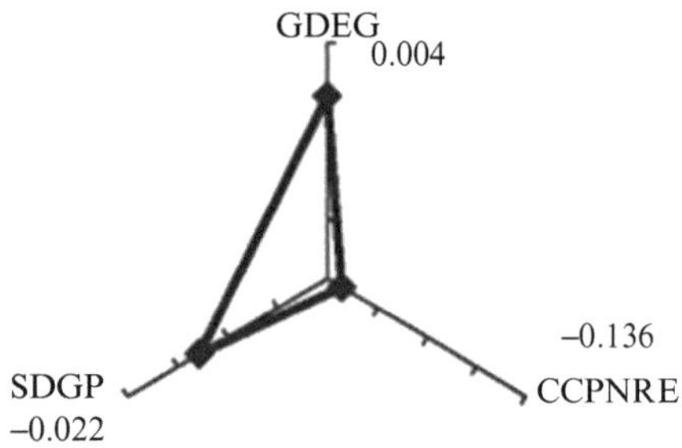

Fig. 9.3 Scores of Tianjin by First-Class Indicators

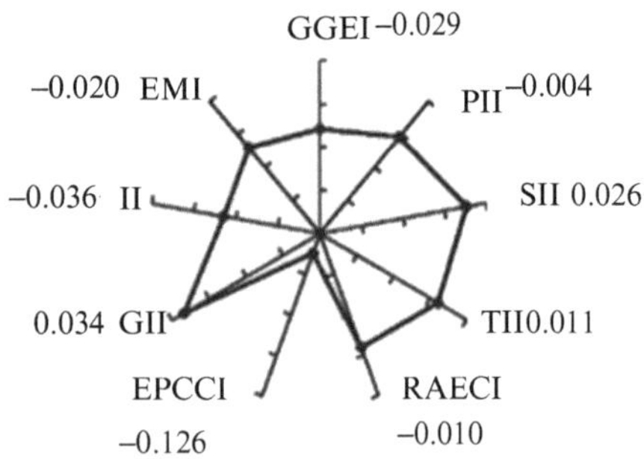

Fig. 9.4 Scores of Tianjin by Second-Class Indicators

Table 9.3 Changes in Tianjin's rankings by First-Class and Second-Class Indicators, 2009–2010

Indicator	2010	2009	Difference	Indicator	2010	2009	Difference
GDI	28	31	3				
GDEG	18	17	−1	RAECI	37	34	−3
GGEI	26	22	−4	EPCCI	35	29	−6
PII	24	23	−1	SDGP	22	32	10
SII	6	6	0	GII	8	20	12
TII	13	14	1	II	30	31	1
CCPNRE	37	30	−7	EMI	25	26	1

Note: A positive value in "Difference" means a rise in ranking

9.2.2 *Changes in Tianjin's GDI Rankings 2009–2010*

According to Table 9.3, in First-Class Indicators, the most obvious change occurred in SDGP where it rose by 10 places. It rose by 1 and 7 places respectively in GDEG and CCPNRE. In Second-Class Indicators, Tianjin rose by 12 in GII and 1 place in TII, II and EMI. It fell by 6, 4, 3, and 1 place in EPCCI, GGEI, RAECI and PII; and t remained the same as those in 2009 in SII.

To further explain the causes of the changes in the rankings by First- and Second-Class Indicators, we put the Third-Class Indicators where a change of more than 3 places occurred from 2009 to 2010 as follows in Table 9.4. Compared with those in 2009, Tianjin both out- and underperformed in ranking in 2010, while the more obvious trend is outperforming the previous year. It rose by 22 places in Harmless treatment of urban household waste, 16 in Ratio of the spending on science, education, culture, and public health to government expenditure, 7 in Ratio of environmental spending to government expenditure, 4 in Industrial SO_2 removal rate and 3 in Proportion of value added of tertiary sector in GDP it dropped in 6 indicators including Ammonia/nitrogen emissions per unit of GDP, Ammonia/nitrogen emissions per capita, Ammonia/nitrogen emissions per unit of land area, Energy consumption per unit of GDP, Labor productivity of the secondary sector and Water resources per capita compared with those in 2009.

Table 9.4 Third-Class Indicators where changes over 3 places occurred by Tianjin, 2009–2010

	Original data for 2009 and 2010			Change in ranking		
Third-Class Indicator	2010	2009	Unit	2010	2009	Difference
Energy consumption per unit of GDP	0.88	0.89	Ton per 10,000 yuan	25	21	−4
Ammonia/nitrogen emissions per unit of GDP	2.54	1.81	Ton per 100 million yuan	23	12	−11
Labor productivity of the secondary sector	16.60	14.42	10,000 yuan per capita	12	9	−3
Proportion of value added of tertiary sector in GDP	45.95	45.27	%	23	26	3
Water resources per capita	93.42	155.54	m^3 per capita	37	34	−3
Ammonia/nitrogen emissions per unit of land area	1.68	1.02	Ton per km^2	35	30	−5
Ammonia/nitrogen emissions per capita	20.13	12.30	Ton per 10,000 persons	32	24	−8
Ratio of environmental spending to government expenditure	1.97	1.19	%	28	35	7
Ratio of the spending on science, education, culture, and public health to government expenditure	25.06	25.05	%	7	23	16
Harmless treatment of urban household waste	100.00	94.31	%	1	23	22
Industrial SO_2 removal rate	63.22	59.73	%	17	21	4

Note: A positive value in "Difference" means a rise in ranking

Green development checkup-Shijiazhuang

No.	Indicator	Unit	Scope	Attribute	2010 average of 38 cities	2010 figure	2009 figure	2010 ranking	2009 ranking	Change in ranking	Source of 2010 data	Chernoff face
1	GDP per capita	Yuan	Whole city	Positive	56,231.37	33,915	30,427.83	32	32	0	Regional Economy; City	
2	Energy consumption per unit of GDP	Ton per 10,000 yuan	Whole city	Negative	0.81	0.87	1.44	24	32	8	Regional Economy; City	☺
3	Electricity consumption per capita in urban areas	kWh per capita	Whole city	Negative	580.70	162.82	125.82	1	1	0	city	
4	CO_2 emissions per unit of GDP			Negative	No data			N/A	N/A	N/A		
5	SO_2 emissions per unit of GDP	Ton per 100 million yuan	Whole city	Negative	43.72	57.01	63.84	29	29	0	Regional Economy; Environment Annual Report	
6	COD emissions per unit of GDP	Ton per 100 million yuan	Whole city	Negative	24.81	37.64	44.46	31	31	0	Regional Economy; Environment Annual Report	
7	Nitrogen oxide emissions per unit of GDP	Ton per 100 million yuan	Whole city	Negative	41.71	56.39	45.66	29	27	−2	Regional Economy; Environment Annual Report	☹
8	Ammonia/nitrogen emissions per unit of GDP	Ton per 100 million yuan	Whole city	Negative	2.63	3.04	3.63	27	28	1	Regional Economy; Environment Annual Report	☺
9	Labor productivity of the primary sector	10,000 yuan per capita	Whole city	Positive	3.03	2.51	2.07	17	17	0	Regional Economy	

(continued)

(continued)

No.	Indicator	Unit	Scope	Attribute	2010 average of 38 cities	2010 figure	2009 figure	2010 ranking	2009 ranking	Change in ranking	Source of 2010 data	Chernoff face
10	Labor productivity of the secondary sector	10,000 yuan per capita	Whole city	Positive	17.91	9.03	8.26	36	33	−3	Regional Economy	☹
11	Water consumption per unit of value added created by industrial enterprises	10,000 tons per 10,000 yuan	Whole city	Negative	0.03	0.05	0.05	34	35	1	Regional Economy; Environment Annual Report	☺
12	Energy consumption per unit of value added created by industrial enterprises			Negative	No data			N/A	N/A	N/A		
13	Utilization rate industrial solid waste	%	Whole city	Positive	85.58	93.40	92.50	19	17	−2	Environment Annual Report	☹
14	Recycling rate of industrial water	%	Whole city	Positive	83.81	95.36	95.21	7	7	0	Environment Annual Report	
15	Labor productivity of the tertiary sector	10,000 yuan per capita	Whole city	Positive	11.40	7.67	7.03	30	27	−3	Regional Economy	☹
16	Proportion of value added of tertiary sector in GDP	%	Whole city	Positive	47.97	40.51	40.15	35	34	−1	City	☹
17	Proportion of tertiary sector employees in the total employed population	%	Whole city	Positive	46.44	35.56	34.86	35	35	0	Regional Economy	

18	Water resources per capita	m^3 per capita	Whole city	Positive	1,026.43	133.35	192.96	35	31	−4	Environment Annual Report; City	☹
19	CO_2 emissions per unit of land area			Negative	No data			N/A	N/A	N/A		
20	CO_2 emissions per capita			Negative	No data			N/A	N/A	N/A		
21	SO_2 emissions per unit of land area	Ton per km^2	Whole city	Negative	11.64	11.43	11.39	26	24	−2	Environment Annual Report; City	☹
22	SO_2 emissions per capita	Ton per 10,000 persons	Whole city	Negative	216.46	184.16	183.08	22	22	0	Environment Annual Report; City	
23	COD emissions per unit of land area	Ton per km^2	Whole city	Negative	7.83	7.55	7.94	26	26	0	Environment Annual Report; City	
24	COD emissions per capita	Ton per 10,000 persons	Whole city	Negative	118.15	121.61	127.51	22	21	−1	Environment Annual Report; City	☹
25	Nitrogen oxides emissions per unit of land area	Ton per km^2	Whole city	Negative	15.00	11.30	8.15	25	20	−5	Environment Annual Report; City	☹
26	Nitrogen oxides emissions per capita	Ton per 10,000 persons	Whole city	Negative	237.70	182.18	130.95	19	14	−5	Environment Annual Report; City	☹
27	Ammonia/nitrogen emissions per unit of land area	Ton per km^2	Whole city	Negative	0.86	0.61	0.65	21	20	−1	Environment Annual Report; City	☹
28	Ammonia/nitrogen emissions per capita	Ton per 10,000 persons	Whole city	Negative	12.63	9.82	10.41	17	16	−1	Environment Annual Report; City	☹

(continued)

(continued)

No.	Indicator	Unit	Scope	Attribute	2010 average of 38 cities	2010 figure	2009 figure	2010 ranking	2009 ranking	Change in ranking	Source of 2010 data	Chernoff face
29	Percentage of the days with air quality at or over level II in a year	%	District	Positive	89.20	87.36	87.09	21	25	4	MEP Data	☺
30	Percentage of days with respirable suspended particulates as the principal pollutants in a year	%	District	Negative	70.81	83.56	80.27	25	24	−1	MEP Data	☹
31	Ratio of environmental spending to government expenditure	%	Whole city	Positive	3.13	2.85	3.30	18	8	−10	China Statistics; City	☹
32	Ratio of the investment in industrial pollution control to GDP	%	Whole city	Positive	0.08	0.03	0.07	21	18	−3	Environment Annual Report; Regional Economy	☹
33	Ratio of the spending on science, education, culture, and public health to government expenditure	%	Whole city	Positive	21.08	20.58	36.98	19	2	−17	China Statistics; City; Regional Economy	☹
34	Area of green land per capita in urban areas	m^2	District	Positive	59.39	36.00	33.89	21	23	2	City	☺
35	Green coverage of urban built-in areas	%	District	Positive	40.04	43.03	41.52	8	13	5	Urban Constr uction	☺

36	Coverage of water supply	%	District	Positive	98.82	100.00	100.00	1	1	0	Urban Constru ction	
37	Treatment rate of urban household wastewater	%	District	Positive	86.16	95.38	83.28	8	20	12	Urban Construction	☺
38	Harmless treatment of urban household waste	%	District	Positive	94.38	100.00	100.00	1	1	0	Urban Construction	
39	Public buses per 10,000 urban residents		District	Positive	15.61	18.29	17.05	6	5	−1	City	☹
40	Industrial SO_2 removal rate	%	Whole city	Positive	57.30	72.92	65.89	10	15	5	Environment Annual Report	☺
41	Industrial wastewater COD removal rate	%	Whole city	Positive	77.86	81.43	83.74	22	21	−1	Environment Annual Report	☹
42	Industrial nitrogen oxide removal rate	%	Whole city	Positive	5.29	0.41	3.48	23	18	−5	Environment Annual Report	☹
43	Industrial waste water ammonia/nitrogen removal rate	%	Whole city	Positive	67.89	73.79	72.70	18	18	0	Environment Annual Report	

Note:
Regional Economy: *China Regional Economy Statistical Yearbook 2011*
City: *China City Statistical Yearbook 2011*
China Statistics: *China Statistical Yearbook 2011*
Urban Construction: *China Urban Construction Statistical Yearbook 2010*
Environment Annual Report: *China Environment Annual Report 2010*
Environmental Yearbook: *China Environmental Statistical Yearbook 2011*
MEP Data: Ministry of Environmental Protection Data Center

9.3 Brief Analysis of Green Development in Shijiazhuang

Shijiazhuang ranked 25th among the 38 participating cities by GDI according to 2010 data, 9 places lower over 2009 (Shijiazhuang ranked 16th in 2009). Following is a brief analysis of its score by each indicator and their changes from 2009 to 2010.

9.3.1 Shijiazhuang's 2010 Scores by GDI

Shijiazhuang scored −0.093 in 2010. From the three First-Class Indicators including GDEG, CCPNRE, and SDGP as shown in Fig. 9.5, Shijiazhuang showed some comparative advantages in terms of SDGP, and it underperformed the national average in GDEG and CCPNRE (Note: the national average value of each indicator is 0).

According to Fig. 9.6, Shijiazhuang surpassed the national average in 3 of Second-Class Indicators in 2010, which were SII, II and EMI; it ranked lower than the national average in GGEI, PII, TII, RAECI, EPCCI and GII.

9.3.2 Changes in Shijiazhuang's GDI Rankings 2009–2010

According to Table 9.5, in First-Class Indicators, the most obvious change occurred in SDGP where a fall by 9 places occurred. It fell by 3 places in CCPNRE, and it remained unchanged in GDEG. In Second-Class Indicators, Shijiazhuang rose by

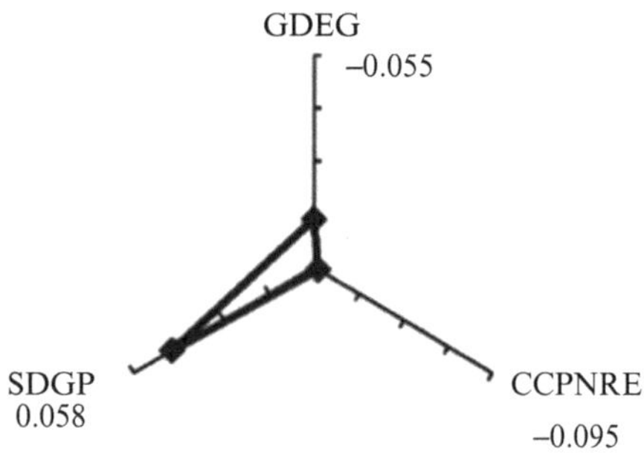

Fig. 9.5 Scores of Shijiazhuang by First-Class Indicators

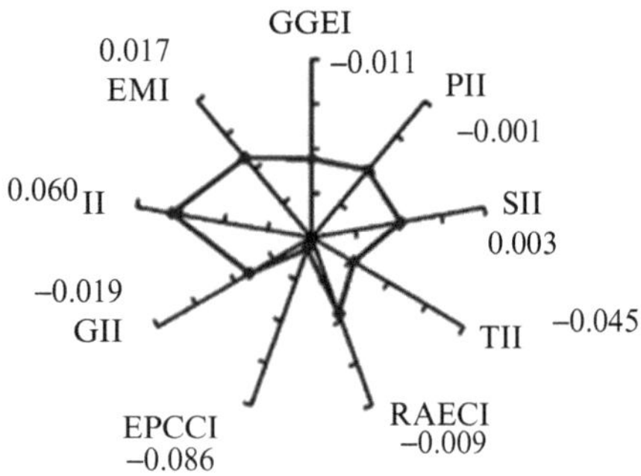

Fig. 9.6 Scores of Shijiazhuang by Second-Class Indicators

Table 9.5 Changes in Shijiazhuang's rankings by First-Class and Second-Class Indicators, 2009–2010

Indicator	2010	2009	Difference	Indicator	2010	2009	Difference
GDI	25	16	−9				
GDEG	26	26	0	RAECI	35	31	−4
GGEI	21	19	−2	EPCCI	28	24	−4
PII	16	17	1	SDGP	15	6	−9
SII	18	16	−2	GII	20	6	−14
TII	35	36	1	II	5	11	6
CCPNRE	29	26	−3	EMI	18	18	0

Note: A positive value in "Difference" means a rise in ranking

6, 1 and 1 place in II, PII and TII; and it fell by 14, 4, 4, 2 and 2 places in GII, RAECI, EPCCI, GGEI and SII. It remained the same by EMI.

To further explain the causes of the changes in the rankings by First- and Second-Class Indicators, we put the Third-Class Indicators where a change of more than 3 places occurred from 2009 to 2010 as follows in Table 9.6. Compared with those in 2009, Tianjin both out- and underperformed in ranking in 2010, while the more obvious trend is underperforming compared with the previous year. It dropped by17 places in Ratio of the spending on science, education, culture, and public health to government expenditure compared with that in 2009, 10 in Ratio of environmental spending to government expenditure, 5 in 3 indicators including Nitrogen oxides emissions per unit of land area, 4 in Water resources per capita and 3 in 3 indicators including Labor productivity of the secondary sector; yet it rose by 5 indicators including Treatment rate of urban household wastewater, Energy consumption per unit of GDP, Green coverage of urban built-in areas, Industrial SO_2 removal rate, Percentage of the days with air quality at or over level II in a year compared with those in 2009.

Table 9.6 Third-Class Indicators where changes over 3 places occurred by Shijiazhuang, 2009–2010

	Original data for 2009 and 2010			Change in ranking		
Third-Class Indicator	2010	2009	Unit	2010	2009	Difference
Energy consumption per unit of GDP	0.87	1.44	Ton per 10,000 yuan	24	32	8
Labor productivity of the secondary sector	9.03	8.26	10,000 yuan per capita	36	33	−3
Labor productivity of the tertiary sector	7.67	7.03	10,000 yuan per capita	30	27	−3
Water resources per capita	133.35	192.96	m^3 per capita	35	31	−4
Nitrogen oxides emissions per unit of land area	11.30	8.15	Ton per km^2	25	20	−5
Nitrogen oxides emissions per capita	182.18	130.95	Ton per 10,000 persons	19	14	−5
Percentage of the days with air quality at or over level II in a year	87.36	87.09	%	21	25	4
Ratio of environmental spending to government expenditure	2.85	3.30	%	18	8	−10
Ratio of the investment in industrial pollution control to GDP	0.03	0.07	%	21	18	−3
Ratio of the spending on science, education, culture, and public health to government expenditure	20.58	36.98	%	19	2	−17
Green coverage of urban built-in areas	43.03	41.52	%	8	13	5
Treatment rate of urban household wastewater	95.38	83.28	%	8	20	12
Industrial SO_2 removal rate	72.92	65.89	%	10	15	5
Industrial nitrogen oxide removal rate	0.41	3.48	%	23	18	−5

Note: A positive value in "Difference" means a rise in ranking

Green development checkup-Taiyuan

No.	Indicator	Unit	Scope	Attribute	2010 average of 38 cities	2010 figure	2009 figure	2010 ranking	2009 ranking	Change in ranking	Source of 2010 data	Chernoff face
1	GDP per capita	Yuan	Whole city	Positive	56,231.37	46,144	44,319.00	22	20	−2	Regional Economy; City	
2	Energy consumption per unit of GDP	Ton per 10,000 yuan	Whole city	Negative	0.81	1.74	1.26	36	29	−7	Regional Economy; City	
3	Electricity consumption per capita in urban areas	kWh per capita	Whole city	Negative	580.70	525.60	438.55	22	21	−1	City	
4	CO_2 emissions per unit of GDP			Negative	No data			N/A	N/A	N/A		
5	SO_2 emissions per unit of GDP	Ton per 100 million yuan	Whole city	Negative	43.72	86.73	100.18	33	34	1	Regional Economy; Environment Annual Report	
6	COD emissions per unit of GDP	Ton per 100 million yuan	Whole city	Negative	24.81	19.19	22.26	18	18	0	Regional Economy; Environment Annual Report	
7	Nitrogen oxide emissions per unit of GDP	Ton per 100 million yuan	Whole city	Negative	41.71	68.26	54.99	33	30	−3	Regional Economy; Environment Annual Report	
8	Ammonia/nitrogen emissions per unit of GDP	Ton per 100 million yuan	Whole city	Negative	2.63	4.03	4.56	30	31	1	Regional Economy; Environment Annual Report	
9	Labor productivity of the primary sector	10,000 yuan per capita	Whole city	Positive	3.03	1.23	1.14	30	30	0	Regional Economy	
10	Labor productivity of the secondary sector	10,000 yuan per capita	Whole city	Positive	17.91	14.57	12.46	14	15	1	Regional Economy	
11	Water consumption per unit of value added created by industrial enterprises	10,000 tons per 10,000 yuan	Whole city	Negative	0.03	0.07	0.08	36	36	0	Regional Economy; Environment Annual Report	

(continued)

(continued)

No.	Indicator	Unit	Scope	Attribute	2010 average of 38 cities	2010 figure	2009 figure	2010 ranking	2009 ranking	Change in ranking	Source of 2010 data	Chernoff face
12	Energy consumption per unit of value added created by industrial enterprises			Negative	No data			N/A	N/A	N/A		
13	Utilization rate industrial solid waste	%	Whole city	Positive	85.58	52.30	48.60	36	35	−1	Environment Annual Report	☹
14	Recycling rate of industrial water	%	Whole city	Positive	83.81	96.89	96.85	1	2	1	Environment Annual Report	☺
15	Labor productivity of the tertiary sector	10,000 yuan per capita	Whole city	Positive	11.40	10.28	9.38	22	19	−3	Regional Economy	☹
16	Proportion of value added of tertiary sector in GDP	%	Whole city	Positive	47.97	53.39	54.43	8	7	−1	City	☹
17	Proportion of tertiary sector employees in the total employed population	%	Whole city	Positive	46.44	53.89	53.68	5	5	0	Regional Economy	
18	Water resources per capita	m^3 per capita	Whole city	Positive	1,026.43	154.79	145.19	33	36	3	Environment Annual Report; City	☺
19	CO_2 emissions per unit of land area			Negative	No data			N/A	N/A	N/A		
20	CO_2 emissions per capita			Negative	No data			N/A	N/A	N/A		
21	SO_2 emissions per unit of land area	Ton per km^2	Whole city	Negative	11.64	17.78	18.50	30	31	1	Environment Annual Report; City	☺
22	SO_2 emissions per capita	Ton per 10,000 persons	Whole city	Negative	216.46	338.81	355.17	32	33	1	Environment Annual Report; City	☺
23	COD emissions per unit of land area	Ton per km^2	Whole city	Negative	7.83	3.93	4.11	11	12	1	Environment Annual Report; City	☺
24	COD emissions per capita	Ton per 10,000 persons	Whole city	Negative	118.15	74.95	78.91	11	10	−1	Environment Annual Report; City	☹

25	Nitrogen oxides emissions per unit of land area	Ton per km^2	Whole city	Negative	15.00	13.99	10.15	27	24	−3	Environment Annual Report; City	☹
26	Nitrogen oxides emissions per capita	Ton per 10,000 persons	Whole city	Negative	237.70	266.66	194.94	31	24	−7	Environment Annual Report; City	☹
27	Ammonia/nitrogen emissions per unit of land area	Ton per km^2	Whole city	Negative	0.86	0.83	0.84	27	27	0	Environment Annual Report; City	
28	Ammonia/nitrogen emissions per capita	Ton per 10,000 persons	Whole city	Negative	12.63	15.76	16.18	27	30	3	Environment Annual Report; City	☺
29	Percentage of the days with air quality at or over level II in a year	%	District	Positive	89.20	83.24	81.04	32	33	1	MEP Data	☺
30	Percentage of days with respirable suspended particulates as the principal pollutants in a year	%	District	Negative	70.81	60.55	78.90	10	20	10	MEP Data	☺
31	Ratio of environmental spending to government expenditure	%	Whole city	Positive	3.13	4.34	3.24	6	11	5	China Statistics; City	☺
32	Ratio of the investment in industrial pollution control to GDP	%	Whole city	Positive	0.08	0.23	0.48	5	3	−2	Environment Annual Report; Regional Economy	☹
33	Ratio of the spending on science, education, culture, and public health to government expenditure	%	Whole city	Positive	21.08	24.12	28.23	9	13	4	China Statistics; City; Regional Economy	☺
34	Area of green land per capita in urban areas		District	Positive	59.39	29.00	27.01	29	30	1	City	☺
35	Green coverage of urban built-in areas	%	District	Positive	40.04	35.75	34.77	32	33	1	Urban Construction	☺
36	Coverage of water supply	%	District	Positive	98.82	100.00	99.66	1	22	21	Urban Construction	☺
37	Treatment rate of urban household wastewater	%	District	Positive	86.16	83.86	70.00	28	30	2	Urban Construction	☺
38	Harmless treatment of urban household waste	%	District	Positive	94.38	100.00	94.81	1	22	21	Urban Construction	☺

(continued)

(continued)

No.	Indicator	Unit	Scope	Attribute	2010 average of 38 cities	2010 figure	2009 figure	2010 ranking	2009 ranking	Change in ranking	Source of 2010 data	Chernoff face
39	Public buses per 10,000 urban residents		District	Positive	15.61	7.76	6.59	36	36	0	City	
40	Industrial SO_2 removal rate	%	Whole city	Positive	57.30	73.01	65.75	8	16	8	Environment Annual Report	
41	Industrial wastewater COD removal rate	%	Whole city	Positive	77.86	85.87	82.05	15	22	7	Environment Annual Report	
42	Industrial nitrogen oxide removal rate	%	Whole city	Positive	5.29	19.91	17.65	2	5	3	Environment Annual Report	
43	Industrial waste water ammonia/nitrogen removal rate	%	Whole city	Positive	67.89	63.96	76.56	25	15	−10	Environment Annual Report	

Note:
Regional Economy: *China Regional Economy Statistical Yearbook 2011*
City: *China City Statistical Yearbook 2011*
China Statistics: *China Statistical Yearbook 2011*
Urban Construction: *China Urban Construction Statistical Yearbook 2010*
Environment Annual Report: *China Environment Annual Report 2010*
Environmental Yearbook: *China Environmental Statistical Yearbook 2011*
MEP Data: Ministry of Environmental Protection Data Center

9.4 Brief Analysis of Green Development in Taiyuan

Taiyuan ranked 23rd among the 38 participating cities by GDI according to 2010 data, 3 places higher over 2009 (Taiyuan ranked 26th in 2009). Following is a brief analysis of its score by each indicator and their changes from 2009 to 2010.

9.4.1 Taiyuan's 2010 Scores by GDI

Taiyuan scored −0.057 in 2010. From the three First-Class Indicators including GDEG, CCPNRE, and SDGP as shown in Fig. 9.7, Taiyuan showed some comparative advantages in SDGP, but underperformed in GDEG and CCPNRE compared with the national average (Note: the national average value of each indicator is 0).

According to Fig. 9.8, Taiyuan surpassed the national average in 3 of Second-Class Indicators in 2010, which were TII, GII, and EMI; yet scored lower than the national average in 6 indicators including GGEI, PII, SII, RAECI, Environmental Pressure and Climate Change and II.

9.4.2 Changes in Taiyuan's GDI Rankings 2009–2010

According to Table 9.7, in First-Class Indicators, the most obvious change occurred in CCPNRE, where Taiyuan rose by 2 places. It rose by 1 place in SDGP; it fell by 1 place in GDEG. From Changes in ranking in Second-Class Indicators, it rose by 5 places in II and 3 in RAECI, EPCCI and Environmental Management Indicator; it fell by 2, 1 and 1 place in GII, GGEI and TII; it remained unchanged by PII and SII as those in 2009.

To further explain the causes of the changes in the rankings by First- and Second-Class Indicators, we put the Third-Class Indicators where a change of more than 3 places occurred from 2009 to 2010 as follows in Table 9.8. Compared with those in 2009, Taiyuan both out- and underperformed in ranking in 2010, while the more

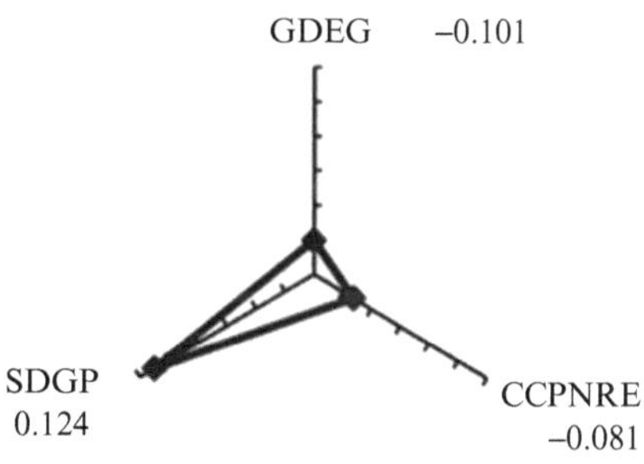

Fig. 9.7 Scores of Taiyuan by First-Class Indicators

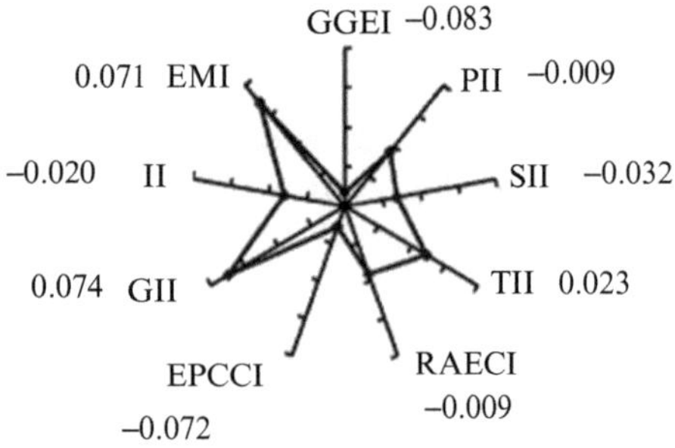

Fig. 9.8 Scores of Taiyuan by Second-Class Indicators

Table 9.7 Changes in Taiyuan's rankings by First-Class and Second-Class Indicators, 2009–2010

Indicator	2010	2009	Difference	Indicator	2010	2009	Difference
GDI	23	26	3				
GDEG	33	32	−1	RAECI	33	36	3
GGEI	34	33	−1	EPCCI	24	27	3
PII	30	30	0	SDGP	7	8	1
SII	32	32	0	GII	5	3	−2
TII	9	8	−1	II	25	30	5
CCPNRE	26	28	2	EMI	5	8	3

Note: A positive value in "Difference" means a rise in ranking

obvious trend is outperforming compared with the previous year. It rose by 21 places in Coverage of water supply and Harmless treatment of urban household waste, 10 in Percentage of days with respirable suspended particulates as the principal pollutants in a year and 8 in Industrial SO_2 removal rate. It rose by varying places in Industrial wastewater COD removal rate and many other indicators. Yet it fell by certain places in 6 indicators including Industrial waste water ammonia/nitrogen removal rate, Energy consumption per unit of GDP and Nitrogen oxides emissions per capita.

Table 9.8 Third-Class Indicators where changes over 3 places occurred by Taiyuan, 2009–2010

	Original data for 2009 and 2010			Change in ranking		
Third-Class Indicator	2010	2009	Unit	2010	2009	Difference
Energy consumption per unit of GDP	1.74	1.26	Ton per 10,000 yuan	36	29	−7
Nitrogen oxide emissions per unit of GDP	68.26	54.99	Ton per 100 million yuan	33	30	−3
Labor productivity of the tertiary sector	10.28	9.38	10,000 yuan per capita	22	19	−3
Water resources per capita	154.79	145.19	m^3 per capita	33	36	3
Nitrogen oxides emissions per unit of land area	13.99	10.15	Ton per km^2	27	24	−3
Nitrogen oxides emissions per capita	266.66	194.94	Ton per 10,000 persons	31	24	−7
Ammonia/nitrogen emissions per capita	15.76	16.18	Ton per 10,000 persons	27	30	3
Percentage of days with respirable suspended particulates as the principal pollutants in a year	60.55	78.90	%	10	20	10
Ratio of environmental spending to government expenditure	4.34	3.24	%	6	11	5
Ratio of the spending on science, education, culture, and public health to government expenditure	24.12	28.23	%	9	13	4
Coverage of water supply	100.00	99.66	%	1	22	21
Harmless treatment of urban household waste	100.00	94.81	%	1	22	21
Industrial SO_2 removal rate	73.01	65.75	%	8	16	8
Industrial wastewater COD removal rate	85.87	82.05	%	15	22	7
Industrial nitrogen oxide removal rate	19.91	17.65	%	2	5	3
Industrial waste water ammonia/nitrogen removal rate	63.96	76.56	%	25	15	−10

Note: A positive value in "Difference" means a rise in ranking

Green development checkup-Hohhot

No.	Indicator	Unit	Scope	Attribute	2010 average of 38 cities	2010 figure	2009 figure	2010 ranking	2009 ranking	Change in ranking	Source of 2010 data	Chernoff face
1	GDP per capita	Yuan	Whole city	Positive	56,231.37	65,518	61,108.00	14	12	−2	Regional Economy; City	☹
2	Energy consumption per unit of GDP	Ton per 10,000 yuan	Whole city	Negative	0.81	1.54	1.65	35	34	−1	Regional Economy; City	☹
3	Electricity consumption per capita in urban areas	kWh per capita	Whole city	Negative	580.70	416.05	308.20	14	9	−5	City	☹
4	CO_2 emissions per unit of GDP			Negative	No data			N/A	N/A	N/A		
5	SO_2 emissions per unit of GDP	Ton per 100 million yuan	Whole city	Negative	43.72	66.16	69.41	31	31	0	Regional Economy; Environment Annual Report	
6	COD emissions per unit of GDP	Ton per 100 million yuan	Whole city	Negative	24.81	24.00	22.51	25	20	−5	Regional Economy; Environment Annual Report	☹
7	Nitrogen oxide emissions per unit of GDP	Ton per 100 million yuan	Whole city	Negative	41.71	83.16	75.63	36	35	−1	Regional Economy; Environment Annual Report	☹
8	Ammonia/nitrogen emissions per unit of GDP	Ton per 100 million yuan	Whole city	Negative	2.63	4.04	3.45	31	27	−4	Regional Economy; Environment Annual Report	☹
9	Labor productivity of the primary sector	10,000 yuan per capita	Whole city	Positive	3.03	2.15	1.80	20	20	0	Regional Economy	

10	Labor productivity of the secondary sector	10,000 yuan per capita	Whole city	Positive	17.91	13.77	12.58	17	13	−4	Regional Economy	☹
11	Water consumption per unit of value added created by industrial enterprises	10,000 tons per 10,000 yuan	Whole city	Negative	0.03	0.03	0.02	24	17	−7	Regional Economy; Environment Annual Report	☹
12	Energy consumption per unit of value added created by industrial enterprises			Negative	No data			N/A	N/A	N/A		
13	Utilization rate industrial solid waste	%	Whole city	Positive	85.58	38.70	26.70	38	38	0	Environment Annual Report	
14	Recycling rate of industrial water	%	Whole city	Positive	83.81	93.08	90.64	13	17	4	Environment Annual Report	☺
15	Labor productivity of the tertiary sector	10,000 yuan per capita	Whole city	Positive	11.40	15.51	14.53	6	4	−2	Regional Economy	☹
16	Proportion of value added of tertiary sector in GDP	%	Whole city	Positive	47.97	58.71	59.16	4	5	1	City	☺

(continued)

(continued)

No.	Indicator	Unit	Scope	Attribute	2010 average of 38 cities	2010 figure	2009 figure	2010 ranking	2009 ranking	Change in ranking	Source of 2010 data	Chernoff face
17	Proportion of tertiary sector employees in the total employed population	%	Whole city	Positive	46.44	44.05	42.94	25	24	−1	Regional Economy	☹
18	Water resources per capita	m^3 per capita	Whole city	Positive	1,026.43	517.42	522.41	24	20	−4	Environment Annual Report; City	☹
19	CO_2 emissions per unit of land area			Negative	No data			N/A	N/A	N/A		
20	CO_2 emissions per capita			Negative	No data			N/A	N/A	N/A		
21	SO_2 emissions per unit of land area	Ton per km^2	Whole city	Negative	11.64	5.92	5.50	12	11	−1	Environment Annual Report; City	☹
22	SO_2 emissions per capita	Ton per 10,000 persons	Whole city	Negative	216.46	446.45	419.34	36	35	−1	Environment Annual Report; City	☹
23	COD emissions per unit of land area	Ton per km^2	Whole city	Negative	7.83	2.15	1.78	5	4	−1	Environment Annual Report; City	☹
24	COD emissions per capita	Ton per 10,000 persons	Whole city	Negative	118.15	161.95	136.00	30	22	−8	Environment Annual Report; City	☹

25	Nitrogen oxides emissions per unit of land area	Ton per km^2	Whole city	Negative	15.00		7.44	5.99	17	14	−3	Environment Annual Report; City	☹
26	Nitrogen oxides emissions per capita	Ton per 10,000 persons	Whole city	Negative	237.70		561.18	456.90	35	36	1	Environment Annual Report; City	☺
27	Ammonia/nitrogen emissions per unit of land area	Ton per km^2	Whole city	Negative	0.86		0.36	0.27	11	5	−6	Environment Annual Report; City	☹
28	Ammonia/nitrogen emissions per capita	Ton per 10,000 persons	Whole city	Negative	12.63		27.26	20.84	38	34	−4	Environment Annual Report; City	☹
29	Percentage of the days with air quality at or over level II in a year	%	District	Positive	89.20		95.60	94.78	10	13	3	MEP Data	☺
30	Percentage of days with respirable suspended particulates as the principal pollutants in a year	%	District	Negative	70.81		42.19	47.40	5	4	−1	MEP Data	☹
31	Ratio of environmental spending to government expenditure	%	Whole city	Positive	3.13		3.66	3.42	10	7	−3	China Statistics; City	☹

(continued)

(continued)

No.	Indicator	Unit	Scope	Attribute	2010 average of 38 cities	2010 figure	2009 figure	2010 ranking	2009 ranking	Change in ranking	Source of 2010 data	Chernoff face
32	Ratio of the investment in industrial pollution control to GDP	%	Whole city	Positive	0.08	0.18	0.14	7	11	4	Environment Annual Report; Regional Economy	
33	Ratio of the spending on science, education, culture, and public health to government expenditure	%	Whole city	Positive	21.08	10.82	21.00	38	38	0	Statistical; City; Regional Economy	
34	Area of green land per capita in urban areas		District	Positive	59.39	22.00	22.26	35	34	−1	City	
35	Green coverage of urban built-in areas	%	District	Positive	40.04	35.69	35.45	33	31	−2	Urban Construction	
36	Coverage of water supply	%	District	Positive	98.82	95.50	95.41	34	33	−1	Urban Construction	
37	Treatment rate of urban household wastewater	%	District	Positive	86.16	77.10	56.96	32	34	2	Urban Construction	
38	Harmless treatment of urban household waste	%	District	Positive	94.38	97.88	95.20	19	19	0	Urban Construction	

39	Public buses per 10,000 urban residents		District	Positive	15.61	15.78	16.99	11	6	−5	City	☹
40	Industrial SO_2 removal rate	%	Whole city	Positive	57.30	73.03	70.83	7	9	2	Environment Annual Report	☺
41	Industrial waste-water COD removal rate	%	Whole city	Positive	77.86	94.17	90.31	3	7	4	Environment Annual Report	☺
42	Industrial nitrogen oxide removal rate	%	Whole city	Positive	5.29	0.00	0.00	31	29	−2	Environment Annual Report	☹
43	Industrial waste water ammonia/nitrogen removal rate	%	Whole city	Positive	67.89	82.48	73.95	11	17	6	Environment Annual Report	☺

Note:
Regional Economy: *China Regional Economy Statistical Yearbook 2011*
City: *China City Statistical Yearbook 2011*
China Statistics: *China Statistical Yearbook 2011*
Urban Construction: *China Urban Construction Statistical Yearbook 2010*
Environment Annual Report: *China Environment Annual Report 2010*
Environmental Yearbook: *China Environmental Statistical Yearbook 2011*
MEP Data: Ministry of Environmental Protection Data Center

9.5 Brief Analysis of Green Development in Hohhot

Hohhot ranked 27th among the 38 participating cities by GDI according to 2010 data, 3 places higher over 2009 (Hohhot ranked 30th in 2009). Following is a brief analysis of its score by each indicator and their changes from 2009 to 2010.

9.5.1 *Hohhot's 2010 Scores by GDI*

Hohhot scored −0.132 in 2010. From the three First-Class Indicators including GDEG, CCPNRE, and SDGP as shown in Fig. 9.9, Hohhot showed some comparative advantages in CCPNRE, yet scored lower than the national average in GDEG and SDGP (Note: the national average value of each indicator is 0).

According to Fig. 9.10, Hohhot surpassed the national average in 3 of Second-Class Indicators in 2010, which were TII, EPCCI and EMI; it ranked lower than the national average in 6 indicators including GGEI, PII, SII, RAECI, GII and II.

9.5.2 *Changes in Hohhot's GDI Rankings 2009–2010*

According to Table 9.9, in First-Class Indicators, the most obvious change occurred in SDGP where it rose by 4 places; it rose by 2 places in CCPNRE; it fell by 2 places

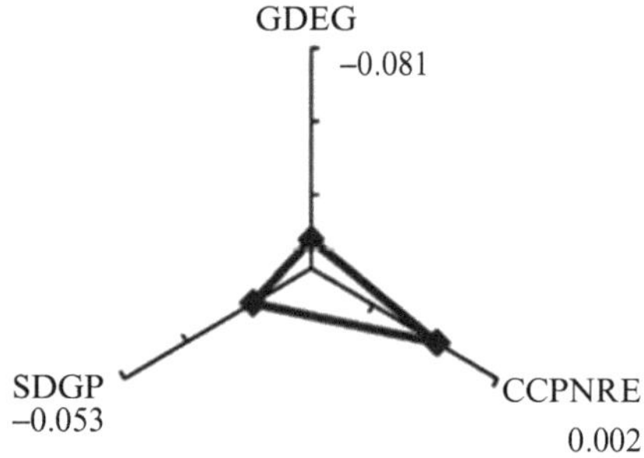

Fig. 9.9 Scores of Hohhot by First-Class Indicators

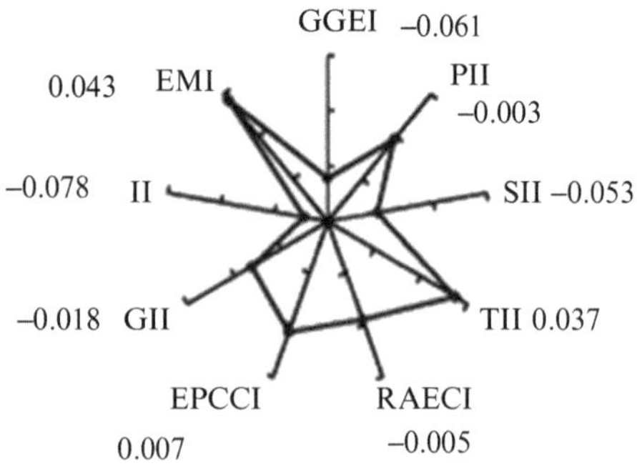

Fig. 9.10 Scores of Hohhot by Second-Class Indicators

Table 9.9 Changes in Hohhot's rankings by First-Class and Second-Class Indicators, 2009–2010

Indicator	2010	2009	Difference	Indicator	2010	2009	Difference
GDI	27	30	3				
GDEG	31	29	−2	RAECI	24	20	−4
GGEI	32	28	−4	EPCCI	13	15	2
PII	19	20	1	SDGP	23	27	4
SII	37	37	0	GII	19	19	0
TII	6	6	0	II	34	34	0
CCPNRE	13	15	2	EMI	9	15	6

Note: A positive value in "Difference" means a rise in ranking

in GDEG. In Second-Class Indicators, Hohhot rose by 6 places in EMI, 2 in EPCCI and 1 in PII; it fell by 4 places in RAECI and GGEI. It remained the same as those in 2009 in SII, GII and II.

To further explain the causes of the changes in the rankings by First- and Second-Class Indicators, we put the Third-Class Indicators where a change of more than 3 places occurred from 2009 to 2010 as follows in Table 9.10. Compared with those in 2009, Hohhot both out- and underperformed in ranking in 2010, while the more obvious trend is outforming compared with the previous year. It rose by 6 places in Industrial waste water ammonia/nitrogen removal rate, 4 in Industrial wastewater COD removal rate. It rose by varying degrees in many other indicators such as Recycling rate of industrial water; it fell in indicators such as COD emissions per capita and Water consumption per unit of value added created by industrial enterprises compared with those in 2009.

Table 9.10 Third-Class Indicators where changes over 3 places occurred by Hohhot, 2009–2010

	Original data for 2009 and 2010			Change in ranking		
Third-Class Indicator	2010	2009	Unit	2010	2009	Difference
Electricity consumption per capita in urban areas	416.05	308.20	kWh per capita	14	9	−5
COD emissions per unit of GDP	24.00	22.51	Ton per 100 million yuan	25	20	−5
Ammonia/nitrogen emissions per unit of GDP	4.04	3.45	Ton per 100 million yuan	31	27	−4
Labor productivity of the secondary sector	13.77	12.58	10,000 yuan per capita	17	13	−4
Water consumption per unit of value added created by industrial enterprises	0.03	0.02	10,000 tons per 10,000 yuan	24	17	−7
Recycling rate of industrial water	93.08	90.64	%	13	17	4
Water resources per capita	517.42	522.41	m^3 per capita	24	20	−4
COD emissions per capita	161.95	136.00	Ton per 10,000 persons	30	22	−8
Nitrogen oxides emissions per unit of land area	7.44	5.99	Ton per km^2	17	14	−3
Ammonia/nitrogen emissions per unit of land area	0.36	0.27	Ton per km^2	11	5	−6
Ammonia/nitrogen emissions per capita	27.26	20.84	Ton per 10,000 persons	38	34	−4
Percentage of the days with air quality at or over level II in a year	95.60	94.78	%	10	13	3
Ratio of environmental spending to government expenditure	3.66	3.42	%	10	7	−3
Ratio of the investment in industrial pollution control to GDP	0.18	0.14	%	7	11	4
Public buses per 10,000 urban residents	15.78	16.99		11	6	−5
Industrial wastewater COD removal rate	94.17	90.31	%	3	7	4
Industrial waste water ammonia/nitrogen removal rate	82.48	73.95	%	11	17	6

Note: A positive value in "Difference" means a rise in ranking

Green development checkup-Shenyang

No.	Indicator	Unit	Scope	Attribute	2010 average of 38 cities	2010 figure	2009 figure	2010 ranking	2009 ranking	Change in ranking	Source of 2010 data	Chernoff face
1	GDP per capita	Yuan	Whole city	Positive	56,231.37	62,357	54,654.00	16	17	1	Regional Economy; City	☺
2	Energy consumption per unit of GDP	Ton per 10,000 yuan	Whole city	Negative	0.81	0.28	0.28	7	4	−3	Regional Economy; City	☹
3	Electricity consumption per capita in urban areas	kWh per capita	Whole city	Negative	580.70	536.02	499.58	25	23	−2	City	☹
4	CO_2 emissions per unit of GDP			Negative	No data			N/A	N/A	N/A		
5	SO_2 emissions per unit of GDP	Ton per 100 million yuan	Whole city	Negative	43.72	24.09	26.47	16	14	−2	Regional Economy; Environment Annual Report	☹
6	COD emissions per unit of GDP	Ton per 100 million yuan	Whole city	Negative	24.81	15.18	15.58	12	10	−2	Regional Economy; Environment Annual Report	☹
7	Nitrogen oxide emissions per unit of GDP	Ton per 100 million yuan	Whole city	Negative	41.71	22.52	25.92	7	12	5	Regional Economy; Environment Annual Report	☺
8	Ammonia/nitrogen emissions per unit of GDP	Ton per 100 million yuan	Whole city	Negative	2.63	1.98	2.37	18	18	0	Regional Economy; Environment Annual Report	
9	Labor productivity of the primary sector	10,000 yuan per capita	Whole city	Positive	3.03	2.95	2.59	9	9	0	Regional Economy	
10	Labor productivity of the secondary sector	10,000 yuan per capita	Whole city	Positive	17.91	27.37	24.12	5	2	−3	Regional Economy	☹
11	Water consumption per unit of value added created by industrial enterprises	10,000 tons per 10,000 yuan	Whole city	Negative	0.03	0.00	0.00	4	2	−2	Regional Economy; Environment Annual Report	☹

(continued)

(continued)

No.	Indicator	Unit	Scope	Attribute	2010 average of 38 cities	2010 figure	2009 figure	2010 ranking	2009 ranking	Change in ranking	Source of 2010 data	Chernoff face
12	Energy consumption per unit of value added created by industrial enterprises			Negative	No data			N/A	N/A	N/A		
13	Utilization rate industrial solid waste	%	Whole city	Positive	85.58	95.70	93.90	14	15	1	Environment Annual Report	☺
14	Recycling rate of industrial water	%	Whole city	Positive	83.81	89.51	88.43	20	19	−1	Environment Annual Report	☹
15	Labor productivity of the tertiary sector	10,000 yuan per capita	Whole city	Positive	11.40	13.60	12.96	10	6	−4	Regional Economy	☹
16	Proportion of value added of tertiary sector in GDP	%	Whole city	Positive	47.97	44.94	45.31	25	25	0	City	
17	Proportion of tertiary sector employees in the total employed population	%	Whole city	Positive	46.44	50.14	48.14	10	12	2	Regional Economy	☺
18	Water resources per capita	m^3 per capita	Whole city	Positive	1,026.43	574.35	389.51	23	24	1	Environment Annual Report; City	☺
19	CO_2 emissions per unit of land area			Negative	No data			N/A	N/A	N/A		
20	CO_2 emissions per capita			Negative	No data			N/A	N/A	N/A		
21	SO_2 emissions per unit of land area	Ton per km^2	Whole city	Negative	11.64	8.39	8.08	18	17	−1	Environment Annual Report; City	☹
22	SO_2 emissions per capita	Ton per 10,000 persons	Whole city	Negative	216.46	151.66	146.66	19	17	−2	Environment Annual Report; City	☹
23	COD emissions per unit of land area	Ton per km^2	Whole city	Negative	7.83	5.29	4.75	19	17	−2	Environment Annual Report; City	☹
24	COD emissions per capita	Ton per 10,000 persons	Whole city	Negative	118.15	95.53	86.30	17	16	−1	Environment Annual Report; City	☹

25	Nitrogen oxides emissions per unit of land area	Ton per km^2	Whole city	Negative	15.00	7.84	7.91	18	19	1	Environment Annual Report; City	☺
26	Nitrogen oxides emissions per capita	Ton per 10,000 persons	Whole city	Negative	237.70	141.77	143.60	14	15	1	Environment Annual Report; City	☺
27	Ammonia/nitrogen emissions per unit of land area	Ton per km^2	Whole city	Negative	0.86	0.69	0.72	22	23	1	Environment Annual Report; City	☺
28	Ammonia/nitrogen emissions per capita	Ton per 10,000 persons	Whole city	Negative	12.63	12.46	13.12	23	26	3	Environment Annual Report; City	☺
29	Percentage of the days with air quality at or over level II in a year	%	District	Positive	89.20	90.11	90.11	19	18	−1	MEP Data	☹
30	Percentage of days with respirable suspended particulates as the principal pollutants in a year	%	District	Negative	70.81	75.07	86.03	19	30	11	MEP Data	☺
31	Ratio of environmental spending to government expenditure	%	Whole city	Positive	3.13	2.05	1.69	26	26	0	China Statistics; City	
32	Ratio of the investment in industrial pollution control to GDP	%	Whole city	Positive	0.08	0.01	0.01	30	36	6	Environment Annual Report; Regional Economy	☺
33	Ratio of the spending on science, education, culture, and public health to government expenditure	%	Whole city	Positive	21.08	20.98	27.52	18	14	−4	China Statistics; City; Regional Economy	☹
34	Area of green land per capita in urban areas	m^2	District	Positive	59.39	50.00	50.75	16	15	−1	City	☹

(continued)

(continued)

No.	Indicator	Unit	Scope	Attribute	2010 average of 38 cities	2010 figure	2009 figure	2010 ranking	2009 ranking	Change in ranking	Source of 2010 data	Chernoff face
35	Green coverage of urban built-in areas	%	District	Positive	40.04	42.01	41.83	13	12	−1	Urban Construction	
36	Coverage of water supply	%	District	Positive	98.82	100.00	100.00	1	1	0	Urban Construction	
37	Treatment rate of urban household wastewater	%	District	Positive	86.16	73.61	78.59	34	27	−7	Urban Construction	☹
38	Harmless treatment of urban household waste	%	District	Positive	94.38	100.00	100.00	1	1	0	Urban Construction	
39	Public buses per 10,000 urban residents		District	Positive	15.61	9.73	9.92	30	34	4	City	☺
40	Industrial SO_2 removal rate	%	Whole city	Positive	57.30	53.16	34.89	24	30	6	Environment Annual Report	☺
41	Industrial wastewater COD removal rate	%	Whole city	Positive	77.86	82.71	86.14	20	16	−4	Environment Annual Report	☹
42	Industrial nitrogen oxide removal rate	%	Whole city	Positive	5.29	0.53	0.51	22	24	2	Environment Annual Report	☺
43	Industrial waste water ammonia/nitrogen removal rate	%	Whole city	Positive	67.89	23.61	27.18	36	36	0	Environment Annual Report	

Note:
Regional Economy: *China Regional Economy Statistical Yearbook 2011*
City: *China City Statistical Yearbook 2011*
China Statistics: *China Statistical Yearbook 2011*
Urban Construction: *China Urban Construction Statistical Yearbook 2010*
Environment Annual Report: *China Environment Annual Report 2010*
Environmental Yearbook: *China Environmental Statistical Yearbook 2011*
MEP Data: Ministry of Environmental Protection Data Center

9.6 Brief Analysis of Green Development in Shenyang

Shenyang ranked 21st among the 38 participating cities by GDI according to 2010 data, 3 places lower over 2009 (Shenyang ranked 18th in 2009). Following is a brief analysis of its score by each indicator and their changes from 2009 to 2010.

9.6.1 Shenyang's 2010 Scores by GDI

Shenyang scored −0.037 in 2010. From the three First-Class Indicators including GDEG, CCPNRE, and SDGP as shown in Fig. 9.11, Shenyang showed some comparative advantages in GDEG, yet scored lower than the national average in CCPNRE and SDGP (Note: the national average value of each indicator is 0).

According to Fig. 9.12, Shenyang surpassed the national average in 5 of Second-Class Indicators in 2010, which were GGEI, PII, SII, TII and II; yet ranked lower than the national average in 4 indicators including RAECI, EPCCI, GII and EMI.

9.6.2 Changes in Shenyang's GDI Rankings 2009–2010

According to Table 9.11, in First-Class Indicators, Shenyang rose by 2 places by GDEG and 1 place in CCPNRE. It dropped by 1 place in SDGP. In Second-Class Indicators, Shenyang experienced a dive by II, 10 places lower than that in 2009.

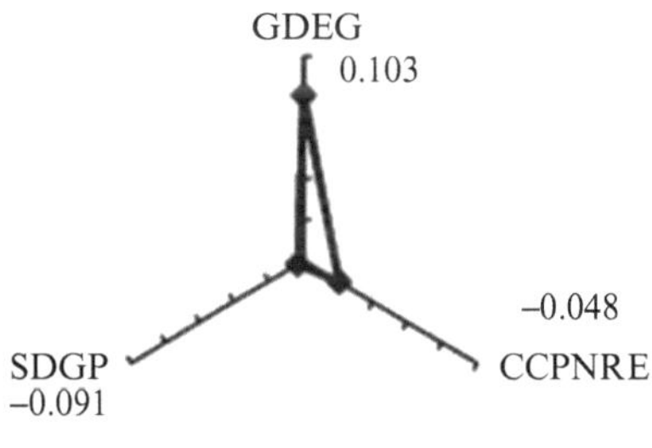

Fig. 9.11 Scores of Shenyang by First-Class Indicators

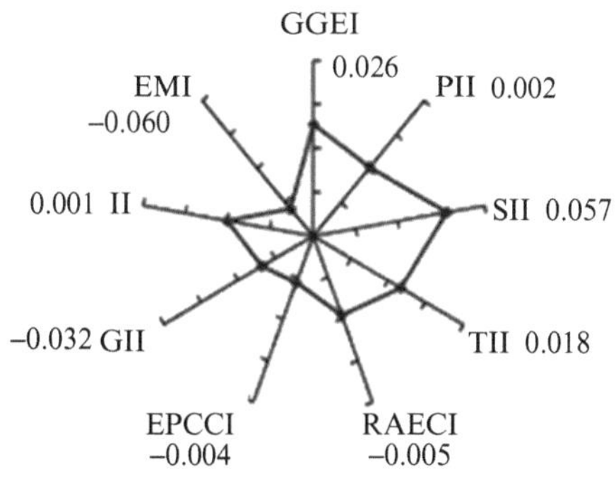

Fig. 9.12 Scores of Shenyang by Second-Class Indicators

Table 9.11 Changes in Shenyang's rankings by First-Class and Second-Class Indicators, 2009–2010

Indicator	2010	2009	Difference	Indicator	2010	2009	Difference
GDI	21	18	−3				
GDEG	4	6	2	RAECI	23	24	1
GGEI	13	12	−1	EPCCI	21	22	1
PII	8	9	1	SDGP	27	26	−1
SII	3	3	0	GII	27	27	0
TII	11	10	−1	II	23	13	−10
CCPNRE	22	23	1	EMI	31	31	0

Note: A positive value in "Difference" means a rise in ranking

It dropped by 1 place in GGEI and TII. It rose by 1 place in PII, RAECI, and EPCCI. Other 3 Second-Class Indicators remained the same as they were in 2009.

To further explain the causes of the changes in the rankings by First- and Second-Class Indicators, we put the Third-Class Indicators where a change of more than 3 places occurred from 2009 to 2010 as follows in Table 9.12. Compared with those in 2009, Shenyang both out- and underperformed in ranking in 2010. It rose by 11, 6, 6, 5, 4 and 3 places by Percentage of days with respirable suspended particulates as the principal pollutants in a year, Ratio of the investment in industrial pollution control to GDP, Industrial SO_2 removal rate, Nitrogen oxide emissions per unit of GDP, Public buses per 10,000 urban residents and Ammonia/nitrogen emissions per capita respectively; it dropped by 7 places by Treatment rate of urban household wastewater compared with that in 2009. It dropped by 4 places by Labor productivity of the tertiary sector, Ratio of the spending on science, education, culture, and public health to government expenditure and Industrial wastewater COD removal rate, 3 places in Energy consumption per unit of GDP and Labor productivity of the secondary sector. The indicators which experienced a rise are of similar number with those which experienced a drop.

Table 9.12 Third-Class Indicators where changes over 3 places occurred by Shenyang, 2009–2010

	Original data for 2009 and 2010			Change in ranking		
Third-Class Indicator	2010	2009	Unit	2010	2009	Difference
Energy consumption per unit of GDP	0.28	0.28	Ton per 10,000 yuan	7	4	−3
Nitrogen oxide emissions per unit of GDP	22.52	25.92	Ton per 100 million yuan	7	12	5
Labor productivity of the secondary sector	27.37	24.12	10,000 yuan per capita	5	2	−3
Labor productivity of the tertiary sector	13.60	12.96	10,000 yuan per capita	10	6	−4
Ammonia/nitrogen emissions per capita	12.46	13.12	Ton per 10,000 persons	23	26	3
Percentage of days with respirable suspended particulates as the principal pollutants in a year	75.07	86.03	%	19	30	11
Ratio of the investment in industrial pollution control to GDP	0.01	0.01	%	30	36	6
Ratio of the spending on science, education, culture, and public health to government expenditure	20.98	27.52	%	18	14	−4
Treatment rate of urban household wastewater	73.61	78.59	%	34	27	−7
Public buses per 10,000 urban residents	9.73	9.92		30	34	4
Industrial SO_2 removal rate	53.16	34.89	%	24	30	6
Industrial wastewater COD removal rate	82.71	86.14	%	20	16	−4

Note: A positive value in "Difference" means a rise in ranking

Green development checkup-Dalian

No.	Indicator	Unit	Scope	Attribute	2010 average of 38 cities	2010 figure	2009 figure	2010 ranking	2009 ranking	Change in ranking	Source of 2010 data	Chernoff face
1	GDP per capita	Yuan	Whole city	Positive	56,231.37	77,704	70,781.00	6	6	0	Regional Economy; City	
2	Energy consumption per unit of GDP	Ton per 10,000 yuan	Whole city	Negative	0.81	0.36	0.44	11	11	0	Regional Economy; City	
3	Electricity consumption per capita in urban areas	kWh per capita	Whole city	Negative	580.70	401.24	366.77	13	13	0	City	
4	CO_2 emissions per unit of GDP			Negative	No data			N/A	N/A	N/A		
5	SO_2 emissions per unit of GDP	Ton per 100 million yuan	Whole city	Negative	43.72	22.28	24.02	12	9	−3	Regional Economy; Environment Annual Report	☹
6	COD emissions per unit of GDP	Ton per 100 million yuan	Whole city	Negative	24.81	11.12	11.88	7	6	−1	Regional Economy; Environment Annual Report	☹
7	Nitrogen oxide emissions per unit of GDP	Ton per 100 million yuan	Whole city	Negative	41.71	24.30	28.35	10	16	6	Regional Economy; Environment Annual Report	☺
8	Ammonia/nitrogen emissions per unit of GDP	Ton per 100 million yuan	Whole city	Negative	2.63	1.25	1.74	9	11	2	Regional Economy; Environment Annual Report	☺
9	Labor productivity of the primary sector	10,000 yuan per capita	Whole city	Positive	3.03	5.03	4.53	5	3	−2	Regional Economy	☹
10	Labor productivity of the secondary sector	10,000 yuan per capita	Whole city	Positive	17.91	21.18	17.79	6	4	−2	Regional Economy	☹
11	Water consumption per unit of value added created by industrial enterprises	10,000 tons per 10,000 yuan	Whole city	Negative	0.03	0.01	0.01	6	6	0	Regional Economy; Environment Annual Report	

12	Energy consumption per unit of value added created by industrial enterprises			Negative	No data			N/A	N/A	N/A		
13	Utilization rate industrial solid waste	%	Whole city	Positive	85.58	94.70	94.90	15	13	−2	Environment Annual Report	☹
14	Recycling rate of industrial water	%	Whole city	Positive	83.81	65.48	55.18	34	36	2	Environment Annual Report	☺
15	Labor productivity of the tertiary sector	10,000 yuan per capita	Whole city	Positive	11.40	10.93	10.13	20	16	−4	Regional Economy	☹
16	Proportion of value added of tertiary sector in GDP	%	Whole city	Positive	47.97	42.43	43.89	28	29	1	City	☺
17	Proportion of tertiary sector employees in the total employed population	%	Whole city	Positive	46.44	51.34	50.59	6	8	2	Regional Economy	☺
18	Water resources per capita	m^3 per capita	Whole city	Positive	1,026.43	669.46	240.94	17	30	13	Environment Annual Report; City	☺
19	CO_2 emissions per unit of land area			Negative	No data			N/A	N/A	N/A		
20	CO_2 emissions per capita			Negative	No data			N/A	N/A	N/A		
21	SO_2 emissions per unit of land area	Ton per km^2	Whole city	Negative	11.64	8.05	7.53	17	16	−1	Environment Annual Report; City	☹
22	SO_2 emissions per capita	Ton per 10,000 persons	Whole city	Negative	216.46	172.81	162.20	20	19	−1	Environment Annual Report; City	☹
23	COD emissions per unit of land area	Ton per km^2	Whole city	Negative	7.83	4.02	3.73	12	10	−2	Environment Annual Report; City	☹
24	COD emissions per capita	Ton per 10,000 persons	Whole city	Negative	118.15	86.23	80.20	16	12	−4	Environment Annual Report; City	☹
25	Nitrogen oxides emissions per unit of land area	Ton per km^2	Whole city	Negative	15.00	8.78	8.89	20	23	3	Environment Annual Report; City	☹
26	Nitrogen oxides emissions per capita	Ton per 10,000 persons	Whole city	Negative	237.70	188.48	191.40	21	23	2	Environment Annual Report; City	☺

(continued)

(continued)

No.	Indicator	Unit	Scope	Attribute	2010 average of 38 cities	2010 figure	2009 figure	2010 ranking	2009 ranking	Change in ranking	Source of 2010 data	Chernoff face
27	Ammonia/nitrogen emissions per unit of land area	Ton per km^2	Whole city	Negative	0.86	0.45	0.55	17	17	0	Environment Annual Report; City	
28	Ammonia/nitrogen emissions per capita	Ton per 10,000 persons	Whole city	Negative	12.63	9.70	11.74	16	22	6	Environment Annual Report; City	☺
29	Percentage of the days with air quality at or over level II in a year	%	District	Positive	89.20	98.90	98.35	5	8	3	MEP Data	☺
30	Percentage of days with respirable suspended particulates as the principal pollutants in a year	%	District	Negative	70.81	41.37	49.59	4	6	2	MEP Data	☺
31	Ratio of environmental spending to government expenditure	%	Whole city	Positive	3.13	1.83	1.59	30	28	−2	China Statistics; City	☹
32	Ratio of the investment in industrial pollution control to GDP	%	Whole city	Positive	0.08	0.02	0.03	26	26	0	Environment Annual Report; Regional Economy	
33	Ratio of the spending on science, education, culture, and public health to government expenditure	%	Whole city	Positive	21.08	18.83	22.75	27	35	8	China Statistics; City; Regional Economy	☺
34	Area of green land per capita in urban areas		District	Positive	59.39	60.00	40.37	8	18	10	City	☺
35	Green coverage of urban built-in areas	%	District	Positive	40.04	45.17	44.75	3	4	1	Urban Construction	☺
36	Coverage of water supply	%	District	Positive	98.82	100.00	100.00	1	1	0	Urban Construction	
37	Treatment rate of urban household wastewater	%	District	Positive	86.16	90.40	90.40	17	9	−8	Urban Construction	☹
38	Harmless treatment of urban household waste	%	District	Positive	94.38	100.00	100.00	1	1	0	Urban Construction	

39	Public buses per 10,000 urban residents		District	Positive	15.61	15.43	15.60	14	8	−6	City	☹
40	Industrial SO_2 removal rate	%	Whole city	Positive	57.30	75.71	74.76	6	5	−1	Environment Annual Report	☹
41	Industrial wastewater COD removal rate	%	Whole city	Positive	77.86	76.38	64.45	29	32	3	Environment Annual Report	☺
42	Industrial nitrogen oxide removal rate	%	Whole city	Positive	5.29	0.19	0.27	28	26	−2	Environment Annual Report	☹
43	Industrial waste water ammonia/nitrogen removal rate	%	Whole city	Positive	67.89	97.43	96.21	2	3	1	Environment Annual Report	☺

Note:
Regional Economy: *China Regional Economy Statistical Yearbook 2011*
City: *China City Statistical Yearbook 2011*
China Statistics: *China Statistical Yearbook 2011*
Urban Construction: *China Urban Construction Statistical Yearbook 2010*
Environment Annual Report: *China Environment Annual Report 2010*
Environmental Yearbook: *China Environmental Statistical Yearbook 2011*
MEP Data: Ministry of Environmental Protection Data Center

9.7 Brief Analysis of Green Development in Dalian

Dalian ranked 7th among the 38 participating cities by GDI according to 2010 data, 1 place higher over 2009 (Dalian ranked 8th in 2009). Following is a brief analysis of its score by each indicator and their changes from 2009 to 2010.

9.7.1 *Dalian's 2010 Scores by GDI*

Dalian scored 0.191 in 2010. From the three First-Class Indicators including GDEG, CCPNRE, and SDGP as shown in Fig. 9.13, Dalian got a relatively balanced score in each of the three indicators, all obviously higher than the national average (Note: the national average value of each indicator is 0).

According to Fig. 9.14, Dalian surpassed the national average in all other 7 of Second-Class Indicators in 2010 except RAECI and GII.

9.7.2 *Changes in Dalian's GDI Rankings 2009–2010*

According to Table 9.13, in First-Class Indicators, Daliang rose by 3 places in GDEG and CCPNRE, and 2 places in Support Degree of Government Policy.

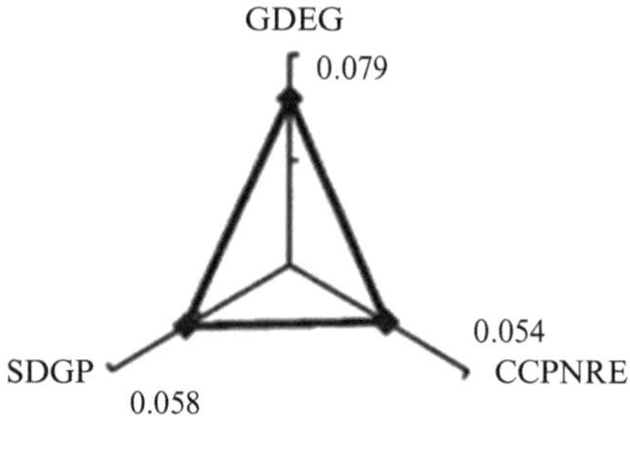

Fig. 9.13 Scores of Dalian by First-Class Indicators

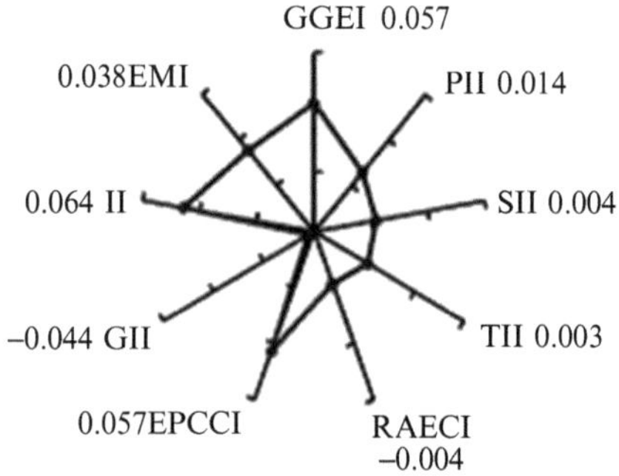

Fig. 9.14 Scores of Dalian by Second-Class Indicators

Table 9.13 Changes in Dalian's rankings by First-Class and Second-Class Indicators, 2009–2010

Indicator	2010	2009	Difference	Indicator	2010	2009	Difference
GDI	7	8	1				
GDEG	7	10	3	RAECI	17	30	13
GGEI	7	9	2	EPCCI	8	11	3
PII	3	3	0	SDGP	14	16	2
SII	16	28	12	GII	34	37	3
TII	15	15	0	II	4	3	−1
CCPNRE	9	12	3	EMI	11	21	10

Note: A positive value in "Difference" means a rise in ranking

In Second-Class Indicators, Dalian dropped by 1 place in II. It remained unchanged in PII and TII. Other 6 Second-Class Indicators ranked higher than those in 2009. It rose by 13, 12 and 10 places respectively in RAECI, SII and EMI. It rose by 3 places in EPCCI and GII. It rose by 2 places in GGEI. Overall, Dalian's rankings in 2010 increased a lot.

To further explain the causes of the changes in the rankings by First- and Second-Class Indicators, we put the Third-Class Indicators where a change of more than 3 places occurred from 2009 to 2010 as follows in Table 9.14. Compared with those in 2009, Dalian generally rose in Third-Class Indicators ranking. Those that risen by over 3 places include Nitrogen oxide emissions per unit of GDP, Water resources per capita, Nitrogen oxides emissions per unit of land area, Ammonia/nitrogen emissions per capita, Percentage of the days with air quality at or over level II in a year, Ratio of the spending on science, education, culture, and public health to government expenditure, Area of green land per capita in urban areas and Industrial wastewater COD removal rate, etc. It dropped by 8, 6, 4, 4 and 3 places in Treatment rate of urban household wastewater, Public buses per 10,000 urban residents, Labor productivity of the tertiary sector, COD emissions per capita and SO_2 emissions per unit of GDP respectively.

Table 9.14 Third-Class Indicators where changes over 3 places occurred by Dalian, 2009–2010

	Original data for 2009 and 2010			Change in ranking		
Third-Class Indicator	2010	2009	Unit	2010	2009	Difference
SO_2 emissions per unit of GDP	22.28	24.02	Ton per 100 million yuan	12	9	−3
Nitrogen oxide emissions per unit of GDP	24.30	28.35	Ton per 100 million yuan	10	16	6
Labor productivity of the tertiary sector	10.93	10.13	10,000 yuan per capita	20	16	−4
Water resources per capita	669.46	240.94	m^3 per capita	17	30	13
COD emissions per capita	86.23	80.20	Ton per 10,000 persons	16	12	−4
Nitrogen oxides emissions per unit of land area	8.78	8.89	Ton per km^2	20	23	3
Ammonia/nitrogen emissions per capita	9.70	11.74	Ton per 10,000 persons	16	22	6
Percentage of the days with air quality at or over level II in a year	98.90	98.35	%	5	8	3
Ratio of the spending on science, education, culture, and public health to government expenditure	18.83	22.75	%	27	35	8
Area of green land per capita in urban areas	60.00	40.37		8	18	10
Treatment rate of urban household wastewater	90.40	90.40	%	17	9	−8
Public buses per 10,000 urban residents	15.43	15.60		14	8	−6
Industrial wastewater COD removal rate	76.38	64.45	%	29	32	3

Note: A positive value in "Difference" means a rise in ranking

Green development checkup-Changchun

No.	Indicator	Unit	Scope	Attribute	2010 average of 38 cities	2010 figure	2009 figure	2010 ranking	2009 ranking	Change in ranking	Source of 2010 data	Chernoff face
1	GDP per capita	Yuan	Whole city	Positive	56,231.37	43,936	37,753.00	25	27	2	Regional Economy; City	☺
2	Energy consumption per unit of GDP	Ton per 10,000 yuan	Whole city	Negative	0.81	0.33	0.37	10	10	0	Regional Economy; City	
3	Electricity consumption per capita in urban areas	kWh per capita	Whole city	Negative	580.70	304.32	267.48	6	5	−1	City	☹
4	CO_2 emissions per unit of GDP			Negative	No data			N/A	N/A	N/A		
5	SO_2 emissions per unit of GDP	Ton per 100 million yuan	Whole city	Negative	43.72	23.90	25.68	15	12	−3	Regional Economy; Environment Annual Report	☹
6	COD emissions per unit of GDP	Ton per 100 million yuan	Whole city	Negative	24.81	20.27	22.39	19	19	0	Regional Economy; Environment Annual Report	
7	Nitrogen oxide emissions per unit of GDP	Ton per 100 million yuan	Whole city	Negative	41.71	47.27	24.36	26	11	−15	Regional Economy; Environment Annual Report	☹
8	Ammonia/nitrogen emissions per unit of GDP	Ton per 100 million yuan	Whole city	Negative	2.63	1.88	2.37	17	19	2	Regional Economy; Environment Annual Report	☺
9	Labor productivity of the primary sector	10,000 yuan per capita	Whole city	Positive	3.03	1.99	1.78	23	21	−2	Regional Economy	☹
10	Labor productivity of the secondary sector	10,000 yuan per capita	Whole city	Positive	17.91	18.96	16.55	7	5	−2	Regional Economy	☹
11	Water consumption per unit of value added created by industrial enterprises	10,000 tons per 10,000 yuan	Whole city	Negative	0.03	0.01	0.01	12	9	−3	Regional Economy; Environment Annual Report	☹
12	Energy consumption per unit of value added created by industrial enterprises			Negative	No data			N/A	N/A	N/A		
13	Utilization rate industrial solid waste	%	Whole city	Positive	85.58	99.60	99.50	2	1	−1	Environment Annual Report	☹

(continued)

(continued)

No.	Indicator	Unit	Scope	Attribute	2010 average of 38 cities	2010 figure	2009 figure	2010 ranking	2009 ranking	Change in ranking	Source of 2010 data	Chernoff face
14	Recycling rate of industrial water	%	Whole city	Positive	83.81	91.81	88.47	16	18	2	Environment Annual Report	☺
15	Labor productivity of the tertiary sector	10,000 yuan per capita	Whole city	Positive	11.40	10.53	9.50	21	18	−3	Regional Economy	☹
16	Proportion of value added of tertiary sector in GDP	%	Whole city	Positive	47.97	40.74	41.49	33	32	−1	City	☹
17	Proportion of tertiary sector employees in the total employed population	%	Whole city	Positive	46.44	37.73	36.53	32	33	1	Regional Economy	☺
18	Water resources per capita	m^3 per capita	Whole city	Positive	1,026.43	584.34	362.99	21	25	4	Environment Annual Report; City	☺
19	CO_2 emissions per unit of land area			Negative	No data			N/A	N/A	N/A		
20	CO_2 emissions per capita			Negative	No data			N/A	N/A	N/A		
21	SO_2 emissions per unit of land area	Ton per km^2	Whole city	Negative	11.64	3.66	3.41	5	5	0	Environment Annual Report; City	
22	SO_2 emissions per capita	Ton per 10,000 persons	Whole city	Negative	216.46	99.59	93.19	8	7	−1	Environment Annual Report; City	☹
23	COD emissions per unit of land area	Ton per km^2	Whole city	Negative	7.83	3.11	2.97	8	8	0	Environment Annual Report; City	
24	COD emissions per capita	Ton per 10,000 persons	Whole city	Negative	118.15	84.46	81.24	15	14	−1	Environment Annual Report; City	☹
25	Nitrogen oxides emissions per unit of land area	Ton per km^2	Whole city	Negative	15.00	7.24	3.24	13	8	−5	Environment Annual Report; City	☹
26	Nitrogen oxides emissions per capita	Ton per 10,000 persons	Whole city	Negative	237.70	196.96	88.40	22	8	−14	Environment Annual Report; City	☹
27	Ammonia/nitrogen emissions per unit of land area	Ton per km^2	Whole city	Negative	0.86	0.29	0.31	6	7	1	Environment Annual Report; City	☺
28	Ammonia/nitrogen emissions per capita	Ton per 10,000 persons	Whole city	Negative	12.63	7.84	8.60	10	10	0	Environment Annual Report; City	
29	Percentage of the days with air quality at or over level II in a year	%	District	Positive	89.20	93.41	93.13	14	14	0	MEP Data	
30	Percentage of days with respirable suspended particulates as the principal pollutants in a year	%	District	Negative	70.81	87.40	79.18	32	21	−11	MEP Data	☹

31	Ratio of environmental spending to government expenditure	%	Whole city	Positive	3.13	3.97	2.08	7	20	13	China Statistics; City	☺
32	Ratio of the investment in industrial pollution control to GDP	%	Whole city	Positive	0.08	0.03	0.08	20	16	−4	Environment Annual Report; Regional Economy	☹
33	Ratio of the spending on science, education, culture, and public health to government expenditure	%	Whole city	Positive	21.08	18.52	25.91	29	17	−12	China Statistics; City; Regional Economy	☹
34	Area of green land per capita in urban areas		District	Positive	59.39	37.00	31.93	20	26	6	City	☺
35	Green coverage of urban built-in areas	%	District	Positive	40.04	38.58	36.11	24	30	6	Urban Construction	☺
36	Coverage of water supply	%	District	Positive	98.82	99.46	99.30	30	26	−4	Urban Construction	☹
37	Treatment rate of urban household wastewater	%	District	Positive	86.16	89.46	88.71	20	12	−8	Urban Construction	☹
38	Harmless treatment of urban household waste	%	District	Positive	94.38	87.45	76.14	31	34	3	Urban Construction	☺
39	Public buses per 10,000 urban residents		District	Positive	15.61	12.22	12.20	23	26	3	City	☺
40	Industrial SO_2 removal rate	%	Whole city	Positive	57.30	36.75	21.32	32	35	3	Environment Annual Report	☺
41	Industrial wastewater COD removal rate	%	Whole city	Positive	77.86	42.87	47.65	36	37	1	Environment Annual Report	☺
42	Industrial nitrogen oxide removal rate	%	Whole city	Positive	5.29	0.00	0.00	31	29	−2	Environment Annual Report	☹
43	Industrial waste water ammonia/nitrogen removal rate	%	Whole city	Positive	67.89	48.30	49.04	32	27	−5	Environment Annual Report	☹

Note:
Regional Economy: *China Regional Economy Statistical Yearbook 2011*
City: *China City Statistical Yearbook 2011*
China Statistics: *China Statistical Yearbook 2011*
Urban Construction: *China Urban Construction Statistical Yearbook 2010*
Environment Annual Report: *China Environment Annual Report 2010*
Environmental Yearbook: *China Environmental Statistical Yearbook 2011*
MEP Data: Ministry of Environmental Protection Data Center

9.8 Brief Analysis of Green Development in Changchun

Changchun ranked 29th among the 38 participating cities by GDI according to 2010 data, 2 places lower over 2009 (Changchun ranked 27th in 2009). Following is a brief analysis of its score by each indicator and their changes from 2009 to 2010.

9.8.1 *Changchun's 2010 Scores by GDI*

Changchun scored −0.164 in 2010. From the three First-Class Indicators including GDEG, CCPNRE, and SDGP as shown in Fig. 9.15, Changchun scored lower than national average in terms of GDEG and SDGP, especially the later which scored −0.157; by GDEG Changchun was similar to the national average (Note: the national average value of each indicator is 0).

According to Fig. 9.16, Changchun surpassed the national average only in SII among other Second-Class Indicators in 2010, which scored 0.035. As to other indicators Changchun scored lower than the national average.

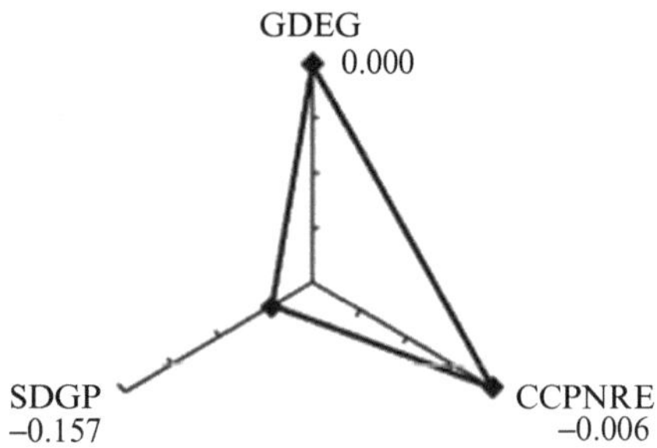

Fig. 9.15 Scores of Changchun by First-Class Indicators

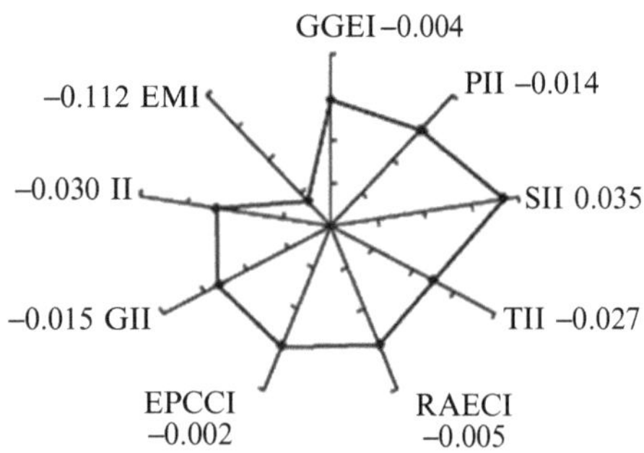

Fig. 9.16 Scores of Changchun by Second-Class Indicators

Table 9.15 Changes in Changchun's rankings by First-Class and Second-Class Indicators, 2009–2010

Indicator	2010	2009	Difference	Indicator	2010	2009	Difference
GDI	29	27	−2				
GDEG	19	15	−4	RAECI	21	25	4
GGEI	20	15	−5	EPCCI	15	9	−6
PII	22	21	−1	SDGP	34	35	1
SII	5	4	−1	GII	18	22	4
TII	32	31	−1	II	29	29	0
CCPNRE	15	10	−5	EMI	37	37	0

Note: A positive value in "Difference" means a rise in ranking

9.8.2 Changes in Changchun's GDI Rankings 2009–2010

According to Table 9.15, in First-Class Indicators, Changchun fell by 5 and 4 places in CCPNRE and GDEG and rose by 1 place in SDGP. In Second-Class Indicators, Changchun only rose by 4 places in RAECI and GII, and it ranked same as those in 2009 in II and EMI. In Third-Class Indicators, Changchun fell by varying degrees, 6 and 5 places in terms of EPCCI and GGEI, and 1 place respectively in PII, SII and TII.

To further explain the causes of the changes in the rankings by First- and Second-Class Indicators, we put the Third-Class Indicators where a change of more than 3 places occurred from 2009 to 2010 as follows in Table 9.16. Compared with those in 2009, Changchun both out- and underperformed in ranking in 2010, while the more obvious trend is underperforming compared with the previous year. It dropped by over 10 places by Nitrogen oxide emissions per unit of GDP, Nitrogen oxides emissions per capita, Ratio of the spending on science, education, culture, and public health to government expenditure and Percentage of days with respirable suspended particulates as the principal pollutants in a year, 15, 14, 12 and 11 places respectively. It dropped by 8 places by Treatment rate of urban household waste water, 5 places in Nitrogen oxides emissions per unit of land area and Industrial waste water ammonia/nitrogen removal rate, 4 in Ratio of the investment in industrial pollution control to GDP and Coverage of water supply, 3 in SO_2 emissions per unit of GDP, Water consumption per unit of value added created by industrial enterprises and Labor productivity of the tertiary sector. There were only 7 indicators in which Changchun rose by over 3 places in ranking.

Table 9.16 Third-Class Indicators where changes over 3 places occurred by Changchun, 2009–2010

	Original data for 2009 and 2010			Change in ranking		
Third-Class Indicator	2010	2009	Unit	2010	2009	Difference
SO_2 emissions per unit of GDP	23.90	25.68	Ton per 100 million yuan	15	12	−3
Nitrogen oxide emissions per unit of GDP	47.27	24.36	Ton per 100 million yuan	26	11	−15
Water consumption per unit of value added created by industrial enterprises	0.01	0.01	10,000 tons per 10,000 yuan	12	9	−3
Labor productivity of the tertiary sector	10.53	9.50	10,000 yuan per capita	21	18	−3
Water resources per capita	584.34	362.99	m^3 per capita	21	25	4
Nitrogen oxides emissions per unit of land area	7.24	3.24	Ton per km^2	13	8	−5
Nitrogen oxides emissions per capita	196.96	88.40	Ton per 10,000 persons	22	8	−14
Percentage of days with respirable suspended particulates as the principal pollutants in a year	87.40	79.18	%	32	21	−11
Ratio of environmental spending to government expenditure	3.97	2.08	%	7	20	13
Ratio of the investment in industrial pollution control to GDP	0.03	0.08	%	20	16	−4
Ratio of the spending on science, education, culture, and public health to government expenditure	18.52	25.91	%	29	17	−12
Area of green land per capita in urban areas	37.00	31.93		20	26	6
Green coverage of urban built-in areas	38.58	36.11	%	24	30	6
Coverage of water supply	99.46	99.30	%	30	26	−4
Treatment rate of urban household wastewater	89.46	88.71	%	20	12	−8
Harmless treatment of urban household waste	87.45	76.14	%	31	34	3
Public buses per 10,000 urban residents	12.22	12.20		23	26	3
Industrial SO_2 removal rate	36.75	21.32	%	32	35	3
Industrial waste water ammonia/nitrogen removal rate	48.30	49.04	%	32	27	−5

Note: A positive value in "Difference" means a rise in ranking

Green development checkup-Harbin

No.	Indicator	Unit	Scope	Attribute	2010 average of 38 cities	2010 figure	2009 figure	2010 ranking	2009 ranking	Change in ranking	Source of 2010 data	Chernoff face
1	GDP per capita	Yuan	Whole city	Positive	56,231.37	36,951	32,053.00	31	30	−1	Regional Economy; City	☹
2	Energy consumption per unit of GDP	Ton per 10,000 yuan	Whole city	Negative	0.81	1.15	1.24	29	28	−1	Regional Economy; City	☹
3	Electricity consumption per capita in urban areas	kWh per capita	Whole city	Negative	580.70	224.24	213.80	3	3	0	City	
4	CO_2 emissions per unit of GDP			Negative	No data			N/A	N/A	N/A		
5	SO_2 emissions per unit of GDP	Ton per 100 million yuan	Whole city	Negative	43.72	22.19	24.59	11	10	−1	Regional Economy; Environment Annual Report	☹
6	COD emissions per unit of GDP	Ton per 100 million yuan	Whole city	Negative	24.81	22.98	26.53	22	21	−1	Regional Economy; Environment Annual Report	☹
7	Nitrogen oxide emissions per unit of GDP	Ton per 100 million yuan	Whole city	Negative	41.71	25.21	28.98	14	17	3	Regional Economy; Environment Annual Report	☺
8	Ammonia/nitrogen emissions per unit of GDP	Ton per 100 million yuan	Whole city	Negative	2.63	1.80	2.51	16	21	5	Regional Economy; Environment Annual Report	☺
9	Labor productivity of the primary sector	10,000 yuan per capita	Whole city	Positive	3.03	2.70	2.60	12	8	−4	Regional Economy	☹
10	Labor productivity of the secondary sector	10,000 yuan per capita	Whole city	Positive	17.91	12.28	9.50	24	27	3	Regional Economy	☺
11	Water consumption per unit of value added created by industrial enterprises	10,000 tons per 10,000 yuan	Whole city	Negative	0.03	0.02	0.03	21	25	4	Regional Economy; Environment Annual Report	☺
12	Energy consumption per unit of value added created by industrial enterprises			Negative	No data			N/A	N/A	N/A		
13	Utilization rate industrial solid waste	%	Whole city	Positive	85.58	89.70	76.30	22	30	8	Environment Annual Report	☺
14	Recycling rate of industrial water	%	Whole city	Positive	83.81	95.94	95.93	5	5	0	Environment Annual Report	

(continued)

(continued)

No.	Indicator	Unit	Scope	Attribute	2010 average of 38 cities	2010 figure	2009 figure	2010 ranking	2009 ranking	Change in ranking	Source of 2010 data	Chernoff face
15	Labor productivity of the tertiary sector	10,000 yuan per capita	Whole city	Positive	11.40	8.90	8.24	24	21	−3	Regional Economy	☹
16	Proportion of value added of tertiary sector in GDP	%	Whole city	Positive	47.97	50.96	51.28	14	15	1	City	☺
17	Proportion of tertiary sector employees in the total employed population	%	Whole city	Positive	46.44	46.14	42.15	18	26	8	Regional Economy	☺
18	Water resources per capita	m^3 per capita	Whole city	Positive	1,026.43	1,504.91	675.57	8	16	8	Environment Annual Report; City	☺
19	CO_2 emissions per unit of land area			Negative	No data			N/A	N/A	N/A		
20	CO_2 emissions per capita			Negative	No data			N/A	N/A	N/A		
21	SO_2 emissions per unit of land area	Ton per km^2	Whole city	Negative	11.64	1.44	1.40	2	2	0	Environment Annual Report; City	
22	SO_2 emissions per capita	Ton per 10,000 persons	Whole city	Negative	216.46	76.95	74.87	4	5	1	Environment Annual Report; City	☺
23	COD emissions per unit of land area	Ton per km^2	Whole city	Negative	7.83	1.49	1.51	3	3	0	Environment Annual Report; City	
24	COD emissions per capita	Ton per 10,000 persons	Whole city	Negative	118.15	79.68	80.76	14	13	−1	Environment Annual Report; City	☹
25	Nitrogen oxides emissions per unit of land area	Ton per km^2	Whole city	Negative	15.00	1.63	1.65	1	1	0	Environment Annual Report; City	
26	Nitrogen oxides emissions per capita	Ton per 10,000 persons	Whole city	Negative	237.70	87.42	88.23	5	7	2	Environment Annual Report; City	☺
27	Ammonia/nitrogen emissions per unit of land area	Ton per km^2	Whole city	Negative	0.86	0.12	0.14	3	3	0	Environment Annual Report; City	
28	Ammonia/nitrogen emissions per capita	Ton per 10,000 persons	Whole city	Negative	12.63	6.24	7.63	7	6	−1	Environment Annual Report; City	☹
29	Percentage of the days with air quality at or over level II in a year	%	District	Positive	89.20	85.71	85.16	26	28	2	MEP Data	☺
30	Percentage of days with respirable suspended particulates as the principal pollutants in a year	%	District	Negative	70.81	90.96	82.74	35	25	−10	MEP Data	☹

31	Ratio of environmental spending to government expenditure	%	Whole city	Positive	3.13	3.27	2.08	16	21	5	China Statistics; City	☺
32	Ratio of the investment in industrial pollution control to GDP	%	Whole city	Positive	0.08	0.00	0.01	38	35	−3	Environment Annual Report; Regional Economy	☹
33	Ratio of the spending on science, education, culture, and public health to government expenditure	%	Whole city	Positive	21.08	19.70	30.78	23	6	−17	China Statistics; City; Regional Economy	☹
34	Area of green land per capita in urban areas		District	Positive	59.39	27.00	25.65	30	32	2	City	☺
35	Green coverage of urban built-in areas	%	District	Positive	40.04	38.38	39.11	25	19	−6	Urban Construction	☹
36	Coverage of water supply	%	District	Positive	98.82	89.17	85.15	38	38	0	Urban Construction	
37	Treatment rate of urban household wastewater	%	District	Positive	86.16	57.18	73.94	37	29	−8	Urban Construction	☹
38	Harmless treatment of urban household waste	%	District	Positive	94.38	82.91	53.93	34	38	4	Urban Construction	☺
39	Public buses per 10,000 urban residents		District	Positive	15.61	10.96	10.55	28	31	3	City	☺
40	Industrial SO_2 removal rate	%	Whole city	Positive	57.30	35.62	34.63	33	31	−2	Environment Annual Report	☹
41	Industrial wastewater COD removal rate	%	Whole city	Positive	77.86	92.10	85.76	6	17	11	Environment Annual Report	☺
42	Industrial nitrogen oxide removal rate	%	Whole city	Positive	5.29	15.60	14.97	4	8	4	Environment Annual Report	☺
43	Industrial waste water ammonia/nitrogen removal rate	%	Whole city	Positive	67.89	98.97	97.40	1	2	1	Environment Annual Report	☺

Note:
Regional Economy: *China Regional Economy Statistical Yearbook 2011*
City: *China City Statistical Yearbook 2011*
China Statistics: *China Statistical Yearbook 2011*
Urban Construction: *China Urban Construction Statistical Yearbook 2010*
Environment Annual Report: *China Environment Annual Report 2010*
Environmental Yearbook: *China Environmental Statistical Yearbook 2011*
MEP Data: Ministry of Environmental Protection Data Center

9.9 Brief Analysis of Green Development in Harbin

Harbin ranked 15th among the 38 participating cities by GDI according to 2010 data, 7 places higher over 2009 (Harbin ranked 22nd in 2009). Following is a brief analysis of its score by each indicator and their changes from 2009 to 2010.

9.9.1 *Harbin's 2010 Scores by GDI*

Harbin scored 0.003 in 2010. From the three First-Class Indicators including GDEG, CCPNRE, and SDGP as shown in Fig. 9.17, Harbin showed some advantages in terms of CCPNRE compared with the national average, yet scored lower than the national average in SDGP (Note: the national average value of each indicator is 0).

According to Fig. 9.18, Harbin surpassed the national average in 4 of Second-Class Indicators in 2010, which were SII, RAECI, EPCCI and EMI; it scored lower than the national average by TII, GII and II; and it was about the same level with the national average in GGEI and PII.

9.9.2 *Changes in Harbin's GDI Rankings 2009–2010*

According to Table 9.17, in First-Class Indicators, the most obvious change occurred in GDEG, where Harbin rose by 4 places in ranking and 2 in CCPNRE;

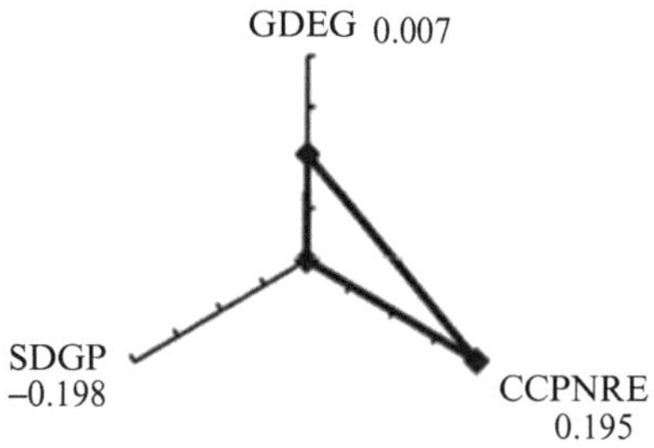

Fig. 9.17 Scores of Harbin by First-Class Indicators

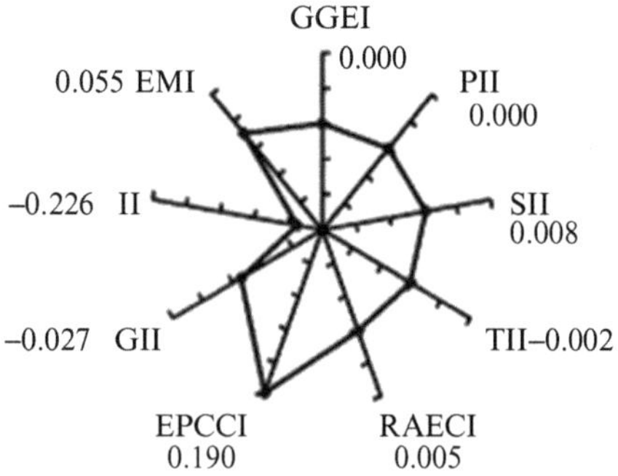

Fig. 9.18 Scores of Harbin by Second-Class Indicators

Table 9.17 Changes in Harbin's rankings by First-Class and Second-Class Indicators, 2009–2010

Indicator	2010	2009	Difference	Indicator	2010	2009	Difference
GDI	15	22	7				
GDEG	16	20	4	RAECI	8	16	8
GGEI	16	23	7	EPCCI	4	6	2
PII	11	8	−3	SDGP	37	36	−1
SII	12	24	12	GII	24	18	−6
TII	18	21	3	II	37	38	1
CCPNRE	4	6	2	EMI	7	12	5

Note: A positive value in "Difference" means a rise in ranking

it fell by 1 place in SDGP. In Second-Class Indicators, Harbin rose by 12, 8, 7, 5, 3, and 2 places and 1 place in SII, RAECI, GGEI, EMI, TII, EPCCI and II respectively; it fell by 6 and 3 places respectively in GII and PII.

To further explain the causes of the changes in the rankings by First- and Second-Class Indicators, we put the Third-Class Indicators where a change of more than 3 places occurred from 2009 to 2010 as follows in Table 9.18. Compared with those in 2009, Harbin had 12 indicators which enjoyed a rise in ranking, among which Industrial wastewater COD removal rate rose by 11 places, Utilization rate industrial solid waste, Water resources per capita and Proportion of tertiary sector employees in the total employed population rose by 8 places; among the 7 indicators which fell in ranking, Ratio of the spending on science, education, culture, and public health to government expenditure, Percentage of days with respirable suspended particulates as the principal pollutants in a year, Treatment rate of urban household wastewater and Green coverage of urban built-in areas suffered a dramatic fall by 17, 10, 8 and 6 places respectively; yet on general, the rising trend of Third-Class Indicators of Harbin was more obvious.

Table 9.18 Third-Class Indicators where changes over 3 places occurred by Harbin, 2009–2010

Third-Class Indicator	Original data for 2009 and 2010			Change in ranking		
	2010	2009	Unit	2010	2009	Difference
Nitrogen oxide emissions per unit of GDP	25.21	28.98	Ton per 100 million yuan	14	17	3
Ammonia/nitrogen emissions per unit of GDP	1.8	2.51	Ton per 100 million yuan	16	21	5
Labor productivity of the primary sector	2.7	2.6	10,000 yuan per capita	12	8	−4
Labor productivity of the secondary sector	12.28	9.5	10,000 yuan per capita	24	27	3
Water consumption per unit of value added created by industrial enterprises	0.02	0.03	10,000 tons per 10,000 yuan	21	25	4
Utilization rate industrial solid waste	89.7	76.3	%	22	30	8
Labor productivity of the tertiary sector	8.9	8.24	10,000 yuan per capita	24	21	−3
Proportion of tertiary sector employees in the total employed population	46.14	42.15	%	18	26	8
Water resources per capita	1,504.91	675.57	m^3 per capita	8	16	8
Percentage of days with respirable suspended particulates as the principal pollutants in a year	90.96	82.74	%	35	25	−10
Ratio of environmental spending to government expenditure	3.27	2.08	%	16	21	5
Ratio of the investment in industrial pollution control to GDP	0	0.01	%	38	35	−3
Ratio of the spending on science, education, culture, and public health to government expenditure	19.7	30.78	%	23	6	−17
Green coverage of urban built-in areas	38.38	39.11	%	25	19	−6
Treatment rate of urban household wastewater	57.18	73.94	%	37	29	−8
Harmless treatment of urban household waste	82.91	53.93	%	34	38	4
Public buses per 10,000 urban residents	10.96	10.55		28	31	3
Industrial wastewater COD removal rate	92.1	85.76	%	6	17	11
Industrial nitrogen oxide removal rate	15.6	14.97	%	4	8	4

Note: A positive value in "Difference" means a rise in ranking

Green development checkup-Shanghai

No.	Indicator	Unit	Scope	Attribute	2010 average of 38 cities	2010 figure	2009 figure	2010 ranking	2009 ranking	Change in ranking	Source of 2010 data	Chernoff face
1	GDP per capita	Yuan	Whole city	Positive	56,231.37	76,074	78,989.00	7	5	−2	Regional Economy; City	
2	Energy consumption per unit of GDP	Ton per 10,000 yuan	Whole city	Negative	0.81	0.73	0.75	19	18	−1	Regional Economy; City	
3	Electricity consumption per capita in urban areas	kWh per capita	Whole city	Negative	580.70	1,201.20	1,092.65	35	35	0	City	
4	CO_2 emissions per unit of GDP			Negative	No data			N/A	N/A	N/A		
5	SO_2 emissions per unit of GDP	Ton per 100 million yuan	Whole city	Negative	43.72	23.36	27.26	14	15	1	Regional Economy; Environment Annual Report	
6	COD emissions per unit of GDP	Ton per 100 million yuan	Whole city	Negative	24.81	14.34	17.52	10	13	3	Regional Economy; Environment Annual Report	
7	Nitrogen oxide emissions per unit of GDP	Ton per 100 million yuan	Whole city	Negative	41.71	29.13	30.12	16	18	2	Regional Economy; Environment Annual Report	
8	Ammonia/nitrogen emissions per unit of GDP	Ton per 100 million yuan	Whole city	Negative	2.63	1.79	2.14	15	16	1	Regional Economy; Environment Annual Report	

(continued)

(continued)

No.	Indicator	Unit	Scope	Attribute	2010 average of 38 cities	2010 figure	2009 figure	2010 ranking	2009 ranking	Change in ranking	Source of 2010 data	Chernoff face
9	Labor productivity of the primary sector	10,000 yuan per capita	Whole city	Positive	3.03	2.67	2.32	14	13	−1	Regional Economy	☹
10	Labor productivity of the secondary sector	10,000 yuan per capita	Whole city	Positive	17.91	16.66	14.17	11	10	−1	Regional Economy	☹
11	Water consumption per unit of value added created by industrial enterprises	10,000 tons per 10,000 yuan	Whole city	Negative	0.03	0.02	0.02	19	20	1	Regional Economy; Environment Annual Report	☺
12	Energy consumption per unit of value added created by industrial enterprises			Negative	No data			N/A	N/A	N/A		
13	Utilization rate industrial solid waste	%	Whole city	Positive	85.58	96.20	95.70	13	11	−2	Environment Annual Report	☹
14	Recycling rate of industrial water	%	Whole city	Positive	83.81	72.35	77.10	32	30	−2	Environment Annual Report	☹
15	Labor productivity of the tertiary sector	10,000 yuan per capita	Whole city	Positive	11.40	16.35	15.23	5	3	−2	Regional Economy	☹
16	Proportion of value added of tertiary sector in GDP	%	Whole city	Positive	47.97	57.28	59.36	5	4	−1	City	☹

17	Proportion of tertiary sector employees in the total employed population	%	Whole city	Positive	46.44	55.92	55.70	4	4	0	Regional Economy	
18	Water resources per capita	m^3 per capita	Whole city	Positive	1,026.43	260.63	296.78	28	29	1	Environment Annual Report; City	☺
19	CO_2 emissions per unit of land area			Negative	No data			N/A	N/A	N/A		
20	CO_2 emissions per capita			Negative	No data			N/A	N/A	N/A		
21	SO_2 emissions per unit of land area	Ton per km^2	Whole city	Negative	11.64	56.48	59.76	38	38	0	Environment Annual Report; City	
22	SO_2 emissions per capita	Ton per 10,000 persons	Whole city	Negative	216.46	254.60	271.45	28	30	2	Environment Annual Report; City	☺
23	COD emissions per unit of land area	Ton per km^2	Whole city	Negative	7.83	34.67	38.39	38	38	0	Environment Annual Report; City	
24	COD emissions per capita	Ton per 10,000 persons	Whole city	Negative	118.15	156.27	174.39	29	31	2	Environment Annual Report; City	☺
25	Nitrogen oxides emissions per unit of land area	Ton per km^2	Whole city	Negative	15.00	70.44	66.03	38	37	−1	Environment Annual Report; City	☹
26	Nitrogen oxides emissions per capita	Ton per 10,000 persons	Whole city	Negative	237.70	317.51	299.90	32	32	0	Environment Annual Report; City	

(continued)

(continued)

No.	Indicator	Unit	Scope	Attribute	2010 average of 38 cities	2010 figure	2009 figure	2010 ranking	2009 ranking	Change in ranking	Source of 2010 data	Chernoff face
27	Ammonia/nitrogen emissions per unit of land area	Ton per km^2	Whole city	Negative	0.86	4.34	4.70	38	38	0	Environment Annual Report; City	
28	Ammonia/nitrogen emissions per capita	Ton per 10,000 persons	Whole city	Negative	12.63	19.56	21.34	31	35	4	Environment Annual Report; City	
29	Percentage of the days with air quality at or over level II in a year	%	District	Positive	89.20	92.03	91.48	16	15	−1	MEP Data	
30	Percentage of days with respirable suspended particulates as the principal pollutants in a year	%	District	Negative	70.81	61.10	70.41	11	13	2	MEP Data	
31	Ratio of environmental spending to government expenditure	%	Whole city	Positive	3.13	1.43	1.14	36	36	0	China Statistics; City	
32	Ratio of the investment in industrial pollution control to GDP	%	Whole city	Positive	0.08	0.05	0.05	16	24	8	Environment Annual Report; Regional Economy	

33	Ratio of the spending on science, education, culture, and public health to government expenditure	%	Whole city	Positive	21.08	24.90	25.03	8	24	16	China Statistics; City; Regional Economy	☺
34	Area of green land per capita in urban areas		District	Positive	59.39	89.00	87.81	6	5	−1	City	☹
35	Green coverage of urban built-in areas	%	District	Positive	40.04	38.15	38.10	26	26	0	Urban Construction上海2010	
36	Coverage of water supply	%	District	Positive	98.82	100.00	100.00	1	1	0	Urban Construction	
37	Treatment rate of urban household wastewater	%	District	Positive	86.16	83.29	88.97	29	11	−18	Urban Construction	☹
38	Harmless treatment of urban household waste	%	District	Positive	94.38	81.86	78.77	35	31	−4	Urban Construction	☹
39	Public buses per 10,000 urban residents		District	Positive	15.61	12.99	12.22	20	25	5	City	☺
40	Industrial SO_2 removal rate	%	Whole city	Positive	57.30	61.23	61.64	20	19	−1	Environment Annual Report	☹
41	Industrial wastewater COD removal rate	%	Whole city	Positive	77.86	92.34	88.48	5	12	7	Environment Annual Report	☺

(continued)

(continued)

No.	Indicator	Unit	Scope	Attribute	2010 average of 38 cities	2010 figure	2009 figure	2010 ranking	2009 ranking	Change in ranking	Source of 2010 data	Chernoff face
42	Industrial nitrogen oxide removal rate	%	Whole city	Positive	5.29	5.96	6.10	11	16	5	Environment Annual Report	
43	Industrial waste water ammonia/nitrogen removal rate	%	Whole city	Positive	67.89	69.63	77.26	21	14	−7	Environment Annual Report	

Note:
Regional Economy: *China Regional Economy Statistical Yearbook 2011*
City: *China City Statistical Yearbook 2011*
China Statistics: *China Statistical Yearbook 2011*
Urban Construction: *China Urban Construction Statistical Yearbook 2010*
Environment Annual Report: *China Environment Annual Report 2010*
Environmental Yearbook: *China Environmental Statistical Yearbook 2011*
MEP Data: Ministry of Environmental Protection Data Center
Note: For Treatment rate of urban household wastewater, Shanghai has done a lot to improve waste water treatment before World Expo 2010, but China Urban Construction Statistical Yearbook 2010 showed that ranking of this indicator fell compared with that in 2009. Our research group has reservations as to this result.

9.10 Brief Analysis of Green Development in Shanghai

Shanghai ranked 26th among the 38 participating cities by GDI according to 2010 data, 3 places lower over 2009 (Shanghai ranked 23rd in 2009). Following is a brief analysis of its score by each indicator and their changes from 2009 to 2010.

9.10.1 Shanghai's 2010 Scores by GDI

Shanghai scored −0.093 in 2010. From the three First-Class Indicators including GDEG, CCPNRE, and SDGP as shown in Fig. 9.19, Shanghai showed some advantages in terms of GDEG; yet it was outperformed by the national average by CCPNRE and SDGP (Note: the national average value of each indicator is 0).

According to Fig. 9.20, Shanghai surpassed the national average in 2 of Second-Class Indicators in 2010, which were TII and EMI, yet scored lower than the national average in 6 indicators including GGEI, SII, RAECI, EPCCI, GII and II; it was of the same level with the national average in PII.

9.10.2 Changes in Shanghai's GDI Rankings 2009–2010

According to Table 9.19, in First-Class Indicators, the most obvious change occurred in CCPNRE, where Shanghai rose by 2 places in ranking; Shanghai rose

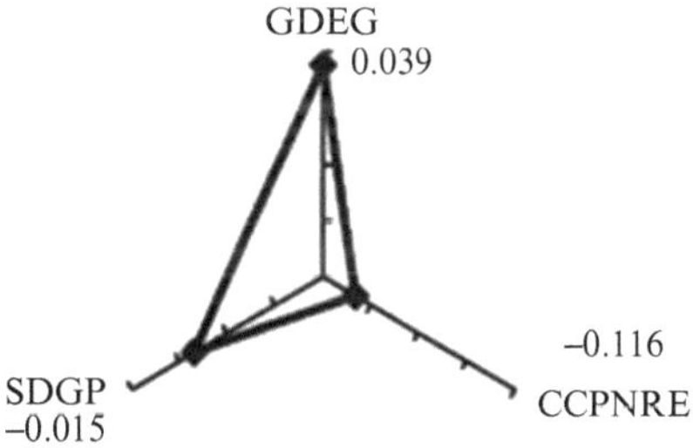

Fig. 9.19 Scores of Shanghai by First-Class Indicators

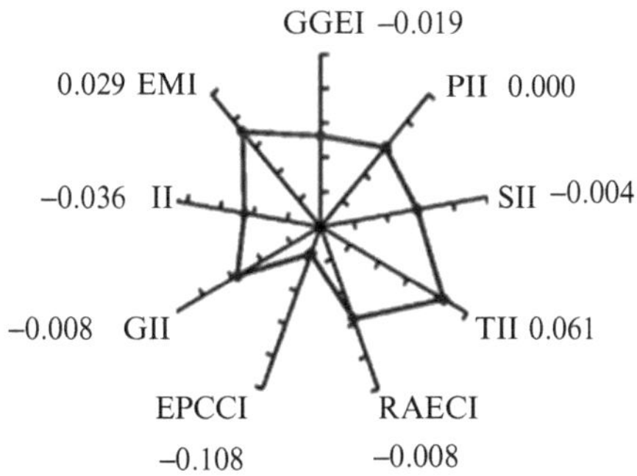

Fig. 9.20 Scores of Shanghai by Second-Class Indicators

Table 9.19 Changes in Shanghai's rankings by First-Class and Second-Class Indicators, 2009–2010

Indicator	2010	2009	Difference	Indicator	2010	2009	Difference
GDI	26	23	−3				
GDEG	12	12	0	RAECI	28	29	1
GGEI	24	17	−7	EPCCI	32	34	2
PII	13	13	0	SDGP	21	22	1
SII	23	20	−3	GII	15	34	19
TII	2	2	0	II	31	22	−9
CCPNRE	33	35	2	EMI	13	14	1

Note: A positive value in "Difference" means a rise in ranking

Table 9.20 Third-Class Indicators where changes over 3 places occurred by Shanghai, 2009–2010

	Original data for 2009 and 2010			Change in ranking		
Third-Class Indicator	2010	2009	Unit	2010	2009	Difference
COD emissions per unit of GDP	14.34	17.52	Ton per 100 million yuan	10	13	3
Ammonia/nitrogen emissions per capita	19.56	21.34	Ton per 10,000 persons	31	35	4
Ratio of the investment in industrial pollution control to GDP	0.05	0.05	%	16	24	8
Ratio of the spending on science, education, culture, and public health to government expenditure	24.90	25.03	%	8	24	16
Treatment rate of urban household wastewater	83.29	88.97	%	29	11	−18
Harmless treatment of urban household waste	81.86	78.77	%	35	31	−4
Public buses per 10,000 urban residents	12.99	12.22		20	25	5
Industrial wastewater COD removal rate	92.34	88.48	%	5	12	7
Industrial nitrogen oxide removal rate	5.96	6.10	%	11	16	5
Industrial waste water ammonia/nitrogen removal rate	69.63	77.26	%	21	14	−7

Note: A positive value in "Difference" means a rise in ranking

by1 place in SDGP. It remained the same by GDEG. In Second-Class Indicators, Shanghai rose by 19, 2, 1 and 1 place in GII, EPCCI, RAECI and EMI, and it fell by 9, 7 and 3 places in II, GGEI and SII. It remained the same as those in 2009 in PII and TII.

To further explain the causes of the changes in the rankings by First- and Second-Class Indicators, we put the Third-Class Indicators where a change of more than 3 places occurred from 2009 to 2010 as follows in Table 9.20. Compared with those in 2009, Shanghai both out- and underperformed in ranking in 2010 with notable oscillations. It dropped by 18 places in Treatment rate of urban household wastewater compared with that in 2009 and 4 in Harmless treatment of urban household waste; it rose by a large margin by Ratio of the spending on science, education, culture, and public health to government expenditure, Ratio of the investment in industrial pollution control to GDP and Industrial wastewater COD removal rate.

Green development checkup-Nanjing

No.	Indicator	Unit	Scope	Attribute	2010 average of 38 cities	2010 figure	2009 figure	2010 ranking	2009 ranking	Change in ranking	Source of 2010 data	Chernoff face
1	GDP per capita	Yuan	Whole city	Positive	56,231.37	65,273	55,290.29	15	16	1	Regional Economy; City	☺
2	Energy consumption per unit of GDP	Ton per 10,000 yuan	Whole city	Negative	0.81	1.08	N/A	27	N/A	N/A	Regional Economy; City	
3	Electricity consumption per capita in urban areas	kWh per capita	Whole city	Negative	580.70	790.17	679.47	31	30	−1	City	☹
4	CO_2 emissions per unit of GDP			Negative	No data			N/A	N/A	N/A		
5	SO_2 emissions per unit of GDP	Ton per 100 million yuan	Whole city	Negative	43.72	26.72	34.89	19	21	2	Regional Economy; Environment Annual Report	☺
6	COD emissions per unit of GDP	Ton per 100 million yuan	Whole city	Negative	24.81	26.63	31.72	28	27	−1	Regional Economy; Environment Annual Report	☹
7	Nitrogen oxide emissions per unit of GDP	Ton per 100 million yuan	Whole city	Negative	41.71	34.61	33.35	22	20	−2	Regional Economy; Environment Annual Report	☹
8	Ammonia/nitrogen emissions per unit of GDP	Ton per 100 million yuan	Whole city	Negative	2.63	0.48	1.47	1	9	8	Regional Economy; Environment Annual Report	☺
9	Labor productivity of the primary sector	10,000 yuan per capita	Whole city	Positive	3.03	2.93	2.82	10	5	−5	Regional Economy	☹

10	Labor productivity of the secondary sector	10,000 yuan per capita	Whole city	Positive	17.91	13.55	11.99	18	17	−1	Regional Economy	☹
11	Water consumption per unit of value added created by industrial enterprises	10,000 tons per 10,000 yuan	Whole city	Negative	0.03	0.05	0.05	35	33	−2	Regional Economy; Environment Annual Report	☹
12	Energy consumption per unit of value added created by industrial enterprises			Negative	No data			N/A	N/A	N/A		
13	Utilization rate industrial solid waste	%	Whole city	Positive	85.58	88.80	91.40	24	20	−4	Environment Annual Report	☹
14	Recycling rate of industrial water	%	Whole city	Positive	83.81	88.10	87.16	23	22	−1	Environment Annual Report	☹
15	Labor productivity of the tertiary sector	10,000 yuan per capita	Whole city	Positive	11.40	12.53	11.59	14	10	−4	Regional Economy	☹
16	Proportion of value added of tertiary sector in GDP	%	Whole city	Positive	47.97	51.85	51.31	12	14	2	City	☺
17	Proportion of tertiary sector employees in the total employed population	%	Whole city	Positive	46.44	50.61	47.37	8	14	6	Regional Economy	☺
18	Water resources per capita	m^3 per capita	Whole city	Positive	1,026.43	587.76	539.13	20	19	−1	Environment Annual Report; City	☹

(continued)

(continued)

No.	Indicator	Unit	Scope	Attribute	2010 average of 38 cities	2010 figure	2009 figure	2010 ranking	2009 ranking	Change in ranking	Source of 2010 data	Chernoff face
19	CO_2 emissions per unit of land area			Negative	No data			N/A	N/A	N/A		
20	CO_2 emissions per capita			Negative	No data			N/A	N/A	N/A		
21	SO_2 emissions per unit of land area	Ton per km^2	Whole city	Negative	11.64	18.42	21.28	32	34	2	Environment Annual Report; City	
22	SO_2 emissions per capita	Ton per 10,000 persons	Whole city	Negative	216.46	192.25	223.35	23	24	1	Environment Annual Report; City	
23	COD emissions per unit of land area	Ton per km^2	Whole city	Negative	7.83	18.36	19.35	36	35	−1	Environment Annual Report; City	
24	COD emissions per capita	Ton per 10,000 persons	Whole city	Negative	118.15	191.61	203.10	36	36	0	Environment Annual Report; City	
25	Nitrogen oxides emissions per unit of land area	Ton per km^2	Whole city	Negative	15.00	23.86	20.35	31	30	−1	Environment Annual Report; City	
26	Nitrogen oxides emissions per capita	Ton per 10,000 persons	Whole city	Negative	237.70	249.01	213.53	28	26	−2	Environment Annual Report; City	
27	Ammonia/nitrogen emissions per unit of land area	Ton per km^2	Whole city	Negative	0.86	0.33	0.90	8	28	20	Environment Annual Report; City	
28	Ammonia/nitrogen emissions per capita	Ton per 10,000 persons	Whole city	Negative	12.63	3.44	9.44	1	11	10	Environment Annual Report; City	

29	Percentage of the days with air quality at or over level II in a year	%	District	Positive	89.20		82.97	86.26	34	26	−8	MEP Data	☹
30	Percentage of days with respirable suspended particulates as the principal pollutants in a year	%	District	Negative	70.81		87.95	83.84	34	28	−6	MEP Data	☹
31	Ratio of environmental spending to government expenditure	%	Whole city	Positive	3.13		1.53	2.29	33	17	−16	China Statistics; City	☹
32	Ratio of the investment in industrial pollution control to GDP	%	Whole city	Positive	0.08		0.06	0.10	14	15	1	Environment Annual Report; Regional Economy	☺
33	Ratio of the spending on science, education, culture, and public health to government expenditure	%	Whole city	Positive	21.08		23.22	23.91	13	28	15	China Statistics; City; Regional Economy	☺
34	Area of green land per capita in urban areas		District	Positive	59.39		141.00	141.47	3	3	0	City	
35	Green coverage of urban built-in areas	%	District	Positive	40.04		44.38	44.11	5	5	0	Urban Construction	
36	Coverage of water supply	%	District	Positive	98.82		100.00	100.00	1	1	0	Urban Construction	

(continued)

(continued)

No.	Indicator	Unit	Scope	Attribute	2010 average of 38 cities	2010 figure	2009 figure	2010 ranking	2009 ranking	Change in ranking	Source of 2010 data	Chernoff face
37	Treatment rate of urban household wastewater	%	District	Positive	86.16	88.82	87.50	21	16	−5	Urban Construction	☹
38	Harmless treatment of urban household waste	%	District	Positive	94.38	78.74	74.88	37	35	−2	Urban Construction	☹
39	Public buses per 10,000 urban residents		District	Positive	15.61	11.27	11.14	27	30	3	City	☺
40	Industrial SO_2 removal rate	%	Whole city	Positive	57.30	84.00	78.65	3	4	1	Environment Annual Report	☺
41	Industrial wastewater COD removal rate	%	Whole city	Positive	77.86	79.42	76.03	25	26	1	Environment Annual Report	☺
42	Industrial nitrogen oxide removal rate	%	Whole city	Positive	5.29	15.02	15.90	5	7	2	Environment Annual Report	☺
43	Industrial waste water ammonia/nitrogen removal rate	%	Whole city	Positive	67.89	91.17	90.71	7	7	0	Environment Annual Report	

Note:
Regional Economy: *China Regional Economy Statistical Yearbook 2011*
City: *China City Statistical Yearbook 2011*
China Statistics: *China Statistical Yearbook 2011*
Urban Construction: *China Urban Construction Statistical Yearbook 2010*
Environment Annual Report: *China Environment Annual Report 2010*
Environmental Yearbook: *China Environmental Statistical Yearbook 2011*
MEP Data: Ministry of Environmental Protection Data Center

9.11 Brief Analysis of Green Development in Nanjing

Nanjing ranked 9th among the 38 participating cities by GDI according to 2010 data, 10 places higher over 2009 (Nanjing ranked 19th in 2009). Following is a brief analysis of its score by each indicator and their changes from 2009 to 2010.

9.11.1 Nanjing's 2010 Scores by GDI

Nanjing scored 0.087 in 2010. From the three First-Class Indicators including GDEG, CCPNRE, and SDGP as shown in Fig. 9.21, Nanjing showed some comparative advantages in GDEG and SDGP, yet scored lower than the national average in CCPNRE (Note: the national average value of each indicator is 0).

According to Fig. 9.22, Nanjing surpassed the national average in 5 of Second-Class Indicators in 2010, which were GGEI, PII, TII, II and EMI, yet scored lower than the national average in 4 indicators including SII, RAECI, EPCCI and GII.

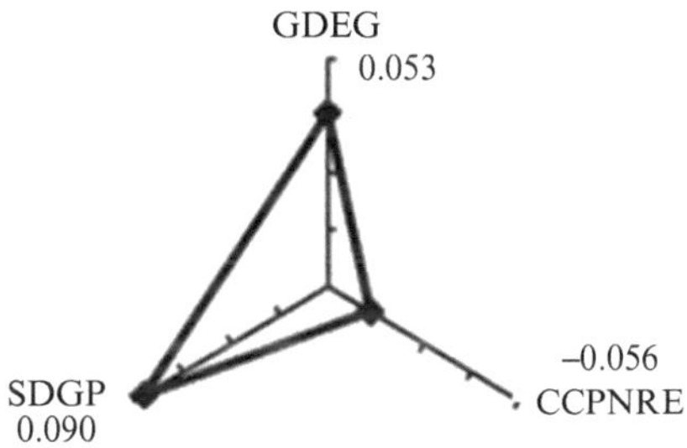

Fig. 9.21 Scores of Nanjing by First-Class Indicators

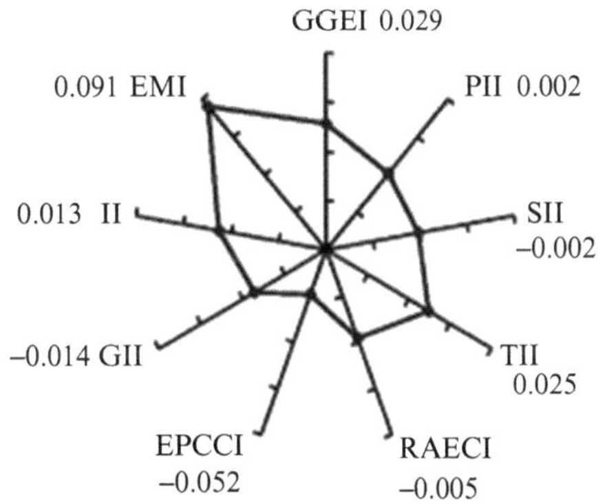

Fig. 9.22 Scores of Nanjing by Second-Class Indicators

Table 9.21 Changes in Nanjing's rankings by First-Class and Second-Class Indicators, 2009–2010

Indicator	2010	2009	Difference	Indicator	2010	2009	Difference
GDI	9	19	10				
GDEG	10	18	8	RAECI	20	19	−1
GGEI	11	25	14	EPCCI	22	33	11
PII	9	5	−4	SDGP	9	10	1
SII	20	19	−1	GII	17	25	8
TII	8	9	1	II	18	10	−8
CCPNRE	23	34	11	EMI	3	6	3

Note: A positive value in "Difference" means a rise in ranking

9.11.2 Changes in Nanjing's GDI Rankings 2009–2010

According to Table 9.21, in First-Class Indicators, the most obvious change occurred in CCPNRE and GDEG, where Nanjing rose by 11 and 8 places in ranking, and it rose by 1 place in SDGP. In Second-Class Indicators, Nanjing rose by 14, 11 and 8 places in GGEI, EPCCI and GII, 3 and 1 place in EMI and TII; it fell by 8 and 4 places in II and PII, and it fell by 1 place in SII and RAECI.

To further explain the causes of the changes in the rankings by First- and Second-Class Indicators, we put the Third-Class Indicators where a change of more than 3 places occurred from 2009 to 2010 as follows in Table 9.22. Compared with those in 2009, Nanjing both out- and underperformed in ranking in 2010, while the more obvious trend is outperforming compared with the previous year. It rose by 20 places in Ammonia/nitrogen emissions per unit of land area, 15 in Ratio of the spending on science, education, culture, and public health to government expenditure, 10 in Ammonia/nitrogen emissions per capita, 8, 6 and 3 places in Ammonia/nitrogen emissions per unit of GDP, Proportion of tertiary sector employees in the total employed population and Public buses per 10,000 urban residents; it fell by 16 and 8 places in Ratio of environmental spending to government expenditure and Percentage of the days with air quality at or over level II in a year. It fell to varying degrees by Percentage of days with respirable suspended particulates as the principal pollutants in a year, Treatment rate of urban household wastewater, Labor productivity of the primary sector, Utilization rate industrial solid waste and Labor productivity of the tertiary sector.

Table 9.22 Third-Class Indicators where changes over 3 places occurred by Nanjing, 2009–2010

Third-Class Indicator	Original data for 2009 and 2010			Change in ranking		
	2010	2009	Unit	2010	2009	Difference
Ammonia/nitrogen emissions per unit of GDP	0.48	1.47	Ton per 100 million yuan	1	9	8
Labor productivity of the primary sector	2.93	2.82	10,000 yuan per capita	10	5	−5
Utilization rate industrial solid waste	88.80	91.40	%	24	20	−4
Labor productivity of the tertiary sector	12.53	11.59	10,000 yuan per capita	14	10	−4
Proportion of tertiary sector employees in the total employed population	50.61	47.37	%	8	14	6
Ammonia/nitrogen emissions per unit of land area	0.33	0.90	Ton per km^2	8	28	20
Ammonia/nitrogen emissions per capita	3.44	9.44	Ton per 10,000 persons	1	11	10
Percentage of the days with air quality at or over level II in a year	82.97	86.26	%	34	26	−8
Percentage of days with respirable suspended particulates as the principal pollutants in a year	87.95	83.84	%	34	28	−6
Ratio of environmental spending to government expenditure	1.53	2.29	%	33	17	−16
Ratio of the spending on science, education, culture, and public health to government expenditure	23.22	23.91	%	13	28	15
Treatment rate of urban household wastewater	88.82	87.50	%	21	16	−5
Public buses per 10,000 urban residents	11.27	11.14		27	30	3

Note: A positive value in "Difference" means a rise in ranking

Green development checkup-Suzhou

No.	Indicator	Unit	Scope	Attribute	2010 average of 38 cities	2010 figure	2009 figure	2010 ranking	2009 ranking	Change in ranking	Source of 2010 data	Chernoff face
1	GDP per capita	Yuan	Whole city	Positive	56,231.37	93,043	83,696.00	3	4	1	Regional Economy; City	☺
2	Energy consumption per unit of GDP	Ton per 10,000 yuan	Whole city	Negative	0.81	0.85	N/A	22	N/A	N/A	Regional Economy; City	
3	Electricity consumption per capita in urban areas	kWh per capita	Whole city	Negative	580.70	483.05	408.28	19	17	−2	City	☹
4	CO_2 emissions per unit of GDP			Negative	No data			N/A	N/A	N/A		
5	SO_2 emissions per unit of GDP	Ton per 100 million yuan	Whole city	Negative	43.72	25.63	33.42	17	18	1	Regional Economy; Environment Annual Report	☺
6	COD emissions per unit of GDP	Ton per 100 million yuan	Whole city	Negative	24.81	14.45	16.66	11	11	0	Regional Economy; Environment Annual Report	
7	Nitrogen oxide emissions per unit of GDP	Ton per 100 million yuan	Whole city	Negative	41.71	33.21	37.57	20	23	3	Regional Economy; Environment Annual Report	☺
8	Ammonia/nitrogen emissions per unit of GDP	Ton per 100 million yuan	Whole city	Negative	2.63	1.05	1.16	7	5	−2	Regional Economy; Environment Annual Report	☹

9	Labor productivity of the primary sector	10,000 yuan per capita	Whole city	Positive	3.03	5.43	4.63	2	2	0	Regional Economy	
10	Labor productivity of the secondary sector	10,000 yuan per capita	Whole city	Positive	17.91	16.31	14.71	3	8	5	Regional Economy	☺
11	Water consumption per unit of value added created by industrial enterprises	10,000 tons per 10,000 yuan	Whole city	Negative	0.03	0.02	0.02	18	19	1	Regional Economy; Environment Annual Report	☺
12	Energy consumption per unit of value added created by industrial enterprises			Negative	No data			N/A	N/A	N/A		
13	Utilization rate industrial solid waste	%	Whole city	Positive	85.58	98.70	98.60	5	5	0	Environment Annual Report	
14	Recycling rate of industrial water	%	Whole city	Positive	83.81	89.82	80.63	19	28	9	Environment Annual Report	☺
15	Labor productivity of the tertiary sector	10,000 yuan per capita	Whole city	Positive	11.40	17.47	15.74	1	1	0	Regional Economy	

(continued)

(continued)

No.	Indicator	Unit	Scope	Attribute	2010 average of 38 cities	2010 figure	2009 figure	2010 ranking	2009 ranking	Change in ranking	Source of 2010 data	Chernoff face
16	Proportion of value added of tertiary sector in GDP	%	Whole city	Positive	47.97	41.38	39.41	30	35	5	City	☺
17	Proportion of tertiary sector employees in the total employed population	%	Whole city	Positive	46.44	39.25	37.47	31	32	1	Regional Economy	☺
18	Water resources per capita	m^3 per capita	Whole city	Positive	1,026.43	403.35	730.03	26	14	−12	Environment Annual Report; City	☹
19	CO_2 emissions per unit of land area			Negative	No data			N/A	N/A	N/A		
20	CO_2 emissions per capita			Negative	No data			N/A	N/A	N/A		
21	SO_2 emissions per unit of land area	Ton per km^2	Whole city	Negative	11.64	23.14	26.63	36	36	0	Environment Annual Report; City	
22	SO_2 emissions per capita	Ton per 10,000 persons	Whole city	Negative	216.46	309.11	357.96	31	34	3	Environment Annual Report; City	☺

23	COD emissions per unit of land area	Ton per km^2	Whole city	Negative	7.83		13.05	13.28	33	31	−2	Environment Annual Report; City	☹
24	COD emissions per capita	Ton per 10,000 persons	Whole city	Negative	118.15		174.32	178.45	32	32	0	Environment Annual Report; City	
25	Nitrogen oxides emissions per unit of land area	Ton per km^2	Whole city	Negative	15.00		29.99	29.94	35	35	0	Environment Annual Report; City	
26	Nitrogen oxides emissions per capita	Ton per 10,000 persons	Whole city	Negative	237.70		400.55	402.46	33	35	2	Environment Annual Report; City	☺
27	Ammonia/nitrogen emissions per unit of land area	Ton per km^2	Whole city	Negative	0.86		0.94	0.92	28	29	1	Environment Annual Report; City	☺
28	Ammonia/nitrogen emissions per capita	Ton per 10,000 persons	Whole city	Negative	12.63		12.62	12.37	24	25	1	Environment Annual Report; City	☺
29	Percentage of the days with air quality at or over level II in a year	%	District	Positive	89.20		90.11	90.11	19	18	−1	MEP Data	☹
30	Percentage of days with respirable suspended particulates as the principal pollutants in a year	%	District	Negative	70.81		75.34	77.50	20	18	−2	MEP Data	☹

(continued)

(continued)

No.	Indicator	Unit	Scope	Attribute	2010 average of 38 cities	2010 figure	2009 figure	2010 ranking	2009 ranking	Change in ranking	Source of 2010 data	Chernoff face
31	Ratio of environmental spending to government expenditure	%	Whole city	Positive	3.13	3.48	3.29	11	9	−2	China Statistics; City	☹
32	Ratio of the investment in industrial pollution control to GDP	%	Whole city	Positive	0.08	0.08	0.11	11	13	2	Environment Annual Report; Regional Economy	☺
33	Ratio of the spending on science, education, culture, and public health to government expenditure	%	Whole city	Positive	21.08	13.90	24.81	35	25	−10	China Statistics; City; Regional Economy	☹
34	Area of green land per capita in urban areas		District	Positive	59.39	58.00	54.14	11	12	1	City	☺
35	Green coverage of urban built-in areas	%	District	Positive	40.04	42.70	42.04	12	11	−1	Urban Construction	☹
36	Coverage of water supply	%	District	Positive	98.82	100.00	100.00	1	1	0	Urban Construction	

37	Treatment rate of urban household wastewater	%	District	Positive	86.16	90.34	87.84	18	15	−3	Urban Construction	☹
38	Harmless treatment of urban household waste	%	District	Positive	94.38	100.00	100.00	1	1	0	Urban Construction	
39	Public buses per 10,000 urban residents		District	Positive	15.61	13.21	12.31	18	24	6	City	☺
40	Industrial SO_2 removal rate	%	Whole city	Positive	57.30	69.18	67.59	12	12	0	Environment Annual Report	
41	Industrial wastewater COD removal rate	%	Whole city	Positive	77.86	87.87	88.79	11	10	−1	Environment Annual Report	☹
42	Industrial nitrogen oxide removal rate	%	Whole city	Positive	5.29	3.83	8.81	14	12	−2	Environment Annual Report	☹
43	Industrial waste water ammonia/nitrogen removal rate	%	Whole city	Positive	67.89	80.40	82.75	12	11	−1	Environment Annual Report	☹

Note:
Regional Economy: *China Regional Economy Statistical Yearbook 2011*
City: *China City Statistical Yearbook 2011*
China Statistics: *China Statistical Yearbook 2011*
Urban Construction: *China Urban Construction Statistical Yearbook 2010*
Environment Annual Report: *China Environment Annual Report 2010*
Environmental Yearbook: *China Environmental Statistical Yearbook 2011*
MEP Data: Ministry of Environmental Protection Data Center

9.12 Brief Analysis of Green Development in Suzhou

Suzhou ranked 14th among the 38 participating cities by GDI according to 2010 data, the same as that in 2009. Following is a brief analysis of its score by each indicator and their changes from 2009 to 2010.

9.12.1 Suzhou's 2010 Scores by GDI

Suzhou scored 0.007 in 2010. From the three First-Class Indicators including GDEG, CCPNRE, and SDGP as shown in Fig. 9.23, Suzhou showed some comparative advantages in terms of GDEG and SDGP; yet it scored lower than the national average in CCPNRE (Note: the national average value of each indicator is 0).

According to Fig. 9.24, Suzhou surpassed the national average in 6 of Second-Class Indicators in 2010, which were GGEI, PII, SII, TII, II and EMI; it scored lower than the national average in RAECI, EPCCI and GII.

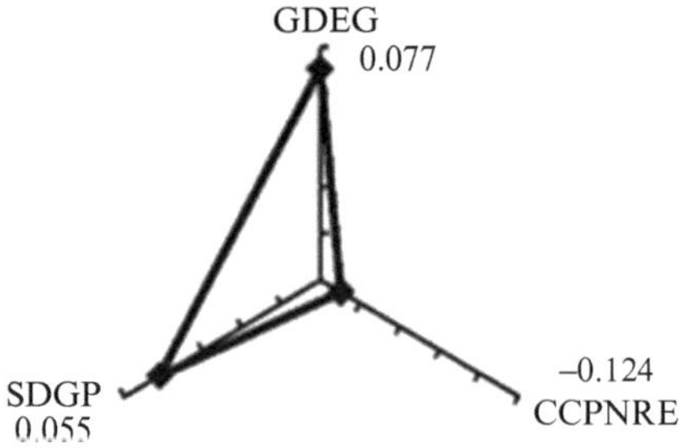

Fig. 9.23 Scores of Suzhou by First-Class Indicators

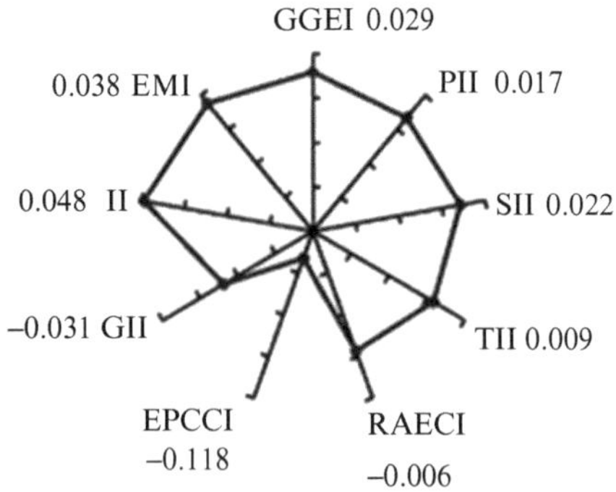

Fig. 9.24 Scores of Suzhou by Second-Class Indicators

Table 9.23 Changes in Suzhou's rankings by First-Class and Second-Class Indicators, 2009–2010

Indicator	2010	2009	Difference	Indicator	2010	2009	Difference
GDI	14	14	0				
GDEG	9	11	2	RAECI	26	14	−12
GGEI	10	11	1	EPCCI	33	32	−1
PII	2	2	0	SDGP	16	7	−9
SII	7	14	7	GII	26	16	−10
TII	14	16	2	II	10	6	−4
CCPNRE	34	33	−1	EMI	10	7	−3

Note: A positive value in "Difference" means a rise in ranking

9.12.2 Changes in Suzhou's GDI Rankings 2009–2010

According to Table 9.23, in First-Class Indicators, the most obvious change occurred in SDGP, 9 places were dropped; it fell by 1 place in CCPNRE; it rose by 2 places in GDEG. In Second-Class Indicators, Suzhou rose by 7 places in SII, 2 in TII, and 1 place in GGEI it fell by 12 places in RAECI, 10 in GII, 4 and 3 places, and 1 place respectively in II, EMI and EPCCI; the ranking of PII remained the same as that in 2009.

To further explain the causes of the changes in the rankings by First- and Second-Class Indicators, we put the Third-Class Indicators where a change of more than 3 places occurred from 2009 to 2010 as follows in Table 9.24. Compared with those in 2009, among the indicators where a change of over 3 places in ranking, those which rose outnumbered those which fell, yet the scale of falls were larger than the scale of the rises. It rose by 9, 6, 5, 5, 3 and 3 places in Recycling rate of industrial water, Public buses per 10,000 urban residents, Labor productivity of the secondary sector, Proportion of value added of tertiary sector in GDP, Nitrogen oxide emissions per unit of GDP and SO_2 emissions per capita; it fell by 12 and 10 places by Water resources per capita and Ratio of the spending on science, education, culture, and public health to government expenditure, and it fell by 3 places in Treatment rate of urban household wastewater.

Table 9.24 Third-Class Indicators where changes over 3 places occurred by Suzhou, 2009–2010

	Original data for 2009 and 2010			Change in ranking		
Third-Class Indicator	2010	2009	Unit	2010	2009	Difference
Nitrogen oxide emissions per unit of GDP	33.21	37.57	Ton per 100 million yuan	20	23	3
Labor productivity of the secondary sector	16.31	14.71	10,000 yuan per capita	3	8	5
Recycling rate of industrial water	89.82	80.63	%	19	28	9
Proportion of value added of tertiary sector in GDP	41.38	39.41	%	30	35	5
Water resources per capita	403.35	730.03	m^3 per capita	26	14	−12
SO_2 emissions per capita	309.11	357.96	Ton per 10,000 persons	31	34	3
Ratio of the spending on science, education, culture, and public health to government expenditure	13.90	24.81	%	35	25	−10
Treatment rate of urban household wastewater	90.34	87.84	%	18	15	−3
Public buses per 10,000 urban residents	13.21	12.31		18	24	6

Note: A positive value in "Difference" means a rise in ranking

Green development checkup-Hangzhou

No.	Indicator	Unit	Scope	Attribute	2010 average of 38 cities	2010 figure	2009 figure	2010 ranking	2009 ranking	Change in ranking	Source of 2010 data	Chernoff face
1	GDP per capita	Yuan	Whole city	Positive	56,231.37	69,828	63,333.16	10	10	0	Regional Economy; City	
2	Energy consumption per unit of GDP	Ton per 10,000 yuan	Whole city	Negative	0.81	0.30	0.33	8	8	0	Regional Economy; City	
3	Electricity consumption per capita in urban areas	kWh per capita	Whole city	Negative	580.70	739.35	665.85	30	29	−1	City	☹
4	CO_2 emissions per unit of GDP			Negative	No data			N/A	N/A	N/A		
5	SO_2 emissions per unit of GDP	Ton per 100 million yuan	Whole city	Negative	43.72	17.52	20.56	6	7	1	Regional Economy; Environment Annual Report	☺
6	COD emissions per unit of GDP	Ton per 100 million yuan	Whole city	Negative	24.81	23.00	26.96	23	23	0	Regional Economy; Environment Annual Report	
7	Nitrogen oxide emissions per unit of GDP	Ton per 100 million yuan	Whole city	Negative	41.71	23.25	23.13	8	10	2	Regional Economy; Environment Annual Report	☺
8	Ammonia/nitrogen emissions per unit of GDP	Ton per 100 million yuan	Whole city	Negative	2.63	1.26	1.52	11	10	−1	Regional Economy; Environment Annual Report	☹

(continued)

(continued)

No.	Indicator	Unit	Scope	Attribute	2010 average of 38 cities	2010 figure	2009 figure	2010 ranking	2009 ranking	Change in ranking	Source of 2010 data	Chernoff face
9	Labor productivity of the primary sector	10,000 yuan per capita	Whole city	Positive	3.03	2.67	2.37	13	12	−1	Regional Economy	☹
10	Labor productivity of the secondary sector	10,000 yuan per capita	Whole city	Positive	17.91	10.08	8.82	33	31	−2	Regional Economy	☹
11	Water consumption per unit of value added created by industrial enterprises	10,000 tons per 10,000 yuan	Whole city	Negative	0.03	0.02	0.02	16	14	−2	Regional Economy; Environment Annual Report	☹
12	Energy consumption per unit of value added created by industrial enterprises			Negative	No data			N/A	N/A	N/A		
13	Utilization rate industrial solid waste	%	Whole city	Positive	85.58	94.10	95.40	16	12	−4	Environment Annual Report	☹
14	Recycling rate of industrial water	%	Whole city	Positive	83.81	73.43	72.43	30	32	2	Environment Annual Report	☺
15	Labor productivity of the tertiary sector	10,000 yuan per capita	Whole city	Positive	11.40	11.50	10.80	18	12	−6	Regional Economy	☹
16	Proportion of value added of tertiary sector in GDP	%	Whole city	Positive	47.97	48.69	49.33	20	19	−1	City	☹

17	Proportion of tertiary sector employees in the total employed population	%	Whole city	Positive	46.44	42.21	40.05	28	30	2	Regional Economy	☺
18	Water resources per capita	m^3 per capita	Whole city	Positive	1,026.43	2,762.99	2,259.21	2	2	0	Environment Annual Report; City	
19	CO_2 emissions per unit of land area			Negative	No data			N/A	N/A	N/A		
20	CO_2 emissions per capita			Negative	No data			N/A	N/A	N/A		
21	SO_2 emissions per unit of land area	Ton per km^2	Whole city	Negative	11.64	5.56	5.83	11	12	1	Environment Annual Report; City	☺
22	SO_2 emissions per capita	Ton per 10,000 persons	Whole city	Negative	216.46	134.56	142.13	14	14	0	Environment Annual Report; City	
23	COD emissions per unit of land area	Ton per km^2	Whole city	Negative	7.83	7.30	7.64	25	25	0	Environment Annual Report; City	
24	COD emissions per capita	Ton per 10,000 persons	Whole city	Negative	118.15	176.63	186.39	33	35	2	Environment Annual Report; City	☺
25	Nitrogen oxides emissions per unit of land area	Ton per km^2	Whole city	Negative	15.00	7.38	6.56	15	16	1	Environment Annual Report; City	☺
26	Nitrogen oxides emissions per capita	Ton per 10,000 persons	Whole city	Negative	237.70	178.53	159.96	18	19	1	Environment Annual Report; City	☺

(continued)

(continued)

No.	Indicator	Unit	Scope	Attribute	2010 average of 38 cities	2010 figure	2009 figure	2010 ranking	2009 ranking	Change in ranking	Source of 2010 data	Chernoff face
27	Ammonia/nitrogen emissions per unit of land area	Ton per km^2	Whole city	Negative	0.86	0.40	0.43	12	12	0	Environment Annual Report; City	
28	Ammonia/nitrogen emissions per capita	Ton per 10,000 persons	Whole city	Negative	12.63	9.67	10.49	14	17	3	Environment Annual Report; City	☺
29	Percentage of the days with air quality at or over level II in a year	%	District	Positive	89.20	86.26	89.56	25	22	−3	MEP Data	☹
30	Percentage of days with respirable suspended particulates as the principal pollutants in a year	%	District	Negative	70.81	83.29	83.29	24	26	2	MEP Data	☺
31	Ratio of environmental spending to government expenditure	%	Whole city	Positive	3.13	2.25	1.96	22	24	2	China Statistics; City	☺
32	Ratio of the investment in industrial pollution control to GDP	%	Whole city	Positive	0.08	0.06	0.13	13	12	−1	Environment Annual Report; Regional Economy	☹

33	Ratio of the spending on science, education, culture, and public health to government expenditure	%	Whole city	Positive	21.08	25.75	30.69	6	7	1	China Statistics; City; Regional Economy	☺
34	Area of green land per capita in urban areas		District	Positive	59.39	35.00	36.53	23	21	−2	City	☹
35	Green coverage of urban built-in areas	%	District	Positive	40.04	39.95	39.94	21	15	−6	Urban Construction	☹
36	Coverage of water supply	%	District	Positive	98.82	100.00	100.00	1	1	0	Urban Construction	
37	Treatment rate of urban household wastewater	%	District	Positive	86.16	95.40	90.02	7	10	3	Urban Construction	☺
38	Harmless treatment of urban household waste	%	District	Positive	94.38	100.00	100.00	1	1	0	Urban Construction	
39	Public buses per 10,000 urban residents		District	Positive	15.61	16.89	18.80	10	2	−8	City	☹
40	Industrial SO_2 removal rate	%	Whole city	Positive	57.30	50.96	46.48	25	26	1	Environment Annual Report	☺
41	Industrial wastewater COD removal rate	%	Whole city	Positive	77.86	80.39	84.25	24	20	−4	Environment Annual Report	☹

(continued)

(continued)

No.	Indicator	Unit	Scope	Attribute	2010 average of 38 cities	2010 figure	2009 figure	2010 ranking	2009 ranking	Change in ranking	Source of 2010 data	Chernoff face
42	Industrial nitrogen oxide removal rate	%	Whole city	Positive	5.29	2.76	3.36	17	19	2	Environment Annual Report	
43	Industrial waste water ammonia/ nitrogen removal rate	%	Whole city	Positive	67.89	61.67	43.74	26	29	3	Environment Annual Report	

Note:
Regional Economy: *China Regional Economy Statistical Yearbook 2011*
City: *China City Statistical Yearbook 2011*
China Statistics: *China Statistical Yearbook 2011*
Urban Construction: *China Urban Construction Statistical Yearbook 2010*
Environment Annual Report: *China Environment Annual Report 2010*
Environmental Yearbook: *China Environmental Statistical Yearbook 2011*
MEP Data: Ministry of Environmental Protection Data Center

9.13 Brief Analysis of Green Development in Hangzhou

Hangzhou ranked 18th among the 38 participating cities by GDI according to 2010 data, 1 place lower over 2009 (Hangzhou ranked 17th in 2009). Following is a brief analysis of its score by each indicator and their changes from 2009 to 2010.

9.13.1 Hangzhou's 2010 Scores by GDI

Hangzhou scored −0.021 in 2010. From the three First-Class Indicators including GDEG, CCPNRE, and SDGP as shown in Fig. 9.25, Hangzhou showed some comparative advantages in terms of GDEG and SDGP, yet scored lower than the national average in CCPNRE (Note: the national average value of each indicator is 0).

According to Fig. 9.26, Hangzhou surpassed the national average in 4 of Second-Class Indicators in 2010, which were GGEI, RAECI, GII and II; yet it scored lower than the national average in SII, TII, EPCCI and EMI; it was about the same level with the national average by PII.

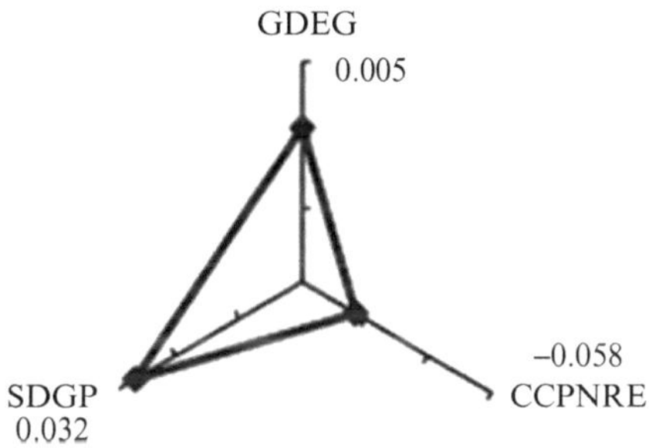

Fig. 9.25 Scores of Hangzhou by First-Class Indicators

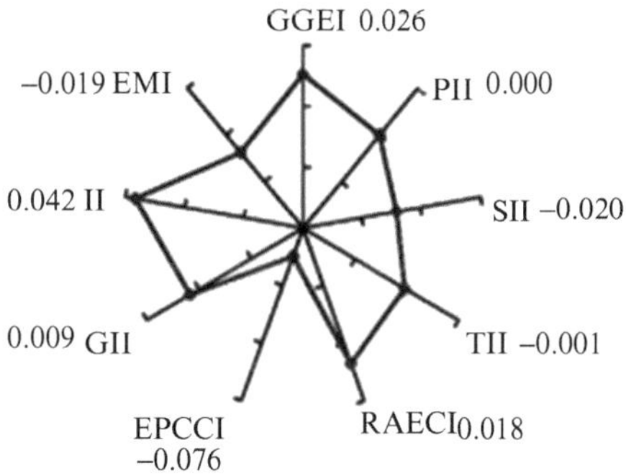

Fig. 9.26 Scores of Hangzhou by Second-Class Indicators

Table 9.25 Changes in Hangzhou's rankings by First-Class and Second-Class Indicators, 2009–2010

Indicator	2010	2009	Difference	Indicator	2010	2009	Difference
GDI	18	17	−1				
GDEG	17	16	−1	RAECI	2	2	0
GGEI	12	13	1	EPCCI	25	25	0
PII	12	12	0	SDGP	17	15	−2
SII	30	31	1	GII	11	9	−2
TII	16	19	3	II	11	8	−3
CCPNRE	24	22	−2	EMI	24	27	3

Note: A positive value in "Difference" means a rise in ranking

9.13.2 *Changes in Hangzhou's GDI Rankings 2009–2010*

According to Table 9.25, in First-Class Indicators, Hangzhou fell by 2 places in CCPNRE and SDGP. It fell by 1 place in GDEG. In Second-Class Indicators, Hangzhou rose by 4, 3 and 1 place in GGEI. Hangzhou rose by 3 places in EMI and TII, and 1 place in GGEI and SII; it remained unchanged by PII, RAECI and EPCCI compared with those in 2009; it fell in rankings of other indicators: 3 places in II and 2 in GII.

To further explain the causes of the changes in the rankings by First- and Second-Class Indicators, we put the Third-Class Indicators where a change of more than 3 places occurred from 2009 to 2010 as follows in Table 9.26. Compared with those in 2009, Hangzhou both out- and underperformed in ranking in 2010, while the more obvious trend is underperforming compared with the previous year. It rose by 3 places in Ammonia/nitrogen emissions per capita, Treatment rate of urban household wastewater and Industrial waste water ammonia/nitrogen removal rate; yet it fell by 8, 6, 6, 4, 4 and 3 places in terms of Public buses per 10,000 urban residents, Labor productivity of the tertiary sector, Green coverage of urban built-in areas, Utilization rate industrial solid waste, Industrial wastewater COD removal rate and Percentage of the days with air quality at or over level II in a year.

Table 9.26 Third-Class Indicators where changes over 3 places occurred by Hangzhou, 2009–2010

	Original data for 2009 and 2010			Change in ranking		
Third-Class Indicator	2010	2009	Unit	2010	2009	Difference
Utilization rate industrial solid waste	94.10	95.40	%	16	12	−4
Labor productivity of the tertiary sector	11.50	10.80	10,000 yuan per capita	18	12	−6
Ammonia/nitrogen emissions per capita	9.67	10.49	Ton per 10,000 persons	14	17	3
Percentage of the days with air quality at or over level II in a year	86.26	89.56	%	25	22	−3
Green coverage of urban built-in areas	39.95	39.94	%	21	15	−6
Treatment rate of urban household wastewater	95.40	90.02	%	7	10	3
Public buses per 10,000 urban residents	16.89	18.80		10	2	−8
Industrial wastewater COD removal rate	80.39	84.25	%	24	20	−4
Industrial waste water ammonia/nitrogen removal rate	61.67	43.74	%	26	29	3

Note: A positive value in "Difference" means a rise in ranking

Green development checkup-Ningbo

No.	Indicator	Unit	Scope	Attribute	2010 average of 38 cities	2010 figure	2009 figure	2010 ranking	2009 ranking	Change in ranking	Source of 2010 data	Chernoff face
1	GDP per capita	Yuan	Whole city	Positive	56,231.37	69,368	60,719.53	11	13	2	Regional Economy; City	☺
2	Energy consumption per unit of GDP	Ton per 10,000 yuan	Whole city	Negative	0.81	1.90	1.85	37	36	−1	Regional Economy; City	☹
3	Electricity consumption per capita in urban areas	kWh per capita	Whole city	Negative	580.70	421.75	366.78	15	14	−1	City	☹
4	CO_2 emissions per unit of GDP			Negative	No data			N/A	N/A	N/A		
5	SO_2 emissions per unit of GDP	Ton per 100 million yuan	Whole city	Negative	43.72	25.71	34.10	18	19	1	Regional Economy; Environment Annual Report	☺
6	COD emissions per unit of GDP	Ton per 100 million yuan	Whole city	Negative	24.81	9.51	11.59	5	5	0	Regional Economy; Environment Annual Report	
7	Nitrogen oxide emissions per unit of GDP	Ton per 100 million yuan	Whole city	Negative	41.71	64.24	56.94	32	31	−1	Regional Economy; Environment Annual Report	☹
8	Ammonia/nitrogen emissions per unit of GDP	Ton per 100 million yuan	Whole city	Negative	2.63	0.77	0.81	3	1	−2	Regional Economy; Environment Annual Report	☹

9	Labor productivity of the primary sector	10,000 yuan per capita	Whole city	Positive	3.03	4.31	2.74	6	6	0	Regional Economy	
10	Labor productivity of the secondary sector	10,000 yuan per capita	Whole city	Positive	17.91	11.35	10.02	29	23	−6	Regional Economy	☹
11	Water consumption per unit of value added created by industrial enterprises	10,000 tons per 10,000 yuan	Whole city	Negative	0.03	0.03	0.04	28	29	1	Regional Economy; Environment Annual Report	☺
12	Energy consumption per unit of value added created by industrial enterprises			Negative	No data			N/A	N/A	N/A		
13	Utilization rate industrial solid waste	%	Whole city	Positive	85.58	89.70	83.50	22	27	5	Environment Annual Report	☺
14	Recycling rate of industrial water	%	Whole city	Positive	83.81	34.62	47.24	38	37	−1	Environment Annual Report	☹
15	Labor productivity of the tertiary sector	10,000 yuan per capita	Whole city	Positive	11.40	13.24	12.82	12	7	−5	Regional Economy	☹
16	Proportion of value added of tertiary sector in GDP	%	Whole city	Positive	47.97	40.15	41.20	36	33	−3	City	☹

(continued)

(continued)

No.	Indicator	Unit	Scope	Attribute	2010 average of 38 cities	2010 figure	2009 figure	2010 ranking	2009 ranking	Change in ranking	Source of 2010 data	Chernoff face
17	Proportion of tertiary sector employees in the total employed population	%	Whole city	Positive	46.44	37.29	30.50	34	38	4	Regional Economy	
18	Water resources per capita	m^3 per capita	Whole city	Positive	1,026.43	1,579.57	1,440.58	6	6	0	Environment Annual Report; City	
19	CO_2 emissions per unit of land area			Negative	No data			N/A	N/A	N/A		
20	CO_2 emissions per capita			Negative	No data			N/A	N/A	N/A		
21	SO_2 emissions per unit of land area	Ton per km^2	Whole city	Negative	11.64	11.30	13.32	25	27	2	Environment Annual Report; City	
22	SO_2 emissions per capita	Ton per 10,000 persons	Whole city	Negative	216.46	193.73	229.57	24	26	2	Environment Annual Report; City	
23	COD emissions per unit of land area	Ton per km^2	Whole city	Negative	7.83	4.18	4.53	14	15	1	Environment Annual Report; City	
24	COD emissions per capita	Ton per 10,000 persons	Whole city	Negative	118.15	71.63	78.05	7	8	1	Environment Annual Report; City	
25	Nitrogen oxides emissions per unit of land area	Ton per km^2	Whole city	Negative	15.00	28.23	22.24	34	32	−2	Environment Annual Report; City	

26	Nitrogen oxides emissions per capita	Ton per 10,000 persons	Whole city	Negative	237.70	483.97	383.32	34	33	−1	Environment Annual Report; City	☹
27	Ammonia/nitrogen emissions per unit of land area	Ton per km^2	Whole city	Negative	0.86	0.34	0.32	9	8	−1	Environment Annual Report; City	☹
28	Ammonia/nitrogen emissions per capita	Ton per 10,000 persons	Whole city	Negative	12.63	5.83	5.47	6	2	−4	Environment Annual Report; City	☹
29	Percentage of the days with air quality at or over level II in a year	%	District	Positive	89.20	86.54	89.84	23	21	−2	MEP Data	☹
30	Percentage of days with respirable suspended particulates as the principal pollutants in a year	%	District	Negative	70.81	75.62	76.16	21	16	−5	MEP Data	☹
31	Ratio of environmental spending to government expenditure	%	Whole city	Positive	3.13	3.23	1.12	17	37	20	China Statistics; City	☺
32	Ratio of the investment in industrial pollution control to GDP	%	Whole city	Positive	0.08	0.01	0.05	33	22	−11	Environment Annual Report; Regional Economy	☹

(continued)

(continued)

No.	Indicator	Unit	Scope	Attribute	2010 average of 38 cities	2010 figure	2009 figure	2010 ranking	2009 ranking	Change in ranking	Source of 2010 data	Chernoff face
33	Ratio of the spending on science, education, culture, and public health to government expenditure	%	Whole city	Positive	21.08	19.03	26.76	26	16	−10	China Statistics; City; Regional Economy	☹
34	Area of green land per capita in urban areas	m^2	District	Positive	59.39	44.00	38.90	17	20	3	City	☺
35	Green coverage of urban built-in areas	%	District	Positive	40.04	38.04	37.83	27	27	0	Urban Construction	
36	Coverage of water supply	%	District	Positive	98.82	100.00	100.00	1	1	0	Urban Construction	
37	Treatment rate of urban household wastewater	%	District	Positive	86.16	85.21	83.97	27	19	−8	Urban Construction	☹
38	Harmless treatment of urban household waste	%	District	Positive	94.38	100.00	100.00	1	1	0	Urban Construction	
39	Public buses per 10,000 urban residents		District	Positive	15.61	15.47	14.63	13	13	0	City	

40	Industrial SO_2 removal rate	%	Whole city	Positive	57.30	86.79	84.68	2	3	1	Environment Annual Report	☺
41	Industrial wastewater COD removal rate	%	Whole city	Positive	77.86	92.44	91.00	4	6	2	Environment Annual Report	☺
42	Industrial nitrogen oxide removal rate	%	Whole city	Positive	5.29	7.74	7.64	9	14	5	Environment Annual Report	☺
43	Industrial waste water ammonia/nitrogen removal rate	%	Whole city	Positive	67.89	96.19	97.75	4	1	−3	Environment Annual Report	☹

Note:
Regional Economy: *China Regional Economy Statistical Yearbook 2011*
City: *China City Statistical Yearbook 2011*
China Statistics: *China Statistical Yearbook 2011*
Urban Construction: *China Urban Construction Statistical Yearbook 2010*
Environment Annual Report: *China Environment Annual Report 2010*
Environmental Yearbook: *China Environmental Statistical Yearbook 2011*
MEP Data: Ministry of Environmental Protection Data Center

9.14 Brief Analysis of Green Development in Ningbo

Ningbo ranked 17th among the 38 participating cities by GDI according to 2010 data, 2 places lower over 2009 (Ningbo ranked 15th in 2009). Following is a brief analysis of its score by each indicator and their changes from 2009 to 2010.

9.14.1 Ningbo's 2010 Scores by GDI

Ningbo scored −0.019 in 2010. From the three First-Class Indicators including GDEG, CCPNRE, and SDGP as shown in Fig. 9.27, Ningbo showed some comparative advantages in SDGP, yet scored lower than the national average in GDEG and CCPNRE (Note: the national average value of each indicator is 0).

According to Fig. 9.28, Ningbo surpassed the national average in 5 of Second-Class Indicators in 2010, which were GGEI, PII, RAECI, II and EMI; it scored lower than the national average in SII, TII, EPCCI and GII.

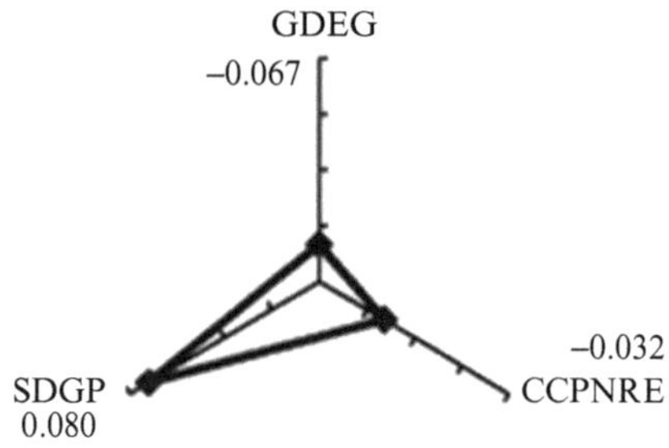

Fig. 9.27 Scores of Ningbo by First-Class Indicators

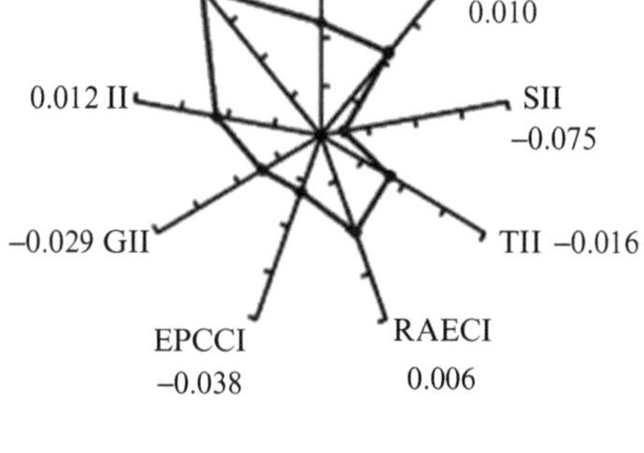

Fig. 9.28 Scores of Ningbo by Second-Class Indicators

Table 9.27 Changes in Ningbo's rankings by First-Class and Second-Class Indicators, 2009–2010

Indicator	2010	2009	Difference	Indicator	2010	2009	Difference
GDI	17	15	−2				
GDEG	28	23	−5	RAECI	6	6	0
GGEI	14	10	−4	EPCCI	19	16	−3
PII	4	6	2	SDGP	11	12	1
SII	38	38	0	GII	25	28	3
TII	28	28	0	II	19	17	−2
CCPNRE	18	16	−2	EMI	3	2	1

Note: A positive value in "Difference" means a rise in ranking

9.14.2 Changes in Ningbo's GDI Rankings 2009–2010

According to Table 9.27, in First-Class Indicators, the most obvious change occurred in GDEG, where Ningbo fell by 5 places in ranking. It fell by 2 places and rose by 1 place in CCPNRE and SDGP respectively. In Second-Class Indicators, Ningbo rose by 2 and 3 places in PII and GII, and 1 place in EMI; it fell by 4, 3 and 2 places in GGEI, EPCCI and II; it remained unchanged in rankings of SII, TII and RAECI compared with those in 2009.

To further explain the causes of the changes in the rankings by First- and Second-Class Indicators, we put the Third-Class Indicators where a change of more than 3 places occurred from 2009 to 2010 as follows in Table 9.28. Compared with those in 2009, Ningbo both out- and underperformed in ranking in 2010, while the more obvious trend is underperforming compared with the previous year. It dropped by 11 places in Ratio of the investment in industrial pollution control to GDP compared with 2009, 10 in Ratio of the spending on science, education, culture, and public health to government expenditure, 8 and 6 in Treatment rate of urban household wastewater and Labor productivity of the secondary sector, and to varying degrees it fell by many other indicators including Labor productivity of the tertiary sector; it rose by leaps and bounds by Ratio of environmental spending to government expenditure, Utilization rate industrial solid waste and Industrial nitrogen oxide removal rate, etc.

Table 9.28 Third-Class Indicators where changes over 3 places occurred by Ningbo, 2009–2010

	Original data for 2009 and 2010			Change in ranking		
Third-Class Indicator	2010	2009	Unit	2010	2009	Difference
Labor productivity of the secondary sector	11.35	10.02	10,000 yuan per capita	29	23	−6
Utilization rate industrial solid waste	89.70	83.50	%	22	27	5
Labor productivity of the tertiary sector	13.24	12.82	10,000 yuan per capita	12	7	−5
Proportion of value added of tertiary sector in GDP	40.15	41.20	%	36	33	−3
Proportion of tertiary sector employees in the total employed population	37.29	30.50	%	34	38	4
Ammonia/nitrogen emissions per capita	5.83	5.47	Ton per 10,000 persons	6	2	−4
Percentage of days with respirable suspended particulates as the principal pollutants in a year	75.62	76.16	%	21	16	−5
Ratio of environmental spending to government expenditure	3.23	1.12	%	17	37	20
Ratio of the investment in industrial pollution control to GDP	0.01	0.05	%	33	22	−11
Ratio of the spending on science, education, culture, and public health to government expenditure	19.03	26.76	%	26	16	−10
Area of green land per capita in urban areas	44.00	38.90	m^2	17	20	3
Treatment rate of urban household wastewater	85.21	83.97	%	27	19	−8
Industrial nitrogen oxide removal rate	7.74	7.64	%	9	14	5
Industrial waste water ammonia/nitrogen removal rate	96.19	97.75	%	4	1	−3

Note: A positive value in “Difference” means a rise in ranking

Green development checkup-Hefei

No.	Indicator	Unit	Scope	Attribute	2010 average of 38 cities	2010 figure	2009 figure	2010 ranking	2009 ranking	Change in ranking	Source of 2010 data	Chernoff face
1	GDP per capita	Yuan	Whole city	Positive	56,231.37	48,312	41,585.00	20	22	2	Regional Economy; City	☺
2	Energy consumption per unit of GDP	Ton per 10,000 yuan	Whole city	Negative	0.81	0.23	0.28	5	5	0	Regional Economy; City	
3	Electricity consumption per capita in urban areas	kWh per capita	Whole city	Negative	580.70	441.10	405.02	17	16	−1	City	☹
4	CO_2 emissions per unit of GDP			Negative	No data			N/A	N/A	N/A		
5	SO_2 emissions per unit of GDP	Ton per 100 million yuan	Whole city	Negative	43.72	17.32	19.22	5	6	1	Regional Economy; Environment Annual Report	☺
6	COD emissions per unit of GDP	Ton per 100 million yuan	Whole city	Negative	24.81	16.56	19.74	15	14	−1	Regional Economy; Environment Annual Report	☹
7	Nitrogen oxide emissions per unit of GDP	Ton per 100 million yuan	Whole city	Negative	41.71	24.80	8.49	11	1	−10	Regional Economy; Environment Annual Report	☹
8	Ammonia/nitrogen emissions per unit of GDP	Ton per 100 million yuan	Whole city	Negative	2.63	1.49	2.32	13	17	4	Regional Economy; Environment Annual Report	☺
9	Labor productivity of the primary sector	10,000 yuan per capita	Whole city	Positive	3.03	1.74	1.51	28	27	−1	Regional Economy	☹

(continued)

(continued)

No.	Indicator	Unit	Scope	Attribute	2010 average of 38 cities	2010 figure	2009 figure	2010 ranking	2009 ranking	Change in ranking	Source of 2010 data	Chernoff face
10	Labor productivity ofthesecondary sector	10,000 yuan per capita	Whole city	Positive	17.91	12.72	9.75	20	26	6	Regional Economy	☺
11	Water consumption per unit of value added created by industrial enterprises	10,000 tons per 10,000 yuan	Whole city	Negative	0.03	0.11	0.12	37	38	1	Regional Economy; Environment Annual Report	☺
12	Energy consumption per unit of value added created by industrial enterprises			Negative	No data			N/A	N/A	N/A		
13	Utilization rate industrial solid waste	%	Whole city	Positive	85.58	98.80	98.70	4	3	−1	Environment Annual Report	☹
14	Recycling rate of industrial water	%	Whole city	Positive	83.81	95.72	95.87	6	6	0	Environment Annual Report	
15	Labor productivity of the tertiary sector	10,000 yuan per capita	Whole city	Positive	11.40	8.24	7.48	26	24	−2	Regional Economy	☹

16	Proportion of value added of tertiary sector in GDP	%	Whole city	Positive	47.97	41.17	42.26	32	31	−1	City	☹
17	Proportion of tertiary sector employees in the total employed population	%	Whole city	Positive	46.44	42.90	39.80	27	31	4	Regional Economy	☺
18	Water resources per capita	m^3 per capita	Whole city	Positive	1,026.43	608.55	358.34	18	26	8	Environment Annual Report; City	☺
19	CO_2 emissions per unit of land area			Negative	No data			N/A	N/A	N/A		
20	CO_2 emissions per capita			Negative	No data			N/A	N/A	N/A		
21	SO_2 emissions per unit of land area	Ton per km^2	Whole city	Negative	11.64	4.73	4.46	7	7	0	Environment Annual Report; City	
22	SO_2 emissions per capita	Ton per 10,000 persons	Whole city	Negative	216.46	67.52	64.29	3	3	0	Environment Annual Report; City	
23	COD emissions per unit of land area	Ton per km^2	Whole city	Negative	7.83	4.52	4.58	17	16	−1	Environment Annual Report; City	☹
24	COD emissions per capita	Ton per 10,000 persons	Whole city	Negative	118.15	64.54	66.03	4	5	1	Environment Annual Report; City	☺

(continued)

(continued)

No.	Indicator	Unit	Scope	Attribute	2010 average of 38 cities	2010 figure	2009 figure	2010 ranking	2009 ranking	Change in ranking	Source of 2010 data	Chernoff face
25	Nitrogen oxides emissions per unit of land area	Ton per km^2	Whole city	Negative	15.00	6.77	1.97	11	4	−7	Environment Annual Report; City	
26	Nitrogen oxides emissions per capita	Ton per 10,000 persons	Whole city	Negative	237.70	96.67	28.39	9	1	−8	Environment Annual Report; City	
27	Ammonia/nitrogen emissions per unit of land area	Ton per km^2	Whole city	Negative	0.86	0.41	0.54	13	16	3	Environment Annual Report; City	
28	Ammonia/nitrogen emissions per capita	Ton per 10,000 persons	Whole city	Negative	12.63	5.79	7.77	5	7	2	Environment Annual Report; City	
29	Percentage of the days with air quality at or over level II in a year	%	District	Positive	89.20	85.16	87.91	28	24	−4	MEP Data	
30	Percentage of days with respirable suspended particulates as the principal pollutants in a year	%	District	Negative	70.81	85.21	87.12	30	32	2	MEP Data	

31	Ratio of environmental spending to government expenditure	%		Whole city	Positive	3.13		2.18	2.07	24	22	−2	China Statistics; City	☹
32	Ratio of the investment in industrial pollution control to GDP	%		Whole city	Positive	0.08		0.00	0.07	37	19	−18	Environment Annual Report; Regional Economy	☹
33	Ratio of the spending on science, education, culture, and public health to government expenditure	%		Whole city	Positive	21.08		16.92	21.19	31	36	5	China Statistics; City; Regional Economy	☺
34	Area of green land per capita in urban areas	m^2		District	Positive	59.39		54.00	50.52	14	16	2	City	☺
35	Green coverage of urban built-in areas	%		District	Positive	40.04		38.82	38.44	23	23	0	Urban Construction	
36	Coverage of water supply	%		District	Positive	98.82		97.22	97.16	31	31	0	Urban Construction	
37	Treatment rate of urban household wastewater	%		District	Positive	86.16		99.81	99.78	2	1	−1	Urban Construction	☹

(continued)

(continued)

No.	Indicator	Unit	Scope	Attribute	2010 average of 38 cities	2010 figure	2009 figure	2010 ranking	2009 ranking	Change in ranking	Source of 2010 data	Chernoff face
38	Harmless treatment of urban household waste	%	District	Positive	94.38	99.97	99.97	17	16	−1	Urban Construction	☹
39	Public buses per 10,000 urban residents		District	Positive	15.61	12.19	12.76	24	20	−4	City	☹
40	Industrial SO_2 removal rate	%	Whole city	Positive	57.30	41.15	36.65	31	29	−2	Environment Annual Report	☹
41	Industrial wastewater COD removal rate	%	Whole city	Positive	77.86	77.41	89.20	27	8	−19	Environment Annual Report	☹
42	Industrial nitrogen oxide removal rate	%	Whole city	Positive	5.29	0.26	10.56	26	11	−15	Environment Annual Report	☹
43	Industrial waste water ammonia/ nitrogen - removal rate	%	Whole city	Positive	67.89	65.89	83.53	24	10	−14	Environment Annual Report	☹

Note:
Regional Economy: *China Regional Economy Statistical Yearbook 2011*
City: *China City Statistical Yearbook 2011*
China Statistics: *China Statistical Yearbook 2011*
Urban Construction: *China Urban Construction Statistical Yearbook 2010*
Environment Annual Report: *China Environment Annual Report 2010*
Environmental Yearbook: *China Environmental Statistical Yearbook 2011*
MEP Data: Ministry of Environmental Protection Data Center

9.15 Brief Analysis of Green Development in Hefei

Hefei ranked 22nd among the 38 participating cities by GDI according to 2010 data, 16 places lower over 2009 (Hefei ranked 6th in 2009). Following is a brief analysis of its score by each indicator and their changes from 2009 to 2010.

9.15.1 *Hefei's 2010 Scores by GDI*

Hefei scored −0.048 in 2010. From the three First-Class Indicators including GDEG, CCPNRE, and SDGP as shown in Fig. 9.29, Hefei showed some comparative advantages in GDEG and CCPNRE; yet scored lower than the national average in SDGP (Note: the national average value of each indicator is 0).

According to Fig. 9.30, Hefei surpassed the national average in 4 of Second-Class Indicators in 2010, which were GGEI, SII, EPCCI and II; it scored lower than the national average in 5 indicators such as PII, TII, RAECI, GII and EMI.

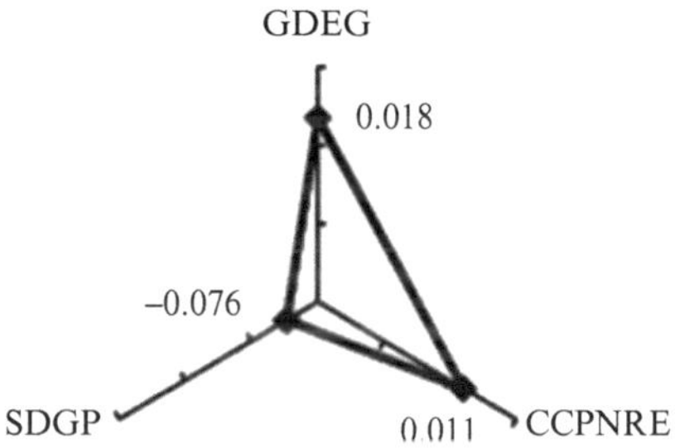

Fig. 9.29 Scores of Hefei by First-Class Indicators

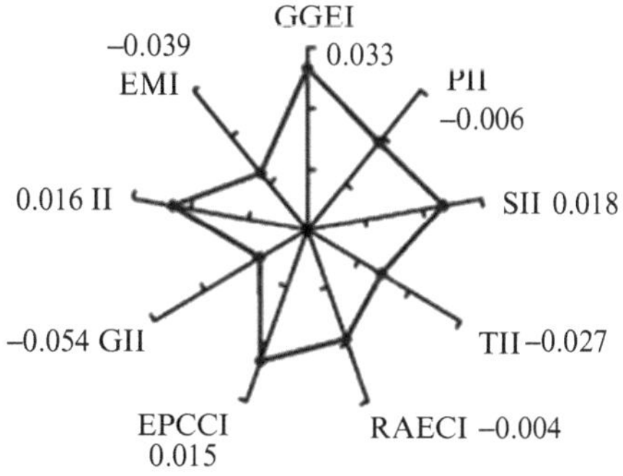

Fig. 9.30 Scores of Hefei by Second-Class Indicators

Table 9.29 Changes in Hefei's rankings by First-Class and Second-Class Indicators, 2009–2010

Indicator	2010	2009	Difference	Indicator	2010	2009	Difference
GDI	22	6	−16				
GDEG	14	8	−6	RAECI	18	26	8
GGEI	9	3	−6	EPCCI	12	5	−7
PII	28	27	−1	SDGP	26	19	−7
SII	10	9	−1	GII	36	35	−1
TII	33	34	1	II	17	14	−3
CCPNRE	12	5	−7	EMI	27	19	−8

Note: A positive value in "Difference" means a rise in ranking

9.15.2 Changes in Hefei's GDI Rankings 2009–2010

According to Table 9.29, in First-Class Indicators, the most obvious change occurred in CCPNRE and SDGP, where Hefei fell by 7 places in ranking; it fell by 6 places in GDEG. In Second-Class Indicators, Hefei rose by 8, 7, and 6 places in EMI, EPCCI and GGEI. Other indicators all suffered slight falls.

To further explain the causes of the changes in the rankings by First- and Second-Class Indicators, we put the Third-Class Indicators where a change of more than 3 places occurred from 2009 to 2010 as follows in Table 9.30. Compared with those in 2009, Hefei both out- and underperformed in ranking in 2010, while the more obvious trend is underperforming compared with the previous year. It rose by 8 places in Water resources per capita and 6 in Labor productivity of the secondary sector, other indicators such as Ammonia/nitrogen emissions per unit of GDP enjoyed slight rises; yet it fell by 19 places by Industrial wastewater COD removal rate compared with that in 2009, 18 in Ratio of the investment in industrial pollution control to GDP, and other indicators such as Industrial nitrogen oxide removal rate and Industrial wastewater ammonia/nitrogen removal rate fell on a large scale.

Table 9.30 Third-Class Indicators where changes over 3 places occurred by Hefei, 2009–2010

	Original data for 2009 and 2010			Change in ranking		
Third-Class Indicator	2010	2009	Unit	2010	2009	Difference
Nitrogen oxide emissions per unit of GDP	24.80	8.49	Ton per 100 million yuan	11	1	−10
Ammonia/nitrogen emissions per unit of GDP	1.49	2.32	Ton per 100 million yuan	13	17	4
Labor productivity of the secondary sector	12.72	9.75	10,000 yuan per capita	20	26	6
Proportion of tertiary sector employees in the total employed population	42.90	39.80	%	27	31	4
Water resources per capita	608.55	358.34	m^3 per capita	18	26	8
Nitrogen oxides emissions per unit of land area	6.77	1.97	Ton per km^2	11	4	−7
Nitrogen oxides emissions per capita	96.67	28.39	Ton per 10,000 persons	9	1	−8
Ammonia/nitrogen emissions per unit of land area	0.41	0.54	Ton per km^2	13	16	3
Percentage of the days with air quality at or over level II in a year	85.16	87.91	%	28	24	−4
Ratio of the investment in industrial pollution control to GDP	0.00	0.07	%	37	19	−18
Ratio of the spending on science, education, culture, and public health to government expenditure	16.92	21.19	%	31	36	5
Public buses per 10,000 urban residents	12.19	12.76		24	20	−4
Industrial wastewater COD removal rate	77.41	89.20	%	27	8	−19
Industrial nitrogen oxide removal rate	0.26	10.56	%	26	11	−15
Industrial waste water ammonia/nitrogen removal rate	65.89	83.53	%	24	10	−14

Note: A positive value in "Difference" means a rise in ranking

Green development checkup-Fuzhou

No.	Indicator	Unit	Scope	Attribute	2010 average of 38 cities	2010 figure	2009 figure	2010 ranking	2009 ranking	Change in ranking	Source of 2010 data	Chernoff face
1	GDP per capita	Yuan	Whole city	Positive	56,231.37	44,000	38,015.00	23	26	3	Regional Economy; City	☺
2	Energy consumption per unit of GDP	Ton per 10,000 yuan	Whole city	Negative	0.81	0.40	0.66	12	15	3	Regional Economy; City	☺
3	Electricity consumption per capita in urban areas	kWh per capita	Whole city	Negative	580.70	474.68	498.96	18	22	4	City	☺
4	CO_2 emissions per unit of GDP			Negative	No data			N/A	N/A	N/A		
5	SO_2 emissions per unit of GDP	Ton per 100 million yuan	Whole city	Negative	43.72	34.37	37.58	25	24	−1	Regional Economy; Environment Annual Report	☹
6	COD emissions per unit of GDP	Ton per 100 million yuan	Whole city	Negative	24.81	17.74	20.60	17	16	−1	Regional Economy; Environment Annual Report	☹
7	Nitrogen oxide emissions per unit of GDP	Ton per 100 million yuan	Whole city	Negative	41.71	43.42	26.11	25	13	−12	Regional Economy; Environment Annual Report	☹
8	Ammonia/nitrogen emissions per unit of GDP	Ton per 100 million yuan	Whole city	Negative	2.63	0.94	1.85	5	14	9	Regional Economy; Environment Annual Report	☺

9	Labor productivity of the primary sector	10,000 yuan per capita	Whole city	Positive	3.03	3.04	2.57	8	10	2	Regional Economy	☺
10	Labor productivity of the secondary sector	10,000 yuan per capita	Whole city	Positive	17.91	11.04	9.01	30	29	−1	Regional Economy	☹
11	Water consumption per unit of value added created by industrial enterprises	10,000 tons per 10,000 yuan	Whole city	Negative	0.03	0.00	0.01	3	5	2	Regional Economy; Environment Annual Report	☺
12	Energy consumption per unit of value added created by industrial enterprises			Negative	No data			N/A	N/A	N/A		
13	Utilization rate industrial solid waste	%	Whole city	Positive	85.58	80.40	94.40	28	14	−14	Environment Annual Report	☹
14	Recycling rate of industrial water	%	Whole city	Positive	83.81	70.44	87.25	33	21	−12	Environment Annual Report	☹
15	Labor productivity of the tertiary sector	10,000 yuan per capita	Whole city	Positive	11.40	9.03	8.33	23	20	−3	Regional Economy	☹
16	Proportion of value added of tertiary sector in GDP	%	Whole city	Positive	47.97	46.06	48.15	22	20	−2	City	☹

(continued)

(continued)

No.	Indicator	Unit	Scope	Attribute	2010 average of 38 cities	2010 figure	2009 figure	2010 ranking	2009 ranking	Change in ranking	Source of 2010 data	Chernoff face
17	Proportion of tertiary sector employees in the total employed population	%	Whole city	Positive	46.44	43.00	40.96	26	28	2	Regional Economy	☺
18	Water resources per capita	m^3 per capita	Whole city	Positive	1,026.43	2,057.59	1,255.64	3	9	6	Environment Annual Report; City	☺
19	CO_2 emissions per unit of land area			Negative	No data			N/A	N/A	N/A		
20	CO_2 emissions per capita			Negative	No data			N/A	N/A	N/A		
21	SO_2 emissions per unit of land area	Ton per km^2	Whole city	Negative	11.64	7.32	7.01	15	14	−1	Environment Annual Report; City	☹
22	SO_2 emissions per capita	Ton per 10,000 persons	Whole city	Negative	216.46	148.99	143.78	18	15	−3	Environment Annual Report; City	☹
23	COD emissions per unit of land area	Ton per km^2	Whole city	Negative	7.83	3.78	3.84	10	11	1	Environment Annual Report; City	☺
24	COD emissions per capita	Ton per 10,000 persons	Whole city	Negative	118.15	76.90	78.80	12	9	−3	Environment Annual Report; City	☹
25	Nitrogen oxides emissions per unit of land area	Ton per km^2	Whole city	Negative	15.00	9.25	4.87	22	12	−10	Environment Annual Report; City	☹

26	Nitrogen oxides emissions per capita	Ton per 10,000 persons	Whole city	Negative	237.70	188.21	99.89	20	11	−9	Environment Annual Report; City	☹
27	Ammonia/nitrogen emissions per unit of land area	Ton per km^2	Whole city	Negative	0.86	0.20	0.35	4	10	6	Environment Annual Report; City	☺
28	Ammonia/nitrogen emissions per capita	Ton per 10,000 persons	Whole city	Negative	12.63	4.09	7.09	2	4	2	Environment Annual Report; City	☺
29	Percentage of the days with air quality at or over level II in a year	%	District	Positive	89.20	96.15	96.70	9	9	0	MEP Data	
30	Percentage of days with respirable suspended particulates as the principal pollutants in a year	%	District	Negative	70.81	62.74	58.36	12	10	−2	MEP Data	☹
31	Ratio of environmental spending to government expenditure	%	Whole city	Positive	3.13	1.64	1.55	32	30	−2	China Statistics; City	☹
32	Ratio of the investment in industrial pollution control to GDP	%	Whole city	Positive	0.08	0.04	0.06	18	21	3	Environment Annual Report; Regional Economy	☺

(continued)

(continued)

No.	Indicator	Unit	Scope	Attribute	2010 average of 38 cities	2010 figure	2009 figure	2010 ranking	2009 ranking	Change in ranking	Source of 2010 data	Chernoff face
33	Ratio of the spending on science, education, culture, and public health to government expenditure	%	Whole city	Positive	21.08	18.72	32.76	28	4	−24	China Statistics; City; Regional Economy	
34	Area of green land per capita in urban areas	m^2	District	Positive	59.39	43.00	40.68	18	17	−1	City	
35	Green coverage of urban built-in areas	%	District	Positive	40.04	40.27	39.25	20	18	−2	Urban Construction	
36	Coverage of water supply	%	District	Positive	98.82	99.86	99.01	23	28	5	Urban Construction	
37	Treatment rate of urban household wastewater	%	District	Positive	86.16	87.10	80.87	24	23	−1	Urban Construction	
38	Harmless treatment of urban household waste	%	District	Positive	94.38	100.00	100.00	1	1	0	Urban Construction	
39	Public buses per 10,000 urban residents		District	Positive	15.61	18.91	14.17	4	16	12	City	
40	Industrial SO_2 removal rate	%	Whole city	Positive	57.30	54.51	50.44	23	23	0	Environment Annual Report	
41	Industrial wastewater COD removal rate	%	Whole city	Positive	77.86	94.89	92.06	2	4	2	Environment Annual Report	

42	Industrial nitrogen oxide removal rate	%	Whole city	Positive	5.29	0.01	0.00	29	29	0	Environment Annual Report	
43	Industrial waste water ammonia/nitrogen removal rate	%	Whole city	Positive	67.89	73.81	58.13	17	26	9	Environment Annual Report	☺

Note:
Regional Economy: *China Regional Economy Statistical Yearbook 2011*
City: *China City Statistical Yearbook 2011*
China Statistics: *China Statistical Yearbook 2011*
Urban Construction: *China Urban Construction Statistical Yearbook 2010*
Environment Annual Report: *China Environment Annual Report 2010*
Environmental Yearbook: *China Environmental Statistical Yearbook 2011*
MEP Data: Ministry of Environmental Protection Data Center

9.16 Brief Analysis of Green Development in Fuzhou

Fuzhou ranked 10th among the 38 participating cities by GDI according to 2010 data, 2 places higher over 2009 (Fuzhou ranked 12th in 2009). Following is a brief analysis of its score by each indicator and their changes from 2009 to 2010.

9.16.1 Fuzhou's 2010 Scores by GDI

Fuzhou scored 0.072in 2010. From the three First-Class Indicators including GDEG, CCPNRE, and SDGP as shown in Fig. 9.31, Fuzhou showed advantages in CCPNRE, yet scored lower than the national average in GDEG and SDGP (Note: the national average value of each indicator is 0).

According to Fig. 9.32, Fuzhou surpassed the national average in 5 of Second-Class Indicators in 2010, which were PII, RAECI, EPCCI, II and EMI; it scored lower than the national average in 4 indicators including GGEI, SII, TII and GII.

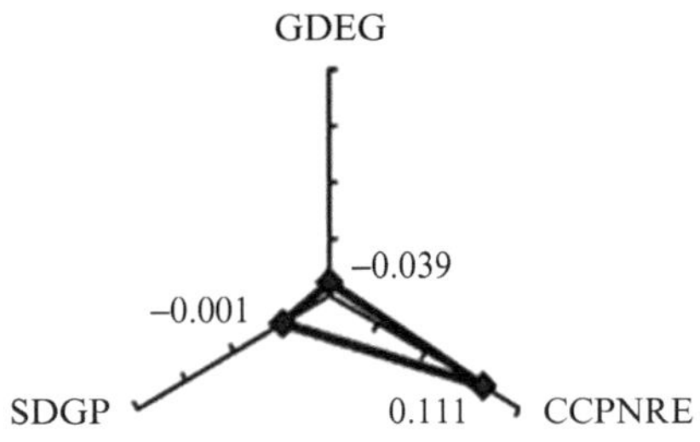

Fig. 9.31 Scores of Fuzhou by First-Class Indicators

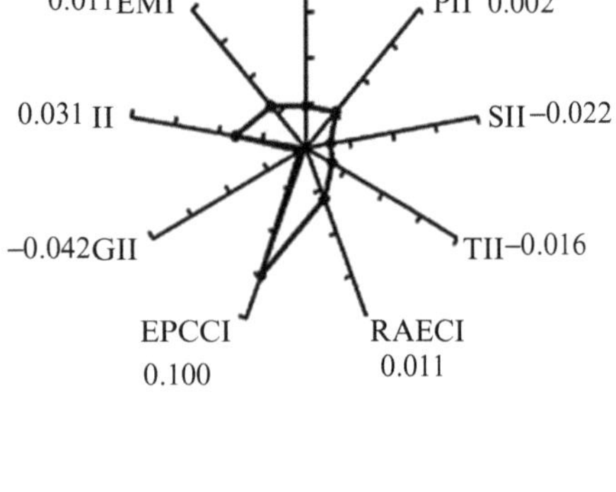

Fig. 9.32 Scores of Fuzhou by Second-Class Indicators

Table 9.31 Changes in Fuzhou's rankings by First-Class and Second-Class Indicators, 2009–2010

Indicator	2010	2009	Difference	Indicator	2010	2009	Difference
GDI	10	12	2				
GDEG	22	19	−3	RAECI	3	9	6
GGEI	19	24	5	EPCCI	7	8	1
PII	7	10	3	SDGP	20	17	−3
SII	31	10	−21	GII	32	14	−18
TII	27	26	−1	II	13	19	6
CCPNRE	7	8	1	EMI	19	23	4

Note: A positive value in "Difference" means a rise in ranking

9.16.2 Changes in Fuzhou's GDI Rankings 2009–2010

According to Table 9.31, in First-Class Indicators, the most obvious change occurred in GDEG and SDGP, where Fuzhou fell by 3 places in ranking, it rose by 1 place in CCPNRE. In Second-Class Indicators, Fuzhou rose by 6 places in RAECI and II, 5 places in GGEI, and 4, 3 and 1 place in EMI, PII, EPCCI; it fell by 21, 18 and 1 place in SII, GII and TII.

To further explain the causes of the changes in the rankings by First- and Second-Class Indicators, we put the Third-Class Indicators where a change of more than 3 places occurred from 2009 to 2010 as follows in Table 9.32. Compared with those in 2009, Fuzhou both out- and underperformed in ranking in 2010 with notable oscillation. It rose by 12 places in Public buses per 10,000 urban residents and 9 in Industrial waste water ammonia/nitrogen removal rate, and many other indicators enjoyed rises on varying degrees; it fell somehow by other indicators such as Nitrogen oxide emissions per unit of GDP compared with that in 2009.

Table 9.32 Third-Class Indicators where changes over 3 places occurred by Fuzhou, 2009–2010

	Original data for 2009 and 2010			Change in ranking		
Third-Class Indicator	2010	2009	Unit	2010	2009	Difference
GDP per capita	44,000.00	38,015.00	Yuan	23	26	3
Energy consumption per unit of GDP	0.40	0.66	Ton per 10,000 yuan	12	15	3
Electricity consumption per capita in urban areas	474.68	498.96	kWh per capita	18	22	4
Nitrogen oxide emissions per unit of GDP	43.42	26.11	Ton per 100 million yuan	25	13	−12
Ammonia/nitrogen emissions per unit of GDP	0.94	1.85	Ton per 100 million yuan	5	14	9
Utilization rate industrial solid waste	80.40	94.40	%	28	14	−14
Recycling rate of industrial water	70.44	87.25	%	33	21	−12
Labor productivity of the tertiary sector	9.03	8.33	10,000 yuan per capita	23	20	−3
Water resources per capita	2,057.59	1,255.64	m^3 per capita	3	9	6
SO_2 emissions per capita	148.99	143.78	Ton per 10,000 persons	18	15	−3
COD emissions per capita	76.90	78.80	Ton per 10,000 persons	12	9	−3
Nitrogen oxides emissions per unit of land area	9.25	4.87	Ton per km^2	22	12	−10
Nitrogen oxides emissions per capita	188.21	99.89	Ton per 10,000 persons	20	11	−9
Ammonia/nitrogen emissions per unit of land area	0.20	0.35	Ton per km^2	4	10	6
Ratio of the investment in industrial pollution control to GDP	0.04	0.06	%	18	21	3
Ratio of the spending on science, education, culture, and public health to government expenditure	18.72	32.76	%	28	4	−24
Coverage of water supply	99.86	99.01	%	23	28	5
Public buses per 10,000 urban residents	18.91	14.17		4	16	12
Industrial waste water ammonia/nitrogen removal rate	73.81	58.13	%	17	26	9

Note: A positive value in "Difference" means a rise in ranking

Green development checkup-Xiamen

No.	Indicator	Unit	Scope	Attribute	2010 average of 38 cities	2010 figure	2009 figure	2010 ranking	2009 ranking	Change in ranking	Source of 2010 data	Chernoff face
1	GDP per capita	Yuan	Whole city	Positive	55,399.15	59,323	68,938.00	17	9	−8	Regional Economy; City	☹
2	Energy consumption per unit of GDP	Ton per 10,000 yuan	Whole city	Negative	0.82	0.57	0.30	15	6	−9	Regional Economy; City	☹
3	Electricity consumption per capita in urban areas	kWh per capita	Whole city	Negative	580.70	1,711.76	1,569.29	38	38	0	City	
4	CO_2 emissions per unit of GDP			Negative	No data			N/A	N/A	N/A		☹
5	SO_2 emissions per unit of GDP	Ton per 100 million yuan	Whole city	Negative	42.67	27.50	28.20	20	16	−4	Regional Economy; Environment Annual Report	☹
6	COD emissions per unit of GDP	Ton per 100 million yuan	Whole city	Negative	24.91	24.69	28.54	26	24	−2	Regional Economy; Environment Annual Report	☹
7	Nitrogen oxide emissions per unit of GDP	Ton per 100 million yuan	Whole city	Negative	40.67	23.33	19.13	9	6	−3	Regional Economy; Environment Annual Report	☹
8	Ammonia/nitrogen emissions per unit of GDP	Ton per 100 million yuan	Whole city	Negative	2.63	2.40	2.40	22	20	−2	Regional Economy; Environment Annual Report	☹

(continued)

(continued)

No.	Indicator	Unit	Scope	Attribute	2010 average of 38 cities	2010 figure	2009 figure	2010 ranking	2009 ranking	Change in ranking	Source of 2010 data	Chernoff face
9	Labor productivity of the primary sector	10,000 yuan per capita	Whole city	Positive	3.00	2.44	1.98	18	18	0	Regional Economy	
10	Labor productivity of the secondary sector	10,000 yuan per capita	Whole city	Positive	18.12	11.80	8.85	27	30	3	Regional Economy	☺
11	Water consumption per unit of value added created by industrial enterprises	10,000 tons per 10,000 yuan	Whole city	Negative	0.03	0.01	0.01	10	12	2	Regional Economy; Environment Annual Report	☺
12	Energy consumption per unit of value added created by industrial enterprises			Negative	No data			N/A	N/A	N/A		
13	Utilization rate industrial solid waste	%	Whole city	Positive	83.42	87.30	90.20	25	24	−1	Environment Annual Report	☹
14	Recycling rate of industrial water	%	Whole city	Positive	82.10	90.43	93.91	18	14	−4	Environment Annual Report	☹
15	Labor productivity of the tertiary sector	10,000 yuan per capita	Whole city	Positive	11.39	11.64	7.90	17	22	5	Regional Economy	☺

16	Proportion of value added of tertiary sector in GDP	%	Whole city	Positive	48.37	49.15	51.56	17	11	−6	City	☺
17	Proportion of tertiary sector employees in the total employed population	%	Whole city	Positive	46.83	40.43	52.36	30	6	−24	Regional Economy	☹
18	Water resources per capita	m^3 per capita	Whole city	Positive	1,040.56	777.98	395.48	15	23	8	Environment Annual Report; City	☺
19	CO_2 emissions per unit of land area			Negative	No data			N/A	N/A	N/A		
20	CO_2 emissions per capita			Negative	No data			N/A	N/A	N/A		
21	SO_2 emissions per unit of land area	Ton per km^2	Whole city	Negative	11.34	33.10	29.49	37	37	0	Environment Annual Report; City	
22	SO_2 emissions per capita	Ton per 10,000 persons	Whole city	Negative	211.11	291.57	264.59	29	29	0	Environment Annual Report; City	
23	COD emissions per unit of land area	Ton per km^2	Whole city	Negative	7.63	29.72	29.85	37	37	0	Environment Annual Report; City	
24	COD emissions per capita	Ton per 10,000 persons	Whole city	Negative	117.25	261.76	267.77	38	38	0	Environment Annual Report; City	

(continued)

(continued)

No.	Indicator	Unit	Scope	Attribute	2010 average of 38 cities	2010 figure	2009 figure	2010 ranking	2009 ranking	Change in ranking	Source of 2010 data	Chernoff face
25	Nitrogen oxides emissions per unit of land area	Ton per km^2	Whole city	Negative	14.61	28.08	20.01	33	29	−4	Environment Annual Report; City	☹
26	Nitrogen oxides emissions per capita	Ton per 10,000 persons	Whole city	Negative	231.68	247.33	179.48	26	22	−4	Environment Annual Report; City	☹
27	Ammonia/nitrogen emissions per unit of land area	Ton per km^2	Whole city	Negative	0.83	2.88	2.51	36	36	0	Environment Annual Report; City	
28	Ammonia/nitrogen emissions per capita	Ton per 10,000 persons	Whole city	Negative	12.50	25.40	22.48	36	36	0	Environment Annual Report; City	
29	Percentage of the days with air quality at or over level II in a year	%	District	Positive	89.45	97.53	98.90	7	7	0	MEP Data	
30	Percentage of days with respirable suspended particulates as the principal pollutants in a year	%	District	Negative	69.76	55.62	54.25	7	9	2	MEP Data	☺
31	Ratio of environmental spending to government expenditure	%	Whole city	Positive	3.14	3.32	2.04	15	23	8	China Statistics; City	☺

32	Ratio of the investment in industrial pollution control to GDP	%	Whole city	Positive	0.09	0.06	0.03	15	27	12	Environment Annual Report; Regional Economy	☺
33	Ratio of the spending on science, education, culture, and public health to government expenditure	%	Whole city	Positive	21.06	23.88	23.81	11	30	19	China Statistics; City; Regional Economy	☺
34	Area of green land per capita in urban areas	m^2	District	Positive	58.13	91.00	80.81	5	6	1	City	☺
35	Green coverage of urban built-in areas	%	District	Positive	39.84	40.40	39.47	18	17	−1	Urban Construction	☹
36	Coverage of water supply	%	District	Positive	98.83	100.00	100.00	1	1	0	Urban Construction	
37	Treatment rate of urban household wastewater	%	District	Positive	86.16	90.10	94.05	19	5	−14	Urban Construction	☹
38	Harmless treatment of urban household waste	%	District	Positive	94.38	96.93	100.00	22	1	−21	Urban Construction	☹
39	Public buses per 10,000 urban residents		District	Positive	15.51	18.66	17.63	5	4	−1	City	☹
40	Industrial SO_2 removal rate	%	Whole city	Positive	57.30	25.30	48.55	37	24	−13	Environment Annual Report	☹

(continued)

(continued)

No.	Indicator	Unit	Scope	Attribute	2010 average of 38 cities	2010 figure	2009 figure	2010 ranking	2009 ranking	Change in ranking	Source of 2010 data	Chernoff face
41	Industrial wastewater COD removal rate	%	Whole city	Positive	76.07	95.78	96.08	1	1	0	Environment Annual Report	
42	Industrial nitrogen oxide removal rate	%	Whole city	Positive	5.24	11.99	52.34	8	1	−7	Environment Annual Report	
43	Industrial waste water ammonia/nitrogen removal rate	%	Whole city	Positive	66.79	72.24	84.32	19	9	−10	Environment Annual Report	

Note:
Regional Economy: *China Regional Economy Statistical Yearbook 2011*
City: *China City Statistical Yearbook 2011*
China Statistics: *China Statistical Yearbook 2011*
Urban Construction: *China Urban Construction Statistical Yearbook 2010*
Environment Annual Report: *China Environment Annual Report 2010*
Environmental Yearbook: *China Environmental Statistical Yearbook 2011*
MEP Data: Ministry of Environmental Protection Data Center

9.17 Brief Analysis of Green Development in Xiamen

Xiamen ranked 24th among the 38 participating cities by GDI according to 2010 data, 14 places lower over 2009 (Xiamen ranked 10th in 2009). Following is a brief analysis of its score by each indicator and their changes from 2009 to 2010.

9.17.1 Xiamen's 2010 Scores by GDI

Xiamen scored −0.059 in 2010. From the three First-Class Indicators including GDEG, CCPNRE, and SDGP as shown in Fig. 9.33, Xiamen showed some comparative advantages in SDGP, yet scored lower than the national average in GDEG and CCPNRE (Note: the national average value of each indicator is 0).

According to Fig. 9.34, Xiamen surpassed the national average in 4 of Second-Class Indicators in 2010, which were SII, GII, II and EMI, yet scored lower than the national average in 5 indicators including GGEI, PII, TII, RAECI and EPCCI.

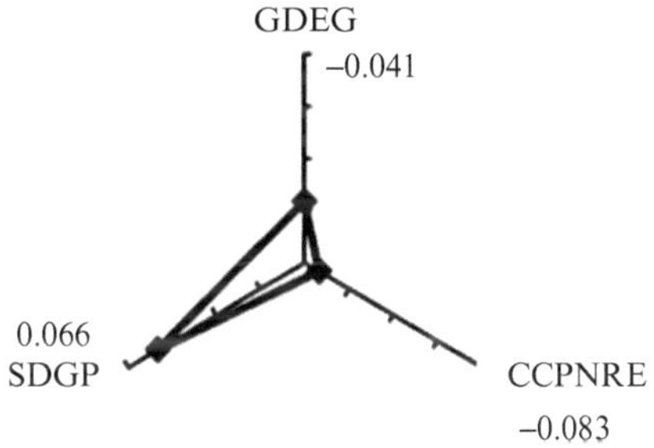

Fig. 9.33 Scores of Xiamen by First-Class Indicators

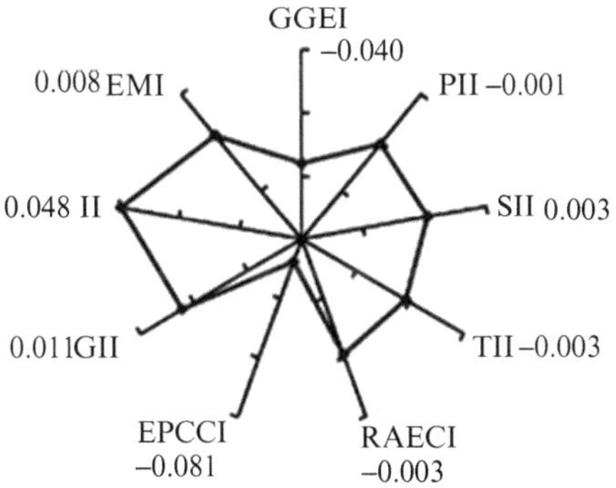

Fig. 9.34 Scores of Xiamen by Second-Class Indicators

Table 9.33 Changes in Xiamen's rankings by First-Class and Second-Class Indicators, 2009–2010

Indicator	2010	2009	Difference	Indicator	2010	2009	Difference
GDI	24	10	−14				
GDEG	23	13	−10	RAECI	15	23	8
GGEI	28	14	−14	EPCCI	27	23	−4
PII	17	18	1	SDGP	13	4	−9
SII	17	15	−2	GII	10	31	21
TII	19	12	−7	II	9	4	−5
CCPNRE	27	24	−3	EMI	20	1	−19

Note: A positive value in "Difference" means a rise in ranking

9.17.2 Changes in Xiamen's GDI Rankings 2009–2010

According to Table 9.33, in First-Class Indicators, the most obvious change occurred in GDEG where Xiamen fell by 10 places in ranking; it fell by 9 places in SDGP and 3 in CCPNRE. In Second-Class Indicators, Xiamen rose by 21, 8 and 1 place in GII, RAECI and PII; it fell by 19 and 14 places in EMI and GGEI. Other indicators suffered from falls by varying degrees.

To further explain the causes of the changes in the rankings by First- and Second-Class Indicators, we put the Third-Class Indicators where a change of more than 3 places occurred from 2009 to 2010 as follows in Table 9.34. Compared with those in 2009, Xiamen both out- and underperformed in ranking in 2010, while the trend of underperforming was notable. It fell by 24 places in Proportion of tertiary sector employees in the total employed population, 21 in Harmless treatment of urban household waste, and dramatic falls occurred in Treatment rate of urban household wastewater etc.; it rose somehow by Ratio of the spending on science, education, culture, and public health to government expenditure and Labor productivity of the tertiary sector etc. compared with that in 2009.

Table 9.34 Third-Class Indicators where changes over 3 places occurred by Xiamen, 2009–2010

Third-Class Indicator	Original data for 2009 and 2010			Change in ranking		
	2010	2009	Unit	2010	2009	Difference
GDP per capita	59,323.00	68,938.00	Yuan	17	9	−8
Energy consumption per unit of GDP	0.57	0.30	Ton per 10,000 yuan	15	6	−9
SO_2 emissions per unit of GDP	27.50	28.20	Ton per 100 million yuan	20	16	−4
Nitrogen oxide emissions per unit of GDP	23.33	19.13	Ton per 100 million yuan	9	6	−3
Labor productivity of the secondary sector	11.80	8.85	10,000 yuan per capita	27	30	3
Recycling rate of industrial water	90.43	93.91	%	18	14	−4
Labor productivity of the tertiary sector	11.64	7.90	10,000 yuan per capita	17	22	5
Proportion of value added of tertiary sector in GDP	49.15	51.56	%	17	11	−6
Proportion of tertiary sector employees in the total employed population	40.43	52.36	%	30	6	−24
Water resources per capita	777.98	395.48	m^3 per capita	15	23	8
Nitrogen oxides emissions per unit of land area	28.08	20.01	Ton per km^2	33	29	−4
Nitrogen oxides emissions per capita	247.33	179.48	Ton per 10,000 persons	26	22	−4
Ratio of environmental spending to government expenditure	3.32	2.04	%	15	23	8
Ratio of the investment in industrial pollution control to GDP	0.06	0.03	%	15	27	12
Ratio of the spending on science, education, culture, and public health to government expenditure	23.88	23.81	%	11	30	19
Treatment rate of urban household wastewater	90.10	94.05	%	19	5	−14
Harmless treatment of urban household waste	96.93	100.00	%	22	1	−21
Industrial SO_2 removal rate	25.30	48.55	%	37	24	−13
Industrial nitrogen oxide removal rate	11.99	52.34	%	8	1	−7
Industrial waste water ammonia/nitrogen removal rate	72.24	84.32	%	19	9	−10

Note: A positive value in "Difference" means a rise in ranking

Green development checkup-Nanchang

No.	Indicator	Unit	Scope	Attribute	2010 average of 38 cities	2010 figure	2009 figure	2010 ranking	2009 ranking	Change in ranking	Source of 2010 data	Chernoff face
1	GDP per capita	Yuan	Whole city	Positive	55,399.15	43,961	39,669.00	24	23	−1	Regional Economy; City	☹
2	Energy consumption per unit of GDP	Ton per 10,000 yuan	Whole city	Negative	0.82	0.84	0.86	21	20	−1	Regional Economy; City	☹
3	Electricity consumption per capita in urban areas	kWh per capita	Whole city	Negative	580.70	302.05	281.06	5	6	1		☺
4	CO_2 emissions per unit of GDP			Negative	No data			N/A	N/A	N/A		
5	SO_2 emissions per unit of GDP	Ton per 100 million yuan	Whole city	Negative	42.67	20.71	19.14	8	5	−3	Regional Economy; Environment Annual Report	☹
6	COD emissions per unit of GDP	Ton per 100 million yuan	Whole city	Negative	24.91	28.29	35.16	29	28	−1	Regional Economy; Environment Annual Report	☹
7	Nitrogen oxide emissions per unit of GDP	Ton per 100 million yuan	Whole city	Negative	40.67	31.87	26.82	19	14	−5	Regional Economy; Environment Annual Report	☹
8	Ammonia/nitrogen emissions per unit of GDP	Ton per 100 million yuan	Whole city	Negative	2.63	2.66	2.76	24	24	0	Regional Economy; Environment Annual Report	

9	Labor productivity of the primary sector	10,000 yuan per capita	Whole city	Positive	3.00	1.68	1.53	29	26	−3	Regional Economy	☹
10	Labor productivity of the secondary sector	10,000 yuan per capita	Whole city	Positive	18.12	17.88	15.13	9	7	−2	Regional Economy	☹
11	Water consumption per unit of value added created by industrial enterprises	10,000 tons per 10,000 yuan	Whole city	Negative	0.03	0.01	0.01	7	7	0	Regional Economy; Environment Annual Report	
12	Energy consumption per unit of value added created by industrial enterprises			Negative	No data			N/A	N/A	N/A		
13	Utilization rate industrial solid waste	%	Whole city	Positive	83.42	93.60	96.90	18	10	−8	Environment Annual Report	☹
14	Recycling rate of industrial water	%	Whole city	Positive	82.10	75.51	75.49	28	31	3	Environment Annual Report	☺
15	Labor productivity of the tertiary sector	10,000 yuan per capita	Whole city	Positive	11.39	5.71	5.08	36	36	0	Regional Economy	
16	Proportion of value added of tertiary sector in GDP	%	Whole city	Positive	48.37	41.25	38.59	31	36	5	City	☺
17	Proportion of tertiary sector employees in the total employed population	%	Whole city	Positive	46.83	50.65	50.87	7	7	0	Regional Economy	

(continued)

(continued)

No.	Indicator	Unit	Scope	Attribute	2010 average of 38 cities	2010 figure	2009 figure	2010 ranking	2009 ranking	Change in ranking	Source of 2010 data	Chernoff face
18	Water resources per capita	m^3 per capita	Whole city	Positive	1,040.56	203.68	980.03	30	12	−18	Environment Annual Report; City	
19	CO_2 emissions per unit of land area			Negative	No data			N/A	N/A	N/A		
20	CO_2 emissions per capita			Negative	No data			N/A	N/A	N/A		
21	SO_2 emissions per unit of land area	Ton per km^2	Whole city	Negative	11.34	5.55	4.50	10	8	−2	Environment Annual Report; City	
22	SO_2 emissions per capita	Ton per 10,000 persons	Whole city	Negative	211.11	82.23	67.16	5	4	−1	Environment Annual Report; City	
23	COD emissions per unit of land area	Ton per km^2	Whole city	Negative	7.63	7.59	8.27	27	27	0	Environment Annual Report; City	
24	COD emissions per capita	Ton per 10,000 persons	Whole city	Negative	117.25	112.34	123.39	20	20	0	Environment Annual Report; City	
25	Nitrogen oxides emissions per unit of land area	Ton per km^2	Whole city	Negative	14.61	8.55	6.31	19	15	−4	Environment Annual Report; City	
26	Nitrogen oxides emissions per capita	Ton per 10,000 persons	Whole city	Negative	231.68	126.57	94.14	12	9	−3	Environment Annual Report; City	
27	Ammonia/nitrogen emissions per unit of land area	Ton per km^2	Whole city	Negative	0.83	0.71	0.65	23	21	−2	Environment Annual Report; City	

28	Ammonia/nitrogen emissions per capita	Ton per 10,000 persons	Whole city	Negative	12.50	10.54	9.68	19	12	−7	Environment Annual Report; City	☹
29	Percentage of the days with air quality at or over level II in a year	%	District	Positive	89.45	93.96	95.05	12	10	−2	MEP Data	☹
30	Percentage of days with respirable suspended particulates as the principal pollutants in a year	%	District	Negative	69.76	69.04	73.42	16	15	−1	MEP Data	☹
31	Ratio of environmental spending to government expenditure	%	Whole city	Positive	3.14	1.47	1.34	35	32	−3	China Statistics; City	☹
32	Ratio of the investment in industrial pollution control to GDP	%	Whole city	Positive	0.09	0.03	0.06	23	20	−3	Environment Annual Report; Regional Economy	☹
33	Ratio of the spending on science, education, culture, and public health to government expenditure	%	Whole city	Positive	21.06	19.96	25.75	22	18	−4	China Statistics; City; Regional Economy	☹
34	Area of green land per capita in urban areas	m^2	District	Positive	58.13	38.00	33.39	19	25	6	City	☹

(continued)

(continued)

No.	Indicator	Unit	Scope	Attribute	2010 average of 38 cities	2010 figure	2009 figure	2010 ranking	2009 ranking	Change in ranking	Source of 2010 data	Chernoff face
35	Green coverage of urban built-in areas	%	District	Positive	39.84	42.76	42.50	11	10	−1	Urban Construction	
36	Coverage of water supply	%	District	Positive	98.83	99.79	100.00	25	1	−24	Urban Construction	
37	Treatment rate of urban household wastewater	%	District	Positive	86.16	75.00	86.07	33	17	−16	Urban Construction	
38	Harmless treatment of urban household waste	%	District	Positive	94.38	100.00	100.00	1	1	0	Urban Construction	
39	Public buses per 10,000 urban residents		District	Positive	15.51	11.75	11.71	26	28	2	City	
40	Industrial SO_2 removal rate	%	Whole city	Positive	57.30	62.99	33.90	18	33	15	Environment Annual Report	
41	Industrial wastewater COD removal rate	%	Whole city	Positive	76.07	40.52	73.53	37	29	−8	Environment Annual Report	
42	Industrial nitrogen oxide removal rate	%	Whole city	Positive	5.24	1.37	1.21	19	20	1	Environment Annual Report	
43	Industrial waste water ammonia/nitrogen removal rate	%	Whole city	Positive	66.79	61.40	34.05	27	33	6	Environment Annual Report	

Note:
Regional Economy: *China Regional Economy Statistical Yearbook 2011*
City: *China City Statistical Yearbook 2011*
China Statistics: *China Statistical Yearbook 2011*
Urban Construction: *China Urban Construction Statistical Yearbook 2010*
Environment Annual Report: *China Environment Annual Report 2010*
Environmental Yearbook: *China Environmental Statistical Yearbook 2011*
MEP Data: Ministry of Environmental Protection Data Center

9.18 Brief Analysis of Green Development in Nanchang

Nanchang ranked 31st among the 38 participating cities by GDI according to 2010 data, 2 places lower over 2009 (Nanchang ranked 29th in 2009). Following is a brief analysis of its score by each indicator and their changes from 2009 to 2010.

9.18.1 Nanchang's 2010 Scores by GDI

Nanchang scored −0.175 in 2010. From the three First-Class Indicators including GDEG, CCPNRE, and SDGP as shown in Fig. 9.35, Nanchang was outperformed by the national average in all three indicators (Note: the national average value of each indicator is 0).

According to Fig. 9.36, Nanchang surpassed the national average in 2 of Second-Class Indicators in 2010, which were SII and II, yet scored lower than the national average 7 indicators including GGEI, PII, TII, RAECI, EPCCI, GII and EMI.

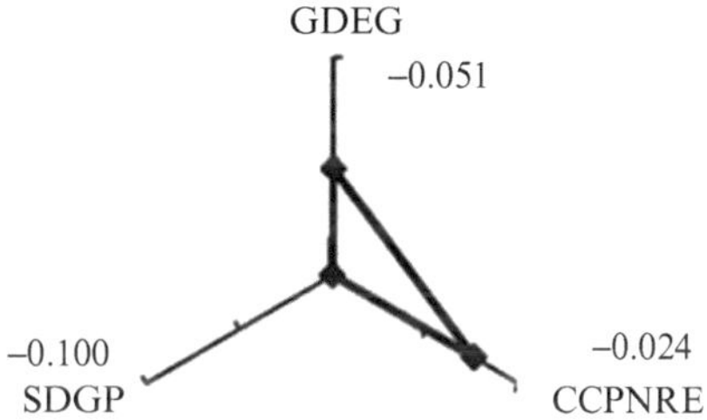

Fig. 9.35 Scores of Nanchang by First-Class Indicators

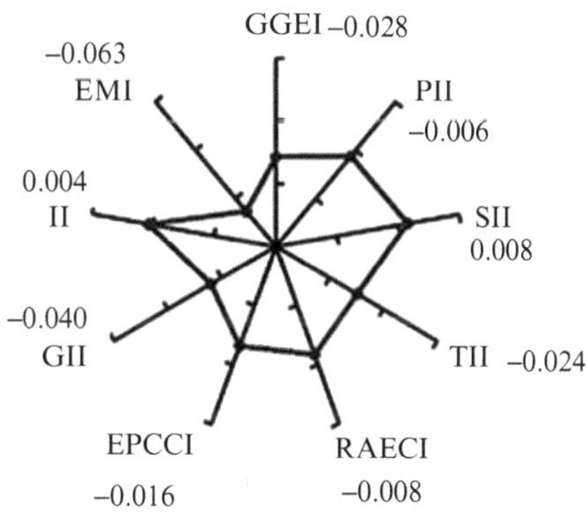

Fig. 9.36 Scores of Nanchang by Second-Class Indicators

Table 9.35 Changes in Nanchang's rankings by First-Class and Second-Class Indicators, 2009–2010

Indicator	2010	2009	Difference	Indicator	2010	2009	Difference
GDI	31	29	−2				
GDEG	25	24	−1	RAECI	30	12	−18
GGEI	25	26	1	EPCCI	17	17	0
PII	29	26	−3	SDGP	30	29	−1
SII	13	11	−2	GII	31	29	−2
TII	30	32	2	II	22	9	−13
CCPNRE	17	17	0	EMI	32	34	2

Note: A positive value in "Difference" means a rise in ranking

9.18.2 Changes in Nanchang's GDI Rankings 2009–2010

According to Table 9.35, in First-Class Indicators, the most obvious change occurred in GDEG and SDGP, where Nanchang fell by 1 place in ranking; it remained unchanged in CCPNRE. In Second-Class Indicators, Nanchang rose by 2 places in TII and EMI, and 1 place in GGEI; it fell by 18 and 13 places in RAECI and II, 3, 2, and 2 places in PII, SII and GII. It remained the same as those in 2009 in EPCCI.

To further explain the causes of the changes in the rankings by First- and Second-Class Indicators, we put the Third-Class Indicators where a change of more than 3 places occurred from 2009 to 2010 as follows in Table 9.36. Compared with those in 2009, Nanchang both out- and underperformed in ranking in 2010, while the more obvious trend is underperforming compared with the previous year. It dropped by 24 places in Coverage of water supply compared with that in 2009, and 18 in Water resources per capita. Other indicators suffered from falls by varying degrees; it rose to a certain extent in Industrial SO_2 removal rate, Area of green land per capita in urban areas and Industrial waste water ammonia/nitrogen removal rate.

Table 9.36 Third-Class Indicators where changes over 3 places occurred by Nanchang, 2009–2010

Third-Class Indicator	Original data for 2009 and 2010			Change in ranking		
	2010	2009	Unit	2010	2009	Difference
SO_2 emissions per unit of GDP	20.71	19.14	Ton per 100 million yuan	8	5	−3
Nitrogen oxide emissions per unit of GDP	31.87	26.82	Ton per 100 million yuan	19	14	−5
Labor productivity of the primary sector	1.68	1.53	10,000 yuan per capita	29	26	−3
Utilization rate industrial solid waste	93.60	96.90	%	18	10	−8
Recycling rate of industrial water	75.51	75.49	%	28	31	3
Proportion of value added of tertiary sector in GDP	41.25	38.59	%	31	36	5
Water resources per capita	203.68	980.03	m^3 per capita	30	12	−18
Nitrogen oxides emissions per unit of land area	8.55	6.31	Ton per km^2	19	15	−4
Nitrogen oxides emissions per capita	126.57	94.14	Ton per 10,000 persons	12	9	−3
Ammonia/nitrogen emissions per capita	10.54	9.68	Ton per 10,000 persons	19	12	−7
Ratio of environmental spending to government expenditure	1.47	1.34	%	35	32	−3
Ratio of the investment in industrial pollution control to GDP	0.03	0.06	%	23	20	−3
Ratio of the spending on science, education, culture, and public health to government expenditure	19.96	25.75	%	22	18	−4
Area of green land per capita in urban areas	38.00	33.39	m^2	19	25	6
Coverage of water supply	99.79	100.00	%	25	1	−24
Treatment rate of urban household wastewater	75.00	86.07	%	33	17	−16
Industrial SO_2 removal rate	62.99	33.90	%	18	33	15
Industrial wastewater COD removal rate	40.52	73.53	%	37	29	−8
Industrial waste water ammonia/nitrogen removal rate	61.40	34.05	%	27	33	6

Note: A positive value in "Difference" means a rise in ranking

Green development checkup-Jinan

No.	Indicator	Unit	Scope	Attribute	2010 average of 38 cities	2010 figure	2009 figure	2010 ranking	2009 ranking	Change in ranking	Source of 2010 data	Chernoff face
1	GDP per capita	Yuan	Whole city	Positive	55,399.15	57,947	50,218.90	18	19	1	Regional Economy; City	
2	Energy consumption per unit of GDP	Ton per 10,000 yuan	Whole city	Negative	0.82	0.87	N/A	23	N/A	N/A	Regional Economy; City	
3	Electricity consumption per capita in urban areas	kWh per capita	Whole city	Negative	580.70	495.68	434.65	20	20	0	City	
4	CO_2 emissions per unit of GDP			Negative	No data			N/A	N/A	N/A		
5	SO_2 emissions per unit of GDP	Ton per 100 million yuan	Whole city	Negative	42.67	22.70	25.92	13	13	0	Regional Economy; Environment Annual Report	
6	COD emissions per unit of GDP	Ton per 100 million yuan	Whole city	Negative	24.91	13.18	15.45	9	9	0	Regional Economy; Environment Annual Report	
7	Nitrogen oxide emissions per unit of GDP	Ton per 100 million yuan	Whole city	Negative	40.67	25.03	27.74	13	15	2	Regional Economy; Environment Annual Report	
8	Ammonia/nitrogen emissions per unit of GDP	Ton per 100 million yuan	Whole city	Negative	2.63	1.33	1.96	12	15	3	Regional Economy; Environment Annual Report	
9	Labor productivity of the primary sector	10,000 yuan per capita	Whole city	Positive	3.00	2.79	2.43	11	11	0	Regional Economy	

10	Labor productivity of the secondary sector	10,000 yuan per capita	Whole city	Positive	18.12		12.58	11.59	21	20	−1	Regional Economy	☹
11	Water consumption per unit of value added created by industrial enterprises	10,000 tons per 10,000 yuan	Whole city	Negative	0.03		0.02	0.03	20	24	4	Regional Economy; Environment Annual Report	☺
12	Energy consumption per unit of value added created by industrial enterprises			Negative	No data				N/A	N/A	N/A		
13	Utilization rate industrial solid waste	%	Whole city	Positive	83.42		97.50	93.90	11	15	4	Environment Annual Report	☺
14	Recycling rate of industrial water	%	Whole city	Positive	82.10		96.06	96.48	4	3	−1	Environment Annual Report	☹
15	Labor productivity of the tertiary sector	10,000 yuan per capita	Whole city	Positive	11.39		12.18	10.45	15	14	−1	Regional Economy	☹
16	Proportion of value added of tertiary sector in GDP	%	Whole city	Positive	48.37		52.62	51.49	10	12	2	City	☺
17	Proportion of tertiary sector employees in the total employed population	%	Whole city	Positive	46.83		44.36	45.46	24	20	−4	Regional Economy	☹
18	Water resources per capita	m^3 per capita	Whole city	Positive	1,040.56		289.70	332.52	27	27	0	Environment Annual Report; City	
19	CO_2 emissions per unit of land area			Negative	No data				N/A	N/A	N/A		

(continued)

(continued)

No.	Indicator	Unit	Scope	Attribute	2010 average of 38 cities	2010 figure	2009 figure	2010 ranking	2009 ranking	Change in ranking	Source of 2010 data	Chernoff face
20	CO_2 emissions per capita			Negative	No data			N/A	N/A	N/A		
21	SO_2 emissions per unit of land area	Ton per km^2	Whole city	Negative	11.34	9.98	10.11	22	22	0	Environment Annual Report; City	
22	SO_2 emissions per capita	Ton per 10,000 persons	Whole city	Negative	211.11	135.17	136.95	15	13	−2	Environment Annual Report; City	
23	COD emissions per unit of land area	Ton per km^2	Whole city	Negative	7.63	5.79	6.03	22	21	−1	Environment Annual Report; City	
24	COD emissions per capita	Ton per 10,000 persons	Whole city	Negative	117.25	78.44	81.64	13	15	2	Environment Annual Report; City	
25	Nitrogen oxides emissions per unit of land area	Ton per km^2	Whole city	Negative	14.61	11.00	10.82	24	25	1	Environment Annual Report; City	
26	Nitrogen oxides emissions per capita	Ton per 10,000 persons	Whole city	Negative	231.68	149.03	146.57	15	16	1	Environment Annual Report; City	
27	Ammonia/nitrogen emissions per unit of land area	Ton per km^2	Whole city	Negative	0.83	0.58	0.77	18	24	6	Environment Annual Report; City	
28	Ammonia/nitrogen emissions per capita	Ton per 10,000 persons	Whole city	Negative	12.50	7.92	10.38	11	15	4	Environment Annual Report; City	
29	Percentage of the days with air quality at or over level II in a year	%	District	Positive	89.45	84.34	80.77	30	34	4	MEP Data	

30	Percentage of days with respirable suspended particulates as the principal pollutants in a year	%	District	Negative	69.76	93.42	94.79	37	37	0	MEP Data	
31	Ratio of environmental spending to government expenditure	%	Whole city	Positive	3.14	3.39	2.81	13	13	0	China Statistics; City	
32	Ratio of the investment in industrial pollution control to GDP	%	Whole city	Positive	0.09	0.07	0.02	12	32	20	Environment Annual Report; Regional Economy	☺
33	Ratio of the spending on science, education, culture, and public health to government expenditure	%	Whole city	Positive	21.06	21.18	25.64	17	19	2	China Statistics; City; Regional Economy	☺
34	Area of green land per capita in urban areas		District	Positive	58.13	34.00	31.49	24	27	3	City	☺
35	Green coverage of urban built-in areas	%	District	Positive	39.84	37.04	36.43	30	29	−1	Urban Construction	☹
36	Coverage of water supply	%	District	Positive	98.83	100.00	99.82	1	20	19	Urban Construction	☺
37	Treatment rate of urban household wastewater	%	District	Positive	86.16	96.65	94.08	6	4	−2	Urban Construction	☹
38	Harmless treatment of urban household waste	%	District	Positive	94.38	90.78	78.03	29	32	3	Urban Construction	☺
39	Public buses per 10,000 urban residents		District	Positive	15.51	12.18	12.55	25	21	−4	City	☹

(continued)

(continued)

No.	Indicator	Unit	Scope	Attribute	2010 average of 38 cities	2010 figure	2009 figure	2010 ranking	2009 ranking	Change in ranking	Source of 2010 data	Chernoff face
40	Industrial SO_2 removal rate	%	Whole city	Positive	57.30	68.01	68.24	13	11	−2	Environment Annual Report	
41	Industrial wastewater COD removal rate	%	Whole city	Positive	76.07	82.83	79.03	19	24	5	Environment Annual Report	
42	Industrial nitrogen oxide removal rate	%	Whole city	Positive	5.24	0.01	0.00	30	29	−1	Environment Annual Report	
43	Industrial waste water ammonia/nitrogen removal rate	%	Whole city	Positive	66.79	92.10	91.02	6	6	0	Environment Annual Report	

Note:
Regional Economy: *China Regional Economy Statistical Yearbook 2011*
City: *China City Statistical Yearbook 2011*
China Statistics: *China Statistical Yearbook 2011*
Urban Construction: *China Urban Construction Statistical Yearbook 2010*
Environment Annual Report: *China Environment Annual Report 2010*
Environmental Yearbook: *China Environmental Statistical Yearbook 2011*
MEP Data: Ministry of Environmental Protection Data Center

9.19 Brief Analysis of Green Development in Jinan

Jinan ranked 19th among the 38 participating cities by GDI according to 2010 data, 5 places higher over 2009 (Jinan ranked 5th in 2009). Following is a brief analysis of its score by each indicator and their changes from 2009 to 2010.

9.19.1 Jinan's 2010 Scores by GDI

Jinan scored −0.029 in 2010. From the three First-Class Indicators including GDEG, CCPNRE, and SDGP as shown in Fig. 9.37, Jinan showed some comparative advantages in terms of GDEG and SDGP, yet scored lower than the national average in CCPNRE (Note: the national average value of each indicator is 0).

According to Fig. 9.38, Jinan surpassed the national average in 5 of Second-Class Indicators in 2010, which were PII, SII, TII, GII and EMI; it was outperformed by the national average in 3 indicators, which were RAECI, EPCCI and II; it was about the same level with the national average in GGEI.

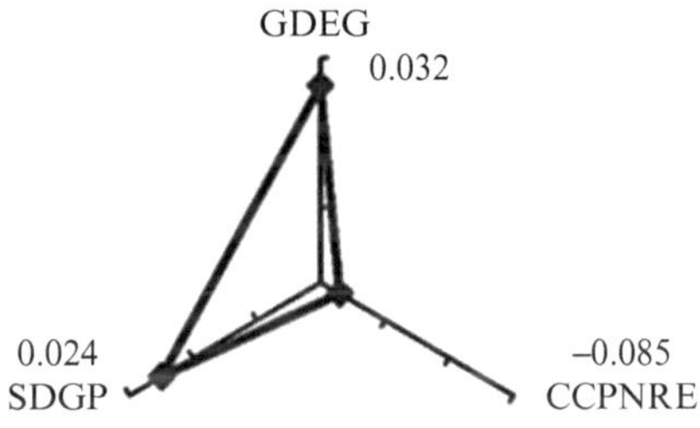

Fig. 9.37 Scores of Jinan by First-Class Indicators

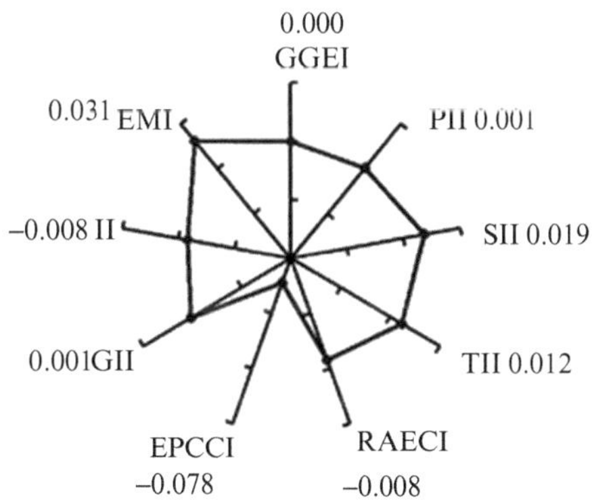

Fig. 9.38 Scores of Jinan by Second-Class Indicators

Table 9.37 Changes in Jinan's rankings by First-Class and Second-Class Indicators, 2009–2010

Indicator	2010	2009	Difference	Indicator	2010	2009	Difference
GDI	19	24	5				
GDEG	13	14	1	RAECI	27	27	0
GGEI	17	18	1	EPCCI	26	28	2
PII	10	11	1	SDGP	19	21	2
SII	9	8	−1	GII	12	21	9
TII	12	13	1	II	24	26	2
CCPNRE	28	29	1	EMI	12	17	5

Note: A positive value in "Difference" means a rise in ranking

9.19.2 Changes in Jinan's GDI Rankings 2009–2010

According to Table 9.37, in First-Class Indicators, the most obvious change occurred in SDGP, where Jinan rose by 2 places in ranking; it rose by 1 place respectively in GDEG and CCPNRE. In Second-Class Indicators, Jinan rose by 9 places in GII, 5 in EMI, 2 in II and EPCCI, and 1 in GGEI, PII and TII; it fell by 1 place in SII; it remained unchanged by RAECI compared with that in 2009.

To further explain the causes of the changes in the rankings by First- and Second-Class Indicators, we put the Third-Class Indicators where a change of more than 3 places occurred from 2009 to 2010 as follows in Table 9.38. Compared with those in 2009, Jinan both out- and underperformed in ranking in 2010 with a notable rising trend. It rose by 20 places in Ratio of the investment in industrial pollution control to GDP, 19 in Coverage of water supply, and rises in most indicators such as Ammonia/nitrogen emissions per unit of land area and Industrial wastewater COD removal rate; yet it fell by 4 places by Proportion of tertiary sector employees in the total employed population and Public buses per 10,000 urban residents compared with that in 2009.

Table 9.38 Third-Class Indicators where changes over 3 places occurred by Jinan, 2009–2010

Third-Class Indicator	Original data for 2009 and 2010			Change in ranking		
	2010	2009	Unit	2010	2009	Difference
Ammonia/nitrogen emissions per unit of GDP	1.33	1.96	Ton per 100million yuan	12	15	3
Water consumption per unit of value added created by industrial enterprises	0.02	0.03	10,000 tons per 10,000 yuan	20	24	4
Utilization rate industrial solid waste	97.50	93.90	%	11	15	4
Proportion of tertiary sector employees in the total employed population	44.36	45.46	%	24	20	−4
Ammonia/nitrogen emissions per unit of land area	0.58	0.77	Ton per km^2	18	24	6
Ammonia/nitrogen emissions per capita	7.92	10.38	Ton per 10,000 persons	11	15	4
Percentage of the days with air quality at or over level II in a year	84.34	80.77	%	30	34	4
Ratio of the investment in industrial pollution control to GDP	0.07	0.02	%	12	32	20
Area of green land per capita in urban areas	34.00	31.49	m^2	24	27	3
Coverage of water supply	100.00	99.82	%	1	20	19
Harmless treatment of urban household waste	90.78	78.03	%	29	32	3
Public buses per 10,000 urban residents	12.18	12.55		25	21	−4
Industrial wastewater COD removal rate	82.83	79.03	%	19	24	5

Note: A positive value in "Difference" means a rise in ranking

Green development checkup-Qingdao

No.	Indicator	Unit	Scope	Attribute	2010 average of 38 cities	2010 figure	2009 figure	2010 ranking	Ranking	Change in ranking	Source of 2010 data	Chernoff face
1	GDP per capita	Yuan	Whole city	Positive	55,399.15	65,812	57,251.15	13	14	1	Regional Economy; City	☺
2	Energy consumption per unit of GDP	Ton per 10,000 yuan	Whole city	Negative	0.82	0.32	0.35	9	9	0	Regional Economy; City	
3	Electricity consumption per capita in urban areas	kWh per capita	Whole city	Negative	580.70	356.78	699.09	9	31	22	City	☺
4	CO_2 emissions per unit of GDP			Negative	No data			N/A	N/A	N/A		
5	SO_2 emissions per unit of GDP	Ton per 100 million yuan	Whole city	Negative	42.67	21.74	24.73	10	11	1	Regional Economy; Environment Annual Report	☺
6	COD emissions per unit of GDP	Ton per 100 million yuan	Whole city	Negative	24.91	8.99	10.55	4	4	0	Regional Economy; Environment Annual Report	
7	Nitrogen oxide emissions per unit of GDP	Ton per 100 million yuan	Whole city	Negative	40.67	15.45	20.40	4	7	3	Regional Economy; Environment Annual Report	☺
8	Ammonia/nitrogen emissions per unit of GDP	Ton per 100 million yuan	Whole city	Negative	2.63	1.56	1.34	14	8	–6	Regional Economy; Environment Annual Report	☹

9	Labor productivity of the primary sector	10,000 yuan per capita	Whole city	Positive	3.00	2.66	2.23	15	14	−1	Regional Economy	☹
10	Labor productivity of the secondary sector	10,000 yuan per capita	Whole city	Positive	18.12	12.51	11.10	22	21	−1	Regional Economy	☹
11	Water consumption per unit of value added created by industrial enterprises	10,000 tons per 10,000 yuan	Whole city	Negative	0.03	0.01	0.01	11	8	−3	Regional Economy; Environment Annual Report	☹
12	Energy consumption per unit of value added created by industrial enterprises			Negative	No data			N/A	N/A	N/A		
13	Utilization rate industrial solid waste	%	Whole city	Positive	83.42	98.30	98.20	8	8	0	Environment Annual Report	
14	Recycling rate of industrial water	%	Whole city	Positive	82.10	89.12	87.59	21	20	−1	Environment Annual Report	☹
15	Labor productivity of the tertiary sector	10,000 yuan per capita	Whole city	Positive	11.39	13.99	12.69	9	8	−1	Regional Economy	☹
16	Proportion of value added of tertiary sector in GDP	%	Whole city	Positive	48.37	46.43	45.40	21	24	3	City	☺

(continued)

(continued)

No.	Indicator	Unit	Scope	Attribute	2010 average of 38 cities	2010 figure	2009 figure	2010 ranking	Ranking	Change in ranking	Source of 2010 data	Chernoff face
17	Proportion of tertiary sector employees in the total employed population	%	Whole city	Positive	46.83	37.68	35.64	33	34	1	Regional Economy	
18	Water resources per capita	m^3 per capita	Whole city	Positive	1,040.56	207.95	155.05	29	35	6	Environment Annual Report; City	
19	CO_2 emissions per unit of land area			Negative	No data			N/A	N/A	N/A		
20	CO_2 emissions per capita			Negative	No data			N/A	N/A	N/A		
21	SO_2 emissions per unit of land area	Ton per km^2	Whole city	Negative	11.34	10.27	10.35	23	23	0	Environment Annual Report; City	
22	SO_2 emissions per capita	Ton per 10,000 persons	Whole city	Negative	211.11	147.73	149.07	17	18	1	Environment Annual Report; City	
23	COD emissions per unit of land area	Ton per km^2	Whole city	Negative	7.63	4.25	4.42	15	14	−1	Environment Annual Report; City	
24	COD emissions per capita	Ton per 10,000 persons	Whole city	Negative	117.25	61.10	63.60	3	3	0	Environment Annual Report; City	
25	Nitrogen oxides emissions per unit of land area	Ton per km^2	Whole city	Negative	14.61	7.30	8.54	14	22	8	Environment Annual Report; City	

26	Nitrogen oxides emissions per capita	Ton per 10,000 persons	Whole city	Negative	231.68	105.01	122.97	10	13	3	Environment Annual Report; City	☺
27	Ammonia/nitrogen emissions per unit of land area	Ton per km^2	Whole city	Negative	0.83	0.74	0.56	24	18	−6	Environment Annual Report; City	☹
28	Ammonia/nitrogen emissions per capita	Ton per 10,000 persons	Whole city	Negative	12.50	10.58	8.07	20	8	−12	Environment Annual Report; City	☹
29	Percentage of the days with air quality at or over level II in a year	%	District	Positive	89.45	90.38	91.21	18	16	−2	MEP Data	☹
30	Percentage of days with respirable suspended particulates as the principal pollutants in a year	%	District	Negative	69.76	78.90	76.44	23	17	−6	MEP Data	☹
31	Ratio of environmental spending to government expenditure	%	Whole city	Positive	3.14	2.42	1.63	21	27	6	China Statistics; City	☺
32	Ratio of the investment in industrial pollution control to GDP	%	Whole city	Positive	0.09	0.02	0.02	27	33	6	Environment Annual Report; Regional Economy	☺

(continued)

(continued)

No.	Indicator	Unit	Scope	Attribute	2010 average of 38 cities	2010 figure	2009 figure	2010 ranking	Ranking	Change in ranking	Source of 2010 data	Chernoff face
33	Ratio of the spending on science, education, culture, and public health to government expenditure	%	Whole city	Positive	21.06	15.87	24.79	33	26	−7	China Statistics; City; Regional Economy	☹
34	Area of green land per capita in urban areas	m^2	District	Positive	58.13	60.00	58.09	8	9	1	City	☺
35	Green coverage of urban built-in areas	%	District	Positive	39.84	43.38	43.38	7	7	0	Urban Construction	
36	Coverage of water supply	%	District	Positive	98.83	100.00	100.00	1	1	0	Urban Construction	
37	Treatment rate of urban household wastewater	%	District	Positive	86.16	88.29	84.64	22	18	−4	Urban Construction	☹
38	Harmless treatment of urban household waste	%	District	Positive	94.38	100.00	100.00	1	1	0	Urban Construction	
39	Public buses per 10,000 urban residents		District	Positive	15.51	16.93	15.57	9	9	0	City	
40	Industrial SO_2 removal rate	%	Whole city	Positive	57.30	64.56	66.44	14	13	−1	Environment Annual Report	☹
41	Industrial wastewater COD removal rate	%	Whole city	Positive	76.07	84.82	85.05	16	19	3	Environment Annual Report	☺

42	Industrial nitrogen oxide removal rate	%	Whole city	Positive	5.24	1.26	0.94	20	22	2	Environment Annual Report	☺
43	Industrial waste water ammonia/nitrogen removal rate	%	Whole city	Positive	66.79	87.52	89.47	9	8	−1	Environment Annual Report	☹

Note:
Regional Economy: *China Regional Economy Statistical Yearbook 2011*
City: *China City Statistical Yearbook 2011*
China Statistics: *China Statistical Yearbook 2011*
Urban Construction: *China Urban Construction Statistical Yearbook 2010*
Environment Annual Report: *China Environment Annual Report 2010*
Environmental Yearbook: *China Environmental Statistical Yearbook 2011*
MEP Data: Ministry of Environmental Protection Data Center

9.20 Brief Analysis of Green Development in Qingdao

Qingdao ranked 8th among the 38 participating cities by GDI according to 2010 data, 1 place higher over 2009 (Qingdao ranked 9th in 2009). Following is a brief analysis of its score by each indicator and their changes from 2009 to 2010.

9.20.1 Qingdao's 2010 Scores by GDI

Qingdao scored 0.109 in 2010. From the three First-Class Indicators including GDEG, CCPNRE, and SDGP as shown in Fig. 9.39, Qingdao showed some comparative advantages in terms of GDEG and SDGP, yet scored lower than the national average in CCPNRE (Note: the national average value of each indicator is 0).

According to Fig. 9.40, Qingdao surpassed the national average in 4 of Second-Class Indicators in 2010, which were GGEI, SII, II and EMI. It scored lower than the national average in TII, RAECI, EPCCI and GII. It remained the same as the national average in PII.

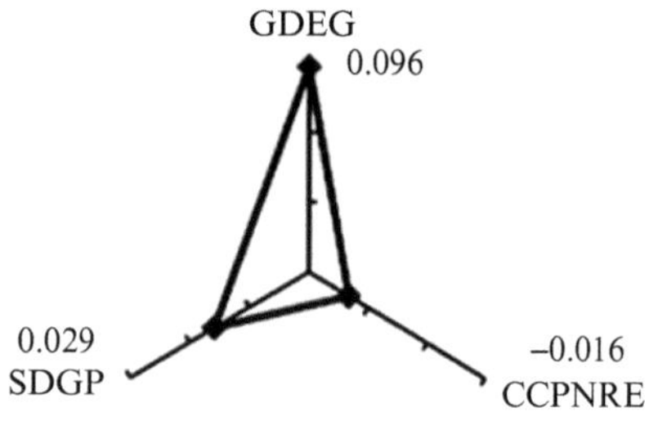

Fig. 9.39 Scores of Qingdao by First-Class Indicators

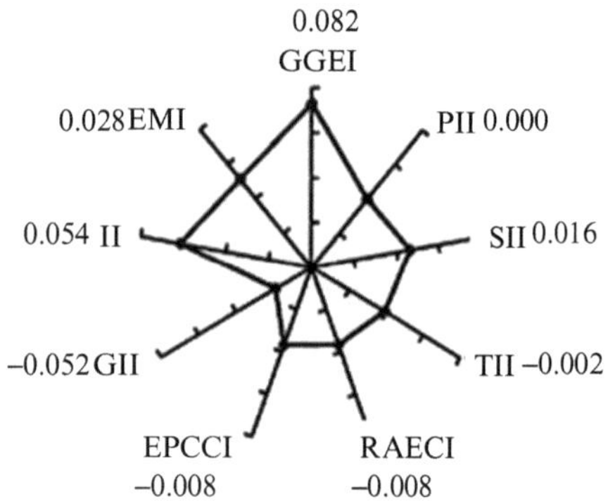

Fig. 9.40 Scores of Qingdao by Second-Class Indicators

Table 9.39 Changes in Qingdao's rankings by First-Class and Second-Class Indicators, 2009–2010

Indicator	2010	2009	Difference	Indicator	2010	2009	Difference
GDI	8	9	1				
GDEG	6	9	3	RAECI	29	35	6
GGEI	4	7	3	EPCCI	16	14	−2
PII	14	14	0	SDGP	18	13	−5
SII	11	7	−4	GII	35	33	−2
TII	17	20	3	II	6	5	−1
CCPNRE	16	14	−2	EMI	14	11	−3

Note: A positive value in "Difference" means a rise in ranking

9.20.2 Changes in Qingdao's GDI Rankings 2009–2010

According to Table 9.39, in First-Class Indicators, Qingdao rose by 3 places in GDEG. It dropped by 5 and 2 places in SDGP and CCPNRE. From changes in ranking, it rose by 6, 3 and 3 places in RAECI, GGEI and TII; it dropped by 4, 3, 2, 2, and 1 place in SII, EMI, EPCCI, GII and II. It remained unchanged by PII as compared with that in 2009.

To further explain the causes of the changes in the rankings by First- and Second-Class Indicators, we put the Third-Class Indicators where a change of more than 3 places occurred from 2009 to 2010 as follows in Table 9.40. Compared with those in 2009, Qingdao both out- and underperformed in ranking in 2010 with dramatic oscillation. It rose by 22 places in Electricity consumption per capita in urban areas and 8 in Nitrogen oxides emissions per unit of land area. It rose by small scales in other indicators such as Water resources per capita. It dropped by 12 places in Ammonia/nitrogen emissions per capita as compared with that in 2009 and 7 in Ratio of the spending on science, education, culture, and public health to government expenditure. It dropped slightly in other indicators such as Ammonia/nitrogen emissions per unit of GDP and Percentage of days with respirable suspended particulates as the principal pollutants in a year.

Table 9.40 Third-Class Indicators where changes over 3 places occurred by Qingdao, 2009–2010

Third-Class Indicator	Original data for 2009 and 2010			Change in ranking		
	2010	2009	Unit	2010	2009	Difference
Electricity consumption per capita in urban areas	356.78	699.09	kWh per capita	9	31	22
Nitrogen oxide emissions per unit of GDP	15.45	20.40	Ton per 100 million yuan	4	7	3
Ammonia/nitrogen emissions per unit of GDP	1.56	1.34	Ton per 100 million yuan	14	8	−6
Water consumption per unit of value added created by industrial enterprises	0.01	0.01	10,000 tons per 10,000 yuan	11	8	−3
Proportion of value added of tertiary sector in GDP	46.43	45.40	%	21	24	3
Water resources per capita	207.95	155.05	m^3 per capita	29	35	6
Nitrogen oxides emissions per unit of land area	7.30	8.54	Ton per km^2	14	22	8
Nitrogen oxides emissions per capita	105.01	122.97	Ton per 10,000 persons	10	13	3
Ammonia/nitrogen emissions per unit of land area	0.74	0.56	Ton per km^2	24	18	−6
Ammonia/nitrogen emissions per capita	10.58	8.07	Ton per 10,000 persons	20	8	−12
Percentage of days with respirable suspended particulates as the principal pollutants in a year	78.90	76.44	%	23	17	−6
Ratio of environmental spending to government expenditure	2.42	1.63	%	21	27	6
Ratio of the investment in industrial pollution control to GDP	0.02	0.02	%	27	33	6
Ratio of the spending on science, education, culture, and public health to government expenditure	15.87	24.79	%	33	26	−7
Treatment rate of urban household wastewater	88.29	84.64	%	22	18	−4
Industrial wastewater COD removal rate	84.82	85.05	%	16	19	3

Note: A positive value in "Difference" means a rise in ranking

Green development checkup-Zhengzhou

No.	Indicator	Unit	Scope	Attribute	2010 average of 38 cities	2010 figure	2009 figure	2010 ranking	2009 ranking	Change in ranking	Source of 2010 data	Chernoff face
1	GDP per capita	Yuan	Whole city	Positive	55,399.15	47,608	44,231.35	21	21	0	Regional Economy; City	
2	Energy consumption per unit of GDP	Ton per 10,000 yuan	Whole city	Negative	0.82	0.60	0.65	16	14	−2	Regional Economy; City	
3	Electricity consumption per capita in urban areas	kWh per capita	Whole city	Negative	580.70	427.89	372.52	16	15	−1	City	
4	CO_2 emissions per unit of GDP			Negative	No data			N/A	N/A	N/A		
5	SO_2 emissions per unit of GDP	Ton per 100 million yuan	Whole city	Negative	42.67	42.05	45.33	26	26	0	Regional Economy; Environment Annual Report	
6	COD emissions per unit of GDP	Ton per 100 million yuan	Whole city	Negative	24.91	15.67	17.11	14	12	−2	Regional Economy; Environment Annual Report	
7	Nitrogen oxide emissions per unit of GDP	Ton per 100 million yuan	Whole city	Negative	40.67	47.49	45.72	27	28	1	Regional Economy; Environment Annual Report	
8	Ammonia/nitrogen emissions per unit of GDP	Ton per 100 million yuan	Whole city	Negative	2.63	2.36	1.81	21	13	−8	Regional Economy; Environment Annual Report	

(continued)

(continued)

No.	Indicator	Unit	Scope	Attribute	2010 average of 38 cities	2010 figure	2009 figure	2010 ranking	2009 ranking	Change in ranking	Source of 2010 data	Chernoff face
9	Labor productivity of the primary sector	10,000 yuan per capita	Whole city	Positive	3.00	1.17	1.03	33	32	−1	Regional Economy	☹
10	Labor productivity of the secondary sector	10,000 yuan per capita	Whole city	Positive	18.12	14.50	11.70	15	18	3	Regional Economy	☺
11	Water consumption per unit of value added created by industrial enterprises	10,000 tons per 10,000 yuan	Whole city	Negative	0.03	0.01	0.02	14	15	1	Regional Economy; Environment Annual Report	☺
12	Energy consumption per unit of value added created by industrial enterprises			Negative	No data			N/A	N/A	N/A		
13	Utilization rate industrial solid waste	%	Whole city	Positive	83.42	83.00	82.60	27	28	1	Environment Annual Report	☺
14	Recycling rate of industrial water	%	Whole city	Positive	82.10	87.58	92.21	24	16	−8	Environment Annual Report	☹
15	Labor productivity of the tertiary sector	10,000 yuan per capita	Whole city	Positive	11.39	8.32	7.82	25	23	−2	Regional Economy	☹
16	Proportion of value added of tertiary sector in GDP	%	Whole city	Positive	48.37	40.74	42.89	33	30	−3	City	☹

17	Proportion of tertiary sector employees in the total employed population	%	Whole city	Positive	46.83		44.65	41.10	23	27	4	Regional Economy ☺
18	Water resources per capita	m^3 per capita	Whole city	Positive	1,040.56		140.36	182.95	34	32	−2	Environment Annual Report; City ☹
19	CO_2 emissions per unit of land area			Negative	No data				N/A	N/A	N/A	
20	CO_2 emissions per capita			Negative	No data				N/A	N/A	N/A	
21	SO_2 emissions per unit of land area	Ton per km^2	Whole city	Negative	11.34		17.81	16.99	31	30	−1	Environment Annual Report; City ☹
22	SO_2 emissions per capita	Ton per 10,000 persons	Whole city	Negative	211.11		179.67	174.26	21	20	−1	Environment Annual Report; City ☹
23	COD emissions per unit of land area	Ton per km^2	Whole city	Negative	7.63		6.64	6.41	24	24	0	Environment Annual Report; City
24	COD emissions per capita	Ton per 10,000 persons	Whole city	Negative	117.25		66.97	65.79	5	4	−1	Environment Annual Report; City ☹
25	Nitrogen oxides emissions per unit of land area	Ton per km^2	Whole city	Negative	14.61		20.11	17.13	28	27	−1	Environment Annual Report; City ☹
26	Nitrogen oxides emissions per capita	Ton per 10,000 persons	Whole city	Negative	231.68		202.92	175.77	23	21	−2	Environment Annual Report; City ☹
27	Ammonia/nitrogen emissions per unit of land area	Ton per km^2	Whole city	Negative	0.83		1.00	0.68	29	22	−7	Environment Annual Report; City ☹

(continued)

(continued)

No.	Indicator	Unit	Scope	Attribute	2010 average of 38 cities	2010 figure	2009 figure	2010 ranking	2009 ranking	Change in ranking	Source of 2010 data	Chernoff face
28	Ammonia/nitrogen emissions per capita	Ton per 10,000 persons	Whole city	Negative	12.50	10.10	6.97	18	3	−15	Environment Annual Report; City	☹
29	Percentage of the days with air quality at or over level II in a year	%	District	Positive	89.45	86.81	88.19	22	23	1	MEP Data	☺
30	Percentage of days with respirable suspended particulates as the principal pollutants in a year	%	District	Negative	69.76	86.58	88.49	31	33	2	MEP Data	☺
31	Ratio of environmental spending to government expenditure	%	Whole city	Positive	3.14	2.00	2.71	27	15	−12	China Statistics; City	☹
32	Ratio of the investment in industrial pollution control to GDP	%	Whole city	Positive	0.09	0.03	0.08	25	17	−8	Environment Annual Report; Regional Economy	☹
33	Ratio of the spending on science, education, culture, and public health to government expenditure	%	Whole city	Positive	21.06	19.98	28.47	21	12	−9	China Statistics; City; Regional Economy	☹
34	Area of green land per capita in urban areas		District	Positive	58.13	22.00	36.14	35	22	−13	City	☹
35	Green coverage of urban built-in areas	%	District	Positive	39.84	34.88	34.54	35	34	−1	Urban Construction	☹

36	Coverage of water supply	%	District	Positive	98.83		100.00	100.00	1	1	0	Urban Construction	
37	Treatment rate of urban household wastewater	%	District	Positive	86.16		97.20	97.18	4	3	−1	Urban Construction	☹
38	Harmless treatment of urban household waste	%	District	Positive	94.38		89.61	86.78	30	27	−3	Urban Construction	☹
39	Public buses per 10,000 urban residents		District	Positive	15.51		9.39	15.53	33	10	−23	City	☹
40	Industrial SO_2 removal rate	%	Whole city	Positive	57.30		30.67	34.54	34	32	−2	Environment Annual Report	☹
41	Industrial wastewater COD removal rate	%	Whole city	Positive	76.07		79.01	75.54	26	27	1	Environment Annual Report	☺
42	Industrial nitrogen oxide removal rate	%	Whole city	Positive	5.24		0.30	0.00	24	29	5	Environment Annual Report	☺
43	Industrial waste water ammonia/nitrogen removal rate	%	Whole city	Positive	66.79		70.57	68.92	20	19	−1	Environment Annual Report	☹

Note:
Regional Economy: *China Regional Economy Statistical Yearbook 2011*
City: *China City Statistical Yearbook 2011*
China Statistics: *China Statistical Yearbook 2011*
Urban Construction: *China Urban Construction Statistical Yearbook 2010*
Environment Annual Report: *China Environment Annual Report 2010*
Environmental Yearbook: *China Environmental Statistical Yearbook 2011*
MEP Data: Ministry of Environmental Protection Data Center

9.21 Brief Analysis of Green Development in Zhengzhou

Zhengzhou ranked 36th among the 38 participating cities by GDI according to 2010 data, 8 places lower over 2009 (Zhengzhou ranked 28th in 2009). Following is a brief analysis of its score by each indicator and their changes from 2009 to 2010.

9.21.1 Zhengzhou's 2010 Scores by GDI

Zhengzhou scored −0.284 in 2010. From the three First-Class Indicators including GDEG, CCPNRE, and SDGP as shown in Fig. 9.41, Zhengzhou scored lower than the national average in all three indicators (Note: the national average value of each indicator is 0).

According to Fig. 9.42, Zhengzhou scored lower than the national average in 9 of Second-Class Indicators in 2010.

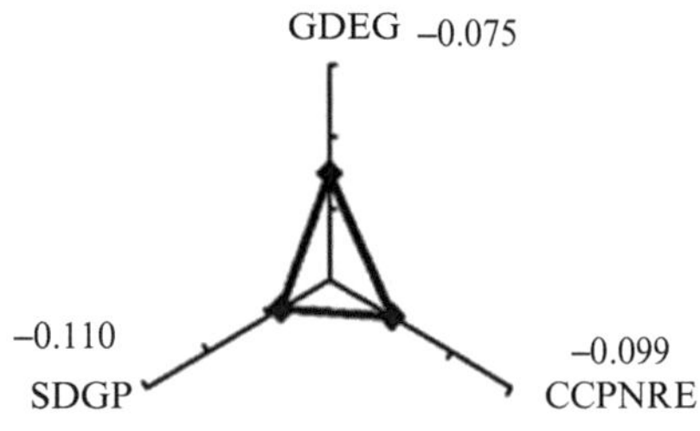

Fig. 9.41 Scores of Zhengzhou by First-Class Indicators

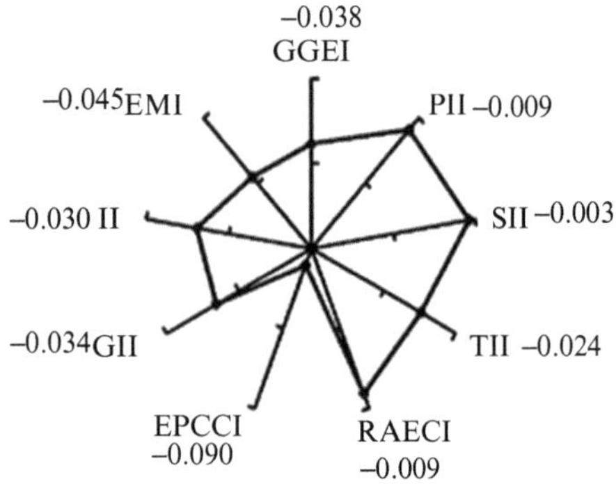

Fig. 9.42 Scores of Zhengzhou by Second-Class Indicators

Table 9.41 Changes in Zhengzhou's rankings by First-Class and Second-Class Indicators, 2009–2010

Indicator	2010	2009	Difference	Indicator	2010	2009	Difference
GDI	36	28	−8				
GDEG	30	25	−5	RAECI	34	32	−2
GGEI	27	21	−6	EPCCI	29	19	−10
PII	33	32	−1	SDGP	31	24	−7
SII	22	18	−4	GII	29	13	−16
TII	31	30	−1	II	28	24	−4
CCPNRE	30	20	−10	EMI	30	28	−2

Note: A positive value in "Difference" means a rise in ranking

9.21.2 Changes in Zhengzhou's GDI Rankings 2009–2010

According to Table 9.41, in First-Class Indicators, Zhengzhou dropped by 10, 7, and 5 places in CCPNRE, SDGP, and GDEG. From changes in ranking, all Second-Class Indicators dropped, 16 in GII, 10 in EPCCI and 6 in GGEI. Other indicators suffered drops to various degrees.

To further explain the causes of the changes in the rankings by First- and Second-Class Indicators, we put the Third-Class Indicators where a change of more than 3 places occurred from 2009 to 2010 as follows in Table 9.42. Compared with those in 2009, Zhengzhou both out- and underperformed in ranking in 2010, while the more obvious trend is underperforming compared with the previous year. It dropped by 23 places in Public buses per 10,000 urban residents, 15 in Ammonia/nitrogen emissions per capita, 13 and 12 in Area of green land per capita in urban areas and Ratio of environmental spending to government expenditure, and drops in indicators such as Ammonia/nitrogen emissions per unit of GDP and Recycling rate of industrial water to various degrees. It rose by 5, 4 and 3 places in Industrial nitrogen oxide removal rate, Proportion of tertiary sector employees in the total employed population and Labor productivity of the secondary sector.

Table 9.42 Third-Class Indicators where changes over 3 places occurred by Zhengzhou, 2009–2010

	Original data for 2009 and 2010			Change in ranking		
Third-Class Indicator	2010	2009	Unit	2010	2009	Difference
Ammonia/nitrogen emissions per unit of GDP	2.36	1.81	Ton per 100 million yuan	21	13	−8
Labor productivity of the secondary sector	14.50	11.70	10,000 yuan per capita	15	18	3
Recycling rate of industrial water	87.58	92.21	%	24	16	−8
Proportion of value added of tertiary sector in GDP	40.74	42.89	%	33	30	−3
Proportion of tertiary sector employees in the total employed population	44.65	41.10	%	23	27	4
Ammonia/nitrogen emissions per unit of land area	1.00	0.68	Ton per km^2	29	22	−7
Ammonia/nitrogen emissions per capita	10.10	6.97	Ton per 10,000 persons	18	3	−15
Ratio of environmental spending to government expenditure	2.00	2.71	%	27	15	−12
Ratio of the investment in industrial pollution control to GDP	0.03	0.08	%	25	17	−8
Ratio of the spending on science, education, culture, and public health to government expenditure	19.98	28.47	%	21	12	−9
Area of green land per capita in urban areas	22.00	36.14		35	22	−13
Harmless treatment of urban household waste	89.61	86.78	%	30	27	−3
Public buses per 10,000 urban residents	9.39	15.53		33	10	−23
Industrial nitrogen oxide removal rate	0.30	0.00	%	24	29	5

Note: A positive value in "Difference" means a rise in ranking

Green development checkup-Wuhan

No.	Indicator	Unit	Scope	Attribute	2010 average of 38 cities	2010 figure	2009 figure	2010 ranking	2009 ranking	Change in ranking	Source of 2010 data	Chernoff face
1	GDP per capita	Yuan	Whole city	Positive	55,399.15	56,367	51,136.00	19	18	−1	Regional Economy; City	☹
2	Energy consumption per unit of GDP	Ton per 10,000 yuan	Whole city	Negative	0.82	1.07	1.12	26	26	0	Regional Economy; City	
3	Electricity consumption per capita in urban areas	kWh per capita	Whole city	Negative	580.70	640.80	580.61	28	26	−2	City	☹
4	CO_2 emissions per unit of GDP			Negative	No data			N/A	N/A	N/A		
5	SO_2 emissions per unit of GDP	Ton per 100 million yuan	Whole city	Negative	42.67	20.81	30.90	9	17	8	Regional Economy; Environment Annual Report	☺
6	COD emissions per unit of GDP	Ton per 100 million yuan	Whole city	Negative	24.91	32.54	38.33	30	30	0	Regional Economy; Environment Annual Report	
7	Nitrogen oxide emissions per unit of GDP	Ton per 100 million yuan	Whole city	Negative	40.67	39.10	45.96	24	29	5	Regional Economy; Environment Annual Report	☺
8	Ammonia/nitrogen emissions per unit of GDP	Ton per 100 million yuan	Whole city	Negative	2.63	2.72	3.43	25	26	1	Regional Economy; Environment Annual Report	☺

(continued)

(continued)

No.	Indicator	Unit	Scope	Attribute	2010 average of 38 cities	2010 figure	2009 figure	2010 ranking	2009 ranking	Change in ranking	Source of 2010 data	Chernoff face
9	Labor productivity of the primary sector	10,000 yuan per capita	Whole city	Positive	3.00	2.66	2.08	16	16	0	Regional Economy	
10	Labor productivity of the secondary sector	10,000 yuan per capita	Whole city	Positive	18.12	14.28	12.93	16	12	−4	Regional Economy	
11	Water consumption per unit of value added created by industrial enterprises	10,000 tons per 10,000 yuan	Whole city	Negative	0.03	0.03	0.04	26	28	2	Regional Economy; Environment Annual Report	
12	Energy consumption per unit of value added created by industrial enterprises			Negative	No data			N/A	N/A	N/A		
13	Utilization rate industrial solid waste	%	Whole city	Positive	83.42	98.60	89.50	6	26	20	Environment Annual Report	
14	Recycling rate of industrial water	%	Whole city	Positive	82.10	93.05	84.38	14	25	11	Environment Annual Report	
15	Labor productivity of the tertiary sector	10,000 yuan per capita	Whole city	Positive	11.39	11.87	10.35	16	15	−1	Regional Economy	

16	Proportion of value added of tertiary sector in GDP	%	Whole city	Positive	48.37	51.44	50.41	13	16	3	City	☺
17	Proportion of tertiary sector employees in the total employed population	%	Whole city	Positive	46.83	50.05	48.98	12	10	−2	Regional Economy	☹
18	Water resources per capita	m^3 per capita	Whole city	Positive	1,040.56	915.71	430.26	13	22	9	Environment Annual Report; City	☺
19	CO_2 emissions per unit of land area			Negative	No data			N/A	N/A	N/A		
20	CO_2 emissions per capita			Negative	No data			N/A	N/A	N/A		
21	SO_2 emissions per unit of land area	Ton per km^2	Whole city	Negative	11.34	10.92	14.14	24	28	4	Environment Annual Report; City	☺
22	SO_2 emissions per capita	Ton per 10,000 persons	Whole city	Negative	211.11	110.97	143.95	11	16	5	Environment Annual Report; City	☺
23	COD emissions per unit of land area	Ton per km^2	Whole city	Negative	7.63	17.08	17.54	35	34	−1	Environment Annual Report; City	☹
24	COD emissions per capita	Ton per 10,000 persons	Whole city	Negative	117.25	173.50	178.57	31	33	2	Environment Annual Report; City	☺
25	Nitrogen oxides emissions per unit of land area	Ton per km^2	Whole city	Negative	14.61	20.52	21.03	29	31	2	Environment Annual Report; City	☺

(continued)

(continued)

No.	Indicator	Unit	Scope	Attribute	2010 average of 38 cities	2010 figure	2009 figure	2010 ranking	2009 ranking	Change in ranking	Source of 2010 data	Chernoff face
26	Nitrogen oxides emissions per capita	Ton per 10,000 persons	Whole city	Negative	231.68	208.50	214.12	24	27	3	Environment Annual Report; City	☺
27	Ammonia/nitrogen emissions per unit of land area	Ton per km^2	Whole city	Negative	0.83	1.43	1.57	32	35	3	Environment Annual Report; City	☺
28	Ammonia/nitrogen emissions per capita	Ton per 10,000 persons	Whole city	Negative	12.50	14.52	15.97	26	29	3	Environment Annual Report; City	☺
29	Percentage of the days with air quality at or over level II in a year	%	District	Positive	89.45	78.02	82.42	36	32	−4	MEP Data	☹
30	Percentage of days with respirable suspended particulates as the principal pollutants in a year	%	District	Negative	69.76	84.38	83.56	28	27	−1	MEP Data	☹
31	Ratio of environmental spending to government expenditure	%	Whole city	Positive	3.14	1.82	1.32	31	34	3	China Statistics; City	☺
32	Ratio of the investment in industrial pollution control to GDP	%	Whole city	Positive	0.09	0.03	0.15	24	9	−15	Environment Annual Report; Regional Economy	☹

33	Ratio of the spending on science, education, culture, and public health to government expenditure	%	Whole city	Positive	21.06	19.38	23.02	24	32	8	China Statistics; City; Regional Economy	☺
34	Area of green land per capita in urban areas	m^2	District	Positive	58.13	30.00	29.64	27	29	2	City	☺
35	Green coverage of urban built-in areas	%	District	Positive	39.84	37.17	37.46	29	28	−1	Urban Construction	☹
36	Coverage of water supply	%	District	Positive	98.83	100.00	99.53	1	23	22	Urban Construction	☺
37	Treatment rate of urban household wastewater	%	District	Positive	86.16	94.96	90.44	10	8	−2	Urban Construction	☹
38	Harmless treatment of urban household waste	%	District	Positive	94.38	85.01	77.95	33	33	0	Urban Construction	
39	Public buses per 10,000 urban residents		District	Positive	15.51	13.45	14.06	17	17	0	City	
40	Industrial SO_2 removal rate	%	Whole city	Positive	57.30	63.82	48.38	16	25	9	Environment Annual Report	☺
41	Industrial wastewater COD removal rate	%	Whole city	Positive	76.07	87.16	85.75	13	18	5	Environment Annual Report	☺

(continued)

(continued)

No.	Indicator	Unit	Scope	Attribute	2010 average of 38 cities	2010 figure	2009 figure	2010 ranking	2009 ranking	Change in ranking	Source of 2010 data	Chernoff face
42	Industrial nitrogen oxide removal rate	%	Whole city	Positive	5.24	0.21	0.18	27	27	0	Environment Annual Report	
43	Industrial waste water ammonia/nitrogen removal rate	%	Whole city	Positive	66.79	57.11	59.46	29	24	−5	Environment Annual Report	

Note:
Regional Economy: *China Regional Economy Statistical Yearbook 2011*
City: *China City Statistical Yearbook 2011*
China Statistics: *China Statistical Yearbook 2011*
Urban Construction: *China Urban Construction Statistical Yearbook 2010*
Environment Annual Report: *China Environment Annual Report 2010*
Environmental Yearbook: *China Environmental Statistical Yearbook 2011*
MEP Data: Ministry of Environmental Protection Data Center

9.22 Brief Analysis of Green Development in Wuhan

Wuhan ranked 34th among the 38 participating cities by GDI according to 2010 data, 1 place higher over 2009 (Wuhan ranked 35th in 2009). Following is a brief analysis of its score by each indicator and their changes from 2009 to 2010.

9.22.1 *Wuhan's 2010 Scores by GDI*

Wuhan scored −0.262 in 2010. From the three First-Class Indicators including GDEG, CCPNRE, and SDGP as shown in Fig. 9.43, Wuhan underperformed compared with the national average in all three indicators (Note: the national average value of each indicator is 0).

According to Fig. 9.44, Wuhan surpassed the national average in 2 of Second-Class Indicators in 2010, which were TII and SII; it ranked lower than the national average in 7 indicators, which were PII, RAECI, EMI, II, GII, GGEI and EPCCI.

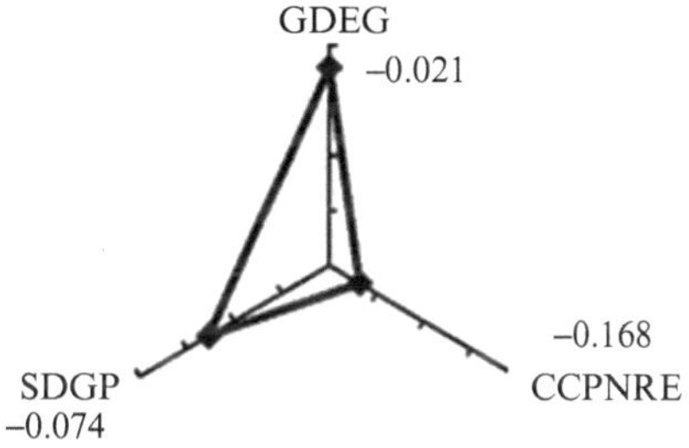

Fig. 9.43 Scores of Wuhan by First-Class Indicators

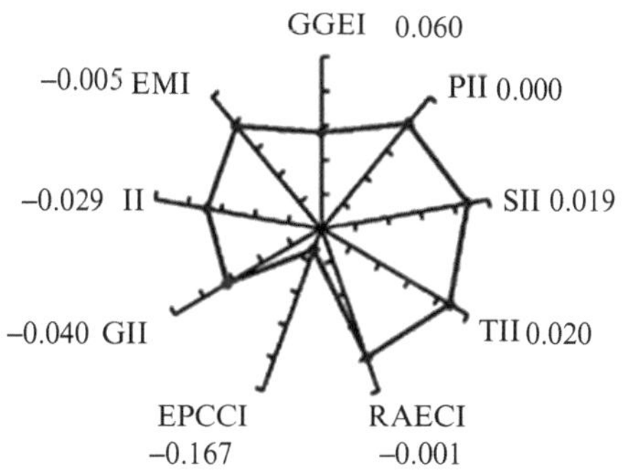

Fig. 9.44 Scores of Wuhan by Second-Class Indicators

Table 9.43 Changes in Wuhan's rankings by First-Class and Second-Class Indicators, 2009–2010

Indicator	2010	2009	Difference	Indicator	2010	2009	Difference
GDI	34	35	1				
GDEG	20	27	7	RAECI	13	22	9
GGEI	31	32	1	EPCCI	37	35	−2
PII	15	16	1	SDGP	25	30	5
SII	8	22	14	GII	30	30	0
TII	10	11	1	II	27	27	0
CCPNRE	38	36	−2	EMI	21	25	4

Note: A positive value in "Difference" means a rise in ranking

9.22.2 Changes in Wuhan's GDI Rankings 2009–2010

According to Table 9.43, in First-Class Indicators, the most obvious change occurred in GDEG, a rise of 7 places; it rose by 5 places in SDGP; it dropped by 2 places in CCPNRE. From changes in ranking, it rose by 14, 9, 4, 1, 1, and 1 place in SII, RAECI, EMI, GGEI, PII and TII; it dropped by 2 places in EPCCI; it remained unchanged in GII and II compared with that in 2009.

To further explain the causes of the changes in the rankings by First- and Second-Class Indicators, we put the Third-Class Indicators where a change of more than 3 places occurred from 2009 to 2010 as follows in Table 9.44. Compared with those in 2009, Wuhan both out- and underperformed in ranking in 2010, while the more obvious trend is outperforming compared with the previous year. It rose by 22 places in Coverage of water supply, 20 in Utilization rate industrial solid waste, and it rose to various degrees in Recycling rate of industrial water and Water resources per capita etc. It however dropped in 4 indicators such as Labor productivity of the secondary sector, Industrial waste water ammonia/nitrogen removal rate compared with that in 2009.

Table 9.44 Third-Class Indicators where changes over 3 places occurred by Wuhan, 2009–2010

	Original data for 2009 and 2010			Change in ranking		
Third-Class Indicator	2010	2009	Unit	2010	2009	Difference
SO_2 emissions per unit of GDP	20.81	30.90	Ton per 100 million yuan	9	17	8
Nitrogen oxide emissions per unit of GDP	39.10	45.96	Ton per 100 million yuan	24	29	5
Labor productivity of the secondary sector	14.28	12.93	10,000 yuan per capita	16	12	−4
Utilization rate industrial solid waste	98.60	89.50	%	6	26	20
Recycling rate of industrial water	93.05	84.38	%	14	25	11
Proportion of value added of tertiary sector in GDP	51.44	50.41	%	13	16	3
Water resources per capita	915.71	430.26	m^3 per capita	13	22	9
SO_2 emissions per unit of land area	10.92	14.14	Ton per km^2	24	28	4
SO_2 emissions per capita	110.97	143.95	Ton per 10,000 persons	11	16	5
Nitrogen oxides emissions per capita	208.50	214.12	Ton per 10,000 persons	24	27	3
Ammonia/nitrogen emissions per unit of land area	1.43	1.57	Ton per km^2	32	35	3
Ammonia/nitrogen emissions per capita	14.52	15.97	Ton per 10,000 persons	26	29	3
Percentage of the days with air quality at or over level II in a year	78.02	82.42	%	36	32	−4
Ratio of environmental spending to government expenditure	1.82	1.32	%	31	34	3
Ratio of the investment in industrial pollution control to GDP	0.03	0.15	%	24	9	−15
Ratio of the spending on science, education, culture, and public health to government expenditure	19.38	23.02	%	24	32	8
Coverage of water supply	100.00	99.53	%	1	23	22
Industrial SO_2 removal rate	63.82	48.38	%	16	25	9
Industrial wastewater COD removal rate	87.16	85.75	%	13	18	5
Industrial waste water ammonia/nitrogen removal rate	57.11	59.46	%	29	24	−5

Note: A positive value in "Difference" means a rise in ranking

Green development checkup-Changsha

No.	Indicator	Unit	Scope	Attribute	2010 average of 38 cities	2010 figure	2009 figure	2010 ranking	2009 ranking	Change in ranking	Source of 2010 data	Chernoff face
1	GDP per capita	Yuan	Whole city	Positive	55,399.15	66,464	56,620.00	12	15	3	Regional Economy; City	
2	Energy consumption per unit of GDP	Ton per 10,000 yuan	Whole city	Negative	0.82	0.17	0.19	2	1	−1	Regional Economy; City	
3	Electricity consumption per capita in urban areas	kWh per capita	Whole city	Negative	580.70	528.12	530.46	24	25	1	City	
4	CO_2 emissions per unit of GDP			Negative	No data			N/A	N/A	N/A		
5	SO_2 emissions per unit of GDP	Ton per 100 million yuan	Whole city	Negative	42.67	20.38	22.75	7	8	1	Regional Economy; Environment Annual Report	
6	COD emissions per unit of GDP	Ton per 100 million yuan	Whole city	Negative	24.91	15.48	21.53	13	17	4	Regional Economy; Environment Annual Report	
7	Nitrogen oxide emissions per unit of GDP	Ton per 100 million yuan	Whole city	Negative	40.67	15.15	14.38	3	2	−1	Regional Economy; Environment Annual Report	
8	Ammonia/nitrogen emissions per unit of GDP	Ton per 100 million yuan	Whole city	Negative	2.63	2.33	2.55	19	22	3	Regional Economy; Environment Annual Report	
9	Labor productivity of the primary sector	10,000 yuan per capita	Whole city	Positive	3.00	1.76	1.50	27	28	1	Regional Economy	

10	Labor productivity of the secondary sector	10,000 yuan per capita	Whole city	Positive	18.12	18.38	15.24	8	6	−2	Regional Economy	☹
11	Water consumption per unit of value added created by industrial enterprises	10,000 tons per 10,000 yuan	Whole city	Negative	0.03	0.01	0.01	8	10	2	Regional Economy; Environment Annual Report	☺
12	Energy consumption per unit of value added created by industrial enterprises			Negative	No data			N/A	N/A	N/A		
13	Utilization rate industrial solid waste	%	Whole city	Positive	83.42	99.70	90.60	1	23	22	Environment Annual Report	☺
14	Recycling rate of industrial water	%	Whole city	Positive	82.10	92.43	94.44	15	11	−4	Environment Annual Report	☹
15	Labor productivity of the tertiary sector	10,000 yuan per capita	Whole city	Positive	11.39	11.28	10.52	19	13	−6	Regional Economy	☹
16	Proportion of value added of tertiary sector in GDP	%	Whole city	Positive	48.37	41.96	44.64	29	28	−1	City	☹
17	Proportion of tertiary sector employees in the total employed population	%	Whole city	Positive	46.83	41.12	40.11	29	29	0	Regional Economy	

(continued)

(continued)

No.	Indicator	Unit	Scope	Attribute	2010 average of 38 cities	2010 figure	2009 figure	2010 ranking	2009 ranking	Change in ranking	Source of 2010 data	Chernoff face
18	Water resources per capita	m^3 per capita	Whole city	Positive	1,040.56	1,654.97	1,476.24	5	5	0	Environment Annual Report; City	
19	CO_2 emissions per unit of land area			Negative	No data			N/A	N/A	N/A		
20	CO_2 emissions per capita			Negative	No data			N/A	N/A	N/A		
21	SO_2 emissions per unit of land area	Ton per km^2	Whole city	Negative	11.34	5.32	5.14	9	10	1	Environment Annual Report; City	
22	SO_2 emissions per capita	Ton per 10,000 persons	Whole city	Negative	211.11	96.48	93.77	7	8	1	Environment Annual Report; City	
23	COD emissions per unit of land area	Ton per km^2	Whole city	Negative	7.63	4.04	4.87	13	18	5	Environment Annual Report; City	
24	COD emissions per capita	Ton per 10,000 persons	Whole city	Negative	117.25	73.28	88.75	9	17	8	Environment Annual Report; City	
25	Nitrogen oxides emissions per unit of land area	Ton per km^2	Whole city	Negative	14.61	3.96	3.25	6	9	3	Environment Annual Report; City	
26	Nitrogen oxides emissions per capita	Ton per 10,000 persons	Whole city	Negative	231.68	71.71	59.27	3	4	1	Environment Annual Report; City	

27	Ammonia/nitrogen emissions per unit of land area	Ton per km^2	Whole city	Negative	0.83	0.61	0.58	20	19	−1	Environment Annual Report; City	☹
28	Ammonia/nitrogen emissions per capita	Ton per 10,000 persons	Whole city	Negative	12.50	11.01	10.52	22	18	−4	Environment Annual Report; City	☹
29	Percentage of the days with air quality at or over level II in a year	%	District	Positive	89.45	92.56	91.21	15	16	1	MEP Data	☺
30	Percentage of days with respirable suspended particulates as the principal pollutants in a year	%	District	Negative	69.76	74.79	79.18	18	21	3	MEP Data	☺
31	Ratio of environmental spending to government expenditure	%	Whole city	Positive	3.14	2.07	1.32	25	33	8	China Statistics; City	☺
32	Ratio of the investment in industrial pollution control to GDP	%	Whole city	Positive	0.09	0.01	0.00	36	38	2	Environment Annual Report; Regional Economy	☺

(continued)

(continued)

No.	Indicator	Unit	Scope	Attribute	2010 average of 38 cities	2010 figure	2009 figure	2010 ranking	2009 ranking	Change in ranking	Source of 2010 data	Chernoff face
33	Ratio of the spending on science, education, culture, and public health to government expenditure	%	Whole city	Positive	21.06	16.90	25.25	32	22	−10	China Statistics; City; Regional Economy	☹
34	Area of green land per capita in urban areas	m^2	District	Positive	58.13	36.00	33.76	21	24	3	City	☺
35	Green coverage of urban built-in areas	%	District	Positive	39.84	36.19	38.38	31	24	−7	Urban Construction	☹
36	Coverage of water supply	%	District	Positive	98.83	100.00	100.00	1	1	0	Urban Construction	
37	Treatment rate of urban household wastewater	%	District	Positive	86.16	90.80	79.43	15	26	11	Urban Construction	☺
38	Harmless treatment of urban household waste	%	District	Positive	94.38	100.00	100.00	1	1	0	Urban Construction	
39	Public buses per 10,000 urban residents		District	Positive	15.51	14.71	14.75	16	12	−4	City	☹

40	Industrial SO_2 removal rate	%	Whole city	Positive	57.30	46.91	42.51	28	27	−1	Environment Annual Report	☹
41	Industrial wastewater COD removal rate	%	Whole city	Positive	76.07	62.25	62.64	32	35	3	Environment Annual Report	☺
42	Industrial nitrogen oxide removal rate	%	Whole city	Positive	5.24	3.72	39.81	15	2	−13	Environment Annual Report	☹
43	Industrial waste water ammonia/nitrogen removal rate	%	Whole city	Positive	66.79	40.51	35.90	34	31	−3	Environment Annual Report	☹

Note:
Regional Economy: *China Regional Economy Statistical Yearbook 2011*
City: *China City Statistical Yearbook 2011*
China Statistics: *China Statistical Yearbook 2011*
Urban Construction: *China Urban Construction Statistical Yearbook 2010*
Environment Annual Report: *China Environment Annual Report 2010*
Environmental Yearbook: *China Environmental Statistical Yearbook 2011*
MEP Data: Ministry of Environmental Protection Data Center

9.23 Brief Analysis of Green Development in Changsha

Changsha ranked 13th among the 38 participating cities by GDI according to 2010 data, 1 place lower over 2009 (Changsha ranked 13th in 2009). Following is a brief analysis of its score by each indicator and their changes from 2009 to 2010.

9.23.1 *Changsha's 2010 Scores by GDI*

Changsha scored 0.044 in 2010. From the three First-Class Indicators including GDEG, CCPNRE, and SDGP as shown in Fig. 9.45, Changsha outperformed other places in terms of GDEG and CCPNRE; yet it performed weaker compared in the national average in SDGP (Note: the national average value of each indicator is 0).

According to Fig. 9.46, Changsha surpassed the national average in 5 of Second-Class Indicators in 2010, which were GGEI, EPCCI, SII, II and RAECI; it scored lower than the national average in 4 indicators such as PII, TII, GII and EMI.

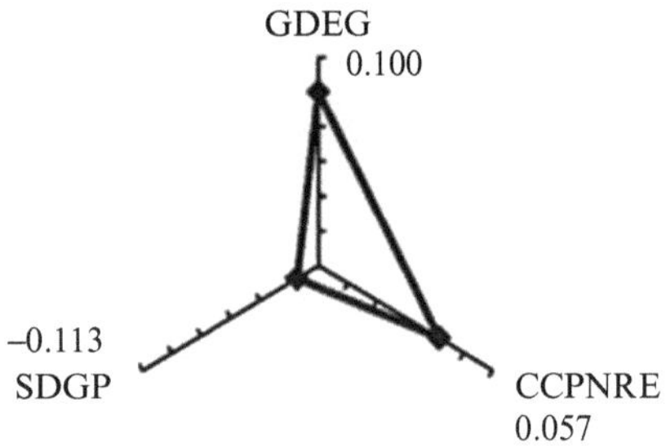

Fig. 9.45 Scores of Changsha by First-Class Indicators

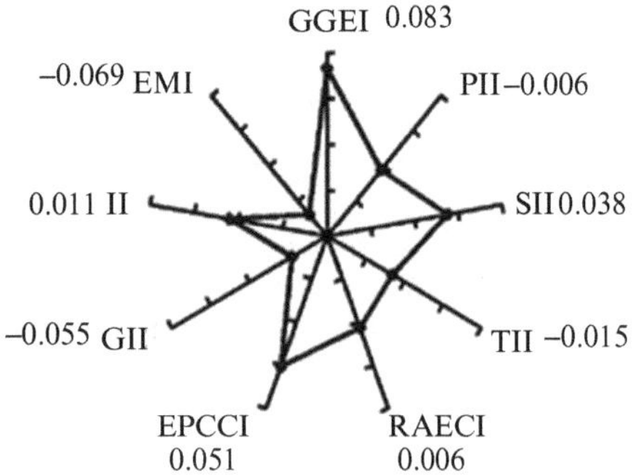

Fig. 9.46 Scores of Changsha by Second-Class Indicators

Table 9.45 Changes in Changsha's rankings by First-Class and Second-Class Indicators, 2009–2010

Indicator	2010	2009	Difference	Indicator	2010	2009	Difference
GDI	13	13	0				
GDEG	5	7	2	RAECI	5	5	0
GGEI	3	5	2	EPCCI	9	12	3
PII	27	28	1	SDGP	32	25	−7
SII	4	5	1	GII	37	36	−1
TII	26	24	−2	II	20	20	0
CCPNRE	8	11	3	EMI	34	24	−10

Note: A positive value in "Difference" means a rise in ranking

9.23.2 Changes in Changsha's GDI Rankings 2009–2010

According to Table 9.45, in First-Class Indicators, the most obvious change occurred in SDGP with a drop of 7 places; it rose by 3 and 2 places in CCPNRE and GDEG. In Second-Class Indicators, Changsha rose by 3, 2, 1 and 1 places in EPCCI, GGEI, PII and SII; it dropped by 1, 2 and 10 places in GII, TII and EMI; it remained unchanged by RAECI and II compared with that in 2009.

To further explain the causes of the changes in the rankings by First- and Second-Class Indicators, we put the Third-Class Indicators where a change of more than 3 places occurred from 2009 to 2010 as follows in Table 9.46. Compared with those in 2009, Changsha both out- and underperformed in ranking in 2010. It rose by 22 places in Utilization rate industrial solid waste, 11 in Treatment rate of urban household wastewater, and to various degrees in many other indicators such as COD emissions per capita; it dropped to some extent in 8 indicators such as Industrial waste water ammonia/nitrogen removal rate, Recycling rate of industrial water and Ammonia/nitrogen emissions per capita.

Table 9.46 Third-Class Indicators where changes over 3 places occurred by Changsha, 2009–2010

	Original data for 2009 and 2010			Change in ranking		
Third-Class Indicator	2010	2009	Unit	2010	2009	Difference
GDP per capita	66,464.00	56,620.00	Yuan	12	15	3
COD emissions per unit of GDP	15.48	21.53	Ton per 100 million yuan	13	17	4
Ammonia/nitrogen emissions per unit of GDP	2.33	2.55	Ton per 100 million yuan	19	22	3
Utilization rate industrial solid waste	99.70	90.60	%	1	23	22
Recycling rate of industrial water	92.43	94.44	%	15	11	−4
Labor productivity of the tertiary sector	11.28	10.52	10,000 yuan per capita	19	13	−6
COD emissions per unit of land area	4.04	4.87	Ton per km^2	13	18	5
COD emissions per capita	73.28	88.75	Ton per 10,000 persons	9	17	8
Nitrogen oxides emissions per unit of land area	3.96	3.25	Ton per km^2	6	9	3
Ammonia/nitrogen emissions per capita	11.01	10.52	Ton per 10,000 persons	22	18	−4
Percentage of days with respirable suspended particulates as the principal pollutants in a year	74.79	79.18	%	18	21	3
Ratio of environmental spending to government expenditure	2.07	1.32	%	25	33	8
Ratio of the spending on science, education, culture, and public health to government expenditure	16.90	25.25	%	32	22	−10
Area of green land per capita in urban areas	36.00	33.76		21	24	3
Green coverage of urban built-in areas	36.19	38.38	%	31	24	−7
Treatment rate of urban household wastewater	90.80	79.43	%	15	26	11
Public buses per 10,000 urban residents	14.71	14.75		16	12	−4
Industrial wastewater COD removal rate	62.25	62.64	%	32	35	3
Industrial nitrogen oxide removal rate	3.72	39.81	%	15	2	−13
Industrial waste water ammonia/nitrogen removal rate	40.51	35.90	%	34	31	−3

Note: A positive value in “Difference” means a rise in ranking

Green development checkup-Guangzhou

No.	Indicator	Unit	Scope	Attribute	2010 average of 38 cities	2010 figure	2009 figure	2010 ranking	2009 ranking	Change in ranking	Source of 2010 data	Chernoff face
1	GDP per capita	Yuan	Whole city	Positive	55,399.15	87,458	89,082.00	4	2	−2	Regional Economy; City	
2	Energy consumption per unit of GDP	Ton per 10,000 yuan	Whole city	Negative	0.82	0.63	0.27	17	3	−14	Regional Economy; City	
3	Electricity consumption per capita in urban areas	kWh per capita	Whole city	Negative	580.70	1,353.22	1,290.45	37	37	0	City	
4	CO_2 emissions per unit of GDP			Negative	No data			N/A	N/A	N/A		
5	SO_2 emissions per unit of GDP	Ton per 100 million yuan	Whole city	Negative	42.67	9.35	11.27	3	4	1	Regional Economy; Environment Annual Report	
6	COD emissions per unit of GDP	Ton per 100 million yuan	Whole city	Negative	24.91	9.84	14.09	6	8	2	Regional Economy; Environment Annual Report	
7	Nitrogen oxide emissions per unit of GDP	Ton per 100 million yuan	Whole city	Negative	40.67	18.49	21.07	5	8	3	Regional Economy; Environment Annual Report	
8	Ammonia/nitrogen emissions per unit of GDP	Ton per 100 million yuan	Whole city	Negative	2.63	0.78	0.90	4	3	−1	Regional Economy; Environment Annual Report	

(continued)

(continued)

No.	Indicator	Unit	Scope	Attribute	2010 average of 38 cities	2010 figure	2009 figure	2010 ranking	2009 ranking	Change in ranking	Source of 2010 data	Chernoff face
9	Labor productivity of the primary sector	10,000 yuan per capita	Whole city	Positive	3.00	2.38	2.16	19	15	−4	Regional Economy	☹
10	Labor productivity of the secondary sector	10,000 yuan per capita	Whole city	Positive	18.12	13.12	11.65	19	19	0	Regional Economy	
11	Water consumption per unit of value added created by industrial enterprises	10,000 tons per 10,000 yuan	Whole city	Negative	0.03	0.02	0.02	15	21	6	Regional Economy; Environment Annual Report	☺
12	Energy consumption per unit of value added created by industrial enterprises			Negative	No data			N/A	N/A	N/A		
13	Utilization rate industrial solid waste	%	Whole city	Positive	83.42	89.80	92.40	21	18	−3	Environment Annual Report	☹
14	Recycling rate of industrial water	%	Whole city	Positive	82.10	50.79	45.29	36	38	2	Environment Annual Report	☺
15	Labor productivity of the tertiary sector	10,000 yuan per capita	Whole city	Positive	11.39	17.27	15.69	4	2	−2	Regional Economy	☹

16	Proportion of value added of tertiary sector in GDP	%	Whole city	Positive	48.37	61.01	60.85	3	3	0	City	
17	Proportion of tertiary sector employees in the total employed population	%	Whole city	Positive	46.83	50.40	48.95	9	11	2	Regional Economy	☺
18	Water resources per capita	m^3 per capita	Whole city	Positive	1,040.56	1,143.60	1,160.18	12	11	−1	Environment Annual Report; City	☹
19	CO_2 emissions per unit of land area			Negative	No data			N/A	N/A	N/A		
20	CO_2 emissions per capita			Negative	No data			N/A	N/A	N/A		
21	SO_2 emissions per unit of land area	Ton per km^2	Whole city	Negative	11.34	12.15	12.93	28	26	−2	Environment Annual Report; City	☹
22	SO_2 emissions per capita	Ton per 10,000 persons	Whole city	Negative	211.11	112.81	121.79	12	11	−1	Environment Annual Report; City	☹
23	COD emissions per unit of land area	Ton per km^2	Whole city	Negative	7.63	12.78	16.17	32	33	1	Environment Annual Report; City	☺
24	COD emissions per capita	Ton per 10,000 persons	Whole city	Negative	117.25	118.68	152.27	21	30	9	Environment Annual Report; City	☺
25	Nitrogen oxides emissions per unit of land area	Ton per km^2	Whole city	Negative	14.61	24.02	24.17	32	34	2	Environment Annual Report; City	☺

(continued)

(continued)

No.	Indicator	Unit	Scope	Attribute	2010 average of 38 cities	2010 figure	2009 figure	2010 ranking	2009 ranking	Change in ranking	Source of 2010 data	Chernoff face
26	Nitrogen oxides emissions per capita	Ton per 10,000 persons	Whole city	Negative	231.68	223.07	227.64	25	30	5	Environment Annual Report; City	☺
27	Ammonia/nitrogen emissions per unit of land area	Ton per km^2	Whole city	Negative	0.83	1.02	1.03	30	31	1	Environment Annual Report; City	☺
28	Ammonia/nitrogen emissions per capita	Ton per 10,000 persons	Whole city	Negative	12.50	9.47	9.69	13	13	0	Environment Annual Report; City	
29	Percentage of the days with air quality at or over level II in a year	%	District	Positive	89.45	97.80	95.05	6	10	4	MEP Data	☺
30	Percentage of days with respirable suspended particulates as the principal pollutants in a year	%	District	Negative	69.76	67.95	58.63	14	11	−3	MEP Data	☹
31	Ratio of environmental spending to government expenditure	%	Whole city	Positive	3.14	2.49	1.07	20	38	18	China Statistics; City	☺
32	Ratio of the investment in industrial pollution control to GDP	%	Whole city	Positive	0.09	0.01	0.02	28	31	3	Environment Annual Report; Regional Economy	☺

33	Ratio of the spending on science, education, culture, and public health to government expenditure	%	Whole city	Positive	21.06	23.82	30.40	12	9	−3	China Statistics; City; Regional Economy	☹
34	Area of green land per capita in urban areas	m^2	District	Positive	58.13	187.00	190.05	2	2	0	City	
35	Green coverage of urban built-in areas	%	District	Positive	39.84	41.96	38.21	14	25	11	Urban Construction	☺
36	Coverage of water supply	%	District	Positive	98.83	99.56	98.94	28	30	2	Urban Construction	☺
37	Treatment rate of urban household wastewater	%	District	Positive	86.16	96.96	81.00	5	21	16	Urban Construction	☺
38	Harmless treatment of urban household waste	%	District	Positive	94.38	91.96	80.17	28	30	2	Urban Construction	☺
39	Public buses per 10,000 urban residents		District	Positive	15.51	17.31	13.42	8	18	10	City	☺
40	Industrial SO_2 removal rate	%	Whole city	Positive	57.30	82.06	90.72	4	1	−3	Environment Annual Report	☹
41	Industrial wastewater COD removal rate	%	Whole city	Positive	76.07	84.22	80.11	17	23	6	Environment Annual Report	☺

(continued)

(continued)

No.	Indicator	Unit	Scope	Attribute	2010 average of 38 cities	2010 figure	2009 figure	2010 ranking	2009 ranking	Change in ranking	Source of 2010 data	Chernoff face
42	Industrial nitrogen oxide removal rate	%	Whole city	Positive	5.24	40.74	13.51	1	10	9	Environment Annual Report	☺
43	Industrial waste water ammonia/nitrogen removal rate	%	Whole city	Positive	66.79	94.09	94.02	5	4	−1	Environment Annual Report	☹

Note:
Regional Economy: *China Regional Economy Statistical Yearbook 2011*
City: *China City Statistical Yearbook 2011*
China Statistics: *China Statistical Yearbook 2011*
Urban Construction: *China Urban Construction Statistical Yearbook 2010*
Environment Annual Report: *China Environment Annual Report 2010*
Environmental Yearbook: *China Environmental Statistical Yearbook 2011*
MEP Data: Ministry of Environmental Protection Data Center

9.24 Brief Analysis of Green Development in Guangzhou

Guangzhou ranked 5th among the 38 participating cities by GDI according to 2010 data, 1 place lower over 2009 (Guangzhou ranked 7th in 2009). Following is a brief analysis of its score by each indicator and their changes from 2009 to 2010.

9.24.1 Guangzhou's 2010 Scores by GDI

Guangzhou scored 0.283 in 2010. From the three First-Class Indicators including GDEG, CCPNRE, and SDGP as shown in Fig. 9.47, Guangzhou showed obvious advantages in GDEG and SDGP; yet it was lower than the national average in CCPNRE (Note: the national average value of each indicator is 0).

According to Fig. 9.48, Guangzhou surpassed the national average in 5 of Second-Class Indicators in 2010, which were GGEI, TII, RAECI, II and EMI; it scored lower than national average in 4 indicators including PII, GII, EPCCI and SII.

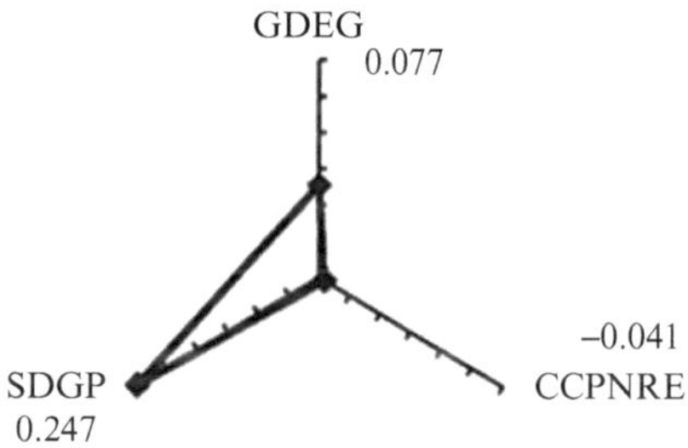

Fig. 9.47 Scores of Guangzhou by First-Class Indicators

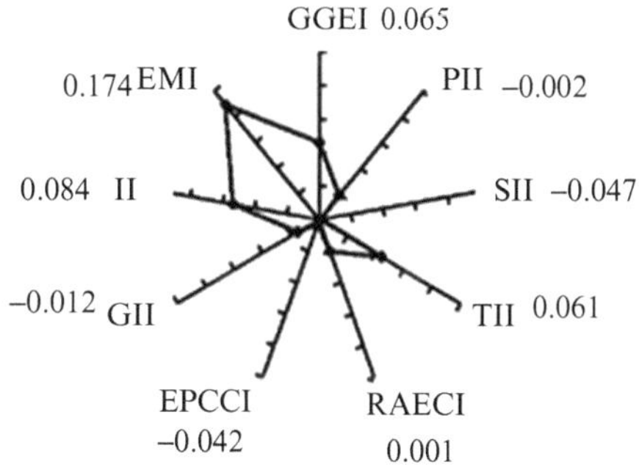

Fig. 9.48 Scores of Guangzhou by Second-Class Indicators

Table 9.47 Changes in Guangzhou's rankings by First-Class and Second-Class Indicators, 2009–2010

Indicator	2010	2009	Difference	Indicator	2010	2009	Difference
GDI	5	7	2				
GDEG	8	3	−5	RAECI	12	11	−1
GGEI	6	2	−4	EPCCI	20	20	0
PII	18	15	−3	SDGP	2	11	9
SII	35	36	1	GII	16	24	8
TII	3	3	0	II	3	15	12
CCPNRE	20	18	−2	EMI	1	4	3

Note: A positive value in "Difference" means a rise in ranking

9.24.2 Changes in Guangzhou's GDI Rankings 2009–2010

According to Table 9.47, in First-Class Indicators, the most obvious change occurred in SDGP with a rise of 9 places; it dropped in 5 and 2 places in GDEG and CCPNRE. In Second-Class Indicators, I rose by 12, 8, 3 and 1 places in II, GII, EMI and SII; it dropped by 1, 3 and 4 places in RAECI, PII and GGEI; it remained unchanged in TII and EPCCI compared with those in 2009.

To further explain the causes of the changes in the rankings by First- and Second-Class Indicators, we put the Third-Class Indicators where a change of more than 3 places occurred from 2009 to 2010 as follows in Table 9.48. Compared with those in 2009, Guangzhou both out- and underperformed in ranking in 2010, while the more obvious trend is outperforming compared with the previous year. It rose by 18 places in Ratio of environmental spending to government expenditure, 16 in Treatment rate of urban household wastewater, and to various degrees in many other indicators including Green coverage of urban built-in areas and Industrial nitrogen oxide removal rate; it dropped to some extent in 6 indicators including Utilization rate industrial solid waste and Ratio of the spending on science, education, culture, and public health to government expenditure.

Table 9.48 Third-Class Indicators where changes over 3 places occurred by Guangzhou, 2009–2010

	Original data for 2009 and 2010			Change in ranking		
Third-Class Indicator	2010	2009	Unit	2010	2009	Difference
Energy consumption per unit of GDP	0.63	0.27	Ton per 10,000 yuan	17	3	−14
Nitrogen oxide emissions per unit of GDP	18.49	21.07	Ton per 100 million yuan	5	8	3
Labor productivity of the primary sector	2.38	2.16	10,000 yuan per capita	19	15	−4
Water consumption per unit of value added created by industrial enterprises	0.02	0.02	10,000 tons per 10,000 yuan	15	21	6
Utilization rate industrial solid waste	89.80	92.40	%	21	18	−3
COD emissions per capita	118.68	152.27	Ton per 10,000 persons	21	30	9
Nitrogen oxides emissions per capita	223.07	227.64	Ton per 10,000 persons	25	30	5
Percentage of the days with air quality at or over level II in a year	97.80	95.05	%	6	10	4
Percentage of days with respirable suspended particulates as the principal pollutants in a year	67.95	58.63	%	14	11	−3
Ratio of environmental spending to government expenditure	2.49	1.07	%	20	38	18
Ratio of the investment in industrial pollution control to GDP	0.01	0.02	%	28	31	3
Ratio of the spending on science, education, culture, and public health to government expenditure	23.82	30.40	%	12	9	−3
Green coverage of urban built-in areas	41.96	38.21	%	14	25	11
Treatment rate of urban household wastewater	96.96	81.00	%	5	21	16
Public buses per 10,000 urban residents	17.31	13.42		8	18	10
Industrial SO_2 removal rate	82.06	90.72	%	4	1	−3
Industrial wastewater COD removal rate	84.22	80.11	%	17	23	6
Industrial nitrogen oxide removal rate	40.74	13.51	%	1	10	9

Note: A positive value in "Difference" means a rise in ranking

Green development checkup-Shenzhen

No.	Indicator	Unit	Scope	Attribute	2010 average of 38 cities	2010 figure	2009 figure	2010 ranking	2009 ranking	Change in ranking	Source of 2010 data	Chernoff face
1	GDP per capita	Yuan	Whole city	Positive	55,399.15	94,296	92,772.00	2	1	−1	Regional Economy; City	☹
2	Energy consumption per unit of GDP	Ton per 10,000 yuan	Whole city	Negative	0.82	0.14	N/A	1	N/A	N/A	Regional Economy; City	
3	Electricity consumption per capita in urban areas	kWh per capita	Whole city	Negative	580.70	798.33	895.13	32	33	1	City	☺
4	CO_2 emissions per unit of GDP			Negative	No data			N/A	N/A	N/A		
5	SO_2 emissions per unit of GDP	Ton per 100 million yuan	Whole city	Negative	42.67	3.39	3.95	2	2	0	Regional Economy; Environment Annual Report	
6	COD emissions per unit of GDP	Ton per 100 million yuan	Whole city	Negative	24.91	2.41	6.09	1	2	1	Regional Economy; Environment Annual Report	☺
7	Nitrogen oxide emissions per unit of GDP	Ton per 100 million yuan	Whole city	Negative	40.67	13.44	17.01	2	3	1	Regional Economy; Environment Annual Report	☺
8	Ammonia/nitrogen emissions per unit of GDP	Ton per 100 million yuan	Whole city	Negative	2.63	0.64	1.10	2	4	2	Regional Economy; Environment Annual Report	☺
9	Labor productivity of the primary sector	10,000 yuan per capita	Whole city	Positive	3.00	17.49	10.79	1	1	0	Regional Economy	
10	Labor productivity of the secondary sector	10,000 yuan per capita	Whole city	Positive	18.12	12.28	10.40	23	22	−1	Regional Economy	☹

11	Water consumption per unit of value added created by industrial enterprises	10,000 tons per 10,000 yuan	Whole city	Negative	0.03	0.00	0.00	1	1	0	Regional Economy; Environment Annual Report	
12	Energy consumption per unit of value added created by industrial enterprises			Negative	No data			N/A	N/A	N/A		
13	Utilization rate industrial solid waste	%	Whole city	Positive	83.42	92.00	90.10	20	25	5	Environment Annual Report	☺
14	Recycling rate of industrial water	%	Whole city	Positive	82.10	48.93	58.24	37	35	−2	Environment Annual Report	☹
15	Labor productivity of the tertiary sector	10,000 yuan per capita	Whole city	Positive	11.39	15.30	13.96	7	5	−2	Regional Economy	☹
16	Proportion of value added of tertiary sector in GDP	%	Whole city	Positive	48.37	52.72	53.25	9	10	1	City	☺
17	Proportion of tertiary sector employees in the total employed population	%	Whole city	Positive	46.83	48.47	45.98	13	17	4	Regional Economy	☺
18	Water resources per capita	m^3 per capita	Whole city	Positive	1,040.56	689.58	715.97	16	15	−1	Environment Annual Report; City	☹
19	CO_2 emissions per unit of land area			Negative	No data			N/A	N/A	N/A		

(continued)

(continued)

No.	Indicator	Unit	Scope	Attribute	2010 average of 38 cities	2010 figure	2009 figure	2010 ranking	2009 ranking	Change in ranking	Source of 2010 data	Chernoff face
20	CO_2 emissions per capita			Negative	No data			N/A	N/A	N/A		
21	SO_2 emissions per unit of land area	Ton per km^2	Whole city	Negative	11.34	15.71	16.31	29	29	0	Environment Annual Report; City	
22	SO_2 emissions per capita	Ton per 10,000 persons	Whole city	Negative	211.11	30.21	36.76	2	2	0	Environment Annual Report; City	
23	COD emissions per unit of land area	Ton per km^2	Whole city	Negative	7.63	11.16	25.13	30	36	6	Environment Annual Report; City	☺
24	COD emissions per capita	Ton per 10,000 persons	Whole city	Negative	117.25	21.46	56.61	1	2	1	Environment Annual Report; City	☺
25	Nitrogen oxides emissions per unit of land area	Ton per km^2	Whole city	Negative	14.61	62.28	70.22	37	38	1	Environment Annual Report; City	☺
26	Nitrogen oxides emissions per capita	Ton per 10,000 persons	Whole city	Negative	231.68	119.77	158.23	11	18	7	Environment Annual Report; City	☺
27	Ammonia/nitrogen emissions per unit of land area	Ton per km^2	Whole city	Negative	0.83	2.98	4.56	37	37	0	Environment Annual Report; City	
28	Ammonia/nitrogen emissions per capita	Ton per 10,000 persons	Whole city	Negative	12.50	5.73	10.28	4	14	10	Environment Annual Report; City	☺
29	Percentage of the days with air quality at or over level II in a year	%	District	Positive	89.45	97.53	99.73	7	4	−3	MEP Data	☹

30	Percentage of days with respirable suspended particulates as the principal pollutants in a year	%	District	Negative	69.76	39.45	48.49	3	5	2	MEP Data	☺
31	Ratio of environmental spending to government expenditure	%	Whole city	Positive	3.14	3.36	3.48	14	6	−8	China Statistics; City	☹
32	Ratio of the investment in industrial pollution control to GDP	%	Whole city	Positive	0.09	0.01	0.02	32	30	−2	Environment Annual Report; Regional Economy	☹
33	Ratio of the spending on science, education, culture, and public health to government expenditure	%	Whole city	Positive	21.06	20.34	28.80	20	10	−10	China Statistics; City; Regional Economy	☹
34	Area of green land per capita in urban areas	m^2	District	Positive	58.13	371.00	391.83	1	1	0	City	
35	Green coverage of urban built-in areas	%	District	Positive	39.84	45.04	45.02	4	2	−2	Urban Construction	☹
36	Coverage of water supply	%	District	Positive	98.83	100.00	100.00	1	1	0	Urban Construction	
37	Treatment rate of urban household wastewater	%	District	Positive	86.16	99.30	68.75	3	31	28	Urban Construction	☺

(continued)

(continued)

No.	Indicator	Unit	Scope	Attribute	2010 average of 38 cities	2010 figure	2009 figure	2010 ranking	2009 ranking	Change in ranking	Source of 2010 data	Chernoff face
38	Harmless treatment of urban household waste	%	District	Positive	94.38	94.60	94.30	25	24	−1	Urban Construction	
39	Public buses per 10,000 urban residents		District	Positive	15.51	103.11	103.02	1	1	0	City	
40	Industrial SO_2 removal rate	%	Whole city	Positive	57.30	55.48	60.35	22	20	−2	Environment Annual Report	
41	Industrial wastewater COD removal rate	%	Whole city	Positive	76.07	89.91	88.41	8	13	5	Environment Annual Report	
42	Industrial nitrogen oxide removal rate	%	Whole city	Positive	5.24	4.10	6.50	13	15	2	Environment Annual Report	
43	Industrial waste water ammonia/nitrogen removal rate	%	Whole city	Positive	66.79	78.47	65.83	14	21	7	Environment Annual Report	

Note:
Regional Economy: *China Regional Economy Statistical Yearbook 2011*
City: *China City Statistical Yearbook 2011*
China Statistics: *China Statistical Yearbook 2011*
Urban Construction: *China Urban Construction Statistical Yearbook 2010*
Environment Annual Report: *China Environment Annual Report 2010*
Environmental Yearbook: *China Environmental Statistical Yearbook 2011*
MEP Data: Ministry of Environmental Protection Data Center

9.25 Brief Analysis of Green Development in Shenzhen

Shenzhen ranked 1st among the 38 participating cities by GDI according to 2010 data, the same as it did in 2009 (Shenzhen ranked 1st in 2009). Following is a brief analysis of its score by each indicator and their changes from 2009 to 2010.

9.25.1 Shenzhen's 2010 Scores by GDI

Shenzhen scored 1.002 in 2010. From the three First-Class Indicators including GDEG, CCPNRE, and SDGP as shown in Fig. 9.49, Shenzhen showed obvious advantages in all three indicators, especially GDEG (Note: the national average value of each indicator is 0).

According to Fig. 9.50, Shenzhen surpassed the national average in 7 of Second-Class Indicators in 2010, which are II, GGEI, EPCCI, PII, SII, TII, and EMI; it scored lower than national average in 2 indicators including RAECI and GII.

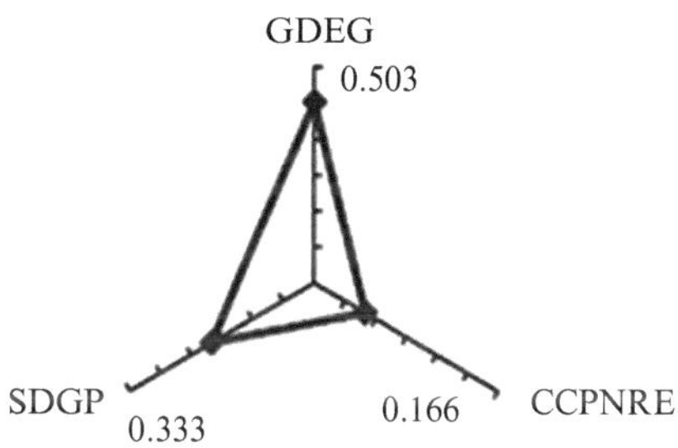

Fig. 9.49 Scores of Shenzhen by First-Class Indicators

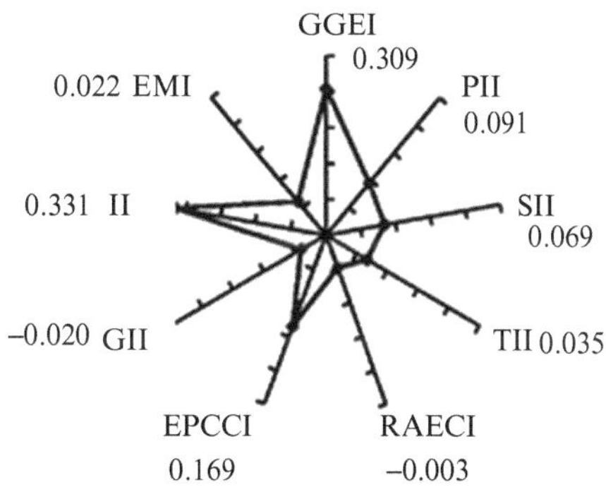

Fig. 9.50 Scores of Shenzhen by Second-Class Indicators

Table 9.49 Changes in Shenzhen's rankings by First-Class and Second-Class Indicators, 2009–2010

Indicator	2010	2009	Difference	Indicator	2010	2009	Difference
GDI	1	1	0				
GDEG	1	1	0	RAECI	16	15	−1
GGEI	1	1	0	EPCCI	6	10	4
PII	1	1	0	SDGP	1	1	0
SII	2	2	0	GII	21	10	−11
TII	7	7	0	II	1	1	0
CCPNRE	6	9	3	EMI	17	20	3

Note: A positive value in "Difference" means a rise in ranking

9.25.2 Changes in Shenzhen's GDI Rankings 2009–2010

According to Table 9.49, Shenzhen rose by 3 places by CCPNRE, and it remained unchanged in SDGP and GDEG, still in the 1st place. From changes in ranking, it rose by 4 and 3 places in EPCCI and EMI; it dropped by 1 and 11 places in RAECI and GII; it remained unchanged in other 5 indicators as compared in 2009.

To further explain the causes of the changes in the rankings by First- and Second-Class Indicators, we put the Third-Class Indicators where a change of more than 3 places occurred from 2009 to 2010 as follows in Table 9.50. Compared with those in 2009, Shenzhen both out- and underperformed in ranking in 2010, while the more obvious trend is outperforming compared with the previous year. It rose by 28 places in Treatment rate of urban household wastewater, 10 places in Ammonia/nitrogen emissions per capita, 7 in Nitrogen oxides emissions per capita, 7 in Industrial waste water ammonia/nitrogen removal rate, 6 in COD emissions per unit of land area, 5 in Utilization rate industrial solid waste, 5 in Industrial wastewater COD removal rate and 4 in Proportion of tertiary sector employees in the total employed population; it dropped to some extent in3 indicators including Percentage of the days with air quality at or over level II in a year, Ratio of environmental spending to government expenditure, Ratio of the spending on science, education, culture, and public health to government expenditure compared with those in 2009.

Table 9.50 Third-Class Indicators where changes over 3 places occurred by Shenzhen, 2009–2010

	Original data for 2009 and 2010			Change in ranking		
Third-Class Indicator	2010	2009	Unit	2010	2009	Difference
Utilization rate industrial solid waste	92.00	90.10	%	20	25	5
Proportion of tertiary sector employees in the total employed population	48.47	45.98	%	13	17	4
COD emissions per unit of land area	11.16	25.13	Ton per km^2	30	36	6
Nitrogen oxides emissions per capita	119.77	158.23	Ton per 10,000 persons	11	18	7
Ammonia/nitrogen emissions per capita	5.73	10.28	Ton per 10,000 persons	4	14	10
Percentage of the days with air quality at or over level II in a year	97.53	99.73	%	7	4	−3
Ratio of environmental spending to government expenditure	3.36	3.48	%	14	6	−8
Ratio of the spending on science, education, culture, and public health to government expenditure	20.34	28.80	%	20	10	−10
Treatment rate of urban household wastewater	99.30	68.75	%	3	31	28
Industrial wastewater COD removal rate	89.91	88.41	%	8	13	5
Industrial waste water ammonia/nitrogen removal rate	78.47	65.83	%	14	21	7

Note: A positive value in "Difference" means a rise in ranking

Green development checkup-Zhuhai

No.	Indicator	Unit	Scope	Attribute	2010 average of 38 cities	2010 figure	2009 figure	2010 ranking	2009 ranking	Change in ranking	Source of 2010 data	Chernoff face
1	GDP per capita	Yuan	Whole city	Positive	55,399.15	77,888	69,890.00	5	8	3	Regional Economy; City	
2	Energy consumption per unit of GDP	Ton per 10,000 yuan	Whole city	Negative	0.82	0.56	0.57	13	12	−1	Regional Economy; City	
3	Electricity consumption per capita in urban areas	kWh per capita	Whole city	Negative	580.70	1,313.35	1,213.33	36	36	0	City	
4	CO_2 emissions per unit of GDP			Negative	No data			N/A	N/A	N/A		
5	SO_2 emissions per unit of GDP	Ton per 100 million yuan	Whole city	Negative	42.67	31.49	34.57	23	20	−3	Regional Economy; Environment Annual Report	
6	COD emissions per unit of GDP	Ton per 100 million yuan	Whole city	Negative	24.91	23.38	26.87	24	22	−2	Regional Economy; Environment Annual Report	
7	Nitrogen oxide emissions per unit of GDP	Ton per 100 million yuan	Whole city	Negative	40.67	80.42	82.78	35	36	1	Regional Economy; Environment Annual Report	
8	Ammonia/nitrogen emissions per unit of GDP	Ton per 100 million yuan	Whole city	Negative	2.63	2.34	2.56	20	23	3	Regional Economy; Environment Annual Report	
9	Labor productivity of the primary sector	10,000 yuan per capita	Whole city	Pcsitive	3.00	3.83	4.06	3	4	1	Regional Economy	

10	Labor productivity of the secondary sector	10,000 yuan per capita	Whole city	Positive	18.12	14.84	12.39	4	16	12	Regional Economy	☺
11	Water consumption per unit of value added created by industrial enterprises	10,000 tons per 10,000 yuan	Whole city	Negative	0.03	0.00	0.00	5	4	−1	Regional Economy; Environment Annual Report	☹
12	Energy consumption per unit of value added created by industrial enterprises			Negative	No data			N/A	N/A	N/A		
13	Utilization rate industrial solid waste	%	Whole city	Positive	83.42	98.20	98.50	9	6	−3	Environment Annual Report	☹
14	Recycling rate of industrial water	%	Whole city	Positive	82.10	62.06	61.03	35	34	−1	Environment Annual Report	☹
15	Labor productivity of the tertiary sector	10,000 yuan per capita	Whole city	Positive	11.39	10.55	9.53	2	17	15	Regional Economy	☺
16	Proportion of value added of tertiary sector in GDP	%	Whole city	Positive	48.37	42.55	44.85	27	27	0	City	
17	Proportion of tertiary sector employees in the total employed population	%	Whole city	Positive	46.83	47.72	48.07	15	13	−2	Regional Economy	☹
18	Water resources per capita	m^3 per capita	Whole city	Positive	1,040.56	1,779.64	2,085.73	4	3	−1	Environment Annual Report; City	☹

(continued)

(continued)

No.	Indicator	Unit	Scope	Attribute	2010 average of 38 cities	2010 figure	2009 figure	2010 ranking	2009 ranking	Change in ranking	Source of 2010 data	Chernoff face
19	CO_2 emissions per unit of land area			Negative	No data			N/A	N/A	N/A		
20	CO_2 emissions per capita			Negative	No data			N/A	N/A	N/A		
21	SO_2 emissions per unit of land area	Ton per km^2	Whole city	Negative	11.34	20.83	20.37	34	33	−1	Environment Annual Report; City	
22	SO_2 emissions per capita	Ton per 10,000 persons	Whole city	Negative	211.11	343.67	342.83	34	32	−2	Environment Annual Report; City	
23	COD emissions per unit of land area	Ton per km^2	Whole city	Negative	7.63	15.46	15.84	34	32	−2	Environment Annual Report; City	
24	COD emissions per capita	Ton per 10,000 persons	Whole city	Negative	117.25	255.14	266.52	37	37	0	Environment Annual Report; City	
25	Nitrogen oxides emissions per unit of land area	Ton per km^2	Whole city	Negative	14.61	53.19	48.78	36	36	0	Environment Annual Report; City	
26	Nitrogen oxides emissions per capita	Ton per 10,000 persons	Whole city	Negative	231.68	877.64	821.00	37	38	1	Environment Annual Report; City	
27	Ammonia/nitrogen emissions per unit of land area	Ton per km^2	Whole city	Negative	0.83	1.55	1.51	33	34	1	Environment Annual Report; City	
28	Ammonia/nitrogen emissions per capita	Ton per 10,000 persons	Whole city	Negative	12.50	25.53	25.35	37	37	0	Environment Annual Report; City	

29	Percentage of the days with air quality at or over level II in a year	%	District	Positive	89.45		100.00	100.00	1	1	0	MEP Data	
30	Percentage of days with respirable suspended particulates as the principal pollutants in a year	%	District	Negative	69.76		38.08	37.50	2	3	1	MEP Data	☺
31	Ratio of environmental spending to government expenditure	%	Whole city	Positive	3.14		14.30	3.26	1	10	9	China Statistics; City	☺
32	Ratio of the investment in industrial pollution control to GDP	%	Whole city	Positive	0.09		0.04	0.05	19	23	4	Environment Annual Report; Regional Economy	☺
33	Ratio of the spending on science, education, culture, and public health to government expenditure	%	Whole city	Positive	21.06		23.97	28.48	10	11	1	China Statistics; City; Regional Economy	☺
34	Area of green land per capita in urban areas	m^2	District	Positive	58.13		55.00	50.82	13	14	1	City	☺
35	Green coverage of urban built-in areas	%	District	Positive	39.84		50.25	44.97	2	3	1	Urban Construction	☺

(continued)

(continued)

No.	Indicator	Unit	Scope	Attribute	2010 average of 38 cities	2010 figure	2009 figure	2010 ranking	2009 ranking	Change in ranking	Source of 2010 data	Chernoff face
36	Coverage of water supply	%	District	Positive	98.83	99.70	98.96	26	29	3	Urban Construction	
37	Treatment rate of urban household wastewater	%	District	Positive	86.16	78.81	53.84	31	37	6	Urban Construction	
38	Harmless treatment of urban household waste	%	District	Positive	94.38	92.34	67.25	27	36	9	Urban Construction	
39	Public buses per 10,000 urban residents		District	Positive	15.51	13.15	12.50	19	23	4	City	
40	Industrial SO_2 removal rate	%	Whole city	Positive	57.30	63.92	70.88	15	8	−7	Environment Annual Report	
41	Industrial wastewater COD removal rate	%	Whole city	Positive	76.07	86.93	91.35	14	5	−9	Environment Annual Report	
42	Industrial nitrogen oxide removal rate	%	Whole city	Positive	5.24	0.26	0.51	25	25	0	Environment Annual Report	
43	Industrial waste water ammonia/nitrogen removal rate	%	Whole city	Positive	66.79	53.91	73.96	30	16	−14	Environment Annual Report	

Note:
Regional Economy: *China Regional Economy Statistical Yearbook 2011*
City: *China City Statistical Yearbook 2011*
China Statistics: *China Statistical Yearbook 2011*
Urban Construction: *China Urban Construction Statistical Yearbook 2010*
Environment Annual Report: *China Environment Annual Report 2010*
Environmental Yearbook: *China Environmental Statistical Yearbook 2011*
MEP Data: Ministry of Environmental Protection Data Center

9.26 Brief Analysis of Green Development in Zhuhai

Zhuhai ranked 11th among the 38 participating cities by GDI according to 2010 data, 14 place lower over 2009 (Zhuhai ranked 25th in 2009). Following is a brief analysis of its score by each indicator and their changes from 2009 to 2010.

9.26.1 Zhuhai's 2010 Scores by GDI

Zhuhai scored 0.061 in 2010. From the three First-Class Indicators including GDEG, CCPNRE, and SDGP as shown in Fig. 9.51, Zhuhai showed obvious advantage in SDGP; it performed relatively weak in GDEG and CCPNRE with scores lower than the national average (Note: the national average value of each indicator is 0).

According to Fig. 9.52, Zhuhai surpassed the national average in 4 of Second-Class Indicators in 2010, which were GII, II, RAECI and PII; it scored lower than the national average in 5 indicators including TII, SII, EMI, GGEI and EPCCI.

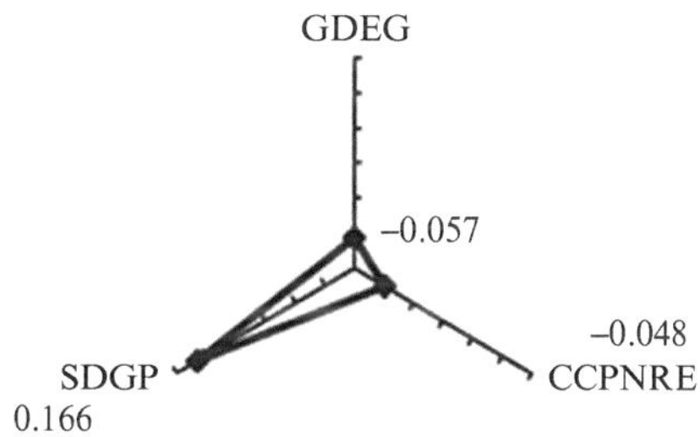

Fig. 9.51 Scores of Zhuhai by First-Class Indicators

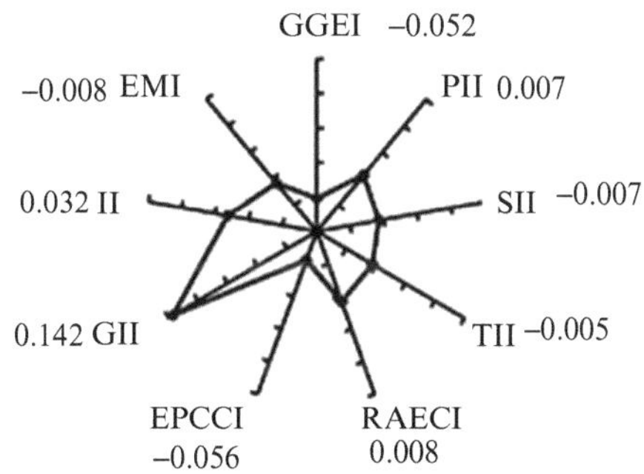

Fig. 9.52 Scores of Zhuhai by Second-Class Indicators

Table 9.51 Changes in Zhuhai's rankings by First-Class and Second-Class Indicators, 2009–2010

Indicator	2010	2009	Difference	Indicator	2010	2009	Difference
GDI	11	25	14				
GDEG	27	21	−6	RAECI	4	3	−1
GGEI	30	29	−1	EPCCI	23	21	−2
PII	5	4	−1	SDGP	3	23	20
SII	25	26	1	GII	2	11	9
TII	20	17	−3	II	12	33	21
CCPNRE	21	21	0	EMI	23	13	−10

Note: A positive value in "Difference" means a rise in ranking

9.26.2 Changes in Zhuhai's GDI Rankings 2009–2010

According to Table 9.51, in First-Class Indicators, the most obvious change occurred in SDGP with a rise of 20 places; it dropped by 6 places GDEG, and it remained unchanged in CCPNRE. From changes in ranking, it rose by 21, 9 and 1 place in II, GII and SII; it dropped by 1, 1, 1, 2, 3 and 10 places in GGEI, PII, RAECI, EPCCI, TII and EMI.

To further explain the causes of the changes in the rankings by First- and Second-Class Indicators, we put the Third-Class Indicators where a change of more than 3 places occurred from 2009 to 2010 as follows in Table 9.52. Compared with those in 2009, Zhuhai both out- and underperformed in ranking in 2010, while the more obvious trend is outperforming compared with the previous year. It rose by 12 places by Labor productivity of the tertiary sector as compared with that in 2009, 12 in Labor productivity of the secondary sector, and it rose by various extent in indicators including Ratio of environmental spending to government expenditure; it dropped to some extent in 5 indicators including SO_2 emissions per unit of GDP, Utilization rate industrial solid waste, Industrial SO_2 removal rate, Industrial wastewater COD removal rate and Industrial waste water ammonia/nitrogen removal rate.

Table 9.52 Third-Class Indicators where changes over 3 places occurred by Zhuhai, 2009–2010

Third-Class Indicator	Original data for 2009 and 2010			Change in ranking		
	2010	2009	Unit	2010	2009	Difference
GDP per capita	77,888.00	69,890.00	Yuan	5	8	3
SO_2 emissions per unit of GDP	31.49	34.57	Ton per 100 million yuan	23	20	−3
Ammonia/nitrogen emissions per unit of GDP	2.34	2.56	Ton per 100 million yuan	20	23	3
Labor productivity of the secondary sector	14.84	12.39	10,000 yuan per capita	4	16	12
Utilization rate industrial solid waste	98.20	98.50	%	9	6	−3
Labor productivity of the tertiary sector	10.55	9.53	10,000 yuan per capita	2	17	15
Ratio of environmental spending to government expenditure	14.30	3.26	%	1	10	9
Ratio of the investment in industrial pollution control to GDP	0.04	0.05	%	19	23	4
Coverage of water supply	99.70	98.96	%	26	29	3
Treatment rate of urban household wastewater	78.81	53.84	%	31	37	6
Harmless treatment of urban household waste	92.34	67.25	%	27	36	9
Public buses per 10,000 urban residents	13.15	12.50		19	23	4
Industrial SO_2 removal rate	63.92	70.88	%	15	8	−7
Industrial wastewater COD removal rate	86.93	91.35	%	14	5	−9
Industrial waste water ammonia/nitrogen removal rate	53.91	73.96	%	30	16	−14

Note: A positive value in "Difference" means a rise in ranking

Green development checkup-Nanning

No.	Indicator	Unit	Scope	Attribute	2010 average of 38 cities	2010 figure	2009 figure	2010 ranking	2009 ranking	Change in ranking	Source of 2010 data	Chernoff face
1	GDP per capita	Yuan	Whole city	Positive	55,399.15	26,330	21,829.00	37	38	1	Regional Economy; City	
2	Energy consumption per unit of GDP	Ton per 10,000 yuan	Whole city	Negative	0.82	0.27	0.32	6	7	1	Regional Economy; City	
3	Electricity consumption per capita in urban areas	kWh per capita	Whole city	Negative	580.70	272.77	246.36	4	4	0	City	
4	CO_2 emissions per unit of GDP			Negative	No data			N/A	N/A	N/A		
5	SO_2 emissions per unit of GDP	Ton per 100 million yuan	Whole city	Negative	42.67	58.46	56.95	30	28	−2	Regional Economy; Environment Annual Report	
6	COD emissions per unit of GDP	Ton per 100 million yuan	Whole city	Negative	24.91	95.93	112.85	38	38	0	Regional Economy; Environment Annual Report	
7	Nitrogen oxide emissions per unit of GDP	Ton per 100 million yuan	Whole city	Negative	40.67	31.00	34.13	17	22	5	Regional Economy; Environment Annual Report	
8	Ammonia/nitrogen emissions per unit of GDP	Ton per 100 million yuan	Whole city	Negative	2.63	3.74	4.41	29	30	1	Regional Economy; Environment Annual Report	
9	Labor productivity of the primary sector	10,000 yuan per capita	Whole city	Positive	3.00	1.20	1.05	31	31	0	Regional Economy	

10	Labor productivity of the secondary sector	10,000 yuan per capita	Whole city	Positive	18.12	9.45	8.22	35	34	−1	Regional Economy	☹
11	Water consumption per unit of value added created by industrial enterprises	10,000 tons per 10,000 yuan	Whole city	Negative	0.03	0.03	0.03	23	22	−1	Regional Economy; Environment Annual Report	☹
12	Energy consumption per unit of value added created by industrial enterprises			Negative	No data			N/A	N/A	N/A		
13	Utilization rate industrial solid waste	%	Whole city	Positive	83.42	94.00	90.70	17	22	5	Environment Annual Report	☺
14	Recycling rate of industrial water	%	Whole city	Positive	82.10	86.03	83.62	26	26	0	Environment Annual Report	
15	Labor productivity of the tertiary sector	10,000 yuan per capita	Whole city	Positive	11.39	6.85	6.27	31	30	−1	Regional Economy	☹
16	Proportion of value added of tertiary sector in GDP	%	Whole city	Positive	48.37	50.21	51.48	15	13	−2	City	☹
17	Proportion of tertiary sector employees in the total employed population	%	Whole city	Positive	46.83	32.61	32.53	38	37	−1	Regional Economy	☹

(continued)

(continued)

No.	Indicator	Unit	Scope	Attribute	2010 average of 38 cities	2010 figure	2009 figure	2010 ranking	2009 ranking	Change in ranking	Source of 2010 data	Chernoff face
18	Water resources per capita	m^3 per capita	Whole city	Positive	1,040.56	1,574.00	2,004.59	7	4	−3	Environment Annual Report; City	
19	CO_2 emissions per unit of land area			Negative	No data			N/A	N/A	N/A		
20	CO_2 emissions per capita			Negative	No data			N/A	N/A	N/A		
21	SO_2 emissions per unit of land area	Ton per km^2	Whole city	Negative	11.34	3.43	2.93	4	3	−1	Environment Annual Report; City	
22	SO_2 emissions per capita	Ton per 10,000 persons	Whole city	Negative	211.11	107.93	93.10	9	6	−3	Environment Annual Report; City	
23	COD emissions per unit of land area	Ton per km^2	Whole city	Negative	7.63	5.63	5.80	21	19	−2	Environment Annual Report; City	
24	COD emissions per capita	Ton per 10,000 persons	Whole city	Negative	117.25	177.10	184.48	34	34	0	Environment Annual Report; City	
25	Nitrogen oxides emissions per unit of land area	Ton per km^2	Whole city	Negative	14.61	1.82	1.75	2	2	0	Environment Annual Report; City	
26	Nitrogen oxides emissions per capita	Ton per 10,000 persons	Whole city	Negative	231.68	57.23	55.80	2	3	1	Environment Annual Report; City	
27	Ammonia/nitrogen emissions per unit of land area	Ton per km^2	Whole city	Negative	0.83	0.22	0.23	5	4	−1	Environment Annual Report; City	

28	Ammonia/nitrogen emissions per capita	Ton per 10,000 persons	Whole city	Negative	12.50	6.90	7.21	8	5	−3	Environment Annual Report; City	☹
29	Percentage of the days with air quality at or over level II in a year	%	District	Positive	89.45	95.60	99.18	10	6	−4	MEP Data	☹
30	Percentage of days with respirable suspended particulates as the principal pollutants in a year	%	District	Negative	69.76	58.63	36.44	9	2	−7	MEP Data	☹
31	Ratio of environmental spending to government expenditure	%	Whole city	Positive	3.14	1.32	2.09	37	19	−18	China Statistics; City	☹
32	Ratio of the investment in industrial pollution control to GDP	%	Whole city	Positive	0.09	0.04	0.24	17	7	−10	Environment Annual Report; Regional Economy	☹
33	Ratio of the spending on science, education, culture, and public health to government expenditure	%	Whole city	Positive	21.06	19.08	25.63	25	20	−5	China Statistics; City; Regional Economy	☹

(continued)

(continued)

No.	Indicator	Unit	Scope	Attribute	2010 average of 38 cities	2010 figure	2009 figure	2010 ranking	2009 ranking	Change in ranking	Source of 2010 data	Chernoff face
34	Area of green land per capita in urban areas	m^2	District	Positive	58.13	137.00	130.75	4	4	0	City	
35	Green coverage of urban built-in areas	%	District	Positive	39.84	40.36	39.65	19	16	−3	Urban Construction	
36	Coverage of water supply	%	District	Positive	98.83	95.10	93.89	35	36	1	Urban Construction	
37	Treatment rate of urban household wastewater	%	District	Positive	86.16	93.27	99.42	11	2	−9	Urban Construction	
38	Harmless treatment of urban household waste	%	District	Positive	94.38	100.00	100.00	1	1	0	Urban Construction	
39	Public buses per 10,000 urban residents		District	Positive	15.51	9.61	10.02	31	33	2	City	
40	Industrial SO_2 removal rate	%	Whole city	Positive	57.30	26.89	25.60	36	34	−2	Environment Annual Report	
41	Industrial wastewater COD removal rate	%	Whole city	Positive	76.07	75.90	70.73	30	30	0	Environment Annual Report	

42	Industrial nitrogen oxide removal rate	%	Whole city	Positive	5.24	1.40	1.21	18	21	3	Environment Annual Report	☺
43	Industrial waste water ammonia/nitrogen removal rate	%	Whole city	Positive	66.79	79.25	79.99	13	12	−1	Environment Annual Report	☹

Note:
Regional Economy: *China Regional Economy Statistical Yearbook 2011*
City: *China City Statistical Yearbook 2011*
China Statistics: *China Statistical Yearbook 2011*
Urban Construction: *China Urban Construction Statistical Yearbook 2010*
Environment Annual Report: *China Environment Annual Report 2010*
Environmental Yearbook: *China Environmental Statistical Yearbook 2011*
MEP Data: Ministry of Environmental Protection Data Center

9.27 Brief Analysis of Green Development in Nanning

Nanning ranked 12th among the 38 participating cities by GDI according to 2010 data, 1 place lower over 2009 (Nanning ranked 11th in 2009). Following is a brief analysis of its score by each indicator and their changes from 2009 to 2010.

9.27.1 Nanning's 2010 Scores by GDI

Nanning scored 0.049 in 2010. From the three First-Class Indicators including GDEG, CCPNRE, and SDGP as shown in Fig. 9.53, Nanning showed some advantages in CCPNRE, and scored lower in GDEG and SDGP (Note: the national average value of each indicator is 0).

According to Fig. 9.54, Nanning surpassed the national average in 3 of Second-Class Indicators in 2010, which were EPCCI, II and RAECI; it scored lower than the national average in 6 indicators including SII, PII, GGEI, TII, EMI and GII.

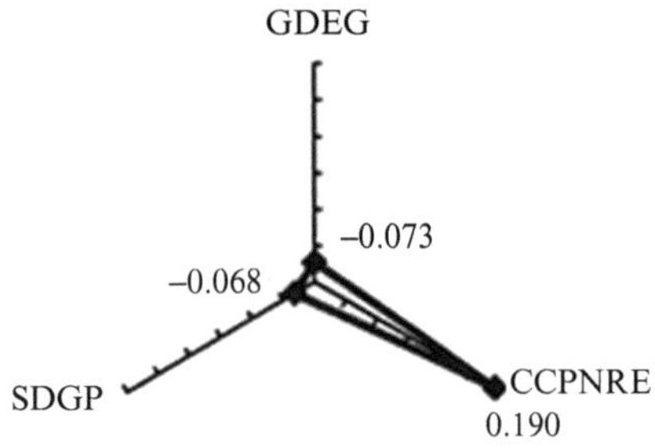

Fig. 9.53 Scores of Nanning by First-Class Indicators

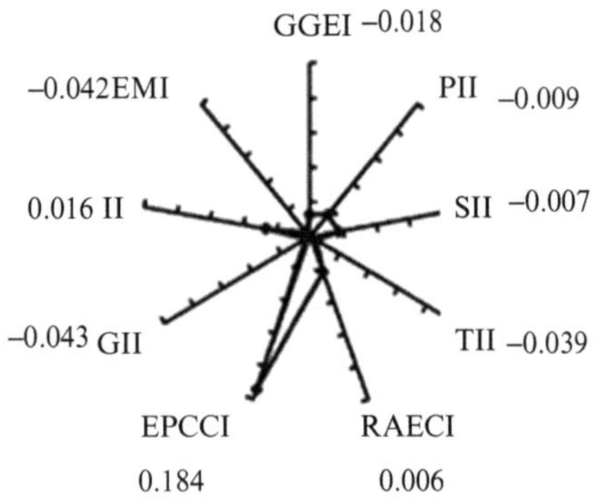

Fig. 9.54 Scores of Nanning by Second-Class Indicators

Table 9.53 Changes in Nanning's rankings by First-Class and Second-Class Indicators, 2009–2010

Indicator	2010	2009	Difference	Indicator	2010	2009	Difference
GDI	12	11	−1				
GDEG	29	33	4	RAECI	7	4	−3
GGEI	23	27	4	EPCCI	5	4	−1
PII	31	31	0	SDGP	24	20	−4
SII	24	29	5	GII	33	15	−18
TII	34	35	1	II	16	12	−4
CCPNRE	5	4	−1	EMI	29	29	0

Note: A positive value in "Difference" means a rise in ranking

9.27.2 Changes in Nanning's GDI Rankings 2009–2010

According to Table 9.53, in First-Class Indicators, the most obvious change occurred in GDEG with a rise of 4 places; it dropped by 4 and 1 place in SDGP and CCPNRE. Judging from changes in ranking, it rose by 5, 4, and 1 place in SII, GGEI and TII; it dropped by 1, 4 and 18 places in EPCCI, RAECI, II and GII; it remained unchanged by PII and EMI.

To further explain the causes of the changes in the rankings by First- and Second-Class Indicators, we put the Third-Class Indicators where a change of more than 3 places occurred from 2009 to 2010 as follows in Table 9.54. Compared with those in 2009, Nanning both out- and underperformed in ranking in 2010, while the more obvious trend is underperforming compared with the previous year. It dropped by 18 places in Ratio of environmental spending to government expenditure, 10 in Ratio of the investment in industrial pollution control to GDP, and to various degrees in many other indicators such as Treatment rate of urban household wastewater; it rose to some extent in 3 indicators which were Industrial nitrogen oxide removal rate, Nitrogen oxide emissions per unit of GDP and Utilization rate industrial solid waste.

Table 9.54 Third-Class Indicators where changes over 3 places occurred by Nanning, 2009–2010

	Original data for 2009 and 2010			Change in ranking		
Third-Class Indicator	2010	2009	Unit	2010	2009	Difference
Nitrogen oxide emissions per unit of GDP	31.00	34.13	Ton per 100 million yuan	17	22	5
Utilization rate industrial solid waste	94.00	90.70	%	17	22	5
Water resources per capita	1,574.00	2,004.59	m^3 per capita	7	4	−3
SO_2 emissions per capita	107.93	93.10	Ton per 10,000 persons	9	6	−3
Ammonia/nitrogen emissions per capita	6.90	7.21	Ton per 10,000 persons	8	5	−3
Percentage of the days with air quality at or over level II in a year	95.60	99.18	%	10	6	−4
Percentage of days with respirable suspended particulates as the principal pollutants in a year	58.63	36.44	%	9	2	−7
Ratio of environmental spending to government expenditure	1.32	2.09	%	37	19	−18
Ratio of the investment in industrial pollution control to GDP	0.04	0.24	%	17	7	−10
Ratio of the spending on science, education, culture, and public health to government expenditure	19.08	25.63	%	25	20	−5
Green coverage of urban built-in areas	40.36	39.65	%	19	16	−3
Treatment rate of urban household wastewater	93.27	99.42	%	11	2	−9
Industrial nitrogen oxide removal rate	1.40	1.21	%	18	21	3

Note: A positive value in "Difference" means a rise in ranking

Green development checkup-Haikou

No.	Indicator	Unit	Scope	Attribute	2010 average of 38 cities	2010 figure	2009 figure	2010 ranking	2009 ranking	Change in ranking	Source of 2010 data	Chernoff face
1	GDP per capita	Yuan	Whole city	Positive	55,399.15	38,731	31,541.00	29	31	2	Regional Economy; City	☺
2	Energy consumption per unit of GDP	Ton per 10,000 yuan	Whole city	Negative	0.82	0.65	0.73	18	17	−1	Regional Economy; City	☹
3	Electricity consumption per capita in urban areas	kWh per capita	Whole city	Negative	580.70	357.46	314.77	10	10	0		
4	CO_2 emissions per unit of GDP			Negative	No data			N/A	N/A	N/A		
5	SO_2 emissions per unit of GDP	Ton per 100 million yuan	Whole city	Negative	42.67	0.82	1.00	1	1	0	Regional Economy; Environment Annual Report	
6	COD emissions per unit of GDP	Ton per 100 million yuan	Whole city	Negative	24.91	20.34	30.34	20	25	5	Regional Economy; Environment Annual Report	☺
7	Nitrogen oxide emissions per unit of GDP	Ton per 100 million yuan	Whole city	Negative	40.67	36.83	39.55	23	24	1	Regional Economy; Environment Annual Report	☺
8	Ammonia/nitrogen emissions per unit of GDP	Ton per 100 million yuan	Whole city	Negative	2.63	3.03	3.91	26	29	3	Regional Economy; Environment Annual Report	☺

(continued)

(continued)

No.	Indicator	Unit	Scope	Attribute	2010 average of 38 cities	2010 figure	2009 figure	2010 ranking	2009 ranking	Change in ranking	Source of 2010 data	Chernoff face
9	Labor productivity of the primary sector	10,000 yuan per capita	Whole city	Positive	3.00	2.01	1.76	21	22	1	Regional Economy	
10	Labor productivity of the secondary sector	10,000 yuan per capita	Whole city	Positive	18.12	7.06	5.87	38	38	0	Regional Economy	
11	Water consumption per unit of value added created by industrial enterprises	10,000 tons per 10,000 yuan	Whole city	Negative	0.03	0.00	0.00	2	3	1	Regional Economy; Environment Annual Report	
12	Energy consumption per unit of value added created by industrial enterprises			Negative	No data			N/A	N/A	N/A		
13	Utilization rate industrial solid waste	%	Whole city	Positive	83.42	97.00	98.70	12	3	−9	Environment Annual Report	
14	Recycling rate of industrial water	%	Whole city	Positive	82.10	75.10	85.00	29	24	−5	Environment Annual Report	
15	Labor productivity of the tertiary sector	10,000 yuan per capita	Whole city	Positive	11.39	6.69	5.98	32	33	1	Regional Economy	
16	Proportion of value added of tertiary sector in GDP	%	Whole city	Positive	48.37	69.58	68.69	2	2	0	City	

17	Proportion of tertiary sector employees in the total employed population	%	Whole city	Positive	46.83	59.80	58.08	3	3	0	Regional Economy	
18	Water resources per capita	m^3 per capita	Whole city	Positive	1,040.56	108.43	112.73	36	37	1	Environment Annual Report; City	☺
19	CO_2 emissions per unit of land area			Negative	No data			N/A	N/A	N/A		
20	CO_2 emissions per capita			Negative	No data			N/A	N/A	N/A		
21	SO_2 emissions per unit of land area	Ton per km^2	Whole city	Negative	11.34	0.20	0.21	1	1	0	Environment Annual Report; City	
22	SO_2 emissions per capita	Ton per 10,000 persons	Whole city	Negative	211.11	2.95	3.08	1	1	0	Environment Annual Report; City	
23	COD emissions per unit of land area	Ton per km^2	Whole city	Negative	7.63	5.05	6.37	18	23	5	Environment Annual Report; City	☺
24	COD emissions per capita	Ton per 10,000 persons	Whole city	Negative	117.25	73.02	93.47	8	18	10	Environment Annual Report; City	☺
25	Nitrogen oxides emissions per unit of land area	Ton per km^2	Whole city	Negative	14.61	9.14	8.30	21	21	0	Environment Annual Report; City	
26	Nitrogen oxides emissions per capita	Ton per 10,000 persons	Whole city	Negative	231.68	132.20	121.86	13	12	−1	Environment Annual Report; City	☹
27	Ammonia/nitrogen emissions per unit of land area	Ton per km^2	Whole city	Negative	0.83	0.75	0.82	26	26	0	Environment Annual Report; City	

(continued)

(continued)

No.	Indicator	Unit	Scope	Attribute	2010 average of 38 cities	2010 figure	2009 figure	2010 ranking	2009 ranking	Change in ranking	Source of 2010 data	Chernoff face
28	Ammonia/nitrogen emissions per capita	Ton per 10,000 persons	Whole city	Negative	12.50	10.89	12.04	21	23	2	Environment Annual Report; City	☺
29	Percentage of the days with air quality at or over level II in a year	%	District	Positive	89.45	100.00	100.00	1	1	0	MEP Data	
30	Percentage of days with respirable suspended particulates as the principal pollutants in a year	%	District	Negative	69.76	18.08	17.81	1	1	0	MEP Data	
31	Ratio of environmental spending to government expenditure	%	Whole city	Positive	3.14	1.87	2.19	29	18	−11	China Statistics; City	☹
32	Ratio of the investment in industrial pollution control to GDP	%	Whole city	Positive	0.09	N/A	N/A	N/A	N/A	N/A	Environment Annual Report; Regional Economy	
33	Ratio of the spending on science, education, culture, and public health to government expenditure	%	Whole city	Positive	21.06	28.11	27.08	4	15	11	China Statistics; City; Regional Economy	☺
34	Area of green land per capita in urban areas	m^2	District	Positive	58.13	23.00	22.83	34	33	−1	City	☹

35	Green coverage of urban built-in areas	%	District	Positive	39.84	44.14	43.78	6	6	0	Urban Construction	
36	Coverage of water supply	%	District	Positive	98.83	100.00	99.77	1	21	20	Urban Construction	☺
37	Treatment rate of urban household wastewater	%	District	Positive	86.16	87.42	77.41	23	28	5	Urban Construction	☺
38	Harmless treatment of urban house-hold waste	%	District	Positive	94.38	100.00	100.00	1	1	0	Urban Construction	
39	Public buses per 10,000 urban residents		District	Positive	15.51	6.98	6.52	37	37	0	City	
40	Industrial SO_2 removal rate	%	Whole city	Positive	57.30	N/A	N/A	N/A	N/A	N/A	Environment Annual Report	
41	Industrial wastewater COD removal rate	%	Whole city	Positive	76.07	92.03	93.41	7	2	−5	Environment Annual Report	☹
42	Industrial nitrogen oxide removal rate	%	Whole city	Positive	5.24	N/A	N/A	N/A	N/A	N/A	Environment Annual Report	
43	Industrial waste water ammonia/nitrogen removal rate	%	Whole city	Positive	66.79	86.50	58.77	10	25	15	Environment Annual Report	☺

Note:
Regional Economy: *China Regional Economy Statistical Yearbook 2011*
City: *China City Statistical Yearbook 2011*
China Statistics: *China Statistical Yearbook 2011*
Urban Construction: *China Urban Construction Statistical Yearbook 2010*
Environment Annual Report: *China Environment Annual Report 2010*
Environmental Yearbook: *China Environmental Statistical Yearbook 2011*
MEP Data: Ministry of Environmental Protection Data Center

9.28 Brief Analysis of Green Development in Haikou

Haikou ranked 2nd among the 38 participating cities by GDI according to 2010 data, 1 place higher over 2009 (Haikou ranked 3rd in 2009). Following is a brief analysis of its score by each indicator and their changes from 2009 to 2010.

9.28.1 Haikou's 2010 Scores by GDI

Haikou scored 0.603 in 2010. From the three First-Class Indicators including GDEG, CCPNRE, and SDGP as shown in Fig. 9.55, Haikou showed obvious advantage in CCPNRE, and were higher than the national average in GDEG and SDGP (Note: the national average value of each indicator is 0).

According to Fig. 9.56, Haikou surpassed the national average in 6 of Second-Class Indicators in 2010, which were EPCCI, GGEI, EMI, TII, II and GII; it ranked slightly lower than 3 indicators which were SII, PII and RAECI.

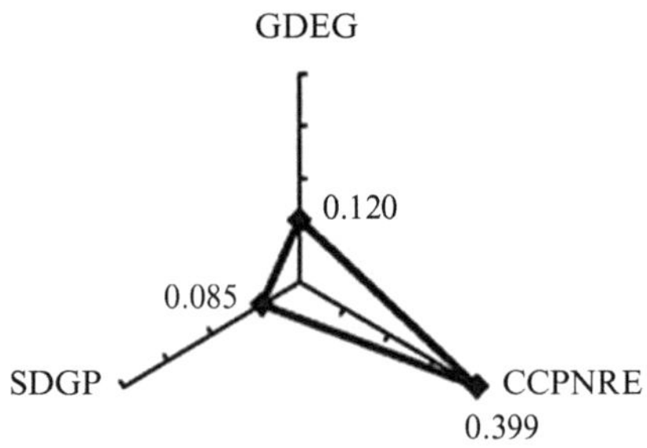

Fig. 9.55 Scores of Haikou by First-Class Indicators

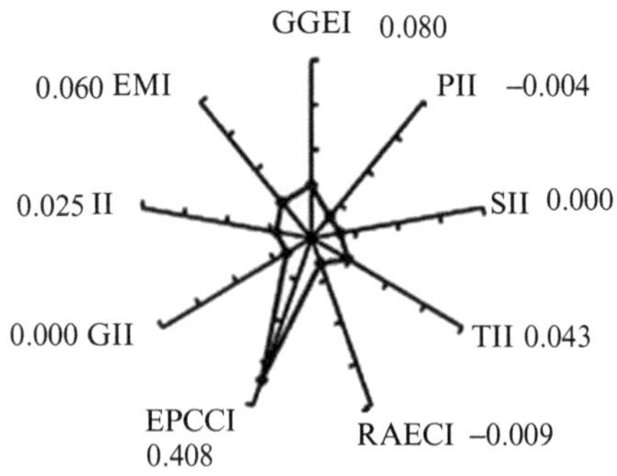

Fig. 9.56 Scores of Haikou by Second-Class Indicators

Table 9.55 Changes in Haikou's rankings by First-Class and Second-Class Indicators, 2009–2010

Indicator	2010	2009	Difference	Indicator	2010	2009	Difference
GDI	2	3	1				
GDEG	3	4	1	RAECI	36	37	1
GGEI	5	8	3	EPCCI	2	2	0
PII	20	22	2	SDGP	10	14	4
SII	19	12	−7	GII	13	23	10
TII	5	5	0	II	15	16	1
CCPNRE	2	2	0	EMI	6	10	4

Note: A positive value in "Difference" means a rise in ranking

9.28.2 Changes in Haikou's GDI Rankings 2009–2010

According to Table 9.55, in First-Class Indicators, the most obvious change occurred SDGP with a rise of 4 places; it dropped by 1 place in GDEG; it remained unchanged in CCPNRE. Judging from changes in ranking, it rose by 10, 4, 3, 2, 1 and 1 place in GII, EMI, GGEI, PII, RAECI and II; it dropped by 7 places in SII; it remained unchanged by TII and EPCCI as compared with that in 2009.

To further explain the causes of the changes in the rankings by First- and Second-Class Indicators, we put the Third-Class Indicators where a change of more than 3 places occurred from 2009 to 2010 as follows in Table 9.56. Compared with those in 2009, Haikou both out- and underperformed in ranking in 2010, while the more obvious trend is outperforming compared with the previous year. It rose by 20 places in Coverage of water supply, 15 in Industrial waste water ammonia/nitrogen removal rate, 11 in Ratio of the spending on science, education, culture, and public health to government expenditure, 10 in COD emissions per capita, 5 in COD emissions per unit of GDP, COD emissions per unit of land area and Treatment rate of urban household wastewater, and 3 in Ammonia/nitrogen emissions per unit of GDP; it dropped to some extent in 4 indicators which were Recycling rate of industrial water, Industrial wastewater COD removal rate, Utilization rate industrial solid waste and Ratio of environmental spending to government expenditure.

Table 9.56 Third-Class Indicators where changes over 3 places occurred by Haikou, 2009–2010

	Original data for 2009 and 2010			Change in ranking		
Third-Class Indicator	2010	2009	Unit	2010	2009	Difference
COD emissions per unit of GDP	20.34	30.34	Ton per 100 million yuan	20	25	5
Ammonia/nitrogen emissions per unit of GDP	3.03	3.91	Ton per 100 million yuan	26	29	3
Utilization rate industrial solid waste	97.00	98.70	%	12	3	−9
Recycling rate of industrial water	75.10	85.00	%	29	24	−5
COD emissions per unit of land area	5.05	6.37	Ton per km^2	18	23	5
COD emissions per capita	73.02	93.47	Ton per 10,000 persons	8	18	10
Ratio of environmental spending to government expenditure	1.87	2.19	%	29	18	−11
Ratio of the spending on science, education, culture, and public health to government expenditure	28.11	27.08	%	4	15	11
Coverage of water supply	100.00	99.77	%	1	21	20
Treatment rate of urban household wastewater	87.42	77.41	%	23	28	5
Industrial wastewater COD removal rate	92.03	93.41	%	7	2	−5
Industrial waste water ammonia/nitrogen removal rate	86.50	58.77	%	10	25	15

Note: A positive value in "Difference" means a rise in ranking

Green development checkup-Chongqing

No.	Indicator	Unit	Scope	Attribute	2010 average of 38 cities	2010 figure	2009 figure	2010 ranking	2009 ranking	Change in ranking	Source of 2010 data	Chernoff face
1	GDP per capita	Yuan	Whole city	Positive	56,231.37	N/A	22,920.00	N/A	36	N/A	Regional Economy; City	
2	Energy consumption per unit of GDP	Ton per 10,000 yuan	Whole city	Negative	0.81	1.16	1.23	30	27	−3	Regional Economy; City	☹
3	Electricity consumption per capita in urban areas	kWh per capita	Whole city	Negative	580.70	219.41	205.39	2	2	0		
4	CO_2 emissions per unit of GDP			Negative	No data			N/A	N/A	N/A		
5	SO_2 emissions per unit of GDP	Ton per 100 million yuan	Whole city	Negative	43.72	117.46	142.65	36	36	0	Regional Economy; Environment Annual Report	
6	COD emissions per unit of GDP	Ton per 100 million yuan	Whole city	Negative	24.81	38.29	45.85	32	33	1	Regional Economy; Environment Annual Report	☺
7	Nitrogen oxide emissions per unit of GDP	Ton per 100 million yuan	Whole city	Negative	41.71	49.02	44.86	28	26	−2	Regional Economy; Environment Annual Report	☹
8	Ammonia/nitrogen emissions per unit of GDP	Ton per 100 million yuan	Whole city	Negative	2.63	4.11	5.12	33	34	1	Regional Economy; Environment Annual Report	☺
9	Labor productivity of the primary sector	10,000 yuan per capita	Whole city	Positive	3.03	N/A	0.82	N/A	35	N/A	Regional Economy	

(continued)

(continued)

No.	Indicator	Unit	Scope	Attribute	2010 average of 38 cities	2010 figure	2009 figure	2010 ranking	2009 ranking	Change in ranking	Source of 2010 data	Chernoff face
10	Labor productivity of the secondary sector	10,000 yuan per capita	Whole city	Positive	17.91	N/A	9.93	N/A	25	N/A	Regional Economy	
11	Water consumption per unit of value added created by industrial enterprises	10,000 tons per 10,000 yuan	Whole city	Negative	0.03	0.03	0.03	25	26	1	Regional Economy; Environment Annual Report	
12	Energy consumption per unit of value added created by industrial enterprises			Negative	No data			N/A	N/A	N/A		
13	Utilization rate industrial solid waste	%	Whole city	Positive	85.58	80.20	79.80	29	29	0	Environment Annual Report	
14	Recycling rate of industrial water	%	Whole city	Positive	83.81	73.08	65.23	31	33	2	Environment Annual Report	
15	Labor productivity of the tertiary sector	10,000 yuan per capita	Whole city	Positive	11.40	N/A	4.34	N/A	37	N/A	Regional Economy	
16	Proportion of value added of tertiary sector in GDP	%	Whole city	Positive	47.97	36.35	37.89	37	37	0	City	
17	Proportion of tertiary sector employees in the total employed population	%	Whole city	Positive	46.44	N/A	34.72	N/A	36	N/A	Regional Economy	

18	Water resources per capita	m^3 per capita	Whole city	Positive	1,026.43	1,472.10	1,391.86	9	7	−2	Environment Annual Report; City	☹
19	CO_2 emissions per unit of land area			Negative	No data			N/A	N/A	N/A		
20	CO_2 emissions per capita			Negative	No data			N/A	N/A	N/A		
21	SO_2 emissions per unit of land area	Ton per km^2	Whole city	Negative	11.64	8.69	9.01	20	20	0	Environment Annual Report; City	
22	SO_2 emissions per capita	Ton per 10,000 persons	Whole city	Negative	216.46	218.70	228.42	26	25	−1	Environment Annual Report; City	☹
23	COD emissions per unit of land area	Ton per km^2	Whole city	Negative	7.83	2.83	2.90	7	7	0	Environment Annual Report; City	
24	COD emissions per capita	Ton per 10,000 persons	Whole city	Negative	118.15	71.30	73.41	6	6	0	Environment Annual Report; City	
25	Nitrogen oxides emissions per unit of land area	Ton per km^2	Whole city	Negative	15.00	3.62	2.83	5	7	2	Environment Annual Report; City	☺
26	Nitrogen oxides emissions per capita	Ton per 10,000 persons	Whole city	Negative	237.70	91.27	71.83	7	5	−2	Environment Annual Report; City	☹
27	Ammonia/nitrogen emissions per unit of land area	Ton per km^2	Whole city	Negative	0.86	0.30	0.32	7	9	2	Environment Annual Report; City	☺
28	Ammonia/nitrogen emissions per capita	Ton per 10,000 persons	Whole city	Negative	12.63	7.65	8.20	9	9	0	Environment Annual Report; City	

(continued)

(continued)

No.	Indicator	Unit	Scope	Attribute	2010 average of 38 cities	2010 figure	2009 figure	2010 ranking	2009 ranking	Change in ranking	Source of 2010 data	Chernoff face
29	Percentage of the days with air quality at or over level II in a year	%	District	Positive	89.20	85.16	82.97	28	31	3	MEP Data	
30	Percentage of days with respirable suspended particulates as the principal pollutants in a year	%	District	Negative	70.81	84.93	86.58	29	31	2	MEP Data	
31	Ratio of environmental spending to government expenditure	%	Whole city	Positive	3.13	3.90	3.80	8	4	−4	China Statistics; City	
32	Ratio of the investment in industrial pollution control to GDP	%	Whole city	Positive	0.08	0.10	0.11	9	14	5	Environment Annual Report; Regional Economy	
33	Ratio of the spending on science, education, culture, and public health to government expenditure	%	Whole city	Positive	21.08	12.84	22.88	36	33	−3	China Statistics; City; Regional Economy	
34	Area of green land per capita in urban areas	m^2	District	Positive	59.39	27.00	59.93	30	8	−22	City	
35	Green coverage of urban built-in areas	%	District	Positive	40.04	40.57	38.48	16	22	6	Urban Construction	

36	Coverage of water supply	%	District	Positive	98.82	94.05	94.60	37	35	−2	Urban Construction	☹
37	Treatment rate of urban household wastewater	%	District	Positive	86.16	91.65	88.36	14	14	0	Urban Construction	
38	Harmless treatment of urban household waste	%	District	Positive	94.38	98.82	95.88	18	18	0	Urban Construction	
39	Public buses per 10,000 urban residents		District	Positive	15.61	4.90	4.16	38	38	0	City	
40	Industrial SO_2 removal rate	%	Whole city	Positive	57.30	62.69	57.10	19	22	3	Environment Annual Report	☺
41	Industrial wastewater COD removal rate	%	Whole city	Positive	77.86	59.29	52.48	33	36	3	Environment Annual Report	☺
42	Industrial nitrogen oxide removal rate	%	Whole city	Positive	5.29	N/A	3.64	N/A	17	N/A	Environment Annual Report	
43	Industrial waste water ammonia/nitrogen removal rate	%	Whole city	Positive	67.89	53.62	47.88	31	28	−3	Environment Annual Report	☹

Note:
Regional Economy: *China Regional Economy Statistical Yearbook 2011*
City: *China City Statistical Yearbook 2011*
China Statistics: *China Statistical Yearbook 2011*
Urban Construction: *China Urban Construction Statistical Yearbook 2010*
Environment Annual Report: *China Environment Annual Report 2010*
Environmental Yearbook: *China Environmental Statistical Yearbook 2011*
MEP Data: Ministry of Environmental Protection Data Center

9.29 Brief Analysis of Green Development in Chongqing

Chongqing ranked 33rd among the 38 participating cities by GDI according to 2010 data, 1 place lower over 2009 (Chongqing ranked 32nd in 2009). Following is a brief analysis of its score by each indicator and their changes from 2009 to 2010.

9.29.1 Chongqing's 2010 Scores by GDI

Chongqing scored −0.244 in 2010. From the three First-Class Indicators including GDEG, CCPNRE, and SDGP as shown in Fig. 9.57, Chongqing showed some comparative advantages in CCPNRE; it ranked lower than the national average in GDEG and SDGP (Note: the national average value of each indicator is 0).

According to Fig. 9.58, Chongqing surpassed the national average in 2 of Second-Class Indicators in 2010, which were RAECI and EPCCI; it ranked lower than 7 indicators which were GGEI, PII, SII, TII, GII, II and EMI.

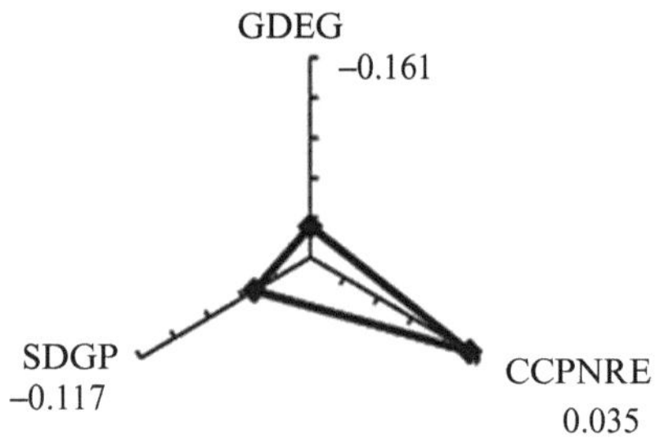

Fig. 9.57 Scores of Chongqing by First-Class Indicators

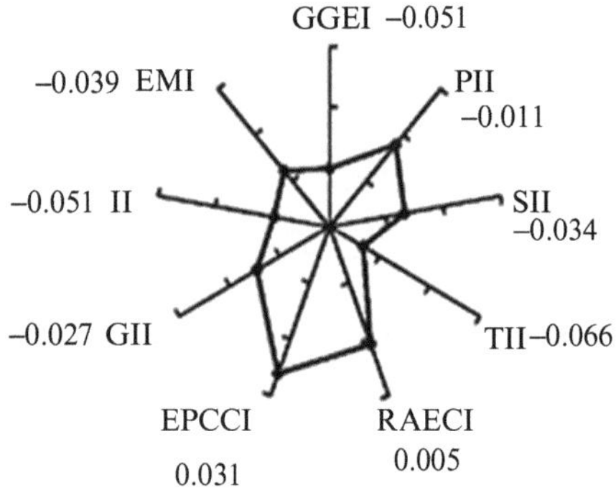

Fig. 9.58 Scores of Chongqing by Second-Class Indicators

Table 9.57 Changes in Chongqing's rankings by First-Class and Second-Class Indicators, 2009–2010

Indicator	2010	2009	Difference	Indicator	2010	2009	Difference
GDI	33	32	−1				
GDEG	36	38	2	RAECI	9	7	−2
GGEI	29	30	1	EPCCI	11	13	2
PII	34	35	1	SDGP	33	31	−2
SII	33	33	0	GII	23	17	−6
TII	37	37	0	II	33	28	−5
CCPNRE	11	13	2	EMI	28	30	2

Note: A positive value in "Difference" means a rise in ranking

9.29.2 Changes in Chongqing's GDI Rankings 2009–2010

According to Table 9.57, in First-Class Indicators, Chongqing rose by 2 places by CCPNRE and GDEG; it dropped by 2 places in SDGP. Judging from changes in ranking, it rose by 2, 2, 1 and 1 place in EPCCI, EMI, GGEI and PII; it dropped by 6, 5 and 2 places in GII, II and RAECI; it remained unchanged by SII and TII as compared with that in 2009.

To further explain the causes of the changes in the rankings by First- and Second-Class Indicators, we put the Third-Class Indicators where a change of more than 3 places occurred from 2009 to 2010 as follows in Table 9.58. Compared with those in 2009, Chongqing both out- and underperformed in ranking in 2010, while the more obvious trend is underperforming compared with the previous year. It dropped by 22 places in Area of green land per capita in urban areas, 4 in Ratio of environmental spending to government expenditure, and 3 in Energy consumption per unit of GDP, Ratio of the spending on science, education, culture, and public health to government expenditure and Industrial waste water ammonia/nitrogen removal rate; it rose on a large scale by 5 indicators which were Green coverage of urban built-in areas, Ratio of the investment in industrial pollution control to GDP, Percentage of the days with air quality at or over level II in a year, Industrial SO_2 removal rate, and Industrial wastewater COD removal rate.

Table 9.58 Third-Class Indicators where changes over 3 places occurred by Chongqing, 2009–2010

Third-Class Indicator	Original data for 2009 and 2010			Change in ranking		
	2010	2009	Unit	2010	2009	Difference
Energy consumption per unit of GDP	1.16	1.23	Ton per 10,000 yuan	30	27	−3
Percentage of the days with air quality at or over level II in a year	85.16	82.97	%	28	31	3
Ratio of environmental spending to government expenditure	3.90	3.80	%	8	4	−4
Ratio of the investment in industrial pollution control to GDP	0.10	0.11	%	9	14	5
Ratio of the spending on science, education, culture, and public health to government expenditure	12.84	22.88	%	36	33	−3
Area of green land per capita in urban areas	27.00	59.93	m^2	30	8	−22
Green coverage of urban built-in areas	40.57	38.48	%	16	22	6
Industrial SO_2 removal rate	62.69	57.10	%	19	22	3
Industrial wastewater COD removal rate	59.29	52.48	%	33	36	3
Industrial waste water ammonia/nitrogen removal rate	53.62	47.88	%	31	28	−3

Note: A positive value in "Difference" means a rise in ranking

Green development checkup-Chengdu

No.	Indicator	Unit	Scope	Attribute	2010 average of 38 cities	2010 figure	2009 figure	2010 ranking	2009 ranking	Change in ranking	Source of 2010 data	Chernoff face
1	GDP per capita	Yuan	Whole city	Positive	56,231.37	41,253	35,215.00	28	28	0	Regional Economy; City	
2	Energy consumption per unit of GDP	Ton per 10,000 yuan	Whole city	Negative	0.81	0.82	0.95	20	22	2	Regional Economy; City	☺
3	Electricity consumption per capita in urban areas	kWh per capita	Whole city	Negative	580.70	367.26	326.96	12	12	0	City	
4	CO_2 emissions per unit of GDP			Negative	No data			N/A	N/A	N/A		
5	SO_2 emissions per unit of GDP	Ton per 100 million yuan	Whole city	Negative	43.72	30.19	37.36	21	23	2	Regional Economy; Environment Annual Report	☺
6	COD emissions per unit of GDP	Ton per 100 million yuan	Whole city	Negative	24.81	25.73	30.51	27	26	−1	Regional Economy; Environment Annual Report	☹
7	Nitrogen oxide emissions per unit of GDP	Ton per 100 million yuan	Whole city	Negative	41.71	11.40	70.36	1	33	32	Regional Economy; Environment Annual Report	☺
8	Ammonia/nitrogen emissions per unit of GDP	Ton per 100 million yuan	Whole city	Negative	2.63	4.09	3.19	32	25	−7	Regional Economy; Environment Annual Report	☹
9	Labor productivity of the primary sector	10,000 yuan per capita	Whole city	Positive	3.03	1.80	1.59	25	25	0	Regional Economy	
10	Labor productivity of the secondary sector	10,000 yuan per capita	Whole city	Positive	17.91	9.54	8.02	34	35	1	Regional Economy	☺

(continued)

(continued)

No.	Indicator	Unit	Scope	Attribute	2010 average of 38 cities	2010 figure	2009 figure	2010 ranking	2009 ranking	Change in ranking	Source of 2010 data	Chernoff face
11	Water consumption per unit of value added created by industrial enterprises	10,000 tons per 10,000 yuan	Whole city	Negative	0.03	0.01	0.01	9	11	2	Regional Economy; Environment Annual Report	☺
12	Energy consumption per unit of value added created by industrial enterprises			Negative	No data			N/A	N/A	N/A		
13	Utilization rate industrial solid waste	%	Whole city	Positive	85.58	99.60	98.90	2	2	0	Environment Annual Report	
14	Recycling rate of industrial water	%	Whole city	Positive	83.81	86.60	81.28	25	27	2	Environment Annual Report	☺
15	Labor productivity of the tertiary sector	10,000 yuan per capita	Whole city	Positive	11.40	8.18	6.93	27	28	1	Regional Economy	☺
16	Proportion of value added of tertiary sector in GDP	%	Whole city	Positive	47.97	50.17	49.59	16	18	2	City	☺
17	Proportion of tertiary sector employees in the total employed population	%	Whole city	Positive	46.44	45.41	44.33	19	22	3	Regional Economy	☺

18	Water resources per capita	m^3 per capita	Whole city	Positive	1,026.43	574.38	563.69	22	18	−4	Environment Annual Report; City	☹
19	CO_2 emissions per unit of land area			Negative	No data			N/A	N/A	N/A		
20	CO_2 emissions per capita			Negative	No data			N/A	N/A	N/A		
21	SO_2 emissions per unit of land area	Ton per km^2	Whole city	Negative	11.64	11.45	12.33	27	25	−2	Environment Annual Report; City	☹
22	SO_2 emissions per capita	Ton per 10,000 persons	Whole city	Negative	216.46	121.36	131.98	13	12	−1	Environment Annual Report; City	☹
23	COD emissions per unit of land area	Ton per km^2	Whole city	Negative	7.83	9.75	10.07	29	28	−1	Environment Annual Report; City	☹
24	COD emissions per capita	Ton per 10,000 persons	Whole city	Negative	118.15	103.41	107.79	19	19	0	Environment Annual Report; City	
25	Nitrogen oxides emissions per unit of land area	Ton per km^2	Whole city	Negative	15.00	4.32	23.22	8	33	25	Environment Annual Report; City	☺
26	Nitrogen oxides emissions per capita	Ton per 10,000 persons	Whole city	Negative	237.70	45.81	248.53	1	31	30	Environment Annual Report; City	☺
27	Ammonia/nitrogen emissions per unit of land area	Ton per km^2	Whole city	Negative	0.86	1.55	1.05	34	32	−2	Environment Annual Report; City	☹
28	Ammonia/nitrogen emissions per capita	Ton per 10,000 persons	Whole city	Negative	12.63	16.44	11.28	28	20	−8	Environment Annual Report; City	☹

(continued)

(continued)

No.	Indicator	Unit	Scope	Attribute	2010 average of 38 cities	2010 figure	2009 figure	2010 ranking	2009 ranking	Change in ranking	Source of 2010 data	Chernoff face
29	Percentage of the days with air quality at or over level II in a year	%	District	Positive	89.20	86.54	86.26	23	26	3	MEP Data	☺
30	Percentage of days with respirable suspended particulates as the principal pollutants in a year	%	District	Negative	70.81	83.84	88.77	26	34	8	MEP Data	☺
31	Ratio of environmental spending to government expenditure	%	Whole city	Positive	3.13	1.30	1.51	38	31	−7	China Statistics; City	☹
32	Ratio of the investment in industrial pollution control to GDP	%	Whole city	Positive	0.08	0.01	0.04	34	25	−9	Environment Annual Report; Regional Economy	☹
33	Ratio of the spending on science, education, culture, and public health to government expenditure	%	Whole city	Positive	21.08	15.35	21.01	34	37	3	China Statistics; City; Regional Economy	☺
34	Area of green land per capita in urban areas	m^2	District	Positive	59.39	31.00	30.95	26	28	2	City	☺

35	Green coverage of urban built-in areas	%		District	Positive	40.04		39.43	38.82	22	21	−1	Urban Construction	☹
36	Coverage of water supply	%		District	Positive	98.82		95.79	97.09	33	32	−1	Urban Construction	☹
37	Treatment rate of urban household wastewater	%		District	Positive	86.16		90.68	88.45	16	13	−3	Urban Construction	☹
38	Harmless treatment of urban household waste	%		District	Positive	94.38		100.00	100.00	1	1	0	Urban Construction	
39	Public buses per 10,000 urban residents			District	Positive	15.61		12.64	14.50	21	14	−7	City	☹
40	Industrial SO_2 removal rate	%		Whole city	Positive	57.30		49.79	62.30	26	18	−8	Environment Annual Report	☹
41	Industrial wastewater COD removal rate	%		Whole city	Positive	77.86		57.93	63.88	34	34	0	Environment Annual Report	
42	Industrial nitrogen oxide removal rate	%		Whole city	Positive	5.29		6.60	0.77	10	23	13	Environment Annual Report	☺
43	Industrial waste water ammonia/nitrogen removal rate	%		Whole city	Positive	67.89		19.56	26.33	37	37	0	Environment Annual Report	

Note:
Regional Economy: *China Regional Economy Statistical Yearbook 2011*
City: *China City Statistical Yearbook 2011*
China Statistics: *China Statistical Yearbook 2011*
Urban Construction: *China Urban Construction Statistical Yearbook 2010*
Environment Annual Report: *China Environment Annual Report 2010*
Environmental Yearbook: *China Environmental Statistical Yearbook 2011*
MEP Data: Ministry of Environmental Protection Data Center

9.30 Brief Analysis of Green Development in Chengdu

Chengdu ranked 30th among the 38 participating cities by GDI according to 2010 data, 6 places higher over 2009 (Chengdu ranked 36th in 2009). Following is a brief analysis of its score by each indicator and their changes from 2009 to 2010.

9.30.1 Chengdu's 2010 Scores by GDI

Chengdu scored −0.172 in 2010. From the three First-Class Indicators including GDEG, CCPNRE, and SDGP as shown in Fig. 9.59, Chengdu showed some advantages by GDEG; yet it ranked lower than the national average CCPNRE and SDGP (Note: the national average value of each indicator is 0).

According to Fig. 9.60, Chengdu surpassed the national average in 3 of Second-Class Indicators in 2010, which were GGEI, SII and EPCCI; yet it ranked lower than the national average in 6 indicators which were PII, TII, RAECI, GII, II and EMI.

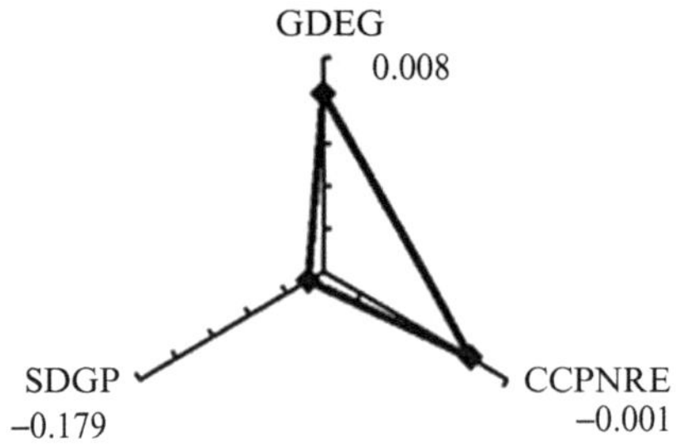

Fig. 9.59 Scores of Chengdu by First-Class Indicators

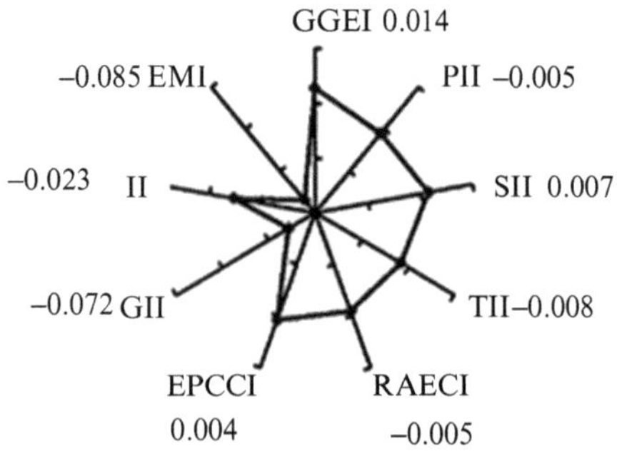

Fig. 9.60 Scores of Chengdu by Second-Class Indicators

Table 9.59 Changes in Chengdu's rankings by First-Class and Second-Class Indicators, 2009–2010

Indicator	2010	2009	Difference	Indicator	2010	2009	Difference
GDI	30	36	6				
GDEG	15	31	16	RAECI	22	18	−4
GGEI	15	31	16	EPCCI	14	31	17
PII	25	25	0	SDGP	36	34	−2
SII	14	21	7	GII	38	38	0
TII	22	25	3	II	26	21	−5
CCPNRE	14	32	18	EMI	36	32	−4

Note: A positive value in "Difference" means a rise in ranking

9.30.2 Changes in Chengdu's GDI Rankings 2009–2010

According to Table 9.59, in First-Class Indicators, the most obvious change occurred in CCPNRE with a rise of 18 places; following is GDEG with a rise of 16 places; it fell by 2 places in SDGP. Judging changes in ranking, it rose by 16, 7, 3 and 17 places by GGEI, SII, TII and EPCCI; it fell by 4, 5 and 4 places by RAECI, II and EMI; it remained unchanged by PII and GII as compared with that in 2009.

To further explain the causes of the changes in the rankings by First- and Second-Class Indicators, we put the Third-Class Indicators where a change of more than 3 places occurred from 2009 to 2010 as follows in Table 9.60. Compared with those in 2009, Chengdu both out- and underperformed in ranking in 2010, while the more obvious trend is outperforming compared with the previous year. It rose by Nitrogen oxide emissions per unit of GDP with a rise of 32 places, and it rose by 8 places in ranking of Percentage of days with respirable suspended particulates as the principal pollutants in a year, and it rose to various extent by many other indicators including Proportion of tertiary sector employees in the total employed population and Ratio of the spending on science, education, culture, and public health to government expenditure; it fell however in 8 indicators including Treatment rate of urban household wastewater, Water resources per capita, Ammonia/nitrogen emissions per capita and Industrial SO_2 removal rate as compared with that in 2009.

Table 9.60 Third-Class Indicators where changes over 3 places occurred by Chengdu, 2009–2010

	Original data for 2009 and 2010			Change in ranking		
Third-Class Indicator	2010	2009	Unit	2010	2009	Difference
Nitrogen oxide emissions per unit of GDP	11.40	70.36	Ton per 100 million yuan	1	33	32
Ammonia/nitrogen emissions per unit of GDP	4.09	3.19	Ton per 100 million yuan	32	25	−7
Proportion of tertiary sector employees in the total employed population	45.41	44.33	%	19	22	3
Water resources per capita	574.38	563.69	m^3 per capita	22	18	−4
Nitrogen oxides emissions per unit of land area	4.32	23.22	Ton per km^2	8	33	25
Nitrogen oxides emissions per capita	45.81	248.53	Ton per 10,000 persons	1	31	30
Ammonia/nitrogen emissions per capita	16.44	11.28	Ton per 10,000 persons	28	20	−8
Percentage of the days with air quality at or over level II in a year	86.54	86.26	%	23	26	3
Percentage of days with respirable suspended particulates as the principal pollutants in a year	83.84	88.77	%	26	34	8
Ratio of environmental spending to government expenditure	1.30	1.51	%	38	31	−7
Ratio of the investment in industrial pollution control to GDP	0.01	0.04	%	34	25	−9
Ratio of the spending on science, education, culture, and public health to government expenditure	15.35	21.01	%	34	37	3
Treatment rate of urban household wastewater	90.68	88.45	%	16	13	−3
Public buses per 10,000 urban residents	12.64	14.50		21	14	−7
Industrial SO_2 removal rate	49.79	62.30	%	26	18	−8
Industrial nitrogen oxide removal rate	6.60	0.77	%	10	23	13

Note: A positive value in "Difference" means a rise in ranking

Green development checkup-Guiyang

No.	Indicator	Unit	Scope	Attribute	2010 average of 38 cities	2010 figure	2009 figure	2010 ranking	2009 ranking	Change in ranking	Source of 2010 data	Chernoff face
1	GDP per capita	Yuan	Whole city	Positive	55,399.15	26,209	24,585.00	38	35	−3	Regional Economy; City	☹
2	Energy consumption per unit of GDP	Ton per 10,000 yuan	Whole city	Negative	0.82	1.10	N/A	28	N/A	N/A	Regional Economy; City	
3	Electricity consumption per capita in urban areas	kWh per capita	Whole city	Negative	580.70	806.92	758.37	33	32	−1	City	☹
4	CO_2 emissions per unit of GDP			Negative	No data			N/A	N/A	N/A		
5	SO_2 emissions per unit of GDP	Ton per 100 million yuan	Whole city	Negative	42.67	167.56	200.65	38	38	0	Regional Economy; Environment Annual Report	
6	COD emissions per unit of GDP	Ton per 100 million yuan	Whole city	Negative	24.91	48.51	56.12	36	36	0	Regional Economy; Environment Annual Report	
7	Nitrogen oxide emissions per unit of GDP	Ton per 100 million yuan	Whole city	Negative	40.67	34.44	17.92	21	5	−16	Regional Economy; Environment Annual Report	☹
8	Ammonia/nitrogen emissions per unit of GDP	Ton per 100 million yuan	Whole city	Negative	2.63	3.38	4.63	28	32	4	Regional Economy; Environment Annual Report	☺
9	Labor productivity of the primary sector	10,000 yuan per capita	Whole city	Positive	3.00	0.83	0.72	36	37	1	Regional Economy	☺
10	Labor productivity of the secondary sector	10,000 yuan per capita	Whole city	Positive	18.12	7.43	6.42	37	37	0	Regional Economy	

(continued)

(continued)

No.	Indicator	Unit	Scope	Attribute	2010 average of 38 cities	2010 figure	2009 figure	2010 ranking	2009 ranking	Change in ranking	Source of 2010 data	Chernoff face
11	Water consumption per unit of value added created by industrial enterprises	10,000 tons per 10,000 yuan	Whole city	Negative	0.03	0.03	0.03	27	27	0	Regional Economy; Environment Annual Report	
12	Energy consumption per unit of value added created by industrial enterprises			Negative	No data			N/A	N/A	N/A		
13	Utilization rate industrial solid waste	%	Whole city	Positive	83.42	56.20	45.80	35	36	1	Environment Annual Report	☺
14	Recycling rate of industrial water	%	Whole city	Positive	82.10	95.28	94.72	8	8	0	Environment Annual Report	
15	Labor productivity of the tertiary sector	10,000 yuan per capita	Whole city	Positive	11.39	5.77	5.45	35	34	−1	Regional Economy	☹
16	Proportion of value added of tertiary sector in GDP	%	Whole city	Positive	48.37	54.18	54.20	6	8	2	City	☺
17	Proportion of tertiary sector employees in the total employed population	%	Whole city	Positive	46.83	46.63	42.83	17	25	8	Regional Economy	☺
18	Water resources per capita	m^3 per capita	Whole city	Positive	1,040.56	1,340.61	1,231.34	10	10	0	Environment Annual Report; City	

19	CO_2 emissions per unit of land area			Negative	No data			N/A	N/A	N/A		
20	CO_2 emissions per capita			Negative	No data			N/A	N/A	N/A		
21	SO_2 emissions per unit of land area	Ton per km^2	Whole city	Negative	11.34	21.33	22.34	35	35	0	Environment Annual Report; City	
22	SO_2 emissions per capita	Ton per 10,000 persons	Whole city	Negative	211.11	462.91	491.11	37	37	0	Environment Annual Report; City	
23	COD emissions per unit of land area	Ton per km^2	Whole city	Negative	7.63	6.17	6.25	23	22	−1	Environment Annual Report; City	☹
24	COD emissions per capita	Ton per 10,000 persons	Whole city	Negative	117.25	134.01	137.35	24	24	0	Environment Annual Report; City	
25	Nitrogen oxides emissions per unit of land area	Ton per km^2	Whole city	Negative	14.61	4.38	2.00	10	5	−5	Environment Annual Report; City	☹
26	Nitrogen oxides emissions per capita	Ton per 10,000 persons	Whole city	Negative	231.68	95.14	N/A	8	N/A	N/A	Environment Annual Report; City	
27	Ammonia/nitrogen emissions per unit of land area	Ton per km^2	Whole city	Negative	0.83	0.43	0.52	15	15	0	Environment Annual Report; City	
28	Ammonia/nitrogen emissions per capita	Ton per 10,000 persons	Whole city	Negative	12.50	9.34	11.33	12	21	9	Environment Annual Report; City	☺
29	Percentage of the days with air quality at or over level II in a year	%	District	Positive	89.45	93.96	95.05	12	10	−2	MEP Data	☹

(continued)

(continued)

No.	Indicator	Unit	Scope	Attribute	2010 average of 38 cities	2010 figure	2009 figure	2010 ranking	2009 ranking	Change in ranking	Source of 2010 data	Chernoff face
30	Percentage of days with respirable suspended particulates as the principal pollutants in a year	%	District	Negative	69.76	56.16	53.42	8	7	−1	MEP Data	☹
31	Ratio of environmental spending to government expenditure	%	Whole city	Positive	3.14	2.65	1.57	19	29	10	China Statistics; City	☺
32	Ratio of the investment in industrial pollution control to GDP	%	Whole city	Positive	0.09	0.28	0.55	4	1	−3	Environment Annual Report; Regional Economy	☹
33	Ratio of the spending on science, education, culture, and public health to government expenditure	%	Whole city	Positive	21.06	21.65	25.54	15	21	6	China Statistics; City; Regional Economy	☺
34	Area of green land per capita in urban areas	m^2	District	Positive	58.13	30.00	26.27	27	31	4	City	☺
35	Green coverage of urban built-in areas	%	District	Positive	39.84	N/A	32.36	N/A	36	N/A	Urban Construction	
36	Coverage of water supply	%	District	Positive	98.83	96.22	95.41	32	33	1	Urban Construction	☺

37	Treatment rate of urban household wastewater	%	District	Positive	86.16	95.20	54.40	9	36	27	Urban Construction	☺
38	Harmless treatment of urban household waste	%	District	Positive	94.38	93.74	95.04	26	20	−6	Urban Construction	☹
39	Public buses per 10,000 urban residents		District	Positive	15.51	9.57	11.57	32	29	−3	City	☹
40	Industrial SO_2 removal rate	%	Whole city	Positive	57.30	81.06	68.96	5	10	5	Environment Annual Report	☺
41	Industrial wastewater COD removal rate	%	Whole city	Positive	76.07	89.48	88.54	9	11	2	Environment Annual Report	☺
42	Industrial nitrogen oxide removal rate	%	Whole city	Positive	5.24	17.42	30.95	3	4	1	Environment Annual Report	☺
43	Industrial waste water ammonia/nitrogen removal rate	%	Whole city	Positive	66.79	67.56	62.02	23	22	−1	Environment Annual Report	☹

Note:
Regional Economy: *China Regional Economy Statistical Yearbook 2011*
City: *China City Statistical Yearbook 2011*
China Statistics: *China Statistical Yearbook 2011*
Urban Construction: *China Urban Construction Statistical Yearbook 2010*
Environment Annual Report: *China Environment Annual Report 2010*
Environmental Yearbook: *China Environmental Statistical Yearbook 2011*
MEP Data: Ministry of Environmental Protection Data Center

9.31 Brief Analysis of Green Development in Guiyang

Guiyang ranked 20th among the 38 participating cities by GDI according to 2010 data, the same as it did in 2009 (Guiyang ranked 20th in 2009). Following is a brief analysis of its score by each indicator and their changes from 2009 to 2010.

9.31.1 Guiyang's 2010 Scores by GDI

Guiyang scored −0.031 in 2010. From the three First-Class Indicators including GDEG, CCPNRE, and SDGP as shown in Fig. 9.61, Guiyang showed obvious advantages by SDGP and CCPNRE; it yet performed weaker than the national average in GDEG (Note: the national average value of each indicator is 0).

According to Fig. 9.62, Guiyang surpassed the national average in 4 of Second-Class Indicators in 2010, which were RAECI, EPCCI, GII and EMI; it ranked lower than the national average in 5 indicators including GGEI, PII, SII, TII and II.

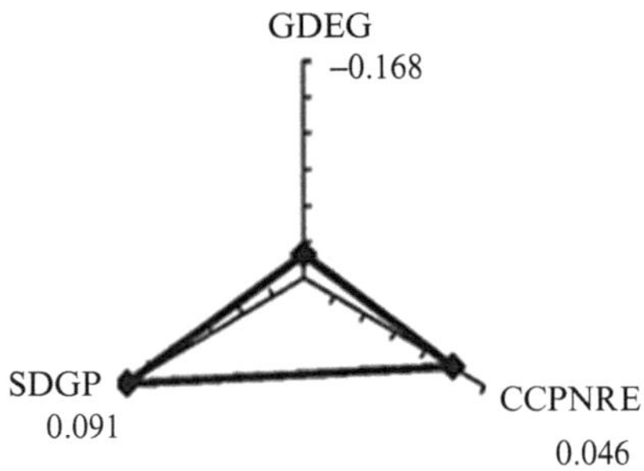

Fig. 9.61 Scores of Guiyang by First-Class Indicators

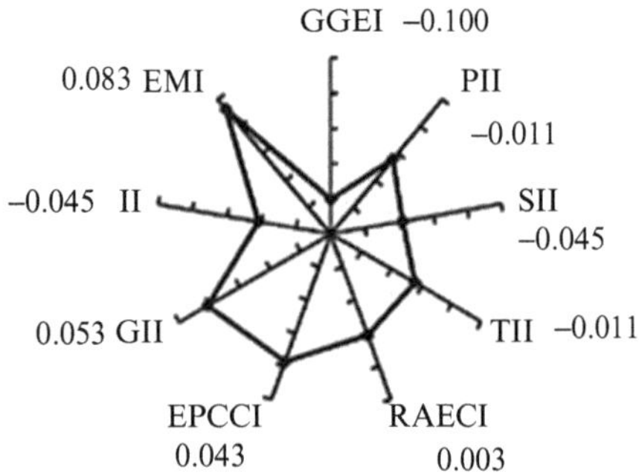

Fig. 9.62 Scores of Guiyang by Second-Class Indicators

Table 9.61 Changes in Guiyang's rankings by First-Class and Second-Class Indicators, 2009–2010

Indicator	2010	2009	Difference	Indicator	2010	2009	Difference
GDI	20	20	0				
GDEG	37	36	−1	RAECI	10	10	0
GGEI	37	34	−3	EPCCI	10	7	−3
PII	36	37	1	SDGP	8	18	10
SII	34	34	0	GII	7	8	1
TII	24	27	3	II	32	35	3
CCPNRE	10	7	−3	EMI	4	5	1

Note: A positive value in "Difference" means a rise in ranking

9.31.2 Changes in Guiyang's GDI Rankings 2009–2010

According to Table 9.61, in First-Class Indicators, the most obvious change occurred in SDGP where it rose by 10 places; it dropped by 1 and 3 places in GDEG and CCPNRE. Judging from changes in ranking, it rose by 3 places in TII and II, and 1 place in PII, GII and EMI; it dropped by 3 places in GGEI and EPCCI; it remained unchanged by SII and RAECI in 2009.

To further explain the causes of the changes in the rankings by First- and Second-Class Indicators, we put the Third-Class Indicators where a change of more than 3 places occurred from 2009 to 2010 as follows in Table 9.62. Compared with those in 2009, Guiyang both out- and underperformed in ranking in 2010. It rose by 27 places in Treatment rate of urban household wastewater, 10 in Ratio of environmental spending to government expenditure, 9 in Ammonia/nitrogen emissions per capita, 8 in Proportion of tertiary sector employees in the total employed population, 6 in Ratio of the spending on science, education, culture, and public health to government expenditure, 5 in Industrial SO_2 removal rate, and 3 in Ammonia/nitrogen emissions per unit of GDP and Area of green land per capita in urban areas; it suffered dramatic drops in 6 indicators including GDP per capita, Nitrogen oxide emissions per unit of GDP and Nitrogen oxides emissions per unit of land area as compared with that in 2009.

Table 9.62 Third-Class Indicators where changes over 3 places occurred by Guiyang, 2009–2010

	Original data for 2009 and 2010			Change in ranking		
Third-Class Indicator	2010	2009	Unit	2010	2009	Difference
GDP per capita	26,209.00	24,585.00	Yuan	38	35	−3
Nitrogen oxide emissions per unit of GDP	34.44	17.92	Ton per 100 million yuan	21	5	−16
Ammonia/nitrogen emissions per unit of GDP	3.38	4.63	Ton per 100 million yuan	28	32	4
Proportion of tertiary sector employees in the total employed population	46.63	42.83	%	17	25	8
Nitrogen oxides emissions per unit of land area	4.38	2.00	Ton per km^2	10	5	−5
Ammonia/nitrogen emissions per capita	9.34	11.33	Ton per 10,000 persons	12	21	9
Ratio of environmental spending to government expenditure	2.65	1.57	%	19	29	10
Ratio of the investment in industrial pollution control to GDP	0.28	0.55	%	4	1	−3
Ratio of the spending on science, education, culture, and public health to government expenditure	21.65	25.54	%	15	21	6
Area of green land per capita in urban areas	30.00	26.27	m^2	27	31	4
Treatment rate of urban household wastewater	95.20	54.40	%	9	36	27
Harmless treatment of urban household waste	93.74	95.04	%	26	20	−6
Public buses per 10,000 urban residents	9.57	11.57		32	29	−3
Industrial SO_2 removal rate	81.06	68.96	%	5	10	5

Note: A positive value in “Difference” means a rise in ranking

Green development checkup-Kunming

No.	Indicator	Unit	Scope	Attribute	2010 average of 38 cities	2010 figure	2009 figure	2010 ranking	2009 ranking	Change in ranking	Source of 2010 data	Chernoff face
1	GDP per capita	Yuan	Whole city	Positive	55,399.15	33,549	28,894.00	33	33	0	Regional Economy; City	
2	Energy consumption per unit of GDP	Ton per 10,000 yuan	Whole city	Negative	0.82	0.56	1.00	14	25	11	Regional Economy; City	
3	Electricity consumption per capita in urban areas	kWh per capita	Whole city	Negative	580.70	577.39	585.61	27	27	0	City	
4	CO_2 emissions per unit of GDP			Negative	No data			N/A	N/A	N/A		
5	SO_2 emissions per unit of GDP	Ton per 100 million yuan	Whole city	Negative	42.67	42.63	55.08	27	27	0	Regional Economy; Environment Annual Report	
6	COD emissions per unit of GDP	Ton per 100 million yuan	Whole city	Negative	24.91	7.67	13.32	2	7	5	Regional Economy; Environment Annual Report	
7	Nitrogen oxide emissions per unit of GDP	Ton per 100 million yuan	Whole city	Negative	40.67	24.90	22.65	12	9	−3	Regional Economy; Environment Annual Report	
8	Ammonia/nitrogen emissions per unit of GDP	Ton per 100 million yuan	Whole city	Negative	2.63	1.26	0.90	10	2	−8	Regional Economy; Environment Annual Report	

(continued)

(continued)

No.	Indicator	Unit	Scope	Attribute	2010 average of 38 cities	2010 figure	2009 figure	2010 ranking	2009 ranking	Change in ranking	Source of 2010 data	Chernoff face
9	Labor productivity of the primary sector	10,000 yuan per capita	Whole city	Positive	3.00	0.89	0.83	35	34	−1	Regional Economy	
10	Labor productivity of the secondary sector	10,000 yuan per capita	Whole city	Positive	18.12	11.87	9.31	26	28	2	Regional Economy	
11	Water consumption per unit of value added created by industrial enterprises	10,000 tons per 10,000 yuan	Whole city	Negative	0.03	0.04	0.04	32	30	−2	Regional Economy; Environment Annual Report	
12	Energy consumption per unit of value added created by industrial enterprises			Negative	No data			N/A	N/A	N/A		
13	Utilization rate industrial solid waste	%	Whole city	Positive	83.42	41.30	39.90	37	37	0	Environment Annual Report	
14	Recycling rate of industrial water	%	Whole city	Positive	82.10	94.94	94.70	9	9	0	Environment Annual Report	
15	Labor productivity of the tertiary sector	10,000 yuan per capita	Whole city	Positive	11.39	5.94	5.18	34	35	1	Regional Economy	

16	Proportion of value added of tertiary sector in GDP	%	Whole city	Positive	48.37	49.01	48.10	18	21	3	City	☺
17	Proportion of tertiary sector employees in the total employed population	%	Whole city	Positive	46.83	45.10	44.17	21	23	2	Regional Economy	☺
18	Water resources per capita	m^3 per capita	Whole city	Positive	1,040.56	1,195.74	1,302.08	11	8	−3	Environment Annual Report; City	☹
19	CO_2 emissions per unit of land area			Negative	No data			N/A	N/A	N/A		
20	CO_2 emissions per capita			Negative	No data			N/A	N/A	N/A		
21	SO_2 emissions per unit of land area	Ton per km^2	Whole city	Negative	11.34	3.92	4.44	6	6	0	Environment Annual Report; City	
22	SO_2 emissions per capita	Ton per 10,000 persons	Whole city	Negative	211.11	142.09	175.68	16	21	5	Environment Annual Report; City	☺
23	COD emissions per unit of land area	Ton per km^2	Whole city	Negative	7.63	0.70	1.07	1	2	1	Environment Annual Report; City	☺
24	COD emissions per capita	Ton per 10,000 persons	Whole city	Negative	117.25	25.55	42.47	2	1	−1	Environment Annual Report; City	☹
25	Nitrogen oxides emissions per unit of land area	Ton per km^2	Whole city	Negative	14.61	2.29	1.83	3	3	0	Environment Annual Report; City	

(continued)

(continued)

No.	Indicator	Unit	Scope	Attribute	2010 average of 38 cities	2010 figure	2009 figure	2010 ranking	2009 ranking	Change in ranking	Source of 2010 data	Chernoff face
26	Nitrogen oxides emissions per capita	Ton per 10,000 persons	Whole city	Negative	231.68	83.00	72.26	4	6	2	Environment Annual Report; City	
27	Ammonia/nitrogen emissions per unit of land area	Ton per km^2	Whole city	Negative	0.83	0.12	0.07	2	2	0	Environment Annual Report; City	
28	Ammonia/nitrogen emissions per capita	Ton per 10,000 persons	Whole city	Negative	12.50	4.20	2.86	3	1	−2	Environment Annual Report; City	
29	Percentage of the days with air quality at or over level II in a year	%	District	Positive	89.45	100.00	100.00	1	1	0	MEP Data	
30	Percentage of days with respirable suspended particulates as the principal pollutants in a year	%	District	Negative	69.76	65.48	69.59	13	12	−1	MEP Data	
31	Ratio of environmental spending to government expenditure	%	Whole city	Positive	3.14	4.85	7.13	5	1	−4	China Statistics; City	

32	Ratio of the investment in industrial pollution control to GDP	%	Whole city	Positive	0.09	0.10	0.14	10	10	0	Environment Annual Report; Regional Economy	
33	Ratio of the spending on science, education, culture, and public health to government expenditure	%	Whole city	Positive	21.06	11.28	22.80	37	34	−3	China Statistics; City; Regional Economy	☹
34	Area of green land per capita in urban areas	m^2	District	Positive	58.13	34.00	40.11	24	19	−5	City	☹
35	Green coverage of urban built-in areas	%	District	Positive	39.84	41.36	38.95	15	20	5	Urban Construction	☺
36	Coverage of water supply	%	District	Positive	98.83	99.69	99.24	27	27	0	Urban Construction	
37	Treatment rate of urban household wastewater	%	District	Positive	86.16	100.00	91.31	1	7	6	Urban Construction	☺
38	Harmless treatment of urban household waste	%	District	Positive	94.38	96.80	94.96	23	21	−2	Urban Construction	☹
39	Public buses per 10,000 urban residents		District	Positive	15.51	20.63	12.84	2	19	17	City	☺
40	Industrial SO_2 removal rate	%	Whole city	Positive	57.30	87.99	87.04	1	2	1	Environment Annual Report	☺

(continued)

(continued)

No.	Indicator	Unit	Scope	Attribute	2010 average of 38 cities	2010 figure	2009 figure	2010 ranking	2009 ranking	Change in ranking	Source of 2010 data	Chernoff face
41	Industrial wastewater COD removal rate	%	Whole city	Positive	76.07	87.18	86.71	12	15	3	Environment Annual Report	☺
42	Industrial nitrogen oxide removal rate	%	Whole city	Positive	5.24	0.00	0.00	31	29	−2	Environment Annual Report	☹
43	Industrial waste water ammonia/nitrogen removal rate	%	Whole city	Positive	66.79	75.34	77.95	16	13	−3	Environment Annual Report	☹

Note:
Regional Economy: *China Regional Economy Statistical Yearbook 2011*
City: *China City Statistical Yearbook 2011*
China Statistics: *China Statistical Yearbook 2011*
Urban Construction: *China Urban Construction Statistical Yearbook 2010*
Environment Annual Report: *China Environment Annual Report 2010*
Environmental Yearbook: *China Environmental Statistical Yearbook 2011*
MEP Data: Ministry of Environmental Protection Data Center

9.32 Brief Analysis of Green Development in Kunming

Kunming ranked 4th among the 38 participating cities by GDI according to 2010 data, the same as it did in 2009 (Kunming ranked 4th in 2009). Following is a brief analysis of its score by each indicator and their changes from 2009 to 2010.

9.32.1 Kunming's 2010 Scores by GDI

Kunming scored 0.401 in 2010. From the three First-Class Indicators including GDEG, CCPNRE, and SDGP as shown in Fig. 9.63, Kunming showed obvious advantages in Carrying Capacity Potential of Natural Resources and SDGP; it ranked lower than the national average by GDEG and Environment (Note: the national average value of each indicator is 0).

According to Fig. 9.64, Kunming surpassed the national average in 4 of Second-Class Indicators in 2010, which were RAECI, EPCCI, II, and EMI; it yet ranked lower than the national average in 5 indicators which were GGEI, PII, SII, TII and GII.

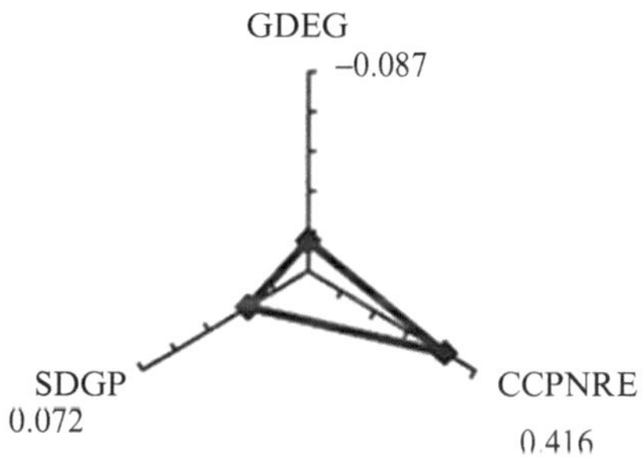

Fig. 9.63 Scores of Kunming by First Class Indicators

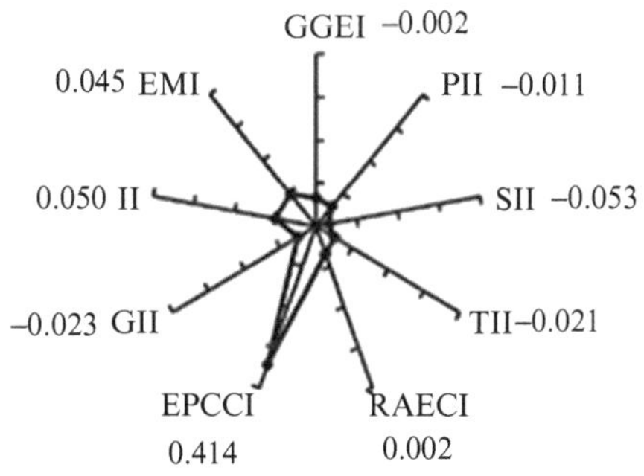

Fig. 9.64 Scores of Kunming by Second-Class Indicators

Table 9.63 Changes in Kunming's rankings by First-Class and Second-Class Indicators, 2009–2010

Indicator	2010	2009	Difference	Indicator	2010	2009	Difference
GDI	4	4	0				
GDEG	32	30	−2	RAECI	11	8	−3
GGEI	18	16	−2	EPCCI	1	1	0
PII	35	34	−1	SDGP	12	5	−7
SII	36	35	−1	GII	22	5	−17
TII	29	29	0	II	7	18	11
CCPNRE	1	1	0	EMI	8	9	1

Note: A positive value in "Difference" means a rise in ranking

9.32.2 Changes in Kunming's GDI Rankings 2009–2010

According to Table 9.63, in First-Class Indicators, the most obvious change occurred in SDGP with a fall of 7 places, and it fell by 2 places by GDEG; it remained unchanged in CCPNRE. Judging from changes in ranking, it rose by 11 and 1 place in II and EMI; it fell by 17 places by GII, and it dropped slightly in PII, SII and RAECI; it remained unchanged by TII and EPCCI in 2009.

To further explain the causes of the changes in the rankings by First- and Second-Class Indicators, we put the Third-Class Indicators where a change of more than 3 places occurred from 2009 to 2010 as follows in Table 9.64. Compared with those in 2009, Kunming both out- and underperformed in ranking in 2010. It rose by 11 places in Energy consumption per unit of GDP, and 5 in COD emissions per unit of GDP, Proportion of value added of tertiary sector in GDP, Green coverage of urban built-in areas. It rose by 3 places in SO_2 emissions per capita. It fell to various extents by Nitrogen oxide emissions per unit of GDP, Ammonia/nitrogen emissions per unit of GDP, Water resources per capita, Ratio of environmental spending to government expenditure, Ratio of the spending on science, education, culture, and public health to government expenditure and Area of green land per capita in urban areas.

Table 9.64 Third-Class Indicators where changes over 3 places occurred by Kunming, 2009–2010

	Original data for 2009 and 2010			Change in ranking		
Third-Class Indicator	2010	2009	Unit	2010	2009	Difference
Energy consumption per unit of GDP	0.56	1.00	Ton per 10,000 yuan	14	25	11
COD emissions per unit of GDP	7.67	13.32	Ton per 100 million yuan	2	7	5
Nitrogen oxide emissions per unit of GDP	24.90	22.65	Ton per 100 million yuan	12	9	−3
Ammonia/nitrogen emissions per unit of GDP	1.26	0.90	Ton per 100 million yuan	10	2	−8
Proportion of value added of tertiary sector in GDP	49.01	48.10	%	18	21	3
Water resources per capita	1,195.74	1,302.08	m^3 per capita	11	8	−3
SO_2 emissions per capita	142.09	175.68	Ton per 10,000 persons	16	21	5
Ratio of environmental spending to government expenditure	4.85	7.13	%	5	1	−4
Ratio of the spending on science, education, culture, and public health to government expenditure	11.28	22.80	%	37	34	−3
Area of green land per capita in urban areas	34.00	40.11	m^2	24	19	−5
Green coverage of urban built-in areas	41.36	38.95	%	15	20	5

Note: A positive value in "Difference" means a rise in ranking

Green development checkup-Xi'an

No.	Indicator	Unit	Scope	Attribute	2010 average of 38 cities	2010 figure	2009 figure	2010 ranking	2009 ranking	Change in ranking	Source of 2010 data	Chernoff face
1	GDP per capita	Yuan	Whole city	Positive	55,399.15	38,343	32,411.00	30	29	−1	Regional Economy; City	☹
2	Energy consumption per unit of GDP	Ton per 10,000 yuan	Whole city	Negative	0.82	0.21	0.22	4	2	−2	Regional Economy; City	☹
3	Electricity consumption per capita in urban areas	kWh per capita	Whole city	Negative	580.70	515.71	431.76	21	19	−2	City	☹
4	CO_2 emissions per unit of GDP			Negative	No data			N/A	N/A	N/A		
5	SO_2 emissions per unit of GDP	Ton per 100 million yuan	Whole city	Negative	42.67	34.07	39.61	24	25	1	Regional Economy; Environment Annual Report	☺
6	COD emissions per unit of GDP	Ton per 100 million yuan	Whole city	Negative	24.91	38.77	49.63	33	34	1	Regional Economy; Environment Annual Report	☺
7	Nitrogen oxide emissions per unit of GDP	Ton per 100 million yuan	Whole city	Negative	40.67	28.33	33.77	15	21	6	Regional Economy; Environment Annual Report	☺
8	Ammonia/nitrogen emissions per unit of GDP	Ton per 100 million yuan	Whole city	Negative	2.63	4.24	4.99	34	33	−1	Regional Economy; Environment Annual Report	☹
9	Labor productivity of the primary sector	10,000 yuan per capita	Whole city	Positive	3.00	1.17	0.88	32	33	1	Regional Economy	☺
10	Labor productivity of the secondary sector	10,000 yuan per capita	Whole city	Positive	18.12	10.16	8.75	31	32	1	Regional Economy	☺

11	Water consumption per unit of value added created by industrial enterprises	10,000 tons per 10,000 yuan	Whole city	Negative	0.03	0.01	0.02	13	13	0	Regional Economy; Environment Annual Report	
12	Energy consumption per unit of value added created by industrial enterprises			Negative	No data			N/A	N/A	N/A		
13	Utilization rate industrial solid waste	%	Whole city	Positive	83.42	98.10	97.80	10	9	−1	Environment Annual Report	☹
14	Recycling rate of industrial water	%	Whole city	Positive	82.10	80.45	78.49	27	29	2	Environment Annual Report	☺
15	Labor productivity of the tertiary sector	10,000 yuan per capita	Whole city	Positive	11.39	8.00	7.37	28	26	−2	Regional Economy	☹
16	Proportion of value added of tertiary sector in GDP	%	Whole city	Positive	48.37	52.20	53.92	11	9	−2	City	☹
17	Proportion of tertiary sector employees in the total employed population	%	Whole city	Positive	46.83	45.00	45.15	22	21	−1	Regional Economy	☹
18	Water resources per capita	m^3 per capita	Whole city	Positive	1,040.56	199.27	300.25	31	28	−3	Environment Annual Report; City	☹

(continued)

(continued)

No.	Indicator	Unit	Scope	Attribute	2010 average of 38 cities	2010 figure	2009 figure	2010 ranking	2009 ranking	Change in ranking	Source of 2010 data	Chernoff face
19	CO_2 emissions per unit of land area			Negative	No data			N/A	N/A	N/A		
20	CO_2 emissions per capita			Negative	No data			N/A	N/A	N/A		
21	SO_2 emissions per unit of land area	Ton per km^2	Whole city	Negative	11.34	8.41	8.54	19	19	0	Environment Annual Report; City	
22	SO_2 emissions per capita	Ton per 10,000 persons	Whole city	Negative	211.11	108.66	111.07	10	10	0	Environment Annual Report; City	
23	COD emissions per unit of land area	Ton per km^2	Whole city	Negative	7.63	9.57	10.70	28	29	1	Environment Annual Report; City	☺
24	COD emissions per capita	Ton per 10,000 persons	Whole city	Negative	117.25	123.67	139.18	23	26	3	Environment Annual Report; City	☺
25	Nitrogen oxides emissions per unit of land area	Ton per km^2	Whole city	Negative	14.61	6.99	7.28	12	18	6	Environment Annual Report; City	☺
26	Nitrogen oxides emissions per capita	Ton per 10,000 persons	Whole city	Negative	231.68	90.35	94.71	6	10	4	Environment Annual Report; City	☺
27	Ammonia/nitrogen emissions per unit of land area	Ton per km^2	Whole city	Negative	0.83	1.05	1.08	31	33	2	Environment Annual Report; City	☹

28	Ammonia/nitrogen emissions per capita	Ton per 10,000 persons	Whole city	Negative	12.50		13.53	13.99	25	27	2	Environment Annual Report; City	☺
29	Percentage of the days with air quality at or over level II in a year	%	District	Positive	89.45		83.24	83.24	32	30	−2	MEP Data	☹
30	Percentage of days with respirable suspended particulates as the principal pollutants in a year	%	District	Negative	69.76		95.89	92.33	38	35	−3	MEP Data	☹
31	Ratio of environmental spending to government expenditure	%	Whole city	Positive	3.14		1.49	1.87	34	25	−9	China Statistics; City	☹
32	Ratio of the investment in industrial pollution control to GDP	%	Whole city	Positive	0.09		0.03	0.02	22	29	7	Environment Annual Report; Regional Economy	☺
33	Ratio of the spending on science, education, culture, and public health to government expenditure	%	Whole city	Positive	21.06		21.21	23.87	16	29	13	China Statistics; City; Regional Economy	☺

(continued)

(continued)

No.	Indicator	Unit	Scope	Attribute	2010 average of 38 cities	2010 figure	2009 figure	2010 ranking	2009 ranking	Change in ranking	Source of 2010 data	Chernoff face
34	Area of green land per capita in urban areas	m^2	District	Positive	58.13	19.00	21.47	38	36	−2	City	☹
35	Green coverage of urban built-in areas	%	District	Positive	39.84	40.43	40.42	17	14	−3	Urban Construction	☹
36	Coverage of water supply	%	District	Positive	98.83	100.00	100.00	1	1	0	Urban Construction	
37	Treatment rate of urban household wastewater	%	District	Positive	86.16	86.41	80.97	25	22	−3	Urban Construction	☹
38	Harmless treatment of urban household waste	%	District	Positive	94.38	97.48	90.30	20	26	6	Urban Construction	☺
39	Public buses per 10,000 urban residents		District	Positive	15.51	12.63	12.53	22	22	0	City	
40	Industrial SO_2 removal rate	%	Whole city	Positive	57.30	43.82	37.04	29	28	−1	Environment Annual Report	☹
41	Industrial wastewater COD removal rate	%	Whole city	Positive	76.07	76.66	74.17	28	28	0	Environment Annual Report	
42	Industrial nitrogen oxide removal rate	%	Whole city	Positive	5.24	0.00	0.00	31	29	−2	Environment Annual Report	☹

43	Industrial waste water ammonia/nitrogen removal rate	%		Whole city	Positive	66.79		41.29	34.89	33	32	−1	Environment Annual Report	☹

Note:
Regional Economy: *China Regional Economy Statistical Yearbook 2011*
City: *China City Statistical Yearbook 2011*
China Statistics: *China Statistical Yearbook 2011*
Urban Construction: *China Urban Construction Statistical Yearbook 2010*
Environment Annual Report: *China Environment Annual Report 2010*
Environmental Yearbook: *China Environmental Statistical Yearbook 2011*
MEP Data: Ministry of Environmental Protection Data Center

9.33 Brief Analysis of Green Development in Xi'an

Xi'an ranked 32nd among the 38 participating cities by GDI according to 2010 data, 1 place higher over 2009 (Xi'an ranked 33rd in 2009). Following is a brief analysis of its score by each indicator and their changes from 2009 to 2010.

9.33.1 Xi'an's 2010 Scores by GDI

Xi'an scored −0.232 in 2010. From the three First-Class Indicators including GDEG, CCPNRE, and SDGP as shown in Fig. 9.65, Xi'an ranked lower than the national average in all three indicators (Note: the national average value of each indicator is 0).

According to Fig. 9.66, Xi'an surpassed the national average only in II while other 8 Second-Class Indicators were lower than the national average.

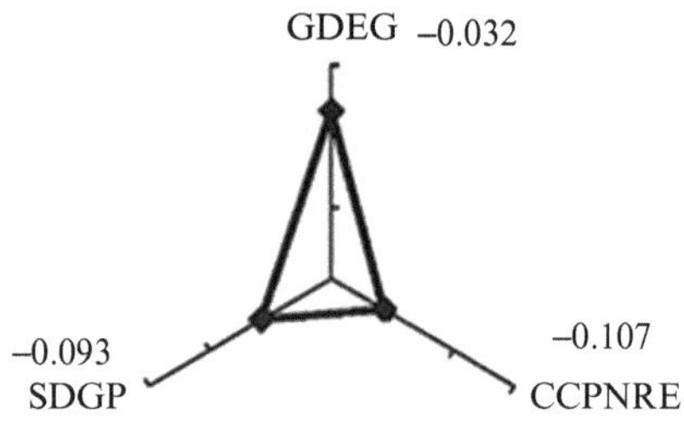

Fig. 9.65 Scores of Xi'an by First-Class Indicators

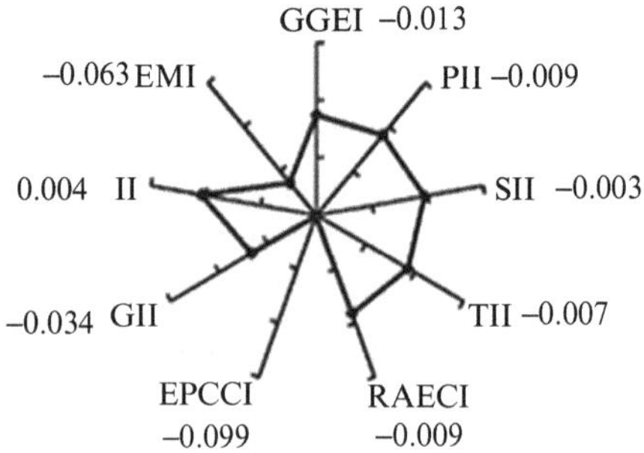

Fig. 9.66 Scores of Xi'an in ranking of Second-Class Indicators

Table 9.65 Changes in Xi'an's rankings by First-Class and Second-Class Indicators, 2009–2010

Indicator	2010	2009	Difference	Indicator	2010	2009	Difference
GDI	32	33	1				
GDEG	21	22	1	RAECI	31	28	−3
GGEI	22	20	−2	EPCCI	30	30	0
PII	32	33	1	SDGP	28	33	5
SII	21	25	4	GII	28	32	4
TII	21	18	−3	II	21	23	2
CCPNRE	31	31	0	EMI	33	33	0

Note: A positive value in "Difference" means a rise in ranking

9.33.2 Changes in Xi'an's GDI Rankings 2009–2010

According to Table 9.65, in First-Class Indicators, the most obvious change occurred in SDGP with a rise of 5 places; it rose by 1 place in GDEG; it remained unchanged by CCPNRE. Judging from changes in ranking, it rose by 4 places in SII and GII, 2 in II and 1 in PII; it fell slightly in GGEI, TII and RAECI; it remained unchanged in EPCCI and EMI as compared with that in 2009.

To further explain the causes of the changes in the rankings by First- and Second-Class Indicators, we put the Third-Class Indicators where a change of more than 3 places occurred from 2009 to 2010 as follows in Table 9.66. Compared with those in 2009, Xi'an both out- and underperformed in ranking in 2010, while the more obvious trend is outperforming compared with the previous year. It rose by 13 places in Ratio of the spending on science, education, culture, and public health to government expenditure, 7 in Ratio of the investment in industrial pollution control to GDP, and it rose to various degrees by Nitrogen oxide emissions per unit of GDP, Nitrogen oxides emissions per unit of land area, Nitrogen oxides emissions per capita and COD emissions per capita; it dropped to some extent by 5 indicators which were Ratio of environmental spending to government expenditure, Water resources per capita, Percentage of days with respirable suspended particulates as the principal pollutants in a year, Green coverage of urban built-in areas and Treatment rate of urban household wastewater.

Table 9.66 Third-Class Indicators where changes over 3 places occurred by Xi'an, 2009–2010

Third-Class Indicator	Original data for 2009 and 2010			Change in ranking		
	2010	2009	Unit	2010	2009	Difference
Nitrogen oxide emissions per unit of GDP	28.33	33.77	Ton per 100 million yuan	15	21	6
Water resources per capita	199.27	300.25	m^3 per capita	31	28	−3
COD emissions per capita	123.67	139.18	Ton per 10,000 persons	23	26	3
Nitrogen oxides emissions per unit of land area	6.99	7.28	Ton per km^2	12	18	6
Nitrogen oxides emissions per capita	90.35	94.71	Ton per 10,000 persons	6	10	4
Percentage of days with respirable suspended particulates as the principal pollutants in a year	95.89	92.33	%	38	35	−3
Ratio of environmental spending to government expenditure	1.49	1.87	%	34	25	−9
Ratio of the investment in industrial pollution control to GDP	0.03	0.02	%	22	29	7
Ratio of the spending on science, education, culture, and public health to government expenditure	21.21	23.87	%	16	29	13
Green coverage of urban built-in areas	40.43	40.42	%	17	14	−3
Treatment rate of urban household wastewater	86.41	80.97	%	25	22	−3

Note: A positive value in "Difference" means a rise in ranking

Green development checkup-Lanzhou

No.	Indicator	Unit	Scope	Attribute	2010 average of 38 cities	2010 figure	2009 figure	2010 ranking	2009 ranking	Change in ranking	Source of 2010 data	Chernoff face
1	GDP per capita	Yuan	Whole city	Positive	55,399.15	30,672	27,904.06	34	34	0	Regional Economy; City	
2	Energy consumption per unit of GDP	Ton per 10,000 yuan	Whole city	Negative	0.82	1.99	2.09	38	37	−1	Regional Economy; City	
3	Electricity consumption per capita in urban areas	kWh per capita	Whole city	Negative	580.70	349.04	306.46	7	7	0	City	
4	CO_2 emissions per unit of GDP			Negative	No data			N/A	N/A	N/A		
5	SO_2 emissions per unit of GDP	Ton per 100 million yuan	Whole city	Negative	42.67	96.87	91.73	35	33	−2	Regional Economy; Environment Annual Report	
6	COD emissions per unit of GDP	Ton per 100 million yuan	Whole city	Negative	24.91	47.03	54.29	35	35	0	Regional Economy; Environment Annual Report	
7	Nitrogen oxide emissions per unit of GDP	Ton per 100 million yuan	Whole city	Negative	40.67	57.35	62.96	31	32	1	Regional Economy; Environment Annual Report	
8	Ammonia/nitrogen emissions per unit of GDP	Ton per 100 million yuan	Whole city	Negative	2.63	5.57	5.68	35	35	0	Regional Economy; Environment Annual Report	
9	Labor productivity of the primary sector	10,000 yuan per capita	Whole city	Positive	3.00	0.83	0.74	37	36	−1	Regional Economy	

(continued)

(continued)

No.	Indicator	Unit	Scope	Attribute	2010 average of 38 cities	2010 figure	2009 figure	2010 ranking	2009 ranking	Change in ranking	Source of 2010 data	Chernoff face
10	Labor productivity of the secondary sector	10,000 yuan per capita	Whole city	Positive	18.12	11.51	9.95	28	24	−4	Regional Economy	☹
11	Water consumption per unit of value added created by industrial enterprises	10,000 tons per 10,000 yuan	Whole city	Negative	0.03	0.04	0.04	30	32	2	Regional Economy; Environment Annual Report	☺
12	Energy consumption per unit of value added created by industrial enterprises			Negative	No data			N/A	N/A	N/A		
13	Utilization rate industrial solid waste	%	Whole city	Positive	83.42	78.90	73.50	30	31	1	Environment Annual Report	☺
14	Recycling rate of industrial water	%	Whole city	Positive	82.10	94.27	94.14	10	13	3	Environment Annual Report	☺
15	Labor productivity of the tertiary sector	10,000 yuan per capita	Whole city	Positive	11.39	6.50	6.16	33	31	−2	Regional Economy	☹
16	Proportion of value added of tertiary sector in GDP	%	Whole city	Positive	48.37	48.84	49.87	19	17	−2	City	☹
17	Proportion of tertiary sector employees in the total employed population	%	Whole city	Positive	46.83	50.14	47.27	11	16	5	Regional Economy	☺

18	Water resources per capita	m^3 per capita	Whole city	Positive	1,040.56	10,149.6	10,148.03	1	1	0	Environment Annual Report; City	
19	CO_2 emissions per unit of land area			Negative	No data			N/A	N/A	N/A		
20	CO_2 emissions per capita			Negative	No data			N/A	N/A	N/A		
21	SO_2 emissions per unit of land area	Ton per km^2	Whole city	Negative	11.34	7.37	6.18	16	13	−3	Environment Annual Report; City	☹
22	SO_2 emissions per capita	Ton per 10,000 persons	Whole city	Negative	211.11	297.94	250.61	30	28	−2	Environment Annual Report; City	☹
23	COD emissions per unit of land area	Ton per km^2	Whole city	Negative	7.63	3.58	3.66	9	9	0	Environment Annual Report; City	
24	COD emissions per capita	Ton per 10,000 persons	Whole city	Negative	117.25	144.64	148.32	26	28	2	Environment Annual Report; City	☺
25	Nitrogen oxides emissions per unit of land area	Ton per km^2	Whole city	Negative	14.61	4.36	4.24	9	11	2	Environment Annual Report; City	☺
26	Nitrogen oxides emissions per capita	Ton per 10,000 persons	Whole city	Negative	231.68	176.38	172.00	16	20	4	Environment Annual Report; City	☺
27	Ammonia/nitrogen emissions per unit of land area	Ton per km^2	Whole city	Negative	0.83	0.42	0.38	14	11	−3	Environment Annual Report; City	☺
28	Ammonia/nitrogen emissions per capita	Ton per 10,000 persons	Whole city	Negative	12.50	17.14	15.52	30	28	−2	Environment Annual Report; City	☹

(continued)

(continued)

No.	Indicator	Unit	Scope	Attribute	2010 average of 38 cities	2010 figure	2009 figure	2010 ranking	2009 ranking	Change in ranking	Source of 2010 data	Chernoff face
29	Percentage of the days with air quality at or over level II in a year	%	District	Positive	89.45	60.71	64.56	38	38	0	MEP Data	
30	Percentage of days with respirable suspended particulates as the principal pollutants in a year	%	District	Negative	69.76	87.40	93.97	32	36	4	MEP Data	
31	Ratio of environmental spending to government expenditure	%	Whole city	Positive	3.14	5.14	2.71	3	14	11	China Statistics; City	
32	Ratio of the investment in industrial pollution control to GDP	%	Whole city	Positive	0.09	N/A	0.34	N/A	5	N/A	Environment Annual Report; Regional Economy	
33	Ratio of the spending on science, education, culture, and public health to government expenditure	%	Whole city	Positive	21.06	26.35	35.07	5	3	−2	China Statistics; City; Regional Economy	

34	Area of green land per capita in urban areas	m^2	District	Positive	58.13	21.00	20.78	37	37	0	City	
35	Green coverage of urban built-in areas	%	District	Positive	39.84	25.02	26.37	38	38	0	Urban Construction	
36	Coverage of water supply	%	District	Positive	98.83	94.96	92.38	36	37	1	Urban Construction	☺
37	Treatment rate of urban household wastewater	%	District	Positive	86.16	57.55	60.00	36	33	−3	Urban Construction	☹
38	Harmless treatment of urban household waste	%	District	Positive	94.38	80.26	80.91	36	29	−7	Urban Construction	☹
39	Public buses per 10,000 urban residents		District	Positive	15.51	10.22	10.06	29	32	3	City	☺
40	Industrial SO_2 removal rate	%	Whole city	Positive	57.30	47.82	74.55	27	6	−21	Environment Annual Report	☹
41	Industrial wastewater COD removal rate	%	Whole city	Positive	76.07	51.87	78.42	35	25	−10	Environment Annual Report	☹
42	Industrial nitrogen oxide removal rate	%	Whole city	Positive	5.24	14.52	14.41	7	9	2	Environment Annual Report	☺

(continued)

(continued)

No.	Indicator	Unit	Scope	Attribute	2010 average of 38 cities	2010 figure	2009 figure	2010 ranking	2009 ranking	Change in ranking	Source of 2010 data	Chernoff face
43	Industrial waste water ammonia/ nitrogen removal rate	%	Whole city	Positive	66.79	60.94	59.53	28	23	−5	Environment Annual Report	☹

Note:
Regional Economy: *China Regional Economy Statistical Yearbook 2011*
City: *China City Statistical Yearbook 2011*
China Statistics: *China Statistical Yearbook 2011*
Urban Construction: *China Urban Construction Statistical Yearbook 2010*
Environment Annual Report: *China Environment Annual Report 2010*
Environmental Yearbook: *China Environmental Statistical Yearbook 2011*
MEP Data: Ministry of Environmental Protection Data Center

9.34 Brief Analysis of Green Development in Lanzhou

Lanzhou ranked 37th among the 38 participating cities by GDI according to 2010 data, 3 places lower over 2009 (Lanzhou ranked 34th in 2009). Following is a brief analysis of its score by each indicator and their changes from 2009 to 2010.

9.34.1 Lanzhou's 2010 Scores by GDI

Lanzhou scored −0.356 in 2010. From the three First-Class Indicators including GDEG, CCPNRE, and SDGP as shown in Fig. 9.67, Lanzhou outperformed other places in terms of all three indicators (Note: the national average value of each indicator is 0).

According to Fig. 9.68, Lanzhou surpassed the national average in 2 of Second-Class Indicators in 2010, which were RAECI and GII; it scored lower than the national average in 7 indicators in GGEI, PII, SII, TII, EPCCI, II and EMI.

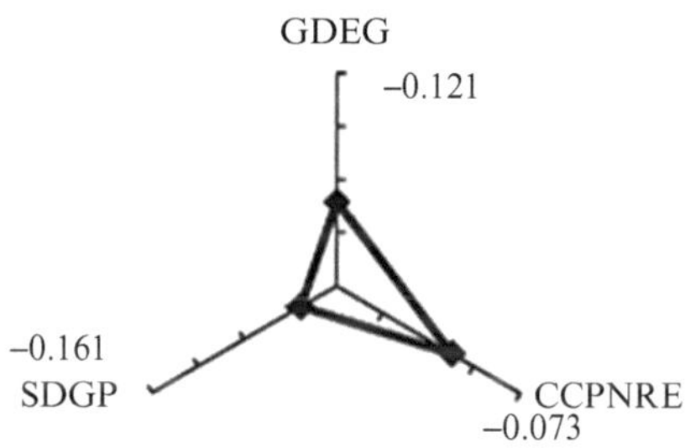

Fig. 9.67 Scores of Lanzhou by First-Class Indicators

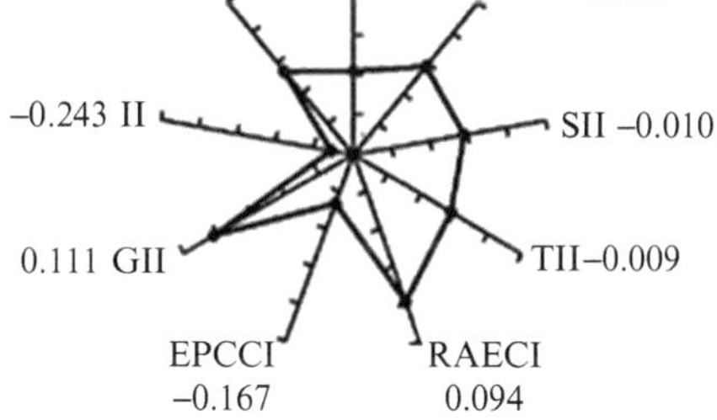

Fig. 9.68 Scores of Lanzhou by Second-Class Indicators

Table 9.67 Changes in Lanzhou's rankings by First-Class and Second-Class Indicators, 2009–2010

Indicator	2010	2009	Difference	Indicator	2010	2009	Difference
GDI	37	34	−3				
GDEG	35	35	0	RAECI	1	1	0
GGEI	35	36	1	EPCCI	38	38	0
PII	37	36	−1	SDGP	35	28	−7
SII	27	30	3	GII	3	2	−1
TII	23	22	−1	II	38	37	−1
CCPNRE	25	25	0	EMI	26	16	−10

Note: A positive value in "Difference" means a rise in ranking

9.34.2 Changes in Lanzhou's GDI Rankings 2009–2010

According to Table 9.67, in First-Class Indicators, the most obvious change occurred in SDGP with a fall of 7 places, and it remained unchanged by GDEG and CCPNRE compared with that in 2009. Judging from changes in ranking, it fell obviously in EMI with a fall of 10 places, and it fell by 1 place in PII, TII, GII and II; it rose by 3 places in TII, 1 in RAECI. It remained unchanged by EPCCI as compared with that in 2009.

To further explain the causes of the changes in the rankings by First- and Second-Class Indicators, we put the Third-Class Indicators where a change of more than 3 places occurred from 2009 to 2010 as follows in Table 9.68. Compared with those in 2009, Lanzhou both out- and underperformed in ranking in 2010. The most dramatic change occurred in Ratio of environmental spending to government expenditure with a drop of 11 places. It rose much in Recycling rate of industrial water, Proportion of tertiary sector employees in the total employed population, Nitrogen oxides emissions per capita, Percentage of days with respirable suspended particulates as the principal pollutants in a year and Public buses per 10,000 urban residents; it fell in 5 indicators which were Labor productivity of the secondary sector, SO_2 emissions per unit of land area, Ammonia/nitrogen emissions per unit of land area, Treatment rate of urban household wastewater and Harmless treatment of urban household waste.

Table 9.68 Third-Class Indicators where changes over 3 places occurred by Lanzhou, 2009–2010

	Original data for 2009 and 2010			Change in ranking		
Third-Class Indicator	2010	2009	Unit	2010	2009	Difference
Labor productivity of the secondary sector	11.51	9.95	10,000 yuan per capita	28	24	−4
Recycling rate of industrial water	94.27	94.14	%	10	13	3
Proportion of tertiary sector employees in the total employed population	50.14	47.27	%	11	16	5
SO_2 emissions per unit of land area	7.37	6.18	Ton per km^2	16	13	−3
Nitrogen oxides emissions per capita	176.38	172.00	Ton per 10,000 persons	16	20	4
Ammonia/nitrogen emissions per unit of land area	0.42	0.38	Ton per km^2	14	11	−3
Percentage of days with respirable suspended particulates as the principal pollutants in a year	87.40	93.97	%	32	36	4
Ratio of environmental spending to government expenditure	5.14	2.71	%	3	14	11
Treatment rate of urban household wastewater	57.55	60.00	%	36	33	−3
Harmless treatment of urban household waste	80.26	80.91	%	36	29	−7
Public buses per 10,000 urban residents	10.22	10.06		29	32	3

Note: A positive value in "Difference" means a rise in ranking

Green development checkup-Xining

No.	Indicator	Unit	Scope	Attribute	2010 average of 38 cities	2010 figure	2009 figure	2010 ranking	2009 ranking	Change in ranking	Source of 2010 data	Chernoff face
1	GDP per capita	Yuan	Whole city	Positive	55,399.15	28,428	22,865.00	35	37	2	Regional Economy; City	
2	Energy consumption per unit of GDP	Ton per 10,000 yuan	Whole city	Negative	0.82	1.54	3.24	34	38	4	Regional Economy; City	
3	Electricity consumption per capita in urban areas	kWh per capita	Whole city	Negative	580.70	351.62	323.00	8	11	3	City	
4	CO_2 emissions per unit of GDP			Negative	No data			N/A	N/A	N/A		
5	SO_2 emissions per unit of GDP	Ton per 100 million yuan	Whole city	Negative	42.67	156.72	178.49	37	37	0	Regional Economy; Environment Annual Report	
6	COD emissions per unit of GDP	Ton per 100 million yuan	Whole city	Negative	24.91	71.44	81.80	37	37	0	Regional Economy; Environment Annual Report	
7	Nitrogen oxide emissions per unit of GDP	Ton per 100 million yuan	Whole city	Negative	40.67	118.18	108.31	37	38	1	Regional Economy; Environment Annual Report	
8	Ammonia/nitrogen emissions per unit of GDP	Ton per 100 million yuan	Whole city	Negative	2.63	9.30	9.63	38	38	0	Regional Economy; Environment Annual Report	
9	Labor productivity of the primary sector	10,000 yuan per capita	Whole city	Positive	3.00	N/A	N/A	N/A	N/A	N/A	Regional Economy	
10	Labor productivity of the secondary sector	10,000 yuan per capita	Whole city	Positive	18.12	N/A	N/A	N/A	N/A	N/A	Regional Economy	

11	Water consumption per unit of value added created by industrial enterprises	10,000 tons per 10,000 yuan	Whole city	Negative	0.03	0.04	0.04	31	31	0	Regional Economy; Environment Annual Report	
12	Energy consumption per unit of value added created by industrial enterprises			Negative	No data			N/A	N/A	N/A		
13	Utilization rate industrial solid waste	%	Whole city	Positive	83.42	83.60	91.90	26	19	−7	Environment Annual Report	☹
14	Recycling rate of industrial water	%	Whole city	Positive	82.10	91.18	86.75	17	23	6	Environment Annual Report	☺
15	Labor productivity of the tertiary sector	10,000 yuan per capita	Whole city	Positive	11.39	N/A	N/A	N/A	N/A	N/A	Regional Economy	
16	Proportion of value added of tertiary sector in GDP	%	Whole city	Positive	48.37	45.05	46.41	24	22	−2	City	☹
17	Proportion of tertiary sector employees in the total employed population	%	Whole city	Positive	46.83	N/A	45.83	N/A	18	N/A	Regional Economy	
18	Water resources per capita	m^3 per capita	Whole city	Positive	1,040.56	597.04	629.58	19	17	−2	Environment Annual Report; City	☹
19	CO_2 emissions per unit of land area			Negative	No data			N/A	N/A	N/A		

(continued)

(continued)

No.	Indicator	Unit	Scope	Attribute	2010 average of 38 cities	2010 figure	2009 figure	2010 ranking	2009 ranking	Change in ranking	Source of 2010 data	Chernoff face
20	CO_2 emissions per capita			Negative	No data			N/A	N/A	N/A		
21	SO_2 emissions per unit of land area	Ton per km^2	Whole city	Negative	11.34	9.86	9.49	21	21	0	Environment Annual Report; City	
22	SO_2 emissions per capita	Ton per 10,000 persons	Whole city	Negative	211.11	342.15	332.02	33	31	−2	Environment Annual Report; City	☹
23	COD emissions per unit of land area	Ton per km^2	Whole city	Negative	7.63	4.50	4.35	16	13	−3	Environment Annual Report; City	☹
24	COD emissions per capita	Ton per 10,000 persons	Whole city	Negative	117.25	155.97	152.16	28	29	1	Environment Annual Report; City	☺
25	Nitrogen oxides emissions per unit of land area	Ton per km^2	Whole city	Negative	14.61	7.44	5.76	16	13	−3	Environment Annual Report; City	☹
26	Nitrogen oxides emissions per capita	Ton per 10,000 persons	Whole city	Negative	231.68	258.01	201.48	30	25	−5	Environment Annual Report; City	☹
27	Ammonia/nitrogen emissions per unit of land area	Ton per km^2	Whole city	Negative	0.83	0.59	0.51	19	14	−5	Environment Annual Report; City	☹
28	Ammonia/nitrogen emissions per capita	Ton per 10,000 persons	Whole city	Negative	12.50	20.31	17.91	33	32	−1	Environment Annual Report; City	☹
29	Percentage of the days with air quality at or over level II in a year	%	District	Positive	89.45	85.71	76.92	26	36	10	MEP Data	☺

30	Percentage of days with respirable suspended particulates as the principal pollutants in a year	%	District	Negative	69.76	92.33	97.26	36	38	2	MEP Data	☺
31	Ratio of environmental spending to government expenditure	%	Whole city	Positive	3.14	5.67	3.52	2	5	3	China Statistics; City	☺
32	Ratio of the investment in industrial pollution control to GDP	%	Whole city	Positive	0.09	0.11	0.47	8	4	−4	Environment Annual Report; Regional Economy	☹
33	Ratio of the spending on science, education, culture, and public health to government expenditure	%	Whole city	Positive	21.06	29.42	23.51	3	31	28	China Statistics; City; Regional Economy	☺
34	Area of green land per capita in urban areas	m^2	District	Positive	58.13	26.00	11.92	32	38	6	City	☺
35	Green coverage of urban built-in areas	%	District	Positive	39.84	35.12	34.80	34	32	−2	Urban Construction	☹
36	Coverage of water supply	%	District	Positive	98.83	99.85	99.35	24	25	1	Urban Construction	☺
37	Treatment rate of urban household wastewater	%	District	Positive	86.16	55.05	54.47	38	35	−3	Urban Construction	☹

(continued)

(continued)

No.	Indicator	Unit	Scope	Attribute	2010 average of 38 cities	2010 figure	2009 figure	2010 ranking	2009 ranking	Change in ranking	Source of 2010 data	Chernoff face
38	Harmless treatment of urban household waste	%	District	Positive	94.38	N/A	66.80	N/A	37	N/A	Urban Construction	
39	Public buses per 10,000 urban residents		District	Positive	15.51	19.06	15.00	3	11	8	City	
40	Industrial SO_2 removal rate	%	Whole city	Positive	57.30	27.63	15.99	35	36	1	Environment Annual Report	
41	Industrial wastewater COD removal rate	%	Whole city	Positive	76.07	10.08	18.86	38	38	0	Environment Annual Report	
42	Industrial nitrogen oxide removal rate	%	Whole city	Positive	5.24	0.00	0.00	31	29	−2	Environment Annual Report	
43	Industrial waste water ammonia/nitrogen removal rate	%	Whole city	Positive	66.79	3.24	22.58	38	38	0	Environment Annual Report	

Note:
Regional Economy: *China Regional Economy Statistical Yearbook 2011*
City: *China City Statistical Yearbook 2011*
China Statistics: *China Statistical Yearbook 2011*
Urban Construction: *China Urban Construction Statistical Yearbook 2010*
Environment Annual Report: *China Environment Annual Report 2010*
Environmental Yearbook: *China Environmental Statistical Yearbook 2011*
MEP Data: Ministry of Environmental Protection Data Center

9.35 Brief Analysis of Green Development in Xining

Xining ranked 38th among the 38 participating cities by GDI according to 2010 data, the same as it did in 2009 (Xining ranked 38th in 2009). Following is a brief analysis of its score by each indicator and their changes from 2009 to 2010.

9.35.1 Xining's 2010 Scores by GDI

Xining scored −0.615 in 2010. From the three First-Class Indicators including GDEG, CCPNRE, and SDGP as shown in Fig. 9.69, Xining scored lower than the national average in all three First-Class Indicators (Note: the national average value of each indicator is 0).

According to Fig. 9.70, Xining surpassed the national average only in GII, and other 8 indicators scored lower than the national average.

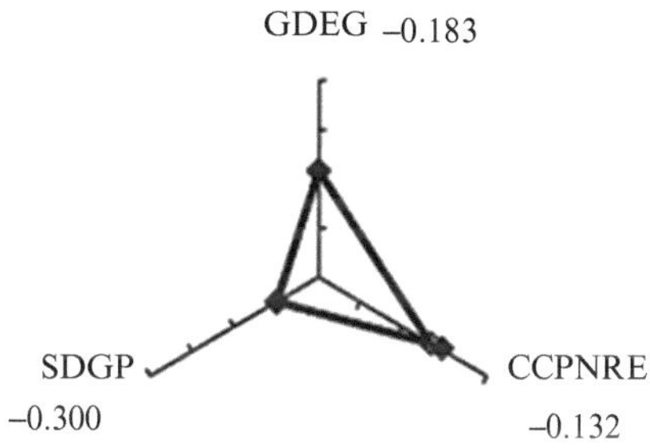

Fig. 9.69 Scores of Xining by First-Class Indicators

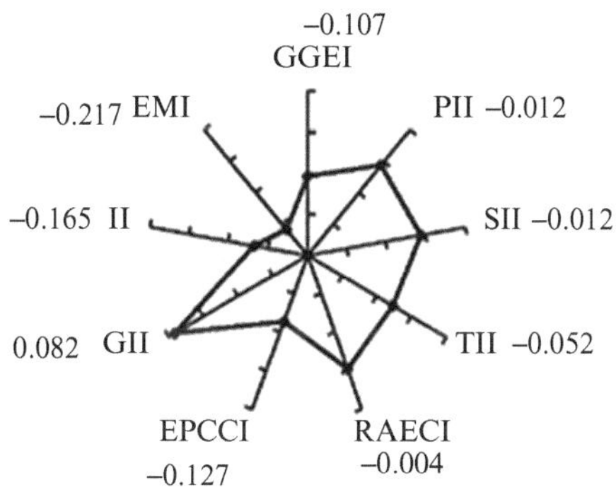

Fig. 9.70 Scores of Xining by Second-Class Indicators

Table 9.69 Changes in Xining's rankings by First-Class and Second-Class Indicators, 2009–2010

Indicator	2010	2009	Difference	Indicator	2010	2009	Difference
GDI	38	38	0				
GDEG	38	37	−1	RAECI	19	17	−2
GGEI	38	38	0	EPCCI	36	36	0
PII	38	38	0	SDGP	38	38	0
SII	29	27	−2	GII	4	7	3
TII	36	33	−3	II	36	36	0
CCPNRE	35	37	2	EMI	38	38	0

Note: A positive value in "Difference" means a rise in ranking

9.35.2 Changes in Xining's GDI Rankings 2009–2010

According to Table 9.69, in First-Class Indicators, Xining dropped by 1 place in GDEG; it rose by 2 places in CCPNRE and it remained unchanged in SDGP. Judging from changes in ranking, it fell by 3 places in TII, 2 in RAECI and it rose by 3 places in GII. It remained unchanged in GGEI, PII, EPCCI, II and EMI compared with that in 2009.

To further explain the causes of the changes in the rankings by First- and Second-Class Indicators, we put the Third-Class Indicators where a change of more than 3 places occurred from 2009 to 2010 as follows in Table 9.70. Compared with those in 2009, Xining both out- and underperformed in ranking in 2010. The most obvious change occurred in Percentage of the days with air quality at or over level II in a year with a rise of 10 places. It rose to some extent in 4 indicators which were Energy consumption per unit of GDP, Electricity consumption per capita in urban areas, Recycling rate of industrial water and Ratio of environmental spending to government expenditure. It worsened in 6 indicators as compared with that in 2009 in 6 indicators which were COD emissions per unit of land area, Nitrogen oxides emissions per unit of land area, Nitrogen oxides emissions per capita, Ammonia/nitrogen emissions per unit of land area and Ratio of the investment in industrial pollution control to GDP.

Table 9.70 Third-Class Indicators where changes over 3 places occurred by Xining, 2009–2010

	Original data for 2009 and 2010			Change in ranking		
Third-Class Indicator	2010	2009	Unit	2010	2009	Difference
Energy consumption per unit of GDP	1.54	3.24	Ton per 10,000 yuan	34	38	4
Electricity consumption per capita in urban areas	351.62	323.00	kWh per capita	8	11	3
Utilization rate industrial solid waste	83.60	91.90	%	26	19	−7
Recycling rate of industrial water	91.18	86.75	%	17	23	6
COD emissions per unit of land area	4.50	4.35	Ton per km^2	16	13	−3
Nitrogen oxides emissions per unit of land area	7.44	5.76	Ton per km^2	16	13	−3
Nitrogen oxides emissions per capita	258.01	201.48	Ton per 10,000 persons	30	25	−5
Ammonia/nitrogen emissions per unit of land area	0.59	0.51	Ton per km^2	19	14	−5
Percentage of the days with air quality at or over level II in a year	85.71	76.92	%	26	36	10
Ratio of environmental spending to government expenditure	5.67	3.52	%	2	5	3
Ratio of the investment in industrial pollution control to GDP	0.11	0.47	%	8	4	−4

Note: A positive value in "Difference" means a rise in ranking

Green development checkup-Yinchuan

No.	Indicator	Unit	Scope	Attribute	2010 average of 38 cities	2010 figure	2009 figure	2010 ranking	2009 ranking	Change in ranking	Source of 2010 data	Chernoff face
1	GDP per capita	Yuan	Whole city	Positive	55,399.15	42,771	38,392.00	27	24	−3	Regional Economy; City	☹
2	Energy consumption per unit of GDP	Ton per 10,000 yuan	Whole city	Negative	0.82	1.39	1.59	33	33	0	Regional Economy; City	
3	Electricity consumption per capita in urban areas	kWh per capita	Whole city	Negative	580.70	358.19	410.85	11	18	7	City	☺
4	CO_2 emissions per unit of GDP			Negative	No data			N/A	N/A	N/A		
5	SO_2 emissions per unit of GDP	Ton per 100 million yuan	Whole city	Negative	42.67	56.45	64.36	28	30	2	Regional Economy; Environment Annual Report	☺
6	COD emissions per unit of GDP	Ton per 100 million yuan	Whole city	Negative	24.91	44.04	44.54	34	32	−2	Regional Economy; Environment Annual Report	☹
7	Nitrogen oxide emissions per unit of GDP	Ton per 100 million yuan	Whole city	Negative	40.67	71.02	72.04	34	34	0	Regional Economy; Environment Annual Report	
8	Ammonia/nitrogen emissions per unit of GDP	Ton per 100 million yuan	Whole city	Negative	2.63	5.93	5.96	37	36	−1	Regional Economy; Environment Annual Report	☹
9	Labor productivity of the primary sector	10,000 yuan per capita	Whole city	Positive	3.00	1.80	1.39	26	29	3	Regional Economy	☺
10	Labor productivity of the secondary sector	10,000 yuan per capita	Whole city	Positive	18.12	15.86	12.48	13	14	1	Regional Economy	☺

11	Water consumption per unit of value added created by industrial enterprises	10,000 tons per 10,000 yuan	Whole city	Negative	0.03	0.04	0.05	33	34	1	Regional Economy; Environment Annual Report	☺
12	Energy consumption per unit of value added created by industrial enterprises			Negative	No data			N/A	N/A	N/A		
13	Utilization rate industrial solid waste	%	Whole city	Positive	83.42	75.40	90.80	31	21	−10	Environment Annual Report	☹
14	Recycling rate of industrial water	%	Whole city	Positive	82.10	89.04	93.61	22	15	−7	Environment Annual Report	☹
15	Labor productivity of the tertiary sector	10,000 yuan per capita	Whole city	Positive	11.39	7.95	6.65	29	29	0	Regional Economy	
16	Proportion of value added of tertiary sector in GDP	%	Whole city	Positive	48.37	44.64	46.13	26	23	−3	City	☹
17	Proportion of tertiary sector employees in the total employed population	%	Whole city	Positive	46.83	47.09	49.12	16	9	−7	Regional Economy	☹
18	Water resources per capita	m^3 per capita	Whole city	Positive	1,040.56	82.62	84.35	38	38	0	Environment Annual Report; City	
19	CO_2 emissions per unit of land area			Negative	No data			N/A	N/A	N/A		
20	CO_2 emissions per capita			Negative	No data			N/A	N/A	N/A		

(continued)

(continued)

No.	Indicator	Unit	Scope	Attribute	2010 average of 38 cities	2010 figure	2009 figure	2010 ranking	2009 ranking	Change in ranking	Source of 2010 data	Chernoff face
21	SO_2 emissions per unit of land area	Ton per km^2	Whole city	Negative	11.34	3.43	3.22	3	4	1	Environment Annual Report; City	☺
22	SO_2 emissions per capita	Ton per 10,000 persons	Whole city	Negative	211.11	196.87	199.66	25	23	−2	Environment Annual Report; City	☹
23	COD emissions per unit of land area	Ton per km^2	Whole city	Negative	7.63	2.68	2.23	6	5	−1	Environment Annual Report; City	☹
24	COD emissions per capita	Ton per 10,000 persons	Whole city	Negative	117.25	153.60	138.20	27	25	−2	Environment Annual Report; City	☹
25	Nitrogen oxides emissions per unit of land area	Ton per km^2	Whole city	Negative	14.61	4.31	3.60	7	10	3	Environment Annual Report; City	☺
26	Nitrogen oxides emissions per capita	Ton per 10,000 persons	Whole city	Negative	231.68	247.70	223.50	27	29	2	Environment Annual Report; City	☺
27	Ammonia/nitrogen emissions per unit of land area	Ton per km^2	Whole city	Negative	0.83	0.36	0.30	10	6	−4	Environment Annual Report; City	☹
28	Ammonia/nitrogen emissions per capita	Ton per 10,000 persons	Whole city	Negative	12.50	20.69	18.48	34	33	−1	Environment Annual Report; City	☹
29	Percentage of the days with air quality at or over level II in a year	%	District	Positive	89.45	90.93	90.11	17	18	1	MEP Data	☺

30	Percentage of days with respirable suspended particulates as the principal pollutants in a year	%	District	Negative	69.76	71.23	78.08	17	19	2	MEP Data	☺
31	Ratio of environmental spending to government expenditure	%	Whole city	Positive	3.14	3.46	4.29	12	3	−9	China Statistics; City	☹
32	Ratio of the investment in industrial pollution control to GDP	%	Whole city	Positive	0.09	0.36	0.25	1	6	5	Environment Annual Report; Regional Economy	☺
33	Ratio of the spending on science, education, culture, and public health to government expenditure	%	Whole city	Positive	21.06	17.93	30.41	30	8	−22	China Statistics; City; Regional Economy	☹
34	Area of green land per capita in urban areas	m^2	District	Positive	58.13	57.00	56.67	12	10	−2	City	☹
35	Green coverage of urban built-in areas	%	District	Positive	39.84	43.03	43.02	8	8	0	Urban Construction	
36	Coverage of water supply	%	District	Positive	98.83	99.48	99.50	29	24	−5	Urban Construction	☹

(continued)

(continued)

No.	Indicator	Unit	Scope	Attribute	2010 average of 38 cities	2010 figure	2009 figure	2010 ranking	2009 ranking	Change in ranking	Source of 2010 data	Chernoff face
37	Treatment rate of urban household wastewater	%	District	Positive	86.16	91.80	46.52	13	38	25	Urban Construction	☺
38	Harmless treatment of urban household waste	%	District	Positive	94.38	100.00	100.00	1	1	0	Urban Construction	
39	Public buses per 10,000 urban residents		District	Positive	15.51	14.77	14.45	15	15	0	City	
40	Industrial SO_2 removal rate	%	Whole city	Positive	57.30	59.72	66.30	21	14	−7	Environment Annual Report	☹
41	Industrial wastewater COD removal rate	%	Whole city	Positive	76.07	82.93	88.05	18	14	−4	Environment Annual Report	☹
42	Industrial nitrogen oxide removal rate	%	Whole city	Positive	5.24	0.00	0.00	31	29	−2	Environment Annual Report	☹
43	Industrial waste water ammonia/nitrogen removal rate	%	Whole city	Positive	66.79	96.46	67.18	3	20	17	Environment Annual Report	☺

Note:
Regional Economy: *China Regional Economy Statistical Yearbook 2011*
City: *China City Statistical Yearbook 2011*
China Statistics: *China Statistical Yearbook 2011*
Urban Construction: *China Urban Construction Statistical Yearbook 2010*
Environment Annual Report: *China Environment Annual Report 2010*
Environmental Yearbook: *China Environmental Statistical Yearbook 2011*
MEP Data: Ministry of Environmental Protection Data Center

9.36 Brief Analysis of Green Development in Yinchuan

Yinchuan ranked 16th among the 38 participating cities by GDI according to 2010 data, 5 places higher over 2009 (Yinchuan ranked 21st in 2009). Following is a brief analysis of its score by each indicator and their changes from 2009 to 2010.

9.36.1 Yinchuan's 2010 Scores by GDI

Yinchuan scored −0.006 in 2010. From the three First-Class Indicators including GDEG, CCPNRE, and SDGP as shown in Fig. 9.71, Yinchuan showed obvious advantages in SDGP, and scored lower than the national average in GDEG and CCPNRE (Note: the national average value of each indicator is 0).

According to Fig. 9.72, Yinchuan surpassed the national average in 3 of Second-Class Indicators in 2010, which were GII, II and EMI; it scored lower than the national average in6 indicators which were GGEI, PII, SII, TII, RAECI and EPCCI.

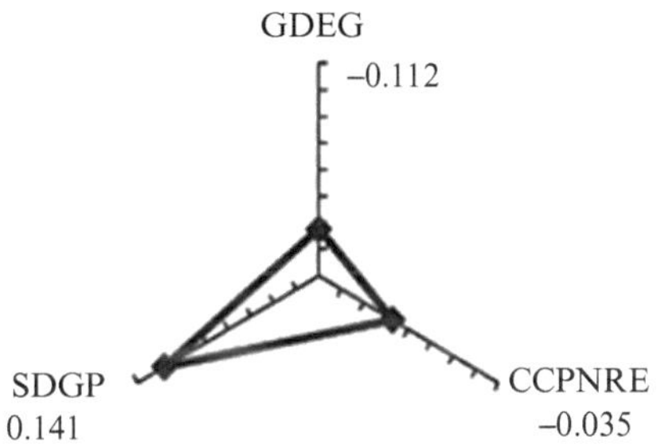

Fig. 9.71 Scores of Yinchuan by First-Class Indicators

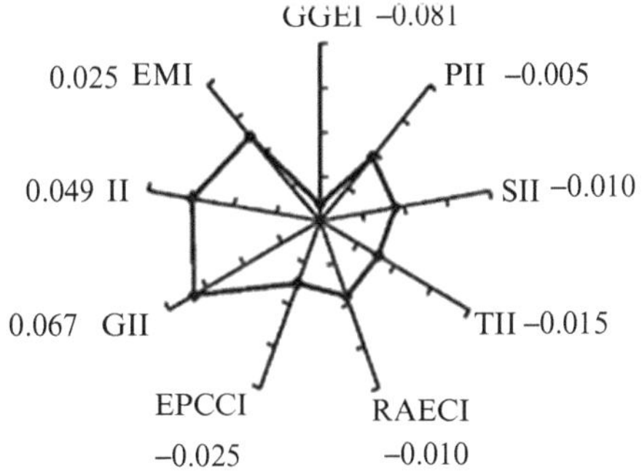

Fig. 9.72 Scores of Yinchuan by Second-Class Indicators

Table 9.71 Changes in Yinchuan's rankings by First-Class and Second-Class Indicators, 2009–2010

Indicator	2010	2009	Difference	Indicator	2010	2009	Difference
GDI	16	21	5				
GDEG	34	34	0	RAECI	38	38	0
GGEI	33	35	2	EPCCI	18	18	0
PII	26	29	3	SDGP	5	9	4
SII	28	13	−15	GII	6	4	−2
TII	25	23	−2	II	8	25	17
CCPNRE	19	19	0	EMI	16	22	6

Note: A positive value in "Difference" means a rise in ranking

9.36.2 Changes in Yinchuan's GDI Rankings 2009–2010

According to Table 9.71, in First-Class Indicators, the most obvious change occurred in SDGP with a rise of 4 places, and it remained unchanged in GDEG and CCPNRE. Judging from changes in ranking, it rose by 17, 6, 3, and 2 places in II, EMI, PII and GGEI; it fell by 15 places in SII, and it fell by 2 places in TII and GII; it remained unchanged in RAECI and EPCCI as compared with that in 2009.

To further explain the causes of the changes in the rankings by First- and Second-Class Indicators, we put the Third-Class Indicators where a change of more than 3 places occurred from 2009 to 2010 as follows in Table 9.72. Compared with those in 2009, Yinchuan both out- and underperformed in ranking in 2010. It rose by 7 places in Electricity consumption per capita in urban areas and 5 in Ratio of the investment in industrial pollution control to GDP. It rose by 3 places in Labor productivity of the primary sector and Nitrogen oxides emissions per unit of land area. Situation worsened in 7 indicators which were Utilization rate industrial solid waste, Ratio of environmental spending to government expenditure, Recycling rate of industrial water, Proportion of tertiary sector employees in the total employed population, Ammonia/nitrogen emissions per unit of land area, GDP per capita and Proportion of value added of tertiary sector in GDP as compared with that in 2009.

Table 9.72 Third-Class Indicators where changes over 3 places occurred by Yinchuan, 2009–2010

	Original data for 2009 and 2010			Change in ranking		
Third-Class Indicator	2010	2009	Unit	2010	2009	Difference
GDP per capita	42,771.00	38,392.00	yuan	27	24	−3
Electricity consumption per capita in urban areas	358.19	410.85	kWh per capita	11	18	7
Labor productivity of the primary sector	1.80	1.39	10,000 yuan per capita	26	29	3
Utilization rate industrial solid waste	75.40	90.80	%	31	21	−10
Recycling rate of industrial water	89.04	93.61	%	22	15	−7
Proportion of value added of tertiary sector in GDP	44.64	46.13	%	26	23	−3
Proportion of tertiary sector employees in the total employed population	47.09	49.12	%	16	9	−7
Nitrogen oxides emissions per unit of land area	4.31	3.60	Ton per km^2	7	10	3
Ammonia/nitrogen emissions per unit of land area	0.36	0.30	Ton per km^2	10	6	−4
Ratio of environmental spending to government expenditure	3.46	4.29	%	12	3	−9
Ratio of the investment in industrial pollution control to GDP	0.36	0.25	%	1	6	5

Note: A positive value in "Difference" means a rise in ranking

Green development checkup-Urumqi

No.	Indicator	Unit	Scope	Attribute	2010 average of 38 cities	2010 figure	2009 figure	2010 ranking	2009 ranking	Change in ranking	Source of 2010 data	Chernoff face
1	GDP per capita	Yuan	Whole city	Positive	55,399.15	43,039	38,249.00	26	25	−1	Regional Economy; City	☹
2	Energy consumption per unit of GDP	Ton per 10,000 yuan	Whole city	Negative	0.82	1.27	N/A	31	N/A	N/A	Regional Economy; City	
3	Electricity consumption per capita in urban areas	kWh per capita	Whole city	Negative	580.70	545.08	528.56	26	24	−2	City	☹
4	CO_2 emissions per unit of GDP			Negative	No data			N/A	N/A	N/A		
5	SO_2 emissions per unit of GDP	Ton per 100 million yuan	Whole city	Negative	42.67	91.36	118.49	34	35	1	Regional Economy; Environment Annual Report	☺
6	COD emissions per unit of GDP	Ton per 100 million yuan	Whole city	Negative	24.91	21.38	35.61	21	29	8	Regional Economy; Environment Annual Report	☺
7	Nitrogen oxide emissions per unit ofGDP	Ton per 100 million yuan	Whole city	Negative	40.67	125.38	94.63	38	37	−1	Regional Economy; Environment Annual Report	☹
8	Ammonia/nitrogen emissions per unit of GDP	Ton per 100 million yuan	Whole city	Negative	2.63	5.61	6.88	36	37	1	Regional Economy; Environment Annual Report	☺

9	Labor productivity of the primary sector	10,000 yuan per capita	Whole city	Positive	3.00	1.98	1.65	7	24	17	Regional Economy	☺
10	Labor productivity of the secondary sector	10,000 yuan per capita	Whole city	Positive	18.12	24.61	19.66	2	3	1	Regional Economy	☺
11	Water consumption per unit of value added created by industrial enterprises	10,000 tons per 10,000 yuan	Whole city	Negative	0.03	0.11	0.12	38	37	−1	Regional Economy; Environment Annual Report	☹
12	Energy consumption per unit of value added created by industrial enterprises			Negative	No data			N/A	N/A	N/A		
13	Utilization rate industrial solid waste	%	Whole city	Positive	83.42	68.20	65.30	32	33	1	Environment Annual Report	☺
14	Recycling rate of industrial water	%	Whole city	Positive	82.10	93.73	96.89	12	1	−11	Environment Annual Report	☹
15	Labor productivity of the tertiary sector	10,000 yuan per capita	Whole city	Positive	11.39	9.06	7.39	3	25	22	Regional Economy	☺

(continued)

(continued)

No.	Indicator	Unit	Scope	Attribute	2010 average of 38 cities	2010 figure	2009 figure	2010 ranking	2009 ranking	Change in ranking	Source of 2010 data	Chernoff face
16	Proportion of value added of tertiary sector in GDP	%	Whole city	Positive	48.37	53.65	57.15	7	6	−1	City	☹
17	Proportion of tertiary sector employees in the total employed population	%	Whole city	Positive	46.83	69.61	69.81	2	2	0	Regional Economy	
18	Water resources per capita	m^3 per capita	Whole city	Positive	1,040.56	427.25	488.41	25	21	−4	Environment Annual Report; City	☹
19	CO_2 emissions per unit of land area			Negative	No data			N/A	N/A	N/A		
20	CO_2 emissions per capita			Negative	No data			N/A	N/A	N/A		
21	SO_2 emissions per unit of land area	Ton per km^2	Whole city	Negative	11.34	7.26	8.38	14	18	4	Environment Annual Report; City	☺
22	SO_2 emissions per capita	Ton per 10,000 persons	Whole city	Negative	211.11	413.26	484.26	35	36	1	Environment Annual Report; City	☺
23	COD emissions per unit of land area	Ton per km^2	Whole city	Negative	7.63	1.70	2.52	4	6	2	Environment Annual Report; City	☺

24	COD emissions per capita	Ton per 10,000 persons	Whole city	Negative	117.25	96.71	145.53	18	27	9	Environment Annual Report; City	☺
25	Nitrogen oxides emissions per unit of land area	Ton per km^2	Whole city	Negative	14.61	9.96	6.69	23	17	−6	Environment Annual Report; City	☹
26	Nitrogen oxides emissions per capita	Ton per 10,000 persons	Whole city	Negative	231.68	567.16	386.74	36	34	−2	Environment Annual Report; City	☹
27	Ammonia/nitrogen emissions per unit of land area	Ton per km^2	Whole city	Negative	0.83	0.45	0.49	16	13	−3	Environment Annual Report; City	☹
28	Ammonia/nitrogen emissions per capita	Ton per 10,000 persons	Whole city	Negative	12.50	25.38	28.13	35	38	3	Environment Annual Report; City	☺
29	Percentage of the days with air quality at or over level II in a year	%	District	Positive	89.45	72.80	71.70	37	37	0	MEP Data	
30	Percentage of days with respirable suspended particulates as the principal pollutants in a year	%	District	Negative	69.76	78.36	79.50	22	23	1	MEP Data	☺

(continued)

(continued)

No.	Indicator	Unit	Scope	Attribute	2010 average of 38 cities	2010 figure	2009 figure	2010 ranking	2009 ranking	Change in ranking	Source of 2010 data	Chernoff face
31	Ratio of environmental spending to government expenditure	%	Whole city	Positive	3.14	3.89	2.99	9	12	3	China Statistics; City	☺
32	Ratio of the investment in industrial pollution control to GDP	%	Whole city	Positive	0.09	N/A	0.01	N/A	34	N/A	Environment Annual Report; Regional Economy	
33	Ratio of the spending on science, education, culture, and public health to government expenditure	%	Whole city	Positive	21.06	22.50	24.06	14	27	13	China Statistics; City; Regional Economy	☺
34	Area of green land per capita in urban areas	m^2	District	Positive	58.13	67.00	66.33	7	7	0	City	
35	Green coverage of urban built-in areas	%	District	Positive	39.84	34.80	34.25	36	35	−1	Urban Construction	☹
36	Coverage of water supply	%	District	Positive	98.83	99.93	99.93	22	19	−3	Urban Construction	☹

37	Treatment rate of urban household wastewater	%	District	Positive	86.16	60.65	60.83	35	32	−3	Urban Construction	☹
38	Harmless treatment of urban household waste	%	District	Positive	94.38	87.40	84.67	32	28	−4	Urban Construction	☹
39	Public buses per 10,000 urban residents		District	Positive	15.51	15.56	16.66	12	7	−5	City	☹
40	Industrial SO_2 removal rate	%	Whole city	Positive	57.30	42.22	15.76	30	37	7	Environment Annual Report	☺
41	Industrial wastewater COD removal rate	%	Whole city	Positive	76.07	81.17	64.26	23	33	10	Environment Annual Report	☺
42	Industrial nitrogen oxide removal rate	%	Whole city	Positive	5.24	0.00	0.04	31	28	−3	Environment Annual Report	☹
43	Industrial waste water ammonia/nitrogen removal rate	%	Whole city	Positive	66.79	90.33	38.22	8	30	22	Environment Annual Report	☺

Note:
Regional Economy: *China Regional Economy Statistical Yearbook 2011*
City: *China City Statistical Yearbook 2011*
China Statistics: *China Statistical Yearbook 2011*
Urban Construction: *China Urban Construction Statistical Yearbook 2010*
Environment Annual Report: *China Environment Annual Report 2010*
Environmental Yearbook: *China Environmental Statistical Yearbook 2011*
MEP Data: Ministry of Environmental Protection Data Center

9.37 Brief Analysis of Green Development in Urumqi

Urumqi ranked 35th among the 38 participating cities by GDI according to 2010 data, 2 places higher over 2009 (Urumqi ranked 37th in 2009). Following is a brief analysis of its score by each indicator and their changes from 2009 to 2010.

9.37.1 Urumqi's 2010 Scores by GDI

Urumqi scored −0.274 in 2010. From the three First-Class Indicators including GDEG, CCPNRE, and SDGP as shown in Fig. 9.73, Urumqi scored lower than the national average in all three indicators (Note: the national average value of each indicator is 0).

According to Fig. 9.74, Urumqi surpassed the national average by SII and TII; it scored lower than the national average in 7 indicators which include GGEI and PII.

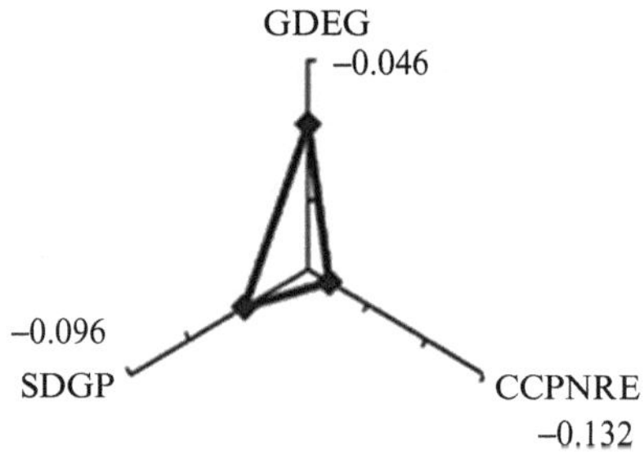

Fig. 9.73 Scores of Urumqi by First-Class Indicators

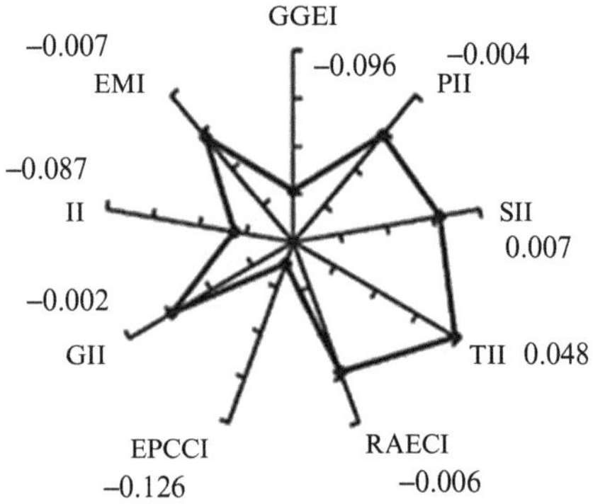

Fig. 9.74 Scores of Urumqi by Second-Class Indicators

Table 9.73 Changes in Urumqi's rankings by First-Class and Second-Class Indicators, 2009–2010

Indicator	2010	2009	Difference	Indicator	2010	2009	Difference
GDI	35	37	2				
GDEG	24	28	4	RAECI	25	21	−4
GGEI	36	37	1	EPCCI	34	37	3
PII	23	24	1	SDGP	29	37	8
SII	15	17	2	GII	14	26	12
TII	4	4	0	II	35	32	−3
CCPNRE	36	38	2	EMI	22	36	14

Note: A positive value in "Difference" means a rise in ranking

9.37.2 Changes in Urumqi's GDI Rankings 2009–2010

According to Table 9.73, in First-Class Indicators, the most obvious change occurred in SDGP with a rise of 8 places; it rose by 4 and 2 places in GDEG and CCPNRE. Judging from changes in ranking, it rose by 14 and 12 places in EMI and GII, and it rose to some extent in GGEI, PII, SII and EPCCI; it dropped by 4 and 3 places in RAECI and II. It remained unchanged in TII.

To further explain the causes of the changes in the rankings by First- and Second-Class Indicators, we put the Third-Class Indicators where a change of more than 3 places occurred from 2009 to 2010 as follows in Table 9.74. Compared with those in 2009, Urumqi both out- and underperformed in ranking in 2010, while the more obvious trend is underperforming compared with the previous year. It rose to a large extent in 11 indicators including Labor productivity of the tertiary sector, and it dropped to some extent in 9 indicators including Recycling rate of industrial water.

Table 9.74 Third-Class Indicators where changes over 3 places occurred by Urumqi, 2009–2010

	Original data for 2009 and 2010			Change in ranking		
Third-Class Indicator	2010	2009	Unit	2010	2009	Difference
COD emissions per unit of GDP	21.38	35.61	Ton per 100 million yuan	21	29	8
Labor productivity of the primary sector	1.98	1.65	10,000 yuan per capita	7	24	17
Recycling rate of industrial water	93.73	96.89	%	12	1	−11
Labor productivity of the tertiary sector	9.06	7.39	10,000 yuan per capita	3	25	22
Water resources per capita	427.25	488.41	m^3 per capita	25	21	−4
SO_2 emissions per unit of land area	7.26	8.38	Ton per km^2	14	18	4
COD emissions per capita	96.71	145.53	Ton per 10,000 persons	18	27	9
Nitrogen oxides emissions per unit of land area	9.96	6.69	Ton per km^2	23	17	−6
Ammonia/nitrogen emissions per unit of land area	0.45	0.49	Ton per km^2	16	13	−3
Ammonia/nitrogen emissions per capita	25.38	28.13	Ton per 10,000 persons	35	38	3
Ratio of environmental spending to government expenditure	3.89	2.99	%	9	12	3
Ratio of the spending on science, education, culture, and public health to government expenditure	22.50	24.06	%	14	27	13
Coverage of water supply	99.93	99.93	%	22	19	−3
Treatment rate of urban household wastewater	60.65	60.83	%	35	32	−3
Harmless treatment of urban household waste	87.40	84.67	%	32	28	−4
Public buses per 10,000 urban residents	15.56	16.66		12	7	−5
Industrial SO_2 removal rate	42.22	15.76	%	30	37	7
Industrial wastewater COD removal rate	81.17	64.26	%	23	33	10
Industrial nitrogen oxide removal rate	0.00	0.04	%	31	28	−3
Industrial waste water ammonia/nitrogen removal rate	90.33	38.22	%	8	30	22

Note: A positive value in "Difference" means a rise in ranking

Green development checkup-Karamay

No.	Indicator	Unit	Scope	Attribute	2010 average of 38 cities	2010 figure	2009 figure	2010 ranking	2009 ranking	Change in ranking	Source of 2010 data	Chernoff face
1	GDP per capita	Yuan	Whole city	Positive	55,399.15	12,1387	87,000.00	1	3	2	Regional Economy; City	
2	Energy consumption per unit of GDP	Ton per 10,000 yuan	Whole city	Negative	0.82	1.34	1.70	32	35	3	Regional Economy; City	
3	Electricity consumption per capita in urban areas	kWh per capita	Whole city	Negative	580.70	525.60	307.77	23	8	−15	City	
4	CO_2 emissions per unit of GDP			Negative	No data			N/A	N/A	N/A		
5	SO_2 emissions per unit of GDP	Ton per 100 million yuan	Whole city	Negative	42.67	75.48	84.19	32	32	0	Regional Economy; Environment Annual Report	
6	COD emissions per unit of GDP	Ton per 100 million yuan	Whole city	Negative	24.91	11.80	5.95	8	1	−7	Regional Economy; Environment Annual Report	
7	Nitrogen oxide emissions per unit of GDP	Ton per 100 million yuan	Whole city	Negative	40.67	N/A	40.09	N/A	25	N/A	Regional Economy; Environment Annual Report	
8	Ammonia/nitrogen emissions per unit of GDP	Ton per 100 million yuan	Whole city	Negative	2.63	1.06	1.31	8	7	−1	Regional Economy; Environment Annual Report	
9	Labor productivity of the primary sector	10,000 yuan per capita	Whole city	Positive	3.00	3.06	2.74	4	7	3	Regional Economy	

(continued)

(continued)

No.	Indicator	Unit	Scope	Attribute	2010 average of 38 cities	2010 figure	2009 figure	2010 ranking	2009 ranking	Change in ranking	Source of 2010 data	Chernoff face
10	Labor productivity of the secondary sector	10,000 yuan per capita	Whole city	Positive	18.12	56.75	59.47	1	1	0	Regional Economy	
11	Water consumption per unit of value added created by industrial enterprises	10,000 tons per 10,000 yuan	Whole city	Negative	0.03	0.04	0.02	29	16	−13	Regional Economy; Environment Annual Report	☹
12	Energy consumption per unit of value added created by industrial enterprises			Negative	No data			N/A	N/A	N/A		
13	Utilization rate industrial solid waste	%	Whole city	Positive	83.42	66.30	56.80	33	34	1	Environment Annual Report	☺
14	Recycling rate of industrial water	%	Whole city	Positive	82.10	96.63	94.56	2	10	8	Environment Annual Report	☺
15	Labor productivity of the tertiary sector	10,000 yuan per capita	Whole city	Positive	11.39	6.71	6.11	11	32	21	Regional Economy	☺
16	Proportion of value added of tertiary sector in GDP	%	Whole city	Positive	48.37	9.76	12.67	38	38	0	City	

17	Proportion of tertiary sector employees in the total employed population	%	Whole city	Positive	46.83	45.18	45.81	20	19	−1	Regional Economy	☹
18	Water resources per capita	m^3 per capita	Whole city	Positive	1,040.56	797.81	935.20	14	13	−1	Environment Annual Report; City	☹
19	CO_2 emissions per unit of land area			Negative	No data			N/A	N/A	N/A		
20	CO_2 emissions per capita			Negative	No data			N/A	N/A	N/A		
21	SO_2 emissions per unit of land area	Ton per km^2	Whole city	Negative	11.34	4.74	4.50	8	9	1	Environment Annual Report; City	☺
22	SO_2 emissions per capita	Ton per 10,000 persons	Whole city	Negative	211.11	1,177.80	1,102.98	38	38	0	Environment Annual Report; City	
23	COD emissions per unit of land area	Ton per km^2	Whole city	Negative	7.63	0.74	0.32	2	1	−1	Environment Annual Report; City	☹
24	COD emissions per capita	Ton per 10,000 persons	Whole city	Negative	117.25	184.07	77.96	35	7	−28	Environment Annual Report; City	☹
25	Nitrogen oxides emissions per unit of land area	Ton per km^2	Whole city	Negative	14.61	N/A	2.14	N/A	6	N/A	Environment Annual Report; City	

(continued)

(continued)

No.	Indicator	Unit	Scope	Attribute	2010 average of 38 cities	2010 figure	2009 figure	2010 ranking	2009 ranking	Change in ranking	Source of 2010 data	Chernoff face
26	Nitrogen oxides emissions per capita	Ton per 10,000 persons	Whole city	Negative	231.68	N/A	525.26	N/A	37	N/A	Environment Annual Report; City	
27	Ammonia/nitrogen emissions per unit of land area	Ton per km^2	Whole city	Negative	0.83	0.07	0.07	1	1	0	Environment Annual Report; City	
28	Ammonia/nitrogen emissions per capita	Ton per 10,000 persons	Whole city	Negative	12.50	16.62	17.22	29	31	2	Environment Annual Report; City	☺
29	Percentage of the days with air quality at or over level II in a year	%	District	Positive	89.45	99.73	99.70	4	5	1	MEP Data	☺
30	Percentage of days with respirable suspended particulates as the principal pollutants in a year	%	District	Negative	69.76	45.75	53.70	6	8	2	MEP Data	☺
31	Ratio of environmental spending to government expenditure	%	Whole city	Positive	3.14	4.91	6.06	4	2	−2	China Statistics; City	☹
32	Ratio of the investment in industrial pollution control to GDP	%	Whole city	Positive	0.09	0.34	0.50	2	2	0	Environment Annual Report; Regional Economy	

33	Ratio of the spending on science, education, culture, and public health to government expenditure	%	Whole city	Positive	21.06	36.66	39.08	1	1	0	China Statistics; City; Regional Economy	
34	Area of green land per capita in urban areas	m^2	District	Positive	58.13	59.00	55.93	10	11	1	City	☺
35	Green coverage of urban built-in areas	%	District	Positive	39.84	42.90	42.77	10	9	−1	Urban Construction	☹
36	Coverage of water supply	%	District	Positive	98.83	100.00	100.00	1	1	0	Urban Construction	
37	Treatment rate of urban household wastewater	%	District	Positive	86.16	92.12	91.81	12	6	−6	Urban Construction	☹
38	Harmless treatment of urban household waste	%	District	Positive	94.38	94.87	94.03	24	25	1	Urban Construction	☺
39	Public buses per 10,000 urban residents		District	Positive	15.51	7.97	12.20	35	26	−9	City	☹
40	Industrial SO_2 removal rate	%	Whole city	Positive	57.30	10.39	10.47	38	38	0	Environment Annual Report	
41	Industrial wastewater COD removal rate	%	Whole city	Positive	76.07	81.66	92.45	21	3	−18	Environment Annual Report	☹

(continued)

(continued)

No.	Indicator	Unit	Scope	Attribute	2010 average of 38 cities	2010 figure	2009 figure	2010 ranking	2009 ranking	Change in ranking	Source of 2010 data	Chernoff face
42	Industrial nitrogen oxide removal rate	%	Whole city	Positive	5.24	0.00	0.00	31	29	−2	Environment Annual Report	
43	Industrial waste water ammonia/nitrogen removal rate	%	Whole city	Positive	66.79	69.61	33.21	22	34	12	Environment Annual Report	

Note:
Regional Economy: *China Regional Economy Statistical Yearbook 2011*
City: *China City Statistical Yearbook 2011*
China Statistics: *China Statistical Yearbook 2011*
Urban Construction: *China Urban Construction Statistical Yearbook 2010*
Environment Annual Report: *China Environment Annual Report 2010*
Environmental Yearbook: *China Environmental Statistical Yearbook 2011*
MEP Data: Ministry of Environmental Protection Data Center

9.38 Brief Analysis of Green Development in Karamay

Karamay ranked 3rd among the 38 participating cities by GDI according to 2010 data, 1 place lower over 2009 (Karamay ranked 2nd in 2009). Following is a brief analysis of its score by each indicator and their changes from 2009 to 2010.

9.38.1 Karamay's 2010 Scores by GDI

Karamay scored 0.403 in 2010. From the three First-Class Indicators including GDEG, CCPNRE, and SDGP as shown in Fig. 9.75, Karamay showed obvious advantages in all three indicators especially in CCPNRE (Note: the national average value of each indicator is 0).

According to Fig. 9.76, Karamay surpassed the national average in 6 of Second-Class Indicators in 2010, which were GGEI, PII, SII, EPCCI, GII and II; it scored lower than the national average in 3 indicators which were TII, RAECI and EMI.

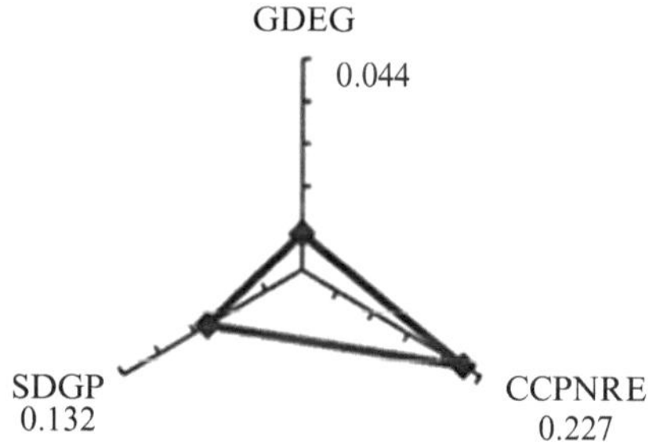

Fig. 9.75 Scores of Karamay by First-Class Indicators

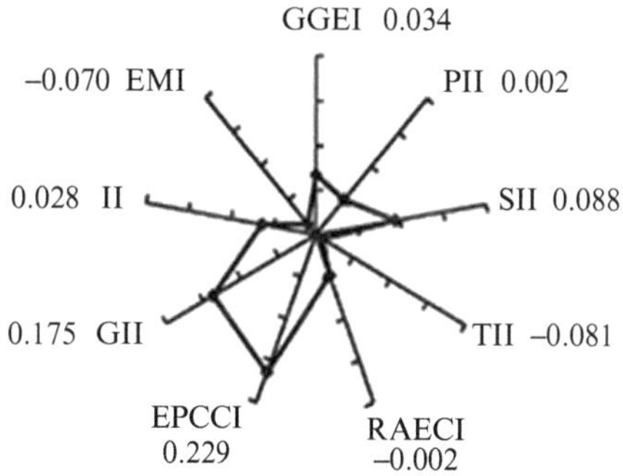

Fig. 9.76 Scores of Karamay by Second-Class Indicators

Table 9.75 Changes in Karamay's rankings by First-Class and Second-Class Indicators, 2009–2010

Indicator	2010	2009	Difference	Indicator	2010	2009	Difference
GDI	3	2	−1				
GDEG	11	5	−6	RAECI	14	13	−1
GGEI	8	4	−4	EPCCI	3	3	0
PII	6	7	1	SDGP	6	3	−3
SII	1	1	0	GII	1	1	0
TII	38	38	0	II	14	7	−7
CCPNRE	3	3	0	EMI	35	35	0

Note: A positive value in "Difference" means a rise in ranking

9.38.2 Changes in Karamay's GDI Rankings 2009–2010

According to Table 9.75, in First-Class Indicators, Karamay dropped by 6 and 3 places in GDEG and SDGP; it remained unchanged in CCPNRE. Judging from changes in ranking, it dropped by 7, 4 and 1 in II, GGEI and RAECI, it rose by 1 place in PII; it remained unchanged by SII, TII, EPCCI, GII and EMI as compared with that in 2009.

To further explain the causes of the changes in the rankings by First- and Second-Class Indicators, we put the Third-Class Indicators where a change of more than 3 places occurred from 2009 to 2010 as follows in Table 9.76. Compared with those in 2009, Karamay both out- and underperformed in ranking in 2010, while the more obvious trend is underperforming compared with the previous year. It dropped by 28 places in COD emissions per capita, 18 in Industrial wastewater COD removal rate, 15 in Electricity consumption per capita in urban areas, 13 in Water consumption per unit of value added created by industrial enterprises, 9 in Public buses per 10,000 urban residents, 7 in COD emissions per unit of GDP, 6 in Treatment rate of urban household wastewater, and it rose to some extent by 4 indicators which were Labor productivity of the tertiary sector, Recycling rate of industrial water, Energy consumption per unit of GDP and Labor productivity of the primary sector as compared with that in 2009.

Table 9.76 Third-Class Indicators where changes over 3 places occurred by Karamay, 2009–2010

	Original data for 2009 and 2010			Change in ranking		
Third-Class Indicator	2010	2009	Unit	2010	2009	Difference
Energy consumption per unit of GDP	1.34	1.70	Ton per 10,000 yuan	32	35	3
Electricity consumption per capita in urban areas	525.60	307.77	kWh per capita	23	8	−15
COD emissions per unit of GDP	11.80	5.95	Ton per 100million yuan	8	1	−7
Labor productivity of the primary sector	3.06	2.74	10,000 yuan per capita	4	7	3
Water consumption per unit of value added created by industrial enterprises	0.04	0.02	10,000 tons per 10,000 yuan	29	16	−13
Recycling rate of industrial water	96.63	94.56	%	2	10	8
Labor productivity of the tertiary sector	6.71	6.11	10,000 yuan per capita	11	32	21
COD emissions per capita	184.07	77.96	Ton per 10,000 persons	35	7	−28
Treatment rate of urban household wastewater	92.12	91.81	%	12	6	−6
Public buses per 10,000 urban residents	7.97	12.20		35	26	−9
Industrial wastewater COD removal rate	81.66	92.45	%	21	3	−18

Note: A positive value in "Difference" means a rise in ranking

Green development checkup-Lhasa

No.	Indicator	Unit	Scope	Attribute	2010 average of evaluated cities	2010 figure	2009 figure	Source of 2010 data
1	GDP per capita	Yuan	Whole city	Positive	55,399.15	23,775	20,264.00	Regional Economy
2	Energy consumption per unit of GDP	Ton per 10,000 yuan	Whole city	Negative	0.82	N/A	N/A	
3	Electricity consumption per capita in urban areas	kWh per capita	Whole city	Negative	580.70	N/A	N/A	
4	CO_2 emissions per unit of GDP			Negative	No data			
5	SO_2 emissions per unit of GDP	Ton per 100 million yuan	Whole city	Negative	42.67	N/A	8.67	
6	COD emissions per unit of GDP	Ton per 100 million yuan	Whole city	Negative	24.91	N/A	32.74	
7	Nitrogen oxide emissions per unit of GDP	Ton per 100 million yuan	Whole city	Negative	40.67	N/A	2.35	
8	Ammonia/nitrogen emissions per unit of GDP	Ton per 100 million yuan	Whole city	Negative	2.63	N/A	2.96	
9	Labor productivity of the primary sector	10,000 yuan per capita	Whole city	Positive	3.00	N/A	N/A	City; Lhasa
10	Labor productivity of the secondary sector	10,000 yuan per capita	Whole city	Positive	18.12	N/A	N/A	City; Lhasa
11	Water consumption per unit of value added created by industrial enterprises	10,000 tons per 10,000 yuan	Whole city	Negative	0.03	N/A	N/A	
12	Energy consumption per unit of value added created by industrial enterprises			Negative	No data			
13	Utilization rate industrial solid waste	%	Whole city	Positive	83.42	1.30	18.70	Environment Annual Report
14	Recycling rate of industrial water	%	Whole city	Positive	82.10	16.91	17.90	Environment Annual Report

15	Labor productivity of the tertiary sector	10,000 yuan per capita	Whole city	Positive	11.39	N/A	N/A	
16	Proportion of value added of tertiary sector in GDP	%	Whole city	Positive	48.37	N/A	64.60	
17	Proportion of tertiary sector employees in the total employed population	%	Whole city	Positive	46.83	N/A	N/A	Lhasa
18	Water resources per capita	m^3 per capita	Whole city	Positive	1,040.56	N/A	N/A	
19	CO_2 emissions per unit of land area			Negative	No data			
20	CO_2 emissions per capita			Negative	No data			
21	SO_2 emissions per unit of land area	Ton per km^2	Whole city	Negative	11.34	N/A	N/A	
22	SO_2 emissions per capita	Ton per 10,000 persons	Whole city	Negative	211.11	N/A	N/A	
23	COD emissions per unit of land area	Ton per km^2	Whole city	Negative	7.63	N/A	N/A	
24	COD emissions per capita	Ton per 10,000 persons	Whole city	Negative	117.25	N/A	N/A	
25	Nitrogen oxides emissions per unit of land area	Ton per km^2	Whole city	Negative	14.61	N/A	N/A	
26	Nitrogen oxides emissions per capita	Ton per 10,000 persons	Whole city	Negative	231.68	N/A	N/A	
27	Ammonia/nitrogen emissions per unit of land area	Ton per km^2	Whole city	Negative	0.83	N/A	N/A	
28	Ammonia/nitrogen emissions per capita	Ton per 10,000 persons	Whole city	Negative	12.50	N/A	N/A	
29	Percentage of the days with air quality at or over level II in a year	%	District	Positive	89.45	98.90	98.90	MEP Data
30	Percentage of days with respirable suspended particulates as the principal pollutants in a year	%	District	Negative	69.76	29.86	35.90	MEP Data
31	Ratio of environmental spending to government expenditure	%	Whole city	Positive	3.14	N/A	2.77	

(continued)

(continued)

No.	Indicator	Unit	Scope	Attribute	2010 average of evaluated cities	2010 figure	2009 figure	Source of 2010 data
32	Ratio of the investment in industrial pollution control to GDP	%	Whole city	Positive	0.09	N/A	N/A	
33	Ratio of the spending on science, education, culture, and public health to government expenditure	%	Whole city	Positive	21.06	N/A	N/A	
34	Area of green land per capita in urban areas		District	Positive	58.13	10.26	94.97	Lhasa
35	Green coverage of urban built-in areas	%	District	Positive	39.84	32.25	32.14	Urban Construction
36	Coverage of water supply	%	District	Positive	98.83	99.22	97.82	Urban Construction
37	Treatment rate of urban household wastewater	%	District	Positive	86.16	N/A	N/A	
38	Harmless treatment of urban household waste	%	District	Positive	94.38	N/A	N/A	
39	Public buses per 10,000 urban residents		District	Positive	15.51	11.64	6.14	Lhasa
40	Industrial SO_2 removal rate	%	Whole city	Positive	57.30	N/A	N/A	
41	Industrial wastewater COD removal rate	%	Whole city	Positive	76.07	8.24	7.00	Environment Annual Report
42	Industrial nitrogen oxide removal rate	%	Whole city	Positive	5.24	N/A	N/A	
43	Industrial waste water ammonia/nitrogen removal rate	%	Whole city	Positive	66.79	25.00	25.00	Environment Annual Report

Note:
Regional Economy: *China Regional Economy Statistical Yearbook 2011*
City: *China City Statistical Yearbook 2011*
China Statistics: *China Statistical Yearbook 2011*
Urban Construction: *China Urban Construction Statistical Yearbook 2010*
Environment Annual Report: *China Environment Annual Report 2010*
Environmental Yearbook: *China Environmental Statistical Yearbook 2011*
MEP Data: Ministry of Environmental Protection Data Center
Lhasa: *Lhasa Statistical Yearbook 2011*

9.39 Brief Analysis of Green Development in Lhasa

In the 2012 GDI system, data of only 11 out of 43 Third-Class Indicators could be obtained from authoritative yearbooks published, and not others, therefore Lhasa was not included in the 38 participating cities this year.

Among the 11 Third-Class Indicators where data were available, 3 belonged to the category of GDEG, one of the First-Class Indicators, which were GDP per capita, Utilization rate industrial solid waste and Recycling rate of industrial water, while the first one belonged to Economic Development Efficiency, one of Second-Class Indicators, and the second and third fell to Second Industry, another Second-Class Indicators. Two indicators belonged to CCPNRE, one of First-Class Indicators, which were Percentage of the days with air quality at or over level II in a year and Percentage of days with respirable suspended particulates as the principal pollutants in a year, which fell into EPCCI, one of Second-Class Indicators; 6 indicators belonged to SDGP, one of the First-Class Indicators, which were Area of green land per capita in urban areas, Green coverage of urban built-in areas, Coverage of water supply, Public buses per 10,000 urban residents, Industrial wastewater COD removal rate and Industrial waste water ammonia/nitrogen removal rate, among which Area of green land per capita in urban areas belonged to Green Investment, one of Second-Class Indicators, and Industrial waste water ammonia/nitrogen removal rate belonged to Environmental Management Indicator, another Second-Class Indicators, and other belonged to the category of II.

A brief analysis within a limited scope can be drawn on green development of Lhasa from data of all indicators of Lhasa in 2009 and 2010 as well as the average of participating cities in 2010. Details are set out in Table 9.77.

9.39.1 Green Development in Lhasa in 2010

Green development in Lhasa in 2010 can be understood from a comparison of indicators of Lhasa in 2010 and the average of participating cities in 2010.

According to Table 9.77, only 3 indicators beat the average of 38 participating cities among the 11 indicators of Lhasa in 2010, which were Percentage of the days with air quality at or over level II in a year, Percentage of days with respirable suspended particulates as the principal pollutants in a year and Coverage of water supply, the first two belonged to the indicator of CCPNRE, and the third one belonged to SDGP. Though with 3 indicators standing advantages as compared to the average of participating cities, the margins of 2 of them were not obvious except Percentage of days with respirable suspended particulates as the principal pollutants in a year, a negatively-correlated indicator. 8 indicators scored lower than the average of 38 participating cities including 3 indicators under GDEG, and 5 indicators under SDGP. Except that the scores of Green coverage of urban built-in areas and Public buses per 10,000 urban residents were slightly lower than the national average, the other 5 indicators had a large difference to the average of participating cities.

Table 9.77 Lhasa's 11 Third-Class Indicators where data are available, 2009–2010

Indicator	Unit	Scope	Attribute	2010 figure	2010 average of evaluated cities	2009 figure
GDP per capita	Yuan	Whole city	Positive	23,775.00	55,399.15	20,264.00
Utilization rate industrial solid waste	%	Whole city	Positive	1.30	83.42	18.70
Recycling rate of industrial water	%	Whole city	Positive	16.91	82.10	17.90
Percentage of the days with air quality at or over level II in a year	%	District	Positive	98.90	89.45	98.90
Percentage of days with respirable suspended particulates as the principal pollutants in a year	%	District	Negative	29.86	69.76	35.90
Area of green land per capita in urban areas	m^2	District	Positive	10.26	58.13	94.97
Green coverage of urban built-in areas	%	District	Positive	32.25	39.84	32.14
Coverage of water supply	%	District	Positive	99.22	98.83	97.82
Public buses per 10,000 urban residents		District	Positive	11.64	15.51	6.14
Industrial wastewater COD removal rate	%	Whole city	Positive	8.24	76.07	7.00
Industrial waste water ammonia/nitrogen removal rate	%	Whole city	Positive	25.00	66.79	25.00

The 11 Third-Class Indicators of Lhasa available indicate that green development of Lhasa in 2010 lagged behind the national average. From the three aspects of green development, Lhasa scored lower than the national average except for CCPNRE.

9.39.2 Changes in Green Development in Lhasa 2009–2010

The change from 2009 to 2010 in green development of Lhasa can be found from the comparison of 2009 and 2010 data. It is clear where the city progressed and where it regressed.

In GDEG, 1 out of 3 indicators progressed as compared with that in 2009, which was GDP per capita; 1 indicator suffered from setback, which was Recycling rate of industrial water; 1 indicator experienced dramatic oscillation between the 2 years, and we deem that this singular value may due to various reasons such as inconsistencies in statistical standards.

In CCPNRE, among the 2 indicators of 2010, the indicator of Percentage of days with respirable suspended particulates as the principal pollutants in a year achieved a dramatic rise. The indicator of Percentage of the days with air quality at or over level II in a year remained unchanged as compared with that in 2009.

In SDGP, except for Area of green land per capita in urban areas which we think a singular value exists, and Industrial waste water ammonia/nitrogen removal rate remained unchanged in 2009, the rest 4 indicators achieved progress, and some progressed a lot, such as Public buses per 10,000 urban residents.

The above analysis indicates that of the 11 Third-Class Indicators where data were available in 2010, except for 2 indicators containing singular values, 6 of the rest 9 indicators progressed as compared with those in 2009, 2 remained unchanged, and only 1 fell behind. It means that though still not as good as the national average, green development of Lhasa in 2010 achieved obvious progress as compared with that in 2009.

Part III
Public Opinions

During the GDI evaluation and at the press conference for the launch of the *China Green Development Index Report*, friends of all sectors, the press in particular, shared the same concern with us that the province and city rankings by the GDI worked out only based on statistical data might differ from what the public think of green development. In light of that, we have conducted the survey on public satisfaction with urban green development for the 2012 report to obtain local residents' opinions on the green development in their city, which will help us to get a full picture of how green development goes in the evaluated cities. This part consists of Chap. 10 Questionnaire Design for the Survey on Public Satisfaction with Urban Green Development and Chap. 11 Survey on Public Satisfaction with Urban Green Development: Results and Analysis. We appreciate comments on the questionnaire design and survey results and would make further improvements.

Chapter 10
Questionnaire Design for the Survey on Public Satisfaction with Urban Green Development

Jiancheng Pan, Junli Zhao, and Yajing Cong

One of the objectives of future economic development of cities is to promote green development. The opinions of urban residents, who are both participants and beneficiaries of urban green development, help us to get a clearer picture of how green development goes in cities. In light of that, we carried out the Survey on Public Satisfaction with Urban Green Development in May 2012, which served as an important supplement to the CGDI evaluation based on statistical data.

First of all, it is essential to design a questionnaire for the public survey, which not only reflects the state of green development but also is closely associated to GDI measurement. The research group held three expert seminars, and China Economic Monitoring and Analysis Center of the National Bureau of Statistics of China also convened several expert seminars and work meetings concerning the design of the questionnaire. Consensus has been reached on respondents' general information, survey area, sampling methods, understandability and accuracy of questions, and satisfaction levels. Multiple drafts concluded into the Questionnaire for the 2012 Survey on Public Satisfaction with Urban Green Development including 19 questions in four parts as shown below:

Questionnaire for the 2012 Survey on Public Satisfaction with Urban Green Development

Screening information
A1 Age of the respondent
Under 18 (survey stops)
2.18–40
3.41–60

Jingya Cong, Xiaoyan Tan and Jingli Xing from the National Bureau of Statistics of China participated in the design, implementation, data calculation and preparation of report.

J. Pan (✉) • J. Zhao • Y. Cong
China Economic Monitoring and Analysis Center, National Bureau of Statistics of China, Beijing, China
e-mail: panjc@stats.gov.cn; zhaojl@stats.gov.cn; congyajing@stats.gov.cn

X. Li and J. Pan (eds.), *China Green Development Index Report 2012: Regional Comparison*, Current Chinese Economic Report Series,
DOI 10.1007/978-3-642-54178-0_10,

4.61 and above
A2 How long has the respondent resided in this city?
1. Less than 6 months (survey stops)
2. Six months to 1 year
3. 1–3 years
4. More than 3 years

General information of the respondent
City (to be provided by the interviewer)
A3 Gender of the respondent (to be provided by the interviewer)
1. Male 2. Female
A4 Do you have the household registration of the city?
1. Yes
2. No
A5 Your educational attainment
1. Junior college or above
2. High school or technical secondary school
3. Middle school

Part 1: Opinion on urban environment
Q1 How do you rate the street sanitation?
1. Good
2. Average
3. Poor
Q2 How do you rate the drinking water of the city?
1. Good
2. Average
3. Poor
Q3 How do you rate the pollution of rivers and lakes in the city?
1. No pollution
2. Little pollution
3. Serious pollution
4. I don't know/care
Q4 How do you rate the air quality in the city?
1. Good
2. Average
3. Poor
Q5 What are the major sources of pollution in the city? (max. three options)
1. Motor vehicle exhaust
2. Cooking fume created by catering facilities
3. Pollutant discharge from plants
4. Household waste
5. Agricultural pollution
6. Electromagnetic radiation pollution
7. Plastic bags/lunch boxes
8. Noises (transport, construction, entertainment facilities, etc)

Q6 How has the urban environment changed in the past three years?
1. It gets better
2. It is the same
3. It gets worse

Part 2: Opinion on urban infrastructure
Q7 How do you rate the greening of the city?
1. Good
2. Average
3. Poor
Q8 How do you rate the number and locations of public leisure facilities?
1. Good
2. Average
3. Poor
Why not satisfied?
1. There are too few
2. They are not located very well
3. Other (please specify)
Q9 How do you rate the household waste disposal in your neighborhood?
1. Good
2. Average
3. Poor
Q10 How do you rate the public transport accessibility in the city?
1. Good
2. Average
3. Poor
Q11 How do you rate the traffic in the city?
1. Good
2. Average
3. Poor
Q12 What means of transport do you usually use?
1. I drive (automobile/motorcycle)
2. I use public transport (bus/subway)
3. I take a taxi
4. I ride a bicycle/battery bicycle or walk
5. Other

Part 3: Opinion on government's green actions
Q13 How do you rate the waste separation facilities in the city?
1. Good
2. Average
3. Poor
Q14 How do you rate the safety of daily foods?
1. Good
2. Average
3. Poor

Q15 Do you know how to file a complaint about environmental problems? (website or telephone)
1. Yes
2. Yes, but I forgot it
3. Not at all
Have you ever filed such a complaint?
1. Yes
2. No (go to Q16)
How do you rate the result of complaint handling?
1. Good
2. Average
3. Poor
Q16 How do you rate the effectiveness of the control of pollution caused by enterprises?
1. Good
2. Average
3. Poor
Q17 How do you rate the importance attached by the government to environmental protection?
1. Good
2. Average
3. Poor

Part 4: General
Q18 In general, how do you rate the city where you live?
1. Good
2. Average
3. Poor
Q19 What is the average monthly income of your family (including salaries and other sources of all family members)?
1. Less than RMB 3,00.
2. RMB 3,000 to 7,00.
3. RMB 7,000 to 12,000
4. More than RMB 12,000

The questions mainly are about the general assessment of residents on the city's environment, infrastructure and government's green actions. Of them, environment includes street sanitation, drinking water, pollution of rivers and lakes, air quality and environmental changes in recent 3 years; infrastructure includes greening, number and locations of public leisure facilities, household waste disposal, public transport accessibility, and traffic; and government's green actions includes waste separation facilities, food safety, awareness of filing complaints about environmental problems, effectiveness of enterprises' pollution control, and importance attached by the government to environmental protection.

The survey covered 38 key cities of China, including 16 eastern cities: Beijing, Tianjin, Shijiazhuang, Shanghai, Nanjing, Suzhou, Hangzhou, Ningbo, Fuzhou,

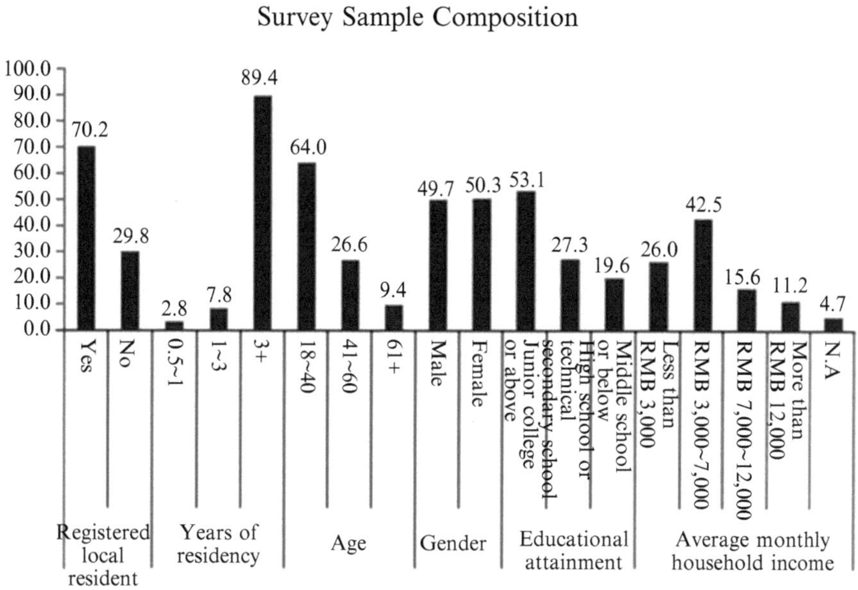

Fig. 10.1 Survey sample composition

Xiamen, Jinan, Qingdao, Guangzhou, Shenzhen, Zhuhai and Haikou; 6 central cities: Taiyuan, Hefei, Nanchang, Zhengzhou, Wuhan and Changsha; 12 western cities: Hohhot, Nanning, Chongqing, Chengdu, Guiyang, Kunming, Xi'an, Lanzhou, Xining, Yinchuan, Urumqi and Karamay; and 4 northeastern cities: Shenyang, Dalian, Changchun and Harbin.

We surveyed by telephone 700 urban residents chosen at random from each city. As shown in Fig. 10.1, from the perspective of household registration, 70.2 % of the respondents are registered in the city and 29.8 % are registered elsewhere. 89.4 % of the respondents have resided in the city for more than 3 years and 10.6 % for 6 months to 3 years.

From the perspective of age, 64.0 % of the respondents are aged 18–40, 26.6 % were aged 41–60 and 9.4 % are aged 61 or above. From the perspective of gender, 49.7 % are men and 50.3 % are women. From the perspective of educational attainment, 53.1 % have received senior college education or above, 27.3 % have received high school or technical secondary school education, and 19.6 % have received middle school education or below. From the perspective of income, 42.5 % of the respondents reported average monthly household income[1] between RMB 3,000 and 7,000, 26.0 % reported less than RMB 3,000, 15.6 % reported RMB 7,000–12,000, and 11.2 % reported more than 12,000. The survey samples are reasonably distributed to well represent city residents in different area and of different groups.

[1] Including salaries and other sources of all family members.

Based on experts' views, we devised the method of measuring public satisfaction with urban green development as follow:

First, score of questions with three options (Good, Average, Poor): the three options are assigned values 1, 0 and −1 respectively, and the core of a question is calculated as: suppose $X_1 = 1$, $X_2 = 0$, $X_3 = -1$, then the score of a question Qj = (N1*X1 + N2*X2 + N3*X3)/N. In the formula, N_i is the number of respondents who had chosen X_i, N is the total number of respondents who had replied the question, and X_i is the value of each option.

Questions with more than three options, such as Q5, Q12, Q18 and Q19 are not accounted to the measurement of satisfaction. They serve as referential indicators for further study.

Second, scores of urban environment, infrastructure and government's green actions are the arithmetic mean of scores of the related questions, i.e.:

Score of urban environment = (Q1 + Q2 + Q3 + Q4 + Q6)/5
Score of urban infrastructure = (Q7 + Q8 + Q9 + Q10 + Q11)/5
Score of government's green actions = (Q13 + Q14 + Q151 + Q16 + Q18)/5

Third, score of the overall satisfaction of city green development is the arithmetic mean of the scores of the above three indicators, ranging from −1 to 1, with 0 as the critical value. A score of positive value means "satisfied", and a score of negative value means "unsatisfied". The higher the value is, the more satisfactory the green development is, and vice versa.

Chapter 11
Survey on Public Satisfaction with Urban Green Development: Results and Analysis

Jiancheng Pan, Junli Zhao, and Degang Jia

The survey shows: the score of overall satisfaction with urban green development is 0.121 and the urban residents generally hold a positive attitude to green development. However, there is still some gap between the state of green development and public expectations. The overall satisfaction varies greatly from city to city, with western cities ranking the highest, eastern and northeastern regions relatively high, and Central China the lowest. Among the indicators of satisfaction, the satisfaction with the urban environment and infrastructure is higher, but residents are dissatisfied with the government's green actions, showing that the government should introduce more targeted and effective policies to support urban green development.

11.1 Urban Residents Are Positive to the State of Green Development, and Satisfaction Varies Greatly from City to City

It shows in the survey on public satisfaction with urban green development in the year of 2012 that the average overall satisfaction with the green development of 38 cities is 0.121 (Table 11.1) and the urban residents are generally positive to the state of green development; however, the satisfaction value is relatively low, indicating some gap between the state of urban green development and the residents' expectations. The inter-city difference is relatively large in the satisfaction with the green development, with the western region ranking the highest, the eastern and northeastern regions relatively high and the central region the lowest.

J. Pan (✉) • J. Zhao • D. Jia
China Economic Monitoring and Analysis Center,
National Bureau of Statistics of China, Beijing, China
e-mail: panjc@gj.stats.cn; zhaojl@gj.stats.cn; jiadg@gj.stats.cn

X. Li and J. Pan (eds.), *China Green Development Index Report 2012: Regional Comparison*, Current Chinese Economic Report Series,
DOI 10.1007/978-3-642-54178-0_11,

Table 11.1 Public satisfaction with urban green development (2012)

Cities	Overall satisfaction with green development		Satisfaction with urban environment		Satisfaction with urban infrastructure		Satisfaction with government's green actions	
	Ranking	Score	Ranking	Score	Ranking	Score	Ranking	Score
Average		0.121		0.233		0.227		−0.098
Karamay	1	0.558	1	0.715	1	0.699	1	0.259
Yinchuan	2	0.308	3	0.487	3	0.425	3	0.013
Xining	3	0.280	2	0.496	8	0.360	7	−0.015
Xiamen	4	0.273	6	0.391	2	0.435	5	−0.007
Hangzhou	5	0.265	4	0.413	7	0.378	4	0.005
Chongqing	6	0.258	10	0.350	4	0.392	2	0.033
Chengdu	7	0.224	12	0.334	9	0.349	6	−0.010
Zhuhai	8	0.220	9	0.359	5	0.391	16	−0.089
Qingdao	9	0.220	5	0.395	11	0.338	14	−0.073
Ningbo	10	0.210	14	0.290	6	0.381	8	−0.041
Changchun	11	0.205	8	0.362	13	0.302	9	−0.047
Nanning	12	0.177	11	0.341	15	0.256	12	−0.067
Dalian	13	0.171	15	0.278	10	0.347	19	−0.113
Suzhou	14	0.161	17	0.238	12	0.308	11	−0.064
Haikou	15	0.148	7	0.380	22	0.189	21	−0.124
Jinan	16	0.125	20	0.198	16	0.255	15	−0.078
Kunming	17	0.123	18	0.226	18	0.218	13	−0.073
Xi'an	18	0.118	16	0.265	20	0.207	20	−0.118
Guiyang	19	0.109	13	0.296	33	0.083	10	−0.050
Shenzhen	20	0.088	28	0.135	14	0.273	25	−0.143
Urumqi	21	0.069	23	0.154	28	0.149	17	−0.097
Shijiazhuang	22	0.064	30	0.117	19	0.215	24	−0.140
Taiyuan	23	0.055	25	0.148	30	0.125	18	−0.108
Fuzhou	24	0.053	26	0.143	25	0.172	30	−0.156
Nanchang	25	0.050	19	0.218	35	0.075	26	−0.145
Shanghai	26	0.047	36	0.065	21	0.203	23	−0.126
Zhengzhou	27	0.044	31	0.109	26	0.169	27	−0.147
Guangzhou	28	0.043	35	0.068	23	0.186	22	−0.125
Nanjing	29	0.039	34	0.070	17	0.222	32	−0.176
Tianjin	30	0.038	32	0.107	24	0.181	31	−0.175
Shenyang	31	0.038	24	0.152	29	0.146	34	−0.185
Harbin	32	0.035	21	0.195	32	0.087	33	−0.176
Beijing	33	0.035	33	0.100	27	0.158	29	−0.153
Hefei	34	0.035	22	0.167	31	0.087	28	−0.150
Changsha	35	0.009	27	0.141	34	0.077	35	−0.192
Hohhot	36	−0.036	29	0.132	36	−0.036	36	−0.203
Wuhan	37	−0.120	37	−0.054	37	−0.080	37	−0.224
Lanzhou	38	−0.137	38	−0.067	38	−0.085	38	−0.257

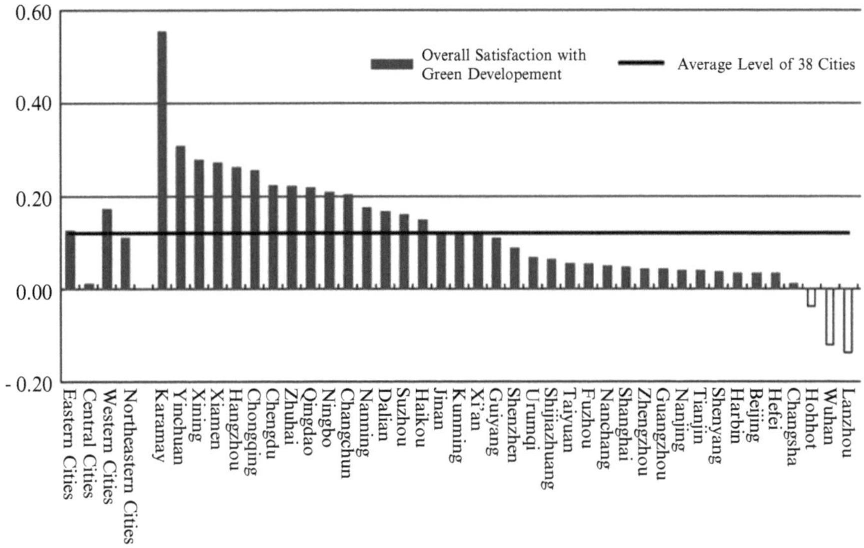

Fig. 11.1 Overall satisfaction with urban green development

By region, the eastern, central, western and northeastern cities score 0.127, 0.012, 0.171 and 0.112 in overall satisfaction with urban green development respectively (Fig. 11.1); the western cities enjoy the highest overall satisfaction but have the greatest inter-city difference with 0.695 between Karamay the highest and Lanzhou the lowest and 0.445 between Yinchuan the second and Lanzhou; among 12 western cities, five of them rank among the top 10, four from 11 to 20 and three from 21 to 38. The eastern cities enjoy a relatively high satisfaction with the score slightly higher than the average of all cities; they have a relatively high inter-city difference with 0.238 between Xiamen the highest and Beijing the lowest; among 16 eastern cities, five of them rank among the top 10, four from 11 to 20 and seven from 21 to 38. The northeastern cities are relatively low, slightly lower than the average level; the inter-city difference is the smallest with 0.170 between Changchun the highest and Harbin the lowest; among the four northeast cities, two of them rank from 11 to 20 and two from 21 to 38.

The central cities have the lowest satisfaction, slightly higher than zero; the inter-city difference is relatively small with 0.175 between Taiyuan the highest and Wuhan the lowest; all the six central cities rank from 21 to 38.

By cities, the inter-city difference is relatively great with 0.445 between Yinchuan the second[1] and Lanzhou the lowest. The overwhelming majority of cities (35) enjoy

[1] ①The scores of Karamay are significantly higher than other cities in terms of the overall satisfaction and three indicators, and even 0.2 higher than the city ranking the second. Therefore, in order to avoid the exaggeration of the inter-city differences, we only compare cities from the second to the 38th in terms of the inter-city difference unless otherwise specified.

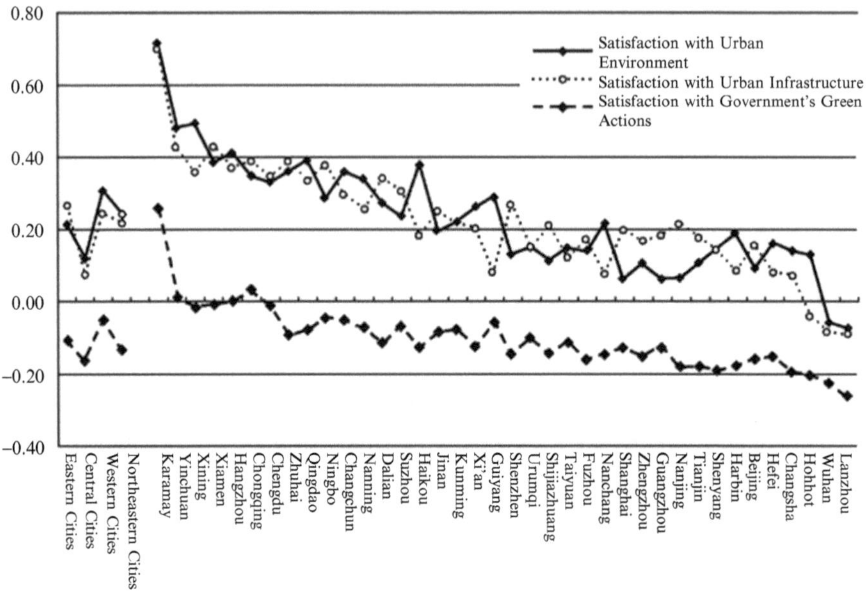

Fig. 11.2 Satisfaction with urban green development by indicators

an overall satisfaction with green development above zero; 17 of them are higher than the average level with Karamay, Yinchuan, Xining, Xiamen, Hangzhou, Chongqing, Chengdu, Zhuhai, Qingdao and Ningbo ranking the top 10; 21 of them are below the average level with three cities—Hohhot, Wuhan and Lanzhou—score negative. All of the top three and two of the lowest three are the western cities, showing great difference of satisfaction among the western cities.

The three indicators under overall satisfaction with urban green development are Satisfaction with Urban Environment, Satisfaction with Urban Infrastructure and Satisfaction with Government's Green Actions, which score 0.233, 0.227 and −0.098 respectively; the inter-city differences in satisfaction with environment and infrastructure are relatively great with 0.563 and 0.520 between the second and the lowest respectively; the inter-city difference in satisfaction with government's green actions is relatively small with 0.290 between the second and the lowest. The survey shows that residents are highly satisfied with the urban environment and infrastructure but generally dissatisfied with the implementation of government's relevant policies and measures.

By regions, the satisfactions with urban environment and infrastructure are much higher than the satisfaction with government's green actions in the eastern, central, western and northeastern cities; in addition, the satisfaction with urban environment is slightly lower than the satisfaction with infrastructure in the eastern cities and slightly higher than that in the central, western and northeastern cities (Fig. 11.2).

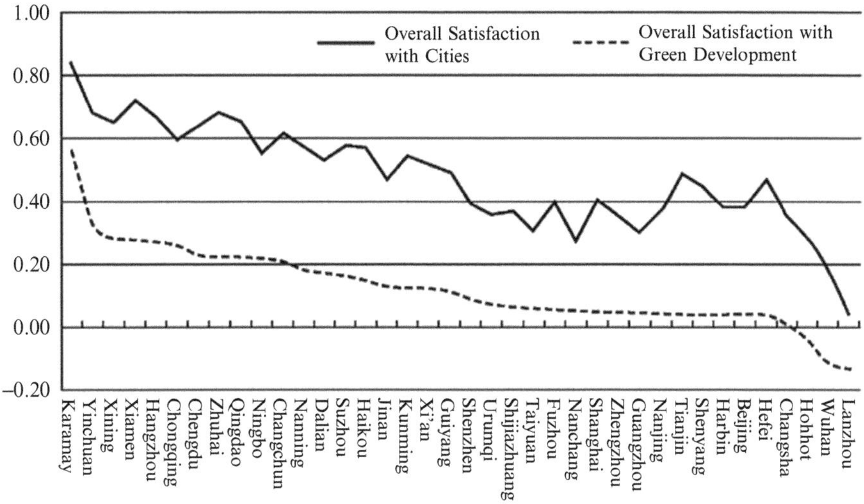

Fig. 11.3 Comparison between the overall satisfaction with cities and the overall satisfaction with green development

By cities, residents in most cities are highly satisfied with the urban environment and infrastructure but dissatisfied with the relevant policies and measures adopted by the government; it is the same case in 38 cities that the satisfactions with environment and infrastructure are much higher than the satisfaction with the government's green actions. The survey shows that the government's policies, failing to offer sufficient support for green development, have a great difference with the urban residents' expectations. It is very necessary for the government to meet the needs of urban residents and take more active measures to promote urban green development.

The survey further shows that the residents are generally very satisfied with the city where they live with 38 cities scoring up to 0.475 in the average of satisfaction, almost three times higher than satisfaction with green development. Among them, 53.7 % of the residents express satisfaction with the city where they live and only 6.1 % clearly express dissatisfaction. Apart from the level of urban green development, the residents' evaluation of the city where they live includes the employment, income, education, medical services and cultural lives with more extensive meanings. Residents' overall satisfaction with the city is much higher than the overall satisfaction with green development (Fig. 11.3), which shows that the government is imperative to promote green development, an area to be strengthened in the development of the city. In addition, the two satisfactions are highly related with the correlation coefficient up to 0.926, indicating the great significance of green development to the overall satisfaction with the city.

11.2 Urban Residents' Satisfaction with the Urban Environment Is Relatively High and the Inter-city Difference Is Relatively Great

Satisfaction with urban environment refers to the residents' comprehensive evaluation of five indicators of the city where they live— street sanitation, drinking water, pollution degree of rivers and lakes, air quality and urban environment changes in the past 3 years. The survey shows that the average satisfaction with the current urban environment of the 38 cities is 0.233 (Fig. 11.4), indicating that residents are relatively positive to the current urban environment, but there is still large room for the improvement of the quality of the urban environment. The inter-city difference is great, characterized by the western economic region having the highest satisfaction, the northeastern and the eastern the relatively high and the central the slightly low.

By areas, satisfactions with the urban environment of the eastern, central, western and northeastern areas are 0.216, 0.121, 0.309 and 0.246 respectively. The western cities enjoy the highest satisfaction and greatest inter-city difference with 0.563 between Xining the second highest and Lanzhou the lowest; among 12 western cities, four of them rank among the top 10, five from 11 to 20, and three from 21 to 38. The northeastern cities have the satisfaction slightly higher than the average with the smallest inter-city difference with 0.210 between Changchun the highest and Shenyang the lowest; among four northeastern cities, one of them ranks among the top 10, one from 11 to 20 and two from 21 to 38. The eastern cities have the satisfaction slightly lower than the average and the relatively great inter-city difference with 0.348 between Hangzhou the highest and Shanghai the lowest; among 16 eastern cities, five of them rank among the top 10, three from 11 to 20 and eight from 21 to 38. The central cities have relatively low satisfaction and small inter-city difference with 0.272 between Nanchang the highest and Wuhan the lowest; among six central cities, one of them ranks from 11 to 20 and five from 21to 38.

By cities, 36 cities have the satisfaction with their environment above zero, showing residents' positive evaluation; 17 of all cities are higher than the average, with Karamay, Xining, Yinchuan, Hangzhou, Qingdao, Xiamen, Haikou, Changchun, Zhuhai and Chongqing ranking the top 10 in order; 21 of them are lower than the average with two cities—Wuhan and Lanzhou—below zero.

Among five indicators of the urban environment, residents are most satisfied with the urban environment changes in the past 3 years, relatively satisfied with the urban drinking water, street sanitation and air quality, and dissatisfied with the pollution degree of urban rivers and lakes (Fig. 11.5).

Residents' satisfaction with the urban environment changes in the past 3 years is 0.578 with up to 69.8 % of the survey respondents considering the urban environment to be better in the past 3 years, 18.2 % unchanged, and 12.0 % worse. By cities, residents' satisfaction with environment changes of all 38 cities are far above zero (Fig. 11.6), of which 17 are higher than the average with Karamay, Xining,

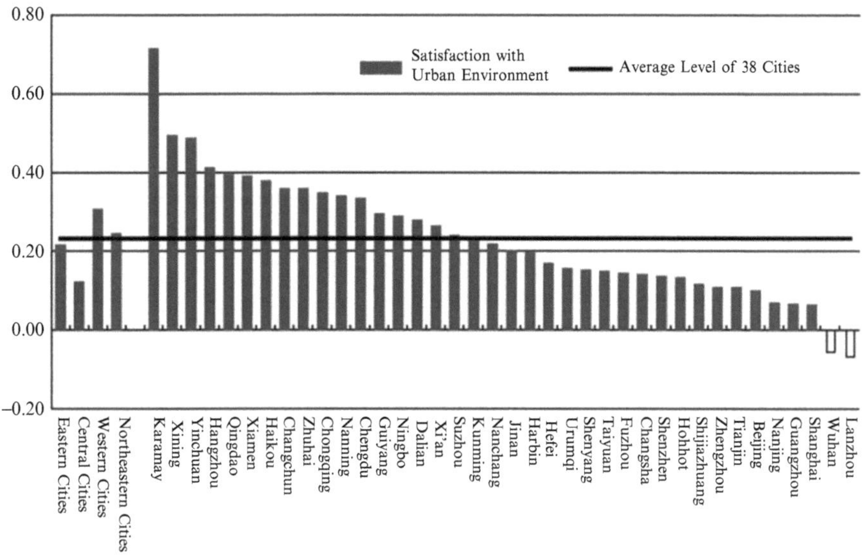

Fig. 11.4 Satisfaction with urban environment

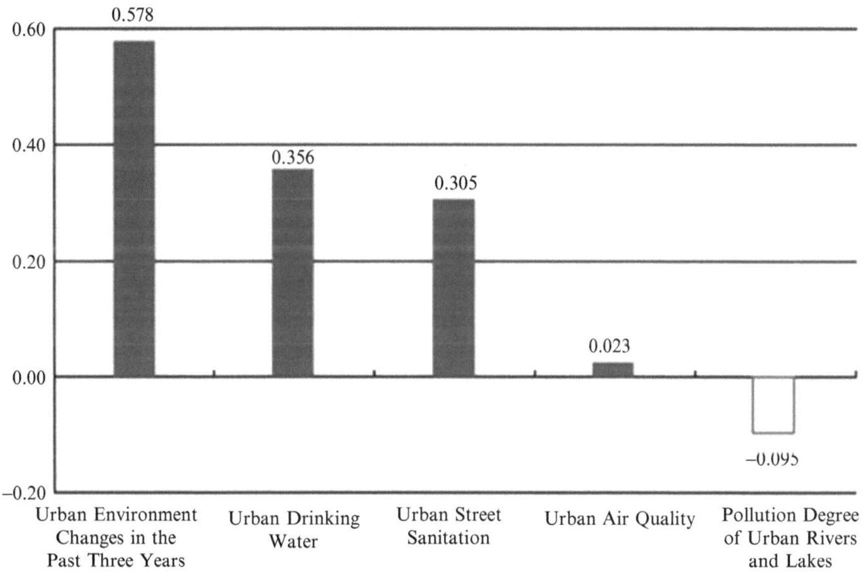

Fig. 11.5 Satisfaction with urban environment by indicators

Taiyuan, Chongqing, Guiyang, Shijiazhuang, Yinchuan, Changchun, Tianjin and Chengdu ranking the top 10 in order; 21 are lower than the average with Nanjing, Zhuhai, Wuhan, Shanghai and Dalian ranking the last five.

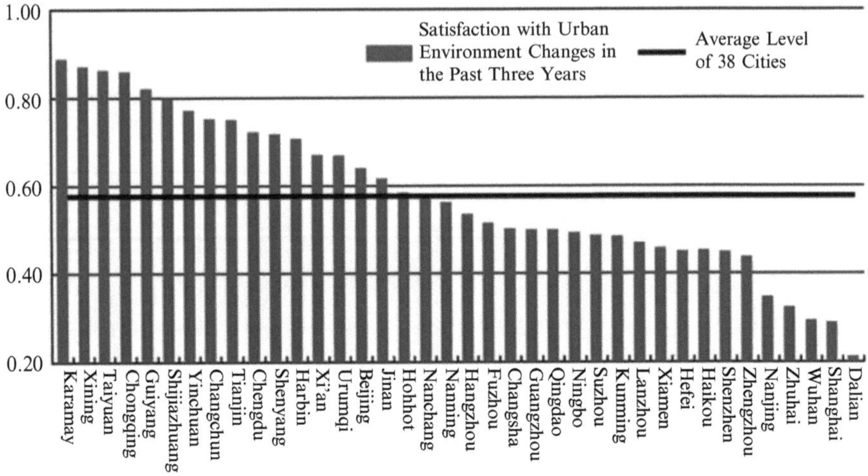

Fig. 11.6 Satisfaction with urban environment changes in the past 3 Years

Satisfaction with urban drinking water is 0.356 with 48.4 % of the survey respondents choosing “satisfied” with the drinking water of the city where they live, 38.7 % “general”, and 12.9 % “dissatisfied”. By cities, residents of the overwhelming majority of the cities (37) express the overall satisfaction with the drinking water and only one city is dissatisfied (Fig. 11.7). Twenty-one of these cities are higher than the average with Karamay, Xining, Yinchuan, Hangzhou, Kunming, Ningbo, Qingdao, Nanjing, Hefei and Xi’an ranking the top 10 in order; 17 are lower than the average with Shijiazhuang below zero.

Satisfaction with urban street sanitation is 0.305 with 40.9 % of the residents considering the streets of the city where they live “clean”, 48.8 % “general” and 10.3 % “dirty”. By cities, residents of the majority of cities (35) express the overall satisfaction with the street sanitation and only three cities are dissatisfied (Fig. 11.8). Seventeen of these cities are higher than the average with Karamay, Xiamen, Hangzhou, Xining, Yinchuan, Zhuhai, Chengdu, Dalian, Nanning and Qingdao ranking the top 10 in order; 21 are lower than the average with three cities—Hohhot, Wuhan and Lanzhou—below zero.

Satisfaction with urban air quality is relatively low, only scoring 0.023 with only 25.4 % of the survey respondents considering the air quality of the city where they live “good”, 51.4 % “general” and 23.2 % “bad”. By cities, residents of 20 cities are satisfied with the urban air quality and 18 dissatisfied (Fig. 11.9). Nineteen of these cities are higher than the average with Haikou, Zhuhai, Karamay, Qingdao, Xiamen, Xining, Yinchuan, Dalian, Guiyang and Nanning ranking the top 10 in order; 19 are lower than the average with Tianjin, Beijing, Nanjing, Wuhan and Lanzhou ranking the last five.

In the five indicators, satisfaction with pollution degree of urban rivers and lakes is the lowest, scoring −0.095 with only 13.5 % of the survey respondents considering the rivers and lakes of the city where they live “unpolluted”, 63.5 % “slightly

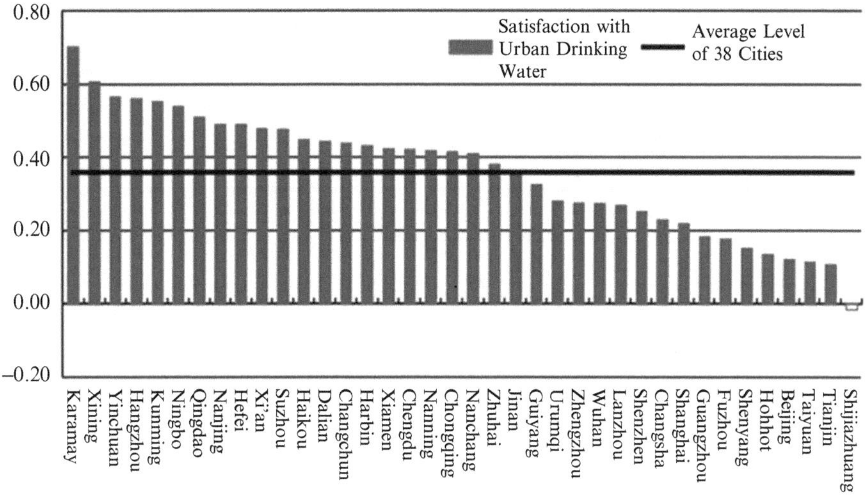

Fig. 11.7 Satisfaction with urban drinking water

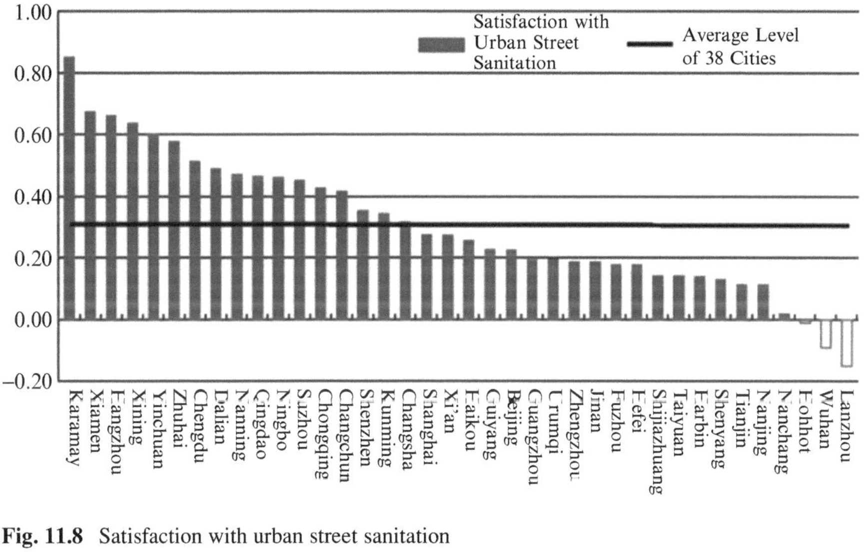

Fig. 11.8 Satisfaction with urban street sanitation

polluted" and 23.0 % "seriously polluted". By cities, the majority of urban residents are dissatisfied with up to 27 cities below zero and only 11 cities satisfaction with pollution degree of urban rivers and lakes above zero (Fig. 11.10). Eighteen of these cities are higher than the average with Karamay, Yinchuan, Qingdao, Hangzhou, Haikou, Xining, Nanning, Xiamen, Changchun and Nanchang ranking the top 10 in order; 20 are lower than the average with Nanjing, Wuhan, Lanzhou, Guangzhou and Kunming ranking the last five.

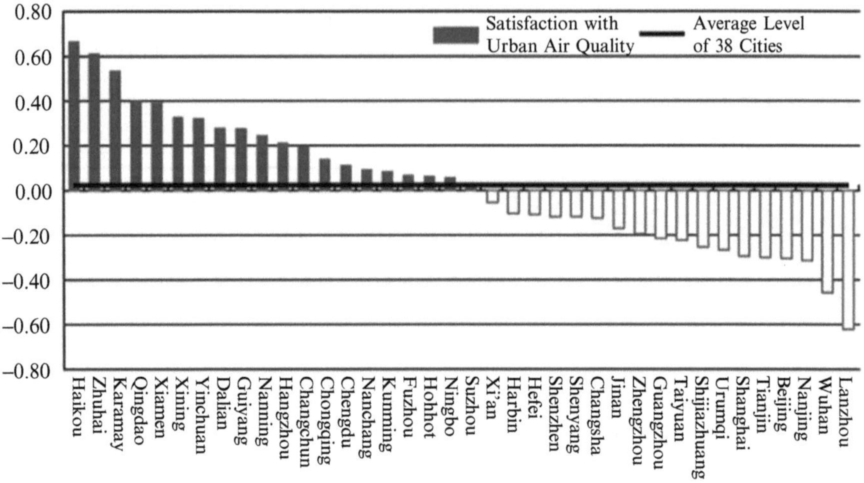

Fig. 11.9 Satisfaction with urban air quality

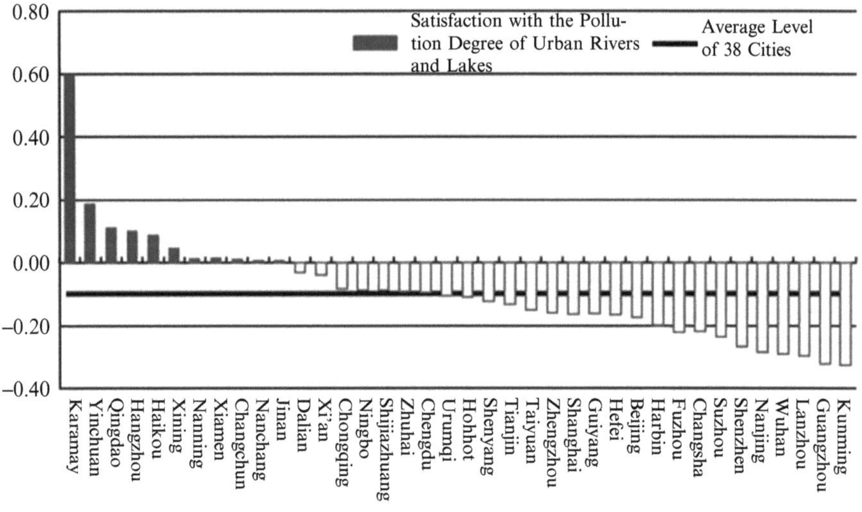

Fig. 11.10 Satisfaction with pollution degree of urban rivers and lakes

For the most polluted aspects of the cities, the survey shows that residents believe that motor vehicle exhaust pollution is the most serious, with 67.3 % choosing this item; the relatively serious pollutions are in order the household waste pollution (34.8 %), noise pollution[2] (26.9 %), industrial waste (26.8 %) and plastic bags or

[2] Including traffic noise, construction noise and entertainment noise etc.

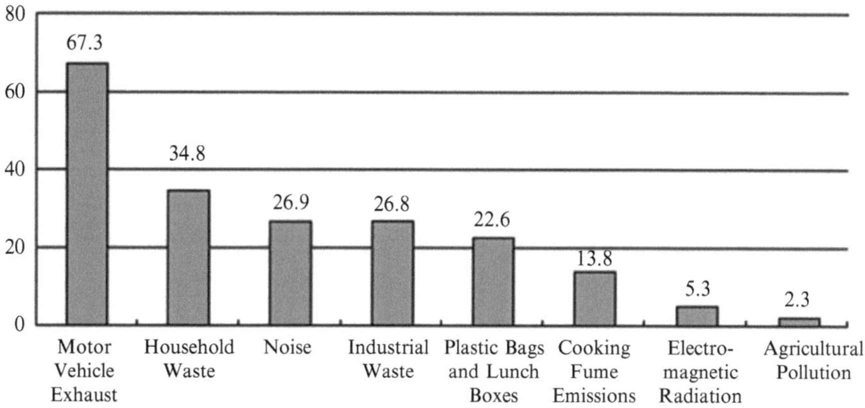

Fig. 11.11 Most seriously polluted areas in 38 cities (%)

plastic lunch boxes pollution (22.6 %), the less selected pollutions are cooking fume pollution (13.8 %), electromagnetic radiation pollution (5.3 %) and agricultural pollution (2.3 %) (Fig. 11.11). By cities, residents of the 38 cities generally consider the urban motor vehicle exhaust pollution the most serious with the choosing all over 50 %; and even higher in Tianjin, Beijing, Shenyang, Wuhan and Shanghai in order with the choosing all over 80 %. For the second serious pollution, most cities are choosing household waste, especially in Guiyang, Hohhot, Haikou, Hefei, Nanchang, Fuzhou, Tianjin, Chongqing and Guangzhou with the choosing proportion all over 40 %; however, some cities like Taiyuan, Dalian, Suzhou, Ningbo, Kunming, Lanzhou, Urumqi and Karamay are considering industrial waste as the second serious pollution, especially in Lanzhou, Suzhou, Ningbo, Guangzhou, Taiyuan, Shenzhen and Urumqi with the choosing all over 35 %. Nanjing and Changsha consider noise as the second serious pollution, while Hefei's choosing of noise pollution closed to household waste. In addition, the overwhelming majority of cities have a very low proportion in choosing cooking fume pollution, electromagnetic radiation pollution and agricultural pollution.

11.3 Satisfaction with Urban Infrastructure Is Relatively High and the Inter-city Difference Is Relatively Great

Satisfaction with urban infrastructure refers to residents' comprehensive evaluation of five indicators of the city where they live—greening, number and distribution of leisure facilities, household waste disposal, convenience of public transport and traffic flow. The survey shows that the average satisfaction with urban infrastructure of 38 cities is 0.227 (Fig. 11.12), indicating that the residents are relatively positive to the current urban infrastructure, but there is still large room for

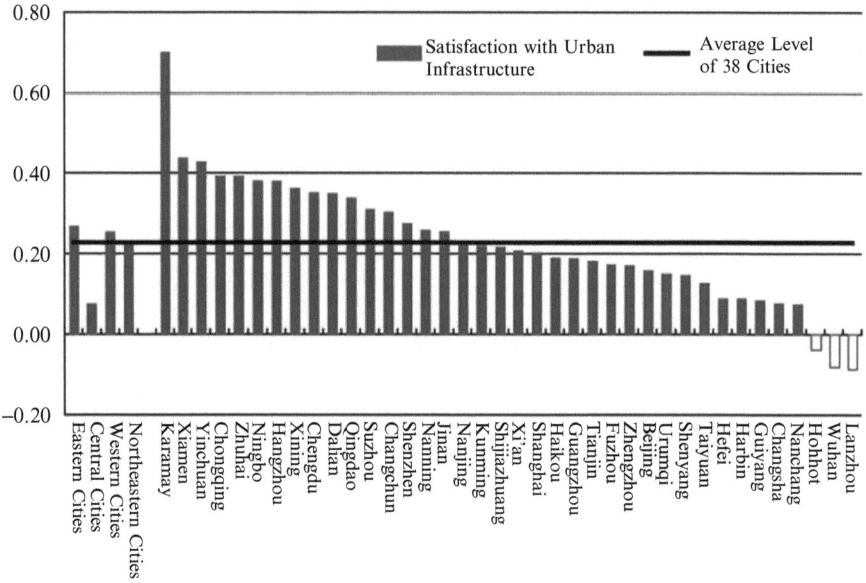

Fig. 11.12 Satisfaction with urban infrastructure

improvement. The inter-city difference is great, characterized by the eastern and the western economic regions having relatively high satisfaction, the northeastern regions lower and the central regions the lowest.

By areas, the satisfactions with urban infrastructure in the eastern, central, western and northeastern cities are 0.268, 0.075, 0.252 and 0.220 respectively. The eastern cities enjoy the highest satisfaction and relatively small inter-city differences with 0.277 between Xiamen the highest and Beijing the lowest; among the 16 eastern cities, four of them rank among the top 10, six from 11 to 20, and six from 21 to 38. The western cities with satisfaction slightly higher than the average. The inter-city difference is relatively great with 0.510 between Yinchuan the second highest and Lanzhou the lowest. Among 12 western cities, five rank among the top 10, three from 11 to 20 and four from 21 to 38. The northeastern cities are slightly lower than the average and the inter-city difference is relatively small with 0.260 between Dalian the highest and Harbin the lowest; among the four northeastern four cities, one ranks among the top 10, one from 11 to 20 and two from 21 to 38. The satisfaction with the central cities is the lowest and the inter-city difference is the smallest with 0.249 between Zhengzhou the highest and Wuhan the lowest, indicating overall level of urban infrastructure in central cities are relatively lower; all the six central cities rank from 21 to 38.

By cities, residents of 35 cities are satisfied with the infrastructure with only three cities below zero. 16 of these cities are higher than the average with Karamay, Xiamen, Yinchuan, Chongqing, Zhuhai, Ningbo, Hangzhou, Xining, Chengdu and

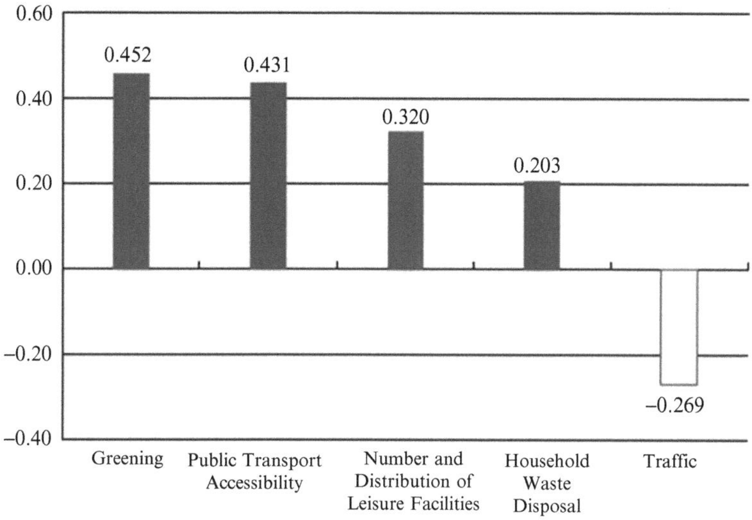

Fig. 11.13 Satisfaction with urban infrastructure by indicators

Dalian ranking the top 10 in order and 22 lower than the average with Hohhot, Wuhan and Lanzhou below zero.

Among the five indicators of urban infrastructure, residents are most satisfied with urban greening, relatively satisfied with public transport accessibility, number and distribution of leisure facilities and household waste disposal and dissatisfied with the traffic flow (Fig. 11.13).

Satisfaction with urban greening is 0.452 with 51.1 % of the respondents considering the greening of the city where they live "good", 42.9 % "general" and 6.0 % "bad". By cities, all the 38 cities enjoy satisfaction with greening above zero (Fig. 11.14), of which 18 are higher than the average of all cities with Karamay, Xiamen, Zhuhai, Hangzhou, Nanning, Ningbo, Dalian, Haikou, Chongqing and Changchun ranking the top 10 in order; 20 are lower than the average with Urumqi, Changsha, Harbin, Wuhan and Lanzhou ranking the last five.

Satisfaction with public transport accessibility is 0.431 with 58.2 % of the survey respondents considering the public transport of the city where they live "convenient", 26.7 % "general" and 15.1 % "inconvenient". By cities, residents of the 38 cities are generally satisfied with the convenience of the public transport of the city where they live (Fig. 11.15), of which 22 are higher than the average of all cities with Karamay, Xiamen, Shanghai, Qingdao, Chongqing, Xining, Shenzhen, Dalian, Beijing and Nanjing ranking the top 10 in order; 16 are lower than the average with Guiyang, Lanzhou, Hefei, Wuhan and Hohhot ranking the last five.

Satisfaction with urban leisure-orientated entertainment places is 0.320 with 45.9 % of the survey respondents "satisfied" with the number and distribution of public leisure facilities such as parks and squares in the city where they live, 40.2 % "general" and 13.9 % "dissatisfied". Among the few residents who are dissatisfied,

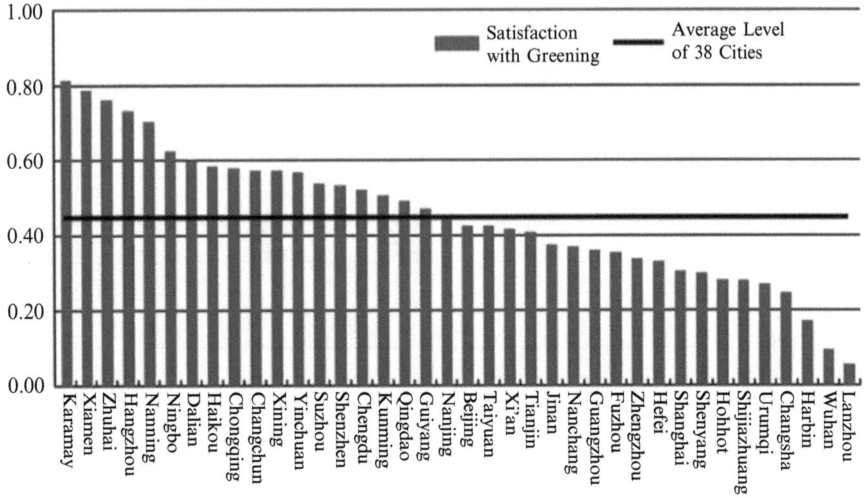

Fig. 11.14 Satisfaction with urban greening

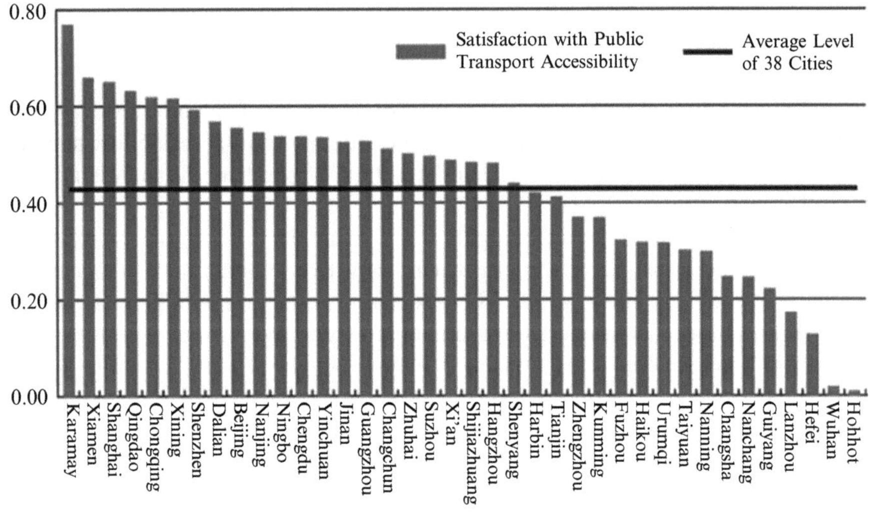

Fig. 11.15 Satisfaction with public transport accessibility

65.2 % think the leisure facilities "too few", 22.1 % "distributed unreasonably" and 12.7 % "too few and distributed unreasonably", "too small in size", "incomplete in facilities" or "bad management", etc.

By cities, all the 38 cities have satisfaction with leisure facilities above zero (Fig. 11.16), of which 19 are higher than the average of all cities with Karamay, Xiamen, Hangzhou, Yinchuan, Dalian, Shijiazhuang, Nanning, Changchun, Xining

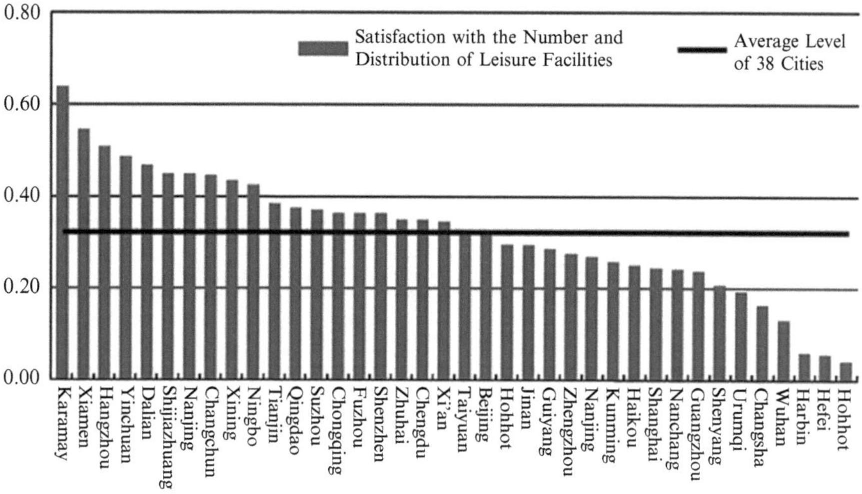

Fig. 11.16 Satisfaction with urban leisure facilities

and Ningbo ranking the top 10 in order; 19 are lower than the average with Changsha, Wuhan, Harbin, Hefei and Lanzhou ranking the last five.

Satisfaction with urban household waste disposal is 0.203 with 40.5 % of the survey respondents "satisfied" with the household waste disposal in the city where they live, 39.4 % "general" and 20.1 % "dissatisfied". By cities, the majority of cities (34) have the satisfaction with household waste disposal above zero with only four cities below zero (Fig. 11.17); 21 of these cities are higher than the average with Karamay, Hangzhou, Chengdu, Jinan, Qingdao, Xiamen, Ningbo, Xining, Dalian and Suzhou ranking the top 10 in order; 17 are lower than the average with four cities—Wuhan, Guiyang, Lanzhou and Hohhot—below zero.

In the five indicators, satisfaction with traffic is the lowest, scoring −0.269 with only 18.5 % of the survey respondents considering the traffic of the city where they live "smooth", 36.2 % "general" and up to 45.3 % "congested". By cities, residents of the majority of the cities (34) are dissatisfied with the traffic flow of the city where they live and only four are satisfied (Fig. 11.18). Four cities which have satisfaction above zero are Karamay, Yinchuan, Chongqing and Zhuhai; among the 21 cities which have satisfaction lower than the average, Nanjing, Shenyang, Taiyuan, Guiyang, Changsha, Nanchang, Beijing, Lanzhou, Wuhan and Hohhot rank the last 10 in order.

As for the ways of daily transportation, the survey shows that nearly half (48.6 %) of the residents choose public transport (bus or subway), followed by private vehicles (cars or motorcycles, 25.1 %) and bicycles, electric bicycles or walking (21.2 %), with taxi having relatively low proportion of choice (4.6 %) and others (0.5 %). By cities, residents' choice with highest proportion in most cities is public transport, and the cities with highest proportion are Xining, Chongqing, Shenzhen, Guangzhou, Xiamen, Wuhan, Zhuhai and Urumqi in order with the

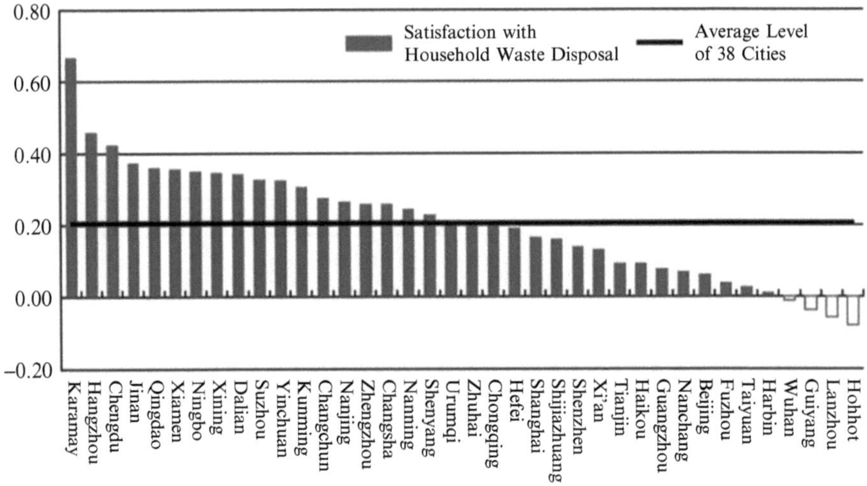

Fig. 11.17 Satisfaction with urban household waste disposal

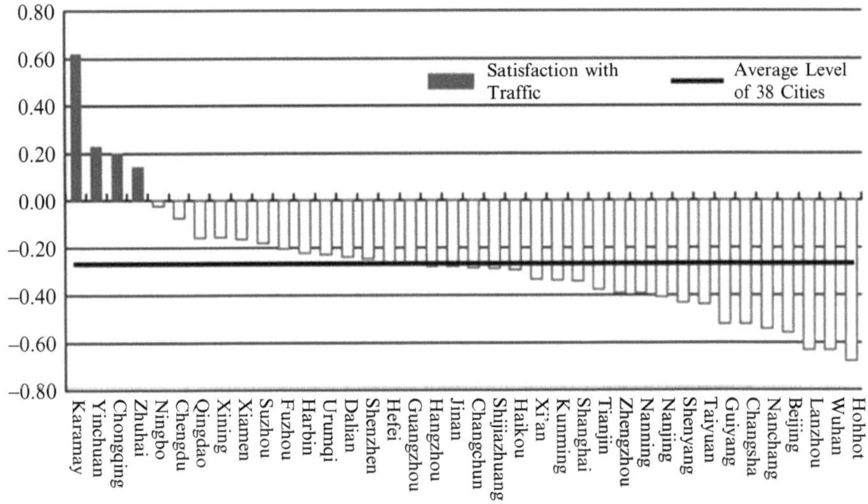

Fig. 11.18 Satisfaction with urban traffic

proportion above 60 %. However, most respondents in Hangzhou, Suzhou, Chengdu and Zhengzhou choose bicycles, electric bicycles or walking with a proportion over 35 %. Most people in Hohhot, Taiyuan and Shijiazhuang choose private vehicles; in addition, the proportion of private vehicles in Shenyang, Beijing, Harbin, Changsha, Dalian and Changchun is relatively high with a proportion near or over 35 %.

11.4 Urban Residents' Satisfaction with Government's Green Actions Is Generally Low

Satisfaction with Government's green actions refers to residents' comprehensive evaluation of five indicators of the city where they live, including waste separation facilities, food safety, knowledge of environmental complaint filing, the effectiveness of industrial waste management and government attention to environmental protection. The survey shows that the average of satisfaction with government's green actions of the 38 cities is −0.098 (Fig. 11.19), indicating that the residents surveyed are generally dissatisfied with the relevant policies and measures taken by the government and there is a long way to go for the government to promote green development.

By regions, the eastern, central, western and northeastern cities score −0.104, −0.161, −0.049 and −0.130 respectively in satisfaction with government's green actions with insignificant inter-region differences. The central cities have the lowest satisfaction; among six central cities, one ranks from 11 to 20 and five from 21 to 38. The northeastern cities follow next; among four northeastern cities, one ranks among the top 10, one from 11 to 20 and two from 21 to 38. The eastern cities are slightly lower than the average; among 16 eastern cities, three rank among the top 10, four from 11 to 20 and nine from 21 to 38. The 12 western cities are slightly higher than the average with six ranking among the top 10, four from 11 to 20 and two from 21 to 38.

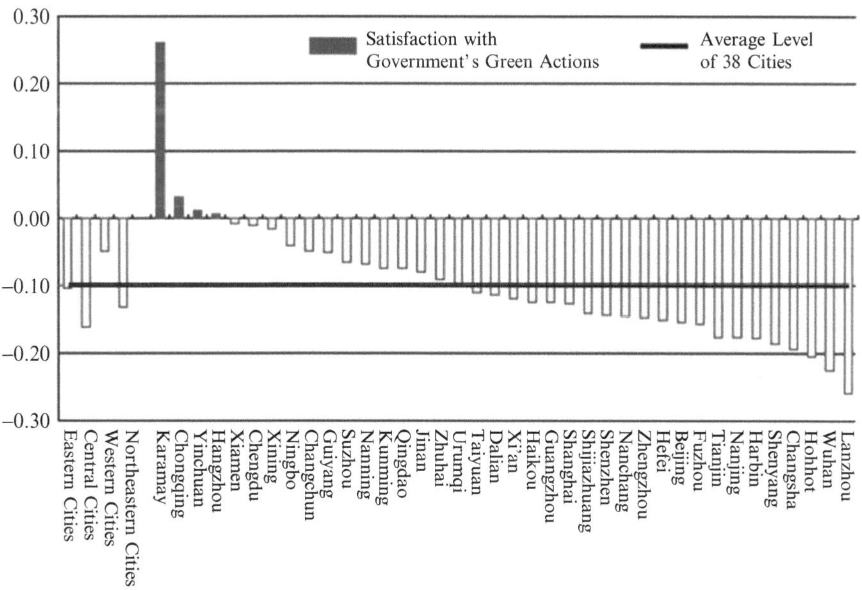

Fig. 11.19 Satisfaction with government's green actions

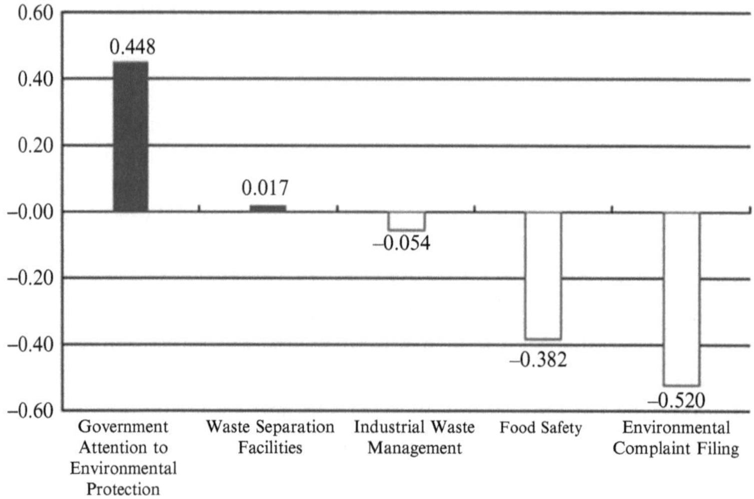

Fig. 11.20 Satisfaction with government's green actions by indicators

By cities, 21 cities have satisfaction with government's green actions lower than the average with Beijing, Fuzhou, Tianjin, Nanjing, Harbin, Shenyang, Changsha, Hohhot, Wuhan and Lanzhou ranking the last 10 in order; 17 are higher than the average, with four cities—Karamay, Chongqing, Yinchuan and Hangzhou above zero.

In the five indicators of government's green actions, the residents are most satisfied with government attention to environmental protection. Their satisfaction with waste separation facilities is relatively low. They are dissatisfied with effectiveness of industrial waste management, food safety, and environmental complaint filing (Fig. 11.20).

Satisfaction with government attention to environmental protection is 0.448; with 55.3 % of the survey respondents considering that the government "empha sizes" the urban environmental protection, 34.2 % choosing "general", and 10.5 % choosing "not emphasizes". By cities, residents of the 38 cities are satisfied with government's environmental protection (Fig. 11.21), of which 21 are higher than the average with Karamay, Xining, Xiamen, Chengdu, Hangzhou, Guiyang, Taiyuan, Yinchuan, Chongqing and Kunming ranking the top 10 in order; 17 are lower than the average with Fuzhou, Hohhot, Nanjing, Wuhan and Lanzhou ranking the last five in order.

Satisfaction with waste separation facilities is 0.017 with 28.3 % of residents surveyed "satisfied" with urban household waste separation facility configuration, 45.0 % "general" and 26.7 % "dissatisfied". By cities, fewer than half of urban residents express satisfaction, that is, 18 cities have satisfaction with waste separation facilities above zero and 20 are below zero (Fig. 11.22). Eighteen of these cities have satisfaction higher than the average with Karamay, Hangzhou, Ningbo, Chongqing, Yinchuan, Xining, Chengdu, Dalian, Xiamen and Jinan ranking the

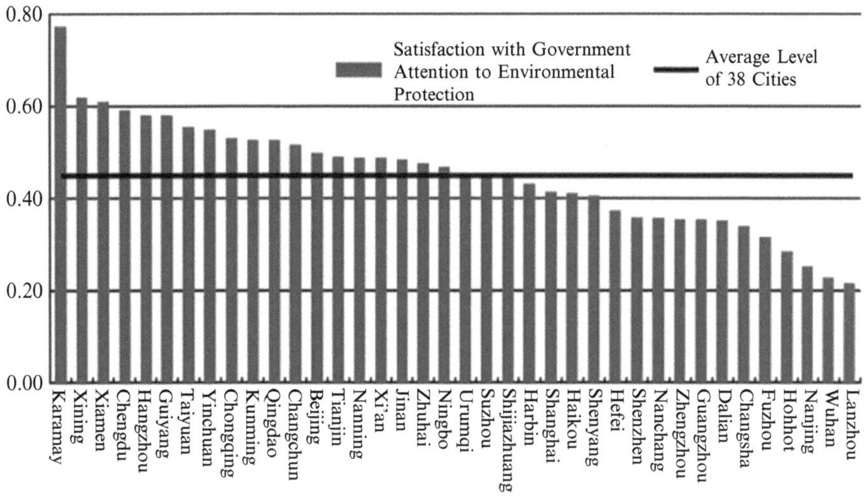

Fig. 11.21 Satisfaction with government attention to environmental protection

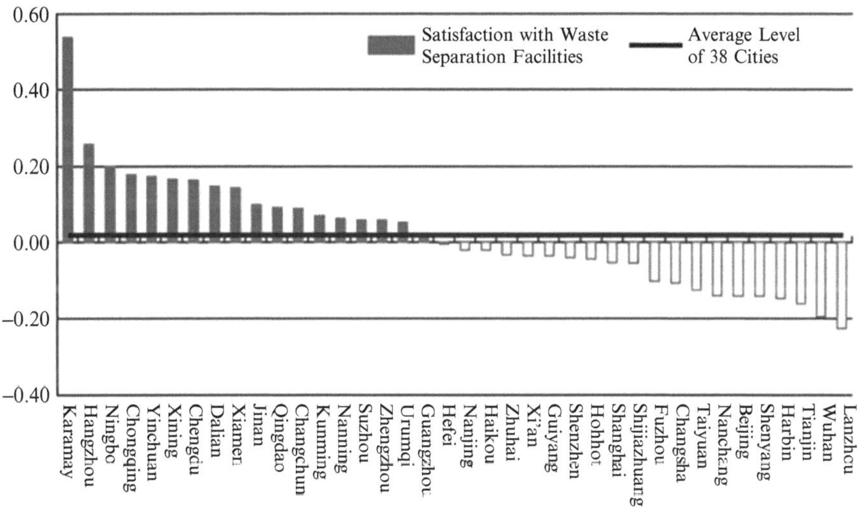

Fig. 11.22 Satisfaction with waste separation facilities

top 10 in order; 20 are lower than the average with Shenyang, Harbin, Tianjin, Wuhan and Lanzhou ranking the last five.

Satisfaction with the effectiveness of industrial waste management is −0.054 with only 12.6 % of the survey respondents considering that the industrial waste management "significantly effective", 69.3 % "generally effective" and 18.1 % "very little effective". By cities, residents of only eight cities are satisfied with the effectiveness of industrial waste management on the whole and up to 30 cities are

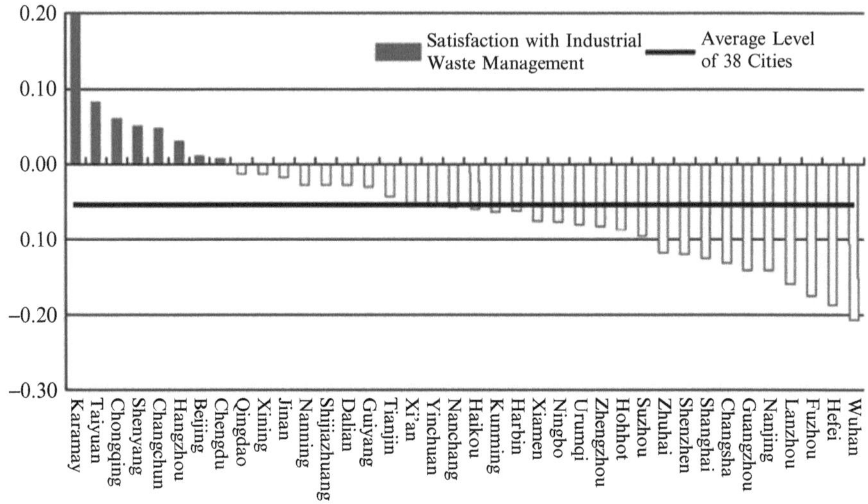

Fig. 11.23 Satisfaction with the effectiveness of industrial waste management

dissatisfied (Fig. 11.23). Among these cities, 18 cities have satisfaction higher than the average and the eight cities expressing satisfaction are Karamay, Taiyuan, Chongqing, Shenyang, Changchun, Hangzhou, Beijing and Chengdu in order; 20 are lower than the average with Nanjing, Lanzhou, Fuzhou, Hefei and Wuhan ranking the last five.

Satisfaction with food safety is −0.382; among these cities, only 15.6 % of the survey respondents "rest assured" of the daily consumed food, 30.5 % choose "general" and up to 53.9 % of the residents choose "worried". By cities, the overwhelming majority of the cities (37) are dissatisfied with daily food safety with only Karamay's satisfaction above zero (Fig. 11.24). 20 of these cities have the satisfaction lower than the average with Dalian, Taiyuan, Beijing, Lanzhou, Shijiazhuang, Changsha, Hohhot, Harbin, Tianjin and Shenyang ranking the last 10 in order; 18 are higher than the average.

Satisfaction with environmental complaint filing is −0.520, indicating an unsmooth communication channel between government agencies and the residents. The survey shows that only 8.5 % of the survey respondents have full knowledge of the environmental complaint filing (website or telephone), 31.0 % "heard, but forget", and up to 60.5 % "do not know at all". By cities, residents of the 38 cities on the whole have little knowledge of environmental complaint filing with satisfaction below zero (Fig. 11.25). Nineteen of these cities are higher than the average with Karamay, Zhuhai, Guiyang, Chongqing, Yinchuan, Guangzhou, Shenzhen, Suzhou, Chengdu and Xiamen ranking the top 10 in order; 19 are lower than the average with Hefei, Urumqi, Beijing, Haikou and Zhengzhou ranking the last five.

The survey further shows that the average rate of residents' environmental complaints of the 38 cities is only 6.0 % (Fig. 11.26), partly because of the little

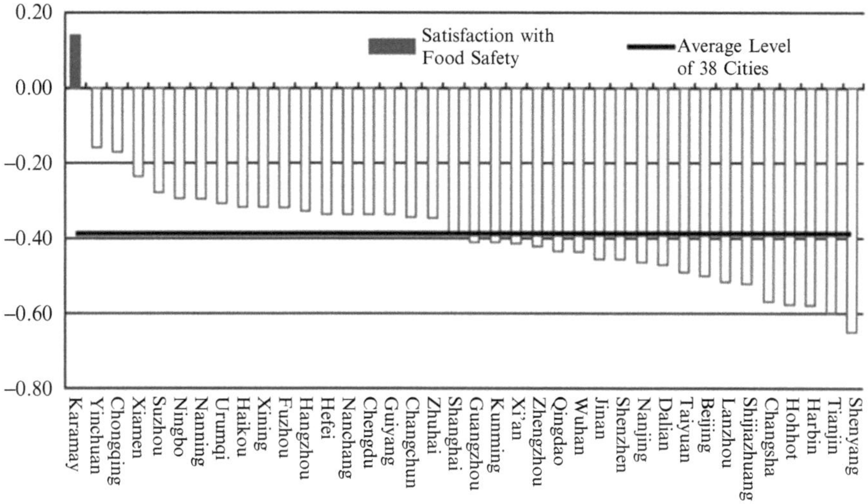

Fig. 11.24 Satisfaction with food safety

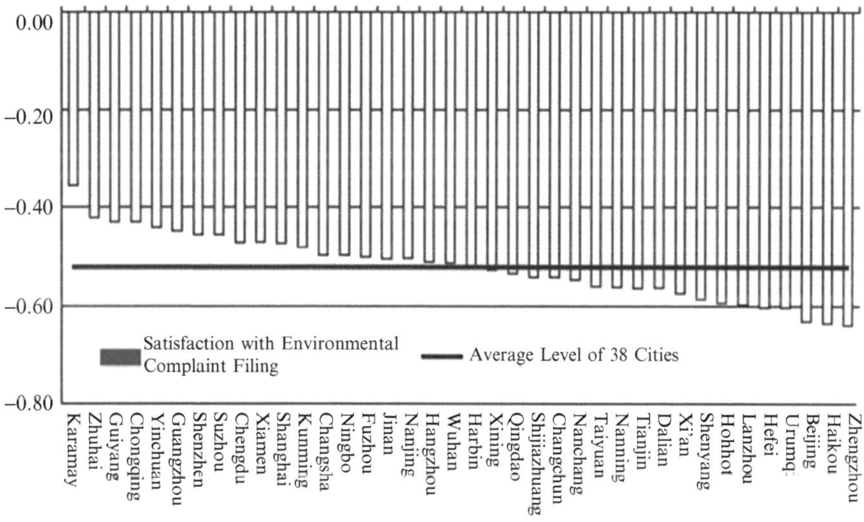

Fig. 11.25 Satisfaction with environmental complaint filing

knowledge of the complaint manners; 18 of these cities are higher than the average with Shenzhen, Nanchang, Xiamen and Changsha ranking the top four with complaint rates from 8 to 9 %; 20 are lower than the average with Hohhot, Ningbo and Fuzhou ranking the last three with the rate of complaints not more than 4.0 %.

Regardless of the low percentage of residents filing environmental complaints, residents of the 38 cities have relatively high dissatisfaction rate of the result of the complaint treatment with an average of 53.8 % (Fig. 11.27); 22 of these cities are

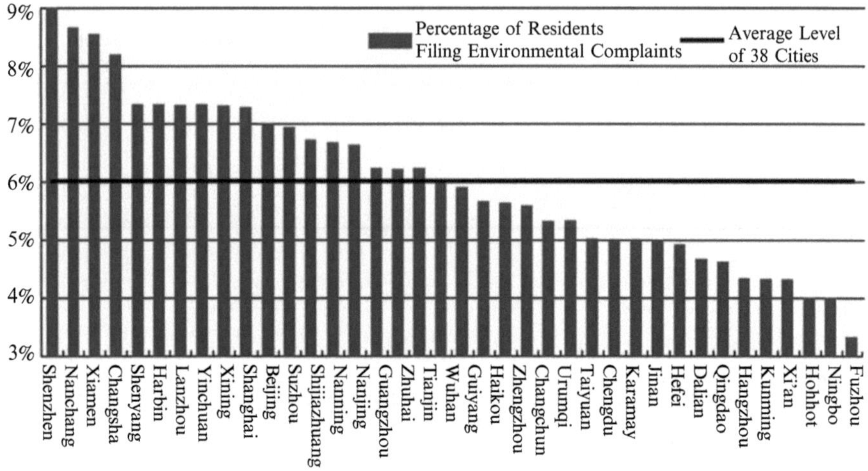

Fig. 11.26 Percentage of residents filing environmental complaints in cities

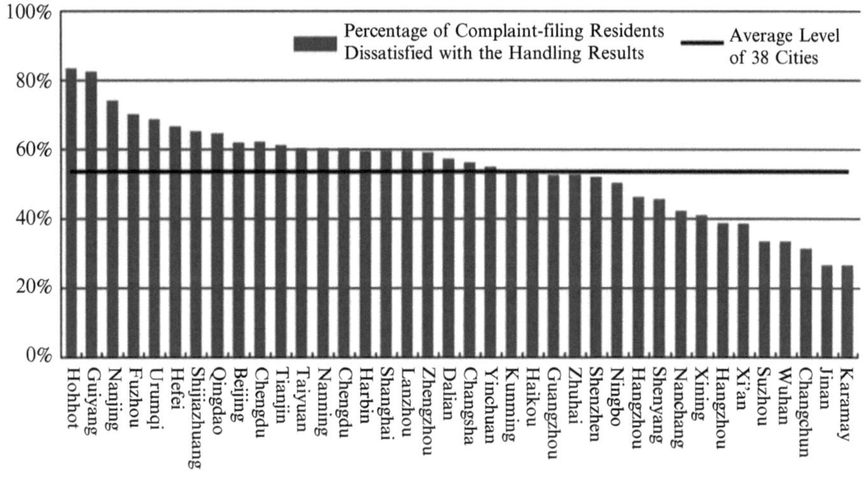

Fig. 11.27 Percentage complaint-filing residents dissatisfied with the handling results in cities

higher than the average with Hohhot, Guiyang and Nanjing ranking the top three with dissatisfaction rate over 70 %; 16 are lower than the average with Jinan and Karamay ranking the last two with dissatisfaction rate no more than 3 %. Generally, the government has a lot to do to respond to complaints from residents and actively improve the urban environment.

11.5 Inspirations from the Survey on Public Satisfaction with Urban Green Development

11.5.1 Public Satisfaction Is an Important Supplement to CGDI

Public satisfaction is the comprehensive reflection of urban residents' subjective judgment, which is a useful supplement to the results of CGDI measurement based on statistical data. It is reflected as follows: First, the urban residents help promote urban green development and are directly influenced by the outcomes of development. Urban green development is closely related to residents' work and life, so the residents' opinions are important reference to the objective evaluation of a city's green development. Second, the public satisfaction survey makes up for the CGDI system's defects in the selection of indicators. Owing to the imperfect statistical system and poor availability of statistical data, there is a lack of GDI indicators for urban green governance such as ecological construction, air quality, urban pollution, traffic congestion and food safety; there is also a lack of relevant indicators to reflect the quality of economic development and the effectiveness of the implementation of government policies. However, public satisfaction survey makes up for the relevant content. The combination of the two approaches helps to provide a full picture of green development.

11.5.2 We Should Look at the Difference Between the Results of Public Satisfaction Survey and GDI Evaluation Correctly

The results of GDI evaluation show that green development is best promoted in eastern areas, relatively good in northeastern and western, and worst in central areas. Seven eastern cities are among the top 10. Prosperous economy and more governments' green investment result in the high ranking of the eastern cities. However, the results of public satisfaction survey show that the overall satisfaction with green development is highest in western areas, relatively high in eastern and northeastern areas, and low in central areas. There are five eastern cities and five western cities among the top 10. The eastern cities are selected mainly for good air quality, little pollution, good urban greening and convenient transport rather than for the most developed economy.

There are several reasons for this phenomenon. First, the index evaluation system of green development is different from public satisfaction survey. The former focuses on published statistics, while the latter attaches importance on the subjective feelings of the public. Second, the information release is unbalanced. For example, though some cities have made great efforts in public facilities and green investment, the special pressure of megacities and the long-term, insignificant and hysteretic achievements, etc. result in the gap with the intuitive feelings. Third, there is difference of development stages between developed areas and the economically backward areas, and the psychological expectations of the public to the cities are very different, which cause the lower public satisfaction in the eastern areas than that of the western areas. Fourth, the small number of the survey samples account for a very small proportion in the total number of residents in cities, especially in megacities, so the conclusion has some limitations.

11.5.3 We Should Attach High Importance to People's Wellbeing and Public Opinions Reflected in Public Satisfaction Survey on Urban Green Development

In the whole process of designing and organizing the questionnaire and acquiring the findings of the survey, we deeply perceive that the green development is inseparable with wellbeing and the effectiveness of the government's green actions has always been highly concerned by the public. The results of this survey tell us that the public are most concerned about the improvement of urban air quality, guarantee of clean urban water, vigorous development of urban public transport system, promotion and popularization of urban household waste separation, and assurance of food safety. Resolution of these problems can greatly improve the level of urban green development and win recognition and support of the public.

11.5.4 Every City Should Choose a Path of Green Development Suitable for Its Own Natural Advantages and Economic Development

By region, the densely populated eastern cities should focus on balancing regional development and controlling population growth by virtue of industrial restructuring in order to avoid excessive concentration of population in large cities; they should also reasonably regulate the spatial distribution of population, reduce the number of commuters and improve the urban traffic conditions through industrial layout and planning of residential areas. When receiving the industrial transfer from the eastern areas, the central cities should avoid the old "control after pollution" mode. Instead, they should moderately take the industrial transfer, and meanwhile accelerate the improvement of the urban infrastructure and environment. The western cities with higher level of green development should select industries adaptable to the green development, maintain reasonable size of cities and keep increasing the environmental carrying capacity; the western cities with lower level of green development should avoid over-exploitation of resources, constrain industrial expansion, occupy the market with high-quality products and thus strengthen the government's ability for green actions.

In summary, the government should be more open and transparent in releasing environmental complaint telephone or website and take initiatives to strengthen communication with the residents so as to solve the environmental problems intensely reflected by the urban residents in a more timely and effective manner.

Part IV
Professors' Forum: Proposals for Green Development

The research on green development is a project requiring cooperation between multiple fields and at multiple levels. It involves many economic and social aspects and needs the joint efforts of the human society. In order to make better and sustainable researches on green development, we have invited professors and scholars in both natural and social sciences who write some chapters or parts of this report to offer proposals for China's green development. Proceeding from their fields of study, the experts focus on hotspot issues, make careful and detailed analyses and provide brilliant and insightful views.[1]

[1] This part contains the full text of these professors and scholars' personal views.

Chapter 12
Manage Beijing's "Big City Disease" and Achieve the Capital's Green Development

Shengzu Gu

The GDI measurement and comparison as well as the public survey of *Green Development Index Report 2012—Regional Comparison* inspires my reflection on the capital's "big city disease". The "big city disease" refers to varieties of drawbacks such as environmental pollution, traffic congestion and resource constraints caused by the excessive concentration of the urban population, industries and transport. It not only brings trouble and inconvenience to the people living in the city, but also has some impact on the operation of the city. Air pollution in big cities is caused by many reasons. The sources resulting in Beijing's PM2.5 include: direct and indirect emissions from motor vehicles (22.2 %); coal pollution (16.7 %); industrial spray volatilization such as automotive and furniture spray-paint (16.3 %); urban dust pollution (15.8 %); rural straw incineration and others (4.5 %); and the regional impact from Beijing's surroundings (24.5 %). Complex causes for air pollution determine the governance of the pollution to be a systematic project. The key to managing the "big city disease" caused by air pollution and realizing the capital's green development lies in the government guidance, clear responsibilities of different aspects and cooperative promotion. We recommend eight measures to be taken as follows.

First, the positioning of the city should be made clear to scientifically develop urban planning, rationally distribute population and optimize regional functions and industrial structure, promote urban structure to turn from heavy to light and effectively reduce burdens of megacities. The unbearable "big city disease" caused by the traffic congestion and environmental pollution in cities especially in megacities with population and industries excessively concentrated must be better treated. The urban planning should be scientifically made to strictly control the population, guide the rational distribution of urban population, and improve the environmental development. The coordinated regional development should be properly promoted,

S. Gu (✉)
School of Economics and Resource Management, Beijing Normal University, Beijing, China
e-mail: npcgub@163.com

X. Li and J. Pan (eds.), *China Green Development Index Report 2012: Regional Comparison*, Current Chinese Economic Report Series,
DOI 10.1007/978-3-642-54178-0_12,

parts of the functions of the central city should be decentralized, and the industrial system and the spatial layout should be optimized so that the production-oriented city can turn into a service-oriented city. The capital should become the model for other cities to manage the air pollution and the key is to reposition the urban functions of Beijing, change the "large and all-inclusive" position of "political, economic, cultural and educational center" and adjust the layout of the city. Functions over-concentrated in the center should be changed. On the basis of reviewing the experience in the relocation of Shoudu Iron and Steel Company and transformation of the former industrial base, some functions should be further transferred out of the center of the city to breed new growth point in the peripheral areas, "organically evacuate" the excessive concentration on the core and relieve the spatial pressure. In this way, a single-center form will turn into a multi-center form with radiation from one central city to the surroundings so that the functions of the large city can be relieved and the portfolio cities of the great Beijing area can be built.

Second, transformation of development mode and economic restructuring should be accelerated to strictly restrain the high-emission industries, promote urban greening and reduce emissions of air pollutants from the sources. The increment should be actively controlled and the stock should be optimized. In the aspect of increment, the environmental entry threshold for industries with high energy consumption, high emission and excess capacity should be further enhanced, and the clean production should be further strictly reviewed and checked. The key enterprises with high energy consumption and pollution should be punished more severely. The environmental management system with "high standards and strict management and control" should be used to force enterprises to speed up technological innovation and industrial upgrading. The urban greening should be actively carried out to control the overall pollutant emissions and effectively prevent and control the air pollution. The efficient, convenient, energy-saving and environmentally friendly transport system should be charted and constructed to relieve the traffic congestion and reduce exhaust emissions. The intelligent transportation should be promoted to improve the transport accessibility of the city and enhance the air quality of the city through management and restraint.

Third, more strict environmental protection system should be established to improve monitoring, early-warning and risk assessment mechanism of air pollution, strengthen environmental supervision system, and improve the response mechanism of air pollution. The regional prevention and control mechanism of air pollution management should be established and promoted to strengthen the organization, coordination and cooperation among regions, establish and improve the joint monitoring and forecasting mechanisms, and reduce the impact of external air pollution. The risk investigation and assessment of air pollution should be promoted to improve the prevention-oriented management system. The emergency management of air pollution should be run well and the contingence plan of heavily polluted weather should be constantly improved.

Fourth, the key projects of air pollution management should be implemented and the management in key areas such as transportation, energy, construction, municipal cleaning should be strengthened to control PM2.5 from the sources.

In the transport sector, the existing transport facilities should be comprehensively integrated to improve the existing road capacity and the micro-circulatory system of road network, reduce road congestion and relieve air pollution.

Fifth, the relevant laws and regulations system of air pollution management should be improved to increase the cost of violating laws and severely punish the illegal air pollution. We should extensively draw on and absorb the successful experience of the developed countries in air pollution management by means of legislation and combine it with China's current conditions of the state and the people to accelerate the amendments of laws such as Environmental Protection Law, Law on the Prevention and Control of Atmospheric Pollution, Cleaner Production Promotion Law, Law on Environmental Impact Assessment, etc. and continuously improve the relevant laws and regulations system of air pollution prevention and control so as to effectively provide the legal basis for strictly controlling pollutant emissions and punishing violations of laws. The illegal emissions of atmospheric pollutants should be punished more severely to raise the cost of violating the laws.

Sixth, the institutional reform of environmental management should be pushed forward to bring the environmental quality indicators into the assessment indicators for all levels of government leaders, establish and improve the environmental accountability system, and ensure the implementation of environmental policies such as energy conservation and emissions reduction through the institutionalized design. The government's responsibility for environmental protection should be further stipulated to make clear and strengthen the rights and responsibilities of the principal government leaders at all levels for the environmental quality maintenance in their regions. The evaluation mechanism of the local government's performance should be reformed to enhance investment, strengthen capacity building of the local environmental monitoring, optimize the layout of monitoring network and promote the development of local green economy.

Seventh, market players should be given economic incentives to control air pollution, and enterprises actively engaged in the air pollution control should be support by tax and financial policies.

Eighth, the public propaganda on the green lifestyle and consumption should be enhanced to guide the public to participate in prevention and control of air pollution. The guidance of public opinions should be strengthened to enhance the public environmental awareness and their ability to participate in environmental protection and air pollution prevention, thus creating a good social atmosphere to improve the air quality.

Professor Gu Shengzu, Ph.D. supervisor of the School of Economics and Resource Management, Beijing Normal University

Chapter 13
Several Prescriptions for Beijing's Urban Disease

XianQiang Mao

Beijing has suffered from a series of "urban diseases": traffic congestion, air pollution, rocketing house prices... The "focuses" emerge in systems and organs of transport, environment (air, water) and housing, but the root cause seems to lie in "population", behind which hide the calamities caused by economic structure and layout, transport and urban planning, etc.

Beijing sets up "barriers" for the current population control mainly based on the household registration system and threshold of purchasing houses. It has no other alternatives but to take these unwise moves. In fact, the control by means of "command" violates the economic laws, and the blockage without channels to relieve the population is doomed to failure.

Here I would write out some prescriptions for the population problem and the correspondent "urban disease" of Beijing and other first-tier megacities:

13.1 Regional Development Should Be Balanced to Reduce the Relative Attraction of Beijing to Population

In my view, most of Beijing's transient population from other places (including the household registered population from other places to Beijing) comes from the less developed areas, including the Northeast, North China, Central China, the Northwest and the Southwest with very few people from the Yangtze River Delta and Pearl River Delta regions. Compared to the surrounding areas, Beijing is too attractive with highly concentrated administrative, economic, educational and health resources.

X. Mao (✉)
School of Environment, Beijing Normal University, Beijing, China
e-mail: maoxo@bnu.edu.cn

X. Li and J. Pan (eds.), *China Green Development Index Report 2012: Regional Comparison*, Current Chinese Economic Report Series,
DOI 10.1007/978-3-642-54178-0_13, © Springer-Verlag Berlin Heidelberg 2015

If it is unrealistic to weaken these absolute advantages in resources, then the balanced regional development should be promoted as soon as possible:

First, public services should be balanced. Beijing is swamped with high learning institutions and high school graduates enjoy the highest rate of college admission in the whole country; there are a lot of famous doctors, medical colleges and super-3A hospitals in Beijing. However, Hebei Province, though the environs of the capital tens of kilometers away, actually has a huge gap, and no wonder people would move to the capital.

Second, powers and financial rights should be appropriately delegated to lower levels for decentralization. Powers are excessively concentrated in ministries and commissions under the State Council and the allocation of the state revenue is over-relied on the "projects". As a result, it becomes the normal atmosphere to "go to ministries for money"; it is a palliative treatment to nominally ban parts of "Beijing Offices" and the flowing population and the vehicles used to "go to ministries for money" are as many as usual. If the local finance were sufficient, the value to go to ministries in Beijing would be much smaller, the roads would be less congested at the Mid-Autumn Festival and on the National Day, and there would be fewer opportunities for corruption.

Third, it is most important to balance the economic development. More growth poles at the national level such as the Yangtze River Delta, Pearl River Delta and Beijing-Tianjin regions should be built, several more large regional centers which can match Beijing, Shanghai and Guangzhou in superiorities of all aspects should be developed, and then the population pressure of Beijing, Shanghai and Guangzhou will be naturally alleviated.

Of course, the balanced development is not to be achieved overnight but in the process of gradual change. We have already seen the labor shortage in the eastern areas. On the contrary, the central and western areas, thanks to the transfer of industries, are attracting a growing number of off-farm workers to work in their hometowns, large or medium cities or small towns, which means that more and more off-farm workers no longer need to drift in the eastern areas and big cities.

13.2 Control Population with Industrial Restructuring

The relocation of Capital Iron and Steel Company (Shougang Group) has brought tens of thousands of people out of Beijing. The short-term loss of GDP is very possible to be offset in population evacuation and relief, environmental improvement, rise in (surrounding) land prices and development of alternative industries, and the long-term benefits will be necessarily achieved. Moreover, people are calling not to "judge heroes only by GDP", so it is fundamental to improve people's wellbeing and build livable cities.

13.3 Spatial Distribution of Population Should Be Rationally Regulated and Controlled and Inter-group Commuters Should Be Reduced Through the Industrial Layout and Residential Settlements Planning

Regardless of the improved housing conditions, people spend more time on the congested roads. It is typical of Huilongguan and Tiantongyuan, the two "sleeping towns" which are hard to go in and out. Neither convenient nor environmentally friendly, many people keep running back and forth like a "pendulum" between the residence and the workplace. Grouped enterprises cannot be too far away from the residence, and the cross-regional and cross-group layout should be avoided so as to reduce the amount of commuting between groups and avoid a lot of commuting demands.

In fact, the population in the central city tends to be aging and the retirement population increases. If measures can be taken to "empty the cage for new birds", i.e., move the elderly out of the city and let young people in the suburbs move in the city, then the amount of commuting and traffic flow can be greatly reduced. Of course, the next question is, why do the elderly want to move out of the city? Therefore, it is required to take measures in terms of living facilities, health care, living conditions, and etc. Wisdom is also needed. I guess the government would take it as a "worst plan" and they would never bother to think about it.

13.4 Commuting Ways Should Be Improved to Reduce the Number of Commuters

This is more like a measure to "treat congestion". Employees of many large units in Beijing have very huge amount of commuting. Beijing Normal University, for example, has the campus inside the 3rd Circle Road (Sanhuan), but most of the young faculty live in Jingshiyuan at the side of the 5th Circle Road (Wuhuan). Most of them have bought private car to go to work and send and collect children for school or kindergarten. Some families have even bought two cars to cope with the restriction of license numbers. Provided that the universities could offer commuting shuttle for the community of their employees, how much congestion would be alleviated for Beijing? Unfortunately, the universities will not do a losing business. Why should they subsidize the private uses with the public funds? Therefore, it is not the leadership of Beijing Normal University who should be blamed, but the government should come up with policies to give financial assistance and force these units to offer shuttles. This is not necessarily unfeasible because Beijing gives astronomical sums of subsidies to buses every year, but many buses are inefficient for they are crowded in rush hours and empty in other times. It may be more target-oriented, practical and efficient if the subsidies are given to commuting shuttles of the units like BNU. The measures recently enacted by Beijing government to treat the congestion contain the ones to encourage the school shuttles, which will be one of the effective measures.

Professor XianQiang Mao, School of Environment, Beijing Normal University

Chapter 14
What Kind of Modernization Do We Need?

Fangjian Liu

In the barbaric times with low level of productive forces, human beings were dependent on the nature and the material wealth grew slowly. The excessive pursuit of wealth would tense social relations and intensify social conflicts. Desires difficult to met would also lead to the spiritual and emotional restlessness. Therefore, the early human societies, from the public to politicians and thinkers, from religion to philosophies, laid stress on holding "destiny" in awe. Material wealth was depreciated while "simplicity" and "plainness" were advocated. The excessive pursuit of wealth was repressed by spirit, future and heaven for the moment. This was the harmony between man and nature at the low level.

With the progress of social production, human beings can change their material existence through their own efforts, thus creating the times when humans make initiative demand on the nature. They therefore have the thought to struggle with the nature. In the West, it is the historical process through the Renaissance, the Reformation, the scientific revolution, the Enlightenment, the Age of Revolution, the Industrial Revolution and the development of industrial society after the rise of the new urban civilization. It is basically characterized by the traditional human and animal powers being replaced with coal, oil, electrical power and other new energies, village and household economic organizations with factories and companies, and natural economy with exchange economy. In such a society, humans do not make material exchange with the nature with their physical strength and simple means of production as in the agricultural society. They have much higher productive forces. The difference here does not only lie in the forms of labor, but in people's economic organizations. The social structure and activities are related to the human spirit and civilization. Driven by the modern science and technology, the industrialization becomes so vigorous that it leaves far away from the traditional society. With the development of automation and computer

F. Liu (✉)
School of Economics, Southwest University of Finance and Economics, Chengdu, China
e-mail: lfj@swufe.edu.cn

X. Li and J. Pan (eds.), *China Green Development Index Report 2012: Regional Comparison*, Current Chinese Economic Report Series,
DOI 10.1007/978-3-642-54178-0_14,

technology, information plays an increasingly important role, so much so that people call it the "information age".

In this historical process, the orientation of market and the drive of profit generate the opening up and outwardness, flow and aggressiveness. The modernization modeled on the modern Western society has the clear-cut features of scientific knowledge determinism and economic determinism; it lays emphasis on materially solving social problems. The core throughout the modern Western spirit is individualism, self-awareness, awareness of rights, for-itself awareness, self-love consciousness or egoism. When investigating the nature, utilizing things and creating the material wealth, human beings have released the repressed worldly desires, and constantly overthrown the customs and traditional concepts. However, over-materialization leads to the endless demand on the nature and brings the ecological crisis; specialization and mechanization dissimilate the productive labor; urbanization results in people's sense of tension and instability. Over-materialization not only tenses the social relations, but also unbalances people's material and spiritual lives, and weakens the emotional and spiritual support for life; though bringing about the prosperity of individuality and the growth of human capacity, the development of individualism leads to the sense of alienation between people and nature, people and society and among peoples.

Li Zehou argues that separation of man and nature and the struggle between man and nature are the human's control and conquest over the nature and their confrontation and struggle with the nature, historically reflecting that the industrial revolution and the modern civilization, unlike the agricultural society in compliance with the nature, transform the nature and create new things with the industry of science and technology. But even at this time, some important thinkers, among whom Marx was the pioneer, have already noticed that during and shortly after the control and conquest over the nature, there is a giant issue of mutual infiltration, transformation and dependence between man and nature. It is based on the new and objective relationship between man and nature arising from conquest and transformation of the nature by the modern industry. This new relationship is no longer the one to damage and destroy the ecological environment for the sake of conquering the nature as in the emerging times of the modern industry, but the one to restore the nature and protect the ecological environment as in the post-industrial era when the material civilization is highly developed; human beings are no longer confronted and conflicted with the nature, and they should be harmonious and integrated with each other; human beings are not only a part of the nature, but the aura and glory of the nature, the real laws and objectives of the nature.

In order to learn and draw on the successful experience of the West to achieve China's modernization, we need to relive the tense relations between man and nature and among the people revealed in the modern Western civilization and our own development. We should also strengthen the emotional and spiritual support for life which has been weakened by over-materialization. This is the green, healthy and sustainable path of China's modernization. In this process, first and foremost, man's role of key actors and dominance must be first established. Only having a clear understanding of the basic questions such as for whom development is carried out, on whom the development relies and how to distribute the fruits of the development, can we attach importance on both the growth of material wealth and the protection of the ecological environment on the issue of the development, on both material and spiritual progress, thus achieving a higher level of harmony between man and nature on the basis of the modern material civilization.

Professor Liu Fangjian, School of Economics, Southwest University of Finance and Economics

Chapter 15
Promote the Development of China's Green Economy Based on the "Deep Green"

Xuemin Liu

Since Ame Naess, the Norwegian philosopher advanced the terminology of "deep ecology", it has gradually replaced the "light green" in leading the world trend, which is a significant leap forward of human understanding of the natural environment. The "deep green" no longer puts simple emphasis on "people-centered" protection of natural environment. On the contrary, it stresses that nature is a totality and the elements of the natural system influence and depend on each other. Every screw and gear of the life is important to the health and development of the nature. This is the result of natural evolution and selection. The maintenance and development of human life depends on the dynamic balance of the whole ecosystem. As a big developing country, China has become one of the major economies in the world. China lays emphasis on the "green" development, and the development of the green economy under the guidance of the thought of "deep green" is vitally important for the global promotion of sustainable development. Therefore, in the future development, we must fulfill the following tasks:

First, we should replace the material resources with the intellectual resources to some extent so as to decouple the economic development from the resource consumption and environmental pollution. Many natural resources are non-renewable in human time scales, and some renewable resources will be gradually depleted under the minimum limit of their reproduction. In the economic development of a country, the natural resources are scarce and they are the bottleneck factors restricting the economic development. In contrast to the material resources, the human intelligence, however, can be regarded as inexhaustible resources with infinite creativity and development potential. Therefore, we should replace scarce natural resources with the intellectual resources to some extent.

Second, we should vigorously develop the cycling economy. Based on the principle of reducing waste and resource consumption, reusing resources and

X. Liu (✉)
College of Resources Science and Technology, Beijing Normal University, Beijing, China
e-mail: liuxuemin@bnu.edu.cn

X. Li and J. Pan (eds.), *China Green Development Index Report 2012: Regional Comparison*, Current Chinese Economic Report Series,
DOI 10.1007/978-3-642-54178-0_15, © Springer-Verlag Berlin Heidelberg 2015

recycling waste and harmlessly treating the resources, the resource consumption will be kept within a threshold value of reproduction of the resources, and the pollutant emissions will do within that of the natural purification so that the "Ark" of the Earth can keep its sustainable development. To develop the recycling economy in the market economy, the key economic actors are connected for the purpose for obtaining benefits, which requires the link of the symbiotic and metabolic business communities with interests. The market laws and ecological laws are equally important to develop the recycling economy.

Third, after the "baptism" of industrialization, China needs to transform the industrial and economic restructure and take the path of light development. There is no strict definition and standard for the light industrial development or "light economy", but this kind of industries definitely have strong external radiation for their high levels of knowledge, high degree of concentration, few resource consumption and small environmental disturbance. Industries in terms of culture, creativity, finance and information belong to the category of "light economy". The light industrial development is the only way to develop the green economy.

Fourth, we should change from the "resource-driven" mode of economic development to the "innovation-driven" mode. The economic development supported by the cheap resources will not last long and cannot be sustainable. Only driven by innovation can the economic development be sustainable. Innovation is the soul of a nation, the inexhaustible motive power for the prosperity of a country. We should explore for the internal driving force of the long-term and stable economic development through innovation of concept, technology, mechanism and system.

Fifth, in order to develop the green economy and pass to the "deep green", we must expand the publicity and "awaken the people". "Awakening the people" is the conclusion drawn by Dr. Sun Yat-sen with the accumulation of four decades of revolutionary experience. However, it is more important to "awaken the leadership" because the market economy to be established in China is dominated by the government, and the behavior of the government officials and leaders plays an important role in the market economy. Only when the leadership is awakened to have a full understanding of the necessity and importance of the development of green economy can they fundamentally change the decision-making to more effectively promote the green economy.

Professor Xuemin Liu, College of Resources Science and Technology, Beijing Normal University

Chapter 16
Precisely Define and Scientifically Evaluate the Energy Output Efficiency

Xuguang Song

Energy is the key factor and important safeguard for the regional sustainable development. Improving the regional energy output efficiency is significant to alleviate the pressure on resources and environment in the economic development and promote the regional sustainable development.

At present, the domestic indicators related to the "energy output efficiency" include energy intensity, energy productivity, efficiency of energy use, energy consumption per unit of GDP, etc. These indicators generally reflect the comparison between energy consumption and the influence on economy and environment, but they are different in connotation for the different research angles and applications.

In order to standardize and promote the application of the indicators for the energy output efficiency, the connotation of the "energy output efficiency" should be further precisely defined. In our view, unlike the indicators such as energy consumption per unit of GDP, the energy output efficiency is a positive index, which reflects the output level of the energy consumption per unit of GDP with GDP as the molecular and the amount of energy consumed to produce the GDP as the denominator. Such a definition enables the index to be more consistent with the connotation of the "resource output efficiency", putting more emphasis on the property of "efficiency". Currently, we will be facing many challenges in the scientific evaluation of China's energy output efficiency. On the one hand, for the lack of a sound energy accounting system, there are problems for China's energy statistics such as incomplete coverage, rough statistical separation, and unscientific statistical reports. There are relatively large gaps for regional energy statistic data, especially the microscopic data; on the other hand, there are big problems in the connection between the output data and the energy consumption data, which makes it hard to deepen China's evaluation on the energy output efficiency to the level of regional structure analysis, thus directly

X. Song (✉)
Institute of National Accounting, Beijing Normal University, Beijing, China
e-mail: songxuguang@bnu.edu.cn

X. Li and J. Pan (eds.), *China Green Development Index Report 2012: Regional Comparison*, Current Chinese Economic Report Series,
DOI 10.1007/978-3-642-54178-0_16,

affecting the effectiveness and sustainability of the subsequent theoretical researches and policy designs.

We believe that the tasks of the following three aspects should now be emphatically done well in order to better evaluate China's energy output efficiency: First, we should improving the platform to acquire and process data on energy input and output, focusing on supplementing the microscopic data of the regional energy inputs and outputs so as to offer support of new data for researches such as the analysis on China's energy input and output, the environmental impact of energy consumption, regional sustainable development, etc.

Second, we should carry out the structural researches on energy output efficiency in terms of industrial structure, energy consumption structure, technological progress based on China's reality of economic and social development. The core factors influencing the energy output efficiency should be analyzed through the combination of energy economic theories and empirical econometrics to determine the impact on the changes of energy output efficiency.

Third, we should make pilot accounting of regional energy output efficiency and make case studies through evaluation methods of regional energy output efficiency. On this basis, the accounting and evaluation of regional energy output should be further integrated to carry out the pilot work such as the cooperation of regional energy and industries, adjustment of energy structure and output capacity, evaluation on the change of economic growth modes, monitoring and assessing energy saving and emissions reduction, etc., thus providing quantitative decision-making basis for the relevant departments to formulate the policies.

Professor Xuguang Song, Institute of National Accounting, Beijing Normal University

Chapter 17
Water and China's Green Development

Hongrui Wang

The green development is essentially the scientific development. Since the Global Summit on Environment and Development passed the *Rio Declaration on Environment and Development* in 1992, many countries of the world have been working on promoting the sustainable development. As for China, it is undoubtedly a challenging task to construct a trinity of social, economic and natural green development so that it can be closely meshed with the Chinese civilization and organically integrated with the road of socialism with Chinese characteristics. In this blueprint, the severe water situation has become one of the major restraining factors. With increasing pressure of water shortage, we must protect water resources as what we do to the arable land. The effective and sustainable utilization of water resources through scientific allocation is the key to guarantee and support China's green and harmonious development.

The water supply for residents can be guaranteed in most places of China, but it does not mean that water resources are sufficient in China. In fact, China is basically characterized by too many people with insufficient water and the uneven spatial and temporal distribution of water resources. At the same time, the in-depth development of industrialization and urbanization results in the long-term increasing growth of water demand in China. There will be a more acute contradiction between water supply and demand and a more severe situation of the water resources.

We should advocate the principle of rational water use, scientific management, integrated development and maintenance of balance, scientifically and rationally develop and utilize the water resources, and thus speed up the process of China's green development.

First, this concept of development should follow the guideline to simultaneously broaden the sources and reduce the expenditure. Broadening sources can meet the needs of social and economic development while reducing expenditure can ensure

H. Wang (✉)
College of Water Sciences, Beijing Normal University, Beijing, China
e-mail: henrywang@bnu.edu.cn

X. Li and J. Pan (eds.), *China Green Development Index Report 2012: Regional Comparison*, Current Chinese Economic Report Series,
DOI 10.1007/978-3-642-54178-0_17,

the sustainable utilization of water resources. In light of broadening sources, apart from the large-scale and long-distance water diversion project, positive and effective measures according to local circumstance should be taken to develop renewable water resources, utilize sea water, and acquire rainwater, thus replacing the more valuable freshwater resources. As for reducing expenditure, the following three aspects can be taken into account: First, reduce water consumption and improve the utilization rate of recycling industrial water and irrigation canals for agricultural water; second, play the role of the economic lever of price reform mechanism to raise public awareness of water conservation; third, strengthen the water resources management. The government is required to establish a scientific and rational regulatory system to formulate policies at the height of the national development strategy, give technical supports, and launch a "water revolution" in the society.

It is reported that No.1 Document 2011 by the central Government and the CCCPC Meeting on Water Conservancy have proposed that the implementation of the most stringent water management system will be taken as the strategic initiative to accelerate the transformation of economic development ways, and the construction of a water-saving society will be the main content of building a resource-saving and environmentally friendly society.

Not long before, the State Council issued *Suggestion on Implementation of the Most Stringent Water Management System* and proposed the objectives of controlling the development and utilization of water resources, controlling the water use efficiency and "three red lines" to limit the pollutant holding in water function zones, thus promoting the economic and social development to be adapted to the carrying capacity of water resources and environment.

On April 20, 2012, the High-level Roundtable on the Construction of Chinese Water Management System sponsored by the Global Water Partnership China Committee was held in Beijing. Chen Lei, Minister of Water Resources laid stress on expediting the implementation of the most stringent water management system, focusing on solving China's increasingly complex water problems, efficiently using and effectively protecting water resources, and ensuring the sustainable development of economy and society.

In summary, the water issues, related to the well-being of people of all nationalities, require the joint treatment of the government and the society. In addition, China should strengthen the international exchanges and cooperation, learn and draw on the advanced international concepts, experience and practices to further enhance China's water resources management, promote the transformation of the traditional water conservancy to the modern water conservancy, and safeguard China's green development through the sustainable utilization of water resources.

Professor Hongrui Wang, College of Water Sciences, Beijing Normal University

Chapter 18
Green Economic Development Is the Strategic Choice to Eliminate the Green Poverty

Qi Zhang

The green economy is a globally concerned topic, the eternal theme of China's sustainable development, and the real challenge facing China in the new era to promote the transformation of the development ways and realize the harmonious natural, economic and social development. In particular, the green economic development in the concentrated and contiguous areas with special difficulties, compared to other places, will meet more severe problems, contradictions and challenges in the green economic development. It is very urgent and necessary to strengthen studies on the green economy, green poverty and alleviation of green poverty.

18.1 Green Poverty: The Important Question Facing the Tough Task of Poverty Alleviation in the New Era

Green Poverty seems to be a new term. Literally it seems to mean that the protection of environment and the development of green economy lead to the poverty and the increase of poverty, but actually it is not completely true. We think that green poverty can be analyzed and understood in two aspects: one refers to the poverty for the lack of green and ecological protection system, such as the human survival difficulties caused by lack of water, lean soil or other abominable natural and ecological environment; the other refers to the poverty caused by inconvenient transportation, unfavorable geographic areas, and backward resource and industrial development though with rich green resources and natural ecosystem. It can be seen that the green poverty is a "two-way" poverty, which can be understood

Q. Zhang (✉)
School of Economics and Resource Management, Beijing Normal University, Beijing, China
e-mail: sxzhangqi@163.com

X. Li and J. Pan (eds.), *China Green Development Index Report 2012: Regional Comparison*, Current Chinese Economic Report Series,
DOI 10.1007/978-3-642-54178-0_18, © Springer-Verlag Berlin Heidelberg 2015

as the positive and reverse green poverty. A careful analysis on 14 concentrated contiguous areas with special difficulties in the main battlefield of China's poverty alleviation during the new decade from 2011 to 2020 shows there are positive, reverse and mixed types of green poverty. For example, Liupanshan Area, Yanshan and Taihang Mountains, Luliang Mountains, Dabie Mountains, and Three Regions in Southern Xinjiang, etc. belong to positive green poverty which is caused by lack of resources; Qinba Mountainous Areas, Wuling Mountains, Wumeng Mountains, the rocky desertification areas in Yunnan, Guangxi and Guizhou, Marginal Mountainous Areas of West Yunnan, Mountainous Areas of Southern Great Xing'an Mountain Peak and Luo Xiao Mountains belong to the reverse green poverty. The Tibetan areas of Sichuan Provinces and the Tibetan Region have both, so they are the mixed green poverty.

18.2 Green Economy Is the Strategic Choice to Eliminate Green Poverty

Either positive or reverse green poverty is fundamentally caused by lack of green development. The positive green poverty is the poverty resulting from the abominable ecological environment for the lack of green, thus making it impossible to carry out the development of green economy. The reverse green poverty is the poverty caused by the impossible development of the green resources as well as the lack of green industries. Despite of the differences, they are the same in the lacking or inefficient green economic development. Therefore, enhancing the green economic development is the strategic choice to solve the green poverty.

First, the green economy is macroscopically a new mode of inclusive economic growth and development conducing to the poor people. The past practice has proved it is hard to meet the strategic requirements for eliminating poverty, balancing areas and groups, and achieving harmonious development in the new era simply through the high-speed and high-consumption industrial development, the non-balanced regional development strategies and the excessive economic growth. On the contrary, such strategies more seriously unbalance regional development, deteriorate poverty, prolong the poverty alleviation, and make the poverty alleviation more difficult and the society more unstable. Implementation of the new inclusive economic growth and development conducive to the poor people g is China's strategic choice for the current and future development; it is the urgent task for China's prolonged stability to accelerate the implementation of policies and systems conducive to the poor people and the restructuring of the green economic system to improve their ability.

Second, the green economic development is a sustainable poverty alleviation strategy, which achieves long-term stability and harmony between poverty alleviation and the economic, social and ecological environment rather than the short-term and temporary harmony. This is the fundamental difference with the economic growth oriented poverty alleviation strategy, directly manifesting the basic properties of green economic development, i.e. the harmony between man and nature, and among the people.

18.3 The Green Poverty Alleviation Is the Key for the Tough Task of the Poverty Alleviation in the New Era

The promotion of the green economic development is not only the strategic choice to eliminate the green poverty, but the key for the tough task of the poverty alleviation in the new era. The strategic planning system of green development in poverty-stricken areas, i.e. the green poverty alleviation system should be established. The key of the green poverty alleviation at least includes the following two points.

First, the ecological compensation is the prerequisite for the development of green economy in the poverty-stricken areas. As mentioned above, both the positive green poverty caused by lack of green resources and the reverse green poverty caused by non-development of green resources result from the difficult implementation of the green economy. Meanwhile, the poverty-stricken areas to develop the green economy are often the main functional areas, the development of which is banned or limited by the state. In such a case, the economic development in the poverty-stricken areas will be strictly constrained by the national policies and institutions. These areas take the responsibility for protecting resources, and thus have to be faced with the consequences of fall in economy, reduction in income and deterioration of poverty. We appeal here that the government must work on developing and implementing the ecological compensation system and regulations so as to compensate for the falling income and living standards on the one hand, and protect their equal right for development on the other. A long delay will cause the growing losses for the poverty-stricken areas.

Second, industrial ecologicalization and ecological industrialization are the most effective way for the poverty alleviation in poverty-stricken areas. To alleviate poverty and achieve prosperity in the poverty-stricken areas will eventually need to be supported by building a sustainable industrial system. Only in this way can poverty alleviation and reduction be sustainable. However, the industrial development in poverty-stricken areas should not copy industrial model in the developed regions. They have to make full use of their own characteristics in order to obtain specific advantages, thus determining the implementation of industrial ecologicalization and ecological industrialization. In other words, the sustainable development of industries is to be achieved and the advantages are to be maintained through ecologicalization of industrial development, and the sustainable ecological protection is to be realized through the ecological industrialization. Otherwise, the traditional industrial development at the cost of the environment, resources and energy brings greater risk to the poor and low-income populations. Therefore, industrial ecologicalization and ecological industrialization are the best choices for the green economic development in the poverty-stricken areas. With non-developed industries and unprotected ecological environment, the poverty will be further deteriorated.

Obviously, poverty is an unavoidable theme in the studies on the green economic development. The researches on characteristics and laws of change of the green poverty, and on the mechanism and policies for the green poverty alleviation are not only indispensable, but more necessary and important.

Professor Zhang Qi, School of Economics and Resource Management, Beijing Normal University

Chapter 19
Economic Concentration Helps the Green Development

Jinshe Liang

Economic concentration is conducive to consumption and emissions reduction.

First, concentration is conducive to the environmental protection administration departments to make regulation over enterprises. In fact, many environmental problems result from the high costs of regulation. One of the important reasons lies in the small market in which the gains cannot make up the losses. With the same amount of expenditure for the regulation, the regulatory costs in the concentrated areas, shared by all enterprises, are relatively low, thereby increasing the regulatory efficiency.

Second, similar enterprises in the concentration areas can share the facilities to treat "the three wastes" (waste gas, waste water and industrial residue), and the recycling economy may generate among other enterprises.

Third, the large labor markets may often form in the concentration areas, which can reduce the labor costs for enterprises and provide some space for them to invest in environmental protection.

Fourth, owing to the technological spillover, enterprises in the concentration areas tend to be more innovative, which is manifested in several aspects. Innovation directly results in the increase of the product value or the reduction of production costs.

Except for the first point, the next three imply that enterprises will pay to leave the concentration areas. Therefore, the benefits in the concentration areas can be used to exchange the consumption and emissions reduction. Setting a relatively low pollutant emission in the concentration areas means higher environmental expenditures compared to the non-concentration areas provided that other conditions are equal. However, some enterprises cannot enjoy the external effects if they leave the concentration areas. When the environmental standards in the concentration areas can be well

J. Liang (✉)
School of Geography, Beijing Normal University, Beijing, China
e-mail: liangjs@bnu.edu.cn

X. Li and J. Pan (eds.), *China Green Development Index Report 2012: Regional Comparison*, Current Chinese Economic Report Series,
DOI 10.1007/978-3-642-54178-0_19,

balanced with the non-concentration areas, enterprises can be guided to carry out a higher level of consumption and emissions reduction with this mechanism.

The above analyses show that the spatial economic layout and regional economic policies can guide the economy to develop towards consumption and emissions reduction by using benefits of concentration. The good regional policies and spatial development guidelines must take the green development of economy into account. If the economy intersperses everywhere, enterprise may seek rent to settle places with low cost of environment, thereby impeding the realization of the environmental benefits of concentration.

Many Chinese cities locate enterprises with serious pollution at the "downstream or downwind" part of the city, which is regarded as a spatial layout in favor of the city in the urban planning. However, many cities thus relax the regulation over the "downstream or downwind" enterprises. In fact, it is a great pity as big cities have great concentration benefits, which can be used to encourage enterprises to make innovation for consumption and emissions reduction. The result will further enhance the competitiveness of the city's development, improve the environment and increase the value of land.

In addition to cities, especially large cities, the large-scale economic corridor is another form of concentration. In mainland China, the total land area of the coastal cities (in 12 provinces, municipalities and autonomous regions) and those along the Yangtze River (Shanghai, Zhejiang, Jiangsu, Anhui, Jiangxi, Hubei, Hunan, Chongqing and Sichuan) account for about 26.8 % of the whole country, the population and water resources about 69.6 % and 59.1 % respectively in 2011, while the GDP about 84.5 %. These areas with the best conditions for development in mainland China have great economic potential. Attention should be paid to the positive interaction between concentration and consumption and emissions reduction.

Professor Jinshe Liang, School of Geography, Beijing Normal University

Chapter 20
The Direction of Modern Agricultural Development Is Green Agriculture

Biliang Hu

Agriculture is the foundation of national economy, and it has been proved by the basic theories and the empirical researches of development economics that agricultural productivity can directly affect the process of industrialization and urbanization and the development of other industries and economic sectors of a country, especially a large one. It is for this reason that most countries of the world, particularly the developing countries, attach great importance to the positive significance of agriculture to promote the overall national economic development, and especially to the positive significance to ensure national food security and control inflation through the development of agriculture.

Meanwhile, it is well known that, compared with the traditional agriculture, one of the important characteristics of the modern agriculture is the use of large amounts of chemical fertilizers, pesticides and other modern elements in order to improve the land productivity, thus increasing the carbon emissions in the agricultural sector and bringing negative impact on the environment. Therefore, if the agriculture needs to sustainably develop in the modern society, we should take the environmental factors into full consideration apart from economic factors.

In addition, agriculture has another important feature compared to other economic sectors, that is, the unity of natural production and economic process. The natural resource conditions (such as the quantity and quality of agricultural land, available water and its quality, etc.) have the direct and decisive significance to the agricultural development. Moreover, many important agricultural resources are non-renewable, which determines that the agricultural development must pay special attention to the effective use of natural resources in order to produce more agricultural products with less natural resources.

Thus it can be seen that an agricultural question is absolutely not a single economic question, but a comprehensive one including economic, resource and

B. Hu (✉)
School of Economics and Resource Management, Beijing Normal University, Beijing, China
e-mail: hubiliang@bnu.edu.cn

X. Li and J. Pan (eds.), *China Green Development Index Report 2012: Regional Comparison*, Current Chinese Economic Report Series,
DOI 10.1007/978-3-642-54178-0_20,

environmental factors, which should be taken into account for the development of modern agriculture. We must strive to increase the food production and reduce the carbon emissions of the agricultural sectors. We should not only maintain the environmentally friendly state of agriculture, but also efficiently use the finite agricultural resources. Combined together, the three factors are actually one question, i.e. the development of green agriculture. Therefore, I believe that the correct direction of the modern agricultural development should be the vigorous development of green agriculture.

Professor Hu Biliang, School of Economics and Resource Management, Beijing Normal University

Chapter 21
Restructure the Public Expenditure of the Government

Heng Yin

At present, China should greatly cut down the government's public expenditure on highways, airports, urban squares, etc. and increase the proportion of education, health and social security. The latter can be regarded as the government's green investment.

The educational investment is the main path to accumulate the human capital. Education can also improve national quality and strengthen social harmony and cohesion, but most families, restrained by liquidity, cannot have enough money to achieve the high return of educational investment. In recent years China has implemented policy to charge high fees on education, especially on higher education, and thus the expenditure on higher education accounts for the majority of the income of average families. The secondary education is the same case. Education is a very heavy burden on ordinary families, especially for the majority of rural families. It is hard to know how many students drop out of school due to the liquidity constraints in China, but we can have some idea from a large amount of poor students in the higher education institutions. However, they are lucky in some sense for they can at least continue their studies. Therefore, the government should increase investment in education, suppress the high tuitions and further relieve the public liquidity constraints on the educational investment to ensure every citizen's access to basic education.

The investment in health is also the important path to accumulate the human capital. In China, many families cannot obtain the health care due to liquidity constraints. In rural areas, people becoming poor or falling back into poverty again for illness is an important reason for poverty. Such a problem is equally prominent in Chinese cities. Money, which can alleviate suffering and save lives, has never become such a realistic and clear-cut alternative to life. Whichever way it is seen from, public

H. Yin (✉)
School of Economics and Business Administration, Beijing Normal University, Beijing, China
e-mail: yheng@bnu.edu.cn

X. Li and J. Pan (eds.), *China Green Development Index Report 2012: Regional Comparison*, Current Chinese Economic Report Series,
DOI 10.1007/978-3-642-54178-0_21,

investment in health should be strengthened to establish the medical insurance system including the rural and urban residents.

Low public expenditure on social security is also a common phenomenon in developing countries. As urbanization is speeding up in China, large numbers of rural surplus labor forces flock to cities and towns, which, with the industrial restructuring and the in-depth reform of enterprises, may raise the unemployment rate. The increase of unemployed population and the deterioration of unequal income distribution require the government to increase public investment in social security.

In short, we believe that the government's public expenditures should be comprehensively restructured. In accordance with the idea of public finance, the government should increase the proportion of public expenditure on education, health, and social security and cut down the subsidies for production and the institutional expenditures which can be compensated through the market. The government's expenditure on education should at least account for one sixth of the total fiscal revenue. Calculated according to the proportion 30 % of fiscal revenue in GDP (an appropriate level recently), the public expenditure on education should make up at least 5 % in GDP; the government's expenditure on health care should account for one sixth of the total fiscal revenue, an equivalent to 5 % of GDP; the government's expenditure on basic social security such as the minimum living allowance and pensions should also account for one sixth of the total fiscal expenditure, an equivalent to 5 % of GDP.

Professor Heng Yin, School of Economics and Business Administration, Beijing Normal University

Chapter 22
Carbon Emission Tax—Collect It or Not? How to Collect It?

Jinshi Liu

The global warming caused by the greenhouse gas emission has laid a significant impact on economic and social development of mankind. To meet this challenge, Denmark first started to collect the carbon emission tax in 1990. Since then, many countries have collected the carbon emission tax on fossil fuel products (such as fuel coal, gasoline and natural gas, etc.) according to their carbon content in order to reduce carbon dioxide emissions and protect the environment. At the beginning of the year of 2012, the incident of the European Union's carbon emission tax on airlines produced strong reactions in the world. Quietly, the topic on when China starts to collect the carbon emission tax is more heatedly discussed.

Should the carbon emission tax be collected? Generally speaking, the collection of the carbon emission tax at the necessary time has become the consensus of all walks of life. It has very important significance for China to establish the carbon emission tax mechanism.

First, in the aspect of environmental protection, the carbon emission tax increases the production cost of high energy-consuming enterprises and forces them to reduce energy consumption and promote energy saving and emissions reduction with advanced technology and management methods so as to deal with the climate changes.

Second, in the aspect of economic development, the carbon emission tax can help save energy, promote economic restructuring and transformation of development ways, establish a resource-saving and environmentally friendly society, and achieve sustainable economic development.

Thank Chen Dengke for offering part of the materials. Of course, responsibilities should be taken by their own authors

J. Liu (✉)
School of Economics, Southwestern University of Finance and Economic, Chengdu, China
e-mail: liujinshi@163.com

X. Li and J. Pan (eds.), *China Green Development Index Report 2012: Regional Comparison*, Current Chinese Economic Report Series,
DOI 10.1007/978-3-642-54178-0_22,

Third, in the aspect of international politics, the establishment of carbon emission tax mechanism suitable for China's conditions can build a responsible international image for China, enhance China's discourse right in the world, and increase the initiative in China's foreign exchanges.

How to collect the carbon emission tax? As early as in 2008, the Chinese Academy for Environmental Planning of Ministry of Environmental Protection issued the report of *China's Policy Outline for Carbon Emission Tax in Response to Climate Change*; in 2009, the Research Institute for Fiscal Science, Ministry of Finance formed the report of *Research on Collection of Carbon Emission Tax*, an active exploration for this question; in March 2012, the Chinese Academy of Social Sciences submitted the *Law on Response to Climate Change (Proposal)* to the National People's Congress, Legislative Affairs Office of the State Council, Ministry of Environmental Protection and National Development and Reform Commission, proposing the collection of carbon emission tax on the sales link. How to scientifically, rationally and equally collect the carbon emission tax is a difficult question and it is necessary to rationally design the carbon emission tax collection mechanism based on China's reality.

First, the collection should advance in due order with a low tax rate at the beginning and a gradual and slight increase later so as to reduce the resistance to the collection of the carbon emission tax and avoid serious impact on the economy; the dynamic mechanism of carbon emission tax should be established and the timely adjustment can be made according to the domestic and international economic development as well as the changes of the international political relations.

Second, it should be integrated with the establishment of ecological compensation mechanism. Differential tax rates can be used for different areas. A relatively high tax rate should be set for areas with fragile ecological environment and for those significant to the national ecological protection. At the same time, transfer payments should be used to support the development of these areas to avoid large gaps in regional development.

Third, the appropriate preferential tax policy on industries and enterprises should be formulated. In the premise of scientifically determining the identification methods of carbon emissions, the differential tax rates for different industries can be implemented. Lower rates can be set to industries to be greatly impacted on their competitiveness and related to the national economy and the people's wellbeing. Tax reduction and exemption can be given to enterprises which actively use technology to reduce emissions, recycle carbon dioxide and reach a certain standard.

Fourth, the carbon emissions have strong inter-provincial and international negative externalities. Therefore, the revenue of carbon emission tax should mainly be concentrated in the central financing, used for coordination at the national or even the international level to support the development of China's cause of energy saving and emissions reduction.

Fifth, the collection of carbon emission tax should be integrated with the reform of energy tax, resources tax and other environmental taxes, thus gradually forming a reasonable environmental tax system. Meanwhile, a comprehensive consideration should be taken to integrate it with the reform of carbon emission rights trading.

Sixth, the pilot projects of carbon emission tax should be actively carried out. The carbon emission tax can first be collected in local areas such as some eastern coastal areas with relatively strong economy, improved on the basis of reviewing experience, and then gradually extended to other places throughout the country.

Jinshi Liu, Associate Professor of the School of Economics, Southwestern University of Finance and Economics

Chapter 23
The Function of PM10 and the Potential Value of PM2.5

Li Ding

We adopted the statistical data from 2003 to 2009 (PM10 data started to be officially announced in 2003), analyzed the PM10 data and the mortality data of lung cancer and respiratory diseases in 29 major cities, and acquired the state of PM10 and its impact on mortality rate of respiratory diseases and lung cancer.

The results indicated that the difference of urban residents' lung cancer mortality between 2002 and 2009 was 9.36 out of every 100,000 people, in which 2.673 people were caused by risk factors and 6.687 people by the different age structures of population. It showed that the aging factor of population contributed greatly to mortality from 2002 to 2009, accounting for 71.4 %, while other factors only 28.6 %. As for the respiratory diseases, the morality in 2009 decreased by 42.49 out of every 100,000 people compared to the statistical base year of 2002, in which risk factors dropped the mortality by 59.81 people, accounting for 140.8 %; aging increased the mortality by 17.32 people, contributing to 40.8 %.

So far the main indicator to measure air pollution has been PM10 and many scholars adopt this indicator when studying air pollution. Although a few cities such as Shanghai and Nanjing began to announce the data of PM2.5, most of them are the observational data in the past 5 years with relatively few test points. Therefore, the study of this paper still took the data of PM10 as a major research benchmark, adopted the high-precision surface modeling[4] to make analysis based on the data of PM10 of 29 cities, and acquired nationwide distribution of PM10 and the national average value based on this algorithm.

The results showed that PM10 was zonally distributed with air quality of the northern areas worse than the southern areas. The northwestern areas, Tianjin and Shandong are the most serious. By national distribution, the air quality distribution

Thank Zhang Yan and He Qingyue for their contribution to this part.

L. Ding (✉)
Institute of Development Research, Southwestern University of Finance and Economics, Chengdu, China
e-mail: liding@swufe.edu.cn

X. Li and J. Pan (eds.), *China Green Development Index Report 2012: Regional Comparison*, Current Chinese Economic Report Series,
DOI 10.1007/978-3-642-54178-0_23, © Springer-Verlag Berlin Heidelberg 2015

has features of spatial aggregation and diffusion, and the simulation results are relative in line with the perceptual cognizance of the general public. It is found through the high-precision surface modeling that PM10 in these 7 years fluctuate around 0.11, the standard value with the highest value in 2006, reaching 0.12. According to the first-level standard value 0.04, second-level standard value 0.05 and third-level standard value 0.10, the reference values of annual mean of the inhalable particulate matter PM10, China's air quality has actually been at the third-level standard based on the simulation results of the data of the 29 major cities.

This chapter used standardized mortality of the respiratory diseases to analyze the correlation with PM10. Although the timeliness between respiratory diseases and air pollution is very quick, the mortality lags at least 1 year after getting ill. Therefore, when selecting the independent variables, we added the PM10 lagging 1 year to build a binary regression for correlation analysis. The results indicated that the fit chart of PM10 and lung cancer mortality was splashingly distributed, showing no typical correlation. And then we continued to fit with data lagging 1 or 2 years behind, showing no good effect. Therefore, the statistical results of the existing PM10 showed no apparent correlation with the lung cancer mortality.

It was found through the static analyses that the aging population laid relatively high impact on the lung cancer morality and the growth rate of predisposing factors impacting the disease morality was far less than the aging population. However, the dynamic analysis is more concerned about the change of trend. In general, lung cancer morality is rising. Today when medical conditions and living standards are highly developed, the predisposing factors are still affecting people's health. By the national distribution of PM10, the air quality in the northern areas is inferior to that of the southern areas, the reasons for which are not only the impact of the dust storms in the northern areas, but far more heavy industries in the northern areas than in the south. Moreover, the national origins of energy are mainly concentrated in the north. Tianjin and Shandong with developed industrially are seriously polluted. The air pollution in many cities, especially in large and medium cities, has been characterized by pollution mixed with smoke and car exhaust. Therefore, to improve the environmental quality, it is important to focus on the main polluted areas to reduce or contain the production and spread of pollution according to the local conditions.

The research on correlation between PM10 and the respiratory diseases mortality proved the impact of air pollution on human health. The research showed that environment was positively correlated with mortality, that is, with the improvement of environmental quality, disease mortality declined. Lung cancer mortality is not well correlated with PM10 for different reasons. Chen Shijie et al. (2003) discovered that the latent period of cancer induced by air pollutants was 7–8 years. Secondly, the environmental indicator of PM10 is unable to measure the real environmental conditions. China's current air quality standards were prepared in 1982 and amended respectively in 1996 and in 2000. Internationally, many countries have adopted PM2.5 as the indicator to measure air pollution. PM2.5 refers to particulates with diameter less than or equal to 2.5 μm, also known as inhalable particulate matters. PM10 can directly go into the bronchi and be engulfed by alveolar macrophages (AM). It was found in human lung autopsy that particulate matters remained in the bronchial walls and caused thickening of bronchial walls and increase of collagenocytes and inflammatory cells Kong Xianghuan and Yin Xuejun (1996). The smaller the particulates are, the greater the harm is to human health. Therefore, compared with PM10, PM2.5 is more correlated with the impact on the diseases. We should accelerate the improvement of environmental monitoring indicator system and lay a foundation for better environmental governance and research.

Li Ding, Associate Professor of the School of Public Administration, Southwestern University of Finance and Economics

Chapter 24
On the Approach to Household Waste Separation in Urban Communities

Fangfang Tang

China's policy related to household waste separation and recycling was first proposed in 1992, but underwent slow development in the following 10 years. The Western developed countries have led the world in the household waste separation and recycling, and have been well-developed in the legal system in environmental protection, technologies of household waste separation and disposal and industrial chain of household waste disposal. However, China has the household waste classified and recycled basically by 400,000 scavengers and cleaners. With the increasing progress of urbanization, the household waste separation and recycling have become a topic receiving much concern.

The following problems exist in the current household waste disposal in China's urban communities.

First, the knowledge of household waste separation has not been effectively popularized and publicized, and in the very little publicity, the separation is ambiguous and abstract without detailed instructions. Many citizens state that they do not understand how to specifically classify household waste. Seeing ambiguous signs on the household waste bins, they more often than not throw the household waste into the nearest bin.

Second, there is the shortage of facilities to recycle the household waste and the industrial chain to classify and recycle household waste has not been systematically formed. Classified or not, the household waste will ultimately be disposed with unified landfill or incineration. Even if the household waste is classified in accordance with the international standards, it will finally be mixed up.

Third, the separation and recycling of household waste are optional with narrow recycling. The spontaneous scavengers and cleaners made an important contribution to household waste separation, but they only collect the "salable" waste. Other recyclable household waste will not be recycled with short-term absence of institutions.

F. Tang (✉)
National Policy Lab & Economics, Finance and Marketing, National School of Development, Peking University, Peking, China
e-mail: fftang@ccer.edu.cn

X. Li and J. Pan (eds.), *China Green Development Index Report 2012: Regional Comparison*, Current Chinese Economic Report Series,
DOI 10.1007/978-3-642-54178-0_24,

Fourth, household waste separation involves too many government departments, which are not effectively coordinated with clear responsibilities. Some environment and hygiene management personnel are not positive to household waste separation. They are not willing to spend energy sorting out household waste. For household waste disposal, they will carry it off as soon as possible and take the "out of sight, out of mind" attitude.

For the problems mentioned above, we can propose the corresponding improvement program as follows:

First, we should strengthen the publicity in the community. For example, we can display the ways of classifying and disposing household waste on the community publicity panels, make lectures on household waste separation, and offer voluntary activities. Television can present more public-interest advertising rather than vague slogan to teach people how to classify household waste and advocate household waste separation. In addition, the education and knowledge generalization of household waste separation can be carried out since childhood. For instance, Japan includes the knowledge of household waste separation in textbooks and even tests on the knowledge of household waste separation.

Second, not only should household waste disposal hardware facilities be built, but the technology of household waste disposal needs to follow up in order to gradually form an industry chain for household waste recycling. Germany has established a complete industrial system for household waste disposal with more than 250,000 employees, covering occupations from engineers, civil servants to ordinary workers.

Third, we should strengthen support and guidance for the spontaneous scavengers and cleaners. Scavengers are not paid by the government so they will not increase the financial pressure. The government can build a standardized recycling mechanism to expand scavengers' disposal aspects so that the government can reduce the economic and environmental costs in its own disposal. Cleaners can be organized and collectively trained on the household waste business, and incentives can be given for specific performances.

Fourth, the department coordination system should be improved and responsibilities of various departments should be clearly defined through laws and regulations. We can draw on the successful experience from foreign countries which have more perfect legislation on household waste separation.

The successful implementation of the household waste separation system cannot be divorced from the residents' active participation, from the strict guarantee of laws and regulations, and from the market mechanism with intrinsic economic incentives. They can be summed up as: publicity goes first with multi-participants; supervision is strengthened with two-way incentives and legal protection.

Professor Fangfang Tang, China Center for Economic Research, Peking University

Chapter 25
Green Management of Household Waste and Source Reduction

Jiang Yuan

It has been the common goal pursued by the household waste management at home and abroad from the terminal disposal based on engineering technical measures to green management of household waste focusing on quantity reduction and reclamation utilization. Therefore, China's urban environmental management should not only introduce new technologies and processes to implement the harmless treatment of household waste, but also pay attention to integrating it with China's conditions, drawing on the existing household waste quantity reduction and reclamation measures of other countries, achieving source reduction of household waste, and truly putting the management of urban household waste into the track of sustainable green management. Therefore, the following measures are recommended to take:

25.1 The Industrial Standards Should Be Formulated to Extensively Carry Out Household Waste Separation and Collection

Household waste separation and collection is the key link in household waste management, not only influencing the effects of quantity reduction, but also determining the quantity and quality of household waste recycling. In order to ensure the purity and quality of the available classified and concentrated items, the household waste management departments should propose the household waste separation system suitable for China's conditions as early as possible and develop norms and standards for separation and collection in order to regulate purchasing

J. Yuan (✉)
College of Resources Science and Technology, Beijing Normal University, Beijing, China
e-mail: jiangy@bnu.edu.cn

X. Li and J. Pan (eds.), *China Green Development Index Report 2012: Regional Comparison*, Current Chinese Economic Report Series,
DOI 10.1007/978-3-642-54178-0_25,

prices and quality and guarantee the sources and quality of raw materials and distribution channels for waste-utilizing enterprises.

25.2 Deposit Policy for Reusable Packaging Should Be Implemented

In view of China's reality that residents are not well aware of bringing their own shopping bags and returning bottles or boxes, it is recommended to implement deposit system for bottles and boxes as well as the charging policy for shopping bags to reduce the white pollution and promote the reuse of packaging. Shops selling goods and consumers using goods should make joint efforts to improve the recycling rate of reusable substances and assume the costs, which fully comply with the environment management principles that those who cause pollution are responsible for cleaning up.

25.3 Enterprises Should Be Encouraged to Develop Recycled Products and the Market for Recycled Products Should Be Cultivated

Various preferential policies should be taken to promote the development, production and management of household waste-recycled products. The household waste-recycled products available for consumers and the environmentally friendly products in favor of household waste reduction should be developed as soon as possible. Meanwhile, various publicity activities should be carried out to make residents have a full understanding of the environmental effects and the significance of purchasing and using environmentally friendly products. The government should play an exemplary role and the proportion of environmentally friendly or recycled products in the government's procurement should be increased.

25.4 Household Waste Charging Method Should Be Adjusted to Differentiate the Charges on Separated and Unseparated Household Waste

All of the China's cities implementing household waste charging policies charge household waste on the average quantity. The industrialization of household waste disposal is the necessary requirement of socialist market economy for the cause of environmental protection, and the rational household waste charging standard is the important prerequisite for the industrialization of household waste disposal. A change from charging on average quantity to PAYT (pay as you throw) and differential charges can restrain the residents' arrangement of household waste and help the household waste management enterprises and the resources reuse enterprises raise funds, develop more resource-recycled products or improve product quality, and ultimately establish the green household waste management system integrating the separation, collection and recycling of household waste and the development and market cultivation of environmentally friendly products.

Professor Jiang Yuan, College of Resources Science and Technology, Beijing Normal University

Chapter 26
The Key Issues of Green Development – Small Acts, Values and Systems

Jiansheng Liu

Green development is the fundamental direction of social development. We must seize the key issues to realize it. The key issues are the start from minor affairs, values and system.

I have still deeply impressed by two things when I was in South Korea in the early 1990s. The first thing was the use of toothpick. After using the toothpick, I habitually threw it in the lunch box. One of the Korean friends took it out for me, while the other even blamed me severely. I was very embarrassed at that time. As their honorable guest, I could not understand why they were so serious on such a minor affair. Later they told me that the surplus food of the meal would be used as feedstuff. A toothpick mixed there would pierce the throat of a pig. Such a case had been specially reported and discussed. I then particularly observed how toothpicks were used every time I had a meal at restaurants in South Korea. They were taken away after used as my friends had done. Contrasted with South Korea 20 years ago, I am deeply impressed for at the elite level in China today, college students and teachers have no such a concept. There are toothpicks, napkins and paper cups in leftover buckets in dining halls of universities. There is no basic public education, knowledge, habits and institutions on household waste separation and recycling economy. The second thing was that no "big" Benz cars which were everywhere in China could be found in Seoul. Almost all cars were made in South Korea and there were only a few "small" (mainly for enterprises to receive foreign guests) and conventional Benz (Big Benz was made for Chinese only). Twenty years later, the big-car culture has been evolved to a disastrous extent in China.

Green development is the fundamental direction for China's current and even future development as well as the national issue. The key to realize it lies in minor affairs and values. The core of green development is to handle several problems: environmental problems, pollution problems and sustainable development problems.

J. Liu (✉)
Institute of Energy Economics, Southwestern University of Finance and Economics, Chengdu, China
e-mail: liujiansheng2004168@sina.com

X. Li and J. Pan (eds.), *China Green Development Index Report 2012: Regional Comparison*, Current Chinese Economic Report Series,
DOI 10.1007/978-3-642-54178-0_26,

The green development of cities, especially the large cities is the core of China's current green development, and the main problems of the urban green development are household waste disposal and many problems caused by automobile uses. If these problems could be solved well, over a half of the problems of the urban green development would be solved. If everyone disposed household waste as Korean disposed toothpicks, household waste would not be a problem but our wealth. If China's automobile culture could be fundamentally adjusted, China's urban green development would be fundamentally changed. It is urgent to carry out the green development in Chinese cities. The traffic congestion and urban pollution caused by Chinese urbanization have developed to an extent over the past 10 years that must be resolved immediately, an extent that could hardly be seen worldwide in the past. The solution to this problem is the special issue for the development of China's mega-cities. As for the key issue—the Chinese urban automobile culture, China must implement the most stringent control and management system over urban automobiles in order to effectively promote the healthy development of China's urbanization, fundamentally solve the urban pollution, control the growth in oil consumption to the maximum degree, and guarantee the national energy security.

China's green development needs to start from big cities, from the capital in particular, and especially from the elite circles in the capital, thus giving the greatest driving effect. For all of these, the key is to lay foundation for green society and green development at the aspects of minor affairs, values and systems.

Professor Jiansheng Liu, Institute of Energy Economics, Southwestern University of Finance and Economics

Chapter 27
"Four-dimensional" Promotion Policy of China's Green Humanistic Development

Baoyuan Li

In the 2010 column of this report, I have clearly pointed out: based on China's actual situation, a developing country with a large population in the development of industrialization and urbanization and market-oriented institutional transformation, following the general international trend of global, digital and flattening green economic development, Chinese economic development should implement the "green humanistic strategy". In accordance with four basic levels of economic development, I further proposed the "four-dimensional and all-round" strategy to promote China's green humanistic development.

First, at the dimension of economic growth, we should adopt the humanistic development strategy "based on non-governmental market-oriented green development and elastically driven by macro-control of green GDP". To have the "green" vitality, the economic growth must "follow the mass line" so as to ensure to the maximum extent the "autonomous selection right" for individuals, the "free interactive space" for the public, and the "natural expansion order" for the market. To this end, the government, when promoting economic growth, must not have the inexplicable "utilitarianism" or "sense of achievement". In the macro-control and market regulation, the most important thing is not the "strength" but the "sense of direction" and the "big policy" under the premise of seizing the general direction and trend. The most significant "humanistic" spirit and "green" performance, to be simply put, is to "believe in the masses and govern without interference". Currently, the most pressing thing to be immediately implemented is to establish and improve the "green GDP" statistical evaluation and early warning indicator system. In my view, the fundamental obstacles or difficulties for its being delayed so long without results as the "multi-step water and electricity price" and other initiatives related to green development are not at the level of "technical operation", but the problem of "conceptual attitude" and "emancipation of mind".

B. Li (✉)
Business School, Beijing Normal University, Beijing, China
e-mail: byli@163.com

X. Li and J. Pan (eds.), *China Green Development Index Report 2012: Regional Comparison*, Current Chinese Economic Report Series,
DOI 10.1007/978-3-642-54178-0_27,

Second, at the restructuring dimension, we should adopt the humanistic development strategy "opening urbanized channels for regional mobility based on the realistic background of industrialized development". Economic development is reflected mainly as industrial and regional situations in the "structure". I propose to determine the right direction, proceed from reality, connect between two tracks, and take the staged progressive road. Specifically, as for the industrial policy, powerful measures must be taken to immediately rationalize the enterprises relying on high energy consumption and intense workforces, especially the low-end primary mining, manufacturing and processing enterprises inducing serious pollution and earning black and even bloody money; the administrative barriers to entry should be completely removed and the administrative and market monopoly should be thoroughly smashed for the dominant or pillar industries which not only accord with the basic direction of green development, but also expand employment and protect laborers' rights; More autonomous, free and relaxed space for development should be given in policy to the sunrise industries which accord with the direction of future green development and can greatly enhance the quality and skills of human resources and the core competitiveness of enterprise. All efforts should be made to support and promote them from several aspects such as finance, taxation and credit. As for the regional policy, any administrative regulations and provisions obvious to segregate urban and rural places, restrict activities in a designated area and discriminate identities must be resolutely and quickly cleaned up and punished; Any administrative acts obstructing the free flow of urban, rural and regional resources, especially the human resources mainly for the vested interests of the departments must be resolutely stopped and the legal and administrative responsibilities must be strictly investigated. In the process of promoting industrialization and urbanization, we should pay special attention to the elastic balance strategy "proceeding from reality and connecting the two tracks", and lay stress of the humanistic green governance on the "dual non-green pollution" (i.e., the black and blood pollution of low-level heavy chemical industry and the heavy pollution of vehicle exhaust and massive construction projects in large and medium cities).

Third, at the dimension of institutional change, we should adopt the humanistic development strategy "unwaveringly adhering to the general direction of market-oriented reform, boldly and resolutely breaking through the roadblocks of the vested interest groups in the old system, and perseveringly pushing forward the political process of democratization". In accordance with the thought of green humanistic development, the market is a natural extension order of human beings and the market-oriented development represents the basic direction of humanism. It should be politically made clear that hindering the reform process, conserving vested interests of sectors and strengthening administrative monopoly barriers with every conceivable means are the worst "non-green" and even "black" performance at the dimension of institutional change, which does not accord with the general direction of the trend of "green humanism" of the institutional change and must be resolutely opposed; at the same time, the general direction of market-oriented reform should be made clear in education, health and housing and other areas with the most serious problems in wellbeing, various administrative monopolies opposing to the general direction of market-oriented reform should be boldly and resolutely removed, and the equivalent relations of good governance with tripartite balance of the government's public functions, citizens' social autonomy and the market economic mechanism should be straightened out as soon as possible.

Fourth, at the dimension of welfare improvement, we should adopt the humanistic development strategy that "all citizens have equal social opportunities for development and fair right to share the fruits of development". We should be truly based on humanistic concept of "development for all and all with development". Under the premise of stimulating the internal motivation of the public to freely and independently conduct market innovation, work for prosperity and develop economy, the government should practically do the following: First, completely abandon various household registration and identity discrimination systems formed in the planned economic institutions, remove the hedge of various systems restricting the educational development and market-oriented free flow of human resources as soon as possible, and maximize fair and relaxed environment of social system; second, enhance the reform of the state-owned large-and middle-size enterprises, institutions, and in particular the government and take effective measures to boldly and resolutely abolish various administrative monopoly barriers; third, establish and improve a whole set of unified and comprehensive national social security system, especially implement the fiscal policies to collect the progressive tax on high income, inheritance tax and real estate tax as soon as possible, and enhance the control on income distribution and wealth gap.

In this way, the Chinese green economic development can truly be "people-oriented, overall, coordinated and sustainable", and then get increasingly closer to the goal of a harmonious society where "prosperity for all has been achieved and everyone has an equal share of the results of reform and development".

Professor Baoyuan Li, School of Economics and Business Administration, Beijing Normal University

Chapter 28
On Ambivalence of China's Emerging Middle Class on Green Consumption

Luozhong Wang

The green consumption with the theme of energy saving, environmental protection and health is the main driving force pulling the green industry and the basic aspect of building green economy. The emerging middle class with early awakening environmental consciousness, high requirements of environmental quality and the fame for China's "environmental pioneers", was once placed on with high hopes in terms of green consumption. But so far, the Chinese middle class has still kept in a contradictory state in green consumption with much talk and little action, many complaints and little self-discipline, philosophy first, action behind, and progress slow. Its root cause is that in the present-day China, the consumer mentality of the emerging middle class at all levels is far away from the requirements of the green consumption.

First, in the consumption involving the survival needs, the green consumption of the middle class is constrained by both price and quality. In recent years, as the issues of toxic toys and furniture and contaminated water and air have been disclosed, the Chinese middle class has increased its environmental awareness in the consumption of clothing, food, shelter, transportation and other necessities of life. However, the energy-saving and environmentally friendly hybrid and electric vehicles, "green buildings", energy-saving lamps and other high-tech products are often higher in price than the similar general goods, which is prohibitive to the price-sensitive middle class. Meanwhile, various types of environmental claims, labeling and standards flooding the market make them at a loss as to what to do. The lack of confidence in the quality of domestic green products makes the middle class reluctant when consuming these products.

Second, in the consumption concerning the development needs, the middle class pays obviously more attention to the economic, social and short-term considerations in consumption choice than to the low-carbon, green and eco-friendly concepts. In a big city like Beijing, many of the middle class on the one hand

L. Wang (✉)
School of Management, Beijing Normal University, Beijing, China
e-mail: bnuwlz@126.com

X. Li and J. Pan (eds.), *China Green Development Index Report 2012: Regional Comparison*, Current Chinese Economic Report Series,
DOI 10.1007/978-3-642-54178-0_28, © Springer-Verlag Berlin Heidelberg 2015

complain the difficult parking, serious traffic jams and poor air quality, and on the other hand actively buy private cars, and even buy more than one in order to avoid the trouble caused by limited license numbers. Such contradictory behaviors are determined by the real development needs of the middle class. As many of the emerging middle class are in the critical start-up and rising period of career, the fast pace of work and overload competitive pressure make them try everything they can to spare time and energy to handle working affairs. Therefore, the traffic congestion in rush hours, inadequate supply in particular times and at particular places, and the inconvenient public transport service system at certain occasions are naturally not the first choice of the middle class. Moreover, in many cases, the emerging middle class needs to show off their economic strength and promotion of social status through the consumption patterns and consumer products in line with the specific social evaluation criteria in order to enter, operate and expand the social circle and contact network helpful to their development. However, these evaluation criteria are not formulated according to the simple, healthy, and eco-friendly environmental philosophy, but the social and economic indicators reflecting the distinction of wealth and status.

Finally, in the consumption relevant to the hedonist needs, the green consumption does not necessarily rank first among many options. In the polarized social structure, resentment to the rich in the field of distribution and the "wealth-chasing" impulse in the field of consumption often coexist with one another. Many of the middle class try their best to imitate the lifestyle of the upper class, and luxurious consumers' goods such as the international famous brand clothes, high fuel consumption, luxury car with large displacement, over-decorated residence and upscale restaurants and clubs are favored by the middle class as the social symbols to attract attention and win respect. The two contradictory orientations of luxury and thrift are often uncoordinatedly mixed together, and many office workers will be driving a BMW and seeking half a free parking place for an hour.

Green consumption, as an ecological-based and high-level rational consuming behavior, is a research project far from being solved even in the Western countries, because it is not the first choice in light of the natural orientation of humanism. Tangibly or intangibly constrained by the consumption environment, stage of economic development, social structure and ways of resource allocation in developing countries like China, the green consumption is rather a kind of luxury than necessity for the emerging middle class; it can be easily accepted but hard implemented; it is the "business of enterprises or the government", but "none of my business". But it is for this reason that this career imperative for the long-term development of human society deserves more attention. "The wind rises from the tip of the water weed." With individuals as the starting point, starting from the minimum affairs such as materials recycling and efficient use of energy, relying on the community and other social grass-root organizations for management, combined with policy guidance of tax regulation, the green consumption is expected to obtain greater space for development.

Luozhong Wang, Associate Professor, School of Management, Beijing Normal University

Chapter 29
Bright Prospects of Green Jobs

Desheng Lai

After 30 years of rapid growth, China is faced with many constraints in population, resources and environment. Therefore, the concepts of sustainable, green, scientific and inclusive development are widely recognized and gradually transformed into practice. The outline of the 12th Five-Year Plan clearly proposed: "We will confront increasing resource and environmental restrictions, thus crisis awareness should be enhanced. We will establish green and low carbon development ideas, focus on energy conservation and emissions reduction, improve incentives and constraint mechanisms, and stimulate the establishment of resource-saving and environmentally friendly production and consumption to strengthen sustainable development and improve ecological standards." It means that China has set the trajectory for its future economic development, which must be green and low carbon. The green and low carbon economic development is destined to be a "creative destruction" to employment: on the one hand, the green industries will create a lot of jobs; on the other hand, the traditional industries with high energy consumption and pollution will gradually be compressed or eliminated, and jobs will be destroyed, thereby generating a large number of unemployed population. Therefore, how to balance the creative destruction is the problem necessary to be seriously taken in the process of transformation of economic development.

Green job is a direction with bright prospects. The International Labor Organization, United Nations Environment Program and the International Trade Union Confederation issued the *Green Jobs Initiative* in 2007, pointing out that the green jobs, also known as green-collar jobs, refer to jobs which can greatly promote the maintenance and repair of environmental quality in terms of agriculture, manufacturing, research and development, administration and services. All of the countries attach great importance to it. For example, during the presidential campaign in 2008, Barack Obama, as the Democratic presidential candidate, promised

D. Lai (✉)
School of Economics and Business Administration, Beijing Normal University, Beijing, China
e-mail: lai@bnu.edu.cn

X. Li and J. Pan (eds.), *China Green Development Index Report 2012: Regional Comparison*, Current Chinese Economic Report Series,
DOI 10.1007/978-3-642-54178-0_29,

to produce five million "green jobs". To reach this goal, the Obama administration, once coming into office, began to give subsidies to all green industries as the former administration. According to statistics, the government spent up to ten billion US dollars supporting a variety of green energy plans every year. In 2011, the Obama administration spent 16 billion US dollars to boost "green jobs". Another example is that in early January 2009, Japan and South Korea announced respectively that they would invest huge amounts of money in green projects to create jobs and stimulate the economic growth. Japan stated that it would implement the credit policy of zero interest rate for environmentally friendly enterprises for the purpose of enlarging the green economic market and creating one million new jobs. South Korea said it would invest 38 billion US dollars in a series of domestic eco-friendly projects in the next 4 years, thus creating 960,000 new jobs.

According to the definition by some Chinese scholars, green jobs include three areas: First, the direct green jobs, such as forestation, environmental protection, etc. Workers on these posts are directly employed for the "green jobs", referred to as "pure green" employment; second, the indirect green jobs, referring to the indirect creation of opportunities for "green jobs" by implementing green production, lifestyles and consumption, etc., such as the manufacturing of materials for solar energy and energy-saving buildings, deepening of recycling economy, etc. Workers on these posts are indirectly employed for the "green jobs", referred to as "pan-green" employment; third, green transformative jobs, referring to green jobs transformed from non-green jobs, such as the control of pollution caused in production, change of energy-saving and environmentally friendly technology in production, etc. Workers originally on posts with high pollution and emissions are changed to green jobs, referred to as "greening" employment. Such transformation involves all aspects of technology, methods, processes of production and the end products Xiaozhi (2011). According to this definition, the green jobs permeate throughout all industries and all aspects of these industries and have huge potential for growth.

However, it is a complex systematic project to turn this potential into reality, which needs the joint efforts of many aspects. The government plays a key role. Governments at all levels should not only support the development of green industries, the creation of green jobs and green entrepreneurship in policy, but also carry out reform and innovation at the institutional level so that enterprises have the momentum to go beyond the traditional mode of economic development, include environmental protection and resource conservation in their production function, pursue the green GDP, and leave a greener world for the future.

Professor Desheng Lai, School of Economics and Business Administration, Beijing Normal University

Chapter 30
"Green Wellbeing" Is the Real Quality Wellbeing

Renwu Tang

"People's wellbeing" is the basis for a harmonious society. It is not only an old topic, but one of the most conspicuous terms in China today. The development of "wellbeing" can be roughly divided into three stages: "solution", "improvement" and "development". China, still in the primary stage of socialism, has just accomplished the task of providing adequate food and clothing and entered the "moderately prosperous" society. Therefore, the "wellbeing" of China is still in the stages of "solution" and "improvement". To solve the problems of wellbeing today, the government has to meet the people's needs for survival rights and development requirements, ensuring that all the people enjoy their rights, employment, medical and old-age care, housing and education.

The "development" of wellbeing is not just the economic growth and the rise of per capita incomes. More importantly, people' sense of happiness will increase after the growth of the national income with good air quality, convenient transportation, blue sky, green water and mountains, clean environment, safe food and harmonious society. Therefore, only the development of "green wellbeing" is the real efficient wellbeing. Specifically, the "green wellbeing" has the following features.

First, it is supported by the concept of green and low carbon development. Although the "green wellbeing" is rich in connotation, the most basic idea is to achieve the economic and social development and the coordination between population, resources and environment through saving resources, protecting environment, reducing energy consumption and greenhouse gas emissions, and promoting low carbon technologies. It is the wellbeing with sustainability supported by resource-saving and environmentally friendly production methods and consumption patterns. In the development of wellbeing, harmony between mankind and society, between mankind and nature is to be achieved.

R. Tang (✉)
School of Management, Beijing Normal University, Beijing, China
e-mail: rwtang@bnu.edu.cn

X. Li and J. Pan (eds.), *China Green Development Index Report 2012: Regional Comparison*, Current Chinese Economic Report Series,
DOI 10.1007/978-3-642-54178-0_30,

Second, it is the wellbeing with the synchronous progress of objective figures and subjective feelings. The "green wellbeing" not only refers to the increase of GDP, but more importantly, the rise of indicators for the people's satisfaction, comfort and happiness, especially the mental joy and spiritual harmony. Can the people be harmonious in heart, happy in spirit and comfortable in life when they eat meat and fish with polluted air, contaminated water, gray environment, and the sun and green to be seen nowhere? The "green wellbeing" is not only manifested by the people's real increase in objective income: they have more money in the pocket, richer food on the table, more spacious houses, more convenient transport, and no worry about education, medical and old-age care; more importantly, it is reflected by the increase of the people's subjective feelings: they feel a happier life, bluer sky, greener water, brighter sun, and more comfortable environment.

Third, it is the sustainable wellbeing. Development is the absolute principle, and the key for China to solve the wellbeing problems relies on its own development, achieving a moderately prosperous society in all respects, building modernization, further improving the people's material and cultural lives, enhancing the comprehensive national strength, and remaining invincible in the volatile global environment. The development of wellbeing with different methods and paths will have distinctly different developmental results. China is a country with serious shortage of resources per capita, with per capita arable land, freshwater and forests accounting for only 32, 27.4 and 12.8 % of the world average level respectively, and per capita reserves of oil, natural gas, iron ore and other resources also significantly lower than the world average level. Coupled with the long-term implementation of the mode of extensive economic growth mainly relying on investment and increase of material inputs, the consumption of energy and other resources increase very rapidly, and the environmental deterioration has become increasingly highlighted. Therefore, "made in China" should turn into "created in China", the method of production at the cost of resource consumption and environmental deterioration should be changed into efficient production mode with high added value, low energy consumption and low pollution. Only by building thc ccological civilization, forming thc cncrgy-saving and environmentally friendly industrial structure, ways of growth and consumption patterns can the sustainable development of "green wellbeing" be ensured.

Fourth, it is wellbeing with resource-saving consumption. "Green wellbeing" is by no means the greedy wellbeing recklessly wasting the natural goods, but the wellbeing treasuring resources and protecting the environment. While enjoying the achievements of the modern civilization, we are creating the bitter fruits poisoning ourselves and consuming the resources of our posterities. Statistics show that the United States with 6 % of the world's population consumes one third of the worldwide resources. The use of the Earth's energy by 200 million population of the United States is equivalent to the use of 20 billion populations of the developing countries. The materials consumed by an American in his life are 60 times as many as an Indian. The maintenance of a consumer society like the United States needs as many resources as of five Earth's. China is a developing country, and its basic national conditions of large population and insufficient per capita resources decide that China should not imitate the road of the United States and other developed countries in the wellbeing development. Private cars should be moderately developed, energy and land should be saved in construction industry, and villas and golf courses must be restrained. Only by establishing a conservation-oriented, green, natural, harmonious and healthy consumption pattern can the development of "green wellbeing" be ensured.

Five, it is the wellbeing putting people first and achieving people's overall development. The ultimate goal of the development of the "green wellbeing" is to achieve people's overall development, including the overall development of people's needs, freedom in personality, talent, interests and moral quality. In the final analysis, it is the achievement of people's overall physical and mental development. Therefore, the development of the "green wellbeing", especially in the era of knowledge and information economy, should make everyone fear no trouble in the rear, lightheartedly live and work in this world, and enjoy warmth and happiness of the life.

Professor Renwu Tang, School of Management, Beijing Normal University

Appendices

Appendix 1 International Comparison of Urban Green Development

Cities are significant achievements of human civilization and the major spatial carrier of modern economic and social development and social activities. At present, economic globalization and regional integration lead to reform of production and organizational modes, and increasing resource and environmental pressures drive cities to green development. From a global perspective, green city has become an important development pattern of world's cities; while from a domestic perspective, cities of China have to be open-minded, learn, compete and cooperate with international cities based on domestic conditions. To get an insight of the development pattern and attributes of world's green cities and facilitate building of green cities in China, we prepared the international comparison framework of urban green development and made comparative analysis on the green development of world's cities. It has to be noted that, despite of extensive efforts made by the research group in selecting cities and collecting indicators, international comparison of regional and city green development is to be further explored, compared with domestic comparison; and due to both subjective and objective restrictions, some representative cities and some important indicators are not included into the measurement system; some key factors affecting city green development are not presented due to indicator and data restrictions; the research methodology is yet to be optimized and cannot adequately reflect the green development level of cities; research findings and rankings are for reference only. We hope these could be improved in future works.

X. Li and J. Pan (eds.), *China Green Development Index Report 2012: Regional Comparison*, Current Chinese Economic Report Series,
DOI 10.1007/978-3-642-54178-0, © Springer-Verlag Berlin Heidelberg 2015

A1.1 Sample Selection

To compare and measure GDI of cities in various countries and regions as accurate as possible, and present objective and scientific research findings, we observed three standards in selection of sample cities: (1) the international significance of the city; (2) the social and economic status and representativeness of the city in the region it lies, and; (3) The accessibility, accuracy and normalization of statistical data of the city. Based on the standards, we selected 100 sample cities, including 46 European cities, 22 North American cities, 18 Asian cities, 7 African cities, 4 South American cities, and 3 Oceanian cities, which covered major developed and developing countries. Many of the cities are well-known as economic, political or cultural centers, and represented various development levels in different parts of the world.

A1.2 Indicators and Source of Data

The framework for international comparison of urban green development is based on the indicator framework for CGDI. The first-class indicators include Green Degree of Economic Growth (GDEG), Carrying Capacity Potential of Natural Resources and Environment (CCPNRE) and Support Degree of Government Policies (SDGP). Considering the difficulty in indicator collection and availability of city statistical data, we included six second-class indicators, namely Green GDP per capita, Environmental liveability, CO_2 emission per capita, Energy consumption of the city, Index of governmental public governance, and Index of environmental governance performance. Based on the measurement methodology for GDI of cities in China and the significance and role of each indicator, the Delphi Technique Method was adopted for weight distribution of the international comparison of city green development indicators (Table A1.1).

International comparison of city green development requires high data quality. Among the second-class indicators, Green GDP per capital, Environmental liveability and CO_2 emission per capita were based on the data from the global urban competitiveness database of Urban Competitiveness Center of CASS, and Energy consumption level of city, Index of governmental public governance, and Index of environmental governance performance were based on data rankings worked out by international organizations. Specifically, Green GDP per capita equaled to city GDP minus damages caused by CO_2 emission. GDP data came from official websites of the cities, national statistics websites, regional statistical reports of EU; Environmental liveability was a synthesized data of average temperature, humidity, sunny days and geographic location to describe the weather friendliness; data of CO_2 emission per capita was based on the database of UN Statistics Division; data of Energy consumption level of city was based on *BP Statistical Review of World Energy*; Index of governmental public governance, developed by

Table A1.1 Indicators for measuring GDI of cities worldwide

No.	First-Class Indicators	Weight (%)	Second-Class Indicators
1	Green Degree of Economic Growth	30	Green GDP per capita
2	Carrying Capacity Potential of Natural Resources and Environment	40	Environmental liveability
			CO_2 emission per capita
			Energy consumption level of the city
3	Support Degree of Government Policies	30	Index of governmental public governance
			Index of environmental governance performance

Note: The content of this table was finalized after discussions at several seminars held by the research group

NGO Global Integrity, evaluates the environment of government public governance and accessibility of public services; Index of environmental governance performance was developed by Yale Center for Environmental Law and Policy of Yale University and Center for International Earth Science Information Network of Columbia University to measure the performance of environmental governance by governments. Please be noted that, because it was hard to collect objective data of cities and the data might be normalized in different ways, the research group used approximate variables for logical prediction or used data of the country when certain variables could not be accessed directly.[1]

A1.3 Measurement Results and Analysis

Based on the indicators in the international CGDI system and by using the methods of measurement for China's CGDI, we have worked out the GDI, GDEG, CCPNRE and SDGP of 100 cities (Table A1.2).

From the GDI measurement results, we found that city green development showed distinct characteristics in terms of development phase and regional distribution. City green development in China also showed its own peculiarity.

First, from the perspective of development phases, there were large gaps of green development of cities. Judging from the measurement results, the top ten cities were New York, Lille, Barcelona, Geneva, Belfast, Wellington, Pusan, Zurich, San Francisco and Torino; the bottom ten were St. Petersburg, Bombay, Harare, Moscow, Delhi, Kiev, Ulan Bator, Mexico City, Kolkata, Rio De Janeiro (Fig. A1.1).

[1] Environmental liveability: see http://www.bestplaces.net/climate; CO_2 emission per capita: see http://un-stats.un.org/unsd/databases.htm; *BP Statistical Review of World Energy:* see http://www.bp.com/productlanding.do?cat-egoryId=9025442\contentId=7047113; Index of governmental public governance: see http://report.gtobalintegrity.org/gtobalIn-de=.cfm; Index of environmental governance performance: see http://epi.yale.edu/

Table A1.2 Results of measuring the GDI of cities worldwide

			GDI		First-Class Indicators GDEG		CCPNRE		SDGP	
City	Country	Continent	Score	Ranking	Score	Ranking	Score	Ranking	Score	Ranking
New York	USA	North America	1.652	1	0.100	33	1.556	1	−0.004	53
Lille	France	Europe	1.474	2	0.610	2	0.628	4	0.236	17
Barcelona	Spain	Europe	1.058	3	−0.010	54	0.987	2	0.081	45
Geneva	Switzerland	Europe	0.947	4	0.829	1	−0.243	87	0.361	1
Belfast	UK	Europe	0.818	5	0.377	6	0.266	11	0.176	23
Wellington	New Zealand	Oceania	0.746	6	0.341	7	0.241	16	0.164	31
Pusan	Korea	Asia	0.640	7	−0.207	75	0.840	3	0.007	50
Zurich	Switzerland	Europe	0.625	8	0.444	5	−0.180	73	0.361	1
San Francisco	USA	North America	0.499	9	0.204	14	0.299	8	−0.004	53
Torino	Italy	Europe	0.492	10	0.063	40	0.309	6	0.119	41
Malmo	Sweden	Europe	0.473	11	0.298	8	−0.130	62	0.305	3
Dublin	Ireland	Europe	0.461	12	0.132	26	0.214	17	0.115	44
Goteborg	Sweden	Europe	0.421	13	0.139	24	−0.023	44	0.305	3
Marseilles	France	Europe	0.396	14	0.053	41	0.108	32	0.236	17
Kyoto	Japan	Asia	0.392	15	0.009	49	0.144	29	0.240	12
Nuremberg	Germany	Europe	0.387	16	0.180	16	−0.070	53	0.277	7
Los Angeles	USA	North America	0.381	17	0.121	30	0.264	12	−0.004	53
Lisbon	Portugal	Europe	0.339	18	0.122	29	0.247	15	−0.030	70
Milan	Italy	Europe	0.338	19	0.036	46	0.183	25	0.119	41
Rome	Italy	Europe	0.320	20	−0.056	61	0.257	13	0.119	41
Brussels	Belgium	Europe	0.313	21	0.468	4	−0.304	93	0.149	33
Lyon	France	Europe	0.307	22	0.181	15	−0.109	58	0.236	17
Nagoya	Japan	Asia	0.304	23	0.047	43	0.017	37	0.240	12
Vancouver	Canada	North America	0.298	24	0.005	50	0.167	27	0.125	38
Kobe	Japan	Asia	0.291	25	−0.013	55	0.063	35	0.240	12
Singapore	Singapore	Asia	0.281	26	0.120	31	−0.064	50	0.225	21

Oslo	Norway	Europe	0.277	27	0.205	13	−0.220	81	0.292	6
Edinburgh	UK	Europe	0.274	28	0.250	10	−0.152	67	0.176	23
Melbourne	Australia	Oceania	0.255	29	−0.051	59	0.321	5	−0.016	68
Sydney	Australia	Oceania	0.245	30	−0.043	58	0.303	7	−0.016	68
Munich	Germany	Europe	0.241	31	0.039	45	−0.075	54	0.277	7
Osaka	Japan	Asia	0.233	32	−0.070	62	0.063	36	0.240	12
Stockholm	Sweden	Europe	0.209	33	0.123	28	−0.220	80	0.305	3
San Diego	Chile	South America	0.189	34	−0.220	76	0.214	18	0.196	22
Paris	France	Europe	0.188	35	0.016	48	−0.064	51	0.236	17
Washington	USA	North America	0.180	36	0.219	12	−0.035	45	−0.004	53
Glasgow	UK	Europe	0.174	37	0.173	19	−0.175	72	0.176	23
Liverpool	UK	Europe	0.173	38	0.223	11	−0.226	84	0.176	23
Boston	USA	North America	0.171	39	0.175	18	0.000	40	−0.004	53
Copenhagen	Denmark	Europe	0.157	40	0.284	9	−0.256	88	0.129	37
Tokyo	Japan	Asia	0.128	41	−0.016	56	−0.096	57	0.240	12
Seattle	USA	North America	0.119	42	0.131	27	−0.008	41	−0.004	53
Hague	Netherlands	Europe	0.108	43	0.150	21	−0.186	75	0.144	34
Seoul	Korea	Asia	0.105	44	−0.184	73	0.282	10	0.007	50
Manila	Philippines	Asia	0.105	45	0.497	3	−0.144	66	−0.249	84
Amsterdam	Netherlands	Europe	0.089	46	0.144	23	−0.199	77	0.144	34
Philadelphia	USA	North America	0.078	47	0.072	38	0.010	38	−0.004	53
Vienna	Austria	Europe	0.077	48	0.067	39	−0.153	69	0.163	32
Pittsburgh	USA	North America	0.061	49	0.179	17	−0.113	61	−0.004	53
Atlanta	USA	North America	0.061	50	0.116	32	−0.051	47	−0.004	53
Hamburg	Germany	Europe	0.053	51	−0.001	53	−0.223	82	0.277	7
Rotterdam	Netherlands	Europe	0.052	52	0.093	35	−0.185	74	0.144	34
Toronto	Canada	North America	0.047	53	−0.026	57	−0.052	48	0.125	38
Chicago	USA	North America	0.026	54	0.043	44	−0.013	43	−0.004	53
Helsinki	Finland	Europe	0.024	55	0.160	20	−0.306	94	0.170	30
London	UK	Europe	0.010	56	0.091	36	−0.256	89	0.176	23

(continued)

Table A1.2 (continued)

			First-Class Indicators							
			GDI		GDEG		CCPNRE		SDGP	
City	Country	Continent	Score	Ranking	Score	Ranking	Score	Ranking	Score	Ranking
Frankfurt	Germany	Europe	0.005	57	0.073	37	−0.345	99	0.277	7
Birmingham	UK	Europe	−0.002	58	0.051	42	−0.228	85	0.176	23
Warsaw	Poland	Europe	−0.009	59	−0.157	71	0.208	20	−0.060	71
Kuala Lumpur	Malaysia	Asia	−0.015	60	−0.162	72	0.149	28	−0.002	52
Denver	USA	North America	−0.018	61	0.144	22	−0.159	70	−0.004	53
Athens	Greece	Europe	−0.044	62	−0.141	69	0.207	21	−0.110	74
Ottawa	Canada	North America	−0.076	63	0.000	52	−0.201	78	0.125	38
Detroit	USA	North America	−0.082	64	0.035	47	−0.113	60	−0.004	53
Berlin	Germany	Europe	−0.098	65	−0.090	65	−0.285	92	0.277	7
Dallas	USA	North America	−0.114	66	0.100	34	−0.210	79	−0.004	53
Manchester	UK	Europe	−0.117	67	−0.052	60	−0.240	86	0.176	23
Madrid	Spain	Europe	−0.135	68	−0.079	63	−0.137	64	0.081	45
Houston	USA	North America	−0.146	69	0.137	25	−0.279	91	−0.004	53
Sao Paulo	Brazil	South America	−0.157	70	−0.254	82	0.208	19	−0.112	75
Tallinn	Estonia	Europe	−0.194	71	−0.123	67	−0.091	56	0.020	47
Minsk	Belarus	Europe	−0.204	72	−0.141	68	−0.079	55	0.017	48
Buenos Aires	Argentina	South America	−0.214	73	−0.195	74	0.127	31	−0.147	77
Vilnius	Lithuania	Europe	−0.297	74	−0.084	64	−0.225	83	0.012	49
Beijing	China	Asia	−0.323	75	−0.291	98	0.191	23	−0.224	83
Phoenix	USA	North America	−0.325	76	0.004	51	−0.325	98	−0.004	53
Budapest	Hungary	Europe	−0.361	77	−0.142	70	−0.153	68	−0.066	72
Djakarta	Indonesia	Asia	−0.387	78	−0.255	84	0.076	33	−0.208	81
Shanghai	China	Asia	−0.435	79	−0.271	87	0.189	24	−0.353	86
Bangkok	Thailand	Asia	−0.437	80	−0.254	83	0.000	39	−0.183	79
Havana	Cuba	North America	−0.477	81	−0.233	77	−0.054	49	−0.190	80
Prague	Czech Republic	Europe	−0.508	82	−0.117	66	−0.307	95	−0.084	73

Durban	South Africa	Africa	−0.555	83	−0.245	81	0.285	9	−0.594	99
Port-au-Prince	Haiti	North America	−0.555	84	−0.310	99	0.167	26	−0.412	94
Panama	Republic of Panama	North America	−0.567	85	−0.286	95	−0.112	59	−0.169	78
Lusaka	Zambia	Africa	−0.576	86	−0.276	91	0.076	34	−0.376	87
Cape Town	South Africa	Africa	−0.590	87	−0.243	79	0.247	14	−0.594	99
Cairo	Egypt	Africa	−0.610	88	−0.266	85	−0.135	63	−0.209	82
Luanda	Angola	Africa	−0.654	89	−0.274	90	0.140	30	−0.520	96
Blantyre	Malawi	Africa	−0.666	90	−0.316	100	0.193	22	−0.543	98
St. Petersburg	Russia	Europe	−0.692	91	−0.274	89	−0.010	42	−0.408	91
Bombay	India	Asia	−0.733	92	−0.288	97	−0.048	46	−0.397	88
Harare	Zimbabwe	Africa	−0.826	93	−0.282	94	−0.069	52	−0.474	95
Moscow	Russia	Europe	−0.828	94	−0.279	93	−0.141	65	−0.408	91
Delhi	India	Asia	−0.872	95	−0.287	96	−0.187	76	−0.397	88
Kiev	Ukraine	Europe	−0.873	96	−0.242	78	−0.308	96	−0.323	85
Ulan Bator	Mongolia	Asia	−0.950	97	−0.267	86	−0.274	90	−0.409	93
Mexico City	Mexico	North America	−0.953	98	−0.244	80	−0.167	71	−0.541	97
Kolkata	India	Asia	−0.984	99	−0.278	92	−0.309	97	−0.397	88
Rio De Janeiro	Brazil	South America	−1.111	100	−0.273	88	−0.727	100	−0.112	75

Note: Figures in this table are calculated based on data from the global urban competitiveness database of Urban Competitiveness Center of CASS, Yale Center for Environmental Law and Policy, Yale University, Center for International Earth Science Information Network, Columbia University, and 2011 Environmental Sustainability Index

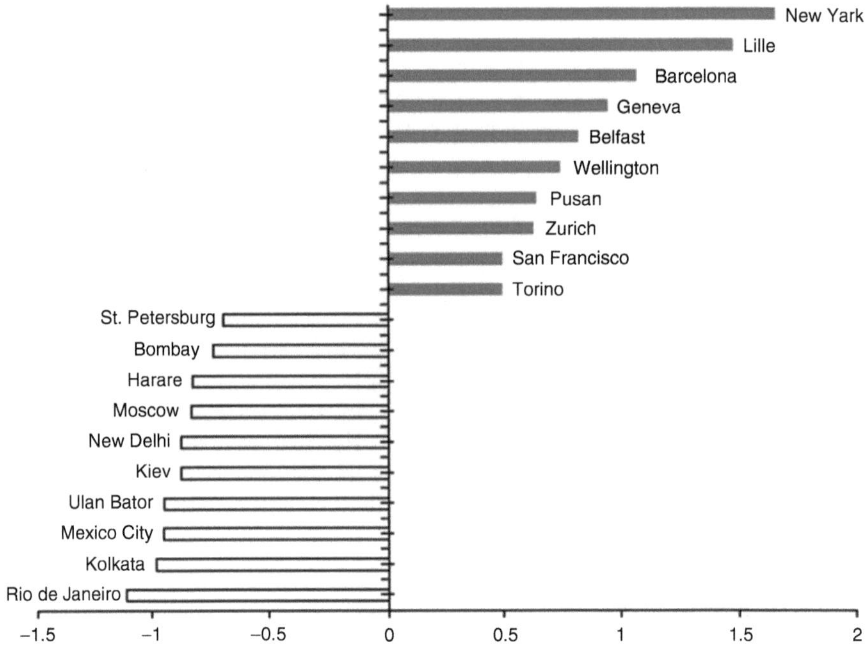

Fig. A1.1 Ranking of world cities by GDI

Generally, large gaps existed in the green development of cities around the world. The development levels of cities usually depended on the economic development of their countries. Cities in developed countries had better green development status. As shown in Fig. A1.1, the top ten cities were mainly from developed European and American countries. While cities in emerging industrial countries and developing countries showed lower development levels. The bottom ten cities were mainly from Russia, India, Mongolia, Mexico and Brazil, where the economic and social development obviously lagged behind European and American countries. From the results we found that, despite the fact that great changed had taken place in world's economic pattern and that emerging countries boasted rapid economic development and increasingly significant roles in international economy and politics, their economic development quality failed to keep up with the development pace, implying their rather backward green development which needed to be expedited for quality and sustainable development.

Second, large regional gaps were found in the green development of cities. The measurement results suggested that, generally, North American, European and Oceanian cities were at the first level, and Asian, South American and African cities at the second level of green development. The former had outstanding overall advantages, higher CCPNRE and SDGP; while the latter extended lower values of all indicators. Meanwhile, there were gaps within each level: cities in Mexico, Panama, Haiti and Cuba all ranked among the bottom ten, of which Mexico City stayed at the last third, far behind cities in USA and Canada; cities in Eastern Europe lagged behind other European cities, or even behind some Asian cities; cities in Eastern Asian stood ahead of Southern Asian counterparts. It was worthy of mentioning that, there was not absolute static advantage. For example, Pusan in Asia ranked No. 7, indicating its high green development. In practice, the gaps suggested dynamic advantages. Cities in different regions or of different types have to find their ways towards green development on the basis of their historical and practical situation.

Third, cities in China were in a critical intermediate phase of green development. Judging from the measurement results, Beijing and Shanghai ranked No.75 and No.79 respectively. Though left far behind cities in developed European and American countries, they ranked ahead of those in emerging industrial and developing countries. This indicated that cities, especially key cities in China, were in a critical intermediate phase of green development. In a world context, they enjoyed a solid foundation for further development, and were possible to catch up with the forerunners. They should learn from the leading cities to further upgrade their green development level, with priority given to CCPNRE. Notably, despite the 30-year rapid economic growth, even the representative cities such as Beijing and Shanghai still suffer backward green development and stay in the middle of the list of the sample cities, suggesting the extremely high cost of the economic growth in cities of China, and the outstanding economic imbalance, inconsistency and unsustainability. There is a long way to high level of green development.

Appendix 2 Analysis of Chengdu's 2009 GDI Ranking

After the *China Green Development Index Report 2011: Regional Comparison* was released in the Great Hall of the People on September 24, 2011, the public was surprised of the low ranking of Chengdu. Reporter Zhu Jianhong from *People's Daily* visited Professor Li Xiaoxi, the leader of the research group.

A2.1 *Traveler's Paradise, Chengdu Is Highly Acknowledged Both at Home and Abroad. However, How Do You Explain That the City Came Only Before the Next to the Last in the* China Green Development Index Report 2011*?*

China Green Development Index Report was first published in 2010. The *Report 2012* for the first time included comparison of cities. Among the 34 evaluated cities,

Chengdu ranked No. 32, which was far from what the public know about the city. I would explain the reasons as follow:

A2.1.1 Reconstruction After May 12 Earthquake

In reference to the World Development Indicators (WDI) of the World Bank, the GDI 2011 of China was based on data of 2009, when Chengdu attached importance to post-quake reconstruction. The low indicator values were due to the severely impaired national economy and social development. Take SDGP which weighed 33 % as an example, Chengdu planned to realize an investment of RMB 400 billion to cope with the reconstruction needs and financial crisis. Of the investment, RMB 60 billion, equaling to the fiscal expenditure of the city in 2009, were allocated to rebuilding of houses. As a result, financial support to green investment and environmental governance was largely reduced, and the SDGP was lower than the national average.

A2.1.2 Overall Arrangement of Urban and Rural Development

The National Pilot Reform District of Comprehensive Supporting Facilities for Overall Arrangement of Urban and Rural Development was approved in Chengdu in 2007, which has made great achievement. However, after establishment of the Pilot Reform District, the Urban Planning of Chengdu city has to expend its coverage from five central urban districts to ten districts including neighboring districts and counties. Compared with other evaluated cities that adopted conventional planning, Chengdu had to include its suburb counties and villages into its statistical system, making significant increase of its administrative area and population, as well as the statistical coverage of the indicators.

In addition, increased administrative area means the industrial and domestic pollutions in counties and villages were also included into the scope of pollution control of the city. This to some extent brought additional green development burden of the city and lowered its GDI ranking.

A2.1.3 Impact of per Capita and per Unit of Land Area Indicators on CCPNRE Ranking

Considering that some provinces have large population and some have large administrative areas, GDI system adopted both per capita and per unit of land area indicators to measure their CCPNRE. Chengdu is relatively weak in CCPNRE, therefore the double indicators increased the weight of its weak indicators and lowered its ranking. Take ammonia nitrogen emissions per capita and per unit of land area, two weak indicators of Chengdu for example: in 2009 Chengdu registered ammonia nitrogen emissions of 12769.5 t, ranking No. 5 in China. While the impact of ammonia nitrogen emissions on the environment was calculated twice because of the double indicators, making the score of the city even lower.

A2.2 *What Are the Low-Ranking Indicators of Chengdu in* China Green Development Index Report 2011*? How Do You Explain the Low Rankings?*

In *China Green Development Index Report 2011*, Chengdu ranked low in GDEG, CCPNRE and SDGP, and specifically in GDP per capita, NO_x emissions per unit of GDP, Labor productivity of secondary sector, Ratio of days with principal pollutants as respirable suspended particulate to the whole year, Removal rate of COD in industrial wastewater, and Removal rate of ammonia nitrogen in industrial wastewater, covering green growth efficiency, reasonable use and conservation of resources and environment, and government's attitude to green development.

According to our research finding and my personal understanding, the low rankings of Chengdu could be explained that: on one hand, as mentioned before, GDI did not reflect the impact of post-quake reconstruction and overall urban and rural arrangement on some indicators of Chengdu; on the other, Chengdu is in an intermediate phase of industrialization with large burden on resources and environment brought by development, which lowered relevant rankings. Moreover, there is a significant gap between the eastern and western regions. Chengdu as a western region is left behind eastern cities in terms of green growth efficiency, green investment, and its rankings in related indicators.

A2.3 *According to Your Knowledge, How Does Chengdu Think of Its Rankings in* China Green Development Index Report 2011*? Did It Take Any Actions in Green Development?*

Chengdu pays great attention on the ranking in *China Green Development Index Report 2011*. Seeing the ranking of 34 evaluated cities, the Publicity Department of Chengdu Municipal Party Committee organized Municipal Development and Reform Commission, Chengdu Urban and Rural Construction Commission, Chengdu Bureau of Statistics, and Chengdu Environmental Protection Bureau to understand our research methodology and concepts, and communicated with the research group concerning relevant issues. Chengdu believes that it supports and is implementing green development as a major economic development trend. Competent authorities of the city pointed out that the research was objective and rational, but some indicators did not reflect the actual status of city, and appreciated further study in this regards. The city also raised pertinent suggestions.

For example, Chengdu Environmental Protection Bureau recommended inclusion of indicators about domestic pollution, the Municipal Development and Reform Commission suggested lowering the relevance of indicators, and Chengdu Urban and Rural Construction Commission advised use of more authoritative data.

Through the communication I learned that Chengdu had more policies and actions concerning green development which were not included into the Report, such as enhanced pollution control and promotion of low-carbon economy. In our future works, we would make the report more inclusive to reflect the green development of cities.

A2.4 How Has Been Chengdu Doing in Recent Years?

Data of 2010 and 2011 tell us that, Chengdu presents good indicators and has made progress in green development. In terms of energy saving and emission reduction, it shared 80 % of the completed volume of Sichuan Province. In 2010, COT emission decreased by 23.6 % and SO_2 by 22.9 % in the city, or respectively 13.6 % and 12.9 % higher than the national standard. In terms of pollution control, its ratio of industrial solid waste utilized reached 99.5 % and recycling rate of industrial water registered 87 % since 2010, far higher than the 2009 data. In terms of industrial structure, it recorded large increase of value added in the secondary and tertiary industries, and the increase of employment rate higher than that of other cities, implying its reasonable industrial structure and good development status.

A2.5 Is There Any Deficit in the Design of City Indicator System in the **China Green Development Index Report 2011***? How Do You Comment the Rationality of the City Rankings?*

Though the 2011 city GDI is newly added in the Report, it has been appraised in several workshops. Therefore the indicator system is designed on a scientific and reasonable basis. First, city GDI observed both green and development philosophy, highlighted the principle of openness, fairness and impartiality, and was based on published yearbooks or data released by competent authorities. Second, indicators in the system have been repeatedly appraised by a more than ten experts in the fields of economy, resources, environment, energy and statistics. Last, the evaluated cities assessed were chosen from the 113 cities subject to the environmental monitoring project of the Ministry of Environmental Protection, and included four municipalities directly under the jurisdiction of the central government, five cities specifically designated in the state plan, and 25 provincial capital cities. In addition, the 2011 city GDI has been reviewed by more than 30 authoritative experts such as Wu Jinglian, Li Yining, Wei Liqun, Liu Shijin, Zhang Xinshi and Niu Wenyuan, to ensure its impartiality.

However, we have realized the deficits through feedback from experts and local authorities. First, the inconsistent quality of data due to the fact that the data sources were limited to authoritative yearbooks and local governments attached different importance to reported data. For example, some cities did not offer complete key indicators. Second, some authorities focused on internal data but we had to use public data. That explains the deviation from the authenticity and objectiveness. Third, we have to commit that the weights of the indicators were to certain extent were subjective, because they were decided by experts by using the Delphi Technique Method.

A2.6 Is There Any New Plan or Idea for the Report of the Next Year?

According to opinions from expert and local government, the report for the next year will be perfected especially the part of city GDI. First, we will include public survey which will be carried out through online survey and field survey in evaluated cities, to review the public opinions and theoretic study. This is what we learn the Chengdu case. Second, we will develop a "green examination form" for each province and city based on the GDI indicator system, to check out their weakness in green development. This is also inspired by the workshop in Chengdu. Third, we will perfect the measurement system according to opinions from expert and local government, through proper adjustment of city indicators and inclusion of additional important cities for more subjective and reasonable rankings. Fourth, we will establish comparable annual "green development progress indicator" for each province and evaluated cities to judge whether they made progress or regression in the reporting year over the previous year.

Appendix 3 PGDI Indicators and Source of Data

A3.1 GDP per Capita

Gross Domestic Product (GDP) refers to the final products at market prices produced by all resident units in a country (or a region) during a certain period of time. For a region, it is called as Gross Regional Product (GRP) or regional GDP. Its calculation formula is as follows:

$$\text{GDP per capita} = \frac{\text{GDP}}{\left(\begin{array}{c}\text{Population at the end of preceding year} + \\ \text{Population at the end of this year}\end{array}\right)/2}$$

Source of Data: *China Statistical Yearbook 2010–2011*, NBS, Beijing, China Statistical Publishing House, 2010–2011.

A3.2 Energy Consumption per Unit of GDP

Total energy consumption refers to the total consumption of energy of various kinds by the production sectors and the households in the country in a given period. It can be divided into three parts: end-use energy consumption; loss during the process of energy conversion; and energy loss.

Energy consumption per unit of GDP refers to the energy consumption per unit of Gross Regional Product in a region in the same reference period, reflecting the increased energy consumption with an additional unit of GDP. The formula is:

$$\text{Energy consumption per unit of GDP} = \text{Total energy consumption}/\text{GDP}$$

Source of Data: *China Statistical Yearbook 2011*, NBS, Beijing, China Statistical Publishing House, 2011.

A3.3 Ratio of Non-fossil Energy Consumption to Total Energy Consumption

Non-fossil energy refers to other energy sources other than coal, oil and natural gas.

The ratio of non-fossil energy consumption to total energy consumption refers to the percentage of non-fossil energy consumption in total energy consumption.

The formula is:

$$\text{Ratio of non-fossil energy consumption to total energy consumption} = \text{Non-fossil energy consumption}/\text{Total energy consumption} * 100\,\%$$

Source of Data: No official data.

A3.4 CO_2 Emissions per Unit of GDP

CO_2 emissions per unit of GDP refer to the ratio of carbon dioxide emissions to GDP in a region in the same reference period. The formula is:

$$CO_2 \text{ emissions per unit of GDP} = CO_2 \text{ emissions}/\text{GDP}$$

Source of Data: No official data.

A3.5 SO_2 Emissions per Unit of GDP

Sulphur dioxide (SO_2) emissions cover SO_2 emissions through industrial activities, non-industrial and other activities, of which emissions through industrial activities refer to volume of sulphur dioxide discharged from fuel burning and production process by enterprises during a given period. The formula is:

$$\begin{aligned}&\text{Industrial } SO_2 \text{ emissions} =\\&\quad SO_2 \text{ discharged from the process of fuel burning} +\\&\quad SO_2 \text{ discharged from the process of production}\end{aligned}$$

Emission through non-industrial and other activities are calculated on the basis of consumption of coal by households and other activities and the sulphur content of coal with the following formula:

$$\begin{aligned}&\text{Emission through non-industrial and other activities} =\\&\quad \text{coals consumed by household andother activities} * \text{Sulphur content} * 0.8 * 2\end{aligned}$$

SO_2 emissions per unit of GDP refer to the ratio of SO_2 emissions to GDP in a region in a given period. The formula is:

$$SO_2 \text{ emissions per unit of GDP} = SO_2 \text{ emissions}/\text{GDP}$$

Source of Data: *China Statistical Yearbook 2010–2011*, NBS, Beijing, China Statistical Publishing House, 2010–2011.

A3.6 COD Emissions per Unit of GDP

Chemical Oxygen Demand (COD) refers to the amount of oxygen required when chemical oxidants are used to oxidize organic pollutants in water. A higher value of COD corresponds to more serious pollution. COD emissions mainly come from wastewater discharged by industry and household, of which COD emissions of the latter refer to the annual amount of COD in the wastewater discharged by urban households, which can be calculated by per capita coefficient as follows:

$$\begin{aligned}&\text{COD emissions in wastewater discharged by urban households} =\\&\quad \text{Coefficient of COD generated through urban non-industrial wastewater} *\\&\quad \text{Urban nonagricultural population} * 365\end{aligned}$$

COD emissions per unit of GDP refer to the ratio of COD emissions to GDP in a region in a given period. The formula is:

$$\text{COD emissions per unit of GDP} = \text{COD}/\text{GDP}$$

Source of Data: *China Statistical Yearbook 2010–2011*, NBS, Beijing, China Statistical Publishing House, 2010–2011.

A3.7 Nitrogen Oxide Emissions per Unit of GDP

Nitrogen oxide emissions per unit of GDP refer to the ratio of nitrogen oxide emissions to GDP in a region in a given period. The formula is:

$$\text{Nitrogen oxide emissions per unit of GDP} = \text{Nitrogen oxide emissions/GDP}$$

Source of Data: *China Statistical Yearbook 2010–2011*, NBS, Beijing, China Statistical Publishing House, 2010–2011; *China Environment Annual Report 2010*, the Ministry of Environmental Protection, Beijing, China Environmental Science Press, 2011.

A3.8 Ammonia/Nitrogen Emissions per Unit of GDP

Ammonia/nitrogen emissions per unit of GDP refer to the ratio of ammonia/nitrogen emissions to GDP in a region in a given period. The formula is:

$$\text{Ammonia/nitrogen emissions per unit of GDP} = \text{Ammonia/nitrogen emissions/GDP}$$

Source of Data: *China Statistical Yearbook 2010–2011*, NBS, Beijing, China Statistical Publishing House, 2010–2011; *China Environment Annual Report 2010*, the Ministry of Environmental Protection, Beijing, China Environmental Science Press, 2011.

A3.9 Electricity Consumption per Capita in Urban Areas

The formula is:

$$\text{Electricity consumption per capita in urban areas} = \text{the amount of electricity consumption in urban areas/annual average urban population}$$

Source of Data: *China City Statistical Yearbook 2011*, NBS, Beijing, China Statistical Publishing House, 2012.

A3.10 Labor Productivity of the Primary Sector

Labor productivity of the primary sector refers to the ratio of value added of primary sector to annual average of employees in primary sector. The formula is:

$$\text{Labor productivity of primary sector} = \\ 2 * \text{Value added of primary sector}/(\text{Employees in primary sector at the end of this year} + \text{Employees in primary sector at the end of preceding year})$$

Source of Data: *China Statistical Yearbook 2011*, NBS, Beijing, China Statistical Publishing House, 2011.

A3.11 Land Productivity

Output ratio of land refers to the output value of crop farming to the sown area of grain crops. The formula is:

$$\text{Land productivity} = \text{Output value of agriculture}/\text{Sown area of grain crops}$$

Source of Data: *China Statistical Yearbook 2011*, NBS, Beijing, China Statistical Publishing House, 2011.

A3.12 Proportion of Water-Saving Irrigated Area in Effectively Irrigated Area

Irrigated area refers to area of land that are effectively irrigated, i.e. relatively level land, where there are water sources or complete sets of irrigation facilities to lift and move adequate water for irrigation purpose under normal conditions. Under normal situations, irrigated area is the sum of watered fields and irrigated fields where irrigation systems or equipment have been installed for regular irrigation purpose. This important indicator reflects drought resistance capacity of the cultivated land in China. The formula is:

$$\text{Proportion of water-saving irrigated area in effectively irrigated area} = \\ 100\,\% * \text{water-saving area}/\text{effectively irrigated area}$$

Source of Data: *China Statistical Yearbook 2011*, NBS, Beijing, China Statistical Publishing House, 2011; *China Water Conservancy Statistical Yearbook 2011*, Ministry of Water Resources, Beijing, China Water Power Press, 2011.

A3.13 Proportion of Effectively Irrigated Area in Cultivated Land Area

Irrigated area refers to area of land that are effectively irrigated, i.e. relatively level land, where there are water sources or complete sets of irrigation facilities to lift and move adequate water for irrigation purpose under normal conditions. Under normal situations, irrigated area is the sum of watered fields and irrigated fields where irrigation systems or equipment have been installed for regular irrigation purpose. This important indicator reflects drought resistance capacity of the cultivated land in China. The formula is:

Area of cultivated land refers to area of land reclaimed for the regular cultivationof various farm crops, including crop-cover land, fallow, newly reclaimed land andland laid idle for less than 3 years.

Source of Data: *China Statistical Yearbook 2011*, NBS, Beijing, China Statistical Publishing House, 2011.

A3.14 Labor Productivity of the Secondary Sector

Labor productivity of the secondary sector refers to the ratio of value added of the secondary sector to annual average of employees in the secondary sector. The formula is:

$$\text{Labor productivity of secondary sector} = 2 * \text{value added of the secondary sector} / (\text{Employees in the secondary sector at the end of this year} + \text{Employees in the secondary sector at the end of preceding year})$$

Source of Data: *China Statistical Yearbook 2011*, NBS, Beijing, China Statistical Publishing House, 2011.

A3.15 Water Consumption per Unit of Value Added Created by Industrial Enterprises

Value added of industry refers to the final results of industrial production of industrial enterprises in money terms during the reference period.

Water consumed by industry refers to water consumed by industrial enterprises for manufacturing, processing, cooling, air-conditioning, purifying, rinsing and so on in process of production, which is measured in terms of new withdrawals of water, excluding reuse of water within the same enterprises.

Water consumption per unit of value added created by industrial enterprises refers to the ratio of water consumed by industry to its value added in a given period. The formula is:

$$\text{Water consumption per unit of value added created by industrial enterprises} = \text{water consumed by industry}/\text{its value added}$$

Source of Data: *China Statistical Yearbook 2011*, NBS, Beijing, China Statistical Publishing House, 2011; *China Regional Economy Statistical Yearbook* 2005–2011, NBS, Beijing, China Statistical Publishing House, 2006–2012.

A3.16 Energy Consumption per Unit of Value Added Created by Industrial Enterprises Above Designated Size

Energy consumption per unit of value added created by industrial enterprises above designated size refers to the ratio of energy consumed by industrial enterprises above designated size to their value added in a region in a given period. The formula is:

$$\text{Energy consumption per unit of value added created by industrial enterprises above designated size} = \text{energy consumed by industrial enterprises above designated size}/\text{their value added}$$

Source of Data: No official data.

A3.17 Utilization Rate of Industrial Solid Waste

Utilization rate of industrial solid waste refers to the percentage of industrial solid waste utilized over industrial solid waste produced (including stocks of the previous years). Its calculation formula is:

$$\text{Utilization rate of industrial solid waste} = 100\,\% * \text{Industrial solid waste utilized}/\big(\text{Industrial solid waste produced} + \text{Stocks of previous utilized}\big)$$

Of which, industrial solid waste produced refers to total volume of solid, semisolid and high concentration liquid residues produced by industrial enterprises from the process of production in a given period, including hazardous waste, slag and ash, gangue, tailings, radioactive residues and other waste, but excluding stones stripped or dug out in mining (gangue and acid or alkaline stones not covered).

A stone is acid or alkaline if the pH value of the water is below 4 or above 10.5, when it is in, or soaked by, the water; Industrial solid waste utilized refers to volume of solid waste from which useful materials may be extracted or which can be converted into usable resources, energy or other materials by means of reclamation, processing, recycling and exchange (including utilizing the stocks of industrial solid waste of the previous years in the years in question, e.g. fertilizers, building materials and road materials. The information concerned shall be collected by the producing units of waste.)

Source of Data: *China Environmental Statistical Yearbook* 2011, the NBS and the Ministry of Environmental Protection, Beijing, China Statistical Publishing House, 2011.

A3.18 Recycling Rate of Industrial Water

Recycling rate of industrial water refers to the ratio of the amount of water re-used in industrial production to total amount of water used in a given period. The formula is:

$$\text{Recycling rate of industrial water} = 100\,\% * \text{Reuse of water}/\left(\text{New withdrawals of water} + \text{reuse of water}\right)$$

Source of Data: *China Environmental Statistical Yearbook* 2011, the NBS and the Ministry of Environmental Protection, Beijing, China Statistical Publishing House, 2011.

A3.19 Ratio of the Output of Six Energy-Intensive Industries to Gross Industrial Output

Ratio of the output of six energy-intensive industries to gross industrial output refers to the percentage of output value of six high energy-bearing industries over gross industrial output value.

Gross industrial output value is the total volume of final industrial products produced and industrial services provided in a given period. It reflects the total achievements and overall scale of industrial production in a given period.

Output value of six energy-intensive industrial sectors refers to the sum of output value of Processing of Petroleum, Coking and Processing of Nuclear Fuel, Manufacture of Raw Chemical Materials and Chemical Products, Manufacture of Non-metallic Mineral Products, Smelting and Pressing of Ferrous Metals, Smelting and Pressing of Non-ferrous Metals, Production and Supply of Electric Power and Heat Power.

Source of Data: *China Industrial Economy Statistical Yearbook 2011*, NBS, Beijing, China Statistical Publishing House, 2011.

A3.20 *Labor Productivity of the Tertiary Sector*

Labor productivity of the tertiary sector refers to the ratio of value added of the tertiary sector to annual average of employees in the secondary sector. The formula is:

$$\text{Labor productivity of the tertiary sector} = 2 * \text{Value added of tertiary sector}/\left(\text{Employees in the tertiary sector at the end of this year} + \text{Employees in the tertiary sector at the end of preceding year}\right)$$

Source of Data: *China Statistical Yearbook 2011*, NBS, Beijing, China Statistical Publishing House, 2011.

A3.21 *Proportion of the Value Added of the Tertiary Sector in GDP*

Proportion of the value added of the tertiary sector in GDP refers to the percentage of value added of the tertiary sector over GDP in a reporting period. The formula is:

$$\text{Proportion of the value added of the tertiary sector} = 100\,\% * \text{Value added of the tertiary sector}/\text{GDP}$$

Source of Data: *China Statistical Yearbook 2011*, NBS, Beijing, China Statistical Publishing House, 2011.

A3.22 *Proportion of Tertiary Sector Employees in the Total Employed Population*

Proportion of tertiary sector employees in the total employed population refers to the percentage of employees of tertiary sector over total employees in a reporting period. The formula is:

$$\text{Proportion of employees of tertiary sector} = 100\,\% * \text{Employees of tertiary sector}/\text{Total employees}$$

Source of Data: *China Statistical Yearbook 2011*, NBS, Beijing, China Statistical Publishing House, 2011.

A3.23 Water Resources per Capita

Total Water Resources refers to total volume of water resources measured as run-off for surface water from rainfall and recharge for groundwater in a given area, excluding transit water.

Water resources per capita refer to run-off for surface water from rainfall and recharge for groundwater shared by each person in a region in a given period. The formula is:

Water resources per capita =
Total water resources of the region/population of the region

Source of Data: *China Statistical Yearbook 2011*, NBS, Beijing, China Statistical Publishing House, 2011.

A3.24 Forest Area per Capita

Forest area refers to the area of forest where trees grow with canopy density above 0.2, including land of natural woods and planted woods, but excluding bush land and thin forest land.

Forest area per capita refers to forest area shared by each person in a region in a given period. The formula is:

Forest area per capita =
Total area of forest of the region/population of the region

Source of Data: *China Statistical Yearbook 2011*, NBS, Beijing, China Statistical Publishing House, 2011.

A3.25 Forest Coverage Rate

Forest coverage rate refers to the ratio of area of afforested land to total land area. Forest area includes the area of trees and bamboo grow with canopy density above 0.2, the area of shrubby tree according to regulations of the government, the area of forest land inside farm land and the area of trees planted by the side of villages, farm houses and along roads and rivers. It is a very important indicator that reflects the status of abundance of forest resource and ecosystem balance and the development level of forestry. The formula for calculating forest coverage rate is as follows:

Forest coverage rate =
100 % * Area of afforested land/Area of total land + 100 % * Area of shrubby tree/Area of total land + 100 % * Area of forest land inside farm land/ Area of total land + 100 % * Area of tree planted by the side of villages, farm houses and along roads and rivers/Area of total land

Source of Data: *China Statistical Yearbook 2011*, NBS, Beijing, China Statistical Publishing House, 2011.

A3.26 Proportion of the Area of Natural Reserves in the Total Area of a Region

Natural reserves refer to certain areas of land, waters or sea that are representative in natural ecological systems or are natural habitats for rare or endangered wild animals or plants, or water conservation zones, or the location of important natural or historical relics, which are demarked by law and put under special protection and management. Nature reserves are designated by the formal approval of governments at and above county level (covering those still existing ones approved by related ministries or Revolutionary Commissions prior to the Sixth Five-Year Plan). Scenic spots and cultural preservation zones are not covered. Proportion of area of natural reserves in total area of a region can be calculated as follows:

Proportion of the area of natural reserves in the total area of a region =
100 % * area of natural reserves / total area of a region

Source of Data: *China Statistical Yearbook 2011*, NBS, Beijing, China Statistical Publishing House, 2011.

A3.27 Proportion of the Area of Wetlands in the Total Area of a Region

Wetlands refer to marshland and peat bog, whether natural or man-made, permanent or temporary; water covered areas, whether stagnant or flowing, with fresh or semi-fresh or salty water that is less than 6 m deep at low tide; as well as coral beach, weed beach, mud beach, mangrove, river outlet, rivers, fresh-water marshland, marshland forests, lakes, salty bog and salt lakes along the coastal areas. Its calculating formula is:

$$\text{Proportion of area of wetlands in total area of a region} = 100\,\% * \text{area of wetlands/total area of a region}$$

Source of Data: *China Statistical Yearbook 2011*, NBS, Beijing, China Statistical Publishing House, 2011.

A3.28 Growing Stock per Capita

Growing stock refers to the total stock volume of trees growing in land, including trees in forest, trees in sparse forest, scattered trees and trees planted by the side of villages, farm houses and along roads and rivers. Its calculating formula is:

$$\text{Growing stock per capita} = \text{Growing stock/year-end population}$$

Source of Data: *China Statistical Yearbook 2011*, NBS, Beijing, China Statistical Publishing House, 2011.

A3.29 CO_2 Emissions per Unit of Land Area

Area under land survey refers to the total area of land, under the land survey, within the jurisdiction of the administrative region, including land for agriculture use, land for construction and unused land. CO_2 emissions per unit of land area in a region can be calculated as follows:

$$CO_2 \text{ emissions per unit of land area} = CO_2 \text{ emissions/Area under land survey}$$

Source of Data: No official data.

A3.30 CO_2 Emissions per Capita

CO_2 emissions per capita can be calculated as follows:

$$CO_2 \text{ emissions per capita} = \text{Total } CO_2 \text{ emissions of the year/average population of the year}$$

Source of Data: No official data.

A3.31 SO_2 Emissions per Unit of Land Area

SO_2 emissions per unit of land area in a region can be calculated as follows:

$$\text{SO}_2 \text{ emissions per unit of land area} = \text{SO}_2 \text{ emissions}/(\text{Area under land survey-Area of desert and Gobi})$$

Source of Data: *China Statistical Yearbook 2011*, NBS, Beijing, China Statistical Publishing House, 2011; *Desert in China*, Wu Zheng, Beijing, the Commercial Press, 1995.

A3.32 SO_2 Emissions per Capita

SO_2 emissions per capita can be calculated as follows:

$$\text{SO}_2 \text{ emissions per capita} = 2 * \text{SO}_2 \text{ emissions of the year}/(\text{Total population at the end of this year} + \text{Total population at the end of preceding year})$$

Source of Data: *China Statistical Yearbook 2011*, NBS, Beijing, China Statistical Publishing House, 2011.

A3.33 COD Emissions per Unit of Land Area

COD emissions per unit of land area can be calculated as follows:

$$\text{COD emissions per unit of land area} = \text{COD emissions}/(\text{Area under land survey-Area of desert and Gobi})$$

Source of Data: *China Statistical Yearbook 2011*, NBS, Beijing, China Statistical Publishing House, 2011; *Desert in China*, Wu Zheng, Beijing, the Commercial Press, 1995.

A3.34 COD Emissions per Capita

COD emissions per capita can be calculated as follows:

$$\text{COD emissions per capita} = 2 * \text{total COD emissions}/(\text{Total population at the end of this year} + \text{Total population at the end of preceding year})$$

Source of Data: *China Statistical Yearbook 2011*, NBS, Beijing, China Statistical Publishing House, 2011.

A3.35 Nitrogen Oxide Emissions per Unit of Land Area

Nitrogen oxide emissions per unit of land area can be calculated as follows:

Nitrogen oxide emissions per capita =
2 * Nitrogen oxide emissions of the year/(Total population at the end of this year + Total population at the end of preceding year)

Ammonia/nitrogen emissions per unit of land area =
Ammonia/nitrogen emissions/(Area under land survey-Area of desert and Gobi)

Consumption of chemical fertilizers per unit of cultivated land area =
Consumption of chemical fertilizer/Area of cultivated land

Nitrogen oxide emissions per unit of land area =
Nitrogen oxide emissions/(Area under land survey-Area of desert and Gobi)

Source of Data: *China Environment Annual Report 2010*, the Ministry of Environmental Protection, Beijing, China Environmental Science Press, 2011; *China Statistical Yearbook 2011*, NBS, Beijing, China Statistical Publishing House, 2011; *Desert in China*, Wu Zheng, Beijing, the Commercial Press, 1995.

A3.36 Nitrogen Oxide Emissions per Capita

Nitrogen oxide emissions per capita can be calculated as follows:

Nitrogen oxides emissions per capita =
Nitrogen oxides emissions/Mid-year population

Source of Data: *China Environment Annual Report 2010*, the Ministry of Environmental Protection, Beijing, China Environmental Science Press, 2011; *China Statistical Yearbook 2011*, NBS, Beijing, China Statistical Publishing House, 2011.

A3.37 Ammonia/Nitrogen Emissions per Unit of Land Area

Ammonia/nitrogen emissions per unit of land area can be calculated as follows:

Ammonia nitrogen emissions per unit of land area =
Ammonia nitrogen emissions/(Area under land survey)

Source of Data: *China Environment Annual Report 2010*, the Ministry of Environmental Protection, Beijing, China Environmental Science Press, 2011; *China Statistical Yearbook 2011*, NBS, Beijing, China Statistical Publishing House, 2011; *Desert in China*, Wu Zheng, Beijing, the Commercial Press, 1995.

A3.38 Ammonia/Nitrogen Emissions per Capita

Ammonia/nitrogen emissions per capita can be calculated as follows:

$$\text{Ammonia/nitrogen emissions per capita} = 2 * \text{Ammonia nitrogen emissions of the year}/(\text{Total population at the end of this year} + \text{Total population at the end of preceding year})$$

Source of Data: *China Environment Annual Report 2010*, the Ministry of Environmental Protection, Beijing, China Environmental Science Press, 2011; *China Statistical Yearbook 2011*, NBS, Beijing, China Statistical Publishing House, 2011.

A3.39 Consumption of Chemical Fertilizers per Unit of Cultivated Land Area

Consumption of chemical fertilizers in agriculture refers to the quantity of chemical fertilizers applied in agriculture in the year, including nitrogenous fertilizer, phosphate fertilizer, potash fertilizer, and compound fertilizer. The consumption of chemical fertilizers is calculated in terms of volume of effective components by means of converting the gross weight of the respective fertilizers into weight containing effective component (e.g. nitrogen content in nitrogenous fertilizer, phosphorous pentoxide contents in phosphate fertilizer, and potassium oxide contents in potash fertilizer). Compound fertilizer is converted in regard to its major components. The formula is:

$$\text{Volume of effective component} = \text{physical quantity} * \text{effective component of certain chemical fertilizers} (\%)$$

Area of cultivated land refers to refers to area of land reclaimed for the regular cultivation of various farm crops, including crop-cover land, fallow, newly reclaimed land and land laid idle for less than 3 years. Consumption of chemical fertilizers per unit of cultivated land area can be calculated as follows:

$$\text{Consumption of chemical fertilizers per unit of area of cultivated land} = \text{Chemical fertilizers consumed}/\text{Area of cultivated land}$$

Source of Data: *China Statistical Yearbook 2011*, NBS, Beijing, China Statistical Publishing House, 2011.

A3.40 Consumption of Pesticides per Unit of Cultivated Land Area

Consumption of pesticides per unit of cultivated land area refers to pesticides consumed by each unit of cultivated land area in a region in a given period, which can be calculated as follows:

$$\text{Consumption of pesticides per unit of cultivated land area} = \text{Pesticides consumed}/\text{Area of cultivated land}$$

Source of Data: *China Environmental Statistical Yearbook 2011*, NBS, the Ministry of Environmental Protection, Beijing, China Statistical Publishing House, 2011; *China Statistical Yearbook 2011*, NBS, Beijing, China Statistical Publishing House, 2011.

A3.41 Nitrogen Oxide Emissions per Capita from Road Transport

Nitrogen oxides emissions per capita from road transport can be calculated as follows:

$$2 * \text{Nitrogen oxide emissions per capita from road transport} = \text{Nitrogen oxides emissions from road traffic}/(\text{Total population at the end of this year} + \text{Total population at the end of preceding year})$$

Source of Data: *China Statistical Yearbook 2011*, NBS, Beijing, China Statistical Publishing House, 2011; *China Environment Annual Report 2010*, the Ministry of Environmental Protection, Beijing, China Environmental Science Press, 2011.

A3.42 Ratio of Environmental Spending to Government Expenditure

Expenditure for environment protection refer to the spending of government on environment protection, including the expense on administration of environment protection, environment monitoring and supervision, pollution control, natural ecology protection, project of virgin forests protection, reforesting farmland, controlling the sources of dust storms, returning pastureland to grassland, returning pastureland to grassland, returning cultivated land to grassland, energy conservation, emissions reduction, comprehensive utilization of renewable energy and resources, etc. Ratio of environmental spending to government expenditure refers to the percentage of expenditure for environment protection over government expenditure. Its formula is:

$$\text{Ratio of environmental spending to government expenditure} = 100\,\% * \text{Expenditure for environment protection}/\text{government expenditure}$$

Source of Data: *China Statistical Yearbook 2011*, NBS, Beijing, China Statistical Publishing House, 2011.

A3.43 Ratio of the Investment in Pollution Control to GDP

The investment in pollution control refers to the formation of investment in fixed assets in the total investment in harnessing pollution and in the construction of urban environment infrastructure facilities. It includes investment in harnessing sources of industrial pollution, investment in environment protection facilities designed concurrently with construction projects, and investment in urban environment infrastructure facilities.

Ratio of the investment in pollution control to GDP refers to the percentage of the investment in pollution control over GDP in a region in a given period. Its formula is:

$$\text{Ratio of the investment in pollution control to GDP} = 100\,\% * \text{the investment in pollution control}/\text{GDP}$$

Source of Data: *China Environmental Statistical Yearbook 2011*, NBS, the Ministry of Environmental Protection, Beijing, China Statistical Publishing House, 2011; *China Statistical Yearbook 2011*, NBS, Beijing, China Statistical Publishing House, 2011.

A3.44 Government Spending per Capita on Rural Water Supply System and Toilet Improvement

Rural population refers to population living in towns and villages under the jurisdiction of counties. Per capita investment of water sanitation and toilet improvement in rural areas can be calculated as follows:

$$\text{Government spending per capita on rural water supply system and toilet improvement} = 2 * \text{investment of water sanitation and toilet improvement in rural areas}/\left(\text{Total rural population at the end of this year} + \text{Total rural population at the end of preceding year}\right)$$

Source of Data: *China Environmental Statistical Yearbook 2011*, NBS, the Ministry of Environmental Protection, Beijing, China Statistical Publishing House, 2011.

A3.45 Investment in Converting Cultivated Land into Forests and Grassland per Unit of Cultivated Land Area

Investment in converting cultivated land into forests and grassland per unit of cultivated land area can be calculated as follows:

$$\begin{aligned}&\text{Investment in converting cultivated land into forests}\\&\quad\text{and grassland per unit of cultivated land area} =\\&\quad\text{Investment in forestry}/\text{cultivated land area}\end{aligned}$$

Source of Data: *China Environmental Statistical Yearbook 2011*, NBS, the Ministry of Environmental Protection, Beijing, China Statistical Publishing House, 2011; *China Statistical Yearbook 2011*, NBS, Beijing, China Statistical Publishing House, 2011.

A3.46 Ratio of the Spending on Science, Education, Culture, and Public Health to Government Expenditure

Expenditure for science refers to the spending of government on science and technology (S&T), including the expense on the administration of S&T, basic research, applied research, research and development, conditions and services of S&T, popularization of social science, science and technology, exchanges and cooperation of S&T, etc.

Expenditure for education refers to the spending of government on education, including the expense on the administration of education, pre-primary education, primary education, secondary education, high school education, regular higher education, primary vocational education, secondary vocational education, technical school education, vocational high school education and higher vocational education, radio and television education, student abroad education, special education, on the job training of cadres, education authorities services, etc.

Expenditure for culture, sport and media refers to the spending of government on culture, cultural heritage, sports, radio, film, television, press and publication, etc.

Expenditure for medical and health care refers to the spending of government on medical and health care, including the expense on administration of medical and health care, medical services, health care, disease prevention and control, health inspection and supervision, women and children's health, rural health care, etc.

Ratio of the spending on science, education, culture, and public health to government expenditure can be estimated as follows:

$$\begin{aligned}&\text{Ratio of the spending on science, education, culture,}\\&\quad\text{and public health to government expenditure} =\\&\quad 100\,\% * \big(\text{Expenditure for science and technology} + \text{Expenditure for education}\\&\quad + \text{Expenditure for culture} + \text{Expenditure for medical and health care}\big)/\\&\quad\text{Local government general budgetary expenditure}\end{aligned}$$

Source of Data: *China Statistical Yearbook 2011*, NBS, Beijing, China Statistical Publishing House, 2011.

A3.47 Area of Green Land per Capita in Urban Areas

Area of green land refers to total area occupied for green projects at the end of the reference period, including park green land, green land attached to institutions, residential quarter green land, production green land, protection green land, and scenic forest land. Area of green land per capita in urban areas can be calculated as follows:

Area of green land per capita in urban areas =
Area of green land in urban areas/annual average urban population

Source of Data: *China Statistical Yearbook 2011*, NBS, Beijing, China Statistical Publishing House, 2011; *China City Statistical Yearbook 2011*, NBS, Beijing, China Statistical Publishing House, 2012.

A3.48 Coverage of Water Supply in Urban Areas

Coverage of water supply in urban areas refers to ratio of urban population with access to tap water to total urban population. The formula is:

Coverage of water supply in urban areas =
100 % * Urban population with access to tapwater/Urban population

Source of Data: *China Statistical Yearbook 2011*, NBS, Beijing, China Statistical Publishing House, 2011.

A3.49 Treatment Rate of Urban Wastewater

Treatment rate of urban wastewater refers to the percentage of wastewater treated over wastewater discharged in urban areas. Its formula is:

Treatment rate of urban wastewater =
100 % * Wastewater treated/Wastewater discharged

Source of Data: *China Environmental Statistical Yearbook 2011*, NBS, the Ministry of Environmental Protection, Beijing, China Statistical Publishing House, 2011.

A3.50 Harmless Treatment Rate of Urban Household Waste

Harmless treatment rate of urban household waste refers to household waste treated over those produced in urban areas. In practical statistics, as it is difficult to estimate the volume of household waste produced, which is replaced with the volume of household waste transported. It is calculated as follows:

$$\text{Harmless treatment rate of urban household waste} = 100\,\% * \text{household waste treated/household waste produced}$$

Source of Data: *China Statistical Yearbook 2011*, NBS, Beijing, China Statistical Publishing House, 2011.

A3.51 Public Buses per 10,000 Urban Residents

Public buses per 10,000 urban residents refers to the number of public transportation vehicles converted in terms of common standards, at the end of the reference period, per 10,000 population in the city district. Its calculation formula is:

$$\text{Public buses per 10,000 urban residents} = 100\,\% * \text{Number of public transportation vehicles/City district population}$$

Source of Data: *China City Statistical Yearbook 2011*, NBS, Beijing, China Statistical Publishing House, 2011.

A3.52 Length of Public Transport Routes per Capita in Urban Areas

Length of public transport routes per capita in urban areas refers to the length of public transit operating routes shared by each person in urban areas, which can be estimated as follows:

$$\text{Length of public transport routes per capita in urban areas} = \text{Length of urban public transit operating routes/annual average urban population}$$

Source of Data: *China Statistical Yearbook 2011*, NBS, Beijing, China Statistical Publishing House, 2011; *China City Statistical Yearbook 2011*, NBS, Beijing, China Statistical Publishing House, 2011.

A3.53 *Ratio of the Rural Residents Benefiting from Water Supply System Improvement to the Total Rural Population*

Ratio of the rural residents benefiting from water supply system improvement to the total rural population refers to population who has benefited from various forms of water improvement projects. Rural population refers to population living in towns and villages under the jurisdiction of counties.

$$\text{Ratio of the rural residents benefiting from water supply system improvement to the total rural population} = 100\,\% * \text{Rural population benefiting from water improvement projects}/\text{Rural population}$$

Source of Data: *China Environmental Statistical Yearbook 2011*, NBS, the Ministry of Environmental Protection, Beijing, China Statistical Publishing House, 2011.

A3.54 *Green Coverage of Urban Built-Up Areas*

Green coverage of urban built-up areas refers to the percentage of green covered area over completed urban area.

Green space in urban built-up areas refers to the total area occupied for green projects at the end of the reference period, including park green land, production green land, protection green land, green land attached to institutions, and other green areas.

Source of Data: *China Statistical Yearbook 2011*, NBS, Beijing, China Statistical Publishing House, 2011.

A3.55 *Newly-Added Afforestation Area of the Year per Capita*

Afforestation refers to the course that acres of forests, trees and shrubs are planted through manual planting on land suitable for afforestation, including barren hills, idle land, sand dunes, non-timber forest land, woodland and "grain for green" land. Newly-added afforestation area of the year per capita can be calculated as follows:

$$\text{Newly-added afforestation area of the year per capita} = 2 * \text{afforestation area of the year}/\left(\text{Total population at the end of this year} + \text{Total population at the end of preceding year}\right)$$

Source of Data: *China Statistical Yearbook 2011*, NBS, Beijing, China Statistical Publishing House, 2011; *China Statistical Yearbook 2010*, NBS, Beijing, China Statistical Publishing House, 2010.

A3.56 Industrial SO_2 Removal Rate

SO_2 emissions through industrial activities refer to volume of sulphur dioxide emission from fuel burning and production process by enterprises during a given period. Volume of industrial SO_2 emissions removed refers to volume of SO_2 removed in waste gas from fuel burning and production process after it being treated by various facilities for control of waste gas.

Industrial SO_2 removal rate refers to the percentage of volume of industrial SO_2 emissions removed over the sum of SO_2 emissions through industrial activities and volume of industrial SO_2 emissions removed. Its calculation formula is:

$$\text{Industrial } SO_2 \text{ removal rate} = 100\,\% * \text{volume of industrial } SO_2 \text{ emissions removed} / \left(SO_2 \text{ emissions through industrial activities} + \text{volume of industrial } SO_2 \text{ emissions removed}\right)$$

Source of Data: *China Statistical Yearbook 2011*, NBS, Beijing, China Statistical Publishing House, 2011.

A3.57 Industrial Wastewater COD Removal Rate

Industrial wastewater COD removal rate refers to the percentage of amount of COD removed in industrial wastewater over the sum of amount of COD discharged in industrial waste and amount of COD removed in industrial wastewater. Its calculation formula is:

$$\text{Industrial wastewater COD removal rate} = 100\% * \text{amount of COD removed in industrial wastewater} / \left(\text{amount of COD discharged in industrial waste} + \text{amount of COD removed in industrial wastewater}\right)$$

Source of Data: *China Environment Annual Report 2010*, NBS, the Ministry of Environmental Protection, Beijing, China Statistical Publishing House, 2010; *China Statistical Yearbook 2011*, NBS, Beijing, China Statistical Publishing House, 2011.

A3.58 Industrial Nitrogen Oxide Removal Rate

Industrial nitrogen oxide emissions refer to volume of nitrogen oxides discharged into the atmosphere generated from production processes by enterprises during a given period. Volume of industrial nitrogen oxide emissions removed refers to volume of nitrogen oxides removed in waste gas from production process after it being treated by various facilities for control of waste gas.

Industrial nitrogen oxide removal rate refers to the percentage of volume of nitrogen oxide emissions removed over the sum of volume of nitrogen oxide emissions and volume of nitrogen oxide emissions removed. Its calculation formula is:

$$\begin{aligned}&\text{Removal rate of ammonia/nitrogen in industrial wastewater} =\\&\quad 100\,\% * \text{amount of ammonia/nitrogen removed in industrial wastewater/}\\&\quad (\text{amount of ammonia/nitrogen removed in industrial waste}+\\&\quad \text{amount of ammonia/nitrogen discharged in industrial wastewater})\end{aligned}$$

$$\begin{aligned}&\text{Removal rate of industrial nitrogen oxide emissions} =\\&\quad 100\,\% \times \text{Volume of nitrogen oxide emissions removed/}\\&\quad (\text{Volume of nitrogen oxide emissions removed}+\\&\quad \text{Volume of nitrogen oxide emissions})\end{aligned}$$

Source of Data: *China Environment Annual Report 2010*, NBS, the Ministry of Environmental Protection, Beijing, China Statistical Publishing House, 2011.

A3.59 Industrial Wastewater Ammonia/Nitrogen Removal Rate

Industrial wastewater ammonia/nitrogen removal rate refers to the percentage of amount of ammonia nitrogen removed in industrial wastewater over the sum of amount of ammonia nitrogen discharged in industrial waste and amount of ammonia nitrogen removed in industrial wastewater. Its calculation formula is:

$$\begin{aligned}&\text{Removal rate of ammonia nitrogen in industrial waste water} =\\&100\% \times \text{Amount of ammonia nitrogen removed in industrial waste water/}\\&(\text{Amount of ammonia nitrogen discharged in industrial waste}+\\&\text{Amount of ammonia nitrogen removed in industrial waste water})\end{aligned}$$

Source of Data: *China Environment Annual Report 2010*, NBS, the Ministry of Environmental Protection, Beijing, China Statistical Publishing House, 2011; *China Statistical Yearbook 2011*, NBS, Beijing, China Statistical Publishing House, 2011.

A3.60 Number of Environmental Emergencies

Environmental emergencies refer to accidents, due to economic or social activities that are contrary to environment protection laws or due to unforeseen factors or natural disasters, that lead to environment pollution, destruction of protected wild animals, plants or nature reserves, damage to human health, economic and property losses, and other negative impacts on the society.

Source of Data: *China Statistical Yearbook 2011*, NBS, Beijing, China Statistical Publishing House, 2011.

Appendix 4 CGDI Indicators and Source of Data

A4.1 GDP per Capita

Gross Domestic Product (GDP) refers to the final products at market prices produced by all resident units in a country (or a region) during a certain period of time. For a region, it is called as Gross Regional Product (GRP) or regional GDP. Its calculation formula is as follows:

$$\text{GDP per capita} = \text{GDP}/\text{annual average population}$$

Source of Data: *China Regional Economy Statistical Yearbook 2011*, NBS, Beijing, China Statistical Publishing House, 2012; *China City Statistical Yearbook 2011*, NBS, Beijing, China Statistical Publishing House, 2011.

A4.2 Energy Consumption per Unit of GDP

Total energy consumption refers to the total consumption of energy of various kinds by the production sectors and the households in the country in a given period. Energy consumption per unit of GDP refers to the energy consumption per unit of Gross Regional Product in a region in the same reference period, reflecting the increased energy consumption with an additional unit of GDP. The formula is:

$$\text{Energy consumption per unit of GDP} = \text{Total energy consumption}/\text{GDP}$$

Source of Data: *China Regional Economy Statistical Yearbook 2011*, NBS, Beijing, China Statistical Publishing House, 2012; *China City Statistical Yearbook 2011*, NBS, Beijing, China Statistical Publishing House, 2011.

A4.3 Electricity Consumption per Capita in Urban Areas

Electricity consumption per capita in urban areas refers to the ratio of electricity consumption by urban households to the annual average urban population in a region in a given period. The formula is:

$$\begin{aligned}&\text{Per capita electricity consumption by urban households} =\\&\quad\text{Electricity consumption by urban households}/\text{Average urban population}\end{aligned}$$

Source of Data: *China City Statistical Yearbook 2011*, NBS, Beijing, China Statistical Publishing House, 2011.

A4.4 CO_2 Emissions per Unit of GDP

CO_2 emissions per unit of GDP refer to the ratio of carbon dioxide emissions to GDP in a region in the same reference period. The formula is:

$$CO_2 \text{ emissions per unit of GDP} = CO_2 \text{ emissions/GDP}$$

A4.5 SO_2 Emissions per Unit of GDP

Sulphur dioxide (SO_2) emissions cover SO_2 emissions through industrial activities and non-industrial activities, of which emissions through industrial activities refer to volume of sulphur dioxide discharged from fuel burning and production process by enterprises during a given period. The formula is:

$$\text{Industrial } SO_2 \text{ emissions} = SO_2 \text{ discharged from the process of fuel burning} + SO_2 \text{ discharged from the process of production}$$

Emission through non-industrial and other activities are calculated on the basis of consumption of coal by households and other activities and the sulphur content of coal with the following formula:

$$\text{Emission through non-industrial and other activities} = \text{coals consumed by household and other activities} \times \text{Sulphur content} * 0.8 * 2$$

SO_2 emissions per unit of GDP refer to the ratio of SO_2 emissions to GDP in a region in a given period. The formula is:

$$SO_2 \text{ emissions per unit of GDP} = SO_2 \text{ emissions/GDP}$$

Source of Data: *China Regional Economy Statistical Yearbook 2011*, NBS, Beijing, China Statistical Publishing House, 2012; *China Environment Annual Report 2010*, the Ministry of Environmental Protection, Beijing, China Environmental Science Press, 2011.

A4.6 COD Emissions per Unit of GDP

Chemical Oxygen Demand (COD) refers to the amount of oxygen required when chemical oxidants are used to oxidize organic pollutants in water. A higher value of COD corresponds to more serious pollution. COD emissions mainly come from wastewater discharged by industry and household, of which COD emissions of the latter refer to the annual amount of COD in the wastewater discharged by urban households, which can be calculated by per capita coefficient as follows:

$$\text{COD emissions in wastewater discharged by urban households} = \text{Coefficient of COD generated through urban non-industrial wastewater} \times \text{Urban nonagricultural population} * 365$$

COD emissions per unit of GDP refer to the ratio of COD emissions to GDP in a region in a given period. The formula is:

$$\text{COD emissions per unit of GDP} = \text{COD}/\text{GDP}$$

Source of Data: *China Regional Economy Statistical Yearbook 2011*, NBS, Beijing, China Statistical Publishing House, 2012; *China Environment Annual Report 2010*, the Ministry of Environmental Protection, Beijing, China Environmental Science Press, 2011.

A4.7 Nitrogen Oxide Emissions per Unit of GDP

Nitrogen oxide emission refers to the volume of nitrogen oxide discharged to the atmosphere during the reference period.

Nitrogen oxides emissions per unit of GDP refer to the ratio of Nitrogen oxide emissions to GDP in a region in a given period. The formula is:

$$\text{Nitrogen oxide emissions per unit of GDP} = \text{Nitrogen oxide emissions}/\text{GDP}$$

Source of Data: *China Regional Economy Statistical Yearbook 2011*, NBS, Beijing, China Statistical Publishing House, 2012; *China Environment Annual Report 2010*, the Ministry of Environmental Protection, Beijing, China Environmental Science Press, 2011.

A4.8 Ammonia/Nitrogen Emissions per Unit of GDP

Ammonia/nitrogen emissions refer to the amount of ammonia/nitrogen in industrial wastewater discharged by enterprises and urban households.

Ammonia/nitrogen emissions per unit of GDP refer to the ratio of ammonia/nitrogen emissions to GDP in a region in a given period. The formula is:

$$\text{Ammonia}/\text{nitrogen emissions per unit of GDP} = \text{Ammonia}/\text{nitrogen emissions}/\text{GDP}$$

Source of Data: *China Regional Economy Statistical Yearbook 2011*, NBS, Beijing, China Statistical Publishing House, 2012; *China Environment Annual*

Report 2010, the Ministry of Environmental Protection, Beijing, China Environmental Science Press, 2011.

A4.9 Labor Productivity of the Primary Sector

Labor productivity of the primary sector refers to the ratio of value added of the primary sector to annual average of employees in the primary sector. The formula is:

$$\text{Labor productivity of the primary sector} = 2 * \text{Value added of the primary sector} / (\text{Employees in primary sector at the end of this year} + \text{Employees in the primary sector at the end of preceding year})$$

Source of Data: *China Regional Economy Statistical Yearbook 2011*, NBS, Beijing, China Statistical Publishing House, 2012.

A4.10 Labor Productivity of the Secondary Sector

Labor productivity of the secondary sector refers to the ratio of value added of the secondary sector to annual average of employees in the secondary sector. The formula is:

$$\text{Labor productivity of the secondary sector} = 2 \times \text{value added of the secondary sector} / (\text{Employees in the secondary sector at the end of this year} + \text{Employees in the secondary sector at the end of preceding year})$$

Source of Data: *China Regional Economy Statistical Yearbook 2011*, NBS, Beijing, China Statistical Publishing House, 2012.

A4.11 Water Consumption per Unit of Value Added Created by Industrial Enterprises

Water consumption per unit of value added created by industrial enterprises refers to the ratio of water consumed by industry to its value added in a given period. Of which value added of industry refers to the final results of industrial production of industrial enterprises in money terms during the reference period; Water consumed by industry refers to water consumed by industrial enterprises for manufacturing, processing, cooling, air-conditioning, purifying, rinsing and so on in process of production, which is measured in terms of new withdrawals of water, excluding reuse of water within the same enterprises. The formula is:

$$\text{Water consumption per unit of value added created by industrial enterprises} = \text{water consumed by industry/its value added}$$

Source of Data: *China Statistical Yearbook 2011*, NBS, Beijing, China Statistical Publishing House, 2012; *China Environment Annual Report 2010,* the Ministry of Environmental Protection, Beijing, China Environmental Science Press, 2011.

A4.12 Energy Consumption per Unit of Value Added Created by Industrial Enterprises

Energy consumption per unit of value added created by industrial enterprises refers to the ratio of energy consumed by industry to its value added in a given period. The formula is:

$$\text{Energy consumption per unit of value added created by industrial enterprises} = \text{energy consumed by industrial enterprises/their value added}$$

Source of Data: *China Regional Economy Statistical Yearbook 2011*, NBS, Beijing, China Statistical Publishing House, 2012; *China Statistical Yearbook 2011*, NBS, Beijing, China Statistical Publishing House, 2011.

A4.13 Utilization Rate of Industrial Solid Waste

Utilization rate of industrial solid waste refers to the percentage of industrial solid waste utilized over industrial solid waste produced (including stocks of the previous years). Its calculation formula is:

$$\text{Utilization rate of industrial solid waste} = 100\,\% * \text{Industrial solid waste utilized}/\left(\text{Industrial solid waste produced} + \text{Stocks of previous utilized}\right)$$

Of which, industrial solid waste produced refers to total volume of solid, semisolid and high concentration liquid residues produced by industrial enterprises from the process of production in a given period, including hazardous waste, slag and ash, gangue, tailings, radioactive residues and other waste, but excluding stones stripped or dug out in mining (gangue and acid or alkaline stones not covered). A stone is acid or alkaline if the pH value of the water is below 4 or above 10.5, when it is in, or soaked by, the water; Industrial solid waste utilized refers to volume of solid waste from which useful materials may be extracted or which can be converted into usable resources, energy or other materials by means of reclamation, processing, recycling and exchange (including utilizing the stocks of industrial solid waste of the previous years in the years in question, e.g. fertilizers, building materials and road materials. The information concerned shall be collected by the producing units of waste.)

Source of Data: *China Environment Annual Report 2010*, the Ministry of Environmental Protection, Beijing, China Environmental Science Press, 2011.

A4.14 Recycling Rate of Industrial Water

The amount of water used in industrial production refers to the amount of water used in industrial and non-industrial activities within enterprises, which covers new withdrawals of water and reuse of water. New withdrawals of water refer to the amount of fresh water used in industrial and non-industrial activities within enterprises in a given period (the amount of fresh water used in non-industrial activities is measured separately, excluding household sewage that is not discharged altogether with household wastewater), which cover their new withdrawals of water from urban running water and their self-supplied water; Reuse of water refers to the amount of water reused by enterprises in a given period, including recycling water, multi-purpose water, and cascade of water (covering water reused after control).

Recycling rate of industrial water refers to the ratio of the amount of water re-used in industrial production to total amount of water used in a given period. The formula is:

$$\text{Recycling rate of industrial water} = 100\,\% \times \text{Reuse of water}/\left(\text{New withdrawals of water} + \text{reuse of water}\right)$$

Source of Data: *China Environment Annual Report 2010*, the Ministry of Environmental Protection, Beijing, China Environmental Science Press, 2011.

A4.15 Labor Productivity of the Tertiary Sector

Labor productivity of the tertiary sector refers to the ratio of value added of the tertiary sector to annual average of employees in secondary sector. The formula is:

$$\text{Labor productivity of the tertiary sector} = 2 * \text{Value added of the tertiary sector}/\left(\text{Employees in the tertiary sector at the end of this year} + \text{Employees in tertiary sector at the end of preceding year}\right)$$

Source of Data: *China Regional Economy Statistical Yearbook 2011*, NBS, Beijing, China Statistical Publishing House, 2012.

A4.16 Proportion of the Value Added of the Tertiary Sector in GDP

Proportion of the value added of the tertiary sector in GDP refers to the percentage of value added of the tertiary sector over GDP in a reporting period.

Source of Data: *China City Statistical Yearbook 2011*, NBS, Beijing, China Statistical Publishing House, 2011.

A4.17 Proportion of Tertiary Sector Employees in the Total Employed Population

Proportion of tertiary sector employees in the total employed population refers to the percentage of employees of tertiary sector over total employees in a reporting period.

Source of Data: *China City Statistical Yearbook 2011*, NBS, Beijing, China Statistical Publishing House, 2011.

A4.18 Water Resources per Capita

Water resources per capita refer to water resources shared by each person in a region in a given period. Of which water resources in a region refers to total volume of water resources measured as run-off for surface water from rainfall and recharge for groundwater in the region, excluding transit water.

Source of Data: *China Environment Annual Report 2010*, the Ministry of Environmental Protection, Beijing, China Environmental Science Press, 2011; *China City Statistical Yearbook 2011*, NBS, Beijing, China Statistical Publishing House, 2011.

A4.19 CO_2 Emissions per Unit of Land Area

CO_2 emissions per unit of land area can be calculated as follows:

$$\text{CO}_2 \text{ emissions per unit of land area} = \text{CO}_2 \text{ emissions/Land area of an administrative region}$$

A4.20 CO_2 Emissions per Capita

CO_2 emissions per capita can be calculated as follows:

$$CO_2 \text{ emissions per capita} = \text{Total } CO_2 \text{ emissions/annual average population}$$

A4.21 SO_2 Emissions per Unit of Land Area

Land area of an administrative region refers to all land area (including water area) within it, which is measured in terms of administrative divisions.

SO_2 emissions per unit of land area in a region can be calculated as follows:

$$SO_2 \text{ emissions per unit of land area} = SO_2 \text{ emissions/Land area of an administrative region}$$

Source of Data: *China Environment Annual Report 2010*, the Ministry of Environmental Protection, Beijing, China Environmental Science Press, 2011; *China City Statistical Yearbook 2011*, NBS, Beijing, China Statistical Publishing House, 2011.

A4.22 SO_2 Emissions per Capita

SO_2 emissions per capita can be calculated as follows:

$$SO_2 \text{ emissions per capita} = SO_2 \text{ emissions/annual average population}$$

Source of Data: *China Environment Annual Report 2010*, the Ministry of Environmental Protection, Beijing, China Environmental Science Press, 2011; *China City Statistical Yearbook 2011*, NBS, Beijing, China Statistical Publishing House, 2011.

A4.23 COD Emissions per Unit of Land Area

COD emissions per unit of land area can be calculated as follows:

$$\text{COD emissions per unit of land area} = \text{COD emissions/Land area of an administrative region}$$

Source of Data: *China Environment Annual Report 2010*, the Ministry of Environmental Protection, Beijing, China Environmental Science Press, 2011; *China City Statistical Yearbook 2011*, NBS, Beijing, China Statistical Publishing House, 2011.

A4.24 COD Emissions per Capita

COD emissions per capita can be calculated as follows:

COD emissions per capita = total COD emissions/annual average population

Source of Data: *China Environment Annual Report 2010*, the Ministry of Environmental Protection, Beijing, China Environmental Science Press, 2011; *China City Statistical Yearbook 2011*, NBS, Beijing, China Statistical Publishing House, 2011.

A4.25 Nitrogen Oxide Emissions per Unit of Land Area

Nitrogen oxide emissions per unit of land area can be calculated as follows:

Nitrogen oxide emissions per unit of land area =
Nitrogen oxide emissions/Land area of an administrative region

Source of Data: *China Environment Annual Report 2010*, the Ministry of Environmental Protection, Beijing, China Environmental Science Press, 2011; *China City Statistical Yearbook 2011*, NBS, Beijing, China Statistical Publishing House, 2011.

A4.26 Nitrogen Oxide Emissions per Capita

Nitrogen oxides emissions per capita can be calculated as follows:

Nitrogen oxide emissions per capita =
Nitrogen oxide emissions/annual average population

Source of Data: *China Environment Annual Report 2010*, the Ministry of Environmental Protection, Beijing, China Environmental Science Press, 2011; *China City Statistical Yearbook 2011*, NBS, Beijing, China Statistical Publishing House, 2011.

A4.27 *Ammonia/Nitrogen Emissions per Unit of Land Area*

Ammonia/nitrogen emissions per unit of land area can be calculated as follows:

$$\text{Ammonia/nitrogen emissions per unit of land area} = \text{Ammonia/nitrogen emissions/Land area of an administrative region}$$

Source of Data: *China Environment Annual Report 2010*, the Ministry of Environmental Protection, Beijing, China Environmental Science Press, 2011; *China City Statistical Yearbook 2011*, NBS, Beijing, China Statistical Publishing House, 2011.

A4.28 *Ammonia/Nitrogen Emissions per Capita*

Ammonia/nitrogen emissions per capita can be calculated as follows:

$$\text{Ammonia/nitrogen emissions per capita} = \text{Ammonia/nitrogen emissions/annual average population}$$

Source of Data: *China Environment Annual Report 2010*, the Ministry of Environmental Protection, Beijing, China Environmental Science Press, 2011; *China City Statistical Yearbook 2011*, NBS, Beijing, China Statistical Publishing House, 2011.

A4.29 *Percentage of Days with Air Quality at or Above Level II in a Year*

Air Pollution Index (API) is defined as a measure of pollution index ranges and corresponding pollutant concentrations in terms of air quality standards and each pollutant's effects on human health and ecological environment. Up to now API adopted in China may be divided into five levels, of which level I means that the air quality is excellent and meets the requirements for air quality in natural reserves, scenic spots and other regions needing special protection, if API is at or below 50; Level II means that the air quality is good, if API is above 50 but less than 100; Level III means that the air quality is lightly polluted, if API is above 100 but less than 200; Level IV means that the air quality is moderately polluted, if API is above 200 but less than 300; Level V means that the air quality is heavily polluted, if API is above 300.

Percentage of days with air quality at or above level II in a year refers to the percentage of days with air quality at and above level II over all days in a year at an administrative region.

Source of Data: Ministry of Environmental Protection Data Center, http://datacenter.mep.gov.cn/

A4.30 Percentage of Days with Respirable Suspended Particulates as the Principal Pollutants in a Year

Principal pollutants refer to the most polluted ones, including sulphur dioxide, nitrogen dioxide and respirable suspended particulate to be measured. Respirable suspended particulate refers to solid matter in the air with diameter from 0.1 to 100 lm that can be suspended in the air, instead of falling onto the ground under the gravity force for long periods of time.

Percentage of days with respirable suspended particulates as the principal pollutants in a year refers to the percentage of days with principal pollutants as respirable suspended particulate over all days in a year at an administrative region.

Source of Data: Ministry of Environmental Protection Data Center, http://datacenter.mep.gov.cn/

A4.31 Ratio of Environmental Spending to Government Expenditure

Expenditure for environment protection refer to the spending of government on environment protection, including the expense on administration of environment protection, environment monitoring and supervision, pollution control, natural ecology protection, project of virgin forests protection, reforesting farmland, controlling the sources of dust storms, returning pastureland to grassland, returning pastureland to grassland, returning cultivated land to grassland, energy conservation, emissions reduction, comprehensive utilization of renewable energy and resources, etc.

Ratio of environmental spending to government expenditure refers to the percentage of expenditure for environment protection over government expenditure. Its formula is:

$$\text{Ratio of environmental spending to government expenditure} = 100\,\% \times \text{Expenditure for environment protection}/\text{Local government general budgetary expenditure}$$

Source of Data: *China Statistical Yearbook 2011*, NBS, Beijing, China Statistical Publishing House, 2011; *China City Statistical Yearbook 2011*, NBS, Beijing, China Statistical Publishing House, 2011.

A4.32 *Ratio of the Investment in Industrial Pollution Control to GDP*

Investment in the control of industrial environmental pollution refers to investment in fixed assets in harnessing industrial wastewater, waste gas, solid waste, noise and other environmental pollution. Ratio of the investment in pollution control to GDP can be calculated as follows:

$$\text{Ratio of the investment in pollution control to GDP} = 100\,\% \times \text{investment in the control of industrial environmental pollution/GDP}$$

Source of Data: *China Environment Annual Report 2010*, the Ministry of Environmental Protection, Beijing, China Environmental Science Press, 2011; *China Regional Economy Statistical Yearbook 2011*, NBS, Beijing, China Statistical Publishing House, 2012.

A4.33 *Ratio of the Spending on Science, Education, Culture, and Public Health to Government Expenditure*

Expenditure for science and technology refers to the spending of government on science and technology (S&T), including the expense on the administration of S&T, basic research, applied research, research and development, conditions and services of S&T, popularization of social science, science and technology, exchanges and cooperation of S&T, etc.

Expenditure for education refers to the spending of government on education, including the expense on the administration of education, pre-primary education, primary education, secondary education, high school education, regular higher education, primary vocational education, secondary vocational education, technical school education, vocational high school education and higher vocational education, radio and television education, student abroad education, special education, on the job training of cadres, education authorities services, etc.

Expenditure for culture, sport and media refers to the spending of government on culture, cultural heritage, sports, radio, film, television, press and publication, etc.

Expenditure for medical and health care refers to the spending of government on medical and health care, including the expense on administration of medical and health care, medical services, health care, disease prevention and control, health inspection and supervision, women and children's health, rural health care, etc.

Ratio of the spending on science, education, culture, and public health to government expenditure can be estimated as follows:

$$\text{Ratio of the spending on science, education, culture, and public health to government expenditure} = 100\,\% * (\text{Expenditure for science and technology} + \text{Expenditure for education} + \text{Expenditure for culture} + \text{Expenditure for medical and health care})/\text{Local government general budgetary expenditure}$$

Source of Data: *China City Statistical Yearbook 2011*, NBS, Beijing, China Statistical Publishing House, 2011; *China Regional Economy Statistical Yearbook 2011*, NBS, Beijing, China Statistical Publishing House, 2012; *China City Statistical Yearbook 2011*, NBS, Beijing, China Statistical Publishing House, 2011.

A4.34 Area of Green Land per Capita

Area of green land refers to total area occupied for green projects at the end of the reference period, including park green land, green land attached to institutions, residential quarter green land, production green land, protection green land, and scenic forest land. Area of green land per capita in urban areas can be calculated as follows:

$$\text{Area of green land per capita} = \text{Area of green land}/\text{permanent population in city districts}$$

Source of Data: *China City Statistical Yearbook 2011*, NBS, Beijing, China Statistical Publishing House, 2011.

A4.35 Green Coverage of Urban Built-In Areas

Green coverage of urban built-in areas refers to the percentage of green covered area over completed urban area at the end of the reference period. Its calculation formula is:

$$\text{Green coverage of urban built-in areas} = 100\,\% \times \text{Ratio of green covered area}/\text{completed urban area}$$

Source of Data: *China Urban Construction Statistical Yearbook 2010*, the Ministry of Housing, Urban and Rural Development, Beijing, China Planning Press, 2011.

A4.36 Coverage of Water Supply in Urban Areas

Coverage of water supply in urban areas refers to ratio of urban population with access to tap water to total urban population. The formula is:

$$\text{Coverage of water supply in urban areas} = 100\,\% \times \text{Urban population with access to tap water/Urban population}$$

Source of Data: *China Municipal Construction Statistical Yearbook 2010*, the Ministry of Housing, Urban and Rural Development, Beijing, China Planning Press, 2011.

A4.37 Treatment Rate of Urban Household Wastewater

Treatment rate of urban household wastewater refers to the percentage of household wastewater treated over domestic wastewater discharged in urban areas. Its formula is:

$$\text{Treatment rate of urban household wastewater} = 100\,\% \times \text{household wastewater treated/household wastewater}$$

Source of Data: *China Municipal Construction Statistical Yearbook 2010*, the Ministry of Housing, Urban and Rural Development, Beijing, China Planning Press, 2011.

A4.38 Harmless Treatment Rate of Urban Household Waste

Harmless treatment rate of urban household waste refers to household waste treated over those produced in urban areas. In practical statistics, as it is difficult to estimate the volume of household waste produced, which is replaced with the volume of household waste transported. It is calculated as follows:

$$\text{Harmless treatment rate of urban household waste} = 100\,\% * \text{household waste treated/household waste produced}$$

Source of Data: *China Urban Construction Statistical Yearbook 2010*, the Ministry of Housing, Urban and Rural Development, Beijing, China Planning Press, 2011.

A4.39 Public Buses per 10,000 Residents

Public buses per 10,000 residents refers to the number of public transportation vehicles converted in terms of common standards, at the end of the reference period, per 10,000 population in the city districts. Its calculation formula is:

$$\text{Public buses per } 10,000 \text{ residents} = 100\,\% * \text{Number of public transportation vehicles} / \text{permanent population in city districts}$$

Source of Data: *China City Statistical Yearbook 2011*, NBS, Beijing, China Statistical Publishing House, 2011.

A4.40 Industrial SO_2 Removal Rate

SO_2 emissions through industrial activities refer to volume of sulphur dioxide emission from fuel burning and production process by enterprises during a given period.

Volume of industrial SO_2 emissions removed refers to volume of SO_2 removed in waste gas from fuel burning and production process after it being treated by various facilities for control of waste gas.

Industrial SO_2 removal rate refers to the percentage of volume of industrial SO_2 emissions removed over the sum of SO_2 emissions through industrial activities and volume of industrial SO_2 emissions removed. Its calculation formula is:

$$\text{Industrial } SO_2 \text{ removal rate} = 100\,\% \times \text{volume of industrial } SO_2 \text{ emissions removed} / \left(SO_2 \text{ emissions through industrial activities} + \text{volume of industrial } SO_2 \text{ emissions removed}\right)$$

Source of Data: *China Environment Annual Report 2010*, the Ministry of Environmental Protection, Beijing, China Environmental Science Press, 2011.

A4.41 Industrial Wastewater COD Removal Rate

Volume of industrial COD emissions removed refers to pure weight of COD removed in industrial wastewater after it being treated by various facilities for control of wastewater.

COD emissions through industrial activities refer to pure weight of COD in industrial wastewater discharged by enterprises during a given period.

Industrial wastewater COD removal rate refers to the percentage of amount of COD removed in industrial wastewater over the sum of amount of COD discharged in industrial waste and amount of COD removed in industrial wastewater. Its calculation formula is:

$$\text{Industrial wastewater COD removal rate} = 100\% * \text{amount of COD removed in industrial wastewater} / \left(\text{amount of COD discharged in industrial waste} + \text{amount of COD removed in industrial wastewater}\right)$$

Source of Data: *China Environment Annual Report 2010*, the Ministry of Environmental Protection, Beijing, China Environmental Science Press, 2011.

A4.42 Industrial Nitrogen Oxide Removal Rate

Volume of industrial nitrogen oxide emissions refers to volume of nitrogen oxide discharged into the atmosphere generated from production processes by enterprises during a given period.

Volume of industrial nitrogen oxide emissions removed refers to volume of nitrogen oxide removed in waste gas from production process after it being treated by various facilities for control of waste gas.

Industrial nitrogen oxide removal rate refers to the percentage of volume of nitrogen oxide emissions removed over the sum of volume of nitrogen oxide emissions and volume of nitrogen oxide emissions removed. Its calculation formula is:

$$\text{Industrial nitrogen oxide removal rate} = 100\% \times \text{Volume of nitrogen oxide emissions removed} / \left(\text{Volume of nitrogen oxide emissions removed} + \text{Volume of nitrogen oxide emissions}\right)$$

Source of Data: *China Environment Annual Report 2010*, the Ministry of Environmental Protection, Beijing, China Environmental Science Press, 2011.

A4.43 Industrial Wastewater Ammonia/Nitrogen Removal Rate

Volume of ammonia nitrogen removed in industrial wastewater refers to pure weight of ammonia nitrogen removed in waste gas from production process after it being treated by various facilities for control of wastewater

Amount of ammonia/nitrogen discharged in industrial waste refers to pure weight of ammonia nitrogen discharged in industrial waste. Industrial wastewater ammonia/nitrogen removal rate refers to the percentage of amount of ammonia/ nitrogen removed in industrial wastewater over the sum of amount of ammonia nitrogen discharged in industrial waste and amount of ammonia/nitrogen removed in industrial wastewater. Its calculation formula is:

$$\begin{aligned}&\text{Industrial wastewater ammonia/nitrogen removal rate} =\\&\quad 100\,\% \times \text{amount of ammonia/nitrogen removed in industrial wastewater/}\\&\quad (\text{amount of ammonia/nitrogen removed in industrial waste}+\\&\quad \text{amount of ammonia/nitrogen discharged in industrial wastewater})\end{aligned}$$

Source of Data: *China Environment Annual Report 2010*, the Ministry of Environmental Protection, Beijing, China Environmental Science Press, 2011.

References

Beatley T (2000) Green urbanism: learning from European cities [M]. Island Press, Washington, DC
Cai Yunlong (2000) The theory of natural resource [M]. Science Press, Beijing
Cao Rongxiang (2000). Global warming: economics, politics and moral of climate change [M]. Social Sciences Document Academic Press, Beijing
China Development Research Foundation (2010) China development report 2010 – new urbanization in China: for a people-centered strategy [R]. People's Publishing House, Beijing
Chinese Society for Urban Studies (2009) China's low carbon eco-city development strategy [M]. China City Press, Beijing
Chen Shijie, Li Xiuyang, Zhou Lianfang (2003) Quantitative study by grey system on the latent period of lung cancer induced by air pollutants. Chin J Epidemiol 24:233–235
Christine Kim et al (2010) Environmental performance index 2010 [C]. Yale University and Columbia University, New Haven
Climate Change & Low Carbon Economy Institute of Renmin University (2010) Low carbon economy [M]. Petroleum Industry Press, Beijing
Cobb C, Halstead T, Rowe J (1995) If the GDP is up, why is America down? [j]. The Atlantic Monthly
Crafts NFR (1997) The human development index and changes in standards of living: some historical comparisons [U]. Eur Rev Econ Hist (1):299–322
Daly H, Cobb J Jr (1989) For the common good: redirecting the economy toward community, the environment, and a sustainable future [M]. Beacon Press, Boston
Department of Comprehensive Statistics of the National Economy, NBS (2009) Compilation of statistics of the sixty years of the People's Republic of China [R]. China Statistical Publishing House, Beijing
Department of Comprehensive Statistics of the National Economy, NBS (2011) China regional economy statistical yearbook 2011 [R]. China Statistical Publishing House, Beijing
Department of Industrial and Transport Statistics, NBS (2011) China industrial economy statistical yearbook 2011. China Statistical Publishing House, Beijing
Donovan N, Halpem D (2002) Life satisfaction: the state of knowledge and implications for government [EB/OL]. United Kingdom Treasury Paper
Giddens A [UK] (2009) The politics of climate change [M]. Social Sciences Document Academic Press, Beijing
Goldsmith E (1972) A blueprint for survival [M]. Penguin Books Ltd., London
Hadwen S, Palmer LJ (1922) Reindeer in Alaska, USDA Bulletin, No. 1089 [R]. US Department of Agriculture, Washington, DC
Hall B, Kerr ML (1991) 1991–1992 green index: a state-by-state guide to the nation's environmental health [M]. Island Press, Washington, DC

X. Li and J. Pan (eds.), *China Green Development Index Report 2012: Regional Comparison*, Current Chinese Economic Report Series,
DOI 10.1007/978-3-642-54178-0, © Springer-Verlag Berlin Heidelberg 2015

Hards Jonathan M, Kennedy S (1999) Carrying capacity in agriculture: global and regional issues [J]. Ecol Econ 29(3):443–461

Kahn [USA] (2008) Green cities [M] (trans: Fanling M). CITIC Publishing House, Beijing

Kong Xianghuan, Yin Xuejun (1996) Comparison of mutagenicity of airborne particulates for strain TA98 with that for its new derivative strains. J Cap Med Univ (4)

Lawn PA (2003) A theoretical foundation to support the index of sustainable economic welfare (ISEW), genuine progress indicator (GPI), and other related indexes [J]. Ecol Econ 44(1):105–118

Leipert C (1987) A critical appraisal of gross national product: the measurement of net national welfare and environmental accounting [J]. J Econ Issues 21(1):357–373

Li Yining (2005) Why is transformation of economic growth mode slow? [J] Price: Theory & Practice

Li Xiaoxi (2009) China: new outlook on development [M]. China Economic Publishing House, Beijing

Li Xiaoxi et al (2009) China economic report for the new century [M]. China Economic Publishing House, Beijing

Li Zehou (2007) Collection of works on history of Chinese thoughts [M]. Tianjin Academy of Social Sciences Press, Tianjin

Li Jianping, Li Minrong, Wang Jinnan (2011) Report on China's provincial environment competitiveness development 2009–2010 [R]. Social Sciences Document Academic Press, Beijing

Lin Yifu, Cai Fang, Li Zhou (1994) China's miracle: development strategy and economic reform [M]. Shanghai People's Publishing House, Shanghai

Ma Shengjie, Yao Xiaoyan (2009) Study on comprehensive evaluation of China's circular economy [M]. China Economic Publishing House, Beijing

Ministry of Water Resources (2011) China water conservancy statistical yearbook 2011 [R]. China Water Power Press, Beijing

NBS (2009–2011) China statistical yearbook 2009–2011 [R]. China Statistical Publishing House, Beijing

NBS, The Ministry of Environmental Protection (2009–2011) China environmental statistical yearbook 2008–2011. China Statistical Publishing House, Beijing

Ni Pengfei, Peter Karl Kresl [USA] (2010) Global urban competitiveness report 2009–2010 [R]. Social Sciences Document Academic Press, Beijing

Nicholson-Lord D (2003) Green cities and why we need them [M]. New Economics Foundation, London

Niu Wenyuan (2007) The overview of China's sustainable development [M]. Science Press, Beijing

OCED (2008) Environmental performance reviews [M] (trans: Cao Dong et al.). China Environmental Science Press, Beijing

OECD (1998) Eco-efficiency [R]. Organisation for Economic Cooperation and Development, Paris

Organization of Urban Socio-Economic Survey, NBS (2011) China city statistical yearbook 2011 [R]. China Statistical Publishing House, Beijing

Qiu Shoufeng (2009) Planning for circular economy: eco-efficiency method and application [M]. Tongji University Press, Shanghai

Ree WE (1992) Ecological footprint and appropriated carrying capacity: what urban economics leaves out [J]. Environ Urban 4(2):121–130

Research Group of Sustainable Development Strategy, CAS (2012) China sustainable development report 2012: China's sustainable development in the shifting global context [R]. Science Press, Beijing

Rijsberman MA, van de Ven Frans HM (2000) Different approaches to assessment of design and management of sustainable urban water system [J]. Environ Impact Assess Rev 20(3):333–345

School of Economics and Resource Management of Beijing Normal University (2008) A report on the development of China's market economy 2008 [R]. Beijing Normal University Press, Beijing

Secretariat of CCICED (2010) CCICED findings on environment and development policies 2007–2009 [R]. China Environmental Science Press, Beijing
State Administration of Environmental Protection (2005) Survey and evaluation of the ecological status of China, integration volume [R]. China Environmental Science Press, Beijing
Scientific Outlook On Development and Sustainable Economic Development Research Base et al (2010) China green development index report 2010: provincial comparison [R]. Normal University Press, Beijing
Scientific Outlook on Development and Sustainable Economic Development Research Base et al (2011) China green development index report 2011: regional comparison [R]. Beijing Normal University Press, Beijing
The Administrative Center for China's Agenda 21, Department for Social Development of the Ministry of Science and Technology (2011) Green development and technological innovation [M]. Science Press, Beijing
The Ministry of Environmental Protection (2011) China environment annual report 2010 [M]. China Environmental Science Press, Beijing
The Ministry of Housing, Urban and Rural Development (2010) China municipal construction statistical yearbook 2010 [R]. China Urban Planning Press, Beijing
The World Bank, Research Group of *World Development Report* (2003) World Development Report 2003 [R]. China Financial and Economic Publishing House, Beijing
The World Bank (2009) World development report 2009: reshaping economic geography [R] (trans: Guangyu H et al.). Tsinghua University Press, Beijing
The World Bank (2011) World development indicators 2011 [M] (trans: Hui W et al.). China Financial and Economic Publishing House, Beijing
The World Bank, Development Research Center of the State Council of the People's Republic of China (2012) China 2030: building a modern, harmonious, and creative high-income society. World Bank; Development Research Center of the State Council, the People's Republic of China, Washington, DC
Tian Hongna (2009) Construction and management of the innovation system for resource-based cities in China [M]. Economic Science Press, Beijing
UNDP (2002) China human development report 2002: making green development a choice [R]. China Financial and Economic Publishing House, Beijing
UNEP (2011a) Towards a green economy: pathways to sustainable development and poverty eradication. UNEP, Nairobi
UNEP (2011b) Towards a green economy, pathways to a sustainable development and poverty eradication – a report for policy makers
Wang Qiuyan (2009) China green development report [R]. China Modern Economic Publishing House, Beijing
Wang Jinnan et al (2009) Green national accounting for China [M]. China Environmental Science Press, Beijing
Wang Weiguang et al (2009) Annual report on climate change actions 2009 [R]. Social Sciences Document Academic Press, Beijing
Wen Jiabao (2012) Report on the work of the government 2012 [R/OL]. http://www.gov.cn/test/2012-03/15/content_2067314.htm
Wu Jinglian (2006) The choice of China growth mode [M]. Yuandong Publishing House, Shanghai
Wu Zheng (2009) Deserts and desert control in China [M]. Science Press, Beijing
Xiaozhi (2011) Green jobs. China Employ (5)
Yang Dongping (2010) China environmental development report 2010 [R]. Social Sciences Document Academic Press, Beijing
YanGeng (2011) Annual report on China's provincial Eco-civilization Index (ECI 2011) [R] (2011) Social Sciences Document Academic Press, Beijing
Zeng Shaojun (2010) Carbon emission reduction: experiences of China – a survey based on clean development mechanism [M]. Social Sciences Document Academic Press, Beijing

Zhang Huanbo (2010) Analysis on climate policies of China, the United States and the European Union [M]. Social Sciences Document Academic Press, Beijing

Zhang Kun Min, Pan Jiahua, Cui Dapeng (2008) Introduction to low carbon economy [M]. China Environmental Science Press, Beijing

Zhang Luqiang (2007) Ecological basis of general circular economy: integration of natural and social sciences [M]. People's Publishing House, Beijing

Zhao Yuan, Hao Lisha, Wang Lishan (2006) Case study on sustainable development [M]. Science Press, Beijing

Zou Shoumin, Wang Jinnan, Hong Yaxiong (2006) Research report on China's environmental protection planning during the 11th five-year plan [R]. China Environmental Science Press, Beijing

Writers by Chapter

Parts	Chapter	Writers
Introduction		Xiaoxi Li, Jiancheng Pan
Part I	Chapter 2	Faqi Shi, Tao Song
	Chapter 3	Mingqing Jiang, Yang Liu
	Chapter 4	Junli Zhao, Jiancong Zhou
	Chapter 5	Faqi Shi, Mingqing Jiang, Hongli Ma, Tao Song, Yang Liu, Jiancong Zhou
Part II	Chapter 6	Youjuan Wang, Lei Zhu, Yilong Shi
	Chapter 7	Yuru Mao, Jiangxue Zhang, Shiyao Liu
	Chapter 8	Xiaolong Chen, Ning Cai, Delong Min
	Chapter 9	Youjuan Wang, Yuru Mao, Xiaolong Chen, Jiangxue Zhang, Ning Cai, Lei Zhu, Yilong Shi, Shiyao Liu, Delong Min
Part III	Chapter 10	Jiancheng Pan, Junli Zhao, Yajing Cong
	Chapter 11	Jiancheng Pan, Junli Zhao, Degang Jia
Part IV	Professors' Forum	Shengzu Gu, Renwu Tang, Desheng Lai, Biliang Hu, Jiang Yuan, Fangjian Liu, Xuguang Song, Xuemin Liu, Qi Zhang, Fangfang Tang, Jinshe Liang, Baoyuan Li, XianQiang Mao, Jiansheng Liu, Heng Yin, Hongrui Wang, Luozhong Wang, Jinshi Liu, Li Ding
Appendices	Appendix 1	Zhao Zheng, Lin Yongsheng, Xiao Yihuan, Zhang Liangliang
	Appendix 2	Xiaoxi Li
	Appendix 3	Faqi Shi, Mingqing Jiang, Tao Song, Yang Liu, Jiancong Zhou
	Appendix 4	Youjuan Wang, Yuru Mao, Xiaolong Chen, Jiangxue Zhang, Ning Cai, Lei Zhu, Yilong Shi, Shiyao Liu, Delong Min

X. Li and J. Pan (eds.), *China Green Development Index Report 2012: Regional Comparison*, Current Chinese Economic Report Series,
DOI 10.1007/978-3-642-54178-0, © Springer-Verlag Berlin Heidelberg 2015

Postscript

From September 2011 to June 2012, the *China Green Development Index Report 2012: Regional Comparison* was completed based on the previous two reports and submitted to the press. The report is a result of the development trends at both home and abroad, great support from all sectors, and dedication of the research group.

Our deepest gratitude goes to Commissioner Ma Jiantang of the National Statistical Bureau (NBS), Secretary Liu Chuansheng and President Zhong Binglin of Beijing Normal University, Secretary Zhao Dewu and President Zhang Zongyi of Southwestern University of Finance and Economics. They are all pleased to preface the book without any hesitation, from which we can feel their encouragement and trust.

China Economic Monitoring and Analysis Center and other departments of NBS have carefully examined and identified the supplements and amendments of the indicators, thereby playing an irreplaceable role. Statistical experts work with high levels of professional standards and commitment with consciousness. Deputy Director Pan Jiancheng provided great support and together with Director Zhao Junli effectively organized the survey of public satisfaction and analysis of the Questionnaire of Public Satisfaction of City Green Development, exhibiting the professional quality of NBS staff including Jia Degang, Cong Jingya, Tan Xiaoyan and Xing Jingli who played important roles in design, implementation, analysis and report drafting. Deputy chief Wang Youjuan, director Faqi Shi, dircctor Mingqing Jiang, director Chen Xiaolong and director Mao Yuru activcly participated in discussions and provided valuable advices for completion of the Report. Once more I would like to extend great appreciation to the organizations that have contributed cooperation, assistance and support to the project.

Gratitude also goes to the experts of the Professors' Forum: they are professor Jiang Yuan of the School of Life Sciences, professor Jinshe Liang of the School of Geography, professor Xuemin Liu of the College of Resources Science and Technology, professor Mao Xianqiang of the School of Environment, professor Hongrui Wang of the College of Water Sciences, professor Renwu Tang and associate professor Luozhong Wang of the School of Management, professors Desheng Lai, Baoyuan Li and Heng Yin of the School of Economics

X. Li and J. Pan (eds.), *China Green Development Index Report 2012: Regional Comparison*, Current Chinese Economic Report Series,
DOI 10.1007/978-3-642-54178-0, © Springer-Verlag Berlin Heidelberg 2015

and Business Administration, professor Xuguang Song of School of National Accounting, professors Hu Biliang and Zhangqi the School of Economics Resource Management from Beijing Normal University, and professors Liu Fangjian, Fangfang Tang, Jiansheng Liu, associate professors Jinshi Liu and Li Ding from Southwestern University of Finance and Economics. Thanks for the valuable proposals for and analysis of China's green development from the experts in natural and social sciences.

Over the past 3 years, I have always been moved by the over 30 evaluation experts of economics, resources, ecology and environment of China. They reviewed the report insightfully in spite of their busy schedule, which benefits the report greatly. Renowned economists Wu Jinglian, Li Yining and Zhang Zhuoyuan gave guiding ideas and practical recommendations which greatly benefited the report; professor Wei Liqun, deputy director of the Literature, History and Learning Committee of CPPCC (Chinese People's Political Consultative Conference), professor Chen Xiwen, deputy director of Central Finance Leading Group Office, Professor Gu Shengzu, deputy director of Internal and Judicial Affairs Committee, Professor Lu Zhongyuan, deputy directors of Development Research Center of the State Council, and Vice Minister Pan Yue of Environmental Protection advised that the report should combine theories with practices to benefit green development of both the central and local governments. Professor Niu Wenyuan and researchers Pan Jiahua and Xia Guang of sustainable development provided valuable suggestions on the indicator system and conclusions concerning resources, ecology and environment. The deputy president of Beijing Normal University, Professor Ge Jianping and deputy president of Southwestern University of Finance and Economics, Professor Bian Huimin, have always been concerned about the progress of our project and have given great support to this report.

Here, I would like to express my appreciation to the teachers and students for their wisdom and labor contributed to the project. They devoted all their efforts and did efficient work to complete the project. Particular thanks are given to Dr. Zhang Jiangxue, Dr. Zhao Zheng and Dr. Lin Yongsheng. As the coordinators of this project they raised important advices during the course of calculation. My postgraduates involved in the entire project and made great contribution in indicator perfection, index calculation, and editing of the review draft. The liaison officers Dr. Tao Song and Dr. Cai Ning effectively helped organize and coordinate input and trial calculation of provincial and city GDI. Dr. Cong Yajing, Dr. Jiang Xin and teacher Rong Tingting offered valuable advices on the calculation. Dr. Xiao Yihuan and Dr. Zhang Liangliang involved the entire process of indicator selection and calculation of international city GDI. Dr. Yang Liu, Master Zhu Lei and Master Zhou Jiancong contributed a lot to selection and calculation of provincial and city GDI, manuscript submission and communication with review experts. I also appreciate the performances of the new members Master Liu Shiyao, Master Shi Yilong and Master Min Delong. Sincere thanks go to the students who worked days and nights.

Here, I would like to thank Wang Ying and Yan Ling, for their management of the funds use and reimbursement. I also appreciate the teachers and students who participated in the conference services several times and in particular those who were responsible for the contact of review experts and manuscript submission. They worked really hard and obtained praise from inside and outside experts.

Last but not least, we appreciate the strong support from the Beijing Normal University Press. For 3 years the Press president, Professor Yang Geng and the editor-in-chief, Ye Zi took great care in the progress of the project, arranged the editing and publishing of the book. As the planning editor of this book, Mr. Hongli Ma involved in the whole process of the discussion and writing in the research team, and did a lot work of guidance and assistance to complete on time the manuscript according to the quality requirements. Ms. Chen Jingsi worked tirelessly, and completed the book editing with high quality.

The 2010 report was recognized at the second China Soft Science Awards. The 2011 Report was covered by many news media agencies including CCTV, Xinhua News Agency and *People's Daily*, and translated into English with the financial support of the 2011 Classic China International Publishing Project launched by the General Administration and Press and Publication of China. I am convinced that the 2012 report will once again draw attention from across China and the world.

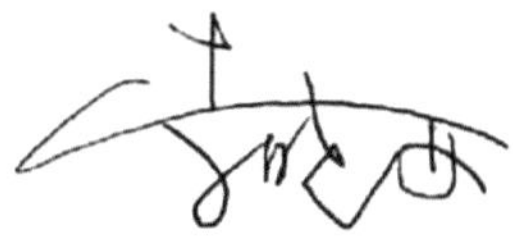

Li Xiaoxi
June 1, 2012

MIX
Papier aus verantwortungsvollen Quellen
Paper from responsible sources
FSC® C105338
FSC
www.fsc.org

If you have any concerns about our products,
you can contact us on
ProductSafety@springernature.com

In case Publisher is established outside the EU,
the EU authorized representative is:
Springer Nature Customer Service Center GmbH
Europaplatz 3, 69115 Heidelberg, Germany

Printed by Libri Plureos GmbH
in Hamburg, Germany